ELEMENTS

OF

CHEMISTRY.

FOR THE

USE OF COLLEGES, ACADEMIES, AND SCHOOLS.

By M. V. REGNAULT.

ILLUSTRATED BY NEARLY SEVEN HUNDRED WOOD-CUTS.

TRANSLATED FROM THE FRENCH,

By T. FORREST BETTON, M.D., M.A.N.S.

FELLOW OF THE COLLEGE OF PHYSICIANS OF PHILADELPHIA, ETC.

AND EDITED WITH NOTES,

By JAMES C. BOOTH,

MELTER AND REFINER U. S. MINT, AND

WILLIAM L. FABER,

METALLURGIST AND MINING ENGINEER.

SECOND EDITION.

TO WHICH IS APPENDED A COMPARATIVE TABLE OF FRENCH AND ENGLISH WEIGHTS AND MEASURES.

IN TWO VOLUMES.—VOL. I.

PHILADELPHIA:
CLARK & HESSER.
1853.

TO

John K. Mitchell, M.D.

PROFESSOR OF INSTITUTES AND PRACTICE OF MEDICINE,
JEFFERSON MEDICAL COLLEGE, PHILADELPHIA.

MY DEAR SIR:

Permit me to offer to you the following translation of a work, on a Science which you once taught with so much advantage to your pupils, as a very feeble mark of gratitude for your unvarying friendship since my boyhood, and a sincere testimonial of the high respect and esteem of,

My dear Sir,

Your very ob't serv't,

And obliged friend,

TH. F. BETTON.

German Town, Phila. Co., April 1, 1853.

TABLE OF CONTENTS OF VOL. I.

COMPARATIVE TABLE

OF

FRENCH AND ENGLISH WEIGHTS AND MEASURES.

THE law of July, 1837, has made the employment of the decimal system compulsory in all calculations after 1840.

A cube of distilled water, measuring a centimetre,* at its greatest density, (*i. e.* 4° of the centigrade, or 39.2° of the Fahrenheit thermometer,) weighs 1 gramme, or 15.438 grains English, which is the unit or standard of the new weights.

The divisions of the gramme are:

The *decigramme* 0.10 = the tenth part of a gramme: or 1.544 of a grain, or 1½ grains, nearly.

The *centigramme* 0.01 = the hundredth part of a gramme: or 0.154 of a grain, or ⅙ of a grain, nearly.

The *milligramme* 0.001 = the thousandth part of a gramme: or 0.015 of a grain, or $\frac{1}{66}$ of a grain, nearly.

The multiples of a gramme are:

The *decagramme*	or 10 grammes	or 154.4 grains	ʒiiss.	nearly.
The *hectogramme*	or 100 grammes	or 1544 grains	℥iiiʒii.	"
The *kilogramme*	or 1,000 grammes	or 15440 grains	℥xxxiiʒi.	"
The *myriagramme*	or 10,000 grammes	or 15440 grains	℔xxvii.	"

The ancient French standard of weight is the pound weight of "marc," which equals 16 ounces, or 500 grammes, (*i. e.* 16 oz. and 39 grs. Troy.)

Grammes are indicated by a comma being placed on the right of the figure, while decigrammes, on the contrary, are placed on the right of the

---

* 0.39371 of an inch.

comma: on the right of the decigrammes are placed the centigrammes: and lastly, at the right of these, the milligrammes. *Ex. gr.*:

1,	= 1 gramme,
0,1	= 1 decigramme,
0,01	= 1 centigramme,
0,001	= 1 milligramme.

		Troy grains.		lb.	oz.	dr.	gr.
Milligramme	=	.0154					
Centigramme	=	.1544					
Decigramme	=	1.5444					
Gramme	=	15.4440					
Decagramme	=	154.4402	=	0	0	2	34.4
Hectogramme	=	1544.4023	=	0	3	1	44.4
Kilogramme	=	15444.0234	=	2	8	1	24
Myriagramme	=	154440.2344	=	26	9	6	0

MEASURES OF CAPACITY.

The *metre* is the unit of length, and is equal to one ten-millionth part of an arc, composed of one-fourth part of the terrestrial meridian, extending from the equator to the pole. The *litre* is the unit of measures of capacity, and is the cube of the tenth part of the metre.

				Wine Measure.		*Eng. Apoth. Measure.* gals.	pts.	oz.	drs.	min.
Millilitre	=	.061028	=	16.2318 minims	=	0	0	0	0	16.3
Centilitre	=	.610280	=	2.7053 fluid drachms	=	0	0	0	2	42
Decilitre	=	6.102800	=	3.3816 fluid ounces	=	0	0	3	3	2
Litre	=	61.028000	=	2.1135 pints	=	0	1	15	1	43
Decalitre	=	610.280000	=	2.6419 gallons	=	2	1	12	1	16
Hectolitre	=	6102.800000			=	22	0	1	4	48
Kilolitre	=	61028.000000			=	220	0	12	6	24
Myrialitre	=	610280.000000			=	2200	7	13	4	48

MEASURES OF LENGTH.

				Miles.	Fur.	Yds.	Ft.	In.
Millimetre	=	.039371						
Centimetre	=	.393710						
Decimetre	=	3.937100						
Metre	=	39.371000	=	0	0	1	0	3.371
Decametre	=	393.710000	=	0	0	10	2	9.710
Hectometre	=	3937.100000	=	0	0	109	1	1.100
Kilometre	=	39371.000000	=	0	4	213	1	11.000
Myriametre	=	393710.00000	=	6	1	156	1	2.000

COMPARISON OF THERMOMETERS.

In *Fahrenheit's* thermometer, which is universally employed in this country and Great Britain, the freezing point of water is placed at 32°, and the boiling point at 212°.

The *Centigrade* thermometer, which has been long used in Sweden under the name of Celsius' thermometer, and is now most generally employed on the continent of Europe, marks the freezing point 0° (*Zero*) and the boiling point 100°.

In *Reaumur's* thermometer, used in France before the Revolution, the freezing point is at zero, and the boiling point at 80°.

In *De Lisle's* thermometer, used in Russia, the graduation begins at the boiling point, which is marked *zero*, while the freezing point is placed at 150°.

It will thus be seen that 180° of Fahrenheit are equal to 100° of the Centigrade, 80° of Reaumur, and 150° of De Lisle; or that 1 degree of the first is equal to $\frac{5}{9}$ of a degree of the second, $\frac{4}{9}$ of the third, and $\frac{5}{6}$ of the last. The degrees of one may therefore be readily converted into an equivalent number of degrees of any other; but in ascertaining their corresponding points upon the different scales, their different modes of graduation must be remembered. Thus, as the zero of Fahrenheit is 32° below the point at which that of the Centigrade and Reaumur is placed, this number must be taken into account in the calculation. The following rules embrace all cases which can occur. De Lisle's thermometer, being seldom or never referred to in works read in this country, is omitted.

1. If any degree on the *Centigrade scale*, either above or below zero, be multipled by 9 and divided by 5, or if any degree of *Reaumur*, above or below zero, be multiplied by 9 and divided by 4, the quotient will, in either case, be the number of degrees above or below 32°, or the freezing point of *Fahrenheit.*

2. The number of degrees between any point of *Fahrenheit's* scale and 32°, if multiplied by 5 and divided by 9, will give the corresponding on

the *Centigrade:* if multiplied by 4 and divided by 9, will give the corresponding point on the scale of *Reaumur.*

3. Any degree of the *Centigrade,* multiplied by 4 and divided by 5, will give the corresponding degree of *Reaumur:* and conversely, any degree of *Reaumur,* multiplied by 5 and divided 4, will give the corresponding degree of the *Centigrade.*

ELEMENTS OF CHEMISTRY.

INTRODUCTION.

§ 1. When we bring the various bodies of nature into juxtaposition, or into contact with each other, several kinds of phenomena result. Sometimes, these phenomena are displayed by important changes in the constitution of the bodies: at other times, on the contrary, the bodies acquire properties more or less fugitive, but which, in nowise, alter their apparent constitution, and do not sensibly change their respective weights. Thus, when a glass rod is rubbed with a piece of cloth, the rod acquires the property of attracting light bodies, such as the down of a quill, small bits of paper, etc., but the glass rod presents no apparent alteration whilst in possession of this property.

When we place a magnet close to, or, better still, in contact with a bar of soft iron, we communicate to the latter the property of attracting objects of iron, but this property vanishes as soon as the magnet is withdrawn.

If we rub with a magnet, not a bar of soft iron, but a bar of steel, the latter acquires the property of attracting objects of iron, even in the absence of the magnet, and preserves this property for some time.

Under these various circumstances, the glass rod, the iron and steel bar, by acquiring new properties, experienced no *sensible* alteration in their constitution, and preserved their weight unchanged.

If we mix together copper filings and pulverized sulphur, we may obtain a very intimate mixture of the two substances. To whatever degree of fineness, however, the particles of each may be reduced, we can always distinguish with a lens or a microscope the particles of the copper from those of the sulphur, and can, therefore, conceive that their mechanical separation is possible. But, if we submit the mixture to the action of heat, a very brilliant phenomenon soon ensues: a brilliant light is evolved, with a great quantity of heat. After the occurrence of this phenomenon, the microscope discovers a complete change in the constitution of the mass: it is impossible to distinguish the particles of copper from those of the sulphur; the particles of the two bodies are in timately united—they have *combined*, and formed a new substance perfectly distinct from its constituent parts.

A piece of iron, exposed to the air, soon becomes covered witl an ocherous coat, commonly called *rust*. If the piece of iron be long exposed to a damp atmosphere, it is so completely transformed into this ocherous substance as to lose all the characteristics of iron. If the iron had been carefully weighed before its exposure, its weight, compared with that of the resulting ocherous mass, would show that the latter was considerably heavier. Under these circumstances, the iron has combined with one of the constituent principles of the air, oxygen; and it has also combined with a portion of water, which always exists in the air in the state of vapour; and the result of these combinations is a new substance entirely different in its properties from those which entered into its composition.

Thus, the various bodies of nature present, when in presence of or contact with each other, two very distinct classes of phenomena: phenomena more or less durable, discovered by no material change in their constitution, and phenomena, on the contrary, which produce an important alteration, and a complete change in their nature and in all their properties.

The former class of these phenomena belongs to Physics: the latter is the province of Chemistry. Thus, we may define *Chemistry to be that portion of the natural sciences which treats of the phenomena resulting from the contact of bodies, when these phenomena effect an entire change in the constitution of these bodies.* But, as it is essential that bodies thus made to react on each other should be clearly described, and their characteristic general properties be previously perfectly well known, chemical science necessarily contains a descriptive part, in which we treat, as it were, of the *description* or *appearance* of each body, by means of which it can always be subsequently recognised.

§ 2. Division of Bodies into Simple and Compound.—Chemists divide bodies into *simple* and *compound bodies*. *Compound bodies* are those from which several substances may be extracted, differing in their properties from each other, and also from the primary body. Thus, common sea salt can be decomposed into two substances, chlorine and sodium; nitre or saltpetre can also be decomposed into potassa and nitric acid. These last two substances are themselves compound: from potassa, we can extract potassium and oxygen; and from nitric acid, oxygen and nitrogen. On the contrary, chlorine, sodium, potassium, oxygen, and nitrogen have never yet been resolved into other principles, and hence have been designated by chemists as simple bodies.

We, therefore, give the name of *simple bodies* to those substances which, although subjected to the various manipulations of the laboratory, are never resolved into other substances. We do not hereby mean to affirm that these bodies are really simple; for it is very possible that the future progress of science will enable us to effect decompositions which resist our present means; and then many, perhaps all, of the bodies now regarded as simple, will be found to be compound.

§ 3. Divisibility of Matter.—Daily experience teaches us that bodies may be reduced into very minute particles; but is this divisibility of matter indefinite, or is it arrested at a certain point, at which the particles are no longer separable by mechanical means? The ancient philosophers discussed this question at length, but without approaching its solution. The researches of modern chemistry have been more successful, and have proved, almost incontestably, that there is a limit to the divisibility of matter. Chemists admit that ultimate analysis shows bodies to be composed of excessively small particles, indivisible by mechanical means; to these they have given the name of *molecules* or *atoms*. The molecules of simple bodies are themselves necessarily simple. The molecules of compound bodies are, on the contrary, compound: but all these complex molecules resemble each other, and are formed in the same manner.

§ 4. Different States of Bodies.—Bodies are presented to us in three different conditions, or states: the *solid state*, the *liquid state*, and the *gaseous state*. Some bodies may be readily obtained in these three different states: thus, water, which is fluid at the ordinary temperature of our latitude, becomes solid, under the form of ice, during the intense cold of winter; whilst, by subjecting it to the action of heat, it is easily made to assume the state of an aeriform fluid, or vapour. The solid and liquid states are common to many bodies; such as the majority of the metals, lead, tin, copper, silver, gold, etc. Some of them, such as iron and platinum, require, in order to pass from the solid to the fluid state, the highest degree of temperature of which our furnaces are capable. Latterly, by means of the voltaic pile, a much greater degree of heat has been obtained, sufficient to render gaseous several of the metals, as gold, silver, copper, etc.

The majority of substances which are gaseous at the ordinary temperature, become fluid when subjected to great pressure and a very low temperature. Hydrogen, oxygen, and nitrogen gas are the only ones which have hitherto resisted liquefaction: but this result cannot be doubted when we shall have attained a greater degree of compression and a more reduced temperature.

The greater part of the gases, which have been liquefied, have been rendered solid by intense cold. It was sufficient to gradually remove the pressure which kept the gas liquefied; the latter then endeavoured to assume the gaseous form: but, to effect this, the absorption of a certain proportion of latent heat, which was abstracted by the gaseous from the fluid parts, was necessary, and thus the temperature of the latter became sufficiently reduced to congeal the fluid.

We may therefore conclude that all natural bodies could assume the three states, were they subjected to favorable conditions of pressure and temperature. We may, however, remark that many solid bodies cannot be liquefied, because they are decomposed when submitted to the action of heat. Thus, carbonate of lime is decomposed at a red heat, by disengaging one of its constituent principles, carbonic acid gas; and at this temperature, it has not undergone fusion. The disengagement of the carbonic acid may be prevented, by enclosing the carbonate of lime in a gun-barrel hermetically sealed: it then fuses at a temperature not much greater than that which effects its decomposition when subjected to the pressure of the atmosphere.

§ 5. Force of Aggregation, or Cohesion.—The force which unites the similar molecules of a simple or of a compound body, is called the *force of aggregation*, or *cohesion*. This force is very great in solid bodies, almost insensible in liquids, and entirely null in elastic fluids. In the latter, the particles, on the contrary, repel each other, and only maintain their actual distances by means of the pressure reacted by the sides of the containing vessel.

§ 6. Chemical Affinity.—The force which unites the simple molecules constituting a molecule of a compound body, bears the name of *chemical affinity*. By virtue of this force, the molecules of simple bodies combine to form compound bodies. Chemical affinity greatly varies, according to the circumstances in which bodies are placed: it is not readily exerted between solid bodies, because the contact of the molecules cannot be perfect. The free exercise of chemical affinity demands the disaggregation of bodies, and, as this disaggregation can only be imperfectly effected by mechanical trituration, they must be reduced to a liquid or gaseous form. *Corpora non agunt, nisi soluta*, was an expression of the old chemists, signifying this fact. In many cases, it is sufficient to liquefy or render gaseous only one of the bodies.

The chemical affinity between two bodies varies greatly, according to temperature. Thus, lime and carbonic acid readily combine at the ordinary temperature to form carbonate of lime, and carbonate of lime decomposes at a red heat, parting with its carbonic acid. At the ordinary temperature, the chemical affinity between lime and carbonic acid is very strong, whilst, at a red heat, it is null.

§ 7. Law of Multiple Proportions.*—When two simple bodies, A and B, combine, 1 molecule of A will combine with 1, 2, 3, 4, ... molecules of B; or, again, 2 molecules of A combine

* First advanced by Dalton, in 1807.

with 1, 2, 3, 4, 5, 7,.... molecules of B; or, lastly, 3 molecules of A may combine with 5, 7,.... molecules of B, and so on. It therefore follows, that, *in the various combinations which a substance* B *may form with the same weight of a substance* A, *the ponderal quantities of the substance* B *will be to each other in rational and commensurable proportions.* This fact, which has been clearly demonstrated by experience, is the principal proof we advance to establish the limited divisibility of matter and the existence of indivisible molecules. Experience even shows that the most simple proportions are those which most frequently occur: we generally find between compound bodies the proportions of 1 : 2, of 1 : 3, of 1 : 4, of 1 : 5, or of 2 : 3, of 2 : 5, of 2 : 7. This law, which governs the proportions in which two bodies combine, is called the *law of multiple proportions.* In our subsequent study of compound bodies, we shall meet with experiments establishing incontestably the truth of this law.

§ 8. Of the different Physical and Organoleptic Characters by which Bodies are distinguished.—In order to specify and describe bodies, we use various characteristics, founded either upon the appearance or physical properties of the bodies, or upon the impressions they produce on our organs. The former are called *physical characters,* the latter have received the name of *organoleptic characters.*

The principal physical characters used in chemistry are—

1st. The various states of the body, that is, the various conditions of temperature and pressure in which the body presents the solid, liquid, or gaseous form.

2d. Its color in these different states.

3d. The nature of its lustre, when this can be specified by comparison. Thus, we say, *metallic, vitreous, resinous* lustre, etc.

4th. Its degree of hardness, if the body be solid; and its greater or less fluidity, if it be liquid.

5th. Its specific gravity or density, that is, the weight of a unit of volume of the body.

6th. The regular or crystalline forms which it assumes.

7th. The appearance of the recent fracture of the body when solid. Thus, we say, *vitreous, crystalline, laminated, granular* fracture, etc.

The organoleptic characters are those impressions produced on the organs of taste, smell, and touch: thus, we mark, by comparison, the taste and smell of substances, and say that a substance is rough, or has an unctuous or greasy feel.

Of the physical characters we have just enumerated, some may be accurately measured or ascertained, and are therefore of great value in defining a substance. Such are, the specific gravity of substances, and the temperature at which they change their condition. The exact appreciation of their crystalline form is also of vast importance: hence, the study of crystalline forms plays an eminent part in the classification of substances and in our modern chemical theories.

§ 9. OF CRYSTALLINE FORMS.—A superficial observation of the different bodies in nature would lead us to suppose that their external form had no regularity, and was susceptible of infinite variation. More attentive study, however, will soon teach us that the majority of them can assume, under certain circumstances, regular* forms, which are always perfectly similar in the various individuals of the same substance. Still further, the majority of substances which appear to us under irregular external forms, present, in their recent fracture, evident indices of a regular or crystalline texture; so that the whole body is merely an aggregation of an infinity of small crystals, dovetailed in each other. These rudimentary crystals are often so small that they can only be distinguished by examining the fracture with a lens or microscope; whence it may be inferred that there are others still smaller, which escape our means of observation.

The crystalline texture of bodies, far from being an exception, is, on the contrary, most frequently to be met with.

The greater part of the substances which we prepare in our laboratories, are capable of being *crystallized*, that is, of assuming regular geometric forms; and we may remark that, when this operation takes place under *identical circumstances*, the forms of the various individual crystals perfectly resemble each other; so much so, as to constitute one of their most certain distinctive characters.

At first sight, the crystalline forms assumed by the various bodies in nature appear to vary *ad infinitum;* but a close study of these various forms has discovered some general laws which they obey, and which considerably lessen their number.

The consideration of the crystalline forms of bodies already occupies an important place in our theories of chemistry. This importance will become greater when the science of crystallography shall be more extended, and when chemists shall define with accuracy the crystalline forms of the bodies which come under their notice. I have thought it necessary to explain here the principles of this science: they merely require of the reader a knowledge of elementary geometry.

PRINCIPLES OF CRYSTALLOGRAPHY.

§ 10. Crystals are terminated by plane faces: and, in general, each plane face corresponds to another, exactly parallel to it, in the crystal; at least, when the crystal is isolated, and regularly

* The science of crystallography has been chiefly established by the brilliant labours of Bergmann, of Romé de Lisle, and of Haüy.

terminated throughout. Most frequently, crystals are imbedded in a solid mass, so that only one summit of the crystal is visible, and only one-half of it can be observed: it is therefore often difficult to verify the proposition just advanced as to the parallelism of the opposite faces; but nearly all imbedded crystals have been sometimes found isolated and perfect, and thus justify the assertion. From analogy, we may therefore infer that such would be the case with all crystals, were they not imbedded, and we may represent them perfect at both extremities.

§ 11. Crystals have always salient and never re-entering angles. Yet, when we observe a mass of a great number of crystals, as, for example, the cavity of a rock, the walls of which are covered with crystals, and called by mineralogists a *geode of crystals*, or a crystallization obtained in the laboratory, we see many re-entering angles, which would seem to invalidate our remark; but these re-entering angles are produced by the junction of two individual crystals, and are never seen in an isolated, individual specimen.

§ 12. CLEAVAGE.—Crystals are not broken with equal readiness in all directions: the fracture generally follows the plane faces. These fractures in the direction of the plane faces may be indefinitely reproduced on the same crystal, parallel to each other, so that the substance may be divided in many laminæ with parallel faces. This is called a *lamellar fracture*. This property of crystals has been long known to lapidaries, who have profited by it, to divide precious stones. Thus, the diamond presents a laminated fracture in four different directions: lapidaries avail themselves of this, to remove the defective portions, and thus abridge, considerably, the cutting of the diamond. They call this operation *cleaving the diamond*. The name of *cleavage* is applied to the parallel faces thus obtained in a crystal by fracture.

The same crystal possesses several directions of cleavage: usually expressed by saying, *many cleavages:* but these cleavages are not always equally easy. Certain cleavages are readily known by the fracture, even when it is accidental: others are obtained only after much care; and even then, often very imperfectly. Thus, carbonate of lime presents three equally easy cleavages, inclined toward each other at an angle of 105° 5′, and, in consequence of which, the substance always breaks into rhombohedrons. Sulphate of lime also presents three cleavages, but one is much more easy than the other two: it follows, therefore, that the crystal tends to separate into laminæ, and, by means of a knife, we can obtain laminæ of exceeding thinness. If these laminæ be broken between the fingers, the other cleavages immediately appear, and give rise to parallelogramic laminæ.

§ 13. FUNDAMENTAL FORMS.—The combination of the planes of cleavage constitutes a geometrical figure, constant in all the individuals of the same crystallized substance: these are called *fundamental forms.*

§ 14. Natural Joints of a Crystal.—The lines in the direction of which the faces of a crystal are divided, are called the *joints.* They are distinguished into *acute* and *obtuse,* according as the faces constituting these joints form with each other an acute or an obtuse angle.

§ 15. Angles of a Crystal.—Three or a greater number of faces, uniting at one point, form a solid angle, which mineralogists term, though improperly, the *angle* of the crystal. The angles are classed according to the number of their faces: thus we say, an angle with 3 faces (fig. 1), with 4 (fig. 2), with 6 (fig. 3), etc. etc.

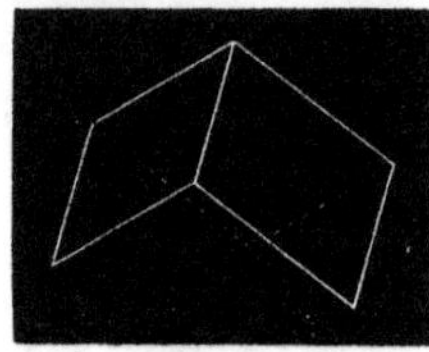
Fig. 1.

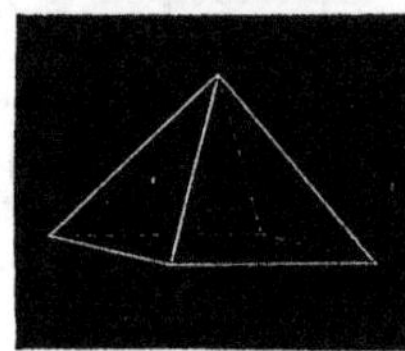
Fig. 2.

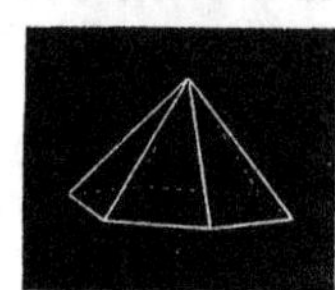
Fig. 3.

§ 16. Simple and Compound Forms.—Sometimes, crystals are only terminated by faces similar to each other. Such are, the regular octahedron, formed by 8 equilateral triangles (fig. 4); the regular hexahedron, or cube, terminated by 6 squares (fig. 5); the hexagonal dodecahedron, formed by 12 isosceles triangles (fig. 6). These are called *simple forms.* We call, on the contrary, *compound,* those forms which include faces of different kinds. Fig. 7 represents a compound form: it is composed of 6 square faces and 8 equilateral triangles. Fig. 8 is also a compound form, and constituted by 6 rectangular faces and 12 isosceles triangles.

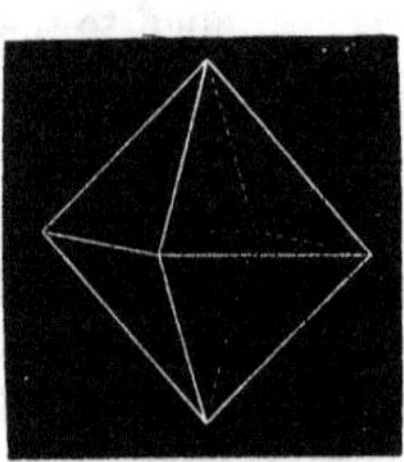
Fig. 4.

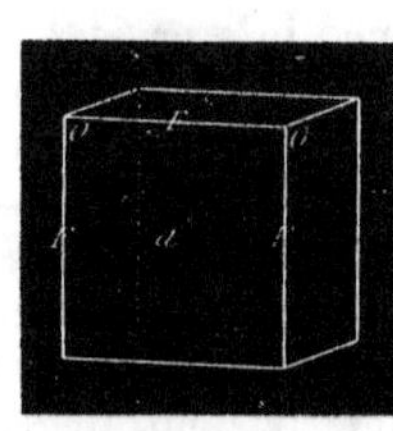
Fig. 5.

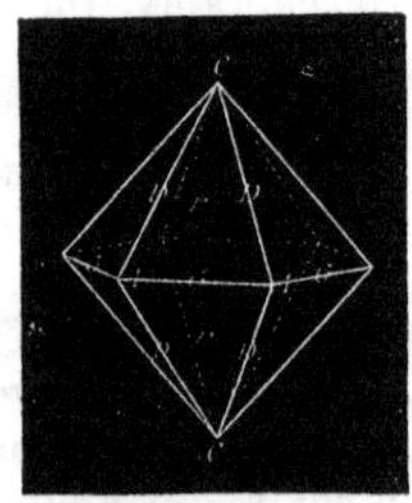
Fig. 6.

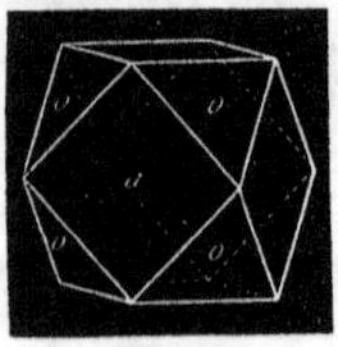

Fig. 7.

If, in a compound crystal, we conceive the faces of the same kind to be extended so as to hide completely the faces of the other kind, we will obtain a simple form. The triangular

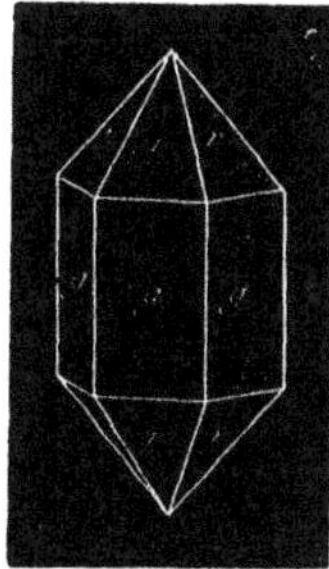

Fig. 8.

faces of fig. 7 being extended, give the regular octahedron (fig. 4). If, on the contrary, we extend the square faces so as to conceal the triangular faces, we will obtain the hexahedron (fig. 5).

Hence we see that compound forms result from the combination of so many simple forms as there are faces of different kinds in those compound forms: we may, therefore, call the compound form of which we have just spoken (fig. 7), a *combination of the octahedron and hexahedron.*

It often happens that, by extending the similar faces of a compound crystal, we obtain an unlimited form, which cannot of itself terminate a crystal. Thus, for example, if we suppose the 6 rectangular faces of fig. 8 to be produced, we will obtain a regular prism with 6 indefinite faces. If, on the contrary, we produce the 12 triangular faces, we obtain a solid, the hexagonal dodecahedron (fig. 6).

It is evident that the faces which form an unlimited solid cannot, of themselves, produce a crystal: they will always appear in combination, either with faces which, being produced, will give a solid, or with faces which, under the same conditions, give open or indefinite forms.

§ 17. Dominant and Secondary Forms.—Generally speaking, in a compound crystal, one of the simple forms constituting it is more developed than the others, and gives the crystal its general aspect: this is then called the *dominant form,* whilst the other forms of the combination are termed *secondary;* their faces are also called *modifying faces.* Thus, figs. 9 and 10 represent combinations of the octahedron with the hexahedron; but in fig. 9 the facets *o* pertaining to the octahedron are more developed than the facets *a* belonging to the hexahedron, and give the crystal an octahedral form: we therefore say that it is an *octahedron modified by the faces of the cube.* On the contrary, in fig. 10, the aspect of the cube predominates, and it will be termed a *hexahedron modified by the faces of the octahedron.*

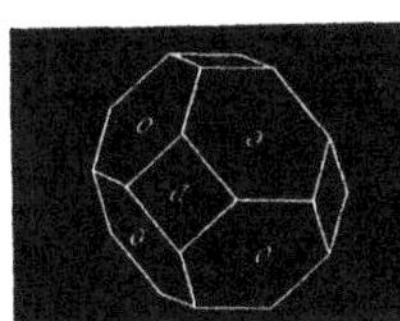

Fig. 9.

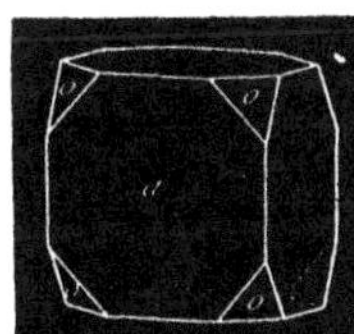

Fig. 10.

§ 18. Truncation.—When, in a combination of several simple forms, an edge or joint of the dominant form is succeeded by a face parallel to this edge, as in fig. 11, the edge is said to be *truncated,* and the modifying face is called *the truncated face,* or *facet of the edge.** This truncated face may incline equally toward

* The edge is also said to be replaced by a plane, either evenly or obliquely; or, as in § 19, by two planes.—*J. C. B.*

both faces of the dominant form which enclose the truncated edge: the truncation is then said to be *right*, or *tangent*, as in fig. 11. In the contrary case, it is said to be *oblique*.

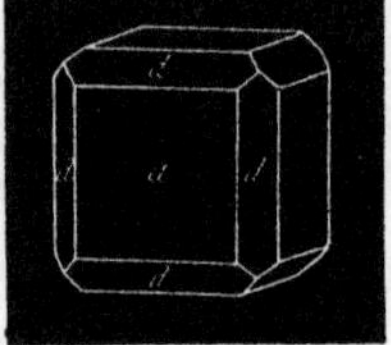

Fig. 11.

Frequently, the angles of the dominant form are truncated, and the faces of the truncation are *right* or *oblique*, according as their inclination to the faces of the dominant form which make the angle is equal or unequal. Fig. 9 represents a regular octahedron, the angles of which are truncated by the faces of the hexahedron: fig. 10 represents a hexahedron the angles of which are truncated by the faces of the octahedron. In both figures, the truncation is right, or tangent.

When an oblique truncated face of an angle inclines equally on the two faces, forming one of the edges of that angle, the truncation is said to *rest symmetrically* on this edge: thus, in fig. 11, the truncated face inclines equally to the two faces: it *rests symmetrically* on the edge. In the contrary case, it is said to *rest obliquely*.

Again, we say that a truncated face *rests symmetrically on a face* of the dominant form, when the line of intersection of these two faces forms equal angles with the two adjacent edges of the dominant form; we say, on the contrary, that it *rests obliquely*, when these angles are unequal.

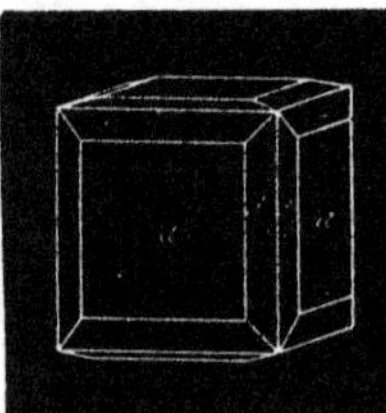

Fig. 12.

§ 19. Bevelment.—The edges of the dominant form are often replaced by two faces parallel to these edges, and equally inclined toward the adjacent faces: in this case, we say that the edge has been beveled. Such is the case in fig. 12, where a bevelment has taken the places of the edges of the hexahedron.

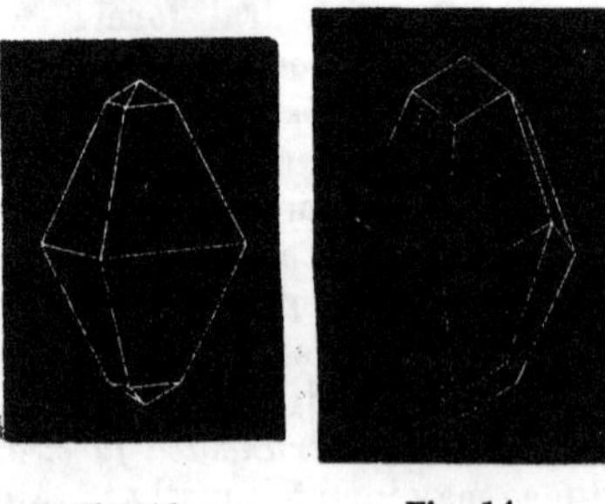

Fig. 13. Fig. 14.

§ 20. Acumination.—An angle of the dominating form is often replaced by another more obtuse angle; the angle is then said to be *acuminated*. Sometimes, the facets of the acumination are equal in number to the faces forming the primitive angle, as in fig. 13: at others, the latter are double, as in fig. 14. The terminal faces rest symmetrically, either on the faces (fig. 13), or on the edges of the angle (fig. 14).

§ 21. Centre of the Crystal.—In all crystals, whether

simple or compound, there is a point at which every right line which passes through and is terminated by the faces of the crystal must be bisected. This point is the *centre of the crystal.*

§ 22. Axes of the Crystal.—In all simple forms, there are certain right lines passing through the centre of the crystal, and around which the faces are symmetrically arranged; these lines have been called the *axes of the crystal.*

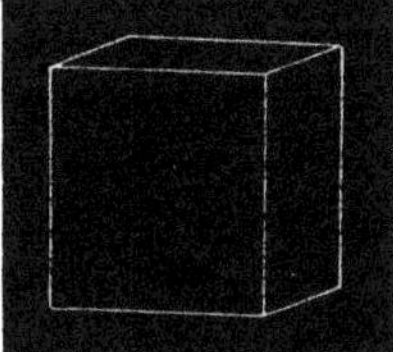
Fig. 15.

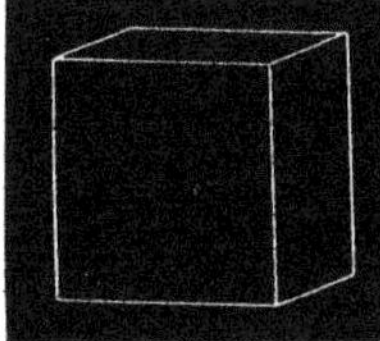
Fig. 16.

Sometimes the crystal has several planes or systems of axes, as the regular hexahedron. In fact, if we connect by lines the centres of the opposite faces (fig. 15), we shall have three right lines possessing the above property, and which, consequently, are axes: we obtain a second system of axes by joining the opposite angles (fig. 16). This gives a system of 4 axes, forming with each other angles of 70° 32′: lastly, if we join, two by two, the centres of the opposite edges (fig. 17), we obtain a system of 6 axes, comprising angles of 60°. All the axes of the hexahedron, which make a part of the same system, are equal to each other.

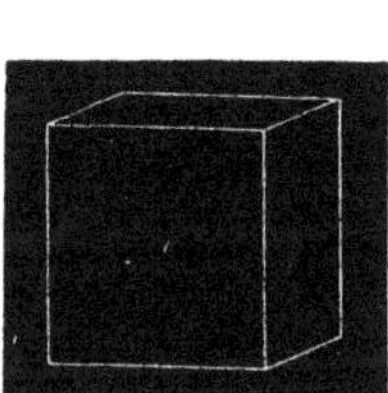
Fig. 17.

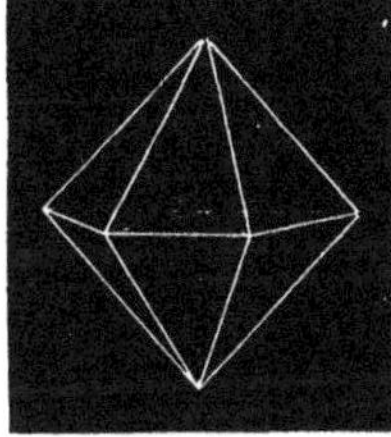
Fig. 18.

Fig. 19.

In the hexagonal dodecahedron (fig. 18), we obtain the axes by joining the opposite angles; and thus have a plane of 3 equal horizontal axes, forming with each other angles of 60°, and a single vertical axis perpendicular to the plane of the three others.

In the oblique rhombic octahedron (fig. 19), the axes are still the lines joining the opposite angles; the three axes of this figure are all unequal and inclined toward each other.

§ 23. Position of the Crystal.—In order to study more readily crystalline forms, it is useful to give to crystals a determinate position; and it has been agreed to place them so that one of their axes shall be vertical. Thus, in the hexadron, we generally adopt, as the plane of axes, that system of three rectangular axes which join the centres of the opposite faces. As these three axes perfectly resemble each other, it is evident that either may be chosen, and that the figure will present exactly the same aspect, whichever axis may be vertical.

When, in the system of axes of a crystal, there is found an axis having no analogue in the system, this axis is always chosen for the vertical position, and is then termed *principal axis;* the others are called *secondary axis.* The hexagonal dodecahedron (fig. 18) is placed so that its single axis may be vertical.

The rhombic octahedron (fig. 19) presenting three unequal axes, either may be chosen as the principal axis: but, the selection once made, it should be continued during the whole study of the crystal.

Neither should the direction of the secondary axis be arbitrary, when we are about to study the various crystals presented by the same substance. In all our figures, the crystals will be placed so that one of the secondary axes shall have the direction of the plane of the figure.

§ 24. Definitions of Systems of Crystallization.—The accurate study of the various compound forms furnished to us by the mineral kingdom has shown that simple forms cannot indiscriminately combine with each other. *We never meet, in the same crystal, simple forms, which have not an identical system of axes.*

Thus, we frequently find the cube and regular octahedron in combination; the rhombohedron is found combined with a regular six-sided prism: but we never see the rhombohedron or six-sided prism combined with the regular octahedron or hexahedron. The rhombohedron and regular six-sided prism have a system of axes composed of 3 similar axes forming with each other angles of 60°, and situated in the same plane, and a fourth axis perpendicular to the other three; whilst, in the cube and regular octahedron, there is found no analogous system of axes.

We give the name of *System of Crystallization* to the collection of the different forms which have similar systems of axes.

Crystallographers have made six systems of crystallization:

1. The first, or regular system of crystallization, is characterized by 3 axes of equal length, and intersecting at right angles.[1]

2. The second system is characterized by 3 perpendicular axes, but two only are of equal length.[2]

3. The third system is characterized by 4 axes, three of which are of equal length, disposed in the same plane, and intersecting at an angle of 60°; the fourth axis is different, and is perpendicular to the system of the three others.[3]

---

[1] This is the *Monometric* or *Tesseral* system of Dana: the *Isometric* of Hausmann: *Tessular* of Mohs and Haidinger: *Tesseral* of Naumann: the *Regular* of G. Rose: the *Cubic* of Dufrenoy.

[2] This is the *Dimetric* system of Dana: *Pyramidal* of Mohs: *Tetragonal* of Naumann: *Monodimetric* of Hausmann: *Quadratic* of Kobell: *Bino-Singulaxe* of Weiss.

[3] This is the *Hexagonal* or *Rhombohedral* system of Dana: the *Rhombohedral* of Mohs: *Hexagonal* of Naumann: *Monotrimetric* of Hausmann. *T. F. B.*

4. The fourth system is characterized by 3 axes, unequal, but intersecting at right angles.[1]

5. The fifth system is characterized by 3 unequal axes: two of these axes intersect obliquely, but the third is perpendicular to the plane of the other two.[2]

6. The sixth system is characterized by 3 unequal axes, which intersect obliquely.[3]

We will now review successively the principal crystalline forms constituting these different systems.

I.—REGULAR SYSTEM OF CRYSTALLIZATION.

§ 25. The forms of this system are characterized by 3 axes of equal length, intersecting at right angles. As we have seen above, other systems of axes are found in these forms; but as these other systems present no new feature, and the regular system of crystallization being completely defined by the three equal and similar axes, we shall consider them alone.

The principal simple forms belonging to this system are—

1st. The *regular octahedron* (fig. 20), formed by 8 equilateral triangles: the edges are equal; the solid angles are equal and have 4 faces. The dihedral angles of the faces are of 70° 32′.

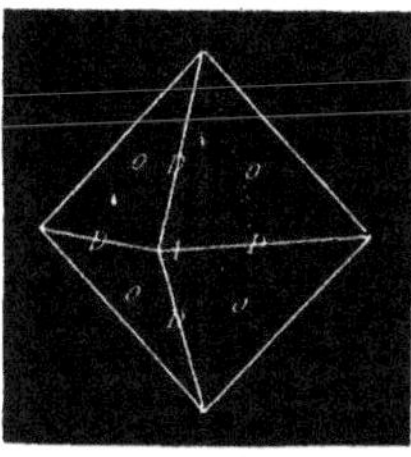

Fig. 20.

The rectangular axes join the opposite angles, and each face divides the three axes in equal lengths. It therefore follows, that if we designate by a the length of these axes, comprised between the centre of the crystal and the point where it meets the faces, we may define the octahedron by saying, that it is the face which divides the three rectangular axes into equal lengths, a. The following formula, which expresses the equality of the three axes, has been agreed upon to represent this face:

$$(a : a : a).$$

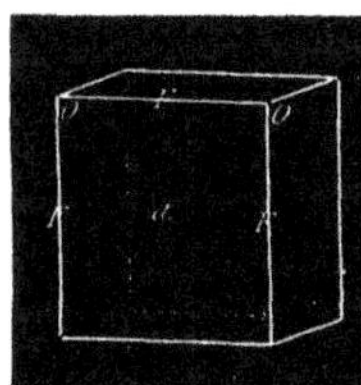

Fig. 21.

2d. The *hexahedron* or *cube* (fig. 21) formed by 6 square faces: the three rectangular axes joining the centres of the opposite faces: each face is perpendicular to one of the axes, and parallel to the other two; so that we may represent each of these faces, and consequently the entire hexahedron, by the formula

$$(a : \infty a : \infty a).$$

[1] This is the *Trimetric* system of Dana: the *Prismatic* of Mohs: the *Rhombic* and *Anisometric* of Naumann: *Binary* of Weiss: *Trimetric* of Hausmann.

[2] This is the *Monoclinic* system of Dana: the *Hemi-prismatic* of Mohs: the *Monoclinohedral* of Naumann: the *Clino-rhombic* of Kobell: the *Augitic* of Haidinger.

[3] This is the *Triclinic* system of Dana: the *Tetarto-prismatic* of Mohs: the *Trichinohedral* of Naumann: the *Clino-rhomboidal* of Kobell: the *Anorthic* of Haidinger. *T. F. B.*

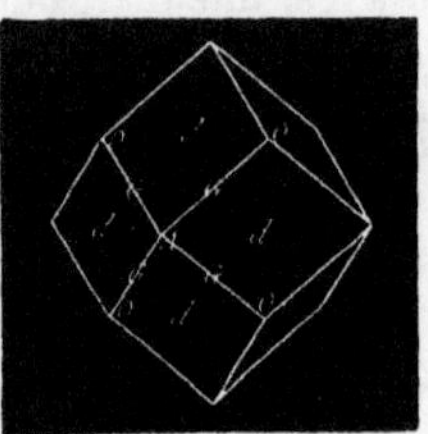

Fig. 22.

3d. The *dodecahedron* (fig. 22), formed by 12 rhombic faces, the angles of which are of 109° 28′, and 72° 32′.

The angles are of two kinds: 6 angles A to 4 faces corresponding in position to the angles of the octahedron, and 8 angles O to 3 faces corresponding to the angles of the hexahedron. Each face of the dodecahedron is parallel to an octahedric axis, and bisects the other two: these faces may be therefore represented by the formula

$$(a : a : \infty\, a.)$$

4th. The *tetrahedron* (figs. 23 and 24) is formed by 4 faces which are equilateral triangles. This solid may be derived from the regular octahedron by supposing the alternate faces of the octahedron to be extended so as to cause the intermediate faces to disappear. As we cause one or other system of alternate faces to disappear, we shall obtain two tetrahedrons (figs. 23 and 24) perfectly equal, but easily distinguished from each other by their position.

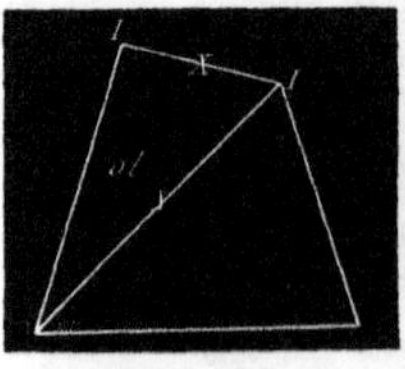

Fig. 23.

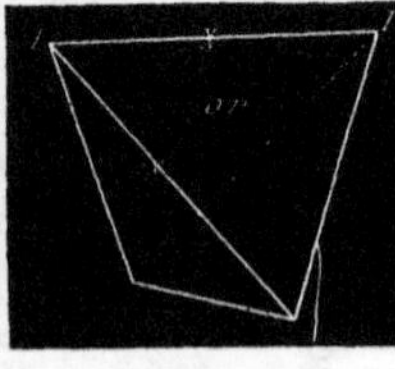

Fig. 24.

This mode of generation of the tetrahedron has given to this form the name of *hemioctahedron*.

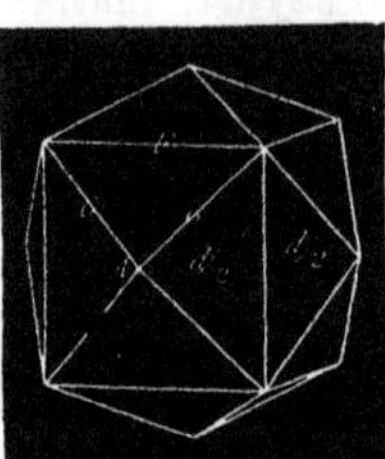

Fig. 25.

5th. The *tetrahexahedron* or *pyramidal hexahedron* (fig. 25) is a solid with 24 faces, the general appearance of which is that of a hexahedron on whose faces 4-sided pyramids have been superimposed.

Most frequently, the height of the 4-sided pyramids implanted on the faces of the hexahedron is equal to one-half of the axis of the hexahedron. Sometimes, however, the ratio between the height of the pyramids and the axis of the hexahedron is more complex, but it is always represented by a very simple rational fraction. Thus, we meet the ratios $\frac{2}{3}$, $\frac{2}{5}$, $\frac{1}{3}$, $\frac{1}{5}$.

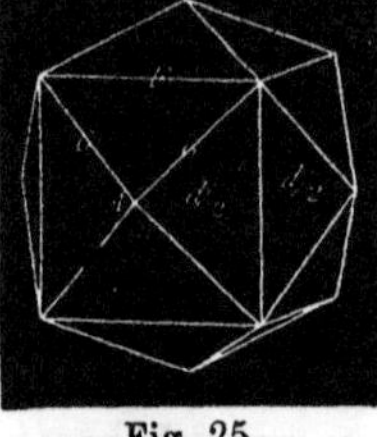

Fig. 26.

If we suppose the alternate faces of the tetrahexahedron to be extended, so as to cause the intermediate faces to disappear, we obtain a figure with 12 pentagonal faces, the *pentagonal dodecahedron* (fig. 26), which may be also called *hemi-tetrahexahedron*, on account of its mode of generation. The same tetrahexahedron may generate two hemi-tetrahexahedrons, according as one or other of the alternate systems of faces is extended. The two figures will be perfectly equal, and differ only in the direction of their faces.

6th. The *trisoctahedron* or *pyramidal octahedron* (fig. 27) is a solid of 24 faces, having the general appearance of a regular octahedron, on the faces of which 3-sided pyramids have been superimposed.

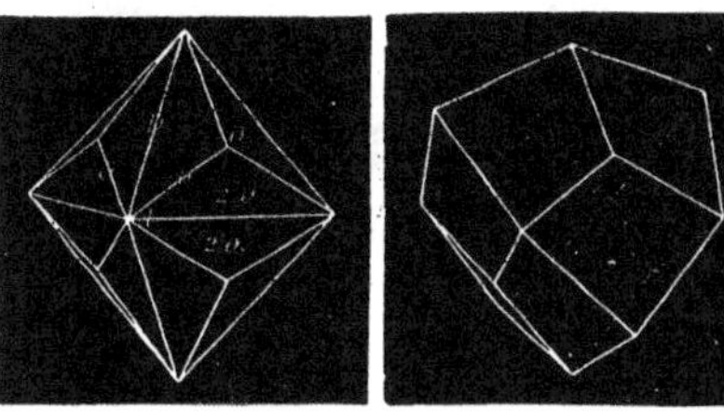

Fig. 27. Fig. 28.

As there are several tetrahexahedrons, presenting different ratios between the elevations of the pyramids and the length of the axes, so there are several trisoctahedrons: the ratios between the elevations of the pyramids and the length of the axes is always represented by very simple fractions, as $\frac{1}{2}$, $\frac{1}{3}$, $\frac{2}{3}$.

By extending the alternate faces of the trisoctahedron we obtain a hemihedric figure (fig. 28), the hemi-trisoctahedron, which has hitherto been but rarely observed.

7th. The *icositetrahedron* (fig. 29) is a solid with 24 faces, 48 edges, and 26 angles. This figure is obtained by supposing the solid angles of the regular octahedron to be replaced by more obtuse 4-sided pyramids, as in fig. 30, and then supposing the faces of these pyramids to be extended so as to cause the faces of the octahedron to entirely disappear. The ratios between the elevations of these pyramids and the length of the axes of the octahedron may be different; so that several icosotretrahedrons may exist: but the ratio is always represented by a very simple rational fraction: hitherto we have discovered only the relations $\frac{1}{2}$ and $\frac{1}{3}$.

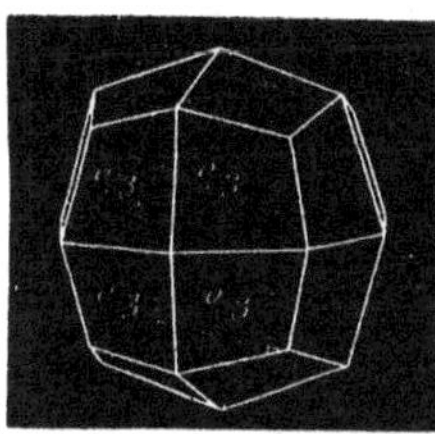

Fig. 29.

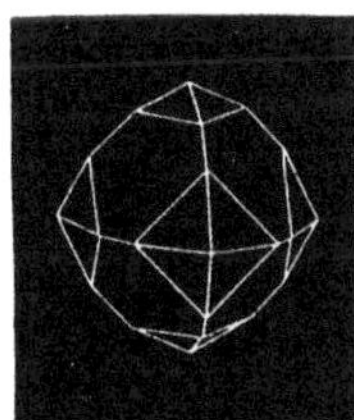

Fig. 30.

Icositetrahedrons are rarely seen in crystals, and are only mentioned here to complete the list.*

§ 26. Compound Forms of the regular System of Crystallization.—The combi-

* The origin assigned for the 24-hedron is for that in figs. 29, 30, or $\frac{o}{3}$ but $\frac{o}{2}$ may be derived from the rhombic 12-hedron by the evenly replacing its edges by a plane. The latter form is common in Garnet, Leucite, Analcime, &c. The general formula for the 24-hedron is $a : a : \frac{1}{m}a$, in which $m = 2$ or 3.—*J. C. B.*

nations of the various simple forms just enumerated give rise to various forms, of which we shall mention the principal.

Figs. 31, 32, and 33 represent three combinations of the regular octahedron and the hexahedron, in which the faces of the octahedron are marked *o*, and those of the hexahedron *a*.

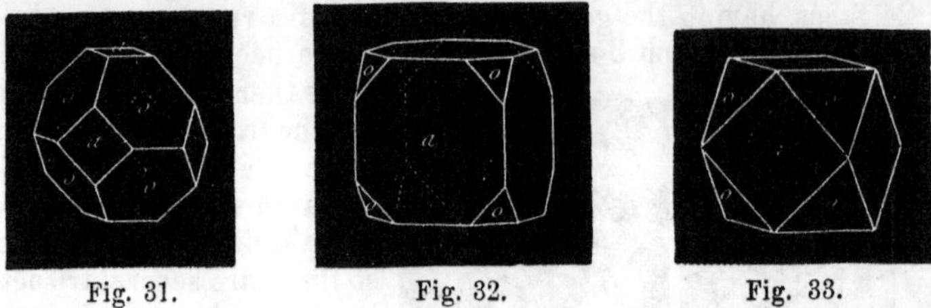

Fig. 31. Fig. 32. Fig. 33.

In fig. 31, the faces of the octahedron predominate: the contrary is true in fig. 32; and lastly, in fig. 33 the two forms are equally developed: this last species has received the name of *cubo-octahedron.**

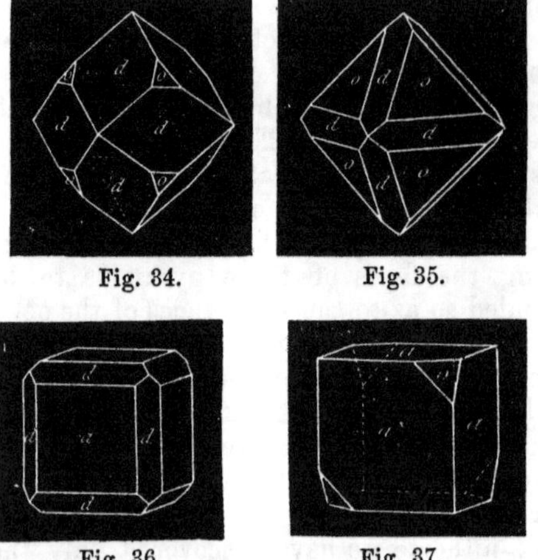

Fig. 34. Fig. 35.

Fig. 36. Fig. 37.

Figs. 34 and 35 represent combinations of the dodecahedron and octahedron. In fig. 35 the faces *o* of the octahedron predominate, whilst in fig. 34 the predominating are the faces *d* of the dodecahedron.

In fig. 36 we find a combination of the hexahedron with the dodecahedron, the hexahedron *a* predominating.

Fig. 37 represents a combination of the hexahedron predominating, with the tetrahedron: it will be seen that of the 8 solid angles of the hexahedron, 4 only are truncated by the faces *o* of the tetrahedron, or *hemi-octahedron.* We find in this combination an exception to the law laid down (§ 10); namely, that, in every regularly terminated crystal, every face has a face parallel to it. In the combination of the hexahedron with the tetrahedron, the facets *o* of the tetrahedron have no parallel facets on the opposite angles of the hexahedron.

* They are also said to be in equilibrium.—*J. C. B.*

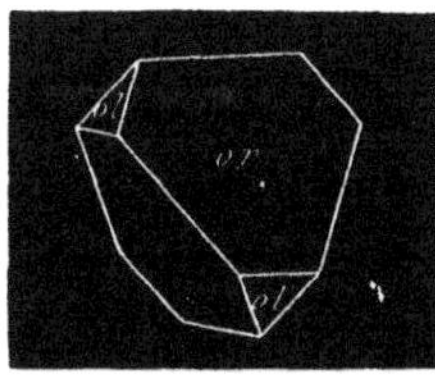

Fig. 38

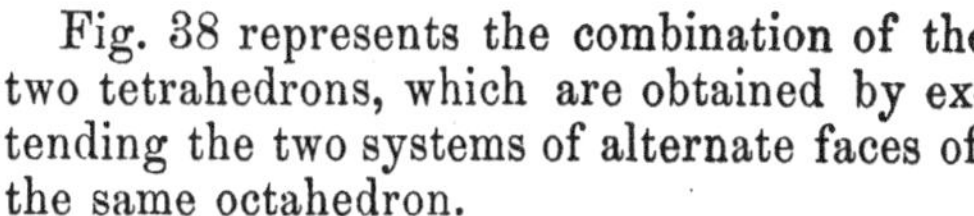

Fig. 38 represents the combination of the two tetrahedrons, which are obtained by extending the two systems of alternate faces of the same octahedron.

The preceding forms result only from the combination of two simple forms of the regular system; but compound forms are sometimes seen more complicated, resulting from the combination of three or more simple forms. Thus, fig. 39 represents the combination of the predominating hexahedron *a*, with the octahedron *o* and the dodecahedron *d*.

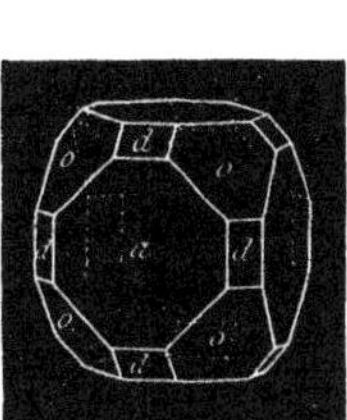

Fig. 39.

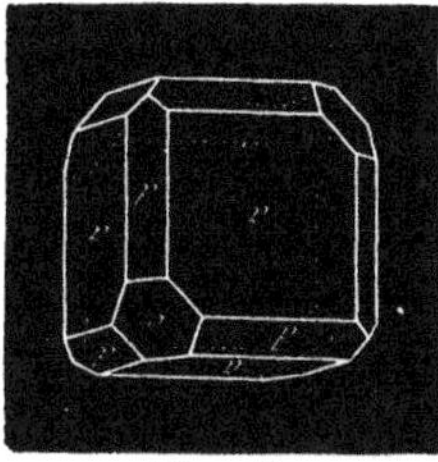

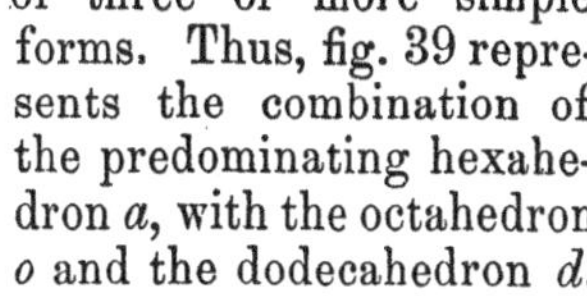

Fig. 40.

Fig. 40 is a combination of the predominating hexahedron *a* with the dodecahedron *d* and the tetrahedron *o*.*

II.—SECOND SYSTEM OF CRYSTALLIZATION.

§ 27. The forms belonging to this system are characterized by 3 rectangular axes, two of which are equal, and the third unequal. We choose the unequal axis as the principal one, and give the crystal such a position as will make this axis vertical. The ratio between the principal axis and the secondary axes may vary very much; and, generally speaking, this relation is complex and irrational.

In the regular system of crystallization, the 3 axes being equal, the faces are symmetrically arranged with reference to the 3 axes. Such is not the case in the second system: the 2 secondary axes being similar, the faces are symmetrically arranged with reference to these two axes, but differently with reference to the principal axis. Therefore we meet in this system faces perpendicular to the principal axis which have no analogues to the 2 secondary axes: and, again, we see faces perpendicular to the 2 secondary

---

* One simple form is entirely omitted in the above enumeration, which has been observed in the Diamond, Garnet, &c., the hexakisoctahedron or solid of 48 triangular planes. It may be viewed as arising from a combination of the 12-hedron, *d*, and the 24-hedron, or 6 × 8-hedron $\frac{o}{2}$, by replacing the edges of this combination evenly by a plane. Its formula is $a : \frac{1}{m}a : \frac{1}{n}$ and 5 different values for *m* and *n* have been observed. This simple form has two hemi-forms, one of which is like the hemioctahedron with a low 6-sided pyramid raised on each plane; the other is formed by supposing a pair of adjacent planes to be extended so as to exclude adjoining pairs of planes. The latter forms a 24-planed solid with trapezoidal planes, but different in appearance from fig. 29, and is termed the hemi-octakishexahedron.—*J. C. B.*

axes which have necessarily no analogue to the principal axis. These faces thus form open prisms, which cannot, of themselves, terminate a crystal. No similar occurrence is found in the regular system of crystallization.

SIMPLE FORMS OF THE SECOND SYSTEM OF CRYSTALLIZATION.—*Octahedrons with a square Base* (fig. 41). The faces of these octahedrons are isosceles triangles: their edges are of two species: 8 terminal edges D, which converge toward the principal axis CC, and 4 lateral edges. A section through these lateral edges, and, consequently, through the secondary axes, gives a square (fig. 41 *a*), and is called the *base of the octahedron.* Sections through the terminal edges give rhombs (fig. 41 *b*).

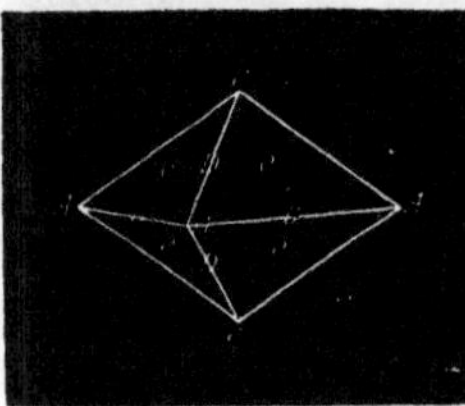

Fig. 41.

In the regular system of crystallization we have but one octahedron: in the second system, on the contrary, we have an infinity of octahedrons with square bases, which differ from each other by the inclination of their faces, or the ratio which the length of the principal axis bears to that of the 2 equal secondary axes; and, in order to define the octahedron, this ratio, or the inclination of the faces, must be given.

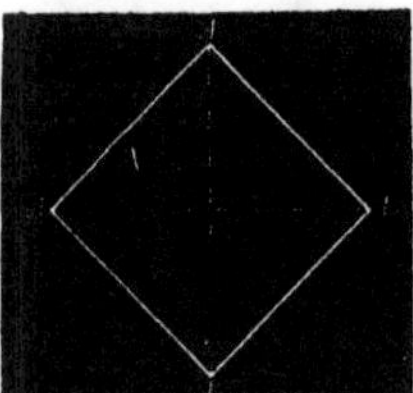

Fig. 41 *a*.

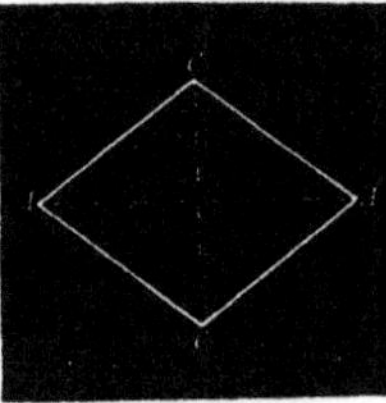

Fig. 41 *b*.

In all octahedrons of the second system of crystallization, the principal axis always joins the apices of the octahedron; but the secondary axis may present two positions, differing either with reference to the lateral edges of the octahedron, or to the sides of the base. These axes may join the opposite angles of the base, as in fig. 42; or the centre of the opposite sides, as in fig. 43. In fact, we thus obtain two octahedrons, with square bases and perfectly equal systems of axes: the octahedron of which the base is fig. 43 has its faces inclined in the same manner as the edges of the octahedron the base of which is fig. 42. We distinguish them by calling the octahedron, of which the base is fig. 42, an *octahedron of the first class*, or *direct octahedron;* and that of which fig. 43 is the base, an *octahedron of the second class*, or *inverse octahedron.*

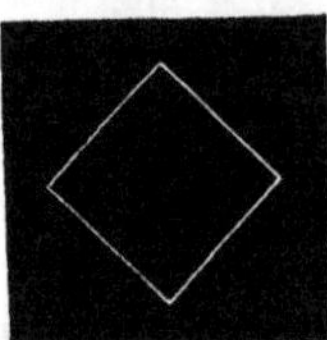

Fig. 42.

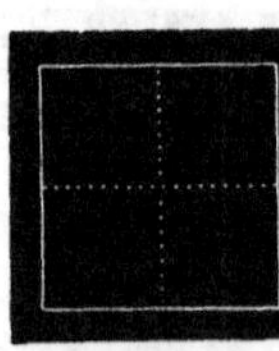

Fig. 43.

When the same substance crystallizes *in octahedrons with square bases*, it does not always present the same octahedron. On the contrary, we often observe several very different octahedrons, but which bear to each other a very simple relation. This relation is thus expressed: *if we reduce these octahedrons to the same base, their elevations or principal axes will bear to each other rational and extremely simple relations.*

One of these octahedrons is chosen as the *principal* or *primitive form;* and that is generally preferred which occurs or which predominates most frequently.* The principal or primitive form is expressed by the formula

$$(a : a : c).$$

The formula of all octahedrons in which the base is situated, with reference to the secondary axes, in the same manner as in the principal octahedron, that is, of all direct, or octahedrons of the first class, then becomes,

$$(a : a : mc):$$

whilst those of the inverse, or octahedron of the second class, in which the inclination of the faces is equal to that presented by the edges of the corresponding octahedrons of the first class, will be

$$(a : \infty a : mc).$$

If an arbitrary value could be assigned to m, the number of these octahedrons would be infinite: but observation has shown, that in the various octahedrons with square bases presented by any one substance, the number m always has a rational and extremely simple rule: thus, the formula of the primitive octahedron being

$$(a : a : c),$$

we always find, in the same substance, octahedrons expressed by,

$$\begin{array}{lcl} (a : a : 2c) & & (a : a : \tfrac{1}{2}c) \\ (a : a : 3c) & \text{or,} & (a : a : \tfrac{1}{3}c) \\ (a : a : 3c) & & (a : a : \tfrac{1}{4}c); \end{array}$$

that is to say, octahedrons which, with equal secondary axes, have a principal axis, 2, 3, 4 times greater, or 2, 3, 4 times smaller, than the principal axis c of the primitive octahedron.

We also find corresponding octahedrons of the second class:

---

* That which is most frequent in a particular mineral species or chemical combination. It is termed the primary or radical 8-hedron.—*J. C. B.*

$$\begin{array}{ccc} (a : \infty a : \ c) & & (a : \infty a : \ c) \\ (a : \infty a : 2c) & \text{or,} & (a : \infty a : \tfrac{1}{2}c) \\ (a : \infty a : 3c) & & (a : \infty a : \tfrac{1}{3}c) \\ (a : \infty a : 4c) & & (a : \infty a : \tfrac{1}{4}c). \end{array}$$

There are, however, still two cases which are often met with in substances belonging to the second system of crystallization, and they are derived from the formulæ

$$(a : a : mc)$$
$$(a : \infty a : mc),$$

by giving m its limited values, that is, by making

$$m = o,$$
$$\text{or,} \quad m = \infty.$$

RIGHT TERMINAL PLANE.—By diminishing the value of m, we obtain octahedrons more and more flattened, and when $m = o$, the octahedron is reduced to its base: we will call this extreme form of the octahedron, the *right terminal plane.* This terminal face can never exist isolated; but it is frequently met with in combination in compound forms. The formula of this face might be $(a : a : 0c)$; but it is generally written $(\infty a : \infty a : mc)$, or simply $(\infty a : \infty a : c)$, and is then considered as the limit of the octahedrons having the principal axis mc, but of which the secondary axes, without losing their equality, may become infinite.

PRISMS WITH SQUARE BASES.—By increasing the value of m in the general formulæ $(a : a : mc)$, $(a : \infty a : mc)$, we obtain octahedrons more and more acute: and, lastly, when $m = \infty$, the octahedrons are changed into two prisms with square bases, of which the bases are, fig. 42, for the prism derived from octahedrons of the first class, and fig. 43, for the prism which is the limit of the octahedrons of the second class. These two prisms cannot, of themselves alone, compose a crystal; but they often terminate a crystal, by combining with the octahedrons or with the right terminal face.

§ 28. COMPOUND FORMS OF THE SECOND SYSTEM OF CRYSTALLIZATION.—When two primitive octahedrons of the first and second class combine, the octahedron d of the second class truncates directly the edges of the octahedron o of the first class, as in fig. 44, which also exhibits the right terminal face c.* Fig. 45 repre-

* In this case (fig. 44) the 8-hedron d has a different value for m than o, being the first more obtuse 8-hedron. In fig. 45, $2d$ is the first more acute 8-hedron than o, since the edges of combination between o and $2d$ are parallel.—*J. C. B.*

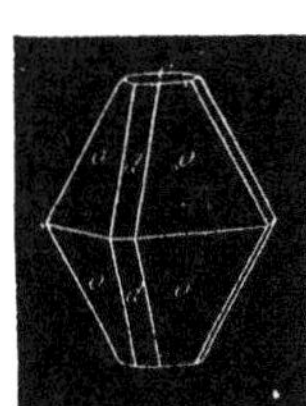

Fig. 44.

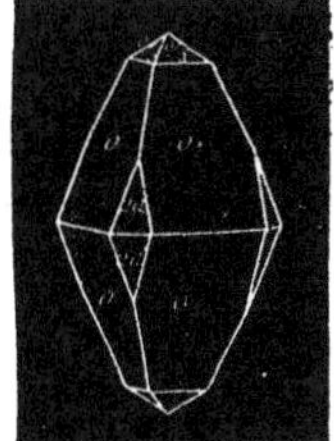

Fig. 45.

sents a combination of the primitive octahedron o, of which the formula is $(a : a : c)$, with the obtuse octahedron $\frac{o}{3}$ of the same class, $\frac{o}{3}$, of which the formula is $(a : a : \frac{1}{3}c)$, and with its first acute octahedron, $2d$, of the second class $(a : a : 2c)$. Fig. 46 gives us a combination of the primitive octahedron o $(a : a : c)$ with the right prism g of the same class $(a : a : \infty c)$. Fig. 47 represents the combination of the same primitive octahedron o $(a : a : c)$ with the right prism a of the second class $(a : \infty a : \infty c)$.

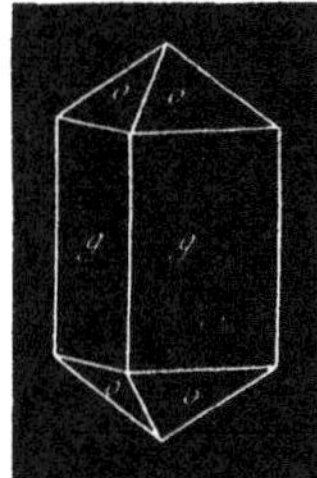

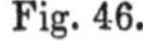

Fig. 46.

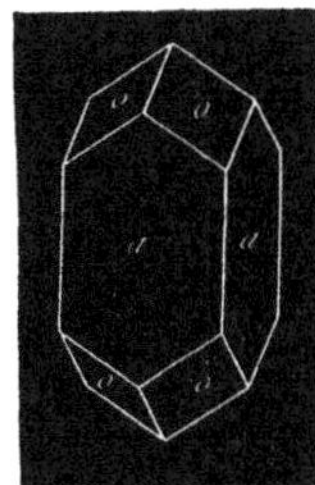

Fig. 47.

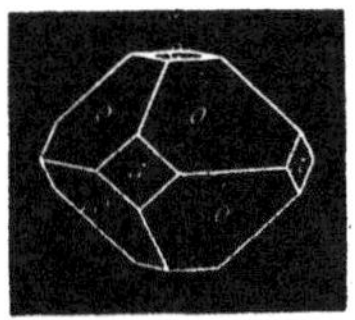

Fig. 48.

In fig. 48, we find a combination of the primitive octahedron o $(a : a : c)$ with the right terminal face c, and with the prism a of second class $(a : \infty a : \infty c)$; the primitive octahedron predominates in the combination.

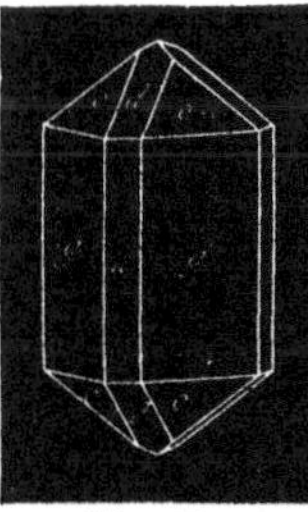

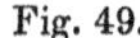

Fig. 49.

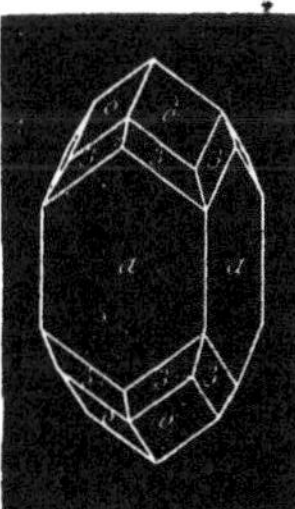

Fig. 50.

Fig. 49 represents a combination of the two right prisms g and a, of which the formulæ are $(a : a : \infty c)$, $(a : \infty a : \infty c)$ with the primitive octahedron o $(a : a : c)$ and the 1st obtuser octahedron d of the second class, $(a : \infty a : c)$; the right prism $(a : a : \infty c)$ predominates in the combination.

Lastly, in fig. 50, we find a combination of the primitive octahedron o $(a : a : c)$, with the di-octahedron 3 of the same class $(a : \frac{1}{3}a : c)$, and the right prism of a of the second class $(a : \infty a : \infty c)$. The prism predominates in the combination.*

* I have taken the liberty of altering the text in this paragraph, as an error has inadvertently crept in. Two simple forms of this system have been omitted, the dioctahedron and its prism. The dioctahedron may be said to arise from the

III.—THIRD SYSTEM OF CRYSTALLIZATION.

§ 29. The forms belonging to the third system of crystallization are characterized by 4 axes, of which 3 are equal, and intersect at angles of 60°: the fourth axis is different, and perpendicular to the other three. This is chosen as the principal axis, and the three axes become secondary. The ratio between the length of the principal axis and that of the secondary axes is indefinite.

It is evident that, in this system of crystallization, the faces are symmetrically disposed with reference to the three secondary axes, whilst they are disposed, with reference to the principal axis, in a manner entirely different from their former arrangement. In the third, as well as in the second and following systems, indefinite forms are met with which cannot, of themselves alone, terminate a crystal.

The following are the principal forms of this system:

Fig. 51.

Hexagonal Dodecahedrons (fig. 51).* These forms have 12 faces, 18 edges, and 8 angles. The faces are isosceles triangles. The edges are of two kinds: 12 terminal D, and 6 lateral G.

The angles also are of two kinds: 2 terminal angles C, which are regular and six-sided, and 6 lateral angles with four sides, which are nearly symmetrical.

A section through the lateral edges gives the *base*, which is a regular hexagon, and contains the three secondary axes. Sections through the two parallel terminal edges give rhombs.

Two classes of dodecahedrons may be distinguished, according to the manner in which the secondary axes are arranged with reference to the base. In the first class, the axes join the angles of the base, as in fig. 52. In the second, the axes join the centre of the opposite side, as in fig. 53.

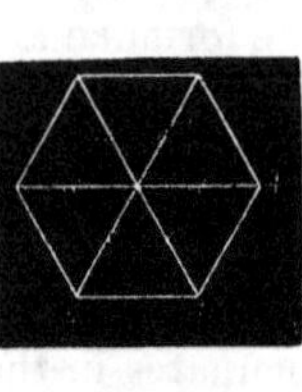

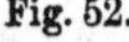

Fig. 52.

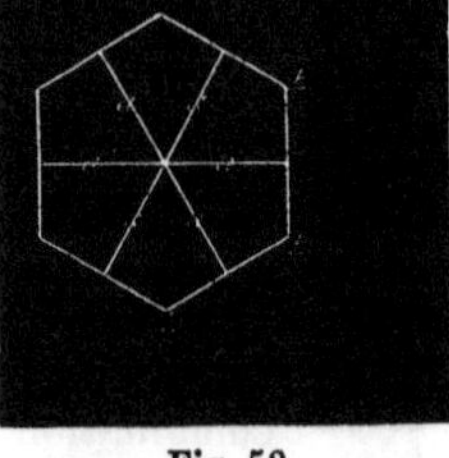

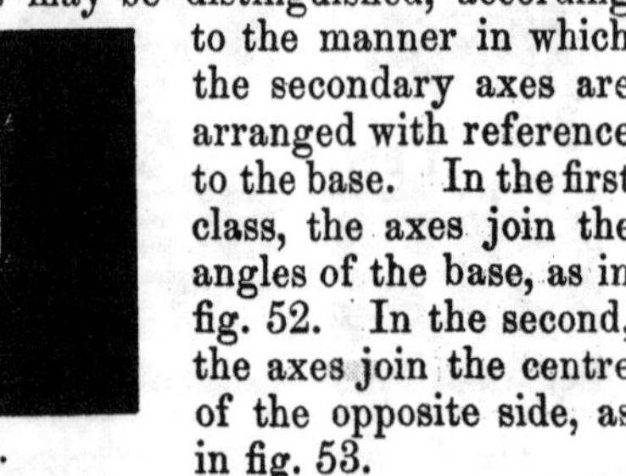

Fig. 53.

8-hedron by bevelling all its terminal edges until the planes of the 8-hedron disappear. It gives an 8-sided pyramid, whose alternate terminal edges are equal, and the adjacent ones unequal. Its formula is $a : na : mc$. It is never isolated, and in combination appears as 3 in fig. 50. The other omitted form is an 8-sided prism, with its alternate angles equal, adjacent unequal. None are represented in the figures, but its planes would appear replacing the edges of combination between a and g, fig. 49.—*J. C. B.*

* They are generally termed *triangular* 12-hedrons, but may be termed hexagonal with reference to the plane of the three axes.—*J. C. B.*

The faces of the direct, or dodecahedrons of the first class, divide the secondary axes, in equal lengths a, and are parallel to the third. The faces of the corresponding inverse, or dodecahedrons of the second class, divide one of the secondary axes, in a length a, and their prolongation divides the other two secondary axes, in the lengths $2a$.

The dodecahedron of the first class is therefore expressed by the formula

$$(a : a : \infty a : c)$$

and the corresponding form of the second class is

$$(2a : a : 2a : c).$$

Besides the two dodecahedrons of which we have just spoken, there may be an infinity of others, belonging to both classes, and of which the formulæ will be

$$(a : a : \infty a : mc) \qquad (2a : a : 2a : mc).$$

But, in one and the same substance, dodecahedrons always bear to each other very simple relations. *If we refer these dodecahedrons to systems of equal secondary axes, their principal axes will bear to each other very simple rational relations : or, in other words, the value of* m *will be* 2, 3, 4, or, $\frac{1}{2}$, $\frac{1}{3}$, $\frac{1}{4}$.

We will, therefore, choose one of these dodecahedrons as the *principal* or *primitive form*, or *type*, and will select that which most frequently occurs, or generally predominates in combinations. By giving to the primitive form the formula

$$(a : a : \infty a : c),$$

the formulæ of dodecahedrons will be—

Dodecah. of 1st class.	Dodecah. of 2d class.
$(a : a : \infty a : c)$	$(2a : a : 2a : c)$
$(a : a : \infty a : 2c)$	$(2a : a : 2a : 2c)$
$(a : a : \infty a : 3c)$	$(2a : a : 2a : 3c)$
$(a : a : \infty a : 4c)$	$(2a : a : 2a : 4c)$
$(a : a : \infty a : \frac{1}{2}c)$	$(2a : a : 2a : \frac{1}{2}c)$
$(a : a : \infty a : \frac{1}{3}c)$	$(2a : a : 2a : \frac{1}{3}c)$
$(a : a : \infty a : \frac{1}{4}c)$	$(2a : a : 2a : \frac{1}{4}c)$

We frequently find, in addition, indefinite forms, which may be considered as the extreme forms of the dodecahedrons, and which are obtained by making $m = o$ or $m = \infty$, in the two general formulæ

$$(a : a : \infty a : mc) \qquad (2a : a : 2a : mc).$$

By making $m=o$, the dodecahedrons are reduced to a single face, parallel and similar to the base. We will call this face the *right terminal plane*. The formula of this face will be, therefore, $(a : a : \infty a : 0c)$, but it is generally written $(\infty a : \infty a : \infty a : mc)$; that is to say, that this face is considered as the limit of the hexagonal dodecahedrons having the principal axis mc, but of which the secondary axes, without losing their equality, have been produced to infinity.

By making $m=\infty$, we obtain two 6-sided prisms, expressed by

$$(2a : a : 2a \; : \infty c)$$
$$(a \; : a : \infty a : \infty c).$$

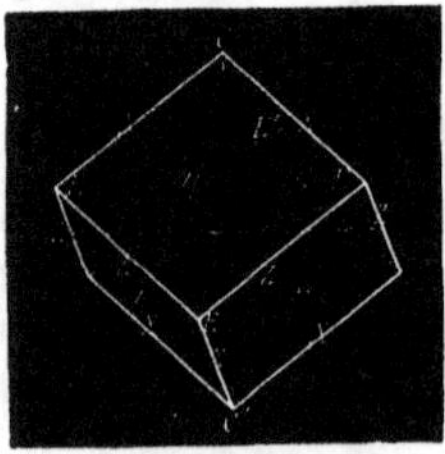
Fig. 54.

Rhombohedrons, or, *Hemidodecahedrons* (fig. 54).—Rhombohedrons have 6 faces, 12 edges, and 8 angles. The faces are rhombs. The edges are of two kinds: 6 terminal X, and 6 lateral. The angles are also of two kinds: 2 regular 3-sided angles C, and 6 lateral 3-sided but irregular angles E.

The principal axis joins the two terminal angles C, whilst the secondary axes join the centre of the opposite lateral edges. Sections passing through the two oblique diagonals CE and C′E′ are rhombs, the planes of which are perpendicular to the faces of the rhombohedron to which these diagonals belong. There are three of these sections in a rhombohedron, and they are called *principal sections*.

The rhombohedron may be considered as being derived from the hexagonal dodecahedron, by a mode of generation similar to that by which we have derived the tetrahedon from the regular octahedron; that is to say, by supposing that the alternate faces of the dodecahedron were produced so as to eclipse the intermediate faces: we then have remaining only the faces of the dodecahedron, pairs of which are parallel. But, as we may choose either system of alternate faces, it is evident that we will obtain two rhombohedrons (figs. 54 and 55) which are perfectly equal, and which would be lost in each other, if one of them of 60° were made to revolve around its principal axis. We shall call these rhombohedrons *direct*, or, *rhombohedrons of the first class;* and *inverse*, or, *rhombohedrons of the second class.*

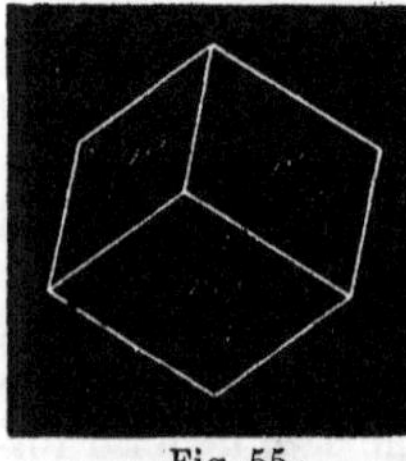
Fig. 55.

As the faces of rhombohedrons coincide with those of the hexagonal dodecahedron, their formulæ will be the same as those of the faces of the dodecahedron: but, in order to distinguish them from the latter, the coefficient $\frac{1}{2}$ is prefixed. Hence, the formula of rhombohedrons of the first class will be

$$\tfrac{1}{2}(a : a : \infty\, a : mc),$$

and that of the second,

$$\tfrac{1}{2}(a' : a' : \infty\, c : mc).$$

We have accented the first two axes, in the latter formula, in order to express that rhombohedrons of the second class divide, when produced, the axes which are directly divided by rhombohedrons of the first class.

The same substance, belonging to the third system of crystallization, often presents several rhombohedrons of the first and of the second class. *If we suppose the secondary axes of these rhombohedrons to be equal, we shall find that the lengths of the principal axes bear to each other rational and simple relations.* One of these rhombohedrons is generally selected as the primitive form, and the others are compared with it.

We shall consider as belonging to the first class, those rhombohedrons of which the faces are arranged in the same manner as the faces of the principal rhombohedron: and to the second class, those of which the faces are arranged in the direction of the edges of the principal rhombohedron.

Rhombohedrons present, like octahedrons of the second system of crystallization, series of figures more obtuse and more acute. Each obtuse rhombohedron of this series has its faces inclined toward the principal axis, in the same manner as the edges of the acute form which immediately follows it; so that each form is the *first acute rhombohedron* of that which precedes it, and the *first obtuse rhombohedron* of that which follows it. The following formulæ express the rhombohedrons of this series:

Principal rhombohedron	....	$(a : a : \infty\, a : c)$
1st obtuse "	....	$(a' : a' : \infty\, a : \frac{1}{2}c)$
2d " "	....	$(a : a : \infty\, a : \frac{1}{4}c)$
3d " "	....	$(a' : a' : \infty\, a : \frac{1}{8}c)$
1st acute "	....	$(a' : a' : \infty\, a : 2c)$
2d " "	....	$(a : a : \infty\, a : 4c)$
3d " "	....	$(a' : a' : \infty\, a : 8c)$.

We sometimes meet, however, rhombohedrons of which the principal axes are 3 or 5 times the length of the principal axis of the primitive rhombohedron.

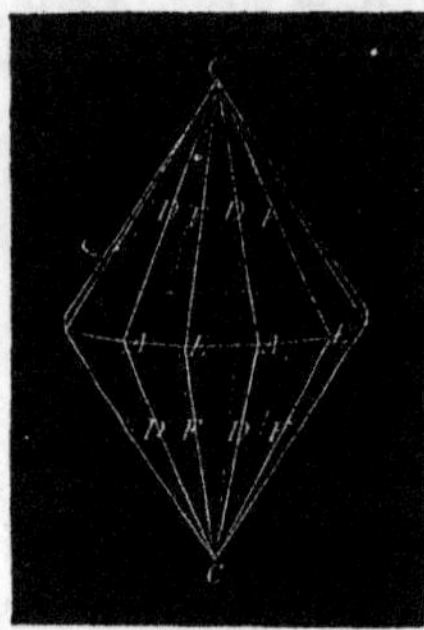
Fig. 56.

Didodecahedrons (fig. 56).—This form has 24 faces: it presents the general appearance of an hexagonal dodecahedron the faces of which are replaced by bevelments, having their edges directed in the same direction as the diagonals of the faces of the dodecahedron. The faces of the didodecahedron are scalene triangles. The 36 edges are of three kinds: 1st, 12 terminal edges D, which correspond, in position, to the terminal edges of the hexagonal dodecahedron of the first class; 2d, 12 terminal edges F, corresponding, in position, to the terminal edges of the dodecahedron of the second class; 3d, 12 lateral edges G, corresponding, two by two, with the lateral edges of the dodecahedron.

The angles are of three kinds: 1st, 2 angles with 12 symmetrical faces C, corresponding to the terminal angles of the octahedron; 2d, 6 lateral 4-sided and symmetrical angles A, corresponding to the lateral angles of the hexagonal dodecahedron of the first class; 3d, 6 lateral 4-sided and symmetrical angles E, corresponding to the lateral angles of the hexagonal dodecahedron of the second class.

The principal axis joins the terminal angles C; the secondary axes join the first lateral angles A.

The most common formula of didodecahedrons is

$$(a : na : pa : mc);$$

the coefficients n, p, m, representing very simple whole numbers, as 1, 2, 3, 4—or very simple fractions, as $\frac{1}{2}$, $\frac{1}{3}$, $\frac{1}{4}$, $\frac{1}{5}$, etc.

Didodecahedrons are never seen in crystals, as predominating forms; but they are frequently met with as modifying faces, in combinations, principally in those in which the 6-sided prism predominates.

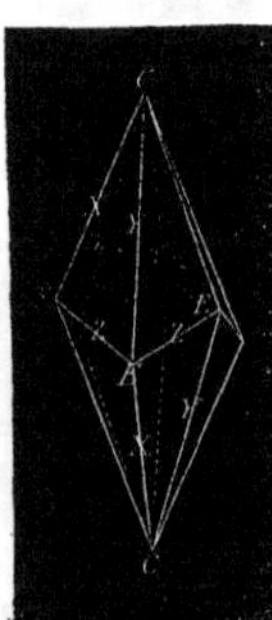
Fig. 57.

Scalenohedrons, or, *Hemididodecahedrons* (fig. 57).—These are the hemihedral forms of didodecahedrons, and are obtained by producing, until they meet the pairs of faces adjacent to the second system of alternate terminal edges (fig. 56). The two scalenohedrons, thus derived from each didodecahedron, have the same ratio of position as the two rhombahedrons derived from the same hexagonal dodecahedron: if one of them of 60° be made to revolve on its principal axis, it will assume the same position as the other. The formulæ of the two scalenohedrons derived from the same didodecahedron $(a : na : pa : mc)$ are

$$\tfrac{1}{2}(a : na : pa : mc)$$
$$\tfrac{1}{2}(a' : na' : pa' : mc).$$

§ 30. Compound Forms of the Third System.—Fig. 58 represents a combination of the primitive dodecahedron r with the first 6-sided prism g.

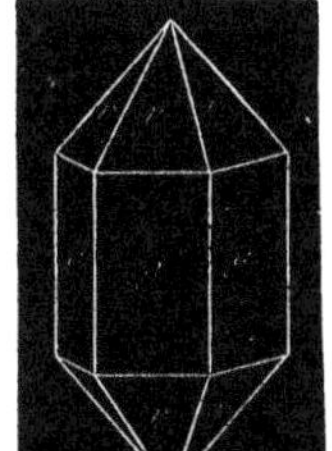
Fig. 58.

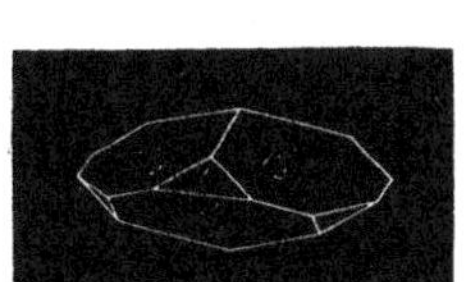
Fig. 59.

Fig. 59 represents a combination of the principal rhombohedron r, of which the formula is $\tfrac{1}{2}(a : a : \infty a : c)$, with its first obtuse rhombohedron $\frac{r'}{2}$, of which the formula is $\tfrac{1}{2}(a' : a' : \infty a : \tfrac{1}{2}c)$: this latter rhombohedron $\frac{r'}{2}$, being the predominating form.

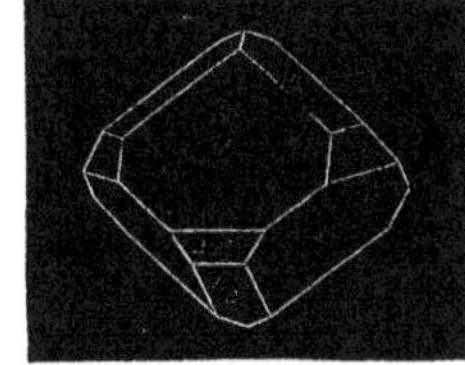
Fig. 60.

Fig. 60 represents a combination of the principal rhombohedron r,

$$\tfrac{1}{2}(a : a' : \infty a : c),$$

with its first obtuse rhombohedron $\frac{r'}{2}$,

$$\tfrac{1}{2}(a' : a' : \infty a : \tfrac{1}{2}c),$$

and with its first acute rhombohedron $2r$,

$$\tfrac{1}{2}(a' : a' : \infty a : 2c),$$

the rhombohedron r predominating.

Fig. 61 represents the combination of the primitive rhombohedron,

$$\tfrac{1}{2}(a : a : \infty a : c),$$

with its second acute rhombohedron $4r$,

$$\tfrac{1}{2}(a : a : \infty a : 4c),$$

the rhombohedron $4r$ predominating.

Fig. 61.

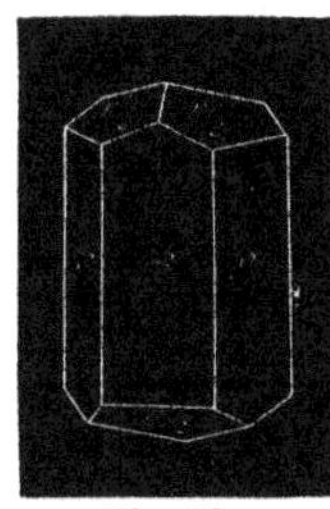
Fig. 62.

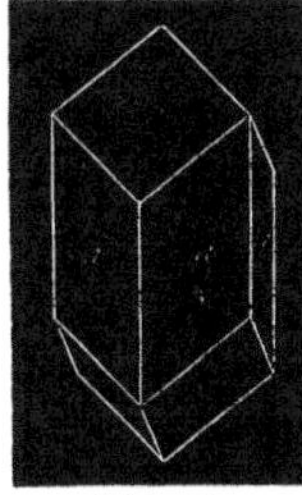
Fig. 63.

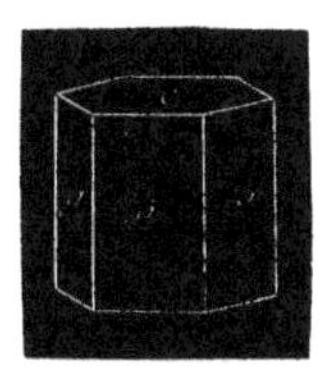
Fig. 64.

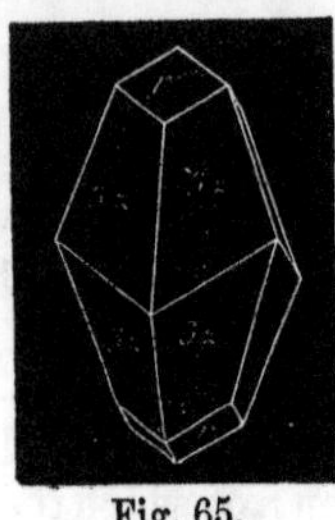
Fig. 65.

Fig. 62 represents a combination of the first 6-sided prism g with a rhombohedron $\frac{r'}{2}$, of the second class.

Fig. 63 represents a combination of the principal rhombohedron r with the second 6-sided prism a.

Fig. 64 shows a combination of the 6-sided prism g with the terminal face c.

Lastly, in fig. 65 is seen a combination of the scalenohedron $3z$, predominating,

$$\tfrac{1}{2}(a : \tfrac{1}{2}a : \tfrac{1}{3}a : c),$$

with the principal rhombohedron r.

IV.—FOURTH SYSTEM OF CRYSTALLIZATION.

§ 31. The forms of the fourth system of crystallization are distinguished by 3 rectangular axes, which are all unequal and of different kinds: it therefore follows, that the choice of the principal axis is entirely arbitrary. The relations of length between the 3 axes are indefinite, and in general are irrational.

The forms of this system are the following:

Simple Forms.—*Right Octahedrons with Rhombic Base* (fig. 66). The faces of these octahedrons are scalene triangles.

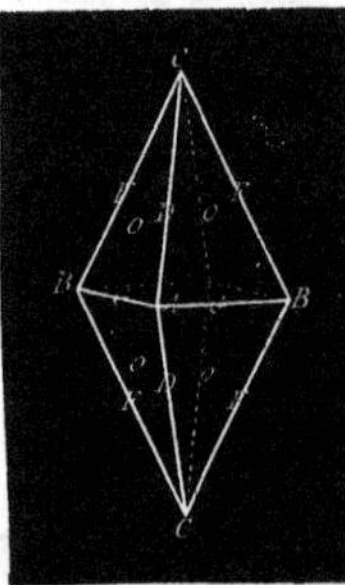
Fig. 66.

The edges are of three kinds: 4 terminal edges D, joining the extremities of the principal with those of the 1st secondary axis; 4 terminal edges F, joining the extremities of the principal with those of the 2d secondary axes; 4 lateral edges C, joining the extremities of the secondary axes.

The angles are of three kinds: 2 terminal angles C, at the extremities of the principal axis; 2 lateral angles A, at the extremities of the 1st secondary axis; 2 lateral angles B, at the extremities of the 2d secondary axis.

Sections made through the terminal edges give rhombs (figs. 67 and 68): the same is true of the section passing through the lateral edges and giving the *base* (fig. 69).

When a substance assumes the form of several octahedrons with rhombic base, all these octahedrons maintain simple relations between the length of their axes.

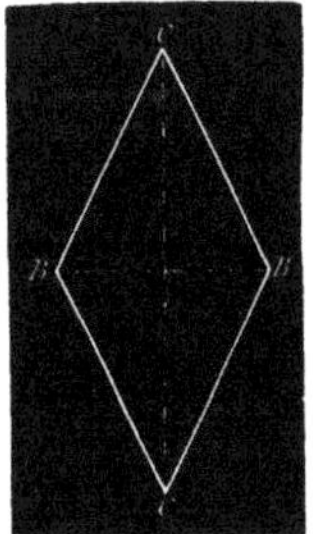
Fig. 67.

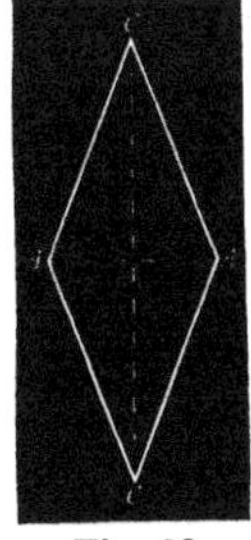
Fig. 68.

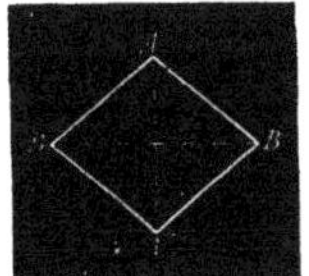
Fig. 69.

The formula of the primitive form is

$$(a : b : c).$$

The other octahedrons which may result from the same form, will then be expressed by

$$\begin{array}{l}(a : b : mc) \\ (a : mb : c) \\ (ma : b : c) \\ (ma : nb : c),\end{array}$$

m and n being very simple rational numbers.

The first three formulæ may be considered as particular cases of the fourth.

The number of octahedrons of the fourth system which *may* be presented in the same substance is therefore still greater than that of the second sytem. But, in reality, this number is *very limited*, and we rarely meet any octahedrons but those which have for formulas

$$\begin{array}{ll}(a : b : c) & \\ (a : b : \tfrac{1}{2}c) & (a : b : 2c) \\ (a : b : \tfrac{1}{4}c) & (a : b : 3c),\end{array}$$

and the extreme forms which are obtained by making m and $n = 0$, or *ad infinitum* in our general formulas.

By making m or $n = 0$, we reduce the octahedron to single faces, perpendicular to one of the axes of the crystal. We thus obtain:

1st. A face perpendicular to the principal axis, by making $c = 0$: the formula of this face should be, therefore, $(ma : nb : 0c)$: we generally give it the formula $(\infty a : \infty b : c)$, which supposes that it is derived from the octahedrons $(ma : nb : c)$ having the axis c, but of which the secondary axes have been produced to infinity.

2d. A face perpendicular to the 1st secondary axis, obtained by supposing $a=0$: the formula of this face should therefore be $(0a : mb : nc)$: it has the formula $(a : \infty b : \infty c)$: that is to say, it is supposed to be derived from the octahedrons $(a : mb : nc)$, having the secondary axis a, and the two axes b and c produced indefinitely.

3d. A face perpendicular to the 2d secondary axis, obtained by making $b=0$: the formula should be, $(ma : 0b : nc)$: it has the formula $(\infty a : b : \infty c)$, and is supposed to be the extreme face of the octahedrons having the axis b, and of which the axes a and c have been produced *ad infinitum.*

By making m or n equal to infinity in the general formula, we obtain three systems of prisms of which the edges are parallel to each of the three axes:

1st. The first system comprises vertical prisms, of which the faces are parallel to the principal axis: their general formula is $(a : mb : \infty c)$: they have the same base as the octahedron from which they are derived. The formula of the vertical prism derived from the primitive octahedron is

$$(a : b : \infty c).$$

2d. The second system comprises horizontal prisms, of which the faces are parallel to the 1st secondary axis, and of which the general formula is $(a : \infty b : mc)$: the formula of the prism derived from the primitive octahedron is

$$(a : \infty b : c).$$

3d. The third system comprises horizontal prisms, of which the faces are parallel to the 2d secondary axis: their general formula will be $(\infty a : mb : c)$, and that of the prism derived from the primitive octahedron is

$$(\infty a : b : c).$$

§ 32. Compound Forms.—The principal compound forms of this system are the following:

(Fig. 70.) Combination of the principal octahedron o with the more obtuse octahedron $\frac{o}{3}$, the terminal face c, and the second horizontal prism f of the principal octahedron.

(Fig. 71.) Combination of the principal octahedron o with its vertical prism g, and the vertical prism $\frac{g}{2}$.

(Fig. 72.) Combination of the principal octahedron o with its first horizontal prism d, and the vertical prism $\frac{g}{2}$.

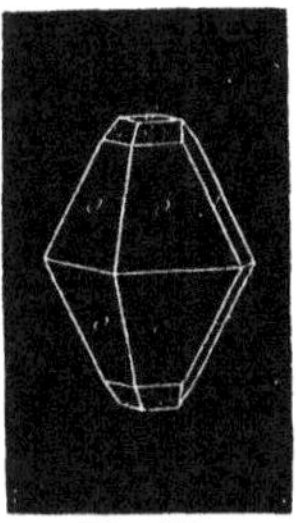
Fig. 70.

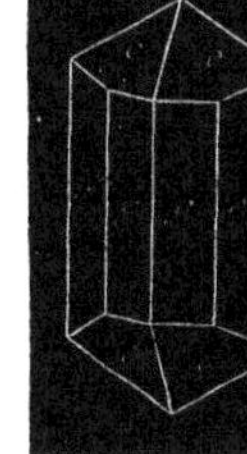
Fig. 71.

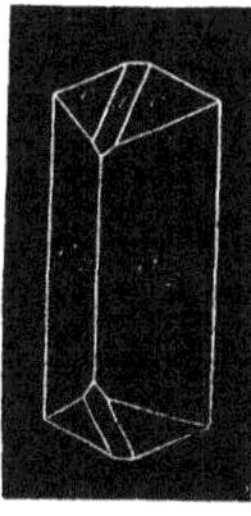
Fig. 72.

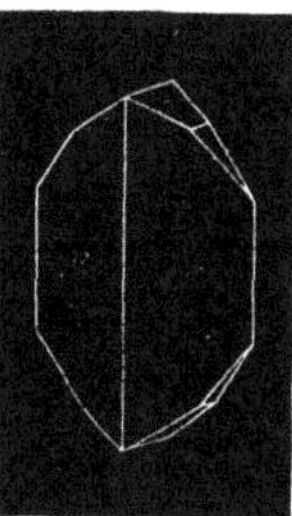
Fig. 73.

(Fig. 73.) Combination of the vertical prism *g* of the primitive form with the 2d horizontal prism *f* of the primitive form, and with a second more acute horizontal prism *2f*.

(Fig. 74.) Combination of the second horizontal prism *f* of the primitive form, the first horizontal prism $\frac{d}{2}$, and the right terminal face *c*.

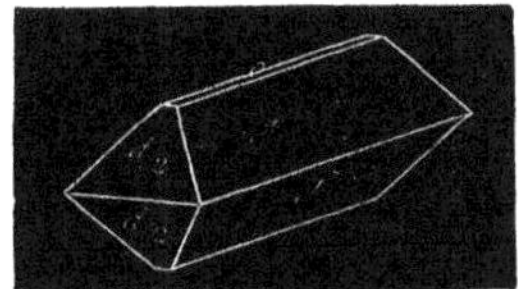
Fig. 74.

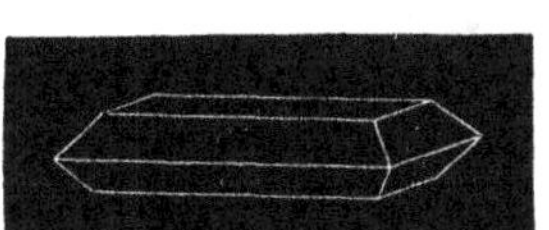
Fig. 75.

(Fig. 75.) The same combination, with the terminal face predominating.

(Fig. 76.) Combination of the 1st vertical prism *g* of the primitive form with the right terminal face *c*, the terminal face predominating.

(Fig. 77.) Combination of the vertical prism *g* of the primitive form, with the first horizontal prism $\frac{d}{2}$ and the terminal face *c*.

(Fig. 78.) Combination of the principal octahedron *o* with the lateral faces *a* and *b*.

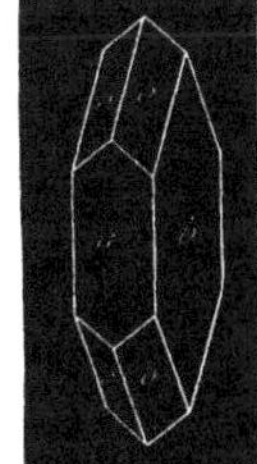

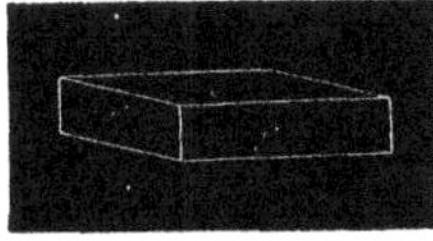

Fig. 76.

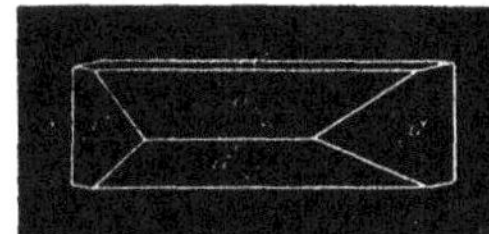
Fig. 77.

Fig. 78.

V.—FIFTH SYSTEM OF CRYSTALLIZATION.

§ 33. The fifth system of crystallization is characterized by 3 unequal axes, two of which are oblique to each other, and the third is perpendicular to the other two. The relations of length between these three axes are absolutely indefinite, and, in general, irrational. Any one of these axes may be chosen as the principal.*

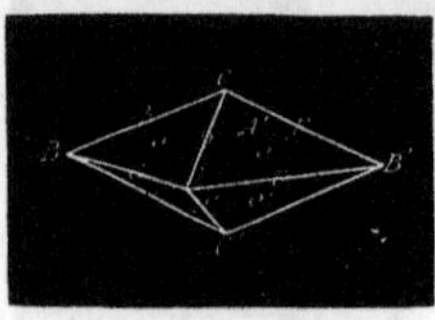

Fig. 79.

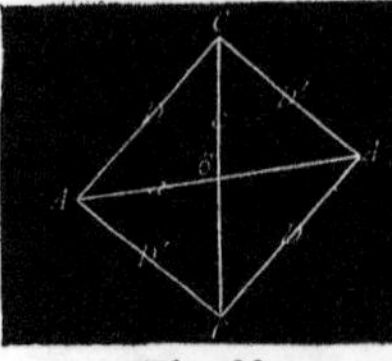

Fig. 80.

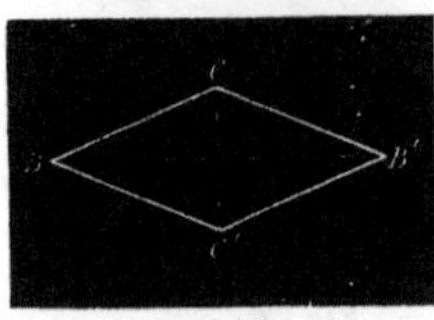

Fig. 81.

Fig. 79 represents an octahedron belonging to this system: one of the oblique axes is taken as the principal axis *c*. The faces are scalene triangles, but they are of two kinds.

The edges are of four kinds: 4 terminal edges, joining the axes *a* and *c*; the opposite axes alone being equal, on account of the obliquity of the axes; 4 terminal edges which join the axes *b* and c, and which are equal, because the two axes *b* and *c* are perpendicular to each other; lastly, 4 lateral edges which join the perpendicular axes *a* and *b*, and which, consequently, are equal to each other.

The section made by the edges D, D′ (fig. 80) is a parallelogram comprising the two oblique axes: it is called the *principal section*.

The section made by the lateral edges give the *base* of the octahedron, which is a rhomb (fig. 81).

In order to perfectly define the octahedron, it is no longer enough to give the length of the three axes: we must also assign the value of the angle δ formed by the oblique axes *b* and *c*.

The octahedron of the fifth system has not all its faces similar; therefore it is not, strictly speaking, a *simple form*. It may be considered as a combination of two oblique prisms, of which the first is formed by the faces BAC, CAB′, BA′C′, and C′A′B′, and the second by the faces BCA′, CA′B′, BAC′, and CA′B′. We may distinguish these two prisms by calling the first *the anterior oblique prism of the octahedron*, and the second, *the posterior oblique prism of the octahedron*. This distinction is necessary, for it frequently happens that, in the compound forms of this system, the octahedrons do not appear entire, but exhibit only one of their oblique prisms; at other times, one of these prisms predominates greatly over the other.

The value of the axes, *a*, *b*, *c* being susceptible of infinite variety, as well as the angle δ of the two oblique axes, it is evident that the fifth system will comprise an infinity of different octahe-

* Properly speaking, the choice of a principal axis is limited to one of the two oblique axes, between which the choice is somewhat arbitrary.—*J. C. B.*

drons. But when one and the same substance presents, in its crystalline form, several octahedrons of the fifth system, it will be found that, in all these octahedrons, the angle δ is the *same*, and that the lengths of the axes a, b, c of one of these octahedrons, always present *commensurable*, and, in general, *very simple relations* with the lengths of the corresponding axes of all the others. So that, if we select one of these octahedrons as a term of comparison, and assign it the formula $(a : b : c)$, all the octahedrons of the same substance will be comprised in the general formula

$$(ma : nb : pc),$$

the quantities m, n, p, being rational numbers, commensurable, and generally very simple, as 2, 3, 4, or $\frac{1}{2}$, $\frac{1}{3}$, $\frac{1}{4}$, &c.

The forms most frequently met with in this system are the extreme forms obtained by successively making $m = \infty$, $n = \infty$, $p = \infty$, or by substituting, successively, $m = 0$, $n = 0$, $p = 0$, in the general formula.

By making $p = \infty$, we obtain vertical prisms, parallel to the principal axis c, and of which the general formula is

$$(a : mb : \infty c),$$

the formula of the principal prism will be

$$(a : b : \infty c).$$

By supposing $n = \infty$, we obtain horizontal prisms, parallel to the 2d secondary axis b, and of which the general formula is

$$(a : \infty b : mc),$$

that of the principal horizontal prism being

$$(a : \infty b : c).$$

Lastly, by making $m = \infty$, we have oblique prisms parallel to the secondary axis a, and of which the general formula is

$$(\infty a : b : mc),$$

the formula of the principal oblique prism being

$$(\infty a : b : c).$$

$p = 0$ gives a terminal face parallel to the axes a and b, to which we may assign the formula $(ma : nb : 0c)$: but we generally write the formula $(\infty a : \infty b : c)$, which supposes this face to be the extreme of the octahedrons $(ma : nb : c)$ having the principal axis c, but of which the secondary axes have been produced to infinity.

$n = 0$ gives a terminal face parallel to the axes a and c, of which the formula would be $(ma : 0b : pc)$: we generally assign to it the formula $(\infty a : b : \infty c)$: this face is then considered as the extreme of the octahedrons $(ma : b : pc)$ having the secondary b, and of which the axes ma and pc have become infinite.

Lastly, $m=0$ gives a terminal face parallel to the axes b and c, of which the formula would be $(0a : nb : pc)$; but to which we ordinarily give the formula $(a : \infty b : \infty c)$, because it is supposed to be derived from the octahedrons $(a : nb : pc)$ which have the secondary axis a, and of which the axes nb and pc have been produced *ad infinitum.*

§ 34. The following are the most simple compound forms met with in this system:

Fig. 82 represents a combination of the perfect primitive octahedron o, o' $(a : b : c)$ with the principal vertical prism g $(a : b \infty c)$.

Fig. 83 is a combination of the perfect principal octahedron o, o' $(a : b : c)$ with the principal vertical prism g $(a : b : \infty c)$, and with the terminal faces b $(\infty a : b : \infty c)$ parallel to the axes a and c.

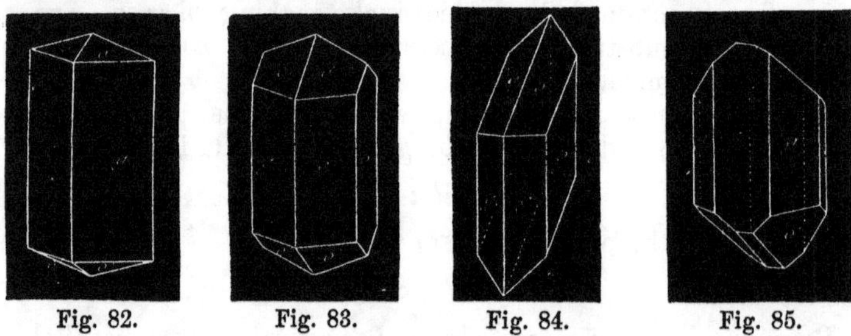

Fig. 82. Fig. 83. Fig. 84. Fig. 85.

Fig. 84 presents a combination of the anterior oblique prism o, o' of the principal octahedron $(a : b : c)$ with its vertical prism g $(a : b : \infty c)$, and with the terminal face b $(\infty a : b : \infty c)$.

Fig. 85 exhibits to us a combination into which enter the posterior oblique prism o' of the principal octahedron $(a : b : c)$, its principal vertical prism g $(a : b : \infty c)$, and the three systems of terminal faces parallel to the axes, namely, the terminal face b parallel to the axes a and c, of which the formula is $(\infty a : b : \infty c)$; the terminal face parallel to the axes b and c, and having for a formula $(a : \infty b : \infty c)$; and, lastly, one oblique face d.

VI.—SIXTH SYSTEM OF CRYSTALLIZATION.

§ 35. The forms of the sixth system of crystallization have 3 unequal axes, oblique, and bearing to each other indefinite relations: the choice of the principal axis is of no moment. It follows, from the inequality and obliquity of the axes, that the forms of this system have not symmetrical faces, and that the parallel faces alone are similar.

Fig. 86 represents an octahedron belonging to this system: the parallel faces alone are equal to each other, so that the faces are of four kinds.

The edges are of six kinds: the anterior terminal D is different

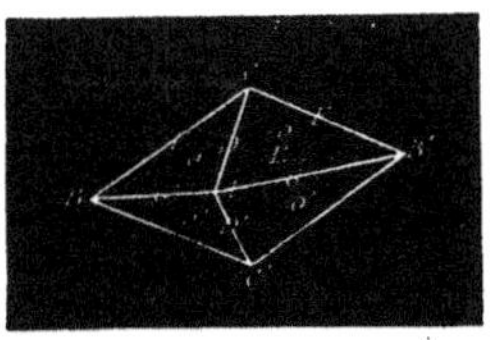

Fig. 86.

from the posterior edge D′: the right terminal F is different from the left terminal edge F′: the right lateral G is different from the left lateral edge G′.

The angles are of three kinds, and formed by unequal edges. Sections made through the terminal or lateral edges are parallelograms.

When the same substance presents several octahedrons, one is chosen as the primitive form: this takes then the formula $(a : b : c)$; but, in order to define it completely, we must assign the value of the angles α, β, γ, which the oblique axes form with each other.

If we then determine the axes of the other octahedrons of the same substance, we shall see that these axes always form with each other the *same angles* α, β, γ, and that their absolute lengths present *very simple* numerical ratios with those of the corresponding axes of the primitive octahedron; so that all these octahedrons may be represented by the formula

$$(ma : nb : pc),$$

m, n, and p being rational, and, in general, very simple numbers.

The octahedrons of this system present four different pairs of parallel faces: they may enter into combinations either by a single pair, or several at a time. It is therefore useful to distinguish each of these pairs by a particular formula. This will be easy, if we preserve the letters a, b, c for the semi-axes on which the positive co-ordinates in analytical geometry are calculated, and, on the contrary, the letters a', b', c' for the portions of the axes directed in the sense of the negative co-ordinates. We can thus represent,

The face A B′C and its parallel by $(a : b : c)$
A B C " " " $(a' : b : c)$
A′B C " " " $(a' : b' : c)$
A′B′C " " " $(a : b' : c)$.

The extreme forms of this system will be obtained by making, successively,

$$p = \infty,\quad n = \infty,\quad m = \infty,$$
$$\text{or,}\quad p = 0,\quad n = 0,\quad m = 0.$$

We will thus obtain three systems of prisms:

Vertical prisms of which the faces are parallel to the principal axis c;

Inclined or oblique prisms having their faces parallel to the axis b;

Inclined prisms having their faces parallel to the axis c, and three terminal faces parallel to each of the three systems of oblique axes taken two by two.

Crystals belonging to this system are often very complex and difficult of accurate definition, because, generally speaking, only one of the pairs of faces of the octahedrons and prisms composing them is visible.

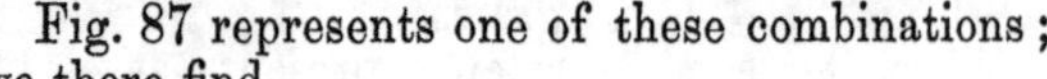

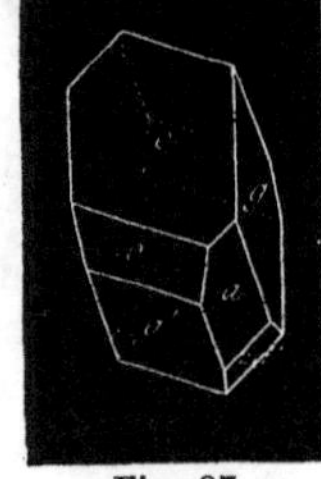

Fig. 87.

Fig. 87 represents one of these combinations; we there find,

1st. The left face of the principal octahedron o;

2d. The oblique terminal face $2d'$;

3d. The right and left faces of the vertical prism g and g' of the principal octahedron;

4th. The terminal face a parallel to the axes a and c;

5th. The terminal face c parallel to the axes a and b.

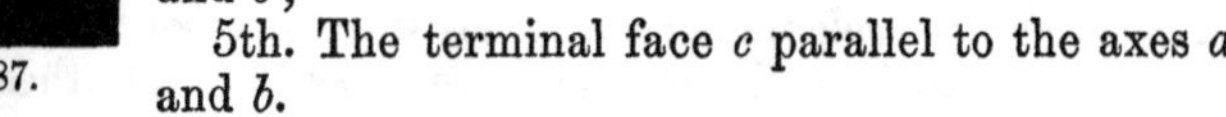

The sixth system of crystallization comprises much fewer crystallized substances than the five preceding systems. The forms of this system are easily recognised by their want of symmetry, but the exact definition of their faces is often very difficult.

HYPOTHESIS OF MOLECULAR DECREMENTS.

§ 35 *a.* The laws of symmetry which exist between all the crystalline forms of the same substance, are very easily explained by starting with certain hypotheses on the form of the crystalline molecules and their mode of grouping. It is useful to study, at this time, these hypotheses, not only because they give us, as it were, material explanation of these laws, but also because, under their guidance, Haüy discovered, by induction, the laws of crystallography, which he afterwards verified by measurement. Let us take a mineral substance, as galena, which crystallizes according to the regular system, and assumes many forms of this system. Let us, in the first case, examine a cubic crystal of galena (fig. 88). If we endeavour to fracture it by violence, or by applying a cutting edge, in various directions, we shall soon find that the crystal cleaves, very readily, in three directions parallel to the faces of the cube, whilst it resists all others. The fragments thus detached from the cubic crystal, as well as the remaining nucleus, have all the forms of rectangular parallelopipedons. This mechanical division may be carried very far, for the little fragments may be further divided, and the microscope will show the most minute dust to be composed of rect-

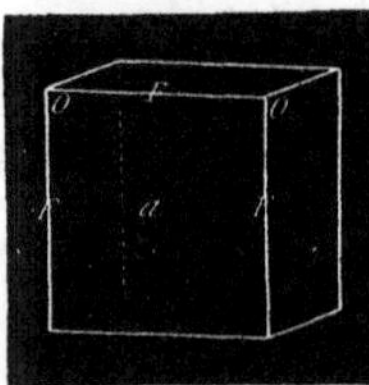

Fig. 88.

tangular parallelopipedons. We are naturally led, by induction, to infer that the ultimate crystalline particles, that is, those which resist cleavage, will affect the same form. These particles are therefore called *integral crystalline molecules*, each one of which is formed of a great number of chemical molecules, separable, perchance, by other mechanical means, and grouped together by means of forces hitherto unexplained.

Let us now take an octahedral crystal of galena (fig. 89). If we endeavour to cleave it in a direction parallel to its faces, we shall not succeed. We obtain, on the contrary, a very ready cleavage in the direction of planes equally inclined toward the 4 faces comprising the solid angles of the octahedron. By effecting these successive cleavages at all the solid angles, we shall soon destroy its octahedral form and obtain a nucleus in the form of a rectangular parallelopipedon, which continued cleavage will diminish, but not alter its cubical form. We therefore conclude that the crystalline molecules of the octahedric crystal, as well as those of the cubic crystals, are small rectangular parallelopipedons.

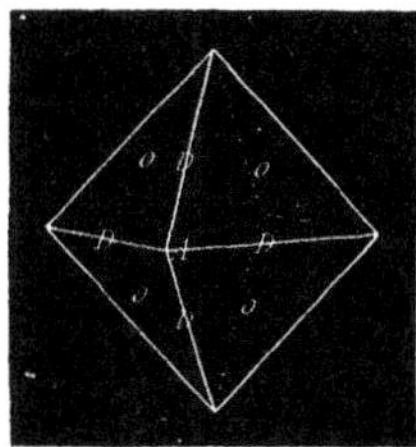

Fig. 89.

Let us select, in the last place, a crystal of galena presenting the form of a rhombic dodecahedron (fig. 90). We shall again find that this crystal does not cleave in a direction parallel to its faces. The only natural cleavages are in the direction of planes equally inclined toward the faces of the 4-sided solid angles A. If we effect successive cleavages on the six 4-sided solid angles, we shall destroy the faces of the dodecahedron, and obtain nuclei having the form of rectangular parallolopipedons, resembling in appearance and the physical properties of their faces the nuclei we obtained from the cubic and octahedric crystals. We are therefore led to conclude that the crystalline molecules composing the dodecahedric crystal have the same form of rectangular parallelopipedons as those of cubic and octahedric crystals.

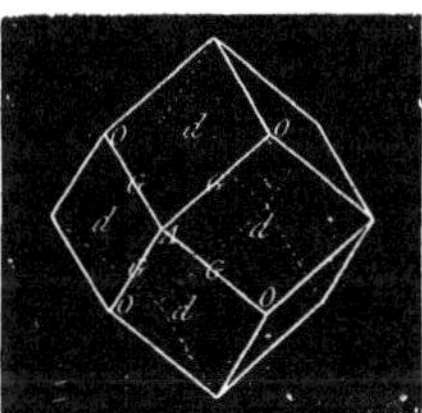

Fig. 90.

But, what is the ratio of the lengths of the sides of this primitive parallelopipedon? We will observe that the three directions of cleavage which lead to this parallelopipedon present no feature distinguishing them from each other: they are equally easy, and the faces they produce have the same lustre. We are therefore induced to admit that the three dimensions of the parallelopipedon are equal, and that it is consequently a cube. The crystalline particles of galena are therefore cubes, and, if induction has not deceived us, we can reproduce, by the juxtaposition of these small elementary cubes, the cube, the octahedron, the rhombic dodecahedron, and, in short, all the crystalline forms of galena. We are about to show that this can be readily effected.

In order to render the fact more apparent, we shall greatly exaggerate the dimensions of the small elementary cubes. This we may do without invalidating the accuracy of the demonstration, for we only consider the tangent planes, the directions of which remain the same, whatever may be the dimensions of the integral crystalline molecules, provided that their forms and mode of grouping be the same. The cubic crystal will be directly formed by the juxtaposition of the elementary cubes. Let us place, on the several faces of the cube *a*, *b*, *c*, *d*, *e*, *f* (fig. 91), strata of cubic

Fig. 91.

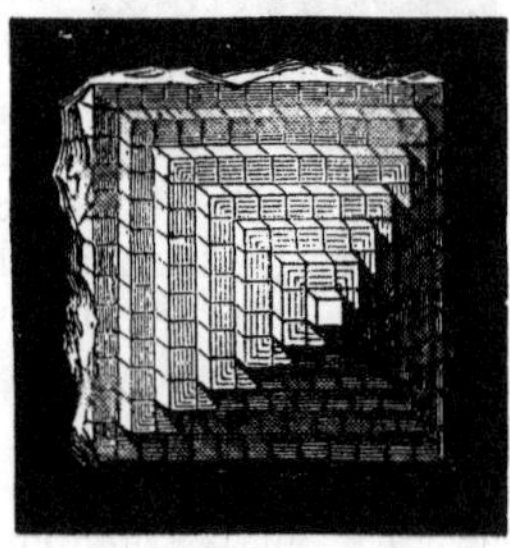
Fig. 91 *a*.

molecules, arranged as they are in the cubic crystal itself; but suppressing, in each stratum, a row parallel to each side of the face of the cube, so that each new stratum shall contain, on each side, one row less than the preceding. It will be readily seen that we thus obtain the rhombic dodecahedron (fig. 90). Fig. 91 proves this fact: in order not to complicate this figure and destroy its general aspect, we have suppressed the lines which mark the separation of the juxtaposed elementary cubes; but we have indicated them on fig. 91 *a*, which represents, on a greater scale, one of the solid angles of the new formation.

By supposing the cubic molecules to be infinitely small, the asperities arising from the subtraction of the rows will disappear, and the faces of the dodecahedron will become perfectly plane. We may therefore say, that *the rhombic dodecahedron is derived from a cube by the decrement, on the faces of the cube, of a row in length and a row in height.*

Let us now suppose that from each new stratum we remove 2, 3, or 4 rows of elementary particles: it is evident that we shall produce, on each face of the cube, 4-sided pyramids, of which the elevations will be $\frac{1}{2}$, $\frac{1}{3}$, or $\frac{1}{4}$ of the axis of the cube, and that we shall obtain the various tetrahedrons (fig. 25) mentioned in § 25.

We shall thus have effected *a decrement of* 1 *row in height, and* 2, 3, *or* 4 *rows in length.*

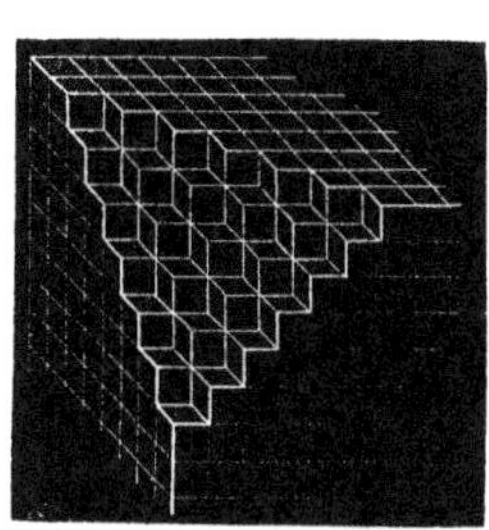

Fig. 92.

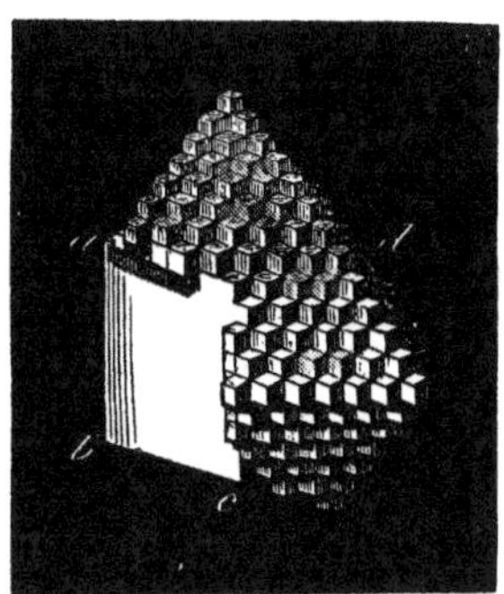

Fig. 93.

Let us now take a large cubic crystal (fig. 92), and, starting from the centre of one of its edges, and symmetrically as regards its conformation, remove a molecule from the first upper stratum, 2 from the second, 3 from the third, we shall obtain a tangent truncation of the solid angle of the cube. Repeating the process on each of the angles, we shall have a regular octahedron (fig. 93) formed by the *decrement of a row in length, and a row in height on the angles of the cube.*

Let us now return to our cube *a, b, c, d, e, f* (fig. 94), and add to its faces additional strata of cubic molecules: but let us make, following the edge *f, e*, a decrement of 2 rows in length and 1 in height, and, following the edge *f, d*, a decrement of 1 row in length and 2 in height, we shall obtain the pentagonal dodecahedron (fig. 94). We have omitted in this figure the lines of separation

Fig. 94.

Fig. 94 *a.*

of the small elementary cubes; but these lines are seen in the fig. 94 *a*, which represents, on a larger scale, the anterior portion of fig. 94. The pentagonal dodecahedron is a hemihedral form, a *hemi-tetrahexahedron* (§ 25): the other hemihedral forms of the regular system are obtained in the same manner, by unsymmetrical decrements on similar edges.

It will be easily seen, without multiplying examples, that we can reproduce, by analogous additions or subtractions, all the figures of the regular system.

§ 35 *b*. It can be shown that all the forms of the second system of crystallization may be constructed with crystalline molecules having the figure of a right parallelopipedon, with a square base, but of which the elevation is not equal to the length of the sides of the base; the ratio between this elevation and the sides of the base being always identical in the same substance, but differing in different substances.

Let us take a crystal having the form of a right prism with a square base, and add to its base strata of crystalline molecules, with a decrement of a row in length and a row in height in the direction of the sides of the base: we shall obtain a square-based pyramid, of which the elevation will present, to the sides of the base, the same ratio as the homologous lengths of the crystalline molecule. Treating the inferior base of the prism in the same manner, we shall obtain a right square-based prism, terminated by two pointings, which, united by their bases, form a square-based octahedron. Assuming this octahedron as the primitive octahedron of the substance, its dimensions will immediately indicate those of the integral crystalline molecule.

We may construct on the same base other 4-sided pyramids, by making decrements of 1 row in length, and 2, 3, or 4 rows in height. We shall thus have octahedrons with square bases, more and more acute, of which the elevations will be 2, 3, or 4 times as great as that of the primitive octahedron. If, on the contrary, we make a decrement of only 1 row in height, and 2, 3, or 4 in length, we shall obtain octahedrons more and more obtuse, of which the elevations will be $\frac{1}{2}$, $\frac{1}{3}$, or $\frac{1}{4}$ of that of the primitive octahedron. We can therefore construct, with the same integral molecule, an indefinite series of obtuse and acute octahedrons of the same class, but which will all possess this property, that, when referred to the same base, their elevations will be to each other as the very simple numbers $1 : 2 : 3 : 4 \ldots$ or $1 : \frac{1}{2} : \frac{1}{3} : \frac{1}{4} \ldots$

Let us now return to our right prism with a square base. Starting from a point in one of its vertical edges, and symmetrically as regards this edge, let us subtract 1 row from the first stratum, 2 from the second, 3 from the third, and so on; in short, let us operate on this prism, as we did upon the cube to obtain the regular octahedron. We shall thus obtain an octahedron which will be the octahedron of the second class of the primitive octahedron, and of which the faces will have the direction of the edges of the latter. By subtracting a row in length and 2, 3, or 4 rows in height, we shall have the series of acute octahedrons of the second class. Lastly, we will obtain a series of obtuse octahedrons of the second class, by subtracting 1 row in height and 2, 3, or 4 rows in length.

§ 35 *c*. A similar mode of generation is applicable to the hexagonal and the most complex systems of crystallization. In the entire, or *holohedral* forms, of the hexagonal system, we must take the regular 6-sided prism as the integral crystalline molecule. By means of this same prism, we can, by suppressing the decrements according to a certain law, construct the hemihedral forms of the same system. It is, perhaps, more easy to consider these last forms as constituted by integral molecules, hemihedral themselves, and having, for example, the form of the primitive rhombohedron. We shall merely show how scalenohedrons may be derived, in this manner, from the primitive rhombohedron having the same lateral edges. Fig. 95 represents this mode of generation of the scalenohedron (fig. 57) of carbonate of lime: this scalenohedron has a principal axis treble of that of the primitive rhombohedron having the same lateral edges, and is frequently found in this substance. It is enough to place, on each face of the primitive rhombohedron *abcde*, strata of molecules similar in form to this rhombohedron, by effecting

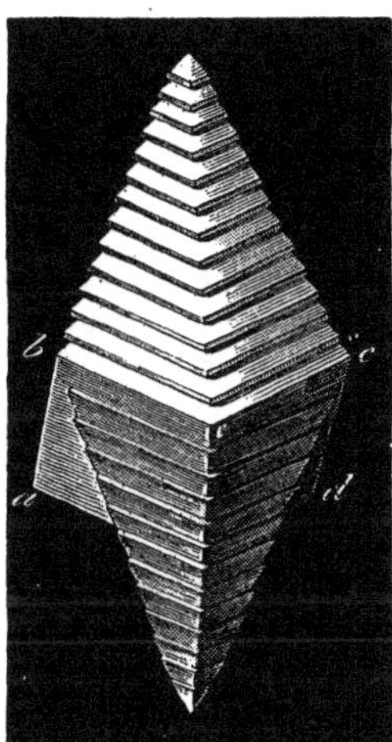

Fig. 95.

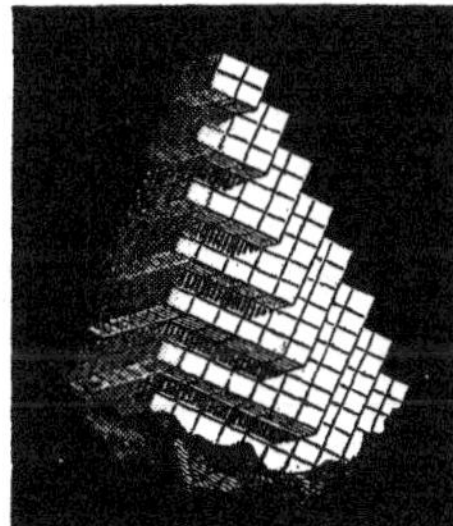
Fig. 95 *a*.

on its lateral edges a decrement of 2 rows in breadth and 1 row in height. The lines of separation of the elementary rhombohedrons are not seen in fig. 95, but they are clearly exhibited in fig. 95 *a*, which shows, on a larger scale, the upper courses of fig. 95.

If we effect a decrement of 1 row in breadth and 1 in height, we should obtain a scalenohedron which, with the same secondary axes, would have a principal axis double of that of the primitive rhombohedron.

§ 35 *d*. In the fourth, fifth, and sixth systems of crystallization, the integral molecule will be a parallelopipedon, of which the elements may be determined from those of the octahedron chosen as the principal. At one time, the small generating solids will be the integral molecule itself; at others, they will be formed by definite aggregation of these molecules. Fig. 96 is an example of the angular decrement of one of the complex generating solids *abcdefg*. The faces thus formed, either on the edges or on the angles, will have different inclinations, which may be indefinitely varied, by varying the mode of composition of the generative solids themselves: but all these faces will present this common character, that the lengths included by them on the homologous axes will be proportional to whole numbers. This is the general law proved by observation, and to which we have already frequently referred.

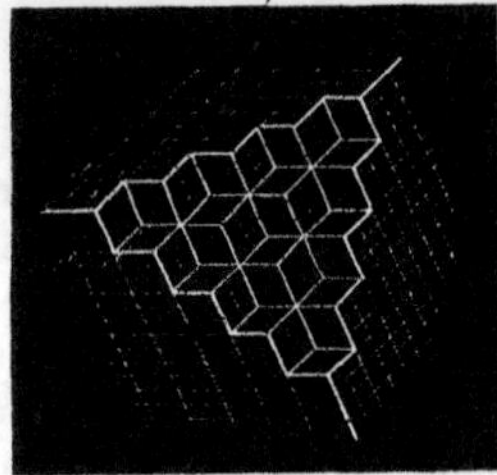

Fig. 96.

DESCRIPTION OF CRYSTALS.

§ 36. We shall now proceed to consider the methods by which we can describe accurately the form of a given crystal. An attentive examination of the crystal and of the symmetry of its modifications will generally show to what system of crystallization it belongs. This superficial description is sufficient when the crystal belongs to the regular system, and it only remains to indicate the simple forms which enter into its composition. This is, however, not the case in all the other systems. It is not enough, then, to indicate the names of the simple forms composing the crystal: it is necessary to give exactly the ratio of the length of the axes of each of the simple forms constituting the crystal, as well as the value of the angles formed by these axes, when they are not rectangles.

The angles of the axes and their ratio of length cannot be measured directly upon the crystal. The only element which admits of direct measurement is the inclination of the various faces to each other. But it is evident that the angles of the axes and their relations of length have an immediate geometrical ratio with the various inclinations of the faces, and that, when the latter are known, the determination of the angles of the axes and their relative lengths becomes a simple problem of geometry.

The limits of this work will not permit us to explain the mode of calculation employed to obtain this result. This calculation is very simple in the rectangular, but somewhat complicated in the oblique system. We would refer the student who is curious in these matters, to the *Treatise on Mineralogy* of M. Dufrénoy, or to the *Crystallography* of M. Miller, translated by M. de Sénarmont,[1] in which he will find the general formulæ which are applied to this calculation, and are remarkable for their great symmetry and ready application to all cases which may occur.

It is not always necessary, in order to accurately define a crystal, to know all its dihedral angles. It is often sufficient to have the value of a few of these angles, for example, when the crystal belongs to one of the most simple of the systems of crystallization. But it is advisable, in all cases, to measure as great a number of angles as possible. When several of these angles are not necessary to the determination of the elements of the crystal, they may be used to verify and correct these elements; all the angles of a crystal presenting, necessarily, geometrical relations to the lengths and directions of its axes.

The chemist who wishes to exactly define a crystal should, therefore, measure all its dihedral angles with the greatest accuracy, noting their value, and the angles. By means of these data, it will be always easy to subsequently determine the elements of the crystal; that is to say, the inclination of the axes, and their relative lengths.

The essential operation, therefore, in determining the nature of a crystal, is the measurement of the inclination of its faces to each other. For this we use instruments called *goniometers*, which are of two kinds,—the *common*, called also *Haüy's goniometer*, and the *reflective goniometer of Wollaston*.

The common goniometer (fig. 97) is composed of a semicircle graduated to degrees, to which are adapted two metallic arms: one of these arms, *ab*, is fixed to the zero of the graduation; the other, *df*, is movable, and marks on the arc the angle of the crystal. In order to measure a dihedral angle, we apply one of its faces to the fixed arm *ab*, in its prolongation, so that the edge of the angle shall be perpendicular to the plane of the arc: the other arm is then moved until its prolongation rests on the other face of the crystal: the angle included between the two arms, and which is seen on the arc, is the angle sought.

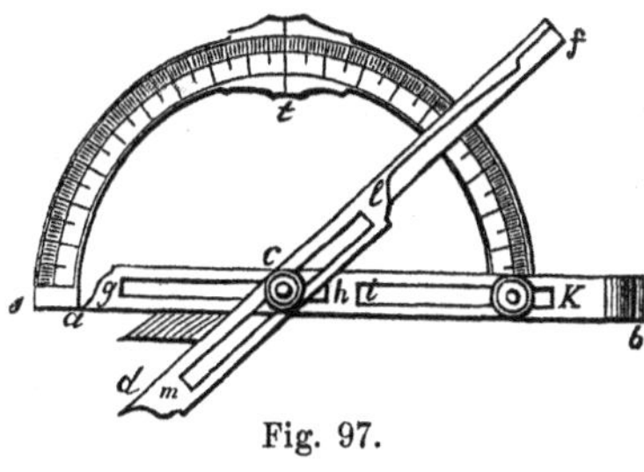

Fig. 97.

The two arms, *ab*, *df*, move in the slits *iK*, *gh*, *lm*, thus allowing us to shorten the branches *ca* and *cd* at pleasure. This is absolutely necessary, for it is sometimes requisite to measure very small crystals, which can only be introduced between the two arms when their branches are very much shortened.

[1] Or to the *System of Mineralogy*, etc., by James D. Dana, A.M. New York, 1850.—*T. F. B.*

This goniometer can give only approximated values; and is then applied with great difficulty to artificial crystals, because the latter, possessing generally but little hardness, are scratched or otherwise injured by the slightest pressure.

The reflective goniometer gives much more accurate results, but is applicable only to crystals possessing a certain degree of lustre. A great number of these goniometers have been constructed: we shall describe that most generally used, and known by the name of *Wollaston's goniometer.*

This instrument (fig. 98) is composed of a vertical arc LL′ graduated on its edge, and of which the horizontal axis is supported by a frame *pqr*. This arc is moved by the wheel *v*. A vernier *uw*, fastened to the extremity of an arm firmly fixed to the frame *pq*, indicates the angle to which the arc has revolved.

Fig. 98.

The axis of the arc is hollow, and is traversed by an inner movable axis *ac*, which is made to turn by means of the wheel *s*. At the extremity *c* of the axis *ac*, is fastened an articulated plate *cgeb*, which supports the crystal *z*. This plate, which is capable of several movements, greatly facilitating the disposition of the crystal, is composed of a semicircle *cge*, jointed at *g*, having at its extremity a hollow cylinder *ef*, split so as to form a spring. This cylinder is traversed by a rod, *bd*, which is turned by the button *b*. The rod *bd* is split at *d*, and into this fissure is introduced a small sheet of brass, to which the crystal is fastened with a little soft wax. The crystal being thus placed on the inner movable axis *ac*, by means of the wheel *s* we can turn it without moving the arc, or turn it simultaneously with the arc, by moving the wheel *v*. The movable parts of the support *cgebd* enable us, without touching the crystal, to approximate it to or remove it from the arc, and to give it various inclinations. This mobility is necessary, for we shall see that it is essential, in order to measure a dihedral crystal, to be able to place the edge of the angle in a direction strictly parallel to the axis of rotation of the arc.

This being done, the instrument is placed upon a table, in front of a house having several well-defined horizontal lines, of which two are chosen as levels. The upper edge of a roof standing out in relief from the sky, answers perfectly for the superior level. The horizontal bar of a window is generally selected for the inferior level.

In the first place, the arc is to be perfectly vertical: this is effected by means of the screws *x*, *x*, *x*, which support the base of the instrument, and an air level. At the same time, the arc is so directed as to be perpendicular to the plane of the house, and, consequently, to the two horizontal lines selected as levels. Then only should the crystal be fixed to the plate, and it is to be placed directly so that the edge of the angle to be measured shall be nearly perpendicular to the plane of the arc. This perpendicularity must afterward be made exact. For this purpose we place the eye very near the crystal, and in such a position as to bring the lower level in the direction of the crystal. The direction of this image reflected should be exactly parallel to the inferior level seen directly. If this condition is not fulfilled, the crystal is to be properly moved, which is easily done by means of the delicate movements of which the instrument is susceptible. One of the faces of the angle will be then perpendicular to the plane of the arc. The edge of the angle will itself be perpendicular to the arc, if the second face of the angle satisfies the same condition as the first. This may be ascertained by operating on the second face as on the first, the eye remaining fixed. Some manipulation is requisite to obtain the union of these two conditions; but a little practice soon renders it easy.

The crystal being properly placed, we proceed to measure the angle. For this purpose we bring the arc to zero of the vernier, by turning the wheel *v*; and, then by the wheel *s*, the crystal is brought into a position in which the eye sees the level reflected on one of its faces, superimposed on the second level seen directly. Then we turn, by the wheel *v*, the arc which necessarily carries in its movement the inner axis *ac*, and, consequently, the crystal, until the eye, which must remain exactly in the same position, sees the upper level reflected on the second face of the crystal, and coinciding with the lower level. The angle which the arc has described, and which is measured by means of the fixed vernier *uw*, is the supplement of the angle of the crystal.

In fact, supposing that *abc* (fig. 99) be the position of our dihedral angle, when the eye, O, of the observer sees the reflection of the

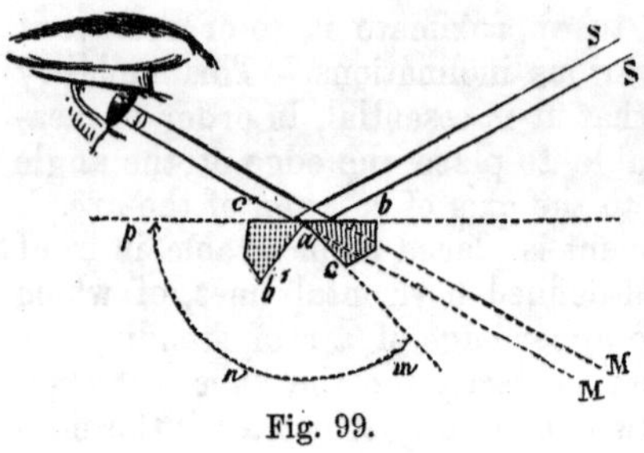

Fig. 99.

upper level S on the face *ab* of the crystal, coinciding with the lower level, M, seen directly, it is evident that, in order that the eye should perceive the same effect on the second face, *ac*, of the angle, the dihedral angle must assume the position *ac'b'*, that is, must describe on the face *ac* the arc *mnp*, which is precisely the supplement of the angle sought.

The reflective goniometer will enable us to measure the angles of a crystal within a few minutes, when the faces of the crystal are perfectly polished. The most essential condition, after the suitable disposition of the crystal, is to keep the eye fixed, if the levels are not at considerable distances. The improvement of this instrument has been attempted by adapting to it a glass provided with a reticula, which should give to the visual ray an invariable direction, and which dispenses with the second level. The focus of the glass should be regulated so as to see clearly the upper level, when the glass is directed toward this level. But this arrangement is of use only when crystals have a high reflecting power, which, unfortunately, is but seldom the case. Some crystals even have a reflecting power so imperfect, that we cannot take for the upper level the edge of a distant roof. In this case, we stand before an open window, of which the upper edge is relieved by the sky, and this edge is assumed as the superior level. A black line, drawn on a sheet of paper fastened to the table which supports the goniometer, may be taken as the inferior level, or even a white thread stretched over this table blackened: we must ascertain that these lines are precisely parallel to the edge of the window.

In some crystals this new arrangement does not suffice, because their faces reflect but slightly. We can sometimes succeed in measuring angles, though with less precision, in a darkened room. We assume as the superior level the light of a wax candle, placed at a certain height, and at some distance from the goniometer; and, for the inferior level, a black line drawn on paper, illuminated by a lamp arranged for this purpose behind the observer. When, during the slow movement of the crystal, the light of the candle, imperfectly reflected by the faces of the crystal, penetrates the eye, it gives the sensation of a flash of lightning, enabling us to make our observations. The height of the plane can also be regulated by a screen. We thus diminish the errors which arise from the angle, always of some extent, under which the observer perceives the height of the flame, when this is not very distant.

Lastly, we can use the reflective goniometer for crystals which do not reflect well, but of which the faces are sufficiently plane, by pasting, either with water or spirits of turpentine, according to the nature of the crystal, small laminæ of mica on those faces.

If this latter method does not answer, we must resort to the common goniometer.

OF THE IMPERFECTIONS OF NATURAL OR ARTIFICAL CRYSTALS.

§ 37. The crystalline forms we have just studied are all perfect and regular: similar perfection is rare in natural crystals or in those obtained in our laboratories. Most generally, crystals are not completely terminated: one of their extremities is imbedded and lost in other crystalline substances. Very often, also, certain faces of the same simple form are much more developed than the others, and the latter appear to have been produced under circumstances which prevented their natural growth.

This inequality in the development of the several faces of the same crystalline form, often changes its general appearance to such a degree as to require some practice in order to recognising its true aspect, especially when it belongs to one of the last crystalline forms. But, amid all the anomalous extensions of the faces, the respective directions remain constantly the same; and if we measure carefully the several angles of the crystal, we can easily construct on paper the regular figure, or the *type* which corresponds to the imperfect crystal. It will suffice, whilst preserving to the various faces of the crystal the directions which have been obtained by the measurement of the angles, to place all the faces of the same kind at equal distances from the centre of the crystal.

We shall give some examples of irregular crystallization; they are to be found in all the systems, even in the regular.

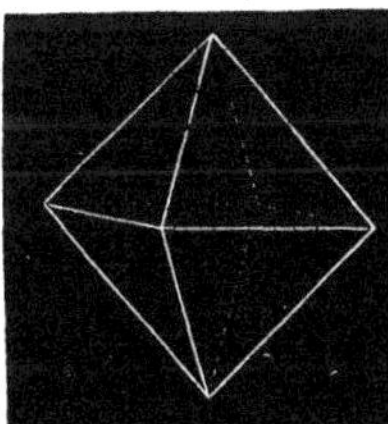

Fig. 100.

The perfect and ordinary form of alum is the regular octahedron (fig. 100); but alum assumes this perfect form only in the same crystals found in the middle of a solution, as, for example, those which are formed at the extremity of a very fine thread suspended in the liquid. Sometimes, also, a very small perfectly regular crystal is formed on one of the faces of a larger one, and is attached to it by an edge or by an angle.

The crystals developed on the sides of the vessel are always dovetailed into each other, and only exhibit some or a portion of their faces free. Fig. 101 gives us an idea of this disposition, and is the exact copy of a mass of alum taken from one of the large tubs used for crystallizing the alum employed in the arts.

If a small regular crystal of alum be placed in a vessel filled with a cold saturated solution of this substance, it will successively increase, but it will assume a very different shape, according to

Fig. 101.

its position in the vessel. If the crystal be at the bottom of the vessel, and nearly on its axis, it grows regularly on all its faces, except that on which it rests. The crystal generally grows more in the horizontal than in the vertical direction, and presents a form analogous to that in fig. 102.

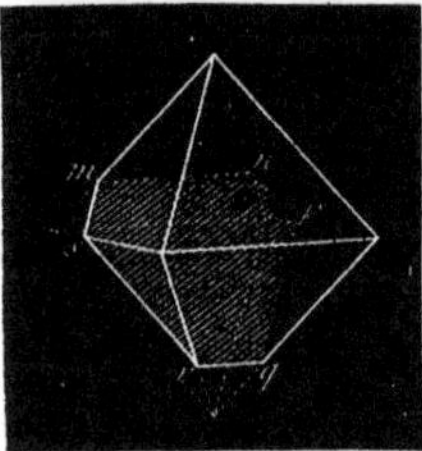

Fig. 102.

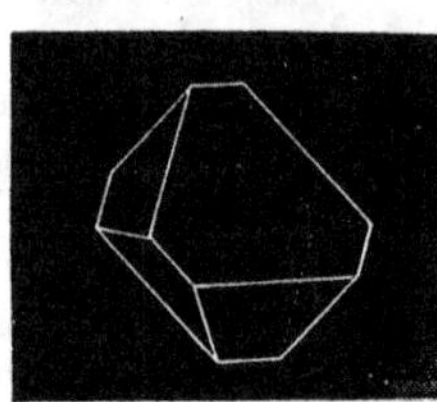

Fig. 103.

The rough surface *mnpqrs* is that which rested on the bottom of the vessel. This form is precisely that which we would have obtained by removing from a regular octahedron a stratum more or less thick, and parallel to one of its faces.

Sometimes, when the crystal takes the form of fig. 103, its increase perpendicularly to the horizontal faces is small, or at least much more feeble than in the other directions; and the two faces which were horizontal in the solution present similar forms.

When the crystal is placed on the bottom, and very near the sides of the vessel, its development is impeded in several directions, and its external configuration becomes more irregular.

We can, however, obtain very large and regularly developed artificial crystals of alum. To do this, we must place a small regular crystal at the bottom of a vessel containing a cold saturated solution of the substance, and turn it daily, so that it may rest on a new face. If it is made to rest alternately on each face, the crystal grows regularly, and may acquire great size without losing its primitive regularity. This regularity, however, is generally only apparent. A large crystal developed under these circumstances is rarely transparent. Its faces are always more or less undulated, and optical examination exhibits a host of internal imperfections.

The smallest crystals are generally the most perfect and best adapted to the measurement of their angles. The determination of their angles by means of Wallaston's goniometer is also more exact, because the slight variations of position which may occur to the observer's eye exert but little influence.

Fig. 104 represents a combination of the octahedron with the hexahedron, frequently found in sulphuret of lead or galena. This mineral often assumes, likewise, the configuration of fig. 105. Its external aspect, at first sight, would lead us to suppose that it belonged to the second system of crystallization; that is, to the system of octahedrons with a square base; but if we measure its dihedral angles, we shall soon find that the faces *o* belong to the regular octahedron. The difference between figs. 105 and 104 is, that in the former, the vertical faces of the hexahedron have become exceedingly developed.

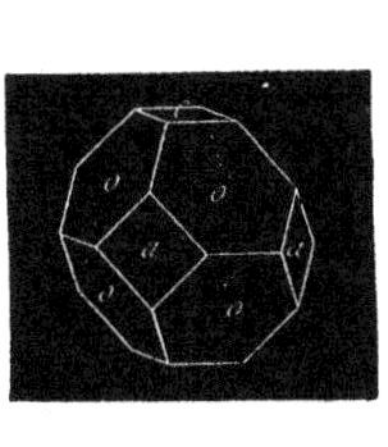

Fig. 104.

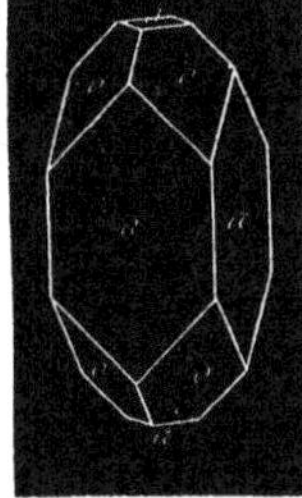

Fig. 105.

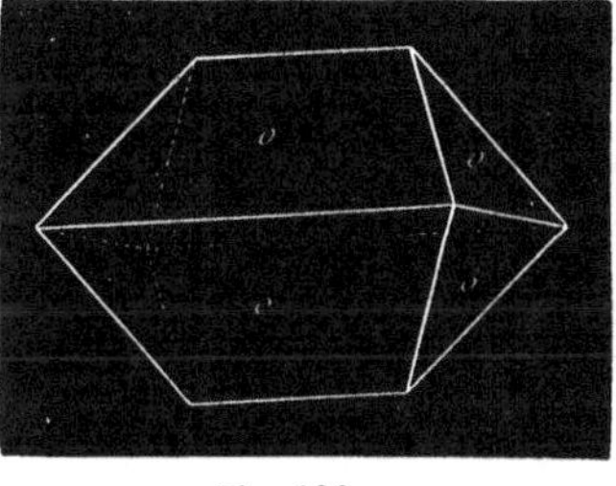

Fig. 106.

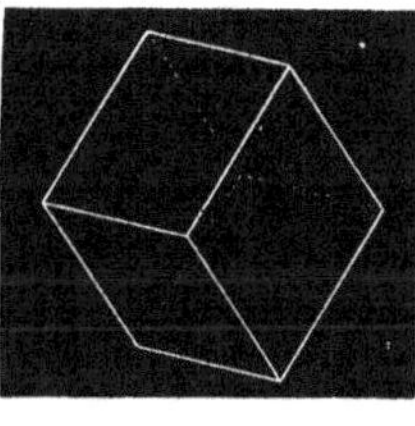

Fig. 107.

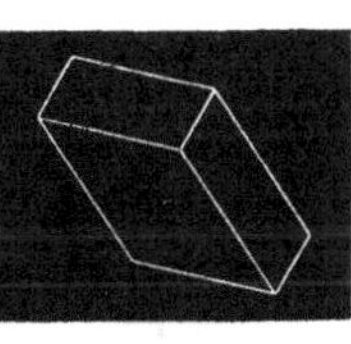

Fig. 108.

Substances which crystallize in regular octahedrons, sometimes appear in the form of fig. 106, which is called the *cuneiform octahedron.* It will be readily seen by the measurement of the angles, that the faces of this crystal belong to a regular octahedron: but 4 of the faces of this octahedron have assumed an anomalous development. In the third or hexagonal system of crystallization, we find many similar anomalies. Carbonate of lime crystallizes as a rhombohedron with an angle of 105° 5′ (fig. 107), and we have seen (§ 12) that this mineral cleaved with the greatest facility, in three directions parallel to the faces of the rhombohedron: we may thus obtain many fundamental forms (fig. 108) having always the same angles, but presenting very different aspects, as they will be more or less flattened. The direction of the principal axis of these rhombohedric fragments is always parallel to the line formed by the equal edges terminating in the same apex.

The ordinary form of quartz is a regular 6-sided prism terminated by a hexagonal dodecahedron. The dihedral angles of the prism are of 120°, and the dihedral angles of the two consecutive faces of the dodecahedron are of 133° 40′. Fig. 109 represents a perfect type of this form. Crystals of quartz, however, rarely exhibit this regularity.

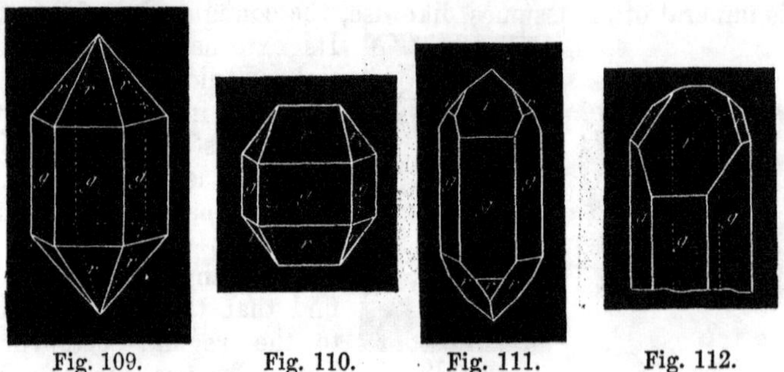

Fig. 109. Fig. 110. Fig. 111. Fig. 112.

Figs. 110, 111, and 112 represent some natural crystals of quartz. They are alterations of the type (fig. 109) produced by the anomalous development of certain faces during the process of crystallization. But, if we measure the angles of these various crystals, the dihedral angles of the faces of the vertical prism will always be found of 120°, and those of the consecutive faces of the pyramids will be of 133° 40′.

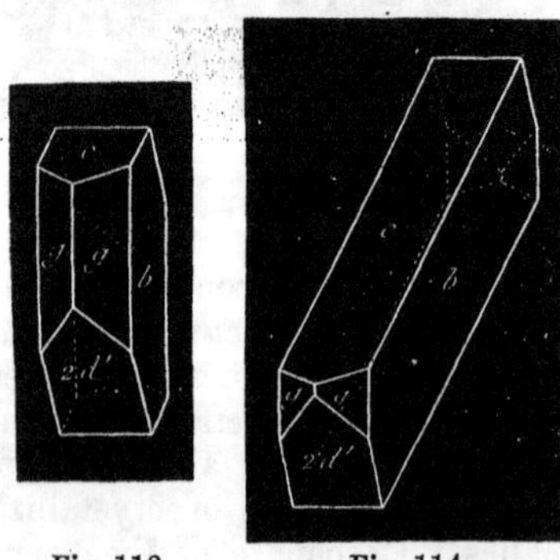

Fig. 113. Fig. 114.

Irregularities of the same kind are found in the most complex systems of crystallization, and sometimes change so entirely the aspect of the configuration, as to require great practice in order to recognise the nature of the different faces. Most frequently, we are obliged to measure the dihedral angles. Some idea may be conceived of the changes which the same form can undergo, from a comparison of figs. 113 and 114, which represent two crystals of feldspar belonging to the fifth system, which have exactly the same faces, but with very different developments.

GROUPING OF CRYSTALS: TRANSPOSITIONS AND HEMITROPISM.

§ 38. We have said that crystals never present re-entering angles, and that angles of this kind were formed only by the contact of two individual crystals. Sometimes this junction is symmetrical, and the groups of crystals then exhibit the regular configuration of figs. 115 and 116.

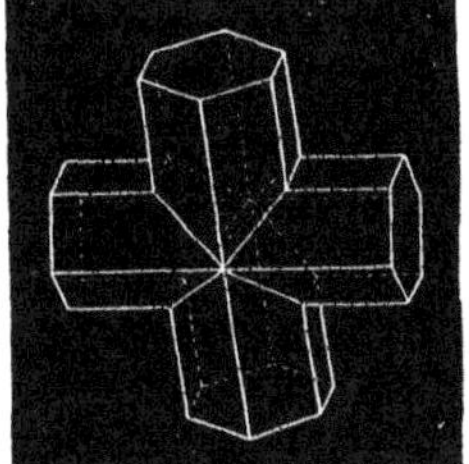

Fig. 115.

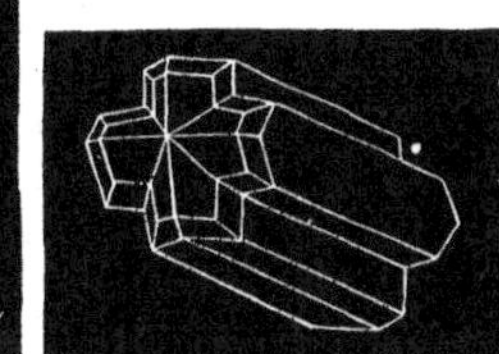

Fig. 116.

In many cases, the junction of crystals is easily recognised; but, in others it is less apparent. Thus, we sometimes see the crystalline form of fig. 117. If we examine separately each half of the crystal made by the plane passing through the edges of the re-entering angle, we shall see that each half belongs to a regular octahedron, and that we may obtain the form of fig. 117 by dividing a regular octahedron (fig. 118) into two equal parts, by a plane *mnpqrs* parallel to the faces of the octahedron, and causing one of the halves of the octahedron to revolve at an angle of 60° on the face of separation, so that *pq*, fig. 118, will coincide with *np*, fig. 117. One of the halves of the octahedron is then said to be transposed.

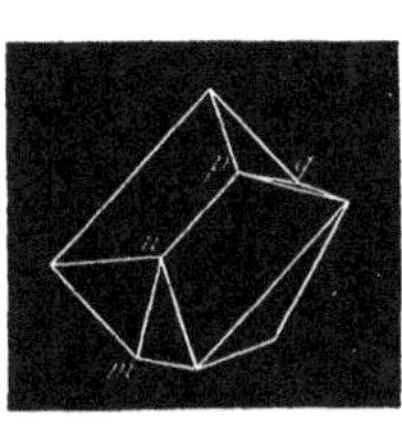

Fig. 117.

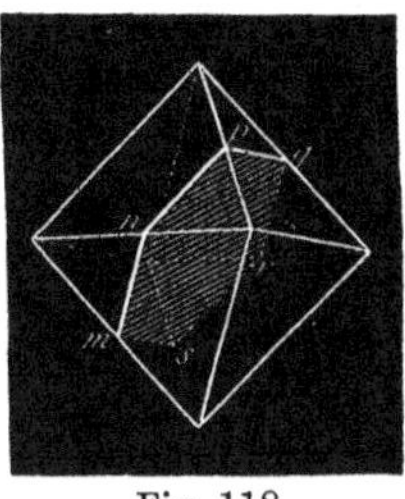

Fig. 118.

Fig. 119 represents a very common form of hydrated sulphate of lime, or gypsum: it is obtained by dividing fig. 120 into 2 equal parts by means of a plane *omnpqr*, and causing one of the halves to make a semi-revolution with reference to the other. We then say that there is *hemitropism*, and the crystal of fig. 119 is called a *hemitrope crystal.**

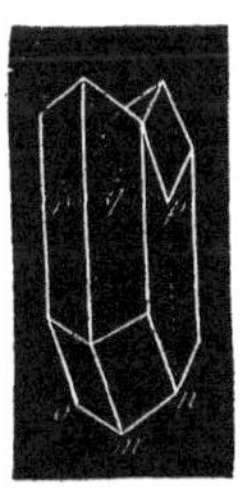

Fig. 119.

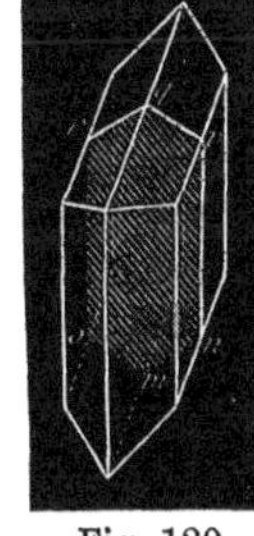

Fig. 120.

* Such crystals are also said to be twinned, or compounded, and on, that is, parallel to, a certain plane. Thus, in the regular system, the octahedron, dodecahedron, and cube may each be compounded on a plane of the octahedron, that is, parallel to that plane.—*J. C. B.*

DIMORPHISM AND POLYMORPHISM.

§ 39. It was for a long time supposed that the same body could only assume crystalline forms derived from one primitive form, according to the rules laid down in the preceding paragraphs: but this proposition is now known not to be exact. Thus, carbonate of lime generally crystallizes in the rhombohedric form, and all its crystals give an elementary cleavage which is a rhombohedron of 105° 5′: but carbonate of lime has been found in forms belonging to the fourth system of crystallization, completely incompatible with rhombohedric cleavage, and is then called by mineralogists *arragonite.*

Sulphur which we crystallize by melting assumes the form of oblique elongated prisms, with rhombic bases, belonging to the fifth system of crystallization. The same substance, crystallized by solution in bi-sulphuret of carbon, takes the form of right octahedrons, with rhombic bases, belonging to the fourth system. Natural crystals of sulphur likewise affect the latter form.

Substances which can thus crystallize according to two different systems, are called *dimorphous;* and the phenomenon itself has received the name of *dimorphism.*

Crystals of the same substance which belong to two different systems, are not only dissimilar in their external appearance, but differ in many other points, and these differences are perceptible even in the finest particles that can be obtained by mechanical means. Thus their hardness and density are different; and they are also differently acted upon by heat and various chemical reagents.

The same substance crystallizes according to two different systems only when the crystallization takes place under dissimilar circumstances, as, for example, at different degrees of temperature. We are therefore forced to admit that the forces by virtue of which molecules are grouped into crystals, vary in their nature and intensity according to the temperature; so that molecules which have been united at a high temperature may come, when the body has returned to the ordinary temperature, under the influence of forces very different from those which govern their crystallization. Thus, we frequently observe that crystals which were formed at a high temperature, and perfectly transparent at the moment of their formation, become in a short time opaque and pulverulent. There is disaggregation, because the molecules have a tendency to a different grouping, by obeying the forces evolved by low temperatures. After this alteration, the lens or microscope will frequently show the mass to be composed of small rudimentary crystals, having the form assumed by the substance when crystallized at the ordinary temperature.

This transformation is very apparent in the crystals of sulphur obtained by melting. These crystals have the form of very elongated prisms of the fifth system: they are of a clear yellow, perfectly transparent, and slightly flexible. At the ordinary temperature, they change entirely in appearance in a few days, lose their transparency, become friable, and, if their dust be examined by the microscope, it will be found to be composed of small crystals belonging to the fourth system, resembling those formed by sulphur when it crystallizes at the ordinary temperature in a solution of bi-sulphuret of carbon. So that whilst these crystals present, externally, the forms of the fifth system, they possess, internally, the crystalline texture and cleavages of the fourth.

At present, we are unacquainted with substances which crystallize in more than two different systems; but it is possible that the same substance, under different conditions, might assume three or a greater number of incompatible forms: it would then be called a *polymorphous substance.*

ISOMORPHISM.

§ 40. The crystalline form of a body is not alone sufficient to distinguish it. If a body crystallizes according to the regular system, it is evidently not defined by saying that it assumes the regular octahedric or the cubic form; for all octahedrons and hexahedrons of the regular system are identical. The same difficulty does not exist in the other systems, for configurations of the same name, belonging to the same system, are far from being similar. We have seen, in fact, that the same substance may assume the form of several octahedrons belonging to the same system of crystallization, but all these octahedrons bear to each other relations by means of which it is easily seen that they belong to the same substance. It is only necessary to measure the various dihedral angles of the crystal, and to deduce from these measurements, by calculation, the angles and relative lengths of its axes: it will be always found that of the octahedrons belonging to the same substance, the angles of the axes are *strictly identical* in all these forms, and that the relative lengths of the homologous axes bear to each other *rational and very simple proportions.* From this, it will be seen that, strictly speaking, the exact determination of the crystalline form of a substance is sufficient to characterize it, when this form does not belong to the regular system.

There is, however, a circumstance which invalidates the proposition just advanced, and which is of the highest importance in chemical theories. It has been seen that substances having a similar chemical composition affect crystalline forms, not absolutely identical, but so nearly resembling each other externally, as to be distinguished only by a very nice measurement of their angles. Thus, the carbonate of lime, or magnesia, of protoxide of iron, of protoxide of manganese, and oxide of zinc, all crystallize in rhombohedrons presenting a rhombohedric cleavage. The angles of these rhombohedrons are—

Of carbonate of lime...........................	105° 5′
" carbonate of magnesia.....................	107° 25′
" carbonate of manganese................	107° 20′
" carbonate of iron..........................	107°
" carbonate of zinc..........................	107° 40′.

Therefore, these angles do not differ sufficiently to permit us to distinguish them by mere inspection.

Again, when substances thus present crystalline forms differing but little from each other, it has been seen that they often replace each other in indefinite proportions, when they crystallize together in the same medium. In fact, we find, in nature, crystals formed of two or a greater number of the preceding carbonates, combined in indefinite proportions. These complex crystals always affect the form of rhombohedrons: the angles of these rhombohedrons are intermediate between those of the rhombohedrons of the simple carbonates which compose them: they approximate nearest to the angles of the rhombohedron pertaining to that carbonate the quantity of which predominates in the crystal.

Sulphate of iron and sulphate of copper, dissolved in water, combine with similar quantities of water, and crystallize in almost identical forms, if the crystallization takes place at a suitable temperature. These temperatures *are not absolutely the same* for both salts, but the difference is very slight. If a crystal of sulphate of copper be placed in a solution of sulphate of iron, at a temperature slightly differing from that at which the sulphate of iron crystallizes under the same form, it will be found to increase in the solution, by assimilating to itself molecules of sulphate of iron. The same crystal, placed in a solution of sulphate of copper, receives an increment of molecules of sulphate of copper, so that we may obtain a complex crystal, composed of alternate strata of sulphate of copper and sulphate of iron. These strata are easily distinguished by their different shades of color when the crystal is fractured.

If we mix the solution of the sulphates of copper and iron, and then slowly evaporate it, we obtain crystals composed at the same time of sulphate of copper and sulphate of iron. The crystals affect forms resembling those of the sulphate of copper, with some slight variation in the angles. The proportion of the two sulphates may be infinitely varied, according to the quantities mixed in the primary solution.

Substances which possess the property of thus crystallizing under forms belonging to the same system, and presenting only slight differences in the absolute value of their angles, and which, moreover, *can replace each other in indefinite proportions*, always forming similar crystals, have received the name of *isomorphous:* the phenomena is called *isomorphism.*

We have said that isomorphous subtances always presented similar compositions. But it is not always easy to make substances presenting similar chemical compositions crystallize under the same form. Thus, carbonate of magnesia and the carbonate of the protoxide of iron crystallize in almost identical rhombohedrons: they have a similar chemical constitution; and we might hence conclude that it would be equally easy to obtain, under identical crystalline forms, sulphate of magnesia and sulphate of iron which have a similar chemical constitution. However, if we mix and evaporate a solution of these two salts, the two sulphates will crystallize separately, according to the forms of different systems. If we analyze the two crystals, we shall find that they do not contain equal quantities of water. The sulphates of iron and magnesia, whilst crystallizing at the same temperature, in the same solution, combine with different quantities of water: they do not present, therefore, similar chemical compositions, and it is not surprising that they assume very different crystalline forms. The example just adduced proves, hence, that the sulphates of iron and magnesia are not isomorphous.

The consideration of isomorphism[1] is of great importance in chemistry: we shall subsequently make frequent use of it to establish the constitution of compound bodies.

CHEMICAL NOMENCLATURE.

§ 41. The number of the different substances found in nature, or artificially obtained in our laboratories, has become so large, that the most retentive memory could not retain the names of all these substances and apply them correctly, if each had a particular appellation, given at random. Chemists therefore soon felt the necessity of inventing a systematic nomenclature, which would enable them to form the names of compound bodies by the combination of the names of the simple bodies constituting them: it is an easy way of recognising, to a certain point, from the name alone, the nature of the compound body, and even some of its most essential properties. Unfortunately, the spirit of this nomenclature bears the impress of the theoretical ideas in vogue at the date of its creation. These ideas have since been greatly modified; the science has advanced rapidly; its domain is not only considerably extended, but it has been studied under new aspects. It follows, therefore, that our chemical nomenclature, although perfectly rational when it was established, no longer harmonizes with the actual state of the science, and, in order to be applicable to our modern ideas, would

[1] The phenomenon of isomorphism was discovered by M. Mitscherlich.

require an entire reformation. So considerable a change should be made with great caution: we should always be liable to discrepancies between the works which preceded and those which follow the adoption of the new nomenclature. A favorable moment must therefore be selected. This moment has not yet arrived; the greater part of our modern chemical theories are now under discussion, and we can hardly hope that at this time the chemists of various countries should agree on a uniform nomenclature—a condition indispensable, however, to the success of the change.

Be this as it may, we shall give the rules of the chemical nomenclature, as they were established in 1787, by a commission of the (French) Academy of Sciences, with some modifications and extensions which have since been added: and we shall point out the principal faults of this nomenclature.

§ 42. At the present day, simple bodies alone bear names which are arbitrary, and given by the caprice of him who discovered or first described their properties. It has been endeavoured to render some of these names significant, by deriving them from a Greek etymology which would recall some of their most characteristic properties. The tendency of this has generally been unfortunate; for, most generally, the point of view at which the body was examined was too exclusive, and bodies have been subsequently discovered presenting similar properties in an equal degree. Thus, to quote but few examples, the word *oxygen* comes from the two Greek words ὀξυς, acid, and γενναω, I generate: it means a *generator of acids*. When this word was selected, it was supposed that oxygen was the only body which could produce acids: now, we know that other bodies possess the same property. *Azote* comes from α privative, and ζωη, life (*which destroys life*): we are now acquinted with many gases which, like azote, are destructive to animal life. We hence conclude that the most insignificant words are the most suitable for simple bodies.

There have been hitherto discovered, sixty-two simple bodies: we give here their names, with the symbols or abridged signs by which chemists have agreed to represent them:

*1.	Oxygen	O
*2.	Hydrogen	H
*3.	Azote or Nitrogen	Az or N*
*4.	Sulphur	S
*5.	Selenium	Se
*6.	Tellurium	Te
*7.	Chlorine	Cl
*8.	Bromine	Br
*9.	Iodine	I

* Az is used by the French, N by other chemists.—*J. C. B.*

*10. Fluorine.................... F
*11. Phosphorus................ P
*12. Arsenic..................... As
*13. Carbon...................... C
*14. Boron........................ B
*15. Silicon...................... Si

*16. Potassium.................. K (from the Latin *Kalium.*)
*17. Sodium...................... Na (from the Latin *Natrium.*)
*18. Lithium..................... Li
*19. Barium...................... Ba
*20. Strontium.................. Sr
*21. Calcium..................... Ca
*22. Magnesium................ Mg
*23. Glucinum................... G
*24. Aluminum.................. Al
25. Zirconium.................. Zr
26. Thorium..................... Th
27. Yttrium...................... Yt
28. Cerium...................... Ce
29. Lanthanum................ La
30. Didymium.................. Di
31. Erbium....................... Er
32. Terbium..................... Te
*33. Manganese................ Mn
*34. Chromium or Chrome.... Cr
35. Tungsten.................... Tg or W (from the German *Wolfram.*)
36. Molybdenum.............. Mo
37. Vanadium.................. Vd
*38. Iron........................... Fe (from the Latin *Ferrum.*)
*39. Cobalt....................... Co
*40. Nickel....................... Ni
*41. Zinc.......................... Zn
*42. Cadmium................... Cd
*43. Copper...................... Cu (from the Latin *Cuprum.*)
*44. Lead.......................... Pb (from the Latin *Plumbum.*)
*45. Bismuth.................... Bi
*46. Mercury.................... Hg (from the Latin *Hydrargyrum.*)
*47. Tin............................ Sn (from the Latin of *Stannum.*)
48. Titanium.................... Ti
49. Tantalum or Columbium. Ta
50. Niobium.................... Nb
51. Ilmenium (?).............. Il
52. Pelopium (?)............... Pp
*53. Antimony.................. Sb (from the Latin *Stibium.*)

*54. Uranium.................... U
*55. Silver........................ Ag (from the Latin *Argentum.*)
*56. Gold.......................... Au (from the Latin *Aurum.*)
*57. Platinum.................... Pt
58. Palladium .... Pd
59. Rhodium.................... R
60. Iridium .... Ir
61. Ruthenium.................. Ru
62. Osmium...................... Os

We have marked with an asterisk (*) the names of the simple bodies which will specially occupy our attention. We shall not dwell so long on the others; the greater part of these are as yet imperfectly known, and, in addition, very rare, and have never been applied to any use in the arts.

Chemists generally agree in dividing simple bodies into two great clases, *metalloids* and *metals.* We will soon explain the characters on which this division has been established.

The class of metalloids comprises the first fifteen simple bodies in our general list: that of the metals comprises all the others.

§ 43. Before treating of the rules which govern the nomenclature of compound bodies, it is necessary to define some of the general terms which are applied to these bodies, which are divided into *acids*, *bases*, and *salts.*

Salts result from the combination of the acids with the bases. When a salt is submitted to the action of the voltaic battery, the combination is decomposed. If the battery be very powerful, the compound is entirely destroyed and resolved into its simple elements. If the battery be weaker, the acid alone separates from the base, and is found at the *positive pole,* and the base at the *negative pole* thereof. Electricities of the same kind repel, those of opposite kinds attract each other. It has been supposed that the molecules of the bodies are either of themselves electrical, or surrounded by an atmosphere of electricity. If this hypothesis be correct, it is evident that the molecule found at the positive pole must possess *negative elecricity,* and the reverse. We therefore admit that, when a salt is decomposed by the galvanic battery, the acid molecule requires negative electricity, and the basal molecule positive electricity; and we say that the acid is the *electronegative element,* and the base the *electropositive element* of the salt.

The manner in which a salt is decomposed by the battery is therefore sufficient to characterize the *acid* and the *basic element.* The acid or electronegative element is that found at the positive pole; and the basal or electropositive element is that found at the negative pole.

When the acid and base are soluble in water, they are distinguished by other properties easily recognised. A great number of organic coloring-matters are changed, in different ways, by acids and bases. The tincture of litmus, as found in commerce, is of a violet blue color. If an acid be added to this tincture, the blue color is immediately changed to a bright red. *Acids, therefore, redden the blue tincture of litmus.*

If we add a solution of a base to the same tincture, the blue color is not altered; but, if we add a sufficient quantity of such a solution to the tincture of litmus, previously reddened by the acid, the red color again becomes blue. *Soluble bases, therefore, restore the blue color of litmus reddened by an acid.*

The yellow tincture of turmeric *is not altered* by acid solutions: *it is reddened* by basic solutions.

The violet tincture of the syrup of violets *is reddened* by acids, and rendered *green* by bases.

It is evident that these characters are of use only in acids and soluble bases. When bodies are insoluble, they can be distinguished only by the manner in which they behave under the influence of the battery, or in which they combine with acid or basic substances the nature of which is not doubtful.

Many substances exert no action on the color of colored reagents; they do not redden the blue tincture of litmus, nor restore this color to a solution previously reddened by an acid. They are called *indifferent*, or *neutral to colored reagents.* Many salts possess this property; in these salts, the reactions which the acid and the base composing them exert on coloring vegetable matter are perfectly neutralized, and they are called *salts neutral to colored reagents.* This state of neutrality depends on the relative forces of the acids and the bases. A very powerful base can never be completely neutralized by a feeble acid, as regards its action on colored reagents. Again, a feeble base cannot entirely destroy the reaction of a very energetic acid on these reagents. It can also be conceived that a salt, which is, as it were, neutral, with one colored reagent, may react upon another more delicate.

There are substances which act the part of acids in relation to very strong bases, and the part of bases in relation to powerful acids. It will therefore be seen, that there is nothing absolute in the definition of acids and bases, since the same substance may, according to circumstances, assume the character of an acid or a base.

§ 44. Of all simple substances in nature, oxygen is the most widely diffused, and forms the greatest number of important combinations. The compounds into which it enters were those first carefully studied by chemists. From this cause the founders of our system of nomenclature devoted peculiar attention to this substance. It may even be said that the exclusive importance they attached to it greatly contributed to render their system defective.

The combinations which oxygen forms with other simple substances are either acids, bases, or neutral bodies. The name of *oxide* has been given to the basic and neutral combinations, and the name of *oxacids*, or simply of *acids*, to acid combinations.

Iron, copper, and lead, form, with oxygen, basic combinations, which are called *oxide of iron*, *oxide of copper*, and *oxide of lead.*

Carbon forms with oxygen a neutral combination, called the *oxide of carbon.*

§ 45. When the rules of our nomenclature were established, it was supposed that the same body, combining with oxygen, could not form more than *two* acid compounds. In order to distinguish them, the word *acid* was immediately preceded by the name of the second substance, which terminated in *ous*, for the lesser quantity of oxygen, and in *ic*, for the greater quantity of the same substance. Thus, two acids were known, resulting from the combination of oxygen and sulphur: the less oxygenated was called *sulphurous acid*, and the more oxygenated, *sulphuric acid.*

At a later period, two new acids resulting from the combination of sulphur and oxygen were discovered: one of these contained less oxygen than sulphurous acid, the second occupied a place between sulphurous and sulphuric acid. It was therefore necessary to modify the general rule, and it was agreed to form the name of the acid less oxygenated than sulphurous acid, by the prefix of the word *hypo* (ὑπό, beneath) and it was called *hyposulphurous acid.* The same rule was applied to the acid intermediate to the sulphuric and sulphurous acids, and it was named *hyposulphuric acid.*

This was a mere temporary relief, and the difficulty was only avoided, for, in latter years, three new combinations of sulphur and oxygen have been discovered: they are all comprised between hyposulphurous and sulphurous acid. In order to name these new compounds, a new rule of nomenclature would be necessary; and chemists are not yet agreed upon this point. Even supposing that it would be practicable, by means of an additional rule, by preserving the first principles of the nomenclature, it is evident that the difficulty would only be postponed, for undoubtedly new combinations of sulphur and oxygen will be discovered.

We are acquainted with five combinations of chlorine with oxygen; four of them have received the following names, in accordance with the rules just given: *hypochlorous acid*, *chlorous acid*, *hypochloric acid*, *chloric acid.*

A fifth combination, found since the discovery of chloric acid, contains more oxygen than the latter. Did we rigorously adopt the primary rules of our nomenclature, this combination would receive the name of *chloric acid*, in lieu of that which now bears it. Now, it can be readily conceived to what serious inconveniences these changes of names would lead: they would necessarily produce great confusion in the science, and give rise to numerous errors. The difficulty has been avoided, by the addition of the prefix *hyper* (from ὑπέρ, above), and thus we say *hyperchloric*, or simply *perchloric acid.* Thus the five combinations of chlorine with oxygen, ranged according to the increasing proportions of oxygen, are,

Hypochlorous acid,
Chlorous acid,
Hypochloric acid,
Chloric acid,
Perchloric acid.

Such are the rules which have hitherto governed chemists in the formation of the nomenclature of the oxacids. The examples just cited, with the remarks thereon, are enough to show how insufficient and defective these rules are, and how desirable it is that they should harmonize with the actual state of our knowledge.

§ 45 *bis.* The same body combining with oxygen, frequently forms several basic or neutral compounds: these are the *oxides.* Experience has shown that, in these different oxides, the proportions of oxygen, combined with the same quantity of the second substance, bear to each other very simple relations, as for example, $\frac{1}{2} : 1 : \frac{3}{2} : 2 : 3 : 4$. Considerations, to be developed hereafter, will determine the choice of the substance to be assumed as containing the proportion 1 of oxygen: this substance is called the *protoxide.* The combination containing the proportion $\frac{3}{2}$ of oxygen takes the name of *sesquioxide:* that containing the proportion 2, is named the *deutoxide* or *binoxide.* The appellations of *tritoxide, quadroxide* are given to the combinations containing 3 or 4 proportions of oxygen. Lastly, the oxides containing less oxygen than the protoxide, are called *suboxides* or *oxidules.**

Thus, manganese forms with oxygen three non-acid combinations or oxides, in which the proportions of oxygen, combined with an equal quantity of manganese, are to each other as $1 : \frac{3}{2} : 2$. These combinations will, therefore, be called *protoxide, sesquioxide, binoxide of manganese.*

The most oxygenated oxide often takes the name of *peroxide:* thus the binoxide of manganese is sometimes called *peroxide of manganese.*

Of the three oxides of manganese, two are bases, the protoxide and sesquioxide: the third, the binoxide or peroxide, is a neutral substance. Some authors have given a different name to the basic combinations, and called the protoxide *manganous* oxide, and the sesquioxide *manganic* oxide. This mode of nomenclature is the same as that adopted for the acids, and is liable to the same objections.

* The strongest basic oxide is now frequently termed oxide, and not protoxide. Deutoxide, tritoxide, &c. were formerly given to the 2d, 3d, &c. oxides, without reference to the exact quantity of oxygen. The German *oxydul* corresponds to our oxide or protoxide, and not to the suboxide.—*J. C. B.*

§46. The rule governing the nomenclature of the salts is extremely simple. The names of salts are formed by combining those of the acid and the base in such a manner that the name of the acid will determine the genus, and the name of the base the species. When the name of the acid terminates in *ic*, the generic name of the salt terminates in *ate*: thus, from sulphuric acids we form *sulphates*, and from phosphoric acid *phosphates*. When the name of the acid terminates in *ous*, the generic name of the salt terminates in *ite*. Thus, sulphurous acid forms *sulphites*, and hyposulphurous acid *hyposulphites*.

The generic name of the acid is followed by that of the base; thus we say, *sulphate of protoxide of manganese*, *sulphate of sesquioxide of manganese*, or, *sulphate of manganous oxide*, *sulphate of manganic oxide*, or, still shorter, *manganous sulphate*, *manganic sulphate*.* We say likewise, *sulphite of protoxide of manganese*, or *manganous sulphite*.

We say, likewise, *sulphite of the protoxide of manganese*, or *manganous sulphite*.

The acid and the base frequently combine in several proportions. Thus, the oxide of potassium, commonly called *potassa*, forms two combinations with sulphuric acid, two *sulphates*. The first does not act on colored reagents, and is named the *neutral sulphate of potassa*, or simply *sulphate of potassa*. The second, or the contrary, exerts a strong acid reaction, and contains, for the same quantity of potassa, a double proportion of sulphuric acid. It is called the *acid sulphate of potassa*, or rather, the *bisulphate of potassa*, the latter name indicating directly the relation between this and the neutral sulphate.

Sometimes the acid and the base form two compounds, in which the quantities of acid, combined with the same quantity of the base, are to each other as 2 : 3 : this happens in carbonic acid and soda. The first compound takes the name of *neutral carbonate of soda*, or simply *carbonate of soda*: the second, that of *sesquicarbonate of soda*.

There are also salts in which the quantity of acid is less than that which exists in the neutral salt: these are called *subsalts*. Thus, the protoxide of iron and the sesquioxide of iron form, with sulphuric acid, neutral sulphates, and the latter basic sulphates or subsalts, which are called the *subsulphates of the sesquioxide of iron*.

Lastly, two salts frequently combine with each other and form compounds more complicated: these compounds are then called *double salts*. The sulphate of alumina and the sulphate of potassa thus form a *double sulphate*, which is called the *double sulphate of alumina and potassa*.

---

* In English, we more frequently say protosulphate, persulphate of manganese, &c.—*J. C. B.*

§ 47. Water is a substance which plays the part of an acid with reference to strong bases, and that of a base with reference to energetic acids: in both cases it forms true salts. The generic name of *hydrates* is given to these salts, in which water acts as an acid: thus we say, *hydrate of potassa, hydrate of the protoxide of iron*, or *ferrous hydrate*. The names of the salts in which water acts as a base should be formed by adding the name of the base to that of the acid, modified as stated in § 46: thus, we ought to say, *sulphate of water, phosphate of water*. Unfortunately, the rule is again forgotten, and we call these compounds *hydrated sulphuric acid, hydrated phosphoric acid*. The same quantity of acid frequently combines with several proportions of water which always bear to each other simple relations: thus, sulphuric acid combines with quantities of water which are to each other as 1 : 2 : 3. These compounds take the name of *protohydrated*, or *monohydrated, bihydrated*, and *trihydrated sulphuric acid*.

§ 48. The combinations of metals with each other have been called *alloys*, which name they still retain in the arts. Thus we say, an *alloy of copper and zinc*, an *alloy of lead and tin*. When mercury is one of the constituents of the alloy, the compound is termed an *amalgam:* an alloy of silver and mercury is called an *amalgam of silver*.

§ 49. The combination of the metalloids with the metals are designated by giving to the metalloids the termination *ide*[1] to mark the genus, and making it precede the name of the metal. Thus, the combination of chlorine and manganese is called the *chloride of manganese;* that of sulphur with iron, the *sulphuret of iron*.

When the metalloid forms with the metallic substance several combinations, experience shows that the quantities of the metalloid combined with the same weight of metal bear to each other simple relations. The nomenclature of these compounds is founded on the rule adopted for the oxides, and we say, *protochloride of manganese, sesquichloride of manganese; protosulphuret, sesquisulphuret*, and *bisulphuret of iron*. When these binary compounds are subjected to the voltaic battery, the metalloid is always found at the positive pole, behaving as an electro-negative element; whilst the metallic substance goes to the negative pole, behaving as an electro-positive element. Therefore, in the compounds, as in the salts, *the electronegative body determines the genus, and the electropositive body defines the species.**

---

[1] And in English, sometimes, of *uret*, as from sulphur we form sulphuret, but the term sulphide is now more frequently used.—*T. F. B.*

* The terms genus and species are not appropriate, for if compounds be classed under the negative constituent, it is the genus, but if under the positive constituent, then the latter becomes the genus. There are no good reasons for classing them under the one constituent more than under the other.—*J. C. B.*

§ 50. Metalloid substances form with each other a great number of combinations, of which the nomenclature follows the same rules as that of the metalloids and metals. Thus we say, *chloride of hydrogen, sulphuret of hydrogen; protochloride, perchloride of sulphur*, etc. The name which determines the genus is always that which refers to the electro-negative element of the compound.

§ 51. Certain combinations of the metalloids with each other are energetic acids, scarcely inferior in activity to the most powerful oxacids; such are the chloride, the fluoride of hydrogen, etc. It was unfortunately deemed necessary to establish a peculiar rule for the nomenclature of these compounds. Supposing that hydrogen played, in these new acids, a part analogous to that of oxygen in the oxacids, the name of *hydracids* was assigned to them. This was a great error: in oxacids, oxygen is the *electronegative element*, while in the hydracids, *hydrogen is constantly the electropositive element.*

Be this as it may, the nomenclature of hydracids is so generally used, that we are obliged to adopt it ourselves. Chloride of hydrogen takes the name of *chlorohydric acid;* the sulphuret of hydrogen that of *sulphohydric acid.* These acids are often called *hydrochloric* and *hydrosulphuric acids;* but these names are more erroneous than the former, because they infringe the general principle, according to which we should always commence the name of the compound by that of the electronegative element.

§ 52. When the combinations of the metalloids with hydrogen are gaseous, and their reaction on colored tests is null or very slight, a name also deduced from an exceptionable rule is frequently assigned to them. Thus, the gaseous combinations of carbon and hydrogen, the gaseous carburets of hydrogen, are called *carburetted hydrogens.* Those of phosphorus with hydrogen, or gaseous phosphurets of hydrogen, are called *phosphuretted hydrogens.* That of sulphur and hydrogen, the acid reaction of which on tinctures is evident though feeble, sulphohydric acid, is often called *sulphuretted hydrogen.* This exceptionable nomenclature is very unfortunate; for, as the gaseous state of substances depends on pressure and temperature, we should, in order to be exact, assign two different names to the same body, according to the circumstances under which they are considered.

§ 53. Certain combinations of sulphur with the metals and metalloids are entirely analogous to the corresponding combinations of oxygen. This analogy was unknown when the rules of the nomenclature were adopted, and no provision was made for it. The acid sulphides, called *sulphacids,* are distinguished from the basic sulphurets, which are called *sulphobases.* The acid sulphides or sulphacids combine with the basic sulphides or sulphobases, and form true salts, called *sulphosalts.* Thus, sulphur and carbon combine, forming the sulphuret of carbon, corresponding in its properties to carbonic acid; and for this reason it is called *sulphocarbonic acid.* In the same way as carbonic acid combines with the basic oxides to form carbonates, sulphocarbonic acid combines with certain basic sulphides or sulphobases to form salts known by the name of *sulphocarbonates.* Thus, sulphocarbonic acid combines with the monosulphide of potassium, and forms a *sulphocarbonate of the monosulphide of potassium*, often called, but improperly, the *sulphocarbonate of potassa.**

Some combinations of chlorine with the metalloids appear also to play the part of acids with reference to certain metallic chlorides. The name of *chloracids* is given to these acid chlorides, and that of *chlorobases* to the basic metallic chlorides. Lastly, the combinations of the chloracids with the chlorobases are called *chloro-salts.* It will be thus seen that, as many metalloids are capable of assuming a part entirely similar to that of oxygen, it is to be regretted that our system of nomenclature is not more precise.

Such are the principal rules of chemical nomenclature adopted by the majority of modern chemists, and which we shall follow in the course of this work. We shall, subsequently, point out some exceptions, consecrated by usage; but these exceptions are, fortunately, very rare, and it will be sufficient to indicate them as they arise.

CHEMICAL FORMULÆ.

§ 54. We gave, in paragraph 42, the list of simple substances hitherto discovered, and opposite to each the sign or symbol by which it has been agreed to represent it. We shall attach a more exact idea to these symbols, and they will serve, not only to recall the nature of a body, but to indicate, in addition, a determinate ponderable quantity, to which we give the name of *chemical equivalent of the body.* It would be impossible to give, at present, a clear and comprehensible definition of chemical equivalents; but we shall explain them successively, as we study the various bodies.

At this time, we shall simply show how, by means of the signs we have adopted for simple bodies, we may compose formulæ representing the composition of compound bodies. These formulæ, termed *chemical formulæ*, are very useful to give tabular forms of chemical reactions: we shall use them from the very commencement of our studies. As we advance, we shall define each, more accurately than we can now do.

The chemical formulæ of binary compounds are formed by placing, after each other, the signs of each of the simple bodies entering into the compound. It has been agreed to place the

* As we say in English, arseniate of iron, meaning arseniate of the oxide of iron, so we say, sulpharseniate of iron, meaning thereby sulpharseniate of sulphuret of iron.—*J. C. B.*

sign of the electropositive element always first. When an electropositive substance R forms several combinations with the same electronegative substance O, experience has shown that, *if we calculate the composition of these various compounds for the same weight of the electropositive body, the ponderable quantities of the electronegative body bear to each other very simple proportions, for example, as the numbers* 1, $\frac{3}{2}$, 2, $\frac{5}{2}$, 3, $\frac{7}{2}$, etc., etc. We therefore give to the *first combination*, to the *protoxide*, the formula RO, and to the other combinations the formulæ $RO\frac{3}{2}$, RO_2, $RO\frac{5}{2}$, RO_3, $RO\frac{7}{2}$, etc., etc.

Thus, manganese forms with oxygen five compounds, of which the first two are basic oxides, the third a neutral oxide, and the last two, most oxygenated, are acids. We therefore write:

Protoxide of manganese........................	MnO
Sesquioxide of manganese........................	$MnO\frac{3}{2}$
Binoxide of manganese	MnO_2
Manganic acid........................	MnO_3
Permanganic acid........................	$MnO\frac{7}{2}$

In these formulæ, the symbols Mn and O not only define the nature of the two bodies, but also indicate their determinate and constant relative weights. We shall subsequently see that, from reasons which we cannot now develop, chemists write the formulæ of the sesquioxide of manganese and of permanganic acid Mn_2O_3, Mn_2O_7, which present the same relations between the ponderable quantities of the manganese and the oxide as the formula $MnO\frac{3}{2}$ and MnO_7.

Sulphur forms with oxygen seven compounds. If we compare the composition of each to the same weight S of sulphur, the pon derable quantities of oxygen entering into these compounds will be to each other as the numbers 1, 1, $\frac{5}{4}$, $\frac{5}{3}$, 2, $\frac{5}{2}$, 3. We will formu larize these compounds as follows:

Hyposulphurous acid........................	SO
Trisulphuretted hyposulphuric acid........................	SO
Bisulphuretted hyposulphuric acid........................	$SO\frac{5}{4}$
Monosulphuretted hyposulphuric acid........................	$SO\frac{5}{3}$
Sulphurous acid	SO_2
Hyposulphuric acid........................	$SO\frac{5}{2}$
Sulphuric acid	SO_3

These, however, are not the formulæ we shall use. We shall in future designate them by the following, which exhibit the same relations between the ponderable quantities of sulphur and oxygen:

Hyposulphurous acid	S_2O_2
Trisulphuretted hyposulphuric acid	S_5O_5
Bisulphuretted hyposulphuric acid	S_4O_5
Monosulphuretted hyposulphuric acid*	S_3O_5
Sulphurous acid	SO_2
Hyposulphuric acid	S_2O_5
Sulphuric acid	SO_3.

The formulæ S_2O_2, S_2O_5 refer to the same bodies as the formulæ SO, $SO\frac{5}{2}$; but the former represent weights double of those represented by the latter. The formula S_4O_5 represents the same body as the formula $SO\frac{5}{4}$, but refers to a quadruple weight. Lastly, the formula S_5O_5 represents a weight five times greater than SO.

We find here, among the compounds of sulphur with oxygen, two combinations, hyposulphurous acid S_2O_2, and trisulphuretted hyposulphuric acid S_5O_5, which present exactly the same proportions between the quantities of sulphur and oxygen which they contain, and have, consequently, the same composition, and yet are *two perfectly distinct substances.* Those substances which, although presenting identical compositions, differ in the aggregate of their properties, are called *isomeric substances.*

The formula of a salt is written by causing the symbol of the acid to follow that of the base, and merely separating them by a point.† Here, also, we write the symbol of the electropositive element first. Thus, the sulphate of the protoxide of manganese is written MnO,SO_3.

If the salt contains several proportions of the acid or the base, the figure representing the number of these proportions, placed as a coefficient, is made to precede the symbol of the element which enters in several proportions. Thus, the weight Mn^2O^3 of the sesquioxyde of manganese forms a sulphate with a weight of

* The names *monosulphuretted*, *bisulphuretted*, and *trisulphuretted hyposulphuric acid*, which we give to the three acids compounded of sulphur and oxygen, and of which the formulæ are S^3O^5, S^4O^5 and S^5O^5, have not been formed according to the rules of nomenclature previously laid down. These names express a relation which exists, *in fact*, between the formulæ of these acids and that of hyposulphuric acid. Indeed, the formula S^3O^5 of monosulphuretted hyposulphuric acid differs from the formula S^2O^5 of hyposulphuric acid, by containing one more S: the formula S^4O^5 of bisulphuretted hyposulphuric acid differs from the formula S^2O^5, containing in addition S^2. Lastly, the formula S^5O^5 of trisulphuretted hyposulphuric acid only differs from the formula S^2O^5 by containing in addition S^3.

† They are more frequently separted by a comma, which we adopt in this translation; and when several compounds are united together, the sign + is inserted; thus the formulæ for alum is written $KO,SO_3+Al_2O_3,3SO_3+24HO$.—*J. C. B.*

sulphuric acid represented by 3 times SO_3; the formula of the salt will be, $Mn_2O_3,3SO_3$.

The formula PbO,NO_5 represents the neutral nitrate (azotate) of lead; and the formula $2PbO,NO_5$ represents a basal nitrate (azotate) of lead which contains, for the same weight of nitric (azotic) acid, a double weight of oxyde of lead.

The formula PbO,NO_5 represents a certain weight of the neutral nitrate (azotate) of lead; if we desire to indicate a double weight of this substance, we write $2(PbO,NO_5)$.

We have seen (§ 40) that, in a neutral salt, a portion of the base could be replaced by an equal quantity of another isomorphous base. We have said, for example, that there was but little difference between the nature of carbonates crystallized in rhombohedrons and that of those presented by carbonate of lime, and that these carbonates differed *chemically* only in having a greater or less proportion of carbonate of lime replaced by *isomorphous* carbonates of magnesia, of protoxide of iron, and protoxide of manganese. The formula of a carbonate thus composed is written,

$$(CaO,MgO,FeO,MnO),CO_2.$$

The preceding remarks on chemical formulæ will suffice for the present: we shall treat more fully of the subject as occasion may require.

DIVISION OF SIMPLE SUBSTANCES INTO METALLOIDS AND METALS.

§ 55. Chemists have generally agreed to divide simple substances into *metalloids* (from μεταλλον, metal, and ειδος, appearance, *which resembles a metal,*) and into *metals;* but it is very difficult to define precisely the characters on which this division is founded.

The metals are opaque, and possess a peculiar lustre, called *metallic.* They are good conductors of heat and electricity. The same properties do not obtain in an equal degree in the metalloids.

This division is therefore founded on properties which are not absolute, and which are more or less developed in the various simple substances; hence it is very vague, and leaves undetermined many simple bodies which may, with equal propriety, be classed among the metals or the metalloids. Thus, in many of its chemical properties, arsenic resembles phosphorus, which is universally placed among the metalloids, and yet, it presents a metallic lustre nearly as decided as that of many of the metals.

Carbon affects various conditions; sometimes it presents more of the characters assigned to the metals; it is wanting in lustre, and is a bad conductor of heat and electricity. At other times, on the contrary, it possesses some of these characters; in the state of graphite, for example, it has a very decided metallic lustre, and charcoal, strongly calcined, conducts electricity moderately well.

The property of being good conductors of heat and electricity belongs eminently to those metals only which have been obtained in masses; and that in consequence of their great fusibility, ductility, or facility with which they are brought into an aggregated form by percussion. Many metals have hitherto been obtained only in a pulverulent state; and then their powers of conducting heat and electricity are very slight.

In the binary compounds of the metals and metalloids, *the metalloids always play the part of the electronegative element.*

The metals and metalloids combine with oxygen. The combinations of the metals with oxygen are most frequently *electropositive oxides* which act as *bases;* and they are those, generally, which contain the most feeble proportions of oxygen. Some more oxygenated compounds play the part of *neutral oxides.* Lastly, the most oxygenated compounds of the metals are often *acids* which form true salts with the basic oxides.

The metalloids, by combining with oxygen, form generally, *neutral oxides,* or *acid combinations.* Some of these combinations, however, act like bases, very feebly, indeed, with reference to strong acids. These same combinations act the part of feeble acids with energetic bases.

It is now seen how correct was our announcement that the division of simple substances into metalloids and metals was vague and uncertain; and it will be readily conceived how difficult it often is to class certain bodies among the metalloids or the metals, inasmuch as, in some of their characters, they may resemble each.

We shall, however, preserve this division, because it is convenient for the purposes of study, and generally adopted by chemists: we shall therefore consider as metalloids the fifteen following simple substances.

1. Oxygen........................ O
2. Hydrogen..................... H
3. Nitrogen...................... N or Az
4. Sulphur........................ S
5. Selenium...................... Se
6. Tellurium..................... Te
7. Chlorine....................... Cl
8. Bromine....................... Br
9. Iodine.......................... I
10. Fluorine....................... F
11. Phosphorus................... P
12. Arsenic........................ As
13. Boron.......................... B
14. Silicon......................... Si
15. Carbon........................ C

ORDER WHICH WILL BE OBSERVED IN THE STUDY OF SUBSTANCES

§ 56. We shall commence the study of substances by that of the metalloids. After each simple substance, we shall examine the combinations which this substance forms with all the preceding simple substances. We shall follow this arrangement except in the numerous combinations which carbon forms with hydrogen, oxygen, and nitrogen. We shall postpone the investigation of these combinations to the end of the work, in a separate part, which we shall call *organic chemistry*. Although the majority of these substances have been drawn from the organic kingdom, this reason alone would not suffice to separate them, in a systematic treatise, from the other combinations formed by carbon; but, in an elementary course, this separation is useful, because the study of the numerous organic combinations is complex and difficult, and it is more advantageous to the student to enter upon it after having become thoroughly acquainted with the principal facts of chemistry.

PART I.

OF THE METALLOIDS.

OXYGEN.

EQUIVALENT = 100 (8. H = 1).

§ 57. OXYGEN* is a colourless, inodorous and tasteless gas. This substance is widely diffused throughout nature, but is not found there pure and isolated. Mixed with nitrogen gas, in the proportion of about $\frac{4}{5}$ nitrogen and $\frac{1}{5}$ oxygen, it constitutes the atmospheric air. It combines with nearly all the other simple substances, and produces a very great number of compounds.

In order to separate the oxygen from the atmospheric air, the nitrogen must be absorbed: that is to say, this latter gas must be combined with a substance which does not act on the oxygen, and which forms with nitrogen a compound, solid or liquid, easily removed. Now, we are unacquainted, at the present time, with any substance which possesses these properties; but we have at our disposal many compounds containing oxygen, which readily part with this gas, wholly or in part, when subjected to a sufficiently elevated temperature.

§ 58. The red oxide of mercury, composed of mercury and oxygen, gives off its oxygen at the temperature of burning alcohol. This substance is placed in a glass tube, *ab*, closed at one end: to the other end is fastened, by means of a cork, a glass tube *cd*, called the *discharging* or *abducting tube*, and having two curvatures, one at *c*, the other at *d*. The bent end of the tube is immersed in a tub, V, filled with water. The portion of the tube *ab* containing the oxide, is heated with an alcohol lamp (fig. 121), or charcoal burning in a small furnace (fig. 122). The air in the tube, dilated by the heat, increases in elastic force: a portion of it soon escapes in the form of bubbles, through the water in the tub V. The oxide, soon reaching the temperature at which it decomposes, separates into its two elements: the mercury condenses in a liquid

* Oxygen was discovered about seventy-five years ago. This honour is generally attributed to Priestley, who announced it in 1774. Nearly at the same time, Scheele and Lavoisier, without having heard of the experiments of the English philosopher, obtained this substance by a different mode.

form in the upper part of the tube, and the oxygen is given off in the form of gas, and passes through the water in the vessel. The

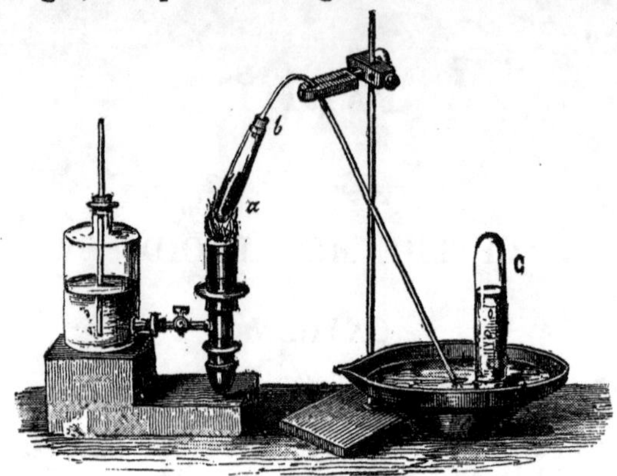

Fig. 121.

first portions of gas which pass over are not collected, as they are mixed with the air which originally filled the tubes. After a few minutes, this air is driven off by oxygen gas, which passes over incessantly.

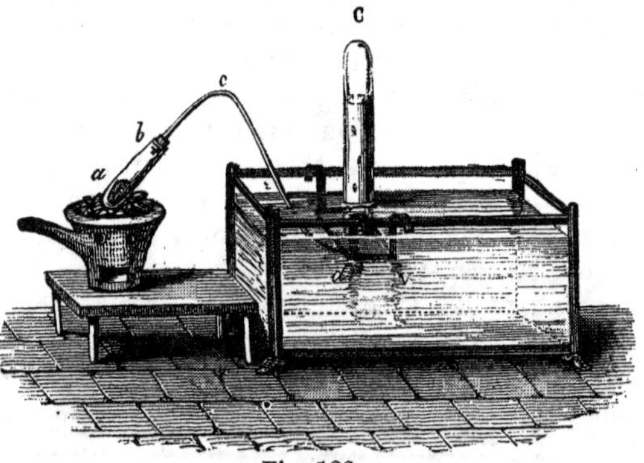

Fig. 122.

In order to collect the gas, we take a bell-glass, C, fill it with water, and applying the flat part of the hand to its opening, invert it in the water of the tub. The bell-glass then remains entirely filled with water, even after the withdrawal of the hand, on account of the atmospheric pressure on the surface of the water in the tub. The bell-glass is placed over the discharging tube, on a small perforated shelf arranged in the tub: if the tub be replaced by an earthen pan, as in fig. 121, the bell-glass is placed on a capsule perforated at *a*, fig. 123, and having a lateral aperture at *u* to allow the passage of the tube *cd*. The bubbles

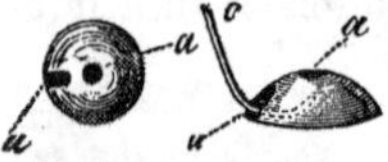

Fig. 123.

of oxygen gas, by reason of their less specific gravity, rise in the water and are collected in the upper part of the bell-glass.

When the pneumatic trough is sufficiently deep, the bell-glasses are filled with water, by simply plunging them in the trough, with the closed extremity downward. The air escapes through the water, and the latter fills the glass, which is then to be inverted and placed on the shelf. This is the most convenient mode when the bell-glasses are very large.

§ 59. The oxide of mercury is too expensive a substance to be used when we wish to obtain a considerable quantity of oxygen gas. But we find in nature another oxide, the peroxide of manganese, which, at a high temperature, parts with a portion of its oxygen, and is converted into another oxide of manganese, containing less oxygen than the peroxide. The decomposition of the peroxide of manganese requires a more elevated temperature than that of the oxide of mercury: nor can it be effected in glass vessels, as they will not bear a sufficient degree of heat. The peroxide of manganese, reduced to powder, is introduced into a stone retort, placed in an earthen furnace F (fig. 124), provided with its *laboratory* L, and afterward covered by the *reverberatory* R. To the neck of the retort is fitted, by means of a cork, the discharging tube *tr*, of which the curved extremity *r* dips into the pneumatic trough. Some hot coals are placed on the grate of the furnace, which is then filled with charcoal: the combustible mass by this means burns slowly, a condition indispensable to the safety of the retort. The peroxide of manganese begins to decompose only at an intense red-heat. The first portions of gas are allowed to escape, as they contain the atmospheric air which was in the retort. The decomposition is finished when the gas passes over no longer, although the fire in the furnace may be brightly burning.

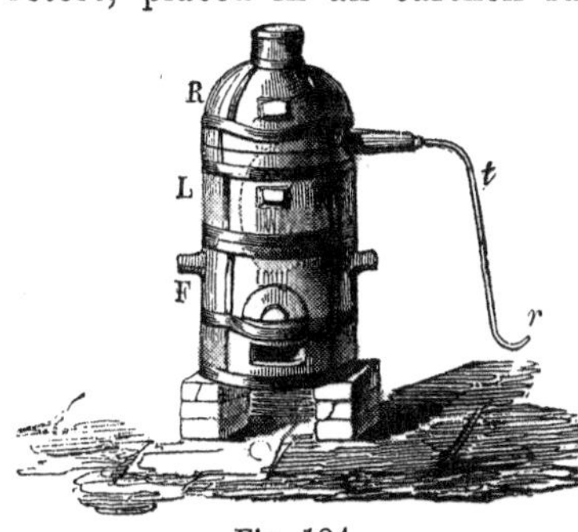

Fig. 124.

100 grains of peroxide of manganese contain

63.36 of manganese,
36.64 of oxygen.

In this decomposition by heat alone, 12^{gr}.22 of oxygen are given off; there remain in the retort 87^{gr}.78 of a brown oxide of manganese, containing 63.36 of manganese and 24.42 of oxygen.

The peroxide of manganese is a mineral substance occurring in lodes in the earth, and is frequently mixed with fragments of the rock composing the walls of the lode. It almost always contains a small quantity of carbonate of lime (limestone). This carbonate of lime is changed, during calcination, into caustic lime, and the carbonic acid gas which is disengaged mixes with and adulterates the oxygen. It is, however, easy to separate them, by dissolving in the water of the trough a small proportion of caustic potash, which absorbs the carbonic acid. We may also collect immediately the oxygen deprived of its carbonic acid, by causing it to pass, when it leaves the retort, through a bottle (fig. 125) with two tubulures containing a solution of caustic potash, and called a *washing apparatus*.*

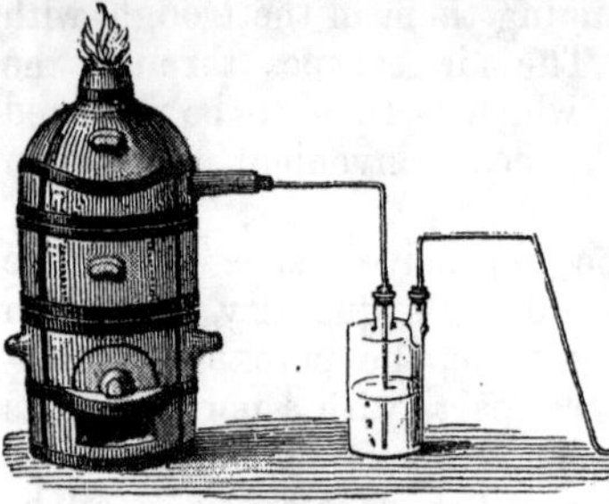

Fig. 125.

§ 60. When we wish to collect a large quantity of gas, the bell-glasses are no longer serviceable, and we use a peculiar receptacle called a *gasometer* (fig. 126). It is composed of a cylindrical copper vessel A, surmounted by a head C, supported by 5 copper pillars. Two of these pillars, *a* and *b*, are hollow, and furnished with stopcocks. The tube *a* empties into the vessel A, close to the upper end. The tube *b* descends, on the contrary, very nearly to the bottom. At *c* is a small tube furnished with a stopcock, and at *d* a larger curved tube, which may be hermetically closed with a cork or a leathern stopper *k*.

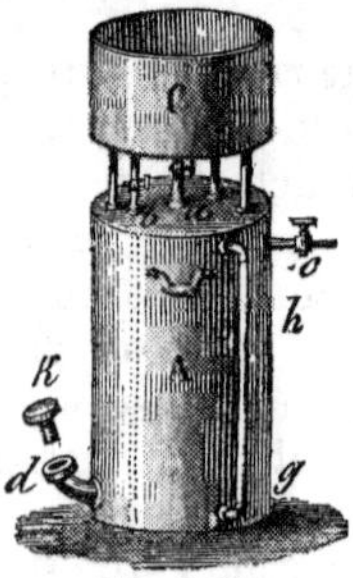

Fig. 126.

The apparatus is first to be filled with water. To do this, we close the stopcock *c*, and the opening of the tube *d*, and pour water into the head C. The water flows into the vessel A by the long tube *b*, and the contained air escapes by the tube *a*: the operation is continued until the vessel A is filled, and then the cocks *a* and *b* are closed.

In order to fill the gasometer with oxygen gas, we uncork the tubulure *d*: the water cannot escape on account of the pressure of the atmosphere. The discharging tube is introduced through this tubulure into the interior of the vessel. As the gas is given off, it collects in the upper part of the vessel A, and the water runs off by the aperture *d*.

The glass tube *gh*, which communicates above and below with the cylinder A, indicates the level of the water therein, and also the quantity of gas it contains. When but little water is left in the cylinder, the discharging tube is removed, and the opening at *d*

* The carbonate may also be removed by previously digesting the pulverized ore with diluted muriatic acid, washing and drying the residue.—*J. C. B.*

closed. The gas may then be retained, at pleasure, in the apparatus.

By opening the cock *b* alone, a portion of water in the head *c* enters, until the gas, compressed into a smaller space, has acquired an elastic force equal to the pressure of the atmosphere exerted on the water in the head, increased by the pressure produced by the column of water comprised between the level of the water in the head, and the level of the water in the vessel A.

In order to fill a bell-glass with oxygen, it is merely necessary to fill the glass with water, and invert it in the head C over the tube *a*. Opening then the cocks *a* and *b*, the gas will escape in bubbles through the tube *a*, and collect in the glass: it will be replaced in the cylinder A by the water which enters by the tube *b*.

§ 61. We have seen that the peroxide of manganese lost by calcination a portion of its oxygen. The same substance loses a much larger portion of this gas when heated with concentrated sulphuric acid, which is one of the most powerful acids known. The peroxide of manganese does not unite with acids. But there is another oxide of manganese, the protoxide, composed of 77.57 of manganese and 22.43 of oxygen, which is a powerful base, and has great affinity for sulphuric acid. It follows from this affinity, that if we heat the pulverized peroxide of manganese with concentrated sulphuric acid, the peroxide loses one-half of its oxygen, and is reduced to a state of protoxide, in which it combines with sulphuric acid to form the sulphate of the protoxide of manganese.

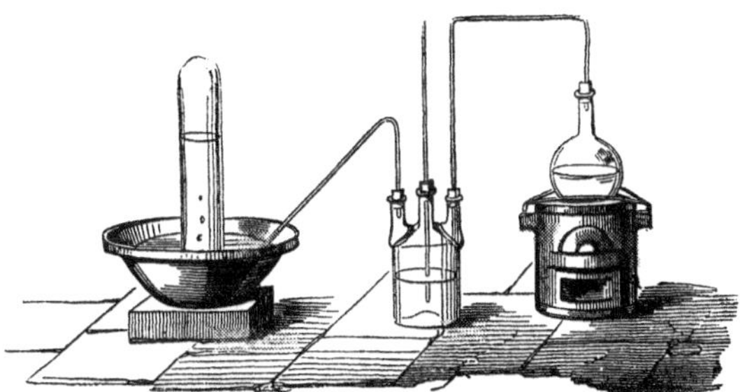

Fig. 127.

The apparatus used for this experiment is composed of a glass balloon (fig. 127), in which is placed the peroxide of manganese finely powdered, and the concentrated sulphuric acid. By means of a cork, a discharging tube is fitted to the neck of the balloon, to conduct the gas beneath a bell-glass placed in the water-trough or in a pan full of water. It is sufficient to heat the balloon with hot coals or an alcohol lamp. When wishing to obtain oxygen gas very pure, we must remember that the natural peroxide of manganese contains nearly always some carbonate of lime. This carbonate, by contact with sulphuric acid, is converted into sulphate of lime, which remains in the retort, and into carbonic acid gas, which is disengaged and mixed with the oxygen. They are, however, easily separated by passing the gas through a washing apparatus containing a solution of potash, as in fig. 127.

§ 62. In the laboratory, a method different from that already explained, and which has the advantage of greater facility, is used to obtain oxygen gas pure and in large quantities. There is found in commerce a salt, the chlorate of potassa, composed of chloric acid and protoxide of potassium or potassa. Chloric acid is a compound of chlorine and oxygen. Chlorate of potassa is easily decomposed by heat; all the oxygen it contains is given off, leaving a compound of chlorine and potassium, the chloride of potassium.

100 grains of chlorate of potassa contain

61.51 chloric acid...................... { 28.88 chlorine, 32.63 oxygen:

38.49 protoxide of potassium....... { 6.53 oxygen, 31.96 potassium.

Hence, 39.16 of oxygen are given off, and there remain

28.88 chlorine, 31.96 potassium } 60.84 chloride of potassium.

The formula we assign to chlorate of potassa is KO,ClO_5, that of chloride of potassium is KCl: we may therefore express the decomposition which takes place in this experiment, as follows:

$$KO,ClO_5 = KCl + O_5 + O;$$

or more commonly,

$$KO,ClO_5 = KCl + 6O.$$

When we want to obtain only a small quantity of oxygen, we introduce the chlorate of potassa into a small glass retort (fig. 128)

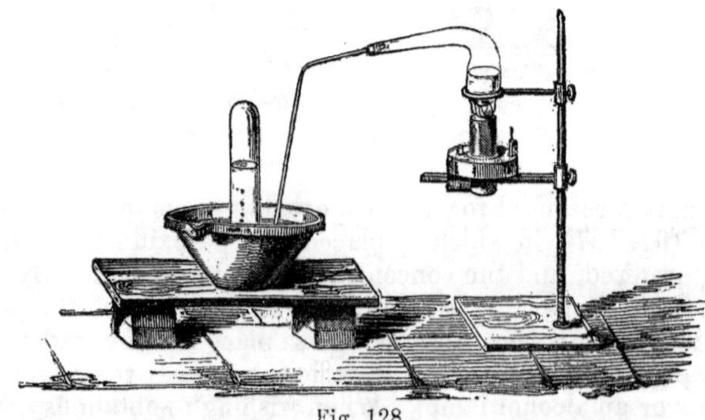

Fig. 128.

heated by charcoal or an alcohol lamp. At first, the chlorate of potassa fuses, and the bubbles announcing its decomposition soon appear. As this decomposition progresses, the substance loses its fluidity, and becomes more and more doughy, and the liberation of the oxygen occurs only by elevating the temperature. Toward the close of the operation, care must be taken that the bottom of the retort, which is chiefly exposed to the action of the heat, does not attain the temperature at which glass softens, for it would then blister, and destroy the experiment.

Chlorate of potassa is now so cheap that it can be used to obtain oxygen gas, even when this is required in large quantities. Still, in this case it is advisable to mix it with an equal weight of peroxide of manganese, or, better still, of oxide of copper, as its decomposition will then be more easily effected. It is also best to use retorts of very hard glass, or to cover the ordinary glass retort with an argillaceous luting,* which enables it to bear heat more readily.†

§ 63. Having described the methods by which oxygen gas is obtained, we will now consider its principal properties.

In its appearance, oxygen gas cannot be distinguished from the atmospheric air; its density is, however, greater than that of the latter. The density of the air being represented by 1.00000, that of oxygen is 1.10563. A litre of atmospheric air in Paris weighs $1^{gm}.2932$, at the temperature of 32° F. and under a pressure equal to a column of mercury of 76 centimetres. Under the same circumstances, a litre of oxygen weighs $1^{gm}.4298$.‡

As gases dilate considerably from elevation of temperature or diminution of pressure, it is absolutely necessary, when we desire to obtain the ratio of density of two gases, to take the ratio of weight of equal bodies of these two gases at the same temperature and under the same pressure. It has been agreed to consider gases, such as they are at a temperature of 32° F. (0° of the centigrade thermometer), or of melting ice, and with an elastic force communicated to them by the pressure exerted by a column of mercury 76 centimetres in height. These we shall hereafter call the *normal conditions of temperature and pressure.*

If all gases presented identical variations of volume for equal changes of temperature and pressure, it is evident that the relations between the weights of equal volumes of these gases, at equal

* This luting is made of 1 part of potter's clay, softened with water, and 2 or 3 parts of sand. Frequently a small quantity of chopped straw or dried horse-dung is added, which renders it more easy of application to the glass.

† When the chlorate of potassa is mixed with about an equal bulk of oxide of manganese or of copper, there is no necessity of luting, a soft soda-glass may be used, and a comparatively low heat is required to evolve all the oxygen; care being requisite rather to reduce than to raise the heat.—*J. C. B.*

‡ 100 cubic inches of air weigh 32.587 grains at 32° F. and 29.92 inches of the barometer (76 centimetres = 29.92 inches B.). Under the same circumstances, 100 cubic inches of oxygen weigh 36.139 grs. The English usually give the weight of 100 cubic inches of gas at 60° F. and 30 inches B.—*J. C. B.*

temperature and pressure, would be constantly the same, whatever might be the absolute volume of this temperature and pressure. We might therefore call the *density of a gas* the ratio between the weight of a certain volume of this gas and that of the same volume of atmospheric air, both gases being at the same temperature and under the same pressure: this temperature and pressure being otherwise of no importance. But experience has proved that this identity of variation exists strictly in no gas. It is very close in some, as, for example, in oxygen, hydrogen, and nitrogen:—in others, it is far from being exact, and can only be approximated when they attain a temperature much greater than that of the atmosphere. It will be therefore necessary to indicate, in these last gases, the temperature and pressure under which their weight has been compared to that of an equal volume of atmospheric air.

Oxygen gas is very sparingly soluble in water. At the ordinary temperature, this fluid dissolves about $\frac{46}{1000}$ of its volume; or, in other words, 1 litre of water dissolves 46 cubic centimetres of oxygen, or 1 kilogramme of water dissolves $64^{\text{milligr}}.4$ of oxygen.*

§ 64. A lighted candle continues to burn in atmospheric air. If we blow it out, the carbonaceous portion remains incandescent for a few moments, but the flame does not spontaneously reappear. If, on the contrary, the candle, still presenting some incandescent points, be plunged into a receiver containing oxygen, it inflames instantly, and burns with great brilliancy. This property is characteristic of this gas, and is constantly made use of in laboratories to detect its presence: we shall see, however, that another gas, the protoxide of nitrogen, possesses it in an equal degree.

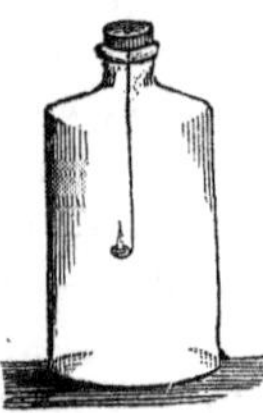
Fig. 129.

The combustion of bodies is much more active in oxygen than in atmospheric air. Thus, a burning coal, when isolated, is promptly extinguished in the air. If we place the same ignited coal in a small porcelain (or copper) cup, fastened to the end of a wire passing through a cork, as in fig. 129, and the cup be plunged into a large receiver filled with oxygen, the coal burns with great brilliancy and activity, and is rapidly consumed.

The combustion of sulphur and phosphorus is much more active in oxygen than in the air. The preceding experiment may be varied by substituting either of these substances for the burning coal. Phosphorus produces a light too brilliant to be endured by the eye.

An iron wire heated to redness soon loses its incandescence in air: but if it be plunged, at a red-heat, into a receiver filled with

* 100 cubic inches of water dissolve 4.6 cubic inches of oxygen, or 100.000 grs. dissolve 6.44 grs. oxygen.—*J. C. B.*

oxygen, it burns with intense brilliancy, throwing off sparks. The experiment is thus performed:—A large-mouthed bottle is filled with oxygen, in the pneumatic trough. In lieu of an iron wire, we take a small blade of steel, such as is used for watch-springs, and which presents more surface than the wire. This blade is annealed; then, having scoured its surface with emery-paper, it is to be twisted into a spiral shape. Its upper end is fixed in a cork which fits the mouth of the bottle (fig. 130): and to the lower end we attach a piece of tinder, which is lighted at the moment of plunging the blade into the bottle. A lively combustion of the tinder ensues, and, in its turn, the steel blade becomes incandescent at the point of contact. The iron takes fire, and burns until it reaches the cork, with great brilliancy, throwing off melted globules of the oxide of iron. It is well to leave a small quantity of water in the bottle, as the incandescent globules of the oxide falling directly on the glass would inevitably break it.

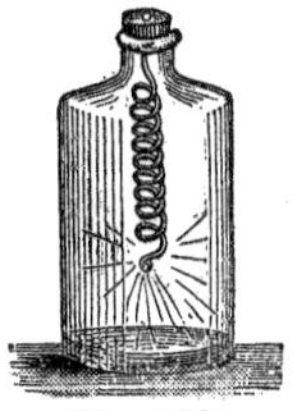

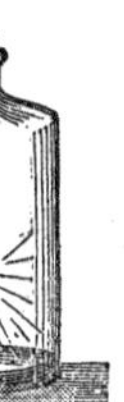

Fig. 130.

These experiments prove that combustion is much more active in oxygen than in atmospheric air. We shall soon see, when treating of nitrogen, that combustion in atmospheric air is owing to the oxygen it contains: oxygen is therefore the *true agent of ordinary combustion.*

Fig. 131.

§ 65. The combustion of bodies in pure oxygen also produces a greater elevation of temperature where the combustion takes place. Thus, for example, we cannot, with an alcohol lamp burning in the open air, generate heat sufficient to melt a platinum wire. Combustion becomes more active when we drive a rapid current of air through the middle of the flame, producing a more complete combustion in a smaller space. For this purpose, we use an instrument called a blowpipe, which consists in a tube bent at right angles and conical internally. The small aperture *b* is placed in the flame. The operator blows through it by the larger opening *a*. The air projected through the blowpipe should not have passed through the lungs: it would be too vitiated, and would not support combustion with sufficient activity. A little practice will soon enable one to breathe through the nose, and use the muscles of the cheeks to blow through the pipe. A continuous jet of air may be thus kept up for ten minutes. The blowpipe is generally made of several pieces which can be separated: a conical tube *ab* (fig. 132), of which the end is inserted in the mouth, or merely placed

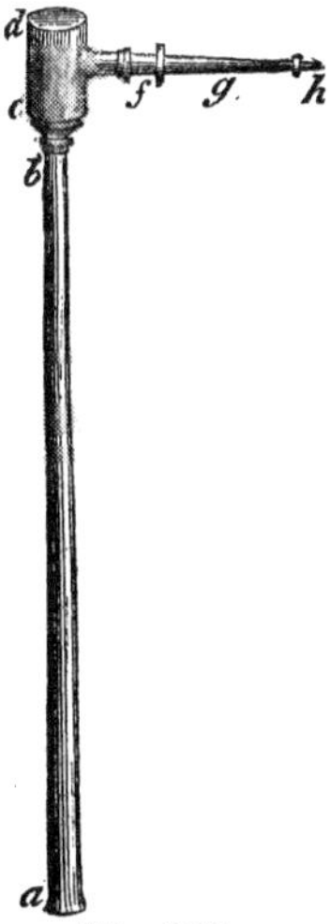

Fig. 132.

against the lips. The extremity *b*, more narrow, is fixed in the cylindrical reservoir *cd*, which serves as a receptacle for air and the moisture deposited by the breath. This cylinder has frequently a small opening in the bottom *d*, closed with a cork, to empty it, when it becomes full of moisture. On one of the sides of this cylinder is the small tube *f*, upon which is fixed the air tube *g*. Small platina tubes, perforated with holes of larger or smaller size, according to the current of air we wish to produce, are frequently added, as at *h*.

When we thus feed an alcohol lamp with a current of air projected by a blowpipe (fig. 133), we obtain at the extremity of the flame, a temperature sufficiently elevated to melt a very fine platinum wire: but if the current of air be replaced by a current of oxygen, we can melt a platinum wire of the diameter of a $\frac{1}{2}$ millimetre ($\frac{2}{100}$ inch). The experiment is easily performed by means of the gasometer described (§ 60). The lateral tubulure *c*, furnished with a stopcock, is intended for this purpose. We fix to its extremity a tube with a small aperture, which is placed in the middle of the flame of the alcohol lamp, and open the stopcocks.

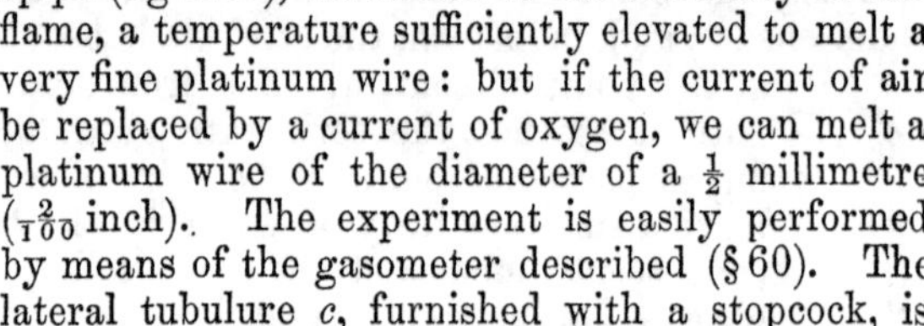

Fig. 133.

When we have no gasometer at our disposal, we may make the experiment with a bladder filled with oxygen gas. For this purpose we soak a bladder in water to render it flexible, and fasten to it a metallic stopcock *r*. In order to fill it with oxygen, we compress it, to expel the air, and then screw the piece *r* (fig. 134) to a copper mounting having a stopcock *s*. This mounting is fastened to the upper part of a bell-glass C, placed in the pneumatic trough and previously filled with oxygen. The cocks are opened and the glass is plunged into the water of the trough. The oxygen contained in the glass is necessarily driven out by the water, into the bladder. If the latter is not full enough, the cocks are closed, the glass is refilled with oxygen, which is again passed into the bladder. The piece *r* is then unscrewed, and a tubulure *t* affixed (fig. 135), which is introduced into the flame, and the jet of oxygen is regulated by the pressure of the arm.

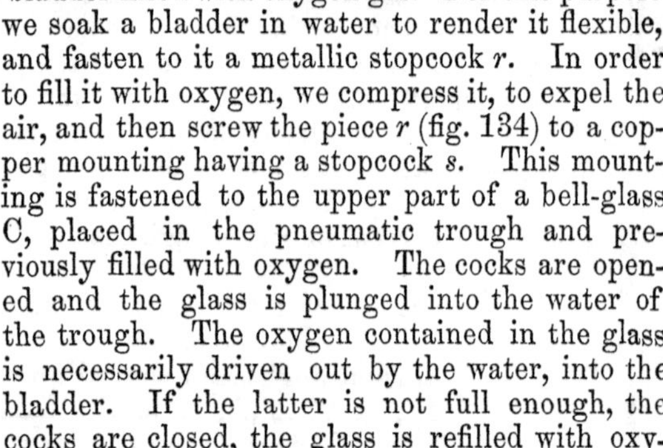

Fig. 134.

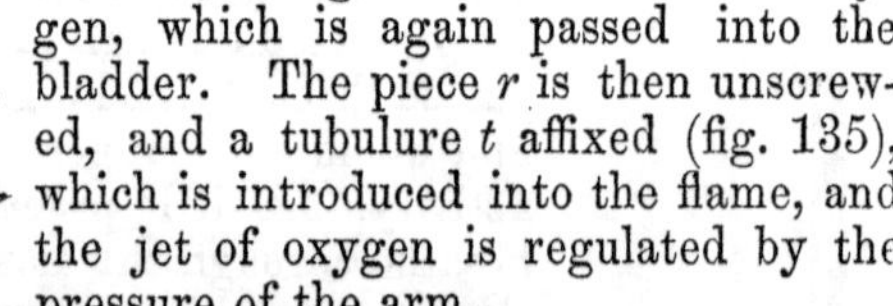

Fig. 135.

§ 66. Oxygen is also the essential element in the respiration of animals. An animal perishes in a few moments, if immersed in air previously deprived of its oxygen.

HYDROGEN.

EQUIVALENT = 12.50 (or 1).

§ 67. Hydrogen* (from ὕδωρ, water, and γεννάω, I generate) is a gas which, as its name imports, enters into the composition of water.

Water is a compound of oxygen and hydrogen. In the laboratory, hydrogen gas is always extracted from water. We have obtained oxygen by decomposing, by heat alone, either the oxide of mercury, the peroxide of manganese, or the chlorate of potassa. An analogous process will not succeed with hydrogen. Water cannot be decomposed by heat alone; but the hydrogen may be separated from the water by heating this fluid with substances which absorb its oxygen. Several metals effect this decomposition. Some, such as potassium and sodium, do it when cold: others, as iron and zinc, require an elevated temperature.

If we introduce into a bell-glass, a fragment of potassium or sodium, it will be seen to rise toward the top of the glass, by virtue of its feeble specific gravity, and an infinity of small bubbles is disengaged from its surface. These bubbles are formed by the hydrogen gas which collects in the upper part of the glass. The metal rapidly disappears by combining with the oxygen of the water: it forms an oxyde which dissolves, and which can be recovered by evaporating the water contained in the bell-glass. In order to make this experiment accurately, a bell-glass is filled with mercury over the mercurial trough, a small quantity of water is

Fig. 136.

introduced into the upper part of the glass, and the fragment of potassium, wrapped in tissue-paper to prevent its combination with

* Hydrogen gas was obtained toward the close of the 17th century; but it was only in 1766, that Cavendish, a celebrated English philosopher, made known its principal properties.

the mercury, is passed in: the potassium rises rapidly through the mercury, until it reaches the water in the bell-glass.

§ 68. In order to decompose water by means of iron, we arrange a porcelain tube in a long furnace, called a *reverberatory furnace* (fig. 136). Into this tube are introduced several bundles of fine iron wire. To one of the ends *a* of the tube, we affix, by means of a cork and a curved tube, a small balloon filled with water; and to the other end, a discharging tube *cd*, which conducts the gas beneath a bell-glass in the pneumatic cistern. The porcelain tube is slowly heated, in order to prevent its fracture from too sudden an elevation of temperature, until it reaches a red-heat. The water in the balloon is then made to boil. The steam passes over the incandescent iron, which deprives it of its oxygen, and the hydrogen is set free and collected in the bell-glass.

§ 69. Iron alone, when cold, will not decompose water: it must be heated to a red-heat. This is not the case when a powerful acid, as the sulphuric, is added to the water. The cause of this decomposition is analogous to that which effects the decomposition of the peroxide of manganese by concentrated sulphuric acid when cold (§ 61). Experience has shown that, *when several bodies are in contact, and that, by the interchange of their elements, new compounds may be formed having great affinity with each other, or possessing, under the circumstances in which they are produced, great fixedness, either isolated or in combination, these new compounds are nearly always formed.* We shall, subsequently adduce several examples in confirmation of this proposition. The present experiment is apposite to the subject. The first combination of the iron with oxygen, the protoxide of iron, is a powerful base, having a great affinity for sulphuric acid. Iron alone, when cold, cannot decompose water; but, in contact with sulphuric acid, its affinity for oxygen is exalted, on account of the affinity of the acid for the protoxide: the water is then decomposed, and the resulting oxide of iron combines with the sulphuric acid to form a salt, the *sulphate of the protoxide of iron.**

The formula of sulphuric acid is SO_3: that of water is HO, as we shall presently see. The reaction may be then expressed by the following equation:

$$Fe+SO_3+HO=FeO,SO_3+H.$$

The process followed in the laboratory is founded on this reaction, but the iron is generally replaced by zinc. Zinc is used, either in the state of the laminated metal found in commerce, and which is cut into small pieces, or in that of granulated zinc. To obtain in the latter form, we melt the metal in an earthen crucible, and

* May it not be, that the dilute acid renders the iron more electropositive, and hence decomposes the water with greater facility?—*J. C. B.*

pour the liquid into a vessel full of water, which divides it into an infinity of small irregular feathered masses, presenting a large surface. The zinc is introduced into a two-mouthed bottle (fig. 137). Through one we pass a discharging tube, which conducts the gas under a bell-glass full of water, and through the other a tube surmounted by a funnel, which descends nearly to the bottom of the bottle. The bottle is first to be about half filled with water through this tube, and then, through the same way, we introduce small quantities of sulphuric acid. Reaction commences as soon as the acid comes in contact with the zinc: the temperature rises, and hydrogen gas is copiously given off. When the disengagement of the gas begins to slacken, we add more sulphuric acid. The sulphate of the protoxide of zinc remains in solution in the fluid, and may be obtained by evaporation. When an apparatus has been used to generate large quantities of hydrogen, it frequently happens that the fluid, on cooling, deposits a considerable quantity of this sulphate in a crystallized form.

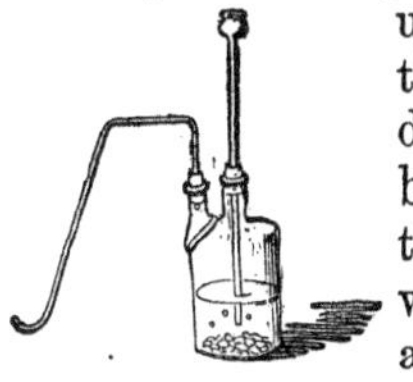
Fig. 137.

§ 70. Hydrogen gas is colourless, and, when perfectly pure, is also inodorous. That prepared in the way just described has always a disagreeable, nauseous smell; but this quality arises from the admixture of a very small quantity of foreign substances, which are to be separated, as will be hereafter explained.

Hydrogen gas has never yet been liquefied by any degree of pressure, assisted by the lowest temperature hitherto produced. It is the lightest gas known; its density is 0.0692, that of the air being 1.0000. A litre of this gas weighs, under the normal conditions of temperature and pressure, $0^{gm}.0896$. Hydrogen gas is, therefore, $14\frac{1}{2}$ times lighter than air: its utility in aeronautics is founded on this property.*

A balloon made of goldbeater's-skin, and 2 or 3 decimetres (8 or 12 inches) in diameter, inflated with hydrogen, will rise in the air.

A volume of 60 cubic metres of hydrogen gas weighs $5^{kil}.58$: an equal volume of atmospheric air weighs, under the same circumstances, $77^{kil}.59$. If, therefore, a balloon of the capacity of 60 cubic metres weighs, with its car and the contents, less than $72^{kil}.21$, it will ascend in the air.†

Soap-bubbles inflated with hydrogen rise in the air, and take fire if they approach very closely a lighted candle. In order to obtain these bubbles, we fill a bladder, provided with a stopcock, with hydrogen gas, and adapt a small tube to the mounting of the bladder; the extremity of this tube is dipped into soapsuds, and

* 100 cubic inches at 60° F. and 29.92 Bar. weigh 2.162 grains.—*J. C. B.*

† 2119 cubic feet (60 cubic meters) of hydrogen weigh $12\frac{1}{3}$ lbs. avoird., and the same bulk of air $171\frac{1}{5}$ lbs., so that if a balloon of that capacity, with its car, &c. weighed less than $158\frac{7}{8}$ lbs., it would ascend.—*J. C. B.*

removed with the liquid drop which adheres to it; then, by opening the stopcock, we obtain soap-bubbles, which separate spontaneously when they are sufficiently large.

§ 71. Hydrogen gas is eminently combustible: it burns in the air with a feeble flame. If we place above this flame a cold body, water, which is the product of combustion, is deposited. This experiment is made either by approximating a lighted taper to the opening of a bell-glass filled with hydrogen, or by adjusting a delicate curved tube to the mouth of the vessel containing the hydrogen (fig. 138). The gas is allowed to pass over for some time, in order to be sure that no atmospheric air remains in the bottle, and then a lighted taper is brought near to the curved tube: the hydrogen gas inflames and burns with a feeble flame. This apparatus is called the *philosopher's lamp.*

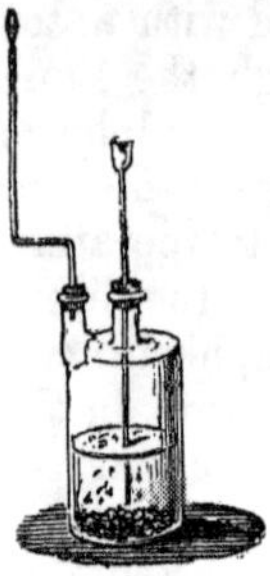

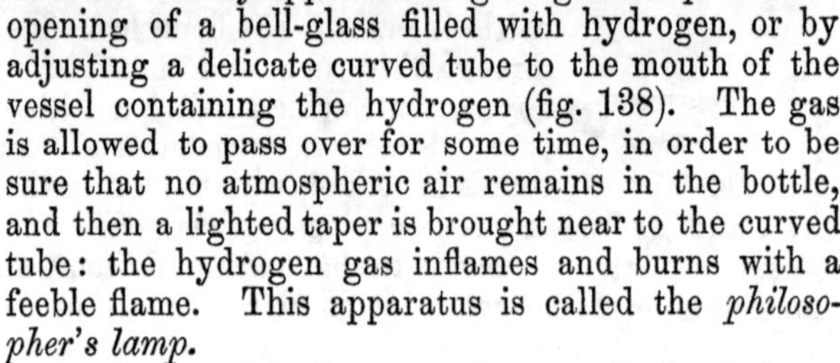

Fig. 138.

A mixture of hydrogen and atmospheric air is explosive. The most powerful possible explosion is a mixture of 2 volumes of hydrogen and 5 volumes of air. This disposition to explode must not be forgotten in making the experiment of the philosopher's lamp. If the air be not completely expelled from the bottle at the moment of lighting the gas, the flame extends to the explosive mixture contained within, the bottle bursts into a thousand pieces, and the operator runs a risk of being seriously injured.

The explosion of a mixture of 2 volumes of hydrogen and 1 volume of oxygen is incomparably more intense than that of a mixture of hydrogen and atmospheric air.

The flame of hydrogen gas is not very brilliant, but it produces a great degree of heat. The heat becomes excessively intense when the combustion is assisted by oxygen gas. The experiment is easily made by the gasometer (fig. 139): it is sufficient to place the tube *c* in the flame of the hydrogen; this flame then becomes much smaller, because the combustion of the gas takes place in a more confined space. The current of oxygen is increased or diminished by opening or closing the stopcock. The proportion of oxygen is most correct when the flame is reduced to its smallest possible size. The flame of hydrogen, fed by oxygen, produces the highest degree of heat hitherto known: it effects the fusion of substances such as lime, which undergo no change in the most elevated temperature which we can produce in our furnaces.

Fig. 139.

Various kinds of apparatus have been invented to effect the combustion of hydrogen by oxygen. Newmann's blowpipe consists of a reservoir B of thick sheet iron (fig. 140), hooped with iron, upon which is mounted a forcing pump P, by means of which the explosive mixture (2 volumes of hydrogen and 1 volume of oxygen) is introduced, under great pressure, into the reservoir. This pump receives, through the tube *t*, the gaseous mixture contained in a bell-glass in the pneumatic cistern, or in a gasometer resembling fig. 139. To do this, we begin by making a vacuum in the reservoir, which can be done with the same pump, merely by changing the action of the valves. When the vacuum is effected, the pump is made to act as a forcing-pump, and the gaseous mixture is forced into the reservoir. This receptacle has a pipe *s*, terminating in a fine point, and furnished with a cock, at the end of which the mixture is inflamed. In order to prevent the flame from extending into the inside of the reservoir, which would occasion a terrible explosion, the pipe is preceded by a brass tube T, of larger diameter, in which are introduced several layers of metallic washers, which cool the gas and prevent the combustion from extending to the reservoir. Notwithstanding this precaution, the apparatus just described has sometimes burst and caused dreadful injuries.

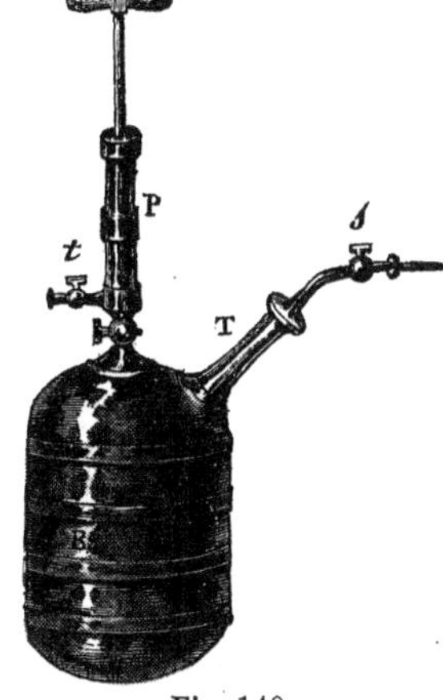

Fig. 140.

We now prefer keeping the gases separate, and mixing them only at a short distance from the orifice of the pipe: thus all danger of explosion is avoided. For this purpose, two gasometers are used, one filled with hydrogen, and the other with oxygen. Two tubes, *r* and *s*, adapted to the tubes *c* of these gasometers, convey the two gases into a single brass tube L (fig. 141), containing a great many layers of metallic washers, and to which is screwed a pipe terminating in a platinum point. The stopcocks *a* of the two gasometers are opened, in such a manner as to admit into the gasometer of hydrogen twice as much water as into the gasometer of oxygen.

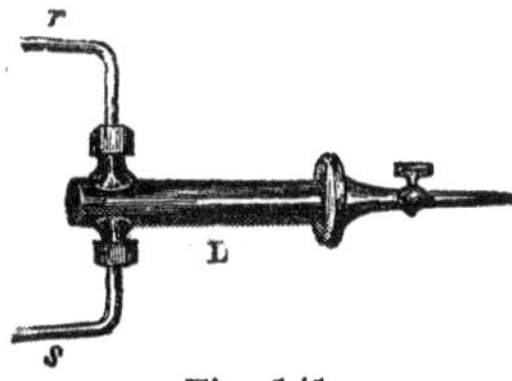

Fig. 141.

When the burning jet is directed upon a small cylinder of chalk, the lime becomes incandescent, and produces a very brilliant light, which has been called *Drummond's light.**

§ 72. Hydrogen, being itself combustible, cannot support the combustion of other combustible substances. In order to prove

* Dr. R. Hare, of Philadelphia, first burned a mixture of the two gases for producing heat and light. Refer to Encyclopedia of Chemistry, art. Blowpipe. Bags of India-rubber cloth are now used to contain the gases for class-experiments, and the jet, fig. 141, adapted to them.—*J. C. B.*

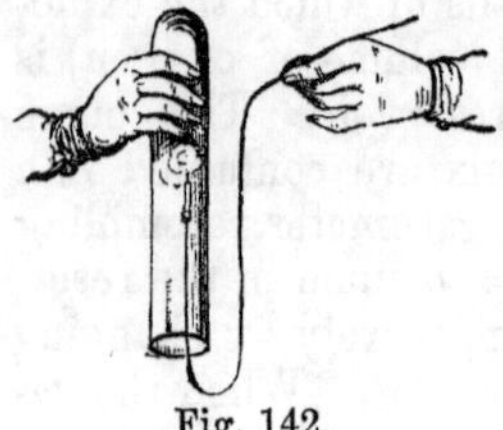
Fig. 142.

this, we close, by means of a small plate of glass, the smoothly-ground aperture of a bell-glass, filled with hydrogen, and placed in the pneumatic trough; the glass thus closed is removed without being inverted: and, on the other hand, we fasten a small wax candle to an iron wire, as represented in fig. 142. The glass is partially opened by withdrawing the plate, and the lighted candle, being introduced into the bell-glass, is immediately extinguished.

§ 73. The zinc of commerce is never absolutely pure; it always contains a small quantity of carbon in combination, and sometimes traces of sulphur and arsenic. When this zinc is dissolved in dilute sulphuric acid, a very small portion of the hydrogen combines with the carbon, and produces a very fetid, oily substance, which communicates a disagreeable odour to the whole quantity of gas. Arsenic and sulphur also combine with a small quantity of hydrogen. The gas may be entirely freed from these foreign bodies, and may be rendered inodorous by allowing it to remain for some time in contact with caustic potassa, which absorbs the oily matter and the combination of sulphur and hydrogen, and subsequently with the perchloride of mercury, or corrosive sublimate, which absorbs the combination of arsenic and hydrogen.

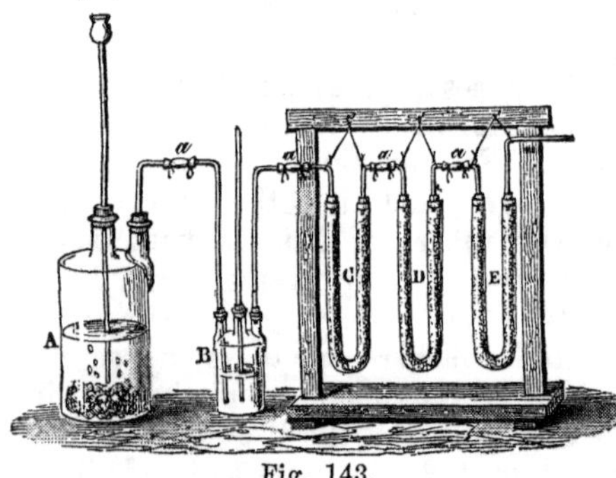

Fig. 143.

In order to obtain readily this result, the gas is made to pass through two long tubes, curved in the shape of the letter U (fig. 143), filled with pieces of pumice-stone, those in tube C saturated with a concentrated solution of caustic potassa, and in D with a solution of the chloride of mercury. The hydrogen leaves this apparatus mixed only with aqueous vapour.

We are often required to operate on dry gases. They are collected, in that case, not over water, but in a mercurial cistern. These cisterns are generally cut out of marble or some solid stone: the smaller ones are of porcelain or cast-iron. They are made of such a shape as to require the least possible quantity of mercury, and still to give, in places, depth sufficient for manipulation. Figs. 144 and 145 represent two vertical sections of mercurial troughs of marble; fig. 144 giving the longitudinal, and fig. 145 the transverse section in the plane *xy* of fig. 144. The line *zu* marks the level of the mercury.

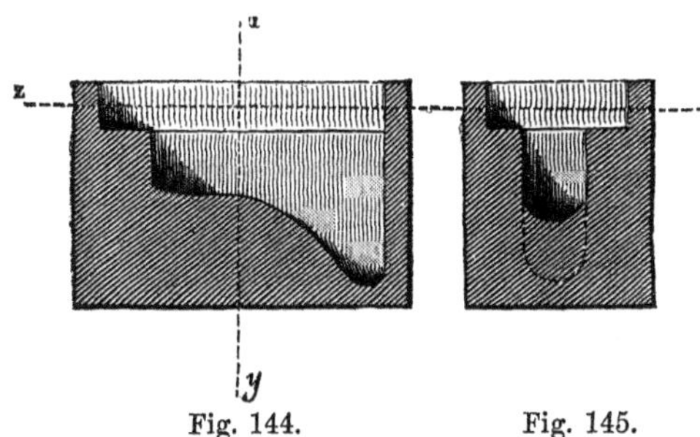

Fig. 144. Fig. 145.

The bell-glasses in which the gases are then collected must be previously well dried. In order to dry a bell-glass or a bottle, it is heated over some coals, turning it in every direction to give it a uniform temperature: and, in addition, air is constantly driven into the interior with a common bellows, to the nozzle of which a glass tube sufficiently long to penetrate to the bottom of the glass has been affixed. The bell-glass is filled with mercury, and inverted in the mercurial, precisely as in the water cistern. In order to dry the gas collected in the glass, we introduce some powerful absorbent of moisture, as a piece of melted chloride of calcium, and let it remain for several hours. At other times, the gas is dried before it is collected, and, for this purpose, is made to pass through a long tube E (fig. 143), filled with pieces of chloride of calcium.

Gases may be likewise perfectly dried by means of concentrated sulphuric acid, a substance extremely absorbent of moisture, and which gives off no sensible vapour at the ordinary temperature. Pumice-stone, previously prepared and saturated with this acid, is introduced into one of the curved tubes. As this stone frequently contains small quantities of chloride, which by contact with sulphuric acid, disengage chlorohydric acid, which would mix with the gas, it is saturated with sulphuric acid, and calcined in an earthen crucible. The chlorides are thus completely decomposed, and changed into sulphates.

§ 74. The inflammation of the explosive mixture of oxygen and hydrogen, or of hydrogen alone, in contact with the air, is not only effected by a lighted taper or an electric spark; it likewise takes place in a cold, in the presence of certain substances, the principal of which is platinum sponge.* If we throw a piece of platinum sponge into an eprouvette containing a mixture of 2 parts of hydrogen and 1 of oxygen, an explosion will instantly ensue. If we project a jet of hydrogen in the air, upon the sponge, this substance becomes incandescent and the gas inflames. The action of the sponge, in this case, has not as yet been clearly explained: but advantage has been taken of it to construct a machine for obtaining fire instantly by means of hydrogen gas.

* The name of *platinum sponge* is given to the spongy mass of metallic platinum obtained by decomposing certain combinations of platinum by heat.

COMBINATIONS OF HYDROGEN AND OXYGEN.

§ 75. We are acquainted with two combinations of hydrogen and oxygen. The first combination, the protoxide, is simply water.*

PROTOXIDE OF HYDROGEN, OR WATER, HO.

§ 76. We have seen (§ 71) that hydrogen, burning in the air, produces water; but in order to make the experiment conclusive, the gas must previously be perfectly dried, for without this precaution it might be alleged that the water arose from the moist gases, and from the solution of which the temperature always rises during the reaction. The apparatus is then arranged as in fig.

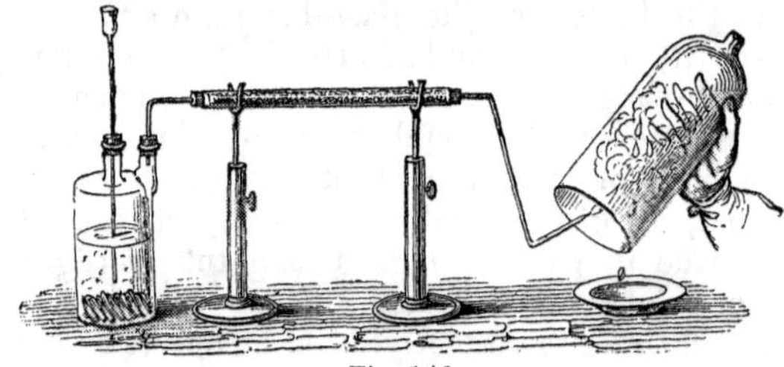

Fig. 146.

146. By holding a tubulated bell-glass slightly inclined, above the flame, the water formed by the combustion trickles down the sides of the glass, and may be collected in a saucer, in any quantity we may desire.

§ 77. Pure water is tasteless and inodorous: under slight pressure it is colourless, but when this pressure is greatly increased, it assumes a very decided greenish tinge.

Water becomes solid in the intense cold of winter. The temperature at which this change takes place is marked 32° on Fahrenheit's thermometer.† If a vessel filled with broken ice or snow be placed in a warm room, the ice soon melts, and, as soon as the fusion has commenced, a thermometer in the vessel marks constantly the same temperature, until the last portions of ice have disappeared. This constant temperature has been selected as one of the fixed points of the thermometer. Water may, however, be reduced below zero without becoming solid, which occurs when it is allowed to get cold in a vessel perfectly quiescent. It has been known to

* Water was considered by the ancients as one of the four elements of nature. It was only toward the close of the eighteenth century that it was ascertained to be composed of hydrogen and oxygen. Priestley first observed that, when hydrogen is burned in an earthen vessel, at the expense of atmospheric air, or of oxygen, a certain quantity of water is deposited on the sides of the vessel. But the composition of water has only been incontestably proved by the almost simultaneous discoveries of Watt, Cavendish, and Lavoisier.

† It is the zero, 0°, of the centigrade and Reaumur's thermometers.

descend to 10.4° F. without congealing: but if the vessel be agitated, or, better still, if a foreign body be introduced therein, icicles immediately form, and the temperature ascends to 32°, and preserves this degree until the whole of the water is solidified. A similar phenomenon occurs in the fusion of all substances.

The transformation of fluid water into ice is, therefore, an actual crystallization, which, however, but rarely gives rise to appreciable crystals: they are aciculæ dovetailed into each other and producing a continuous transparent mass. Crystalline forms may, however, be sometimes recognised in the small icicles which form in muddy water. When the temperature of the air is below 32°, the moisture is precipitated in the form of snow or hoar-frost. Each flake of snow is the union of many crystals. With a good lens, the elementary crystals, which are regular 6-sided, elongated prisms, may be recognised, grouped in stars around a centre, so as always to form angles of 60° and 120°. Nos. 2, 3, 4, 5, 6, 7, 8 of fig. 147, represent some of the most simple of these groupings. Hoar-frost frequently appears in less complicated forms, and we sometimes find perfectly regular hexahedral spangles (No. 1). The crystalline form of ice belongs, therefore, to the hexagonal system.

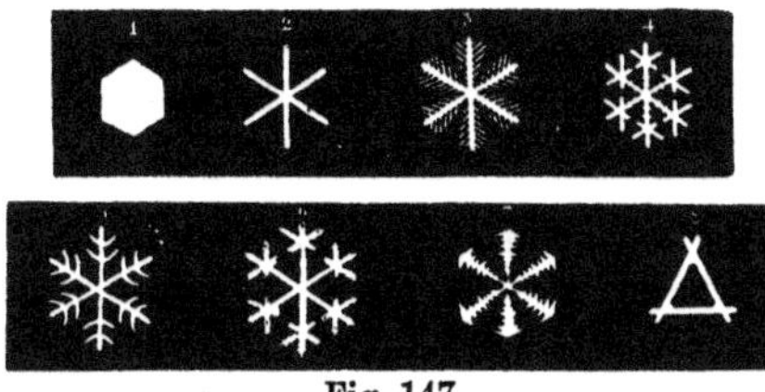
Fig. 147.

Water increases in volume by congelation, so that the density of fluid is greater than that of solid water. Fluids and solids increase in volume, *expand*, by raising their temperature: water is an exception, for a few degrees above 32°. Between 32° and 39½°, water, instead of expanding, contracts; about 39½°, it presents a minimum of volume, and, consequently, a *maximum of density*. Above 39½°, to as high a degree as has been observed, it expands regularly. It has been agreed to assume as unity the density of water at 39½°, and compare with it that of other solids or fluids.* The density of ice is therefore represented by 0.94. The force with which water expands in congelation is irresistible, and sufficient to burst the thickest bomb-shell. Very tenacious but porous stones frequently split during the winter, when the water contained in their pores is frozen.

§ 78. Water readily assumes the gaseous state: the temperature at which this change takes place depends on the pressure of the atmosphere. The second fixed point of Fahrenheit's thermometer is marked 212° (100° of the centigrade), the tempera-

* In England and the United States, we generally assume water at 60° as the unit of density.—*J. C. B.*

ture at which water boils under the pressure of 29.92 inches (760^{mm}) of mercury. The temperature at which this ebullition takes place diminishes with pressure; thus, in the vacuum of an air-pump, water will boil under a superstratum of ice.

Water assumes the aeriform state when the temperature is over 212°, and the pressure less than 29.92 bar. We shall subsequently see how we may ascertain experimentally the weight of a certain volume of this vapour, and compare it with an equal volume of atmospheric air at the same temperature and under the same pressure: this relation is called the *density of the vapour of water* (*steam*). If we ascertain its numeric value for temperatures above 212°, and successively increasing, we shall find that, from about 266°, this relation remains sensibly constant for all the higher temperatures, and that it is represented by the fraction 0.622. We shall therefore adopt this value for the density of the vapour of water. We shall hereafter define, in the same manner, the densities of other vapours.

Water gives off an appreciable vapour into the air: the formation of this vapour is the more abundant as the air is drier, that is, is less *saturated* with the vapour of water, and the temperature is higher. It is then said that water *evaporates* in the air.

The air always contains a certain quantity of the vapour of water. It is very near its *point of saturation* in rainy weather and in winter; and, on the contrary, very far from it during the hot days of summer. Certain substances possess the property of absorbing the water of the air, even when it is not saturated, and of dissolving in this water. These substances are said to be *deliquescent*, such as chloride of calcium, potassa, etc. On the contrary, other substances containing water, readily part with a portion of it to the surrounding air, if the latter is not saturated, and fall into powder: these are called *efflorescent*. Sulphate of soda belongs to this list. It is evident that no substance is efflorescent, in an atmosphere saturated with moisture, and that all soluble bodies are, on the contrary, deliquescent.

It sometimes happens, however, that substances *effloresce* by absorbing the moisture of the air. This occurs in crystallized or melted substances, which have an affinity for water, and form with it new deliquescent combinations. Melted sulphate of soda, exposed to a damp atmosphere, absorbs water and falls into powder.

§ 79. The most limpid river and spring water is not pure: this can be always ascertained by evaporation, a residuum remaining in the vessel. Rain-water is nearly pure, but, as it generally falls on roofs before being collected, it always dissolves a small quantity of foreign bodies. Water is purified by distillation. As large quantities of distilled water are used in the laboratory, this process is conducted on a large scale, in an apparatus called a *still*. The still (fig. 148) is composed of a copper kettle A, set in

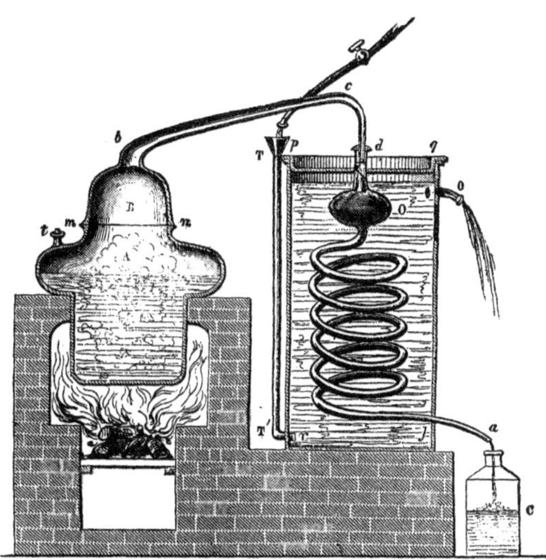

Fig. 148.

a brick furnace, and to which is fitted a head or capital B, terminated in a curved pipe *bcd*, which leads to a worm, contained in a large cylinder of metal or wood, *pqrj*, kept filled with water.* The extremity of the worm terminates at *a* outside of the cylinder. The water to be distilled is introduced into the kettle at *t*. As the water in the cylinder, which serves as a refrigerator, is necessarily heated by the condensation of the vapour in the worm, it must be occasionally renewed. This is most easily effected by means of a reservoir containing cold water, which is slowly carried by the outer tube TT′ to the lower part of the cylinder. In this way, the cold water is always at the bottom, and the heated water escapes by the tube *o* at the upper part. The supply of cold

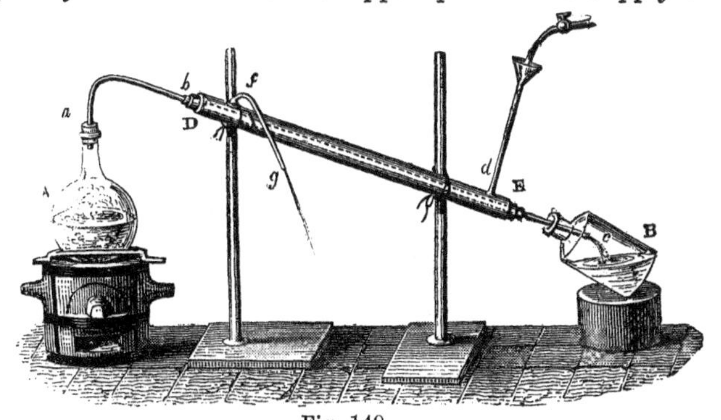

Fig. 149.

* The head, pipe, and worm should be of solid tin.—*J. C. B.*

water may be so regulated that the heated water shall escape at nearly the boiling point, and be reconducted into the kettle, thus avoiding unnecessary waste.

We are sometimes required, in the laboratory, to distil very volatile fluids, the vapour of which must be refrigerated, so as to occasion no loss. We then use one of the apparatuses (figs. 149 and 150).

In fig. 149, the balloon A contains the fluid to be distilled. The glass tube *abc* serves as a worm: it is held in a tin tube or cooler DE, by corks which should close water-tight: the end of the tube enters a bottle to receive the distilled liquid. The cooler has a funnel at *d* through which cold water enters, and at *f* a curved tube by which the heated water escapes.

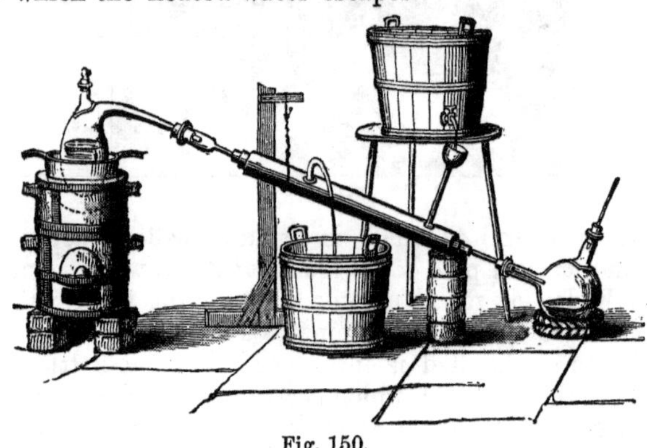

Fig. 150.

In fig. 150, the fluid to be distilled is introduced into a retort, the neck of which enters a larger tube luted to the refrigerator.

When we have but a small quantity of liquid to distil, we may contrive an apparatus, merely with glass tubes and corks, as represented in fig. 151.

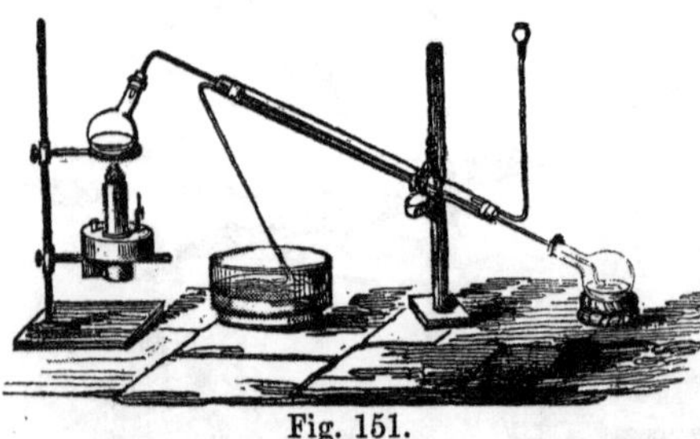

Fig. 151.

§80. Water dissolves a great number of solid and liquid substances, which, generally speaking, dissolve in greater quantities as the temperature is more elevated; so that if a hot saturated solution of these substances be allowed to cool, a portion of the substance crystallizes. To obtain the rest of the solution, the water must be evaporated. This is done by placing the solution in a porcelain saucer over hot coals, or, better still, an alcohol lamp. The operation requires care when we desire not to lose the slightest quantity of the matter in solution, as is the case in chemical analyses. The solution should not be heated to ebullition, because the bubbles of vapour which form on the heated bottom of the saucer burst on the surface, and infallibly throw out from the saucer small quantities of the solution. Fluids are frequently evaporated in a

Fig. 152.

water-bath (fig. 152): the porcelain saucer containing the solution to be evaporated, is placed upon another larger copper one partly filled with water and heated by an alcohol lamp. Sometimes, we do not put any water into the copper vessel: the porcelain saucer is then heated in an air-bath which causes a very regular evaporation. Lastly, in laboratories where there are many solutions to evaporate at once, all the saucers are put in the same sand-bath, heated by wood or coal.

It frequently happens that evaporation is required to be performed slowly and at a low temperature. The saucer is then placed on a larger glass capsule, containing concentrated sulphuric acid, and the whole is covered with a bell-glass (fig. 153). The sulphuric acid absorbs the moisture of the air as fast as it is abstracted from the solution. The evaporation is more rapid if the saucers are placed under the receiver of an air-pump from which the air is exhausted.

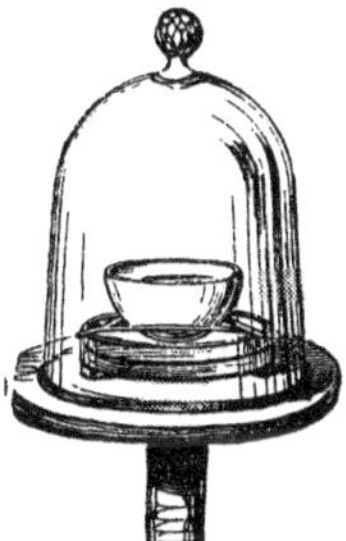

Fig. 153.

§ 81. Water dissolves gases equally. The solubility of the same gas in water increases with the diminution of temperature and pressure exerted on the solution by the undissolved portion of the gas.

When a certain volume of water is surrounded by a limited atmosphere of gas, the water dissolves such a portion of it, that this portion of gas, occupying a volume equal to that of the fluid, possesses an elastic force which is the same constant fraction $\frac{1}{m}$ of the pressure exerted by the undissolved gas on the solution. This fraction is entirely independent of the absolute value of the pressure: we shall suppose it to be $\frac{1}{n}$ for nitrogen, and $\frac{1}{n'}$ for oxygen. Thus, when 1 litre of water is surrounded by an unlimited atmosphere of oxygen, it dissolves a portion of the gas such, that this gas, occupying the volume of 1 litre, will have the density proper to it under a pressure of $\frac{1}{n'}\,h$; h representing the pressure of the undissolved oxygen gas on the liquid. If, in a second experiment, the pressure of the undissolved gas is $\frac{h}{5}$, the litre of dissolved oxygen will have the density proper to it under the pressure of $\frac{1}{n'}.\frac{h}{5}$. Hence its absolute weight will be 5 times smaller in the second case than in the first.

Where water is in contact with an atmosphere formed by the mixture of two or more gases, it dissolves of each a quantity precisely equal to that which it would have dissolved if in contact with an atmosphere of this gas alone, exerting a pressure equal to the fraction of the total pressure, proper to it in the gaseous mixture.

Thus water, in contact with the air, dissolves a quantity of nitrogen equal to that it would dissolve if in contact with an atmosphere consisting wholly of this gas, exerting a pressure equal to $\frac{4}{5}$ of that of the atmosphere, that is, $\frac{1}{n}.\frac{4}{5}$, and a quantity of oxygen $\frac{1}{n'}.\frac{1}{5}$ equal to that which it would dissolve if in contact with an atmosphere of pure oxygen exerting a pressure 5 times less than that of the atmosphere. Consequently, 1 litre of water dissolves, on contact with the air, 1 litre of oxygen with the density proper to it under a pressure of $\frac{1}{n'}.\frac{1}{5}h$: and 1 litre of nitrogen with the density proper to it under a pressure of $\frac{1}{n}.\frac{4}{5}h$. If we wish to bring these gases under the ordinary pressure of the atmosphere, it must be remembered that the volumes of the gases are inversely as the pressure exerted upon them. Consequently, 1 litre of water dissolves, on contact with the air, a fraction $\frac{1}{n'}.\frac{1}{5}$ of a litre of oxygen: and a fraction $\frac{1}{n}.\frac{4}{5}$ of a litre of nitrogen, and, therefore, a total volume of gas represented by $\frac{1}{n'}.\frac{1}{5}+\frac{1}{n}.\frac{4}{5}$.

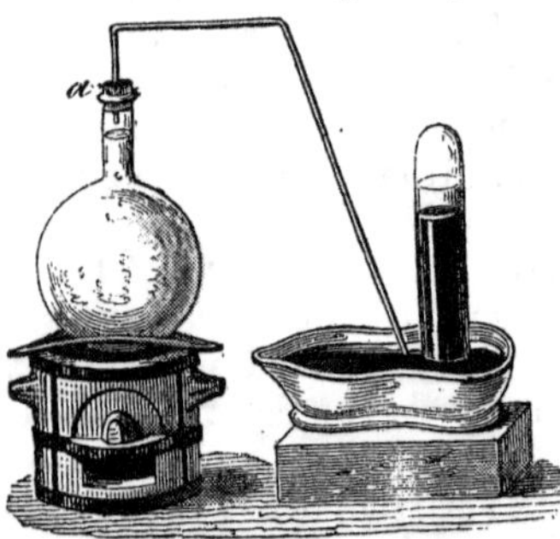

Fig. 154.

The whole volume of the gas dissolved may be easily ascertained by means of the following experiment. Fill a glass balloon (fig. 154) entirely with water; fill also the discharging tube; then insert the stopper *a* into the neck of the balloon: the displaced water escapes by the tube, and the apparatus is perfectly filled with water. Pass the curved end of the tube under a bell-glass filled with mercury, and apply heat to the balloon. When the temperature of the water approaches 40° or 50°, little bubbles are seen to disengage from the sides of the balloon. If the water be made to boil, for a few minutes, the vapour drives the disengaged air into the bell-glass. We measure the volume of air thus collected, and compare it to that of the water from which it arose.

§ 82. Water combines with a great number of substances. With powerful acids it acts the part of a feeble base; and, on the contrary, that of a feeble acid with powerful bases.

Water combines with a great number of salts when these are crystallized in their aqueous solutions; the same salt frequently combines with very different proportions of water, according to the temperature at which crystallization takes place.

§ 83. ANALYSIS OF WATER.—Let us now ascertain the relative proportions in which hydrogen and oxygen combine to form water. To do this, we introduce into the same bell-glass, over mercury, the well-known volumes of these gasses, and apply heat to the mixture. The two gases combine in determinate proportions and form water, which condenses on the sides of the bell-glass. As that gas which is in excess does not entirely disappear, we measure the remainder and ascertain the volumes of the two gases which have combined.

To perform this experiment, we must procure bell-glasses marked into equal divisions and intended to measure gases. Such glasses may be bought, but it is better to divide them ourselves, when we wish to be very exact. We select a bell of very pure glass, of 1 or 2 centimetres ($\frac{1}{2}$ to $\frac{3}{4}$ inch) diameter internally, and 2 or 3 decimetres (8 to 12 inches) in length. It is placed vertically, the closed end downward. We then make a measure or gauge A (fig. 155) with a piece of closed tube, the edges of which are very accurately ground, so that the mouth of the tube may be exactly closed with the small plate of polished glass B. The gauge is then over-filled with mercury, the excess of which is driven off by the glass plate, or *obturator*, applied to its mouth. This measure is poured into the bell-glass to be divided, and the air-bubbles which adhere to its sides are carefully removed. This being done, a mark is made on the glass at the level of the mercury, a second measure poured in, another mark made, and so on.

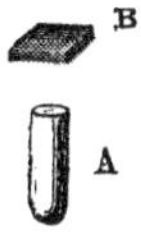

Fig. 155.

It is evident that the spaces between the marks on the glass correspond to equal capacities: and if the bell-glass be not too irregular, it may be granted that they preserve the same diameter in each of the spaces. These spaces may be made to vary in size, according to that of the gauge.

After this preliminary gauging of the bell-glass, it is to be emptied, and covered with a thin coat of the common liquid varnish of the copper engravers. The bell-glass is then placed in a dividing machine, and, by means of an iron point, we mark, on the coat of varnish, divisions arranged in such a manner that each space between two consecutive marks of the gauging shall contain the same number of equal divisions. A larger mark is made at each fifth division, to facilitate its reading, and figures are marked at every tenth. The divisions are then painted with hydrofluoric acid in solution. This acid possesses the property of dissolving glass: and consequently attacks the surface of the bell-glass from which the varnish has been removed, and leaves the divisions engraved thereon.

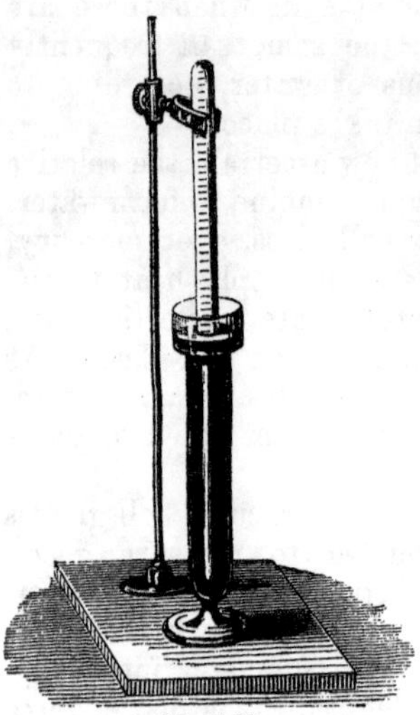

Fig. 156.

When we purchase graduated bell-glasses, they should be verified, if required for exact experiments. This is easily done by means of small gauges resembling those with which we have just measured the bell-glass, or by pouring into the glass quantities of mercury which have been accurately weighed. It is evident that, if the glass be correctly graduated, the volumes occupied by the quantities of mercury should be proportional to their weight.

The bell-glass being accurately graduated, we introduce a certain volume of hydrogen, exactly weighed, taking care to plunge the glass into the mercury until the level of this metal is the same within and without. It is more convenient to make this measurement as in fig. 156, in a glass eprouvette, in which we can more readily level the mercury and read the division. A certain quantity of oxygen gas is then introduced into the same bell-glass. The mixture is then introduced into an apparatus called a *eudiometer*, and which is so arranged that an electric spark can be passed into its interior. The eudiometer (fig. 157) is composed of very thick glass, having at its upper part an iron mounting *a* passing through the thickness of the tube, and hermetically cemented to the opening. On the side of the glass, at *b*, a second hole is bored, in which is cemented a strong iron wire, which penetrates nearly to the upper mounting. The outer extremity of this wire is hooked. The eudiometer, filled with mercury, is inverted over the mercurial trough and the mixture of the gases introduced. The surface of the glass is rubbed several times with a hot rag. The mixture is then exploded by means of a galvanic battery applied at *a* and *b*.

Fig. 157.

At the moment of combustion, a great quantity of heat is disengaged, producing considerable dilatation of the gases, and therefore the gaseous mixture should only half fill the eudiometer, else a part of it would infallibly be projected from the tube. This loss is prevented by closing the opening of the eudiometer with a valved stopper A. At the moment of explosion, there is an increase of elastic force in the apparatus, and the dish *i* is closely applied to the surface of the stopper, so that nothing can escape. As soon as the heat is dissipated, which soon occurs, the water condenses in liquid drops on the sides of the eudiometer, and then occupies a volume 2000 times less than that of the gases from which it sprang. The tension in the apparatus is then lessened, the valve *i* rises, and the mercury enters the eudiometer.

If the gases disappear entirely, it is a proof that the quantities introduced were exactly in the proportion proper to form water: which happens if we have introduced exactly 1 volume of oxygen and 2 volumes of hydrogen. In general, one of these gases is in excess, the gaseous residuum is then passed into the graduated bell-glass, measured, and its return ascertained by the application of a lighted taper; if it burns, the residuum is hydrogen.

Suppose that we introduce into the eudiometer

100 measures of hydrogen,
75 measures of oxygen:

we shall find, after combustion, 25 of oxygen. Therefore, 100 of hydrogen have combined with 50 of oxygen, or 2 volumes of hydrogen and 1 of oxygen.

The same experiment may be made over the water-trough, but then we cannot ascertain the nature of the product of combustion. When we use the water-trough, the mountings of the eudiometer should be of brass. There is also a water-eudiometer (fig. 158) which is readily used. It is composed of a thick glass cylinder AB, intended to contain the mixture: this cylinder is fitted below into a brass mounting BC, having a stopcock at S. A funnel C allows the introduction of the gas. The glass cylinder communicates above with a second funnel D, into which we put water. A stopcock R permits or cuts off the communication. A graduated glass tube EF is screwed to the bottom of the cup D. Lastly, at *v*, the metallic mounting A is perforated by a hole, into which a glass tube has been cemented, traversed by the metallic rod *t*, which is thus isolated from the metallic mounting and nearly approximated to it internally.

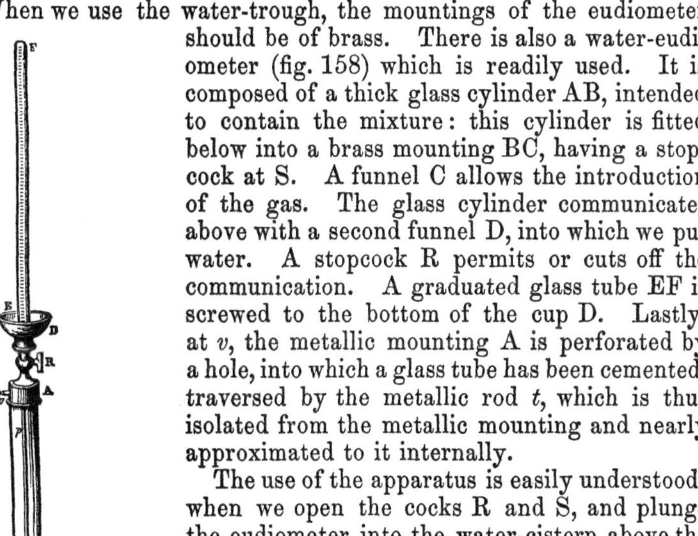

Fig. 158.

The use of the apparatus is easily understood: when we open the cocks R and S, and plunge the eudiometer into the water-cistern above the cup D, it fills with water: we close the cock R and raise the eudiometer. Measure in the graduated tube EF the hydrogen and oxygen, and introduce the mixture into the eudiometer through the funnel C. The mixture is then exploded as before, by means of the button *t*, and at the moment of explosion the cock S must be closed to prevent the escape of the gas.

The remaining gas is now to be measured: this is easily done in the graduated tube EF. To do this, we fill the tube with water, and invert it in the cup D, where it is screwed. By opening the cock R, the gas will pass into the tube EF. To measure it, we unscrew the tube, and plunge it into the water-cistern, so as to establish a coincidence of level externally and internally.

Fig. 159.

The greatest difficulty of eudiometric analyses performed over mercury is owing to the extravasation of the gases: but it may be avoided by using eudiometers divided into equal parts. In order to construct such eudiometers, we select a glass tube closed at one end, of above 10 or 15 millimetres ($\frac{1}{3}$ to $\frac{1}{2}$ inch) in diameter internally, and 1 or 2 millimetres (.04 to .08 inch) in thickness. We bore two small holes *a* and *b* in the tube (fig. 159) by means of a small steel drill in a turning-lathe, keeping the spot moistened with turpentine. We can thus pierce the tube without any risk of breaking it. We then cement to these holes pieces of platinum wire, which are brought nearly to touch each other inside of the glass.

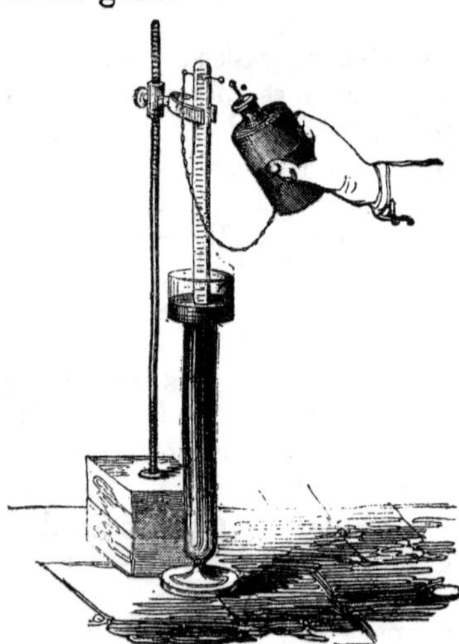

Fig. 160.

We may also solder the platinum wire to the glass, by means of an enameller's lamp. This is preferable when the walls of the glass are not very thick.

The tube is then divided into equal divisions. The walls of this eudiometer being generally thinner than those of the ordinary eudiometer, it is prudent not to hold it in the hand at the moment of explosion, but to fix it in a support (fig. 160).

We may also use another arrangement, which has the advantage of requiring only a small quantity of mercury. The eudiometer has the shape of a tube curved like the letter U. In order to fill it with mercury, it is made to assume the position of fig. 161, and then that of fig. 162: the closed leg A remains filled with mercury. The two gases are introduced by passing into the open leg B the discharging tubes of the gasometers, and causing them to ascend into the leg A. The volumes of the gases introduced, and of the residuum after combustion, are measured in the eudiometer itself, by carefully bringing the

Fig. 161. 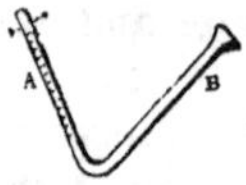 Fig. 162.

mercury to the same level in both legs, which is readily done by abstracting or adding the metal with a pipette.

We shall describe hereafter, in a chapter devoted to the analysis of gaseous mixtures, an eudiometric apparatus more perfect than those just explained, and which furnishes us with very exact results.

§ 84. Water therefore results from the combination of 2 volumes of hydrogen and 1 of oxygen: hence, we can easily deduce the composition of water in weight, since we know the densities of these two gases. In fact, 1 volume of air weighing 1.0000,

1 volume of oxygen weighs	....	1.1056
2 " hydrogen "	2×0.0692 ...... =	0.1384
The water produced weighs	....	1.2440

In order to obtain the quantity of hydrogen and oxygen which forms 100 grammes of water, we make the proportions

$$1.2440 : 1.1056 : : 100 : x,$$
$$\text{whence } x = 88.87.$$
$$1.2440 : 0.1384 : : 100 : y,$$
$$\text{whence } y = 11.13;$$

therefore, 100 parts of water contain 11.13 hydrogen,
88.87 oxygen,
100.00

When 2 volumes of hydrogen combine with 1 volume of oxygen, what is the value of the vapour of water resulting from the combination? If the 2 volumes of hydrogen, combining with 1 of oxygen, formed only a single volume of vapour of water, the density of this vapour would be 1.244. But direct experiment has given, for this density, a value one-half less, that is, 0.622: therefore, 2 volumes of hydrogen combining with 1 of oxygen, have produced, not 1, but 2 volumes of vapour of water.

§ 85. We cannot avoid calling the attention of the student to the simplicity of the relations presented by the volumes of the two combining gases, and the vapour of water resulting from their combination, instead of the complicated and infinitely variable relations which might have occurred. This is not a fortuitous circumstance, peculiar to the case under consideration. We shall also recognise very simple relations in the combinations of the other elementary gases. The study of such combinations has discovered this law[1] of nature: *When two elementary gases combine, their volumes have to each other very simple numerical ratios, and the volume of the resulting compound, considered in the gaseous state, bears also a very simple ratio to the sum of the volumes of the gases which entered into the combination.*

[1] Discovered by M. Gay-Lussac.

§ 86. Another method, still more exact than the eudiometer, has been employed to determine directly the weight of hydrogen and oxygen which combine to form water. Several metallic oxides, heated in a current of hydrogen gas, give off their oxygen, and are reduced to a metallic state. This oxygen, combining with the hydrogen, forms water which can be weighed. The loss in weight of the metallic oxide, gives the weight of the oxygen entering into the water. The difference between the two weights gives the hydrogen.

It is necessary to use in this experiment pure and perfectly dry hydrogen: it is prepared by means of the apparatus described (§ 73), and represented by ABCDE (fig. 163). The oxide of copper is introduced into a strong glass balloon F, with two necks. This balloon communicates with another G, intended to collect the

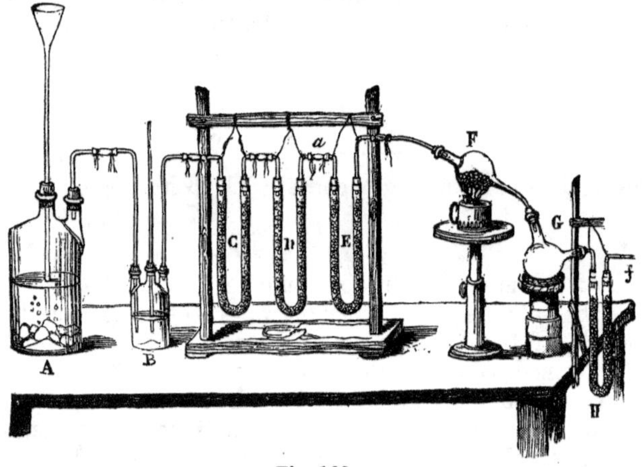

Fig. 163.

greater part of the water formed in the experiment: it is succeeded by a tube H, filled with pumice-stone soaked in concentrated sulphuric acid, and which absorbs the last portions of water. Before making the experiment, we weigh with the greatest nicety the balloon F, empty and very dry; then the same balloon with the oxide of copper perfectly dried. The difference between the two weights gives that of the contained oxide. The balloon G and the tube H are also weighed. The apparatus being arranged, the hydrogen gas is slowly generated, and continued for a long time, in order completely to drive the air out of the apparatus. When it is completely filled with hydrogen, the balloon F is heated by an alcohol lamp. The combustion of the hydrogen with the oxygen of the oxide of copper soon commences, and the water trickles down the sides of the balloon G: the last particles of water formed condense in the tube H, which the hydrogen in excess must traverse before passing out into the air. The experiment is continued until the oxide of copper is completely reduced to the state of metallic copper. The balloon G is then allowed to cool, in the midst of the current of hydrogen; then the portion of the apparatus to the left is separated from the caoutchouc *a*. The balloons GF and the tube H are then filled with hydrogen, and if weighed in this state, the difference between their weights before and after the experiment would depend, not only on the substances which they have condensed during the reaction, but also on the excess of weight of the air which originally filled the apparatus, over the hydrogen which has replaced it. The apparatus must therefore be restored to its primitive condition, and again be filled with atmospheric air. For this purpose, we secure, by means of caoutchouc, the extremity *f* of the tube H (fig. 163) to the tube *s* of fig. 164. This tube communicates with the upper part of the aspirator V, filled with water. At I is a tube filled with pumice-stone, which prevents the vapour of the water in the jar V from penetrating into the tube H, and increasing its weight. By opening the stopcock *r*, the water flows out, and is replaced by air which enters at *a* (fig. 163), is deprived of its moisture in the tube E filled with pumice-stone soaked in sulphuric acid, traverses the apparatus FGH, and drives out the hydrogen from it. If we maintain a nearly regular current of air, it will be sufficient to cause the tube to descend into the water to a certain distance above the level whence the water flows; the jar then acts the part of a Mariotte's jar, and the discharge is nearly regular, so long as the level of the water does not reach the end of the tube. We weigh separately, first the balloon F, then the receiver G, with the tube H. The difference between the weight of the balloon F, containing the oxide of copper, before the experiment, and its weight when containing the metallic copper, gives the weight of the oxygen in the water. The increased weight of the receiver G and the tube H gives the weight of the water formed.

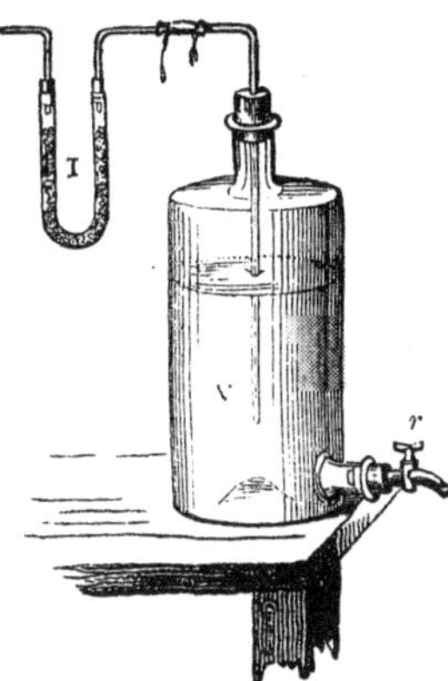

Fig. 164.

The most exact experiments made in this way, have shown that 100 parts of water contain,

Hydrogen	11.11.
Oxygen	88.89.
	100.00.

§ 87. In the experiment just described, as well as that performed in the eudiometer, we ascertain the composition of water by finding the volumes or weights of the separate elements which enter into it: we thus make what is called the *synthesis* of water. But we frequently ascertain the composition of compound bodies by an inverse method. These bodies are decomposed, so as to ascertain the weight of their elements, either by really isolating these elements, or uniting them in combinations of which the composition is known. This process is called *analysis*.

We have described (§ 68) an experiment by which water is decomposed, by passing its vapour through a porcelain tube heated to redness and containing metallic iron. If, in this experiment, we measure the volume of hydrogen gas disengaged, and from this measure deduce the weight of this gas: if, on the other hand, we ascertain the weight of the oxygen which combined with the iron, by weighing the latter before and after the experiment,—we shall have obtained by *analysis* the composition of water. But this experiment is not sufficiently exact.

The composition of water may be determined exactly, by *analysis*, by means of the voltaic pile. If we plunge the two poles of a battery terminating in platinum wire into water slightly acidulated with sulphuric acid, we shall see small bubbles of gas along each wire. These gases may be collected in separate bell-glasses, and we shall find that the gas disengaged at the positive pole is oxygen, and that collected at the negative pole is hydrogen, and that the volume of the latter is precisely double that of the oxygen. The experiment is generally performed in the apparatus represented in fig. 165. The bottom of a wine-glass is pierced with two very small holes, through which the platinum wires are passed. To close them completely some melted mastic is poured into the glass. The glass is filled with acidulated water, and a small graduated bell-glass is placed over each wire. In order to effect the decomposition of the water, it will be enough to bring the platinum wires in communication with the two wires of the battery. The addition of a small quantity of sulphuric acid renders the water a better conductor of electricity, and consequently facilitates its decomposition.

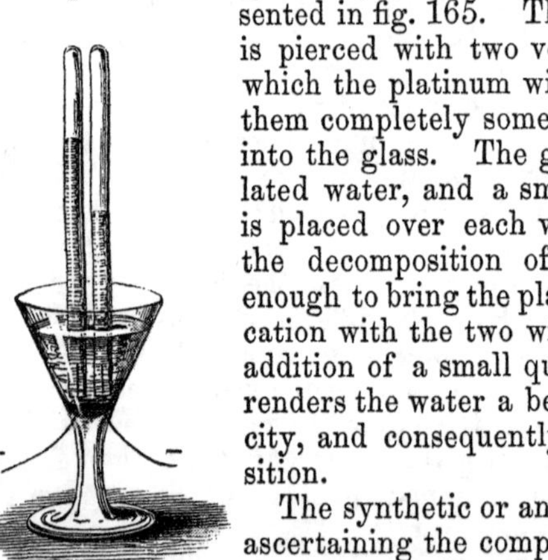

Fig. 165.

The synthetic or analytic method is used for ascertaining the composition of bodies, according as one or the other mode appears more applicable to the case.

§ 88. We frequently express the composition of water in another manner. Instead of inquiring how much hydrogen and oxygen are in 100 parts of water, we ask how much hydrogen is required to form water with 8 parts of oxygen, and say,

	8 of oxygen combine
with........................	1 of hydrogen
and form....................	9 of water.

The quantities 8 of oxygen and 1 of hydrogen are called *equivalent quantities*, or *chemical equivalents;* and we have *agreed* to assign as the *equivalent of water* the number 9, which is the quantity of water containing the quantities 8 of oxygen and 1 of hydrogen. In the same manner, if we consider these bodies in the gaseous state, 1 volume of oxygen *is equivalent* to 2 volumes of hydrogen in the formation of water; and we say that the *equivalent* of oxygen in volume is 1 volume, and the *equivalent* of hydrogen is 2 volumes. From the above definition, the equivalent of the vapour of water is therefore 2 volumes, since it requires 2 volumes of vapour of water to give 1 of oxygen and 2 of hydrogen.

We shall adopt the letter O to express the equivalent of oxygen, that is the weight 8 of oxygen, and the letter H to express the equivalent of hydrogen, or its weight 1. The equivalent of water, that is the weight 9 of water, will be represented by HO. Thus, the characters, H, O, and HO recall not only the nature of the bodies they represent (§ 54), but also the determinate weight of those bodies, or *their equivalents.*

Lastly, the composition of water is expressed in another manner which deserves to be mentioned, because it is used by many chemists.

It is admitted that bodies are formed of molecules, indivisible by mechanical means, and which are called *atoms.* Let us suppose that, when two bodies combine, an atom of one of these bodies unites to 1, 2, 3, 4, 5... atoms of the second, or 2 atoms of the first with 3, 5, 7, 9... of the second. The law of the combination of gases according to simple proportions, a law demonstrated by experiment, will merely be a consequence of the preceding hypotheses, if we admit that the number of atoms contained in equal volumes of the different gases bear to each simple proportions. Let us advance the most plain hypothesis, and admit that *equal volumes of all the elementary gases contain the same number of atoms.* Experiment has shown that 1 volume of oxygen combines with 2 of hydrogen to form water: we can therefore say that 1 atom of oxygen combines with 2 of hydrogen to form 1 atom of water. But the proportions between the ponderable quantities of oxygen, hydrogen, and water, as ascertained by experiment are as the numbers 8 : 1 : 9; we may therefore say that the proportions between the weights of the atom of oxygen, the atom of hydrogen, and the atom of water are those of the numbers 8 : $\frac{1}{2}$: 9, or even, absolutely, that the weight of the atom of oxygen, or

the *atomic* weight of	oxygen is..............................	8
	hydrogen..............................	$\frac{1}{2}$
	water	9

If we adopt the characters H and O to represent the atomic weight of hydrogen and oxygen, it is evident that the atomic formula of water will be H_2O.

The double atom of hydrogen is often represented by the character H. The formula of water is then HO. Many chemists represent the atoms of oxygen by an equal number of points placed above the character which expresses the substance combined with the oxygen: thus, they write water H.

We shall exclusively adopt the notation of equivalents in the present work.

BINOXIDE OF HYDROGEN, HO_2.

§ 89. Hydrogen can combine with a quantity of oxygen greater than that necessary to form water. The second combination has received the name of *binoxide of hydrogen*, or *oxygenated water*.[1] We have seen (§ 64) that by heating the peroxide of manganese with concentrated sulphuric acid, the peroxide is brought to a state of protoxide, which combines with the sulphuric acid, and the oxygen is given off. Other peroxides undergo similar decomposition, when cold, and in contact with dilute acids: but then the oxygen which is freed is not given off, but remains in combination with the water: this is the case with the peroxides of barium, strontium, and potassium. The peroxide of barium is used for the preparation of oxygenated water. This peroxide is rubbed with water in a porcelain mortar, so as to form a liquid paste: and this paste is gradually added to a mixture of 1 part of ordinary chlorohydric acid, and 3 parts of water, contained in a porcelain capsule, and constantly stirred with a glass rod. The peroxide of barium dissolves without the disengagement of any gas: chloride of barium, water, and oxygen, which remains in combination with the water, are formed.

Binoxide of Barium. { Oxygen .... Binoxide of hydrogen.
Protoxide of barium or baryta .... { Barium .... Chloride of barium.
Oxygen .... Water.
Chlorohydric acid ... { Hydrogen .... Water.
Chlorine .... Chloride of barium.

The substances brought into contact are the binoxide of barium, of which the formula is BaO_2, and chlorohydric acid, which we write HCl. The water of the hydrate of the binoxide of barium is separated in combination with one-half of the oxygen of the binoxide, and consequently in the state of binoxide of hydrogen, which dissolves in the surrounding water. The products of the reaction are the chloride of barium BaCl, and the binoxide of hydrogen which, as we shall presently see, we should write HO_2. We may therefore express the reaction by the following equation:

$$BaO_2 + HCl = BaCl + HO_2.$$

[1] Also called peroxide of hydrogen, and discovered by Thenard in 1818.

When the chlorohydric acid is nearly saturated by the baryta, we pour into the solution sulphuric acid, which precipitates the barium in the state of insoluble sulphate of baryta, and the chlorohydric acid is again formed in the liquid.

Chloride of barium...... { Chlorine.................. / Barium..
Water...................... { Oxygen... >Baryta... / Hydrogen................
Sulphuric acid..
> Chlorohydric acid. Sulphate of baryta.

$$BaCl + HO + SO_3 = BaO,SO_3 + HCl.$$

Toward the close, the sulphuric acid is added dropwise, in order not to be in excess. The sulphate of baryta is separated by a fine filter, and we obtain a liquid identical with the original acid liquid, except that it contains a certain quantity of binoxide of hydrogen. We can treat this fluid like the original acid fluid, and dissolve it in an additional quantity of binoxide of barium, until it is saturated with chlorohydric acid, and then again precipitate the baryta by sulphuric acid. After this second operation, the acid solution contains twice as much binoxide of hydrogen as after the first. When these operations have been repeated frequently enough, we obtain a liquid well charged with binoxide of hydrogen, but which contains chlorohydric acid, of which it must be freed. To do this, we add, gradually, some sulphate of silver. Chloride of silver, which precipitates, is formed; and sulphuric acid, which is dissolved in the liquid.

Chlorohydric acid....... { Chlorine.......... .... / Hydrogen....
Sulphate of silver....... { Oxygen. ...... >Water. / Silver .... / Sulphuric acid.
> Chloride of silver.

$$AgO,SO_3 + HCl = AgCl + SO_3 + HO.$$

The sulphuric acid is precipitated, in its turn, by a solution of baryta, which is added dropwise, so as to use only the quantity absolutely necessary. The liquid is again filtered, and placed under the receiver of the air-pump, above a large capsule containing concentrated sulphuric acid. We may thus obtain the binoxide of hydrogen in a state of great concentration, and even of entire purity.

A condition essential to the success of the experiment is to keep the vessel containing the acid liquid in ice, whilst we dissolve the binoxide of barium in it, in order that the fluid may not become heated, which would decompose a great portion of the binoxide of hydrogen. The precipitates of sulphate of baryta which are successively separated, contain a considerable quantity of fluid: we must squeeze them carefully in a cloth, so as to lose as little fluid as possible. It is also well to add, from time to time, a few drops of chlorohydric acid, to replace that which is lost in all these manipulations.

The experiment may be much simplified as follows:—After having, for the first time, saturated the solution of chlorohydric acid with the binoxide of barium, we add an additional quantity of concentrated chlorohydric acid; then a second dose of binoxide of barium, which gives an additional quantity of binoxide of hydrogen and chloride of barium. By exposing the solution to a very low temperature, a great portion of the chloride of barium crystallizes: it is separated by pouring the fluid into another vessel. We again add chlorohydric acid, then the binoxide of barium, and so on. We thus obtain a fluid highly charged with binoxide of hydrogen, and never containing more than the quantity of chloride of barium which it can hold in solution at a very low temperature. This quantity is not great, if we take care, at the close, to plunge the solution into a freezing mixture of pounded ice and sea-salt, in which the temperature falls to 14°. In order to separate the chloride of barium which remains in the fluid, we add, gradually, the sulphate of silver, which precipitates, at once, the chlorine in the state of chloride of silver, and the barium in the state of sulphate of baryta. These precipitates are separated, and the fluid is evaporated under the receiver of an air-pump.

§ 90. The binoxide of hydrogen, reduced to its maximum of concentration, is a colourless fluid, of a syrupy consistence, and possessing a peculiar odour. Its density is 1.453. It has never been solidified at any temperature. This fluid is not very fixed, and decomposes spontaneously at a temperature of 59° to 68°. When heated, its decomposition is very rapid, and sometimes takes place with an explosion. The binoxide of hydrogen dissolved in water is more fixed, and does not decompose until the liquid is heated to 104° to 122°.

The ready decomposition of the binoxide of hydrogen by heat, renders its analysis very simple. We weigh a certain quantity of the binoxide, dissolve it in water, boil the solution, and collect the oxygen which is given off. Now, it will be remembered that this quantity of oxygen is precisely equal to that which exists in the quantity of water arising from the decomposition of the binoxide, and which is formed by subtracting the weight of the oxygen collected from the weight of the binoxide submitted to analysis.

This analysis is performed in the apparatus represented in fig. 166. The solution of the binoxide of hydrogen is put into the small flask A, to which is fixed a curved tube *bcd*, of which the curved end descends into a cylinder C full of mercury, but so that the end *d* of the tube may be above the level of the mercury. Before fitting the cork to the neck of the small bottle, we pass over the tube *cd* a graduated tube B, which descends into the test-glass, until the tube *d* nearly reaches its top: the tube B is held

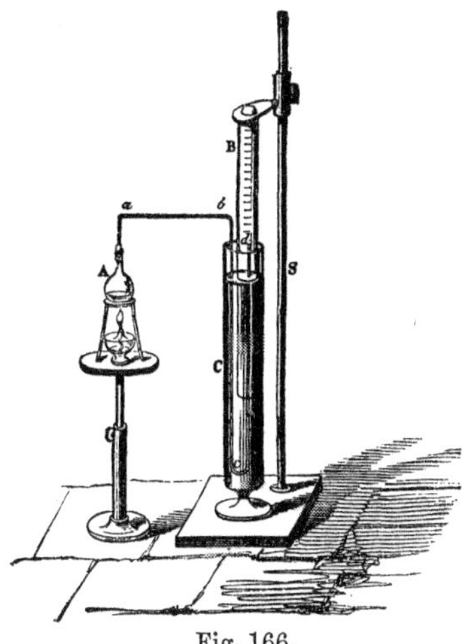

Fig. 166.

in this position by the support S. The cork is then fitted, and the level of the mercury within and without the tube exactly adjusted, which is readily done by abstracting or adding, with a pipette, a small quantity of mercury in the test-glass C: lastly, we note to what division the mercury rises.

The balloon is heated: as the oxygen disengages, the bell-glass is raised, so as to maintain an equal pressure within and without. When the water has boiled for a few moments, decomposition is completed. The apparatus is allowed to assume the ordinary temperature, the level of the mercury is established, and the division it has reached marked down: the increase of volume of gas in the bell-glass represents the volume of disengaged oxygen.

We have just seen that the binoxide of hydrogen produces, when decomposed by heat, quantities of water and oxygen such that the oxygen disengaged is precisely equal to that which exists in the water which has become free. Now, water consists of 1 equivalent of hydrogen and 1 of oxygen, and we write it HO: the binoxide of hydrogen is therefore considered as consisting of 1 equivalent of hydrogen and 2 of oxygen, and its chemical formula should be HO_2.

Solutions of the binoxide of hydrogen being more fixed when they contain some hydrochloric acid, a small quantity of this acid is generally allowed to remain, when we wish to preserve them.

The binoxide of hydrogen parts with its oxygen readily to a number of substances, converting metallic oxides into peroxides. It bleaches the tincture of litmus like chlorine. A drop on the skin makes a white mark.

§ 91. The solution of binoxide of hydrogen in contact with certain substances exhibits some very remarkable phenomena. With gold, platina, and silver finely divided, or certain metallic oxides, such as the peroxide of manganese, peroxide of lead, etc., it decomposes with effervescence by giving off oxygen, whilst the substances which affected the decomposition undergo no change. These substances acted by their presence, but did not enter chemically into the reaction. This mysterious action is called *action of presence* or *catalysis;* we shall find it again in several phenomena. It is proper to remark that substances act, in these cases, with more energy in proportion to their division, for the oxygen only disengages from the surface.

If we add a few drops of sulphuric acid to oxygenated water which is decomposing from the presence of silver or of peroxide of manganese, the evolution of the gas is immediately arrested, but reappears if the acid is saturated by a base. Salts do not effect the decomposition of oxygenated water.

Metallic oxides easily reduced, as the oxides of silver, gold, and platinum, exhibit a very remarkable phenomenon with oxygenated water; which is not only decomposed, but the oxides themselves part with their oxygen and return to the metallic state.

The ready decomposition of oxygenated water by the peroxide of manganese furnishes a simple method of determining by approximation the richness of a solution of binoxide of hydrogen. We fill a small graduated bell-glass with mercury, and, with a pipette, pass a small quantity of the solution to the top of it. We mark the number of divisions it occupies, and introduce some finely divided peroxide of manganese, wrapped in tissue-paper. Decomposition ensues as soon as the powder reaches the fluid. The volume of the oxygen disengaged, compared with the volume of the solution which has produced it, gives the richness or strength of the fluid.

NITROGEN, OR AZOTE.*

EQUIVALENT = 175.0.

§ 92. We have seen that atmospheric air supports combustion only by means of the oxygen it contains. When the oxygen of the air has been absorbed by the combustible substance, there remains a gas in which all combustion is immediately extinguished. This gas is *nitrogen*, or *azote*. We float on the surface of the water of a cistern (fig. 167) a large cork, on which is placed a small porcelain capsule containing a bit of phosphorus, to which fire is communicated by a taper, and the capsule is immediately covered with a large bell-glass, immersed a short distance in the water. Combustion continues in the confined volume of air, until the oxygen has entirely disappeared in consequence of its combination with phosphorus. From this combination results phosphoric acid, which dissolves in the water. When the gas has cooled, after the extinction of the phosphorus, we find that its volume has considerably decreased, and is reduced to about $\frac{4}{5}$.

Fig. 167.

If we require only a small quantity of nitrogen gas, we may deprive the air of its oxygen by means of phosphorus at the ordinary temperature. It is sufficient to allow a stick of phosphorus to remain for twenty-four hours in a bell-glass filled with air, over the pneumatic cistern.

Copper, heated to redness, also deprives air very perfectly of its oxygen. A current of pure nitrogen can readily be procured from the gasometer described (§ 60), by introducing some copper turnings into a hard glass tube *ef* (fig. 168), one of the ends of which, *e*, is made to communicate with the tube *c* of the gasometer, and to the other end *f* a discharging tube is fitted, which allows the gas to be collected. As atmospheric air always contains a small quantity of carbonic acid, and is moreover saturated with water in the gasometer, if we wish to obtain perfectly pure nitrogen, it is necessary, before it reaches the tube filled with copper turnings, to pass it first through a tube T containing pumice-stone soaked in caustic potassa, which absorbs the carbonic acid, and a

* The name *nitrogen* (which generates nitre) has been given to this gas, because it forms an acid with oxygen, nitric, also called azotic acid, which, combining with potassa, forms the nitrate of potassa, commonly called *nitre*, or saltpetre.

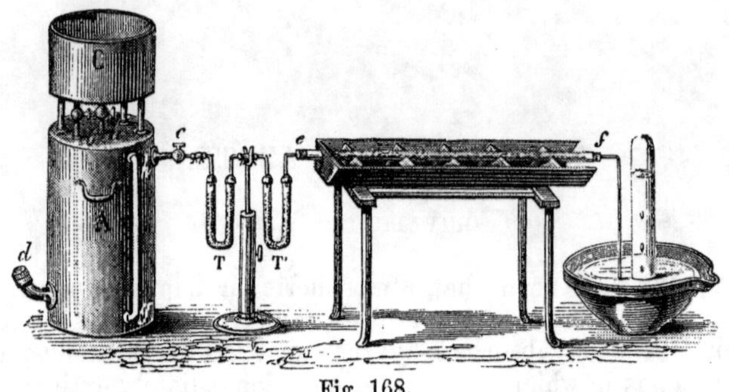

Fig. 168.

second tube T′ filled with pumice-stone imbued with sulphuric acid, which absorbs the water. The glass tube *ef*, containing the copper, is arranged on a small sheet-iron furnace, which permits of its being raised to a red-heat: the tube is wrapped with a sheet of foil, to prevent its losing its shape.

Nitrogen is often obtained, in the laboratory, quite as pure, by another method—the decomposition of ammonia by chlorine. Ammonia is a compound of hydrogen and nitrogen: chlorine combines with hydrogen to form chlorohydric acid, which, in its turn, combines with the undecomposed ammonia, to form the chlorohydrate of ammonia, which remains in solution in the water. The nitrogen, being set free, is disengaged. The flask (fig. 169) contains a mixture of peroxide of manganese and chlorohydric acid: the chlorine disengaged in this reaction passes into a tubulated bottle, half filled with a solution of ammoniacal gas in water: it instantly loses its yellow colour, and an infinity of little bubbles of nitrogen, which may be collected when the atmospheric air has been entirely expelled from the apparatus, escape from the fluid.

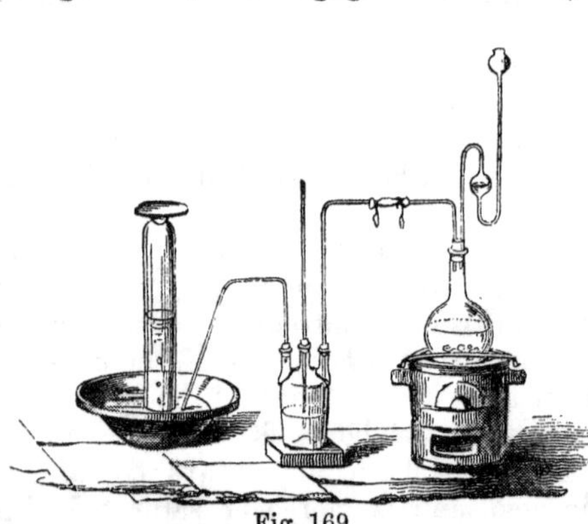
Fig. 169.

This experiment is free from danger so long as the ammoniacal solution contains an excess of ammonia: but, if the disengagement of chlorine be continued after the ammonia has been entirely changed into a chlorohydrate, the chlorine acts on the chlorohydrate of ammonia, and gives rise to an extremely dangerous compound, which we shall meet again under the name of *chloride of nitrogen*. This substance appears under the form of yellow oily drops, and its formation should be carefully avoided, as it is one of the most explosive substances known.

We also obtain very pure nitrogen, and in large quantities, by boiling in a flask a concentrated solution of the nitrite of ammonia, which decomposes into water and nitrogen. The composition of nitrite of ammonia is represented by the formula NH_3HO,NO_3: it contains the elements of 4 equivalents of water and 2 of nitrogen. In fact, we have $NH_3HO,NO_3=4HO+2N$.

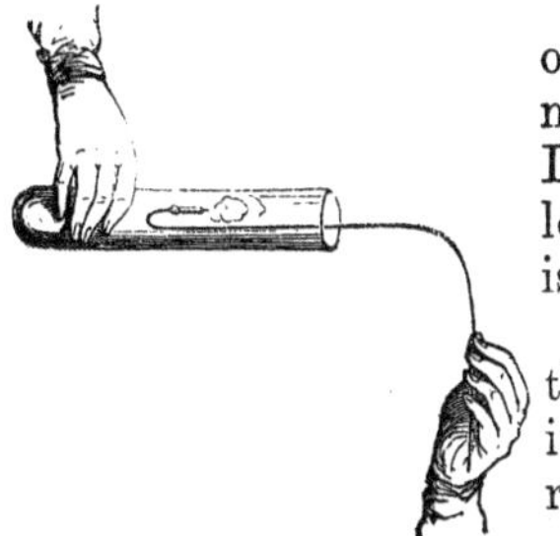

Fig. 170.

§ 93. Nitrogen is a colourless, inodorous and tasteless gas, which thus far has never been liquefied under any pressure. Its density is 0.9713, that is, something less than that of the air. A lighted taper is instantly extinguished in it (fig. 170).

Animals cannot live in nitrogen, and they perish for want of oxygen, which is indispensable to respiration; hence it has received the name *azote* from some chemists (from α privative, and ζωή, life). Nevertheless, this gas exerts no deleterious influence on their organs, since $\frac{4}{5}$ of the atmosphere consist of it.

Water dissolves a very small quantity of nitrogen, about $\frac{25}{1000}$ of its volume: or, in other words, 1 litre of water dissolves 25 cubic centimetres, or 1 kilogramme of water dissolves $0^{gm}.031$ of nitrogen.

ATMOSPHERIC AIR.

§ 94. Atmospheric air consists essentially of a mixture of oxygen and nitrogen, in proportions identical throughout the globe. It contains in addition, a very small quantity of carbonic acid gas and a variable quantity of vapour of water. Air contains, moreover, but in scarcely appreciable quantities, some other gases or vapours, arising from the decomposition of animal and vegetable matter.

§ 95. We will describe the various methods by which the composition of atmospheric air may be exactly determined.* This

* Air was considered by the ancients as one of the four elements of nature. This opinion reigned undisturbed until toward the close of the eighteenth century.

Lavoisier first proved, incontestably, that air was a mixture of two gases, possessing different properties, and nearly determined their proportions. The following is the experiment which led this illustrious and unfortunate chemist to this result (*Traité élémentaire de Chimie*, tom. I. p. 35, ed. 2d):

"I took a matrass containing about 36 cubic inches, with a very long neck, 6 or 7 lines interior diameter, and bent it as in fig. 171, so that it could be set in a furnace MN, whilst the end O of the neck opened under a bell-glass PQ in a mercurial cistern RS. I introduced into the matrass 4 ounces of very pure mer-

analysis consists of two operations performed separately. The object of the first is to determine the carbonic acid and the water;

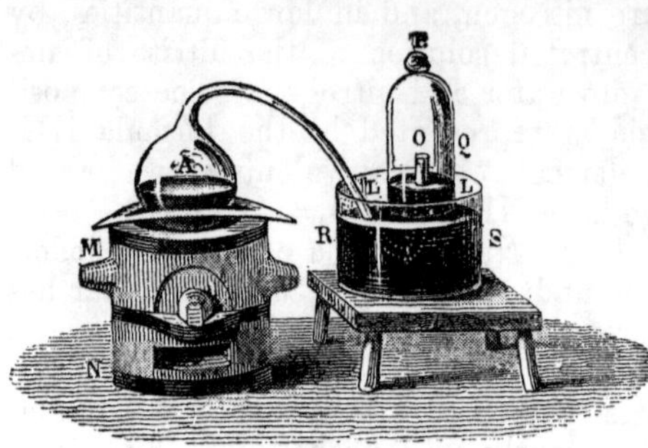

Fig. 171.

cury; then, sucking with a siphon which I passed under the bell-glass PQ, I raised the mercury to LL. I marked this height carefully by pasting a strip of paper over it, and observed exactly the barometer and thermometer.

"Things being thus prepared, I lighted the fire in the furnace MN, and kept it up for nearly 12 days, so that the mercury was heated nearly to the boiling point.

"Nothing remarkable occurred on the first day: the mercury, though not boiling, was constantly evaporating: it coated the inside of the vessels with drops, at first very small, but which gradually increased, and, when they had acquired a certain size, fell spontaneously to the bottom of the vessel, and joined the balance of the mercury. On the second day, I saw swimming on the surface of the mercury small red particles, which, for 4 or 5 days, increased in number and size, after which they ceased enlarging, and remained absolutely in the same state. After 2 days, seeing that the *calcination* of the mercury (oxidation of the mercury) progressed no longer, I extinguished the fire, and allowed the vessels to cool. The volume of air, contained as well in the matrass as in its neck and under the empty part of the bell-glass, reduced to a pressure of 28 inches, and to the temperature of 19°, was, before the operation, of about 55 cubic inches. After the operation, the pressure and temperature being the same, there remained only 42 to 43 inches: there was consequently a diminution of volume of nearly one-sixth. On the other hand, having carefully collected the red particles which formed, and separated them as much as possible from the liquid mercury with which they were coated, they were found to weigh 45 grains.

"The air which remained after this operation was reduced to $\frac{5}{6}$ of its volume by the calcination of the mercury, and was no longer fit for respiration or combustion; for animals perished in it in a few moments, and a candle was as rapidly extinguished as if plunged into water.

"I took the 45 grains of red matter which had formed during the operation, and introduced them into a small glass retort, to which was adapted an apparatus calculated to receive the liquid and aeriform products which might separate: having lighted the fire in the furnace, I observed that as the red matter became heated, its colour became more intense. When the retort subsequently approached incandescence, the red matter gradually began to lose its volume, and in a few minutes entirely disappeared: at the same time, $41\frac{1}{2}$ grains of liquid mercury collected in the receiver, and 7 or 8 cubic inches of an elastic fluid much more fitted to support life and combustion passed under the bell-glass.

"Having introduced a portion of this air into a glass tube of an inch in diameter, and plunging a candle therein, it burned with a dazzling flame; and charcoal, instead of burning quietly, as in ordinary air, burned with a flame and sort of decrepitation, like phosphorus, and a brilliant light which the eye could hardly endure.

"A little reflection on this experiment will show us that the mercury, by calcining, absorbs the salubrious and respirable portion of the air, and that the remaining portion is a kind of mephitis, incapable of supporting animal life and combustion. Atmospheric air is, therefore, composed of two elastic fluids of different, and, as it were, of opposite natures.

"This important truth is proved by recombining the two elastic fluids thus

and of the second, to determine the proportions of hydrogen and nitrogen in the air, when freed from its carbonic acid and aqueous vapour.

Fig. 172 represents the apparatus by means of which we ascertain very accurately the quantity of carbonic acid and vapour of water which exists in the atmosphere.

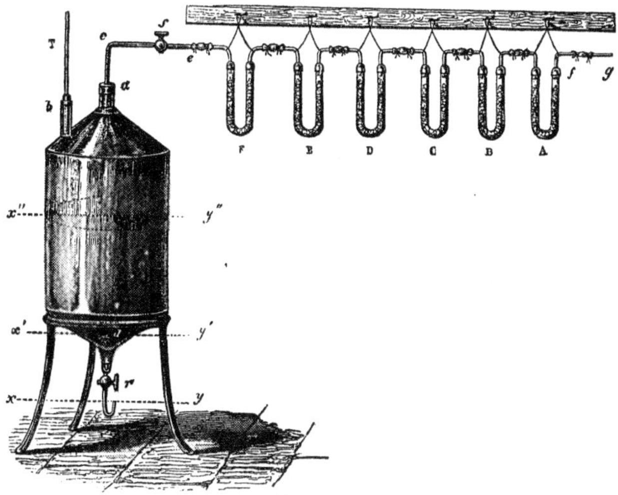

Fig. 172.

A cylindrical vessel V, of galvanized sheet-iron, containing 50 to 100 litres (11 to 22 gallons), is supported by a tripod over a large tub capable of holding all the water contained in the cylinder V. This cylinder has, at its lower part, a stopcock *r*, furnished with a tube about a decimetre (4 inches) in length, and curved at its end. Two tubes, *a* and *b*, are attached to the vessel. In the central tube *a*, we fasten hermetically, by means of a metallic stopper and soft wax, a metallic tube *ad* open at both ends: this tube is curved at *c*, and has a stopcock *s*. In the lateral tube *b*, we introduce a thermometer T, the bulb of which should descend toward the middle of the vessel V.

The capacity of the vessel V may be very exactly ascertained. To do this, we take a balloon (fig. 173) of the capacity of about 10 litres ($2\frac{1}{5}$ gallons), on the neck of which is engraved a horizontal line *a*; the balloon is filled with water to this line, and weighed.

---

separately obtained, that is, the 42 inches of mephitis or non-respirable air, and the 8 cubic inches of respirable air, we thus recompose an air resembling that of the atmosphere, and nearly as fitted for combustion, respiration, and the calcination of metals."

Lavoisier adds that the proportion of respirable gas formed by his experiment, is probably a little too feeble, because he could not combine it perfectly with the mercury.

The vessel is then emptied very accurately of water, and again weighed, and the difference gives the weight of the water. It is easy to show that if the balloon be several times filled and emptied in the same manner and at the same temperature, we shall always obtain within a small fraction the same weight P of water. The vessel V is completely filled with water at the same temperature, the thermometer T adjusted, and the tube *ad*. The stopcock *s* being opened, the cock *r* is opened, and water allowed to flow into the balloon (fig. 173) as far as the level *a*; the cock *r* is then closed, and the balloon emptied precisely in the same manner as it had been gauged. This operation is repeated until the vessel V is entirely emptied. We thus find that the balloon has been filled a certain number of times *n*, and, in the last operation, if it is not completely filled, the water it contains is weighed. Suppose there remains a weight of water *p*: it is evident that the vase V contained a weight of water represented by $nP+p$. If the water were at the temperature of $+39\frac{1}{2}°$, the weight $nP+p$, in kilogrammes, would represent the capacity V of the vessel in litres. But this water is generally at a temperature *t*, at which it possesses a density somewhat less than at $39\frac{1}{2}°$: this density δ, for any temperature *t*, is found in all works on physics; the capacity of the vase V in litres will therefore be represented by

Fig. 173.

$$V=\frac{nP+p}{\delta}.$$

In order to determine the quantities of carbonic acid and vapour of water which exist in the air, we fill the vase V with water, and attach to the tube *c* a series of tubes, A, B, C, D, E, F. The tubes A, B, E, F, are filled with large pieces of pumice-stone soaked in concentrated sulphuric acid; the tubes C, D, with pumice-stone soaked in a concentrated solution of caustic potash: lastly, to the last tube A, we adapt a long tube *fg*, which passes out into the external atmosphere which we are about to analyze.

The curved tubes, containing the pumice-stone, are closed at both ends with good corks pierced by smaller curved tubes, as in fig. 172. The corks should be covered with sealing-wax, which renders them very smooth. We are thus more certain of a hermetical closure; and the corks not being exposed to the air, cannot change in weight, by absorbing or giving off moisture during the experiment. The tubes are joined together by means of small caoutchouc tubes, strongly tied on with silk thread.

The two tubes A and B are weighed together; and likewise the three tubes, C, D, and E. It is unnecessary to weigh the tube F, as it remains attached to the apparatus, and is of no use, except to prevent the vapour of water disengaged from the vessel V from passing into the tube E.

The apparatus being thus arranged, the water is allowed to flow from the vessel V, which is called an *aspirator*. This discharge can only take place so long as bubbles of air reach this vessel by the tube *ad*: the discharge of the water will, moreover, have an equal velocity, because it will take place under the pressure of the column of water comprised between the level xy of the lower orifice and the level $x'y'$ of the orifice of the tube *ad*. In fact, the tube *ad* is entirely filled with air, and communicates freely with the atmosphere, from the connection of the tubes A, B, C, D, E, F; consequently, on the whole level stratum $x'y'$ which passes through the orifice *d*, there is a pressure equal to that of the external atmosphere. In the stratum xy, the pressure which expels the water is equal to the pressure of the atmosphere, increased by the pressure produced by the column of water between the levels xy and $x'y'$. The pressure which opposes this discharge is that of the external atmosphere: the discharge will therefore take place under the pressure produced by the column of water comprised between the levels $x'y'$ and xy, and will be the more rapid for a uniform opening of the cock *r*, as the column of water between xy and $x'y'$ is greater.

The flow of water taking place only under the pressure of the column comprised between the levels xy and $x'y'$, it is evident that this flow will be strictly constant whilst the level of the water in V is above the stratum $x'y'$. This is not the case with the air: it will enter more rapidly as the level of the water descends in the vessel V. Let us suppose that this level has reached the stratum $x''y''$, the pressure on the stratum $x'y'$ is equal to that of the external atmosphere; at an indefinite moment it equals the elastic force of the gas in the upper part of the vessel V, and, in addition, the weight of the liquid column comprised between the levels $x''y''$ and $x'y'$. Thus, by supposing the vessel to be perfectly cylindrical, so that the level of the water may descend regularly, by reason of the constant discharge of the fluid, the air which will enter the apparatus during a minute will go on increasing: for, it must not only fill the vacuum, always the same, made by the discharge of the water, but likewise must constantly increase the elastic force of the internal air, so that this force, added to the pressure of the liquid column comprised between the planes $x''y''$ and $x'y'$, and which always goes on diminishing, equals the pressure of the external atmosphere at the level $x'y'$.

Absolute regularity of the current of air which traverses our apparatus is not indispensable to the success of the present experiment; we must, however, call attention to this circumstance, for this regularity is necessary for other experiments, and it is proper to show that we do not obtain it by the arrangement just described.

The external air, therefore, traverses, before reaching the vase V, the series of tubes A, B, C, D, E, F. In the two tubes A and

B it deposits its moisture; in the tubes C and D its carbonic acid. But as the gas arriving in the latter tubes is completely dry, and as the solution of caustic potassa gives off a sensible quantity of vapour of water, we have placed, after the tubes C and D, the tube E, filled with pumice-stone soaked in sulphuric acid, which retains this small quantity of water.

When the aspirator is perfectly empty, we mark the height H of the barometer and the temperature t of the thermometer T. The curved tubes are detached; A, B weighed together, as likewise C, D, E. The increased weight of these two systems of tubes gives in A and B the quantity of vapour of water, and in C, D, E, that of carbonic acid, existing in the atmospheric air which has traversed the apparatus. We must now ascertain the weight of this air from the data of the experiment.

The volume of air filling the aspirator is V; but this air is saturated with vapour at the temperature t. Let us designate by f the maximum elastic force of the vapour of water at this temperature t. The elastic force of the dry air which has entered the apparatus is $H-f$: a quantity of atmosphere has therefore entered our apparatus such that it occupies, after having entirely parted with its vapour of water and its carbonic acid, a volume V, at a temperature t, and under a pressure $H-f$. The weight P of this air, dried and deprived of carbonic acid, is therefore

$$P = V \cdot 1^{gm}.2932 \cdot \frac{1}{1+0.00367.t} \cdot \frac{H-f}{0.760}.$$

Let us suppose that the weight of the carbonic acid found is p, and the weight of the vapour of water is p'; we shall conclude from our experiment that a weight $P+p+p'$ of atmospheric air, under the conditions in which we have analyzed it, contains p of carbonic acid, and p' of vapour of water: and we may calculate by a simple proportion the quantities of carbonic acid and water found in 100 parts of this atmospheric air.

It is important that the pumice-stone in the tubes should be in large fragments, and merely wetted with the oil of vitriol, in order that an excess of this liquid may not accumulate at the lower part of the curved tubes. The external air ought to pass freely through all these tubes: for, otherwise, at the end of the experiment, the air which fills the aspirator V might have an elastic force much inferior to that of the external air.

We turn upward the pipe terminating the stopcock r, in order that, after the discharge, the curved part may remain filled with water, and prevent the entrance of air into the vessel V.

Experiment has shown that free atmospheric air contains quantities of carbonic acid, varying from 4 to 6 ten thousandths. The quantity of vapour of water is much more irregular, owing to temperature and its state of saturation.

§ 96. Let us now suppose the air to be deprived of its carbonic acid and its vapour of water, and see how we shall ascertain the proportions of oxygen and nitrogen it contains. This may be done by several methods, of which we shall describe the most perfect.

Many substances absorb the oxygen of the air, even at ordinary temperatures. It is therefore sufficient, in order to analyze the air, to introduce a certain quantity of air into a graduated bell-glass, measure this volume very accurately, under given conditions, introduce the absorbing substance, and allow it to remain in the bell-glass until the volume of the gas no longer decreases sensibly, and lastly, to measure again with great exactness the remaining volume, which must be pure nitrogen.

Phosphorus is the absorbing substance best adapted to this purpose. The experiment is performed as follows:

Melt some phosphorus under water, and then run it into bullet-moulds, always under water at about 104°. Introduce into the cavity of the mould, whilst the phosphorus is yet fluid, a platinum wire twisted into a curl at the end. The mould is then plunged into cold water to solidify the phosphorus, and we have a small ball of phosphorus firmly fixed to the end of the platinum wire.

This being done, we introduce into a graduated bell-glass placed over mercury, a certain volume of air, which is carefully measured. The inside of the bell-glass must still be somewhat damp. Although it may have been carefully wiped, and no drops of water be visible, the air intended for analysis will be saturated with moisture by the small quantity of water given off by the sides of the bell-glass.

Let t be the external temperature, H the height of the barometer, f the tension of the vapour of water corresponding to the temperature t, and which will be found in a small table annexed to this work.

The volume V of the gas already observed would be, were it dry, at the temperature of 32°, and under the pressure of $0^{m}.760$,

$$V. \frac{1}{1+0.00367.t} . \frac{H-f}{0.760}.$$

The ball of phosphorus is introduced into the gas (fig. 174), which is easily done by means of the platinum wire to which it is attached, and allowed to remain until the gas no longer diminishes in volume. This sometimes requires more than twenty-four hours. Absorption proceeds more rapidly by placing the bell-glass in the sunshine. When the absorption is completed, the phosphorus is withdrawn, and the volume of gas remaining measured, after it has acquired the temperature t' of the surrounding air. Let us suppose that this volume is V′, the barometric pressure H′: lastly, that the elastic force of the saturated vapour of water at the temperature t' is f': the volume occupied by this air, deprived of its

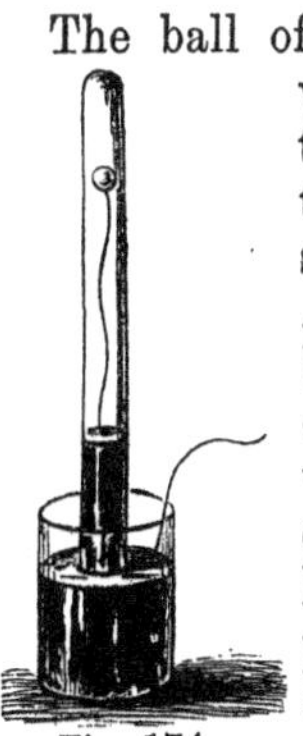

Fig. 174.

moisture, at the temperature of 32° and under the normal pressure of 0^{m}.760, will be

$$V'.\frac{1}{1+0.00367.t'}.\frac{H'-f'}{0.760}.$$

This, therefore is the volume of nitrogen found in a volume $V.\frac{1}{1+0.00367.t}.\frac{H-f}{0.760}$. of dry atmospheric air: whence may be immediately deduced the volume of nitrogen and oxygen in 100 parts of atmospheric air.

The air may likewise be analyzed by employing substances which do not absorb oxygen at the ordinary temperature, but which, when strongly heated, combine actively with this body.

The experiment may also be arranged so as to weigh at the same time the oxygen which has combined with the absorbing substance, and the nitrogen which remains free.

By performing the experiment in the following manner, we may obtain great accuracy (fig. 175): *ab* is a glass tube difficult of

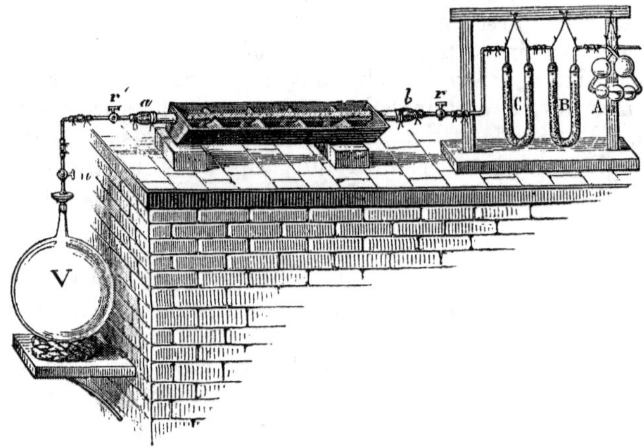

Fig. 175.

fusion, filled with metallic copper, and arranged over a long sheet-iron furnace, so that it may be heated throughout its whole length. The stopcocks *r* and *r'* are fitted to the ends of this tube.

The extremity *a* of the tube is brought into communication with a balloon V holding about 20 litres (5 galls.), having a stopcock *u* : and the extremity *b* communicates with an apparatus ABC.

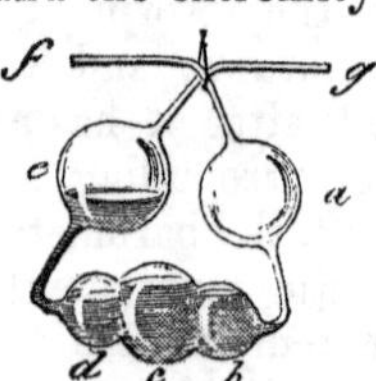

Fig. 176.

The apparatus A, figured on a larger scale in fig. 176, is intended to absorb the carbonic acid of the air. This apparatus, called *Liebig's potassa bulbs*, from the illustrious chemist who contrived it, consists of three bulbs, *b*, *c*, *d*, arranged on the same axis, and two bulbs *a* and *e* placed above, and communicating with the first by narrow tubes. A concentrated solution of potassa is introduced, so as to entirely fill the three lower bulbs. If, then, we slowly exhaust the air by the tube *g*, the external air enters at *f*, and traverses the solution of potassa, passing successively through the bulbs; lastly, in order to reach the bulb *e*, it must pass through a new column of solution of potassa. The gas therefore remains much longer in contact with the potassa than if it were to traverse a straight and unbroken column of fluid, and consequently will be in the most favourable conditions for the absorption of carbonic acid.

The tube B (fig. 175) is filled with pieces of pumice-stone soaked in a concentrated solution of caustic potassa: it is intended to absorb the last portions of carbonic acid gas which might have escaped from the apparatus A.

Lastly, the tube C, filled with pumice-stone soaked in sulphuric acid, completely desiccates the air.

This being done, the tube *ab* is exhausted as perfectly as possible, and the stopcock *r* and *r'* closed. This tube, when exhausted of air, is weighed, which weight is represented by *p*. The balloon V is also weighed under the same circumstances: let its weight be P.

The apparatus is then put in order and the tube *ab* heated to redness. The stopcock *r'* is then opened: the external air enters the tube *ab* after having traversed the series of tubes ABC, which deprive it of its carbonic acid and watery vapour: this air gives off its oxygen to the heated metallic copper, and the nitrogen remains isolated. The stopcock *u* of the balloon is opened, and the stopcock *r* very slightly, so that the gas enters very slowly the balloon V. The rate of its passage can moreover be estimated by the bubbles which traverse the bulbed receiver A: the bubbles or gas should go over one at a time. When the passage of the bubbles becomes slower, which necessarily happens when the difference between the elastic force of the gas in the balloon and that of the external air diminishes, the stopcock *r* is further opened. At the end of the operation, it is opened completely. As soon as the gas ceases to form, the stopcocks *r*, *r'* and *u* are closed, the coals removed, and the apparatus taken to pieces.

The balloon is weighed: let P' be its weight: P'—P is evidently the weight of the nitrogen which has entered it.

Weigh the tube *ab*: let p' be its weight: $p'-p$ will be the weight of the oxygen which has combined with the metallic copper, increased by the quantity of nitrogen in this tube. This last quantity is easily ascertained by again making a vacuum in the tube, and finding its weight p''; $p'-p''$ is then the nitrogen which has been withdrawn by the air-pump, and $p''-p$ the quantity of oxygen combined with the metallic copper. We therefore find a weight of nitrogen

$$(P'-P)+(p'-p''),$$

and a weight of oxygen $\qquad p''-p,$

forming a weight of dry atmospheric air deprived of its carbonic acid, represented by

$$(P'-P)+(p'-p'')+(p''-p)=(P'-P)+(p'-p).$$

It will, therefore, be easy to ascertain, by a proportion, the weights of oxygen and nitrogen which enter into 100 parts by weight of atmospheric air; and as we know the densities of oxygen and nitrogen, we may equally deduce the composition of the air by volume.

§ 97. Great care must be taken in weighing the balloon V, if we wish to be very exact. This operation is necessarily done in the air: now, we know that a body immersed in a fluid loses of its weight a portion equal to the weight of the fluid it has displaced. The volume of air displaced by the balloon is the same in both cases: if, therefore, the air were of the same density in both cases, the difference $P'-P$ would not be affected by this circumstance, and would give exactly the weight of the nitrogen which has entered the balloon. But if the air has changed between the two weighings, in consequence of variations of temperature or barometric pressure, the quantity of air displaced will not be the same, and the difference $P'-P$ will no longer correctly represent the weight of nitrogen in the balloon. It is difficult to calculate the correction in the value of $P'-P$, but we can experiment so as to guard against this cause of error.

Glass balloons, and in general all large vessels, should be weighed by hooking them beneath the dishes of the balance (fig. 177).

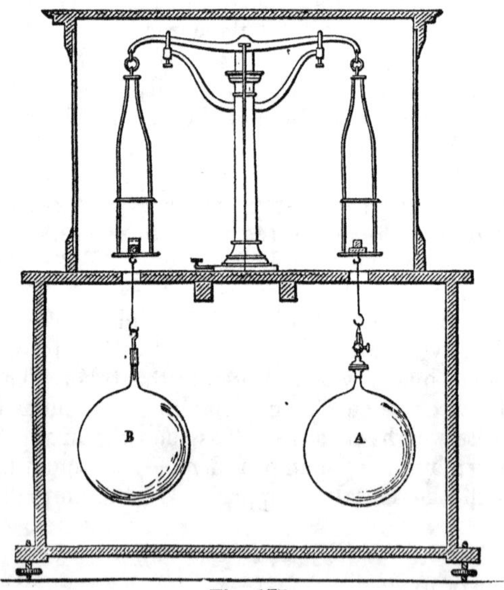

Fig. 177.

Instead of balancing the balloon hooked beneath one of the dishes, by means of ordinary weights placed in the other, it is balanced by a second balloon hermetically closed, and exactly resembling the first. This second balloon is hooked to the other dish of the balance, so that it floats in the same stratum of air as the first. The two balloons displacing the same volume of air, it is evident that all variations which occur in the air affect them exactly in the same manner, and that the difference of weight $P'-P$ between these two weights will be independent of their variations.

It now remains to us to point out how to arrange two balloons which displace exactly the same volume of air.

In order to do this, we ascertain exactly the volume of air displaced by the balloon A, which is to serve for the experiment. For this purpose, this balloon is completely filled with water, and it is weighed immersed in water having exactly the same temperature as that which fills it. The apparent weight of the balloon filled with water is so slight that it may be ascertained by hooking it beneath one of the dishes. We withdraw the balloon from the water and weigh it again, but in the air, after having wiped it dry. For this second operation, we use a strong ordinary balance. The difference between the two weights will be evidently the weight of water displaced by the external volume of the balloon.

A second balloon B, having nearly the same capacity as A, is selected, and the weight of water its external volume displaces ascertained as before. Let us suppose that the external volume of the second balloon is rather smaller than that of the first furnished with a stopcock: we fasten to the neck of the balloon B, with common cement, a brass mounting terminating in a hook intended to suspend the balloon beneath the balance. Let us suppose that the weight of water displaced by this mounting, added to the weight we previously found for the water displaced by the external volume of the balloon B, be less by n grammes than the weight of water displaced by the balloon A: it will be sufficient to append to the balloon B a small glass tube closed at both ends, which exactly displaces n cubic centimetres of water.

If the balloon B is, with its mounting, much lighter than the balloon A, we introduce into it, before closing it hermetically, a quantity of mercury sufficient to balance the balloon A with a very small addition. Fig. 177 represents the two balloons hooked under the dishes of a Fortin's balance. The balance should be contained in a closet of thin wood, to shield it from currents of air. We are thus certain that both float in strata of air of the same temperature, and that they are not unequally influenced by the presence of the experimenter. The oscillations of the balance may also be observed, from a distance, with a spy-glass.

§ 98. Atmospheric air may be also very exactly analyzed by means of the eudiometer.

We introduce into the eudiometer, previously wiped dry, a certain volume V of atmospheric air: the temperature is t, the barometric pressure H, and the elastic force of the saturated vapour is f at the temperature t. The volume of dry air will be, therefore, at 32°, and under the pressure $0^m.760$,

$$V.\frac{1}{1+0.00367.t}\cdot\frac{H-f}{0.760}=V_0.$$

A volume of hydrogen gas is then introduced somewhat less than that of the air, and we measure anew the volume V' of the gas: the temperature and pressure will not have sensibly changed in the interval, and we shall have the same values for t, H, and f. But let us suppose, for greater generalization, that these quantities have become t', H', and f': the volume of the dry gaseous mixture would be, at 32°, under the normal pressure of $0^m.760$,

$$V'.\frac{1}{1+0.00367.t}\cdot\frac{H'-f'}{0.760}=V'_0.$$

V'_0-V_0 will therefore be the volume of dry hydrogen under normal conditions.

An electric spark is passed through; the oxygen of the air burns a volume of hydrogen double of itself, and the product of the combustion condenses in the state of liquid water, of which the volume is of no importance with relation to the volume of the gases which have produced it. When the eudiometer acquires the same temperature as the surrounding air, the volume of the remaining gases is weighed. Let us suppose that this volume be V'', the barometric pressure H'', the temperature t'' and f'', the elastic force of saturated vapour corresponding to the temperature t'': the volume of the dry gaseous mixture will be, at 32°, and under the pressure $0^m.760$,

$$V''.\frac{1}{1+0.00367.t''}\cdot\frac{H''-f''}{0.760}=V''_0.$$

$V''_0-V'_0$ is therefore the volume of the dry oxygen and hydrogen gases, under normal conditions, which have combined.

$\frac{V''_0-V'_0}{3}$ will be the volume of oxygen,

$2\frac{V''_0-V'_0}{3}$ will be the volume of hydrogen.

We conclude, hence, that a volume V_0 of atmospheric air contains a volume $\frac{V''_0-V'_0}{3}$ of oxygen, and a volume $V_0-\frac{V''_0-V'_0}{3}$ of nitrogen.

The eudiometric analysis of the air gives very exact results when this analysis is carefully conducted. But, when we desire very great exactness, it is best to employ a eudiometer of peculiar construction, such as was mentioned in § 83; and which we will describe in the fourth part of this course, when treating of the analysis of compounds and gaseous mixtures.

It has been ascertained, by a great number of analyses, that atmospheric air contains, on an average, in volume

Oxygen	20.90
Nitrogen	79.10
	100.00

or in weight,

Oxygen	23.10
Nitrogen	76.90
	100.00

The constitution of the air collected in various localities, and at different heights in the atmosphere, affords scarcely any sensible variations.

It is very easy to collect a small quantity of air in any given locality, by means of small tubes, drawn out at both ends, and containing 30 or 40 cubic centimetres (2 or 2½ cub. in.). They are to be filled with air by a bellows, and the points closed by the flame of an alcohol lamp. The air contained in these tubes may be preserved for an indefinite time and analyzed in the laboratory by the eudometric process.

§ 99. The great constancy observed in the constitution of the air, has led some chemists to regard atmospheric air, not as a mixture of oxygen and nitrogen, but as an actual chemical combination of these gases. We shall give the principal reasons which prove this opinion to be erroneous, and that oxygen and nitrogen are merely mixed in atmospheric air.

Experiment has shown that two gases always combine in simple ratio of volumes. Now, the simple proportion which most closely approaches the direct analyses of the atmospheric air is the following:

$\frac{1}{5}$ of oxygen	or oxygen	20.00
$\frac{4}{5}$ of nitrogen	or nitrogen	80.00
		100.00

The discrepancy between these numbers and the results of analysis cannot be attributed to the error of experiment, since analyses of the air, made in various ways, have always led to the same result.

Heat is always disengaged in the combination of two gases: now there is no appreciable change of temperature when we mix oxygen and hydrogen; and if these gases are mixed in the proportions constituting the air, we obtain a gaseous mixture absolutely identical with our atmosphere.

But the most convincing proof that air is a simple mixture of oxygen and nitrogen, is in the manner in which atmospheric air behaves with water. We have seen (§ 81) that water which has been for a long time in contact with air always contains a certain quantity of gas in solution, and have described the mode by which this gas may be separated and collected. If the atmospheric air be a compound of oxygen and nitrogen, the gases dissolved in water should present the same composition as the atmosphere, and contain

20.90..oxygen,
79.10 ....nitrogen.

If, on the contrary, air is only a simple mixture of these two gases, as oxygen and nitrogen are not equally soluble, the composition of the dissolved gases will be different from that of the air, and may even be calculated by the rule pointed out (§ 81).

Let us admit, for the sake of clearness, that air is formed of $\frac{1}{5}$ oxygen and $\frac{4}{5}$ nitrogen, the fractions of solubility being $\frac{1}{n'}$ for oxygen and $\frac{1}{n}$ for nitrogen, the gases will be found dissolved in water in the proportions

$$\frac{1}{5}.\frac{1}{n'} \text{ of oxygen,}$$

$$\frac{4}{5}.\frac{1}{n} \text{ of nitrogen;}$$

$$\text{or, } \frac{1}{n'}=0.046, \qquad \frac{1}{n}=0.025,$$

we shall have in the dissolved gases,

Oxygen.......	$\frac{1}{5}$.0.046......	0.0092......	31.5
Nitrogen......	$\frac{4}{5}$.0.025......	0.0200......	68.5
		0.0292	100.0.

Now, the direct analysis of this gaseous mixture extracted from water has given

Oxygen 32.0
Nitrogen 68.0
100.0.

Which agrees, as nearly as possible, with the composition we have calculated, founded on the law of solubility of the gases, and the presumption that the atmospheric air is a mixture of nitrogen and oxygen.

COMPOUNDS OF NITROGEN AND OXYGEN.

§ 100. We are acquainted with five definite combinations of nitrogen and oxygen:

1. The protoxide of nitrogen;
2. The deutoxide of nitrogen;
3. Nitrous or azotous acid;
4. Hyponitric or hypazotic acid;
5. Nitric or azotic acid.

To which the following formulæ have been assigned:

1. Protoxide of nitrogen...... NO or AzO;
2. Deutoxide of nitrogen...... NO_2 " AzO_2;
3. Nitrous acid .... NO_3 " AzO_3;
4. Hyponitric acid............ NO_4 " AzO_4;
5. Nitric acid .... NO_5 " AzO_5.

NITRIC ACID, NO_5 OR AzO_5.

§ 101. Nitric acid is obtained by heating saltpetre or nitrate of potassa with concentrated sulphuric acid. Nitric acid being more feeble and volatile than sulphuric, is separated from its combination and passes over in distillation. Nitrate of potassa is also called *nitre*, whence azotic acid was originally called *nitric*. This name is in very general use at this day, although it does not harmonize with the rules of our chemical nomenclature.

Nitric acid has not been yet obtained free from water, or *anhydrous.** The most concentrated contains 14 per cent. of water: it has a density of 1.522, and boils at 186.8°. If a small quantity of water be added to this acid, and the mixture be distilled, the first portions which pass over contain more real acid than the fluid which remains in the retort. If we observe a thermometer plunged into the boiling fluid, we will see the temperature continually rise, until it reaches 253.4°. Here it remains stationary, and the fluid which distils presents a constant composition: it contains 40 per cent. of water.

If, on the contrary, we add considerable water to the most concentrated acid, and distil this new mixture in a tubulated retort provided with a thermometer, this instrument will at first mark about 212°, but the temperature will gradually rise to 253.4°, and remain stationary until the end of the distillation. The first portions are nearly pure water: the succeeding contain a greater quantity of acid; so that the fluid in the retort becomes more and more concentrated, until it contains only 40 per cent. of water. Now, experiment has proved that all homogeneous compounds which are not decomposed by ebullition, boil at a constant temperature under the same pressure. When a liquid thus presents a constant temperature during the distillation it undergoes in consequence of boiling under the same pressure, it is regarded as homogeneous, and is said to be *a compound of definite proportions*.

The liquid acid, formed of 60 per cent. of pure nitric acid, and 40 of water, presents the characters of a compound with definite proportions. The density of this acid is 1.42.

---

* M. Deville has since succeeded in preparing anhydrous nitric acid by passing dry chlorine over dry nitrate of silver. It forms transparent, colourless crystals, of a right rhombic form, fusing at 85°, boiling at 113°, and decomposing near the latter point.

In the first hydrate of nitric acid, the proportion of the oxygen of the water to the oxygen contained in the pure acid is as 1 to 5; its formula is therefore

$$NO_5+HO.$$

In the second hydrate, this proportion is as 4 to 5, and the formula is

$$NO_5+4HO.$$

§ 102. The first hydrate NO_5+HO congeals at $-58°$. When pure it is colourless, but soon turns yellow when exposed to the light. This agent decomposes nitric acid, leaving oxygen and hyponitric acid NO_4, which remains dissolved in the undecomposed acid. Nitric acid NO_5+HO is therefore a not very stable compound: it is easily decomposed by heat, for a few successive distillations decompose a large proportion of it. If the vapour of nitric acid be driven through a highly heated porcelain tube, the acid is completely decomposed into nitrogen and oxygen. If the tube be less heated, the products of decomposition are oxygen and hyponitric acid.

When we endeavour to deprive nitric acid NO_5+HO of the water it contains, it is decomposed into oxygen and nitrous acid: which happens when it is distilled with four times its weight of concentrated sulphuric acid or with anhydrous phosphoric acid, both of which have great affinity for water.

Nitric acid NO_5+HO has a marked affinity for water: it becomes heated when mixed with this fluid, and fumes in a moist atmosphere. This last property has given to this hydrate the name of *fuming nitric acid*, and depends on the monohydrated nitric acid NO_5+HO possessing a greater tension of vapour, at equal temperatures, than nitric acids containing larger proportions of water. It therefore follows that when the fumes of the monohydrated acid reach the damp air, and there combine with an additional quantity of water, the more hydrated acid cannot remain entire in the state of an invisible vapour in the air, and a considerable portion of it precipitates in the form of mist.

The second hydrate NO_5+4HO is much more fixed than the first: it is neither decomposed by the influence of light alone, nor by repeated distillations. By distilling it with about its weight of concentrated sulphuric acid, $\frac{3}{4}$ of its water may be removed, and the first hydrate NO_5+HO then passes by distillation. It is proper not to use a great excess of sulphuric acid, for a considerable portion of nitric acid would be decomposed.

§ 103. Nitric acid is easily decomposed by many substances, to which it yields a portion of its oxygen. Carbon and sulphur decompose it at the boiling temperature: and many metals at the ordinary temperature. It is an active agent of oxidation daily employed in the laboratory.

Nitric acid, at its maximum of concentration, being much less fixed than the more dilute acid, ought to be a more energetic agent of oxidation. It is so, in fact, as regards the majority of substances: thus, sulphur, phosphorus, and carbon are much more rapidly acted on by the first hydrate NO_5+HO, than by the more dilute acids. The contrary, however, obtains with many metals: thus, iron and tin, which are readily acted on by slightly dilute nitric acid, exhibit but little reaction in this acid at its maximum of concentration; but this reaction becomes very energetic when a small quantity of water is added.

Nitric acid destroys the majority of animal substances; it stains the skin yellow, and also imparts this hue to wool. Advantage is taken of this property in dyeing.

§ 104. Nitrogen and oxygen may combine under the influence of the electric spark, so as to produce nitric acid, the presence of water, or, better still, of water and a powerful base together, being necessary to produce the effect. To prove this, we arrange a curved tube (fig. 178) filled with mercury, so that the two open ends may be plunged into two separate vessels filled with mercury. We introduce into the upper part of the tube a small quantity of air and solution of potassa: and, lastly, establish a communication with the mercury in one of the vessels and the plate of an electrical machine, which is steadily turned, whilst the other vessel communicates with the earth by means of a small iron chain. We thus pass through the tube a series of electric sparks, which effect the combination of the nitrogen and oxygen. After the passage of a great number of sparks, the alkaline solution contains a certain quantity of nitrate of potassa.

Fig. 178.

§ 105. We have said that nitric acid was obtained by the distillation of saltpetre with sulphuric acid. In this process there are several circumstances worthy of remark.

Potassa forms two combinations with sulphuric acid; one neutral and the other acid. The latter contains twice as much sulphuric acid as the first. The neutral combination is anhydrous; its formula is therefore KO,SO_3: the acid combination contains, on the contrary, a certain quantity of water, with which it does not part under 392°: its formula is $KO,2SO_3+HO$, written thus $\begin{pmatrix} KO,SO_3 \\ HO,SO_3 \end{pmatrix}$; and is considered, in this last case, as a double salt formed by the combination of the neutral sulphate of potassa KO,SO_3 with the sulphate of water HO,SO_3.

If we add to one equivalent of saltpetre, KO,NO_5, two equivalents of monohydrated sulphuric acid $2(SO_3+HO)$, we may form

$\begin{pmatrix}KO,SO_3\\HO,SO_3\end{pmatrix}$ and NO_5+HO, or HO,NO_5, that is, the bisulphate of potassa and monohydrated nitric acid, which in fact takes place, and distillation will separate the acid. The following are the most suitable proportions for the success of the operation:

$$100 \text{ nitrate of potassa......} \begin{cases} 46.61 \text{ potassa,} \\ 53.39 \text{ nitric acid,} \end{cases}$$

$$96.8 \text{ sulphuric acid ....} \begin{cases} 79.1 \text{ sulphuric acid,} \\ 17.7 \text{ water,} \end{cases}$$

which will give 62.29 of monohydrated nitric acid.

But, if we add only one equivalent of concentrated sulphuric acid HO,SO_3 to one equivalent of nitrate of potassa KO,NO_5, the reaction becomes much more complicated; only $\frac{1}{2}$ an equivalent of nitrate of potassa is then decomposed, giving $\frac{1}{2}$ an equivalent of monohydrated nitric acid, $\frac{1}{2}(NO_5+HO)$, which distils over, and there remain in the retort a $\frac{1}{2}$ equivalent of acid sulphate of potassa, $\frac{1}{2}\begin{pmatrix}KO,SO_3\\HO,SO_3\end{pmatrix}$, and $\frac{1}{2}$ equivalent of undecomposed nitrate of potassa, $\frac{1}{2}(KO,NO_5)$. If we increase the temperature, there is a reaction between the acid sulphate of potassa and the undecomposed nitrate of potassa: neutral sulphate of potassa is formed, and, consequently, a $\frac{1}{2}$ equivalent of monohydrated nitric acid becomes free: but as the temperature at which monohydrated acid then forms is sufficient to decompose it, we only obtain reddish brown vapours, and no nitric acid.

In the laboratory, fuming nitric acid is obtained by placing in a glass retort equal parts of nitrate of potassa and sulphuric acid: the acid should be introduced by means of a long-necked funnel (fig. 179), so that it may not touch the sides of the neck of the retort; without this precaution, during the distillation, a small

Fig. 179. Fig. 180.

quantity of sulphuric would be mixed with the nitric acid. The neck of the retort is introduced with a matrass (fig. 180) which is corked by a continuous current of cold water. No corks should be used in the construction of the apparatus, for nitric acid attacks cork very readily, and the latter might even take fire therefrom.

In the first stage of the reaction, reddish vapours form, arising from the decomposition of the first portions of nitric acid which become free. These necessarily come into contact with a large quantity of concentrated sulphuric acid which has not yet reacted; they must therefore decompose into nitrous vapours and oxygen. By the application of a proper degree of heat, the greater part of the nitric acid distils over without alteration. The close of the operation is announced by copious reddish vapours filling the retort: the distillation must then be stopped and the product condensed in the receiver separated. This new appearance of nitrous vapours is easily explained: nearly the whole of the nitrate of potassa is decomposed, and, in order that the sulphuric acid may react on the last portions of this salt, it is necessary that the matter in the retort should assume a certain fluidity, which is given only by great elevation of temperature, sufficient, in all cases, to decompose the last portions of nitric acid which become free.

The acid collected is not pure: it is coloured yellow by the dissolved nitrous acid, and may also contain a small quantity of sulphuric acid introduced during distillation. To purify it, it must be shaken with a small quantity of finely powdered nitrate of lead, and then distilled in a retort; the first portions containing the nitrous acid being collected, the receiver is changed, and the pure nitric acid collected. The operation should be arrested before all the acid is distilled, for the last portions may contain some nitrous acid, generated because the sides of the retort, being no longer bathed by fluid, may become so heated as to decompose the nitric acid.

In manufactories, the glass retort is replaced by a cast-iron cylinder (figs. 181 and 182) closed in by two flat plates, which are adjusted by means of bolts. Two of these cylinders are arranged alongside of each other in the same furnace, so that both ends are in a line with the front wall of the furnace. The anterior end has, toward the top, a tube *d* (fig. 182) introduced into a curved adapter by which the vapours are led into the first three-mouthed stone-ware receiver. Two of these receivers are placed side by side, each communicating with one of the two connected cylinders. These receivers also communicate with each other, by means of a curved tube of stone-ware uniting two of their mouths. Their third mouth corresponds with a series of two-mouthed receivers placed in a series.*

Fig. 181.

* Two-mouthed jars are more generally employed, the acid fumes merely passing over the surface of the water, where a large proportion is absorbed in the first jars, and the remainder is taken up before it leaves the series.—*J. C. B.*

Fig .182.

The back plate of the cylinders being removed, the proper quantity of saltpetre is introduced, and the plate replaced. The concentrated sulphuric acid is poured in by a cast-iron funnel E (fig. 183), fitted to a tube *c*, which is then closed by a stopper of earthen-ware.

Fig. 183.

When the cylinders are charged, the joints are luted with clay, and they are heated as regularly as possible. The operation being terminated, the back plate of the cylinder is taken off, and the sulphate of potassa removed by iron scrapers.

The acid condensed in the first receivers is necessarily impure, and contains a considerable quantity of sulphuric acid. This impure acid is used in the manufacture of sulphuric acid, as we shall see hereafter. The succeeding receivers contain the acid of commerce. This acid is more or less concentrated: it contains a certain quantity of nitrous acid, and frequently some chlorine, arising from the impurity of the nitre used in the process. The last receivers contain a very weak acid.

The receivers are not empty at the beginning of the operation. The first generally contains the very dilute acid solution formed in the last receivers of a preceding process, and which thus acquires the strength required in commerce. In the last, on the contrary, pure water is introduced, in order to obtain a complete condensation of the nitrous vapours.

§ 106. The nitric acid of commerce is sufficiently pure for the greater part of the uses of the laboratory. We sometimes, however, require a very pure acid, as in analytical researches. Now, as the acid of commerce generally contains some chlorine and sulphuric acid, it may be purified by agitating it with a small quantity of a concentrated solution of nitrate of silver, and then distilling it in a glass retort, in an apparatus resembling that of fig. 180.*

§ 107. *Analysis of Nitric Acid.*—In order to ascertain the

* A tolerably pure acid, *i. e.* free from chlorine, may be obtained by simply heating the strong acid gently, whereby the chlorine passes off together with some nitric acid.—*J. C. B.*

quantity of nitric acid contained in an acid diluted with water, we proceed in the following manner:—We weigh accurately 10 grammes (about 150 grs.) of this acid in a glass flask containing about 200 cubic centimetres (12 cubic inches), and then add a certain quantity of water. We weigh, also very accurately, 100 grammes (1500 grs.) of very dry and finely powdered oxide of lead, and pour this oxide into the flask. The oxide of lead combines with the nitric acid, and the water becomes free. The water can then be driven off by heat. The last operation demands some caution: the flask must be kept inclined, as in fig. 184, so that nothing may be projected without the vessel. When the matter appears dry, we continue the heat, and introduce as far as the centre of the flask a glass tube fas-

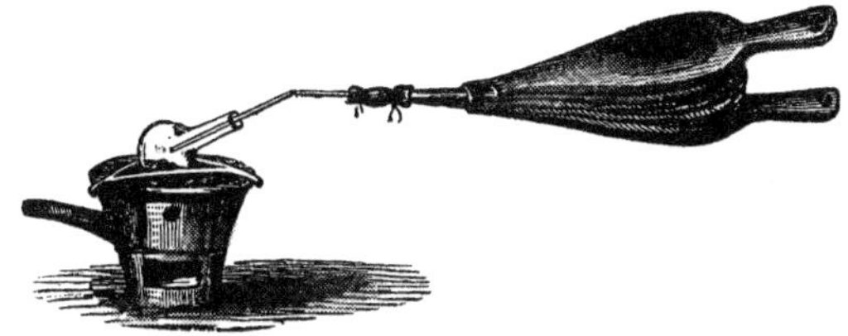

Fig. 184.

tened to the nozzle of a bellows. By blowing gently, the current of air drives off the last portions of the vapour of water. Care must be taken not to heat the flask too much, lest the nitrate of lead be decomposed, which is indicated by the appearance of reddish vapours.

When the flask has cooled, it is weighed, and as we know the weight of the empty flask, we deduct from it the weight P of the oxide of lead and anhydrous nitric acid. P—100 is, therefore, the quantity of anhydrous nitric acid contained in the 10 grammes of dilute acid.

This process is founded on the circumstance of the oxide of lead being an anhydrous base, and the nitrate of lead not containing any water in combination. The weight of the oxide of lead added should also be greater than that which would form, with nitric acid, a neutral nitrate; for, otherwise, the nitric acid would not be entirely retained, and a portion would be volatilized.

§ 108. The composition of anhydrous nitric acid is determined as follows:

We first begin by ascertaining the weight of nitric acid contained in a known weight of crystallized neutral nitrate of lead. To do this, we weigh exactly 10 grammes of the oxide of lead, and pour upon it a quantity of nitric acid, such that, after the complete transformation of the oxide of lead into a nitrate, there shall remain an excess of free acid. It is evaporated and perfectly dried. This latter operation may be done in a small glass balloon (§ 107), by which the quantity of water contained in the hydrated acid is ascertained. The neutral nitrate of lead remains alone: it is weighed: let P be its weight; P—10 is therefore the weight of nitric acid contained in a weight P of neutral nitrate of lead. We thus find that 10 grammes of nitrate of lead contain

Oxide of lead............................	$6^{gm}.738$
Nitric acid................................	$3^{gm}.262$
	$10^{gm}.000.$

We then take a tube *ab* (fig. 185) of very strong glass, of about 60 centimetres (24 inches) in length and 12 millimetres (½ inch) in diameter, closed at one end: we place at the bottom about 10 grammes of bicarbonate of soda, and, above, a few centimetres in

Fig. 185.

length of metallic copper. Again, we weigh very exactly 10 grammes of nitrate of lead, which are introduced into the tube *ab*, immediately above the layer of metallic copper: and, lastly, the tube is filled with copper turnings. We fit to the open end *a*, by means of a cork, a curved tube *acd*, which plunges into a small mercurial tub V, and arrange the tube *ab* over a sheet-iron furnace which allows us to heat its whole length.

The tube *ab* is filled with air, which must be expelled. To effect this, we apply heat to the closed end of the tube; the bicarbonate of soda parts with a portion of its carbonic acid, which expels the air through the mercury. We can readily ascertain if the air is entirely driven out, by collecting some of the gas in a bell-glass, and observing if it is perfectly absorbed by a solution of potassa. If this absorption is complete, it is evident that the air has been entirely expelled and replaced by carbonic acid.

We then remove the coals which heated the bicarbonate of soda, and heat to redness all the anterior part of the tube containing the metallic copper. We then place some coals near the part containing the nitrate of lead, so as to slowly decompose this salt, and collect the gases evolved in a large bell-glass C, over the mercury, to the top of which we have passed a certain quantity of a concentrated solution of potassa. The volatile products arising from the decomposition of the nitrate of lead pass over the heated copper, which seizes upon their oxygen, and the nitrogen alone reaches the bell-glass.

When the nitrate of lead is entirely decomposed, the tube remains filled with nitrogen, which must be also driven into the bell-glass. For this purpose, we again heat the extremity *b* of the tube, which still contains some undecomposed bicarbonate of soda. This salt again gives off carbonic acid, which drives all the nitrogen out of the tube. The carbonic acid which reaches the bell-glass at the same time with the nitrogen, is absorbed by the alkaline solution: so that, at the close of the experiment, we find in the glass all the nitrogen arising from the decomposition of 10 grammes of nitrate of lead. We then measure, exactly, the gas collected. To do this, we transfer it to a graduated bell-glass over the pneumatic cistern, and carefully measure its volume saturated with the vapour of water, after having levelled the water in the bell-glass with the general level of the cistern. Suppose

V to represent the cubic centimetres occupied by the gas:

t its temperature:

f the elastic force of the vapour of water at $t°$:

H the height of the barometer at the moment of measuring the gas.

The number V_0 of cubic centimetres, occupied by the gas at the temperature of 32°, and under the normal pressure of $0^m.760$, will be

$$V_0=V.\frac{1}{1.0.00367.t}.\frac{H-f}{0.760}.$$

If this volume were air, it would weigh

$$V_0.\ 0^{gm}.001293.$$

But, as it is nitrogen gas, which weighs less than air in the ratio of $\frac{0.9713}{1.0000}$, the weight of nitrogen will be

$$p=V_0.\ 0^{gm}.001293.\ 0.9713=V_0.\ 0^{gm}.001256.$$

We infer from this experiment that 10 grammes of nitrate of lead, or $3^{gm}.262$ of anhydrous nitric acid, contain $0^{gm}.845$ of nitrogen.

We hence conclude that 100 of nitric acid contain

Nitrogen	25.93
Oxygen	74.07
	100.00

Or in volume,

1 volume of nitrogen, which weighs	0.9713
2½ of oxygen	2.7640
making	3.7353

In fact, from the proportion

3.7353 of nitric acid : 0.9713 of nitrogen :: 100 of nitric acid : x, we find x=25.99, nearly the proportion of nitrogen found by experiment in 100 of nitric acid.

All the other combinations of nitrogen with oxygen are easily obtained by the decomposition of nitric acid under given conditions.

PROTOXIDE OF NITROGEN, NO.

§ 109. When nitric acid acts on a metal, the protoxide or deutoxide of nitrogen is evolved, according to the nature of the metal. Zinc dissolves in dilute nitric acid, disengaging a mixture of protoxide and deutoxide of nitrogen; but if we allow this gaseous mixture to remain some time in contact with damp zinc or iron filings, the deutoxide of nitrogen is decomposed and changed in protoxide, yielding a portion of its oxygen to the metal.

The protoxide of nitrogen can be much more readily prepared. We heat the nitrate of ammonia in a small glass retort (fig. 186),

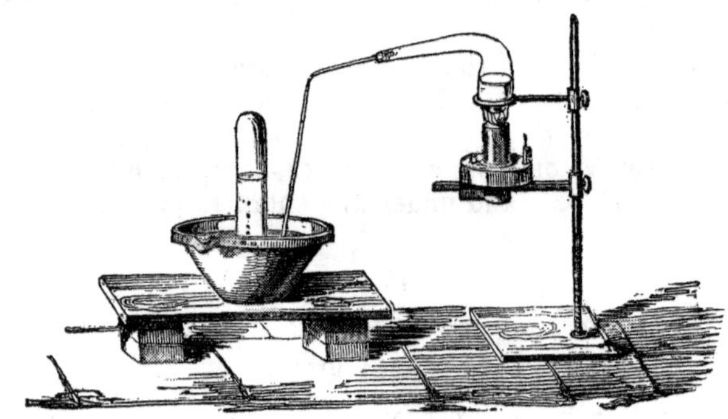

Fig. 186.

provided with a curved tube: the substance at first melts, then boils, and disengages a large quantity of gas, which may be collected either over mercury or water. The retort must be gradually heated, so as not to disengage the gas too rapidly. The nitrate of ammonia disappears and is changed into protoxide of nitrogen and water. The formula of nitrate of ammonia is NH_3HO,NO_5: by heat, it is changed into 2 equivalents of protoxide of nitrogen, 2NO, and 4 equivalents of water, 4HO. We have, in fact,

$$NH_3HO,NO_5=2NO+4HO.$$

§ 110. The protoxide of nitrogen is a colourless, inodorous, and tasteless gas, of a density of 1.527. It liquefies at 32° under a pressure of about 30 atmospheres. It solidifies at 148° below zero.

It undergoes no change by contact with the air. An incandescent coal continues to burn in this gas with a bright light, as in oxygen. A taper having some burning points is rekindled when plunged into the protoxide of nitrogen, and burns with a very brilliant flame. This property, distinctive of oxygen, may cause it to be confounded with the protoxide of nitrogen.

Sulphur, if burning feebly, is extinguished when plunged into a vessel filled with protoxide of nitrogen: but when the burning surface is of some extent, its combustion is very rapid.

Phosphorus burns in the protoxide of nitrogen with a very brilliant white light.

We shall not be surprised that the combustion of substances is more energetic in the protoxide of nitrogen than in atmospheric air, when we remember that the one-half of the volume of the former, and only one-fifth of that of the latter is oxygen. But, in atmospheric air, the oxygen and nitrogen are merely mixed, whilst, in the protoxide of nitrogen, they are combined: the combustible body must therefore be in conditions under which it can destroy this combination; and that it may continue to burn in protoxide of nitrogen, its temperature must generally be elevated.

We have seen that atmospheric air supported animal life only from the oxygen it contains. The phenomenon of respiration appears to consist essentially in a sort of combustion of the organic matters by oxygen, a combustion which evolves carbonic acid and vapour of water. The essential functions of respiration can be carried on equally well in an atmosphere of protoxide of nitrogen; for many animals can live several hours in this gas. However, a prolonged continuance in this gas will give rise to disturbance sufficient to produce death.

The protoxide of nitrogen, inhaled by man, produces a species of intoxication, accompanied, it is said, by agreeable sensations. It was found to possess this property at an early period of its discovery, and hence received the name of *exhilarating gas*. When this experiment is made, the gas should be perfectly pure, as it often contains some chlorine, which would violently affect the respiratory organs. The chlorine is owing to the nitrate of ammonia sometimes containing small portions of chlorohydrate of ammonia.

We have said that the protoxide of nitrogen liquefied at 32° under a pressure of 30 atmospheres. The liquid protoxide of nitrogen may be obtained by compressing the gas in a strong metallic reservoir surrounded by ice, by means of an air-pump. By opening the stopcock of the reservoir, after having inserted it, a portion of the liquid reassumes the gaseous state, but cools the rest to such a degree that it does not volatilize, and even assumes, in part, the solid state, forming a white snow. The liquid part may be collected in a tube, and kept in this state for more than half an hour.

When a metal is plunged into this fluid, it produces a noise similar to that resulting from the immersion of red-hot iron in water. Mercury produces the same effect, and rapidly congeals, forming a metal resembling silver in its physical properties. Potassium, which rapidly decomposes the gaseous protoxide of nitrogen under the influence of heat, is not changed by the contact of the liquid protoxide. Carbon, sulphur, phosphorus, and iodine belong to the same category. The temperature of liquid protoxide of nitrogen at the ordinary atmospheric pressure is very low, and supposed to be $-148°$. It descends much lower when placed beneath the receiver of an air-pump, which is rapidly exhausted, a portion of it then congealing into a white snow. If we place in the protoxide, which is evaporated in the vacuum of an air-pump, a small tube hermetically sealed and containing some liquid protoxide, the latter freezes and forms a perfectly limpid solid mass.

§ 111. The protoxide of nitrogen is easily analyzed as follows: A certain given volume of gas is measured in a graduated glass, placed over mercury, and introduced into a tube curved as in fig. 187. A piece of potassium, fastened to a wire, is passed into the curve of the tube, and heated by an alcohol lamp. Energetic combustion ensues, the potassium decomposes, the protoxide of nitrogen seizes upon its oxygen, and sets free the nitrogen. At the moment of decomposition, the glass must be firmly held in the hand, lest it might be projected from the cistern. When the tube has cooled, the gas is again passed into the graduated glass, and its volume will be found to be unchanged by decomposition. We hence conclude that the protoxide of nitrogen contains exactly its volume of nitrogen.

Fig. 187.

If we deduct from the weight of a volume 1 of the protoxide of nitrogen or from the density of this gas......... =1.527
the weight of a volume 1 of nitrogen or its density =0.972
there remain........................ 0.555

very nearly equal to $\frac{1 \cdot 1056}{2}$ or 0.5528, or the half of the density of oxygen gas.

1 volume of protoxide of nitrogen therefore contains

1 volume of nitrogen...............	0.972
½ " of oxygen................	0.552
	1.524

If we make the proportion

$$1.524 : 0.972 :: 100 : x,$$

x will be the weight of the nitrogen contained in 100 grammes of protoxide of nitrogen: we then have

Nitrogen..............................	63.77
Oxygen..............................	36.23
	100.00

§ 112. The analysis of the protoxide of nitrogen may also be made in the eudiometer, by means of hydrogen gas. Suppose that we have introduced into the eudiometer

	100	measures of protoxide of nitrogen
	150	" of hydrogen
Total...	250	

Let us pass an electric spark through, and again measure the volume of gas: we shall find it reduced to 150 measures; 100 have therefore disappeared. If the nitrogen and oxygen were merely mixed, instead of being combined with condensation, we might deduce the composition of the gas from the volume which has disappeared: but that is impossible, and we must ascertain directly the quantity of hydrogen which has served to burn the oxygen of the protoxide. This quantity will be known, if we know how much hydrogen remains in the 150 divisions of gas after the explosion. To ascertain this volume, we will introduce into the eudiometer 50 divisions of oxygen, making in all 200, and pass an electric spark. After the explosion there remain only 125 divisions of gas; 75 have therefore disappeared, formed of hydrogen and oxygen in the proportions constituting water, that is, 50 of hydrogen and 25 of oxygen.

Thus, in the 150 parts of gas which remained after the first electric spark, there were 50 parts of hydrogen, and consequently 100 parts of nitrogen. Now, as we have introduced, from the first, 150 parts of hydrogen, and only find 50, 100 parts have been burned by the oxygen of the protoxide of nitrogen: 100 parts of this gas, therefore, contain

100 parts of nitrogen
50 " of oxygen.

DEUTOXIDE OF NITROGEN, NO_2.

§ 113. This compound is obtained by dissolving metals in nitric acid properly diluted. We generally use copper or mercury. Copper affords pure deutoxide of nitrogen, provided the temperature be not allowed to rise too high during the reaction, and the acid be sufficiently diluted.

The operation is effected in the same apparatus as that used for making hydrogen gas. Copper turnings are placed in the bottom of a two-mouthed bottle A (fig. 188), and covered with a

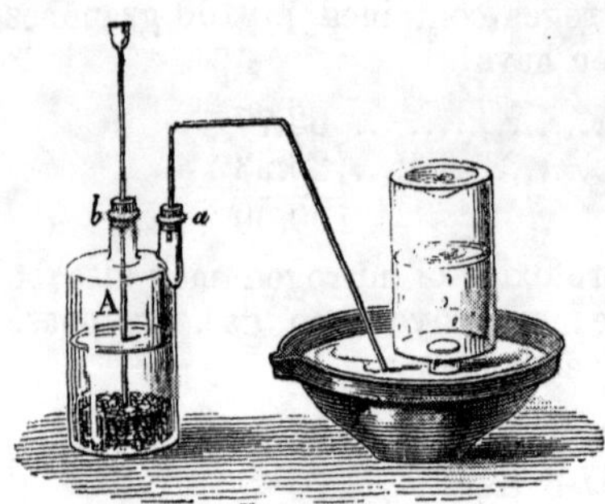

Fig. 188.

layer of water. A discharging-tube is fitted to one of the mouths *a*, and to the other *b* a straight tube terminating in a funnel, acting as a safety-tube, and through which the nitric acid is slowly and gradually added. The gas may be collected over mercury or water. Water dissolves $\frac{1}{20}$ of its volume.

Very pure deutoxide of nitrogen may be obtained by heating the nitrate of potassa KO,NO_5 with a solution of the protochloride of iron FeCl, in an excess of chlorohydric acid.

$$6FeCl+KO,NO_5+4HCl=NO_2+3(Fe_2Cl_3)+KCl+4HO.$$

To make this preparation, we take two equal volumes of chlorohydric acid: we heat one with iron filings, to change it into protochloride of iron, and add it to the other volume of acid. The nitrate of potassa is then treated with this mixture.

§ 114. The deutoxide of nitrogen is a colourless gas which has hitherto borne the greatest degree of pressure without liquefaction. Its density is 1.039.

When mixed with the air, it immediately gives off reddish vapours, absorbing, in this case, oxygen, and changing into hyponitric acid: the vapours have a strongly acid reaction.

The deutoxide of nitrogen has of itself no acid reaction, as is easily shown by the following experiment. We collect some deutoxide of nitrogen in a glass, over mercury, and pass into the glass some tincture of litmus, which preserves its blue colour. But, if we introduce some bubbles of oxygen, the tincture is reddened immediately.

A taper presenting some points of ignition does not inflame when plunged into this gas; but an incandescent coal burns with great brilliancy.

Phosphorus may be melted in deutoxide of nitrogen without taking fire; whilst, in the air, this always happens. But inflamed phosphorus continues to burn longer and with more brilliancy in this gas than in the open air. The light may be compared to that of burning phosphorus in oxygen.

Burning sulphur is extinguished in the deutoxide of nitrogen.

The deutoxide of nitrogen is therefore a less active agent of combustion than the protoxide; and yet, for the same quantity of nitrogen, it contains twice as much oxygen. This shows that the nitrogen and oxygen are combined with much more energy in the deutoxide than in the protoxide, since more powerful affinities are necessary to effect the decomposition.

The deutoxide of nitrogen is absorbed by a solution of the sulphate of the protoxide of iron, and then acquires a very deep brown-colour. This reaction may be used to separate the protoxide from the deutoxide of nitrogen.

The deutoxide of nitrogen is largely dissolved in concentrated nitric acid, but there is a reciprocal decomposition: the deutoxide takes from the nitric acid a portion of its oxygen, and the two substances pass into the state of hyponitric acid. The liquid assumes a brown hue, which is deeper and deeper in proportion to the formation of hyponitric acid. When nitric acid is more diluted with water, it is more fixed, and a smaller quantity of acid decomposes. Lastly, when nitric acid is greatly diluted, it is no longer decomposed by the deutoxide of nitrogen.

These solutions of hyponitric acid in nitric acid more or less concentrated present very various colours. With monohydrated nitric acid, the liquid is brown: with a more diluted acid, it is yellow. Acid of a density of 1.35 is green; that of 1.25 becomes clear blue; and, lastly, acid of a density less than 1.15 is colourless.

This experiment is generally made in the following manner. To a large two-mouthed bottle (fig. 189), in which the deutoxide of nitrogen is produced, a series of three-mouthed bottles are fitted,

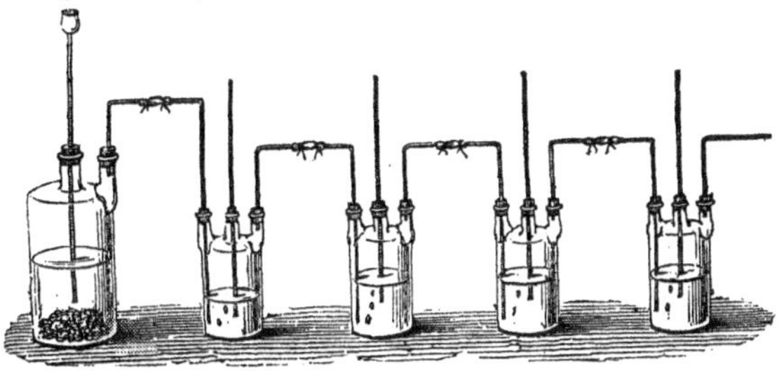

Fig. 189.

and arranged as in the wood-cut. This apparatus has received the name of *Woolf's bottles.** In the first two bottles we place the

* We frequently adopt, in our chemical apparatus, tubes arranged in a peculiar manner, and called *safety-tubes*. Their object is to prevent explosion and the mixture of the fluids contained in the various vessels composing it.

Theory of the safety-tubes.—Let us suppose a flask A (fig. 190) in which there is an evolution of chlorine gas, by the reaction of chlorohydric acid on the peroxide of manganese: let B be a test-glass filled with a solution of potassa, on which we desire the chlorine to act, and for which it has a great affinity. We lead the chlorine by the discharging-tube *abc* to the bottom of the test-glass B. As long as the chlorine is freely furnished by the flask A, the operation goes on regularly, and bubbles of gas pass through the solution of potassa. The elastic force of the gas, in the balloon A, equals the pressure of the external atmosphere on the solution of potassa, increased by the pressure of a column of most concentrated nitric acid; in the third, nitric acid more diluted, having a density of 1.45; in the fourth, acid of 1.35; in the fifth, acid of 1.25; and lastly, in the sixth, acid of 1.10.

The first bottle is originally of a brown colour; but, as the

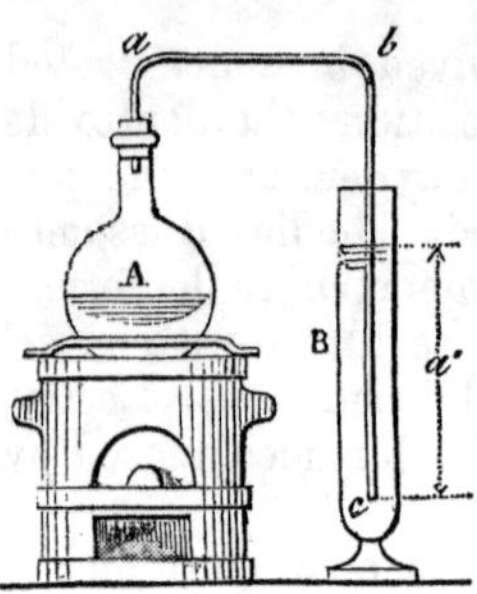

Fig. 190.

solution of potassa equal in height to the distance between the level of the fluid in the test-glass and the extremity c of the discharging-tube. The pressure of the external atmosphere is measured by the height H of a column of mercury which is in equilibrium with it, or in other words, by the height of the mercury in the barometer. The pressure of the column a' of a solution of potassa may be expressed by a column of mercury which would produce an equivalent pressure. If we designate by x the height of this column, by d' and δ the densities, compared with water, of the solution of potassa and of the mercury, we shall evidently have

$$x\delta = a'd' \text{ whence } x = a'\frac{d'}{\delta}.$$

The elastic force of the gas in the interior of the flask will be therefore expressed by a column of mercury of which the height is $H + a'\frac{d'}{\delta}$.

Let us suppose that the evolution of chlorine ceases in the flask A, either because the quantity of chlorohydric acid is exhausted, or because the flask has become too cool. The solution of potassa contained in the discharging-tube bc, continues to absorb the chlorine contained in the flask A: the elastic force of the gas in the apparatus gradually diminishes, and the constant pressure of the atmosphere on the fluid in the test-glass will drive this fluid into the tube bc. If the operator be present, he may save the experiment by quickly uncorking the flask A; but if he be absent, the solution of potassa will soon ascend to the top of the discharging-tube, and, the absorption of the chlorine by the potassa continuing, the greater part of the solution of potassa may pass into the flask A. *Absorption* is then said to have taken place, and the experiment fails.

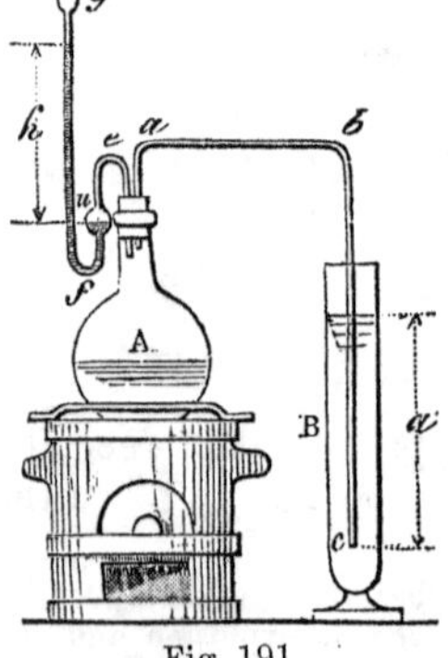

Fig. 191.

It is impossible that an accident of this nature can occur, if we adjust to the flask A, and in the same cork, a curved tube efg having a bulb u, as represented in fig. 191. Into this tube is poured a small quantity of the same fluid as that in the flask, which in this experiment would be chlorohydric acid. When the operation goes on regularly, and the gases are disengaged at the extremity c of the discharging-tube, the elastic force of the internal gas is represented by $H + a'\frac{d'}{\delta}$. The chlorohydric acid will therefore ascend in the leg fg of the curved tube, until the column, elevated above the level of the fluid in the bulb u, the height of which we represent by h, equals the elastic force of $H + a'\frac{d'}{\delta}$, diminished by the pressure H of the atmosphere, for this latter pressure is also exerted on the top of the column h. If d represent the density of the chlorohydric acid compared with water, a column of mercury exerting the same pressure as the column h of chlorohydric acid would be expressed by $h\frac{d}{\delta}$. We should therefore have

$$h\frac{d}{\delta} = a'\frac{d'}{\delta} \text{ whence } h = a'\frac{d'}{d}.$$

deutoxide of nitrogen constantly carries water which condenses in this first bottle, the acid it contains changes colour successively. The second bottle assumes a brown tinge; the third becomes yellow; the fourth, blue; the sixth is colourless.

Let us now suppose that the disengagement of the gas ceases, and that, in consequence of the absorption of the chlorine by the solution of potassa, the elastic force of the gas in the flask A becomes less than that of the atmosphere: it will be seen, that if the various parts of the apparatus are properly proportioned, no absorption of the solution of potassa into the flask A is to be feared. In fact, as the elastic force of the gas in this flask becomes less than that of the atmosphere, the solution of potassa will rise in the tube *bc;* but, at the same time, the chlorohydric acid will descend in the leg *fg* of the curved tube. If the fluid reaches the lowest point *f* before the solution of potassa reaches the summit *b* of the discharging-tube, the atmospheric air will enter by the curved tube and prevent the interior elastic force from being weakened. Absorption will therefore be impossible, and the operation cannot fail of success.

The bulb *u* of the curved tube is intended to prevent, by its great relative capacity, the level of the fluid from rising high in leg *fe*, in consequence of the introduction of the fluid previously contained in the leg *fg:* the air therefore passes into the apparatus, where the internal elastic force has become very slightly inferior to that of the atmosphere.

This bulb is also useful, because it contains the quantity of fluid necessary to completely fill the leg *fg*, when the elastic force of the internal gas becomes much greater than that of the atmosphere. Moreover, this elastic force cannot increase indefinitely: it cannot surpass the pressure of the external atmosphere by a quantity greater than that which balances the fluid column contained in the leg *fg*: for then this column would be projected from the tube, and the internal gas would communicate freely with the atmosphere.

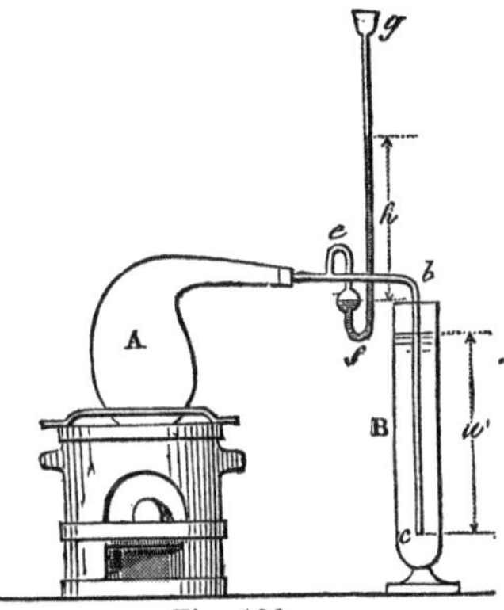

Fig. 192.

This last circumstance frequently occurs in the experiment we have selected as an example. The tube *bc* is often closed by the deposit of crystallized matter formed by the reaction of the chlorine on the potassa. The gas continuing to be disengaged in the flask A, its elastic force continually increasing, if it find no other exit, as in fig. 190, this force will soon be sufficient to burst the flask.

The addition of the curved tube removes the danger: and it is therefore with great justice called a *safety-tube.*

This tube has still another use. It enables us to add, as required, portions of hydrochloric acid, without uncorking the flask.

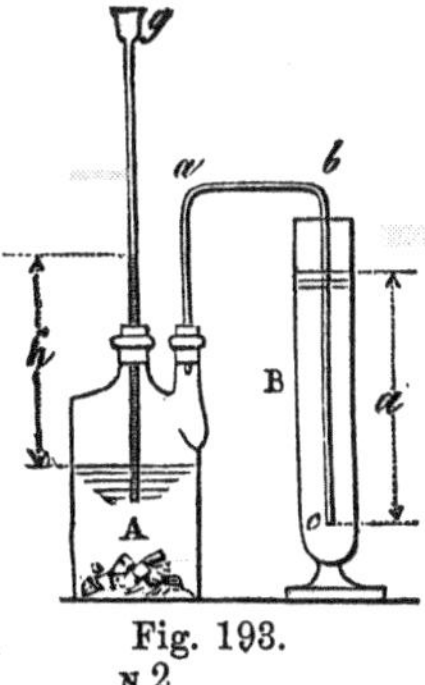

Fig. 193.

When the vessel in which the gas is generated is a retort with but one opening, we use a discharging-tube, to which is attached a tube shaped like the letter S, as in fig. 192. This tube then acts as a safety-tube only; it cannot be used for the introduction of the fluid necessary for reaction. This arrangement is called *Welter's tube*, from its inventor. We can place in this tube any liquid which exerts no chemical actiŏn on the gas.

The vessel used for chemical reaction is often a two-mouthed bottle (fig. 193), as in the preparation of hydrogen gas and the deutoxide of nitrogen. We then use,

§ 115. The analysis of the deutoxide of nitrogen is made by potassium in a curved bell-glass, in the same way as that of the protoxide. After the decomposition, we find the volume of gas reduced by one-half. Thus 1 volume of deutoxide contains a $\frac{1}{2}$ volume of nitrogen.

---

as a safety-tube, a simple straight tube, surmounted by a funnel, and its lower end passing below the surface of the liquid.

Let us now suppose that we wish to pass the same gas, successively, through a series of bottles containing solutions, different or identical, which can absorb it. We use the arrangement represented in fig. 194. A is the flask in which the

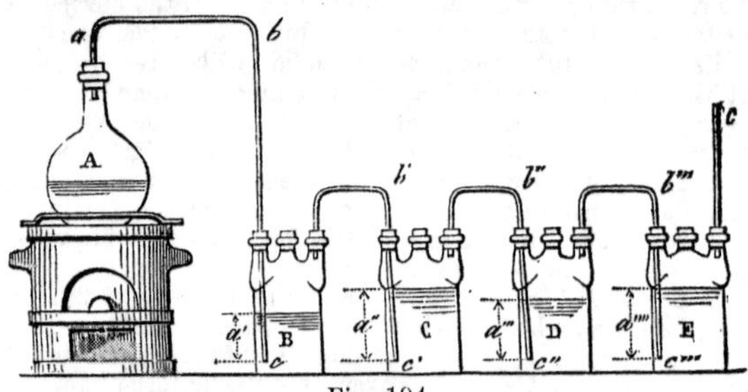

Fig. 194.

chlorine is generated, and the three-mouthed bottles B, C, D, E, contain the solutions intended to absorb the gas. Let us suppose that the evolution of the chlorine be such that the bubbles of gas traverse the fluid of the four bottles, and let us inquire what is the elastic force possessed by the gas in each of these bottles.

The pressure of the atmosphere is freely exerted, by the tube *o* open at both ends, on the surface of the fluid contained in the bottle E. The gas in the bottle E has therefore an elastic force equal to that of the external atmosphere, which we suppose represented by a column H of mercury.

In the bottle D, the pressure on the surface of the fluid is equal to the pressure H of the bottle E, increased by a column of mercury balancing the column a'''' of the liquid E, which the gas should depress in the discharging-tube, to escape by the opening c''''. If d'''' represent the density, compared with water, of the fluid E, the column of mercury balancing the column a'''' of the liquid E is expressed by $a''''\frac{d''''}{\delta}$. The elastic force of the gas in the bottle D is therefore expressed by

$$H+a''''\frac{d''''}{\delta}.$$

In the bottle C, the pressure on the surface of the fluid is equal to the pressure $H+a''''\frac{d''''}{\delta}$ of the gas in the bottle D, augmented by the column of mercury balancing the column a'''' of the fluid D, which the gas must depress to pass from C into D. This column of mercury is expressed by $a'''\frac{d'''}{\delta}$, if d''' be the density of the fluid D. The elastic force of the gas in the bottle C is therefore

$$H+a'''\frac{d'''}{\delta}+a''''\frac{d''''}{\delta}.$$

The pressure on the surface of the fluid in the bottle B is equal to the pressure $H+a'''\frac{d'''}{\delta}+a''''\frac{d''''}{\delta}$ of the gas in the bottle C, increased by the column of mercury balancing the column a'' of the fluid C. This column of mercury is expressed

Deducting from the density of the deutoxide =	1.039
one-half the density of nitrogen $\frac{0.972}{2}$..........	0.486
there remain..................................	0.553

---

by $a''\frac{d''}{\delta}$, if d'' represent the density of the fluid C compared with water. The elastic force of the atmosphere of the bottle B is therefore

$$H+a''\frac{d''}{\delta}+a'''\frac{d'''}{\delta}+a''''\frac{d''''}{\delta}.$$

Lastly, the elastic force of the gas in the flask A, is equal to the elastic force of the bottle B, that is to say $H+a''\frac{d''}{\delta}+a'''\frac{d'''}{\delta}+a''''\frac{d''''}{\delta}$, increased by a column of mercury which balances the column a' of the fluid B. This column of mercury is expressed by $a'\frac{d'}{\delta}$, a' being the density of the fluid B, compared with water. The elastic force of the gas in the flask A is therefore expressed by

$$H+a'\frac{d'}{\delta}+a''\frac{d''}{\delta}+a'''\frac{d'''}{\delta}+a''''\frac{d''''}{\delta}.$$

Thus, when the gas passes freely through the fluids of the bottles B, C, D, and E, we shall have as the elastic forces of the gases:

In E............... H

D.............. $H+a''''\frac{d''''}{\delta}$

C.............. $H+a'''\frac{d'''}{\delta}+a''''\frac{d''''}{\delta}$

B................ $H+a''\frac{d''}{\delta}+a'''\frac{d'''}{\delta}+a''''\frac{d''''}{\delta}$

In the flask A................ $H+a'\frac{d'}{\delta}+a''\frac{d''}{\delta}+a'''\frac{d'''}{\delta}+a''''\frac{d''''}{\delta}.$

Let us now suppose that the evolution of gas ceases in the flask A, during the absence of the operator, the absorption of the gas continuing to take place in the bottles B, C, D, E, the fluid in B will pass into the flask A, that of C into B, that of D into C, and lastly, that of E into D. The experiment will therefore fail.

If, on the contrary, in consequence of chemical reaction, one of the discharging-tubes, bc, $b'c'$, $b''c''$, $b'''c'''$, becomes closed, the elastic force of the gas in the apparatus will increase indefinitely, and one of the bottles preceding the closed tube may burst. The flask A generally explodes, because it presents less resistance.

This danger will be entirely avoided if we arrange the apparatus as in fig. 195; that is, if we adjust to the flask A, a safety-tube curved in the shape of the letter S, and insert into the third mouth of the bottles straight safety tubes s', s'', s''', s'''', dipping slightly into the fluid. There will be then no danger of explosion: for if the internal gases acquire great elastic force, they will eject the fluids through the safety-tubes, and the gases will communicate freely with the atmosphere.

Neither can absorption take place: for, if the elastic force in any one of the bottles becomes inferior to that of the external atmosphere by a quantity equal to that which balances the small column of fluid comprised between the level of the fluid in the bottle and the lower extremity of the safety-tube, the atmospheric air will enter the bottle through this tube, and prevent the internal elastic force from becoming more feeble. The fluids can therefore rise only to a slight distance in the discharging-tubes, and can never pass from one bottle to another.

which is about one-half the density $\frac{1.1056}{2}$ of oxygen.

1 volume of deutoxide of nitrogen contains, therefore,

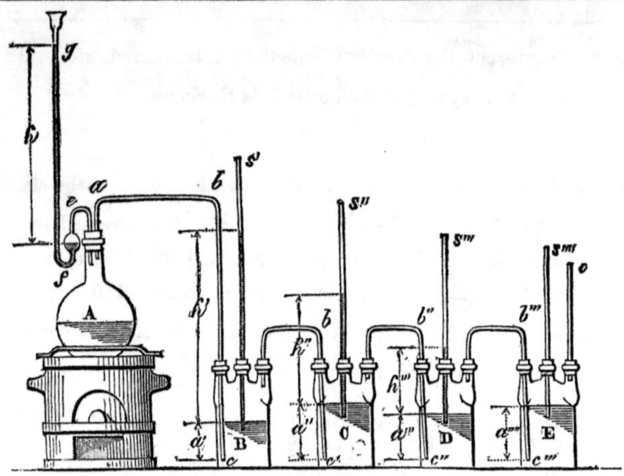

Fig. 195.

The heights h, h', h'', h''', of the fluid in the safety-tubes, are easily calculated.

The column h''' of the fluid, in the safety-tube of the bottle D, equals a column of mercury of the height of $h''' \frac{d'''}{\delta}$; it also balances the elastic force of the gas in the bottle D, of which the value is $H + a'''' \frac{d''''}{\delta}$, diminished by the pressure H of the external atmosphere, which acts equally on the top of the column h'''; we have therefore

$$h''' \frac{d'''}{\delta} = a'''' \frac{d''''}{\delta}, \text{ whence } h''' = a'''' \frac{d''''}{d'''}.$$

The column h'' of the fluid in the safety tube of the bottle C, equals a column of mercury of the height $h'' \frac{d''}{\delta}$, and it balances the elastic force of the gas in the bottle C, diminished by the pressure of the external atmosphere. We have therefore

$$h'' \frac{d''}{\delta} = a''' \frac{d'''}{\delta} + a'''' \frac{d''''}{\delta}$$

whence

$$h'' = a''' \frac{d'''}{d''} + a'''' \frac{d''''}{d''}.$$

According to the same reasoning, the height h' of the fluid in the safety-tube of the bottle B, is represented by

$$h' = a'' \frac{d''}{d'} + a''' \frac{d'''}{d'} + a'''' \frac{d''''}{d'}.$$

Lastly, the height h, which expresses the difference between the level of the fluid in the two legs of the curved tube affixed to the flask A, will be, calling d the density of the solution of chlorohydric acid, compared with water,

$$h - a' \frac{d'}{d} + a'' \frac{d''}{d} + a''' \frac{d'''}{d} + a'''' \frac{d''''}{d}.$$

It is evident that the safety-tubes, in the bottles, should be longer as they are nearer to the flask A, in which the gas is generated.

The apparatus in fig. 195, is called *Woolf's apparatus.*

½ vol. of nitrogen	0.486
½ vol. of oxygen	0.552
	1.038

without condensation, and its composition by weight is,

Nitrogen	46.66
Oxygen	53.34
	100.00

This gas may also be analyzed by hydrogen in the eudiometer, as was explained (§ 112) in the case of the protoxide.

Nitrous Acid, NO_3.

§ 116. It is difficult to obtain nitrous acid in a state of purity. It may be prepared by means of the following compound, hyponitric acid, which may be considered as a combination of nitric with nitrous acid NO_5+NO_3; hyponitric acid, cooled in a glass tube, is added to a quantity of water sufficient to form, with nitric acid, the hydrate NO_5+4HO. The fluid separates into two strata, the inferior of which, consisting of nitrous acid, is of a deep-blue colour; the superior is green, and consists of a solution of nitrous acid in the second hydrate of nitric acid, NO_5+4HO. Nitrous acid is eminently volatile, for it boils about 32°. It is, nevertheless, impossible to distil it without alteration; for it easily changes into the deutoxide of nitrogen, which is disengaged, and into hyponitric acid, which remains. If, therefore, we heat gently the inferior stratum of nitrous acid in a retort, a great deal of deutoxide of nitrogen is disengaged, which carries with it a small quantity of undecomposed nitrous acid, which may be condensed in an excessively cold receiver: the temperature rises gradually in the retort from 32° to 82.4°. The fluid which then remains in the retort is pure hyponitric acid.

Nitrous acid may also be obtained isolated, by passing through a tube curved in U, cooled in a refrigerating mixture, a current of gas composed of 4 volumes of deutoxide of nitrogen and 1 volume of oxygen. The refrigerating mixture should be made of pounded ice and crystallized chloride of calcium: this lowers the temperature to −40°. A blue fluid condenses in the tube thus cooled. If the oxygen be in greater proportion, hyponitric acid is formed: and even with the proportions of the two gases just indicated, a considerable quantity of this last compound is always formed.

Nitrous acid is also frequently formed when we cause nitric acid to react on certain organic substances, such as starch; but, in this case, it is always largely mixed with hyponitric acid.

Nitrous acid mixes with cold water, but as soon as the temperature is slightly elevated, it decomposes. The deutoxide of nitrogen is disengaged, and the water contains nitric acid.

Nitrous acid may be readily obtained in combination with the bases. When we heat carefully the nitrate of potassa in a strong glass retort, we shall see that from the earliest stage of decomposition, oxygen alone is disengaged; and at a later period alone, and a higher temperature, a mixture of oxygen and nitrogen passes over. During the first stage of decomposition, the nitrate of potassa KO,NO_5, is changed into nitrite of potassa KO,NO_3; so that, if we arrest the decomposition at the moment when the gas which passes over contains the nitrogen, the substance in the retort is principally nitrite of potassa. This substance is treated with alcohol, which dissolves the nitrite of potassa, and leaves the nitrate undecomposed. By pouring into the solution of nitrite of potassa a solution of nitrate of silver, we obtain a white precipitate of the nitrite of silver.

§ 117. The composition of nitrous acid may be deduced from the analysis of the nitrite of silver, of which the formula is AgO,NO_3. 10 grammes of nitrite of silver are calcined, $7^{gm}.013$ of metallic silver remain. Now, as $7^{gm}.013$ of silver correspond to $7^{gm}.532$ of oxide of silver which existed in the nitrite, the weight of the nitrous acid in the 10 grammes of the nitrite is, therefore, $2^{gm}.468$.

By another experiment, we decompose in a glass tube 10 grammes of nitrite of silver by metallic copper, as detailed for the analysis of the nitrate of lead (§ 108), and collect the nitrogen which is disengaged.

We conclude from this experiment that $2^{gm}.468$ of nitrous acid contain

Nitrogen	0.910
Oxygen	1.558
	2.468

consequently, 100 of nitrous acid contain

Nitrogen	36.84
Oxygen	63.16
	100.00

which gives

1 volume of nitrogen	0.9713
1½ " oxygen	1.6584
	2.6297

Making the proportion 2.6297 : 0.9713 : : 100 : x, we find for the quantity of nitrogen contained in 100 parts of nitrous acid

$$x=36.93,$$

differing very slightly from the quantity found by direct experiment.

Hyponitric Acid, NO_4.

§ 118. We have seen (§ 105) that, in the preparation of nitric acid, copious reddish vapours are given off at the commencement and close of the operation. This especially occurs when an equivalent of concentrated sulphuric acid is made to react on an equivalent of nitrate of potassa: one-half of the nitric acid, which is not disengaged except at a high temperature, is decomposed into hyponitric acid and oxygen: the hyponitric acid is dissolved in the monohydrated nitric acid which has passed over unchanged.

By carefully distilling the nitric acid obtained under these circumstances, and keeping the receiver very cold, we may separate a considerable quantity of hyponitric acid.

This product is also obtained in the form of reddish vapours, by mixing together the deutoxide of nitrogen and excess of oxygen.

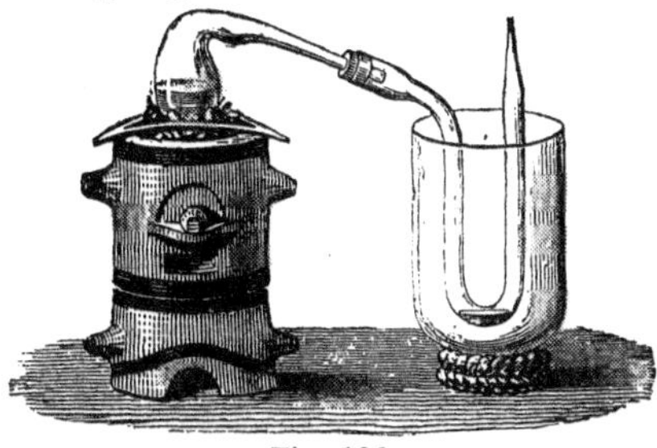

Fig. 196.

But the best way of preparing hyponitric acid is by heating in a strong glass retort (fig. 196), some nitrate of lead previously well dried to deprive it of its hygrometric water, for it does not contain any water of combination. This retort is made to communicate with a receiver properly cooled, in which the hyponitric acid is condensed.

§ 119. Hyponitric acid is an orange-coloured fluid, of the density of 1.42. It boils at +82.4°, and solidifies at 8°. Its vapour is intensely red, having a density of 1.72.

Hyponitric is not an acid *per se*, for it does not produce a hyponitrate by combining with bases: there always forms, in this case, a mixture of nitrate and nitrite: it is therefore more proper to consider this substance as a combination of nitric with nitrous acid. We have, in fact, $2NO_4 = NO_5 + NO_3$.*

Hyponitric acid may be regarded as corresponding to the monohydrated nitric, in which nitrous acid replaces the equivalent of water. We have seen, in fact, that water decomposes hyponitric acid: hydrated nitric acid is formed and the nitrous acid is liberated.

Nitrous acid acts the part of a feeble base with many strong acids. It combines with sulphuric acid, and furnishes a crystalline combination $NO_3,2SO_3$, which is obtained as follows:—We mix, in a tube previously drawn out, liquid sulphurous and hyponitric acid, and then close the tube hermetically. In a few days the tube

* Some chemists term it *peroxide of nitrogen;* others, *nitroso-nitric acid.—J. C. B.*

may be opened; the two substances have combined, and the solid product may be heated to 392°, when it fuses. At a higher temperature, it distils without alteration.

In this experiment, the hyponitric acid NO_4 yields a portion of its oxygen to the sulphurous acid SO_2, which it changes into sulphuric acid SO_3, passing itself into the state of nitrous acid NO_3; but the half only of this acid combines with the sulphuric acid formed, and produces the combination $NO_3,2SO_3$: the other half of the nitrous acid remains liquid. The following equation represents the reaction:

$$2SO_2+2NO_4=NO_3,2SO_3+NO_3.$$

This compound dissolves without change in concentrated sulphuric acid; but it takes the water from the more aqueous sulphuric acid, and is then transformed into a hydrate, which is frequently deposited in crystals. These crystals sometimes form in the manufacture of sulphuric acid on a large scale, as we shall soon see. By contact with pure water, or very diluted sulphuric acid, the combination is destroyed, and the sulphuric and nitrous acids become free.

The colour of hyponitric acid varies with the temperature: it is of an orange-red at 59°, yellow at 32°, and at −4° almost colourless.

Hyponitric acid is decomposed by contact with water into nitric and nitrous acid. Now, we have seen that nitrous acid dissolves in nitric acid in proportions varying according to the state of concentration, and furnished fluids of different colours. It therefore follows, that if we decompose hyponitric acid, by mixing it with a small quantity of water, monohydrated nitric acid NO_5+HO is formed, which dissolves a large quantity of nitrous acid, and imparts a brown or yellow colour to the fluid. If the proportion of water be increased, the nitric acid becomes more diluted and dissolves less of the nitrous: the fluid then becomes green. With still more water, the fluid is blue. Lastly, by still increasing the quantity of water, the fluid remains colourless. In all cases, a greater or less quantity of reddish vapours are disengaged.

§120. *Analysis of Hyponitric Acid.*—We place a certain quan-

Fig. 197.

tity of this acid in a curved tube *efg*, drawn out at both ends, as represented in fig. 197. This tube has been weighed when empty, and again after the introduction of the fluid and sealing its ends hermetically: the increase in weight is the weight of the substance introduced. One of the pointed ends is fitted to a tube *ab*, filled with metallic copper, of which the end *a* has been drawn out, and it is there fastened by means of caoutchouc. Into the other open end *b* a cork is inserted, furnished with a curved tube, which allows us to collect the gas over a small mercurial trough. The air contained in the tube *ab* is completely driven off, by means of a current of carbonic acid from an apparatus (fig. 198), fitted to the pointed end *a* of the tube, before the vessel containing the hyponitric acid is adapted to it. We then heat to redness the tube *ab*, and break off the pointed end of this vessel by pressing it against the sides of the tube *ab*. The acid immediately distils over, its vapour is decomposed by contact with the heated copper, and nitrogen gas is disengaged and collected in the bell-glass C. In order to decompose the last remains of this substance, and drive all the nitrogen into the bell-glass, the apparatus furnishing the carbonic acid is fitted (fig. 198), by means of caoutchouc, to the other end of the vessel, which end is then broken. A current of carbonic acid thus traverses the whole apparatus, and drives the last remains of nitrogen into the bell-glass C. This gas is measured in the manner we described for the analysis of the nitrate of lead (§ 108).

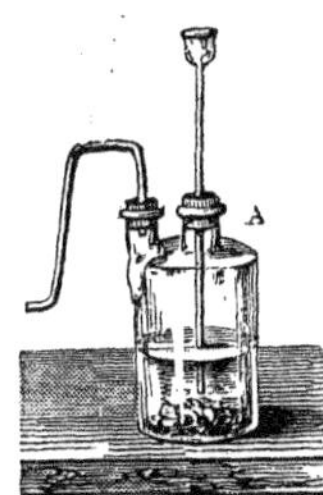

Fig. 198.

We thus find hyponitric acid to be composed of

Nitrogen	30.43
Oxygen	69.57
	100.00

or in volume,

½ volume of nitrogen	0.4856
1 " oxygen	1.1056
	1.5912

forming 1 volume of hyponitric acid: for the density of its vapour has been found to be 1.62 by direct experiment. This is but little more than the sum first obtained. Moreover, if we make the proportion

$$1.5912 : 0.4856 :: 100 : x,$$

we have, for the quantity of nitrogen contained in 100 parts of hyponitric acid

$$x=30.51,$$

which differs but little from that found above.

RECAPITULATION OF THE COMBINATIONS OF NITROGEN WITH OXYGEN.

§ 121. We have found these combinations to be composed as follows:

1. *Protoxide of nitrogen*......1 volume of nitrogen combined with a ½ volume of oxygen, forming 1 volume of protoxide of nitrogen.
2. *Deutoxide of nitrogen*......1 volume of nitrogen combined with 1 volume of oxygen, forming 2 volumes of deutoxide of nitrogen.
3. *Nitrous acid*................1 volume of nitrogen combined with 1½ volumes of oxygen. We do not know what would be the volume of nitrous acid in the gaseous state, for it has not yet been studied, on account of its very ready decomposition.
4. *Hyponitric acid*............1 volume of nitrogen combined with 2 volumes of oxygen, forming 2 volumes of hyponitric acid gas.
5. *Nitric acid*..................1 volume of nitrogen combined with 2½ volumes of oxygen. The volume of gaseous nitric acid produced is unknown, because this acid has not yet been obtained isolated.

The first circumstance worthy of remark is, that in all these compounds the oxygen and the nitrogen combine in *extremely simple proportions.* 1 volume of nitrogen takes ½, 1, 1½, 2, and 2½ volumes of oxygen. Moreover, the volumes of compound gaseous bodies, when they can be examined in this state, bear very simple proportions to the volumes of the component gases. We have here, therefore, a clear confirmation of the general law announced before (§ 85).

In the protoxide of nitrogen, 1 volume of nitrogen, combined with a ½ volume of oxygen, has produced one volume of protoxide: or, in other words, 2 volumes of nitrogen and 1 of oxygen have produced 2 volumes of protoxide: thus the 3 volumes of the component gases have been reduced to 2: there has been a condensation of ⅓.

So also in hyponitric acid: 1 volume of nitrogen and 2 of oxygen furnish 2 volumes of gaseous hyponitric acid: the condensation is therefore the same as in the protoxide.

Now, we have seen (§ 84) that 2 volumes of hydrogen combine with 1 of oxygen, and produce 2 volumes of vapour of water, thus presenting the same amount of condensation as the two preceding cases.

Chemists are therefore led, by analogy, to advance as a law, that, *when 2 volumes of a simple gas combine with 1 volume of another simple gas, the resulting gaseous combination occupies 2 volumes.* We do not consider this law as proven, inasmuch as it is based upon only three examples; but we shall take care, as opportunity offers, to point out the additional examples which confirm it.

In the deutoxide of nitrogen, 1 volume of nitrogen is combined with 1 volume of oxygen, and gives 2 volumes of deutoxide of nitrogen. Thus, the volume of gas here formed is equal to the volume of the component gases, and there is no condensation. We shall, hereafter, meet combinations of simple gases in equal volumes without condensation: so that we may admit, by analogy, until well ascertained facts prove that the law is not general, that, *when two simple gases combine in equal volumes, combination takes place without condensation, that is, the volume of the gaseous compound is equal to the sum of the volumes of the component gases.*

If we refer the composition of the various combinations of nitrogen with oxygen, not to 1 volume of nitrogen, but to 2 volumes of this gas, we shall have

1. Protoxide of nitrogen	2 vols. nitrogen,	1 vol. oxygen,	making	2 vols.	protoxide
2. Deutoxide of nitrogen	2 "	2 "	"	4 "	binoxide
3. Nitrous acid..........	2 "	3 "	"	"	unknown
4. Hyponitric acid......	2 "	4 "	"	4 "	hyponitric gas
5. Nitric acid............	2 "	5 "	"	"	unknown.

The volumes of oxygen which combine with 2 volumes of nitrogen follow therefore the ratio of the whole numbers, 1 : 2 : 3 : 4 : 5; that is to say, in the simplest possible proportions. Let us consider these 2 volumes of nitrogen as *unity*, and call this unity the *equivalent in volume of nitrogen*; and lastly, give to this equivalent the character N. As we have already called the *equivalent of oxygen* 1 volume of this gas, and designated it by the letter O, the five compounds of oxygen and nitrogen will evidently be represented by

1. Protoxide of nitrogen...... NO equivalent 2 volumes.
2. Deutoxide of nitrogen..... NO_2 equivalent 4 volumes.
3. Nitrous acid................. NO_3 equivalent volumes unknown.
4. Hyponitric acid........... NO_4 equivalent 4 volumes.
5. Nitric acid.................. NO_5 equivalent volumes unknown.

We have seen (§ 111) that 100 parts of protoxide of nitrogen in weight contain

Nitrogen..	63.63
Oxygen..	36.37
	100.00

Instead of referring this compound to 100 parts of protoxide of nitrogen, let us refer it to 8 parts of oxygen; that is, to that weight to which we gave the name of *equivalent in weight* of oxygen.* We shall then have

1. Protoxide of nitrogen......... Nitrogen 14
Oxygen 8
making..................... 22 protoxide of nitrogen.

Let us now refer the composition of all the other combinations of nitrogen with oxygen to the weight 14 of nitrogen; we shall find them represented in this very simple and easily remembered manner:

2. Deutoxide of nitrogen......... Nitrogen 14
Oxygen 16
making..................... 30 deutoxide of nitrogen.

3. Nitrous acid................... Nitrogen 14
Oxygen 24
making..................... 38 nitrous acid.

4. Hyponitric acid............... Nitrogen 14
Oxygen 32
making..................... 46 hyponitric acid.

5. Nitric acid...................... Nitrogen 14
Oxygen 40
making..................... 54

Let us give a particular name to this weight 14 of nitrogen, and call it the *equivalent in weight of nitrogen:* we shall have for the composition of these various combinations,

1. Protoxide of nitrogen.......... N=14
O= 8
NO=22=equivalent in weight of protoxide of nitrogen.

2. Deutoxide of nitrogen......... N=14
2O=16
NO_2=30=equivalent in weight of deutoxide of nitrogen.

3. Nitric acid .... N=14
3O=24
NO_3=38=equivalent in weight of nitrous acid.

---

* Having adopted the hydrogen scale in this translation, we have altered the following numbers to those of that scale.—*J. C. B.*

4. Hyponitric acid................ $N=14$
$4O=32$
$NO_4=\overline{46}$=equivalent in weight of hyponitric acid.

5. Nitric acid......................... $N=14$
$5O=40$
$NO_5=\overline{54}$=equivalent in weight of nitric acid.

By choosing the weight 14 of nitrogen, to refer to it the composition of these various combinations, we have obtained this result, that the weights of oxygen which combine with this weight of nitrogen to form the various compounds, are multiples, by the simple numbers 1, 2, 3, 4, 5, of the weight 8 of oxygen, that we have already taken as unity, and that we have called the equivalent of oxygen. We might have chosen as unity any other weight of nitrogen, and referred to it the composition of the other combinations; but it is easily seen that none of these weights would have given numbers so simple and readily remembered as the one we have chosen. This great simplicity induced us to take the weight 14 of nitrogen, and give it the name of the *equivalent of nitrogen*. We shall subsequently see that other reasons will justify the selection.

Let us now see how we will express the composition of the various combinations of oxygen with nitrogen in the *atomic theory*.

We have supposed that all simple gases contained, in equal volumes, the same number of atoms; we therefore say,

In the protoxide of nitrogen	2 atoms of nitrogen	combine with	1 atom of oxygen
In the deutoxide of nitrogen	2 atoms of nitrogen	"	2 atoms of oxygen
In nitrous acid	2 atoms of nitrogen	"	3 atoms of oxygen
In hyponitric acid.............	2 atoms of nitrogen	"	4 atoms of oxygen
In nitric acid	2 atoms of nitrogen	"	5 atoms of oxygen,

and, if we adopt the character N to represent 1 atom of nitrogen, the formula representing 1 atom of these compounds will be,

Protoxide of nitrogen.............................. N_2O
Deutoxide of nitrogen............................. N_2O_2
Nitrous acid... N_2O_3
Hyponitric acid..................................... N_2O_4
Nitric acid.. N_2O_5

or, again, if we represent the double atom N_2 by the character $\bar{N}$, and the number of atoms of oxygen by an equal number of points placed above the character N,

Protoxide of nitrogen.................................. $\dot{\bar{N}}$
Deutoxide of nitrogen.................................. $\ddot{\bar{N}}$

Nitrous acid.. $\overset{\cdot\cdot\cdot}{\not{N}}$

Hyponitric acid...................................... $\overset{::}{\not{N}}$

Nitric acid.. $\overset{:\cdot:}{\not{N}}$

The weight of the atom of nitrogen will, moreover, be one-half of its equivalent, that is, 7.

COMBINATIONS OF NITROGEN WITH HYDROGEN.

AMMONIA, NH_3.

§ 122. Hydrogen and nitrogen form a gaseous compound known under the name of *ammonia.* This name, given by the chemists of an early period, has been preserved by those of modern days, although it forms an exception to the principles of our nomenclature.

Hydrogen and nitrogen do not combine directly when they are in the gaseous state. Nevertheless, if we pass a great number of electric sparks through a mixture of these two gases, especially in the presence of acid vapours, a combination takes place, and the formation of a small quantity of ammonia ensues. A phenomenon of this nature probably produces the nitrate of ammonia found in the rain-water of storms.

The two gases combine, readily, when they come in contact wth each other, in their nascent state, in a liquid. A piece of iron which rusts in the air almost always gives rise to a small quantity of ammonia. The stratum of water which covers the iron dissolves the gases of atmospheric air; the oxygen of the air unites with the metal, and forms the oxide of iron: the pellicle of oxide forms with the metal a voltaic element powerful enough to decompose water. The oxygen, thus liberated, unites with a new portion of iron, and the nascent hydrogen, finding nitrogen in solution in the water, forms with it ammonia. This formation is also facilitated by the carbonic acid of the air.

When we dissolve zinc in nitric acid diluted with water, the liquid is afterward found to contain a considerable quantity of nitrate of ammonia. Its formation is thus explained: by dissolving zinc in nitric acid, much diluted with water, hydrogen gas is disengaged, and the nitrate of the oxide of zinc is formed; the reaction being the same as that which takes place on the contact of zinc and sulphuric acid diluted with water. If, however, we treat the zinc with concentrated nitric acid, the zinc oxidizes at the expense of a portion of the nitric acid, the nitrate of zinc is again formed, and nitrogen and the oxides of nitrogen are disengaged. Lastly, if we treat the zinc with nitric acid of medium concentration, both reactions take place at once; the zinc oxidizes as much at the expense of the oxygen of the water as at that of the oxygen of a portion of the nitric acid, and a mixture of hydrogen and nitrogen is evolved. The two gases thus meeting in their nascent state, in the liquid, combine, and form ammonia. We find, therefore, in this case, a large quantity of nitrate of ammonia in the solution. A still greater quantity of ammonia is obtained by dissolving the zinc in a mixture of dilute sulphuric and nitric acids. We first pour in the diluted sulphuric acid, and then add, drop by drop, the nitric acid until the evolution of hydrogen gas ceases entirely; the zinc continues to dissolve, without disengaging hydrogen, which remains entire, in the fluid, in the state of ammonia.

We shall, subsequently, meet with many similar facts. Gases which do not combine when in the gaseous state, frequently do so when they become free in the same solution. They are then said to combine in their nascent state.

Animal substances, calcined in close vessels, give off, by distillation, a considerable quantity of carbonate of ammonia. This carbonate of ammonia being dissolved in chlorohydric acid, is thus changed into chlorohydrate of ammonia, or the *sal ammoniac* of commerce.

Ammoniacal gas is prepared by heating in a small matrass (fig. 199) a mixture of 1 part of powdered sal ammoniac, and 2 parts of quicklime.

Chlorohydrate of ammonia........	Ammonia		Ammonia.
	Chlorohydric acid.	Hydrogen.	
		Chlorine...	Water.
Lime................	Oxygen................................		Chloride of calcium.
	Calcium................................		

There are formed chloride of calcium, water, and ammoniacal gas,

$$NH_3,HCl+CaO=NH_3+CaCl+HO:$$

the water is retained by the excess of quicklime, which is very attractive of moisture. As the temperature rises, however, especially toward the close of the experiment, and as, consequently, a portion of the water may be driven off, when we wish to have the gas perfectly dry, it is necessary to pass it through a tube filled with pieces of caustic potassa, which absorb the last traces of moisture. The chloride of calcium cannot be used here, because, when *cold*, it absorbs a great quantity of ammoniacal gas.

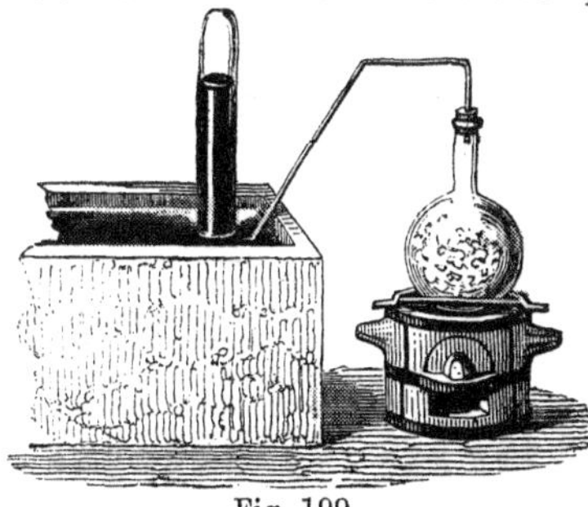

Fig. 199.

The disengagement of ammonia commences even in cold, during the mixture of the lime with the sal ammoniac.

§ 123. Ammonia is a colourless gas, of a sharp and pungent

odour, exciting tears. Its density is 0.597. It is a very powerful alkali, and, as it is gaseous, it has been called the *volatile alkali.* It restores the blue colour of litmus reddened by an acid, and neutralizes the most powerful acids, such as the sulphuric.

Ammoniacal gas is very soluble in water, the solution taking place almost instantly, as is proved by the following experiment: Fill a bell-glass over the mercurial cistern with perfectly pure ammonia, pass a porcelain saucer under the bell-glass, remove it with the saucer filled with mercury, and deposit them carefully in a vessel filled with water, so as to let the saucer rest on the bottom of the vessel. Hitherto the gas in the bell-glass has been in contact with the mercury alone, but if we suddenly raise the bell-glass, still keeping its lower rim under water, the mercury, from its great gravity, falls to the bottom of the vessel, the water ascends into the bell-glass, and the ammonia is so rapidly absorbed as to fill the bell-glass instantly with the water. If the gas is perfectly pure, the water strikes the top of the bell-glass with such violence as frequently to break it. When this experiment is made, therefore, we should be careful to cover the bell-glass with a thick cloth, to avoid the danger. The presence of a single bubble of air in the gas will, by its elasticity, considerably diminish the violence of the shock, and prevent the breaking of the glass.

A piece of ice introduced into a bell-glass containing ammonia, melts immediately by dissolving the ammonia. Cold water dissolves about 500 times its volume of this gas. Heat completely drives the ammonia from this solution, and, after boiling, it contains scarcely any traces of it. The solution of ammonia is prepared in a Woolf's apparatus (fig. 200). Introduce into a large balloon,

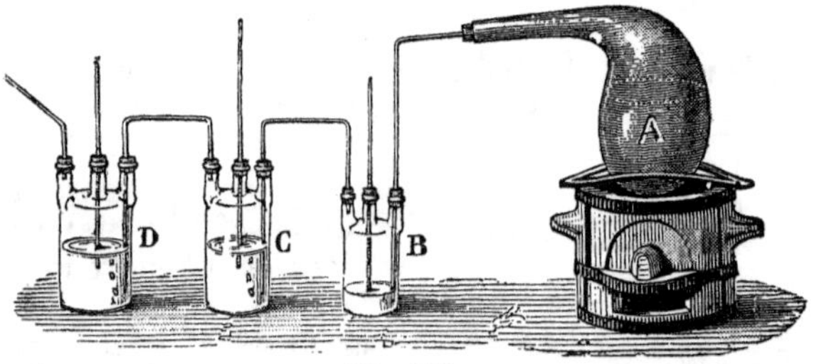

Fig. 200.

or a retort A, a mixture of sal ammoniac and lime. We do not take quicklime, as in the preparation of gaseous ammonia, but slacked lime; and even add, frequently, to the mixture a small quantity of water, which assists the reaction between the two substances. The gas first passes through a small washing-bottle B, containing very little water, and then enters the bottles C and D, which are three-fourths filled with water: as the solution of ammonia is lighter than pure water, we must be careful, if we wish to obtain a saturated solution, to pass the tubes to the bottom of the bottles.

Ammoniacal gas liquefies at —40° under the ordinary pressure of the atmosphere, or at a temperature of 50° under a pressure of 6½ atmospheres. It is easily obtained fluid in the following manner: We expose some pulverized chloride of silver, in the cold, to a current of dry ammoniacal gas: the chloride of silver absorbs a large quantity of ammonia. When it is well saturated, it is placed in a curved tube *abc* (fig. 201), the open end of which *c* is then hermetically sealed. It will then be sufficient to heat, in a water-bath, the temperature of which has been gradually raised, the extremity *a* containing the ammoniacal chloride of silver. This substance melts at about 100°, boils, and completely parts with its ammonia, which is condensed in the part *c* of the tube which has been cooled with ice: the ammonia is then in the state of a colourless very movable fluid, of a density of 0.76. If the chloride be allowed to cool, the liquid ammonia gradually disappears, being reabsorbed by the chloride of silver: so that the experiment may be indefinitely repeated with the same apparatus.

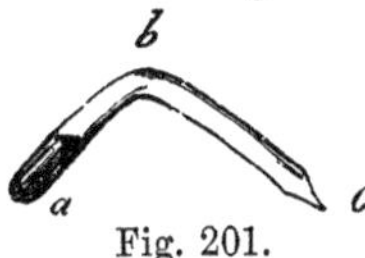

Fig. 201.

In manufactories, the glass balloon is replaced by a cast-iron retort or cylinder built in a furnace; and, toward the close, the temperature is carried high enough to melt the chloride of calcium, which facilitates its removal from the apparatus. It is well to replace the chlorohydrate of ammonia by the sulphate, which is cheaper; but in this case we must add a small quantity of water, and make the mixture exactly, because the sulphate of ammonia is not like the hydrochlorate, and reaction then takes place only by contact.

If we pass ammoniacal gas through a porcelain tube, heated to redness, it is partially decomposed. This decomposition is greatly assisted by placing in the tube, iron, copper, or platinum wire. The metal is of no account in the chemical reaction; it merely *acts by its presence:* nevertheless, the iron and copper absorb, in this case, a small quantity of oxygen, and become very brittle; but the platinum undergoes no change.

If we project a current of ammoniacal gas, by a small aperture, into an atmosphere of pure oxygen, we may inflame this current, and the gas will continue to burn with a yellow flame; ammoniacal gas, however, is not sufficiently combustible to burn in the air.

§ 124. Ammoniacal gas is also decomposed by the electric spark; but the decomposition takes place only at the point of the spark, so that a great number of sparks are necessary to decompose the gas completely. If the experiment be made in a graduated eudiometer, the volume of the gas will be found to increase continually until it reaches double the volume of the ammoniacal gas employed. This experiment shows, therefore, that the decomposition of ammoniacal gas gives a double volume of a mixture of hydrogen and nitrogen.

It is then easy to determine by eudiometric analysis the proportions of the two distinct gases. Suppose that we introduce into the eudiometer 100 parts of the mixture and 50 of oxygen, and pass an electric spark through: we find the volume reduced to 37.5; 112.5 of a mixture of hydrogen and oxygen have therefore disappeared in the proportions constituting water, that is, 75 of hydrogen and 37.5 of oxygen. Therefore, 100 parts of the gaseous mixture contain 75 of hydrogen and 25 of nitrogen. These 25 parts of nitrogen may be isolated, either by introducing into the bell-glass a globule of phosphorus, which absorbs the 12.5 oxygen, or by making the eudiometric analysis, by hydrogen, of the mixture of oxygen and nitrogen. Now, the 100 parts of the mixture proceed from 50 parts of ammoniacal gas: therefore 50 parts of ammoniacal gas contain 75 of hydrogen, and 25 of nitrogen; in other words, 1 volume of ammoniacal gas is formed of $1\frac{1}{2}$ volumes of hydrogen and a $\frac{1}{2}$ volume of nitrogen.

The weight of $1\frac{1}{2}$ volumes	of	hydrogen is	0.1038
The weight of $\frac{1}{2}$	"	nitrogen	0.4856
The weight of 1	"	ammonia	0.5894

Direct experiment has given 0.5896, which differs but slightly.

In order to deduce thence the composition of 100 parts of ammonia, we make the proportions

$$0.5894 : 0.1038 :: 100 : x;$$

which gives for the quantity of hydrogen

$$x=17.61.$$

$$0.5894 : 0 : 4856 :: 100 : y;$$

we thence deduce for the quantity of nitrogen

$$y=82.39.$$

100 parts of ammonia therefore contain

Hydrogen	17.61
Nitrogen	82.39
	100.00.

Let us refer this composition to the equivalent of nitrogen, that is, to 14 of nitrogen, as we did for the compounds of oxygen with nitrogen: it will suffice to make the proportions

$$82.39 : 17.61 :: 14 : x;$$

$$\text{whence } x=37.40;$$

and we obtain

Nitrogen	14	
Hydrogen	3	
making	17	of ammonia.

We observe that 3 is exactly the treble of 1, which we called the equivalent weight of hydrogen; so that we may write the composition of ammonia as follows:

$$\begin{aligned} N &= 14 \\ 3H &= 3 \\ NH_3 &= \overline{17} \end{aligned}$$

which will be the equivalent weight of ammonia.

The numbers 14 and 1, which we have chosen as unity for nitrogen and hydrogen, and have called their *equivalent weights*, therefore possess also this property of expressing the composition of ammonia in the simplest manner possible.

We have seen that 1 volume of ammoniacal gas contains a ½ volume of nitrogen and 1½ volumes of hydrogen; consequently, 4 volumes of ammoniacal gas contain 2 volumes of nitrogen and 6 of hydrogen. Now, 2 volumes of nitrogen represent 1 equivalent in volume of nitrogen; 6 volumes of hydrogen represent 3 equivalents in volume of hydrogen. Consequently, after the composition in volume that we have assigned to ammoniacal gas, we may say that ammonia is formed of 1 equivalent of nitrogen and 3 of hydrogen, and that the equivalent of ammonia in volume is represented by 4 volumes.

According to the atomic theory, the formula of ammonia will be N_2H_6 or NH_3.

Ammoniacal gas combines directly, in the cold, with chlorohydric acid gas, producing the chlorohydrate of ammonia, or sal ammoniac. By mixing 100 parts of ammoniacal gas and 100 parts of chlorohydric acid gas, we shall find the gases to disappear entirely, leaving a white powder of sal ammoniac deposited on the sides of the bell-glass. Thus chlorohydric and ammoniacal gases combine in equal volumes.

Chlorine decomposes ammonia at the ordinary temperature: the result of the decomposition is chlorohydrate of ammonia and nitrogen: the reaction takes place between 8 volumes of ammoniacal gas and 3 volumes of chlorine.

We have

3 vols. chlorine		6 vols. chlorohydric acid	Chlorohydrate of ammonia.
2 " ammonia	1 vol. nitrogen.... / 3 vols. hydrogen..		
6 vols. ammonia			

$$4NH_3+3Cl=3(NH_3,HCl)+N.$$

This experiment is made in the following manner: Pour into a long tube closed at one end, a solution of chlorine in water, so as to fill $\frac{9}{10}$ of the tube, and completely fill it with a solution of ammonia. Close the opening of the tube with the finger, and invert it. The solution of ammonia, which is lighter, ascends in the tube, and bubbles of nitrogen are immediately disengaged. Advantage is sometimes taken of this reaction in the laboratory, in the preparation of this gas: we have described the process previously (§ 92).

Ammonia presents, in contact with many substances, very curious reactions, which are, in general, too complex to be mentioned here. We shall return to them hereafter.

ADDITION TO THE COMBINATIONS OF NITROGEN WITH OXYGEN.

Anhydrous Nitric Acid, NO_5.

§ 124 *bis.* We said (§ 101) that anhydrous nitric acid had not hitherto been procured in an isolated state. This important substance has just been obtained, and is prepared by treating very dry nitrate of silver heated to 122° or 140° with chlorine: this compound is changed into chloride of silver, and white prismatic crystals of *anhydrous nitric acid* are deposited on the cold sides of the apparatus. The oxygen of the oxide of silver is disengaged, as well as nitrous vapours and the oxygen arising from the decomposition of a portion of the nitric acid.

Anhydrous nitric acid melts at 85°, and boils at about 115.° At a temperature slightly elevated above its boiling point, it decomposes into oxygen and hyponitric acid.

SULPHUR.

EQUIVALENT S=16 (200 O=100).

§ 125. Sulphur is a substance found very abundantly in nature, sometimes isolated, and sometimes in combination with a great number of metals. Sulphur, when alone, is sometimes found perfectly pure and in very regular crystals: but most frequently it is intimately mixed with earthy substances. We shall soon see how it is separated from these substances and obtained in the two states found in commerce.

Sulphur may be obtained in three states. At the ordinary temperature it is solid: if heated above 232°, it melts, and furnishes a very limpid canary-yellow fluid: the pieces of unmelted sulphur remain at the bottom of the vessel, thus proving that sulphur increases in bulk or dilates in passing from the solid to the liquid state. Water presents the contrary phenomenon, ice being lighter than water: the latter, passing from the solid to the liquid state, contracts instead of dilating. Sulphur passes suddenly from the liquid to the solid state, without becoming doughy, and is thus most favourable for crystallization. The phenomenon of crystallization of sulphur may be readily observed in a glass tube. When the temperature falls to about 232°, the particles of sulphur, in solidifying, will be seen to form needles, which start from one side and shoot through the liquid mass. New needles are implanted in the crystals already formed, and so on, until the whole mass is solidified. If we do not wait for the completion of the solidification, and pierce the solid crust which forms on the surface, the remainder of the fluid may be poured off, and the crystals exposed. We may, in this way, obtain beautiful crystals by melting a quantity of sulphur in an earthen vessel, and cooling it very slowly. When a solid crust has formed on the surface, it is perforated, and the balance of the liquid poured off. When the mass has become cold, we separate carefully the upper crust, keeping the vessel inverted, for fear of injuring the crystals which line the sides. These crystals are long brilliant prisms, of the same colour as the liquid sulphur.

The predominating form of the crystals of sulphur obtained by fusion is an oblique prism with a rhombic base, in which the principal axis is inclined at an angle of 85° 54′ to the base, and the obtuse angle of the base is 90° 32′. This form belongs to the fifth system of crystallization.

Sulphur may be crystallized at a low temperature, by dissolving it in a volatile liquid. The sulphuret of carbon is the most appropriate. If we expose a solution of sulphur in sulphuret of carbon to the air, the liquid evaporates rapidly, and the sulphur, not finding sufficient sulphuret of carbon to keep it in solution, is slowly deposited, in the midst of the liquid, in regular crystals, differing totally from those which form in melted sulphur. We remarked upon this point in the introduction (§ 39).

Sulphur, crystallized by solution, presents exactly the same form and appearance as the natural article sometimes found in very large and perfectly pure crystals. The most ordinary form of these crystals is that of fig. 70: the predominating form is a right octahedron with a rhombic base, belonging to the fourth system of crystallization (fig. 66). The fracture of these crystals is vitreous and conchoidal. Their density is 2.07.

The crystals which are deposited in the melted sulphur are transparent and slightly elastic; but they soon lose these properties and become opaque and friable. They are then of a clearer yellow. We assigned the cause of this change (§ 39).

It sometimes happens, however, that by dissolving in sulphuret of carbon sulphur which has been recently melted, the liquid left to spontaneous evaporation deposits at the same time crystals belonging to both systems. It is easy to distinguish the right octahedrons with rhombic bases, which generally predominate, and the oblique prisms with rhombic bases. The mixture becomes much more evident when we leave the crystals untouched for several days. The octahedric crystals remain transparent and preserve their colour, whilst the oblique prismatic crystals become opaque, friable, and of a yellow straw-colour. We cannot here (as we have done in § 39) explain the dimorphism of the sulphur by the difference of temperature at which crystallization took place, since the two incompatible forms have been developed in the same medium. It is probable that these two forms have some reference to the two states of ordinary sulphur and soft sulphur, of which we are about to speak; for, by dissolving soft sulphur in sulphuret of carbon, we obtain a greater number of prismatic mingled with the octahedral crystals.

Melted sulphur is perfectly limpid, and of a clear yellow: if it is further heated, its colour becomes deeper, and at the same time it loses its fluidity. At 320° it flows with difficulty, and its colour passes from yellow to brown. At 392° it is so tenacious that the vessel containing it may be inverted without its escaping: its colour is then of a deep brown. If the temperature is carried still higher, the sulphur recovers its fluidity, still preserving its brown colour. Lastly, at 750° it boils, and may be distilled. Distillation is performed in a glass retort, furnished with a receiver. The sulphur is introduced into the retort, which is heated by coals. The sulphur at first melts, and then passes through the various stages we have indicated, and lastly boils. The vapour is driven into the beak of the retort, when it first condenses in the form of a very fine powder, which is called *flowers of sulphur.* But the distillation continuing, the temperature rises in the beak, and soon exceeds 232°, the degree at which sulphur melts, and the vapours condense only in the fluid state. If the sulphur subjected to distillation contains non-volatile foreign substances, they remain in the retort. The colour of the vapour of sulphur is yellowish-brown, and its density has been found to be 6.654.

If we heat sulphur in a crucible to a temperature higher than 392°, and then pour it out, in a small stream, into an earthen vessel filled with cold water, we obtain a spongy, brown, soft and elastic mass, which retains its softness for some time: it then gets harder, and in a few days the sulphur assumes its ordinary hardness, but its colour continues deeper. *Soft* sulphur becomes hard in a few minutes if, instead of allowing it to remain at the ordinary temperature, it is heated to about 212°: the change ensues suddenly, with a spontaneous evolution of heat: for soft sulphur heated to 212°, elevates its temperature to 230°.

Sulphur is a combustible substance, and burns with a bluish flame, giving out the well-known suffocating smell, which needs no description. The sulphur combines with the oxygen of the air, and gives rise to a gaseous compound, *sulphurous acid gas.*

§ 126. Native sulphur is frequently found in volcanic countries: it impregnates the ashes of certain extinguished craters called *solfaterras.* But it is principally found in irregular masses in the midst of the bituminous marls, strata of gypsum, and lime, found in the chalky formation. The mines of Sicily, which are of this character, are the most important in the world, and furnish nearly all the sulphur consumed in the arts. This native sulphur is merely mixed with earthy matter. The rich ores are heated in large kettles until the sulphur melts: the earthy matter falls to the bottom of the kettle: the sulphur is taken out with ladles and poured into sheet-iron vessels, from which, when cool, it is easily removed. It is thus exported, under the name of *crude sulphur.*

The earthy residuum taken from the kettle is then subjected, with the poorer ores, to distillation. The sulphurous earth is placed in earthen pots (fig. 202) holding about 5 gallons. At the

Fig. 202.

upper part of these pots is an opening, which is closed during the operation, and by which the pots are charged and emptied. A bent earthen tube conveys the distilled sulphur into other similarly shaped pots, which act as receivers. At the bottom of these pots is an aperture, which is occasionally opened to allow the sulphur to run into buckets of water. The pots containing the sulphurous earth are placed in two rows on a long furnace, called a *galley furnace*.

This first distillation is very imperfectly performed; the sulphur thus obtained containing 10 or 15 per cent. of earthy matter. Hence it is still called in commerce *crude sulphur*.

The crude sulphur is subjected to a second distillation conducted with great care. The apparatus (fig. 203) in which it is per-

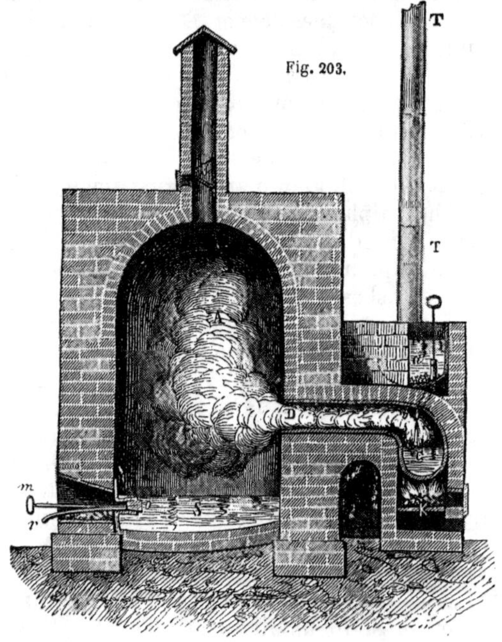

Fig. 203.

formed, consists of a cast-iron kettle CD, which acts as a retort, and a large chamber of brick-work, serving as a receiver. The kettle is placed over a furnace, at K. Formerly, a cast-iron door served to charge the kettle with sulphur, and to extract the residuum, but, in modern times, the distillation is continuous. The vapour of sulphur which rises from the kettle, is conveyed by the pipe D into the chamber A, where it condenses in the form of very fine powder, which is the flowers of sulphur. The chamber is furnished with valves *s* which allow the internal heated air to escape, and prevent the entrance of the external air.

With this apparatus, we may obtain either flowers of sulphur or roll sulphur. The vapour of sulphur, by condensing, heats the chamber, which soon attains a temperature greater than 232°, so that the sulphur cannot condense in the solid state, but remains liquid on the floor of the chamber. If, therefore, we wish to obtain flowers of sulphur, the chamber should be made as large as possible, and the distillation be occasionally suspended, in order to allow the walls to cool. If, on the contrary, we wish to obtain liquid sulphur, we operate with a small room, and do not interrupt the process.

In order to charge the kettle C, it was formerly necessary to remove the door, which was a serious inconvenience, and frequently caused explosions by the mixture of the atmospheric air with the highly-heated vapour of sulphur. This danger is now avoided by placing outside of the furnace a second kettle M, which is heated by the hot air of the furnace before it reaches the chimney. This kettle communicates with the first by means of a pipe *v*. The kettle M is charged with crude sulphur, which melts in it and deposits a portion of the foreign matter, so that the sulphur enters the kettle C already purified by a kind of *decantation*.

The flowers of sulphur are withdrawn from the chamber, after the operation, through a lateral door. The melted sulphur flows out by a small gutter *r* (fig. 203), of which the aperture *o* is closed by a stopper: it is received in moulds of pine wood (fig. 204), moistened but well wiped, and takes the shape of conical sticks: this is the *stick* or *roll sulphur* of commerce. By cooling in the moulds, the sulphur first crystallizes at its periphery, and then gradually toward its axis: it also undergoes some contraction, as is manifested by the cavity filled with confused needles, which are always seen in the end of the stick occupying the upper part of the mould.

Flowers of sulphur almost always exhibit a slight acid reaction with litmus paper, which is due to the presence of a very small quantity of sulphuric acid, and can be removed by repeated washings.

Fig. 204.

COMBINATIONS OF SULPHUR WITH OXYGEN.

§ 127. Sulphur forms a great number of compounds with oxygen. Seven of these are now well ascertained, and they are all acid, viz.:

1. Hyposulphurous acid .... S_2O_2*
2. Trisulpho-hyposulphuric acid .... S_5O_5
3. Bisulpho-hyposulphuric acid .... S_4O_5
4. Monosulpho-hyposulphuric acid .... S_3O_5
5. Sulphurous acid .... SO_2

* The names given by Berzelius to the above are, for 1, Dithionous; 2, Pentathionic; 3, Tetrathionic; 4, Trithionic; and 6, Dithionic acids.—*J. C. B.*

6. Hyposulphuric acid.............................. S_2O_5
7. Sulphuric acid.................................... SO_3

We shall commence with the study of sulphurous acid, because this substance is used in the preparation of nearly all the other compounds of sulphur and oxygen.

SULPHUROUS ACID, SO_2.

§ 128. Sulphurous acid is formed when sulphur is burned in oxygen or in the open air. In the laboratory, several processes are used in its preparation.

A mixture of 6 parts of powdered peroxide of manganese, and 1 part of flowers of sulphur, is heated in a small glass retort (fig. 205): the sulphurous acid gas is made to traverse a small washing-bottle, which retains a small quantity of the sulphur volatilized by the heat and carried over by the current of gas. In this experiment, the sulphur burns at the expense of a portion of the oxygen of the peroxide of manganese: sulphurous acid gas, which is the product of combustion, is disengaged, and the protoxide of manganese remains in the retort.

Fig. 205.

Sulphurous acid is also obtained by decomposing sulphuric acid by a metal which removes a portion of its oxygen, but which does not decompose water when in contact with active acids. Mercury or copper is used for this purpose. The more oxidable metals, such as iron or zinc, would at the same time decompose the water always contained in concentrated sulphuric acid, and sulphurous acid gas and hydrogen would be disengaged together. The mercury or copper-turnings are placed in a flask (fig. 206), concentrated sulphuric acid added, and heated with a few coals. The gas must be passed through a washing-bottle containing some water, which absorbs the vapour of sulphuric acid. If we wish to obtain the gas perfectly dry, we adapt to the bottle a tube containing chloride of calcium. This gas must be collected over mercury, as it is very soluble in water.

Fig. 206.

§ 129. Sulphurous acid is a colourless gas, having a smell resembling that of burning sulphur. It acts energetically on the respiratory organs, exciting cough and a sensation of suffocation. Its effects are not dangerous when breathed in small quantities. Its density is 2.247.

Sulphurous gas liquefies, under the ordinary pressure, at about 14°. It is therefore easy to prepare it in a liquid state in the laboratory, it being merely necessary to pass the gas well dried through a bulb A (fig. 207), placed in a refrigerating mixture of ice and sea-salt, or of ice and chloride of calcium. When the bulb is sufficiently filled, the ends *a* and *b* of the tube are closed by the blowpipe. If we prefer preserving the liquid sulphurous acid in glass tubes, we take tubes closed at one end and elongated in the middle, as in fig. 208; the upper part A forming the funnel. The acid being poured into this funnel, the first drop which enters the cavity B volatilizes and expels the air, so that if we afterward plunge B into the refrigerating mixture, the vapours of sulphurous acid are condensed in it, and it is filled with liquid acid. The tube is filled to three-fourths of its capacity, and then sealed by the blowpipe at *a*, the end B still remaining in the mixture.

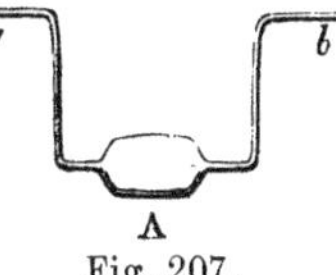

Fig. 207.

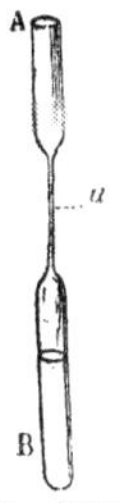

Fig. 208.

Sulphurous acid liquefies at the temperature of 59°, under the pressure of about 2 atmospheres. Liquid sulphurous acid is colourless, and very volatile: its density is 1.42. When it volatilizes in the air, it produces a considerable reduction of temperature. If liquid sulphurous acid be poured on the bulb of a thermometer wrapped in muslin or cotton, the cold produced is sufficient to congeal the mercury. If the same experiment be made on an alcohol thermometer, it falls to —58° or —76°, according to the temperature of the air. A still greater degree of cold may be obtained, by blowing on the wet bulb, or by keeping it under the receiver of an air-pump whilst the vacuum is made.

Sulphurous acid gas, like all gases which at ordinary temperature are near their liquefying point, varies in a striking manner from the law of Mariotte. For the same increase of pressure, the volume of sulphurous acid decreases more rapidly than that of the air. The difference is greater as the temperature is lower, and becomes very small at temperatures greater than 86°.

§ 130. The composition of sulphurous acid gas is easily ascertained by synthesis. Introduce into a balloon (fig. 209) filled with oxygen gas and placed over mercury, a small cup containing a piece of sulphur, and fastened to the end of a wire; the sulphur is then ignited by means of a burning-glass. The sulphur burns, and converts a portion of the oxygen

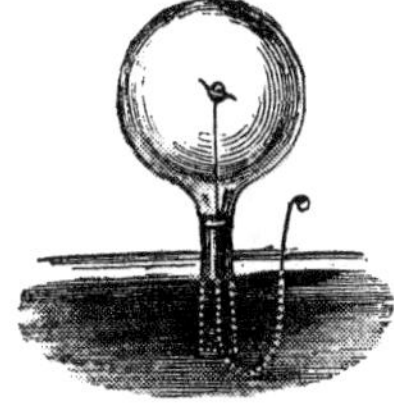
Fig. 209.

into sulphurous acid gas. We find that the volume of gas has not changed in consequence of this combustion, and hence conclude that sulphurous acid gas contains a volume of oxygen equal to its own. This single fact will give the composition of sulphurous acid gas. In fact, if from the weight of 1 volume of sulphurous acid gas, represented by its density........................ 2.247
we deduct the weight of 1 vol. of oxygen.................. 1.106
there remain.. 1.141
which represent nearly $\frac{1}{6}$ of a volume of vapour of sulphur $= \frac{6.654}{6} = 1.109$.

Thus, 1 volume of sulphurous acid gas is composed of 1 volume of oxygen and $\frac{1}{6}$ of a volume of vapour of sulphur.

By a simple proportion, we find for its composition by weight

Sulphur	50.87
Oxygen	49.13
	100.00

Let us refer the composition of gaseous sulphurous acid to a volume $\frac{1}{3}$ of vapour of sulphur, which we shall adopt as an *equivalent volume* of the gaseous sulphur, for reasons to be hereafter stated: we can say, 2 volumes of sulphurous gas contain $\frac{1}{3}$ of a volume of vapour of sulphur and 2 volumes of oxygen; and consequently, 1 equivalent of sulphurous acid, represented by 2 volumes, contains 1 equivalent of vapour of sulphur ($\frac{1}{3}$) and 2 equivalents of oxygen, 2 volumes. The formula of sulphurous acid will therefore be SO_2.

We shall also see, hereafter, that we shall adopt the weight 16 as the *equivalent weight* of sulphur. By referring the composition of sulphurous acid to this weight 16 of sulphur, we say that sulphurous acid is composed of

1 eq. sulphur	16
2 " oxygen	16
1 " sulphurous acid	32

whence we infer, for the composition in weight,

Sulphur	50.00
Oxygen	50.00
	100.00

A great difference will be observed between the preceding theoretic composition, and that deduced from the direct experiment. This is because the densities admitted for sulphurous acid gas and the vapour of sulphur do not exactly agree with the circumstances in which these bodies observe the laws of permanent gases.

§ 131. Sulphurous acid gas cannot be decomposed by heat alone, since it is formed, at a very high temperature, by the combustion of sulphur.

Well-dried oxygen and sulphurous acid do not act on each other at the ordinary temperature, but if a mixture of the two gases be passed through a heated tube containing platinum sponge, they combine and form anhydrous sulphuric acid.

When a solution of sulphurous acid in water is exposed to the air, oxygen is absorbed and sulphuric acid formed. This circumstance renders the preparation, and especially the preservation, of a pure solution of sulphurous acid very difficult. In order to prepare this solution, the bottle must be nearly filled with recently boiled water, and the gas passed rapidly through, so as to avoid as much as possible the entrance of the air. When the solution is saturated, the bottle is corked and inverted.

Water thus dissolves about 50 times its volume of sulphurous acid gas. Heat expels this gas entirely from its solution, and if boiled for a few moments, the latter contains no traces of the gas.

In order to obtain the solution of sulphurous acid economically, concentrated sulphuric acid is heated with charcoal, or even with wood. A mixture of sulphurous and carbonic acid gas is disengaged. The presence of the latter gas does no injury, whether we wish to dissolve the sulphurous gas in water or combine it with the bases. Carbonic acid, at first absorbed by water, or the salifiable bases, is afterward driven off as the solution becomes saturated with sulphurous acid.

Hydrogen when cold does not act on sulphurous acid, but if a mixture of the two gases be passed through a porcelain tube heated to redness, the sulphurous acid is decomposed, water forms, and sulphur is deposited.

Sulphurous acid and sulphuretted hydrogen do not react when the two gases are dry ; but, when their solutions are mixed, they mutually decompose each other, water being formed, and sulphur deposited.

Sulphurous acid is a weak acid, its combinations with the bases being easily decomposed by powerful acids, such as sulphuric, chlorohydric acid, etc.; but it expels carbonic acid from the carbonates.

The majority of organic colouring matters are changed or discoloured by sulphurous acid, the acid sometimes removing the oxygen from the colouring matter, and leaving it colourless: sometimes only combining with the colouring matter, forming a colourless compound. This last effect is seen in rose-leaves, but the leaf thus discoloured recovers its colour when dipped into weak sulphuric acid.

Advantage is taken of this property in bleaching silk and woollen stuffs. The damp goods being suspended in a close chamber in which sulphur is burned, the sulphurous acid gas condenses on them, and destroys the colouring matter. The bleaching of linen and cotton is effected by means of chlorine; but this substance cannot be used in wool or silk, because it destroys their texture.

Sulphurous acid is also used to remove the red stains of fruit upon linen. To do this, the linen is moistened and held over a piece of burning sulphur, or some burning matches. The linen must be then well washed, so as to remove the altered colouring matter, as without this precaution the spot might reappear.

§ 132. Dry chlorine and sulphurous acid do not act on each other in the diffused light; but, if exposed to an intense solar light, the gases combine and form a colourless liquid compound, which is very volatile, and purified by distillation over mercury, which retains the excess of chlorine. The density of this fluid is 1.66; it boils at 77°. The density of its vapour is 4.665. It has an exceedingly sharp and suffocating smell, and results from the combination of equal volumes of chlorine and sulphurous acid, so that its formula is SO_2Cl. Water decomposes it rapidly, sulphuric and chlorohydric acids being formed.

$$SO_2Cl+2HO=SO_3,HO+HCl.$$

The two gases, when moist, react immediately on each other, producing chlorohydric and sulphuric acids.

Sulphurous acid.... } Sulphuric acid.
Water { Oxyen..... }
Water { Hydrogen } Chlorohydric acid.
Chlorine............. }

Sulphuric Acid, SO_3.

§ 133. We have seen (§ 131) that sulphurous acid dissolved in water absorbed oxygen from the air, and was changed into sulphuric acid. This transformation is easily effected by energetic oxidizing substances, such as concentrated nitric acid. If a current of sulphurous acid gas be passed through concentrated nitric acid heated to ebullition, the sulphurous is entirely condensed in the form of sulphuric acid, and the nitric passes into the state of hyponitric acid.

Sulphuric acid may be also obtained by heating sulphur with nitric acid; but a long time is required to completely oxidize the sulphur.

By these two processes, we obtain a mixture of sulphuric acid, nitric acid, and water. This mixture is distilled in a glass retort: nitric acid more or less mixed with water passes over at first; the temperature in the retort gradually rises, and reaches at last 617°. It then remains stationary, and there passes over a very acid homogeneous fluid, composed of sulphuric acid and water, which is called *concentrated sulphuric acid* or *oil of vitriol.* We shall now study its properties.

§ 134. Concentrated sulphuric acid is a fluid of oleaginous consistence, the density of which at 59° is 1.843; it boils at 617°. It is inodorous. The tension of its vapour is not appreciable at the ordinary temperature; and, in fact, we may allow two saucers to remain for several days under the receiver of an air-pump, the one containing concentrated sulphuric acid, and the other a solution of chloride of barium, without the latter becoming cloudy. Now, if sulphuric acid gave off any sensible vapour, this vapour, coming in contact with the solution of the chloride of barium, would decompose it, and form an insoluble sulphate of baryta, which would precipitate in the form of a white powder.

Concentrated sulphuric acid congeals at −30°.

Sulphuric is one of the most powerful acids known, for it deeply reddens litmus, even when diluted with 1000 times its weight of water. Assisted by heat, it expels the majority of the acids from their compounds. This last property depends both on the activity of the acid and its property of boiling only at a very high temperature; and it is from this latter reason that sulphuric acid, when heated, drives off the chlorohydric and nitric acids. But it is again expelled, under the influence of heat, by phosphoric and boracic acids. These acids are nevertheless weaker than sulphuric acid at the ordinary temperature; but they are also much less volatile.

The distillation of concentrated sulphuric acid in a glass retort is a dangerous operation, on account of the commotion produced in the liquid when boiling, and which is sometimes sufficient to elevate the retort, and thus render it liable to break when falling down again on its support. The ebullition becomes more regular if bits of platinum wire be introduced into the retort. The bubbles of vapour are then disengaged not on the sides of the vessel, but at the ends of the wire. However, the distillation of sulphuric acid can only be safely carried on in glass retorts, by heating the liquid on the sides and not from the bottom. The retort is placed in a circular wire-furnace, as in fig. 210, the coals being arranged

Fig. 210.

around it, and the bottom remaining free. In order to prevent the vapours from condensing on the top of the retort, it is covered with a sheet-iron hood A, which rests on the furnace, and is cut out to allow the passage of the beak of the retort. The ebullition of the fluid then takes place against the sides of the retort, without any very violent commotion.

Concentrated sulphuric acid has a powerful affinity for water. It readily absorbs the vapour of water contained in the air, and hence its frequent use in the laboratory to dry gases. Its affinity for water is such, that it frequently causes the formation of water in organic substances, at the expense of the oxygen and hydrogen they contain. In this way it carbonizes the corks of the bottles in which it may be kept. Cork, like the greater part of vegetable substances, is a compound of carbon, hydrogen, and oxygen. Concentrated sulphuric acid removes a portion of the hydrogen and oxygen to form water, with which it unites, and the carbon forms with the balance of the hydrogen and oxygen a brown substance, giving the cork the appearance of having been charred.

When concentrated sulphuric acid is poured into water, the acid falls through the liquid, like a syrup, to the bottom of the vessel, and forms a distinct layer, which slowly dissolves in the supernatant water; but, if the fluids are agitated, they dissolve immediately with a great evolution of heat.

It is dangerous to pour water into concentrated sulphuric acid. A portion of the water, uniting with the acid, disengages a great quantity of heat, which may instantly convert the remainder of the water into vapour, and consequently project the acid from the vessel. We should therefore mix these liquids by pouring the acid in a small stream into the water, while stirring the latter.

Concentrated sulphuric acid, when brought into contact with ice or snow, melts it immediately. The affinity of the acid for water causes the melting of the ice, and the latter, passing into the liquid state, absorbs a great quantity of heat, which it can only receive from the mixture. On the other hand, the combination of sulphuric acid with water evolves heat. The temperature will therefore be elevated or depressed, as either of these effects may predominate. If we shake together rapidly 4 parts of concentrated acid with 1 part of pounded ice, the temperature will rise to 100°: but if we mix 1 part of acid with 4 of ice, the temperature will frequently fall to —4°.

§ 135. The composition of sulphuric acid may be ascertained in the following manner:

Weigh exactly, in a small glass flask, 5 grammes of sulphur, on which highly-concentrated nitric acid is poured. By heating it moderately, the sulphur is changed into sulphuric acid, which remains mixed with the excess of nitric acid and water. When the sulphur has entirely disappeared, boil for some time; the nitric acid and a portion of the water are disengaged, and there remains in the matrass only a mixture of water and sulphuric acid. In order to find the actual quantity of sulphuric acid in the mixture, it is to be combined with an anhydrous base, with which it will form an anhydrous sulphate. The base, which is generally chosen, is the protoxide of lead, which can be easily obtained pure. A certain quantity of this oxide is weighed, 50 grammes, for example (the quantity should be greater than is required to saturate the acid), and poured into the flask; the sulphuric acid combines with a portion of the oxide of lead, sulphate of lead is formed, and the water set free. The water is driven off by heating the flask, and the latter completely desiccated by blowing in a current of air with a bellows arranged as in (§ 107). The flask is weighed after cooling, and we find a weight of 62.5

Deduct the quantity of oxide of lead added.........	50.0
The weight of the sulphuric acid remains............	12.5

Five grammes of sulphur therefore produce 12gm.50 of sulphuric acid.

By operating in this way, a small quantity of the sulphuric acid may be lost during ebullition; for, above 212°, the tension of the vapour of this acid is very sensible.

The composition of sulphuric acid may be ascertained in another way, free from this source of error. Five grammes of sulphur are again transformed into sulphuric acid by means of nitric acid; but the operation is performed in a small glass retort furnished with a receiver. The small quantity of sulphuric acid which escapes is then condensed in the receiver.

When the transformation of the sulphur into sulphuric acid is completed, instead of driving off the excess of nitric acid by heat, which would occasion a small loss of sulphuric acid, we add water, and pour into the liquid, heated to boiling, a solution of chloride of barium. A precipitate of sulphate of baryta is formed, completely insoluble in water, which is collected on a small filter, carefully washed with boiling water, until the wash-water is no longer clouded by sulphuric acid. The filter is then dried, and calcined in a small platinum crucible. The sulphate of baryta is thus perfectly dried; the filter is burned, leaving only some ashes which are too trifling to be noticed, if the filter is small. The crucible is weighed, the matter it contains emptied, and it is again weighed. The difference represents the weight of the sulphate of baryta. This weight will be 36gm.45: now, experiment has shown that 100 parts of sulphate of baryta contain

Sulphuric acid....................................	34.29
Baryta..	65.71
	100.00

consequently, 36.45 of sulphate contain 12.50 of sulphuric acid.

The following is a third method of ascertaining, by synthesis, the composition of sulphuric acid.

We find in nature the sulphuret of lead PbS, perfectly pure and well crystallized, and called *galena* by mineralogists. We weigh, in a flask, a small quantity of this sulphuret reduced to a very fine powder (10 grammes for example), and treat it with concentrated nitric acid, which changes it into the sulphate of the oxide of lead PbO,SO_3. We know that the transformation is perfect when the gray metallic powder of the sulphuret of lead is entirely changed into a white powder. It is then evaporated to dryness, and the residuum in the flask dried, as above (§ 107). We then find that the 100 grammes of sulphuret of lead produce 12.676 of sulphate of lead; the increase of weight represents the oxygen absorbed by the sulphur and the lead, to change the former into sulphuric acid, and the latter into oxide of lead. We shall see, hereafter, that, in all the neutral sulphates, the proportion of oxygen contained in the base is $\frac{1}{3}$ of that contained in the acid: consequently $\frac{3}{4}$. $2^{gm}.676=2^{gm}.007$ represents the quantity of oxygen absorbed by the sulphur to transform it into sulphuric acid.

The composition of the sulphate of lead is easily determined by synthesis. We weigh in a platinum crucible 10 grammes of oxide of lead, and pour upon it an excess of sulphuric acid, which changes the oxide into a sulphate. The excess of acid is then driven off by heating the crucible over an alcohol lamp to redness. We again weigh the crucible, after cooling, and obtain the weight of the sulphate of lead. This weight will be $13^{gm}.585$: we hence conclude that 10 grammes of oxide of lead combine with $3^{gm}.585$ of sulphuric acid; or, in other words, that the sulphate of lead is composed of

Sulphuric acid	$3^{gm}.585$ or	26.39
Oxide of lead	$10^{gm}.000$	73.61
	$13^{gm}.585$	100.00

$12^{gm}.676$ of sulphate of lead consequently contain $3^{gm}.345$ of sulphuric acid, which itself contains $2^{gm}.007$ of oxygen.

We therefore arrive at this final result, that $3^{gm}.345$ of sulphuric acid contain $2^{gm}.007$ of oxygen and $1^{gm}.338$ of sulphur, or that anhydrous sulphuric acid is formed of

Sulphur	40.00
Oxygen	60.00
	100.00

Or, if we refer this compound to the weight 16 of sulphur, which represents its equivalent,

Sulphur	16
Oxygen	24
	40

which corresponds to 1 equivalent of sulphur and 3 equivalents of oxygen: the formula of anhydrous sulphuric acid is therefore S_3O, and its equivalent 40.

The composition of sulphuric acid may be equally established by analysis. If we pass concentrated sulphuric acid in vapour through a porcelain tube heated to redness, it separates into water which becomes free, and a mixture of sulphurous acid gas and oxygen. We find that these gases are exactly in the proportion of 2 volumes of sulphurous acid gas and 1 of oxygen. Now, 2 volumes of sulphurous acid gas contain $\frac{1}{3}$ of a volume of vapour of sulphur and 2 volumes of oxygen; sulphuric acid therefore contains:

$\frac{1}{3}$ of a volume of vapour of sulphur, weighing......	2.218
3 " oxygen..............................	3.318
	5.536

which gives for the percentage composition of sulphuric acid,

Sulphur..	40.06
Oxygen..	59.94
	100.00

This composition differs but little from that obtained by synthesis. It is, however, proper to remark that the analytic method just described is less exact than the synthetic methods previously explained. It requires, in fact, 1st. The measurement in volume of two gases; a measurement which is always inaccurate, especially for sulphurous acid gas which departs so remarkably from the law of Mariotte: 2d. It rests on the density of the vapour of sulphur, of which we only know the approximate value, because its experimental appreciation is accompanied by very great difficulties.

§ 136. Concentrated sulphuric acid, which has hitherto alone occupied our attention, is not an anhydrous acid: it contains a certain quantity of water, which it is important to ascertain exactly. We weigh, in a small flask, 100 grammes of very pure and fine powdered protoxide of lead, and pour on it carefully, by means of a pipette, a given quantity of acid which we wish to analyze. (This quantity should always be less than that necessary to convert the whole of the oxide of lead used into a sulphate.) We again weigh the flask, and find its weight to be P: the increase of weight (P—100) gives the quantity of concentrated acid to be experimented on. We add a small quantity of water, to assist the combination of the sulphuric acid with the oxide of lead; then evaporate the water and dry, as has been stated (§ 107). By again weighing the balloon, we find a weight P′, consisting of the 100 grammes of oxide of lead and the anhydrous sulphuric acid contained in the weight (P—100) of concentrated acid: (P—P′) therefore represents the weight of water contained in this acid.

We find, in this manner, that 100 parts of concentrated sulphuric acid contain 18.3 of water and 81.7 of acid.

If we refer this composition to the weight 40 of red sulphuric acid, which represents its equivalent, we find

Sulphuric acid	40
Water	9
Concentrated sulphuric acid	49

These numbers give, for the percentage composition,

Sulphuric acid	81.64
Water	18.36
	100.00

Now, 9 represents precisely 1 equivalent of water (§ 88); therefore, concentrated sulphuric acid contains 1 equivalent of water and 1 equivalent of dry sulphuric acid, and its formula should be written SO_3+HO, or SO_3,HO. The equivalent of concentrated sulphuric acid is 49.

Monohydrated sulphuric acid is not the only compound of definite proportions that sulphuric acid can form with water. If we add to concentrated sulphuric acid a weight of water equal to that which it already contains, we obtain a second hydrate SO_3+2HO, which crystallizes, in large crystals, at a temperature approaching 32°. We know that crystallization always announces a definite combination. These crystals continue so long as the temperature does not rise above 44° or 46°. In the laboratory, we frequently see these crystals in the bottles of the sulphuric acid of commerce, for it is rarely at its maximum of concentration, and, during the winter, a portion separates in the state of the crystallized hydrate SO_3+2HO.

When we mix water and concentrated sulphuric acid, the volume of the mixture is always less than the sum of the volumes of the fluids mixed: we then say that there is *contraction*. Let v represent the volume of the concentrated acid, v' that of the water, and V the volume of the fluid after mixing, the fraction $\frac{V}{v+v'}$ is called the *fraction of contraction*. This value of this fraction is smallest in the mixture of sulphuric acid and water corresponding to the formula SO_3+3HO, and has induced chemists to look upon this hydrate as a third definite compound of sulphuric acid and water.

If we heat to ebullition the various hydrates of sulphuric acid in a tubulated retort furnished with a thermometer, we find that the hydrate SO_3+HO is the only one presenting a uniform boiling point: the other hydrates give off their water, and the temperature of the boiling point rises successively till it reaches 617°, which is the boiling point of the concentrated acid. The acid SO_3+HO is therefore the only hydrate which distils without change.

§ 137. A peculiar sulphuric acid is prepared in the arts, and known under the name of *German sulphuric acid*, or *Nordhausen acid*. This acid, the preparation of which will be explained hereafter, consists of a solution of anhydrous sulphuric acid in monohydrated acid SO_3+HO. If Nordhausen sulphuric acid be carefully heated in a glass retort, it separates into anhydrous sulphuric acid, which is disengaged in the form of vapour, and monohydrated acid, which remains in the retort. If this vapour be collected in a small long-necked matrass, cooled by a refrigerating mixture, it condenses in long, white, brilliant needles, forming masses resembling asbestos. Anhydrous sulphuric acid melts at about 77°, and boils between 86° and 95°; its vapour is colourless. It has a powerful attraction for water, so that if a small quantity of it be thrown into this liquid, a sound is produced resembling that of plunging a red-hot iron in water. The combination of anhydrous sulphuric acid with water disengages a great quantity of heat, and hence it follows, that when the anhydrous sulphuric acid comes in contact with the water, a high temperature is developed, which vapourizes the contiguous particles of water, but the vapour is immediately condensed by the adjacent strata of cold water. The production of vapour, followed by immediate condensation, is the cause of the hissing, which also occurs when a highly heated body, red-hot iron, for instance, is plunged into water. If we let fall a drop of water into a bottle containing anhydrous sulphuric acid, an explosion ensues with the production of light.

Anhydrous sulphuric acid exposed to the air gives off dense white fumes. Its vapour, at the ordinary temperature, possesses considerable tension; for it then closely approximates the temperature of 95°, at which it boils under the ordinary pressure of the atmosphere. On the other hand, the vapour of monohydrated sulphuric acid SO_3,HO, has scarcely any sensible tension under the same circumstances. It therefore follows, that if anhydrous sulphuric acid be exposed to the air, it will give off vapour copiously, which immediately combines with the vapour of water of the atmosphere, forming a hydrated acid, which is precipitated in the form of mist. The fumes given off in the air by monohydrated nitric acid were explained in the same manner (§ 102). The same is true of all other substances, gaseous or volatile, which fume when exposed to the air.

§ 138. Anhydrous sulphuric acid may be obtained immediately, by strongly heating the bisulphate of soda $NaO,2SO_3$, which parts with one-half of its sulphuric acid at a temperature not sufficiently elevated to decompose the acid.

Three parts of recently calcined, and consequently anhydrous, neutral sulphate of soda, are mixed with two of concentrated sulphuric acid, and gradually heated to a dull red. The substance swells at first, losing water, and then melts, when it is cast into plates, which are broken, and the pieces immediately introduced into an earthen retort, furnished with a receiver cooled by means of ice. By being carefully heated, one-half of the sulphuric acid distils in the anhydrous state, and condenses in the receiver. The residuum in the retort is neutral sulphate of soda, and may be again treated with ordinary sulphuric acid, thus serving indefinitely for the preparation of anhydrous sulphuric acid.

Anhydrous sulphuric acid may also be obtained by passing a mixture of sulphurous acid gas and oxygen through a tube containing platinum sponge and heated to redness. The oxygen and sulphurous acid gases, which do not act on each other when passed through a heated tube, combine, on the contrary, if the tube contain very finely-divided platinum; and yet the metal undergoes no change during the experiment. We have here again an instance of that mysterious and hitherto unexplained influence which certain bodies exert by their presence on chemical combinations or decompositions,—an influence which has received the name (§ 91) of *action of presence*, or *catalysis*.

When the Nordhausen acid is cooled below 32°, it deposits crystals belonging to a hydrate containing less water than the monohydrated sulphuric acid, and having a formula $2SO_3+HO$.

The sulphates of the various bases act very differently under the influence of heat. Sulphates containing very powerful bases, as potassa, soda, baryta, or lime, are unchanged, except at the highest temperature. The sulphates formed by more feeble bases, as the metallic oxides, are decomposed at a temperature more or less elevated. Generally speaking, sulphuric acid, in such a case, is decomposed into sulphurous acid and oxygen. A portion of this latter gas frequently combines with the metallic oxide, causing it to pass into a higher state of oxidation. The sulphates formed by some peroxides, the peroxide of iron, for example, decompose at so low a temperature that the sulphuric acid may escape without decomposition. On this last property is founded the preparation of the Nordhausen sulphuric acid.

We obtain incidentally, in several metallurgic processes, principally in the treatment of the ores of copper, large quantities of the sulphate of the protoxide of iron, called in commerce *green vitriol*. The formula of this salt is

$$FeO,SO_3+7HO.$$

Subjected to heat, the sulphate of iron loses at first 6 equivalents of water; the 7th is disengaged only at a more elevated temperature. If heated still higher, the protoxide of iron changes into a peroxide at the expense of the sulphuric acid, by absorbing a quantity of oxygen equal to one-half of that which the protoxide already contains; one-half of the sulphuric acid is thus decomposed and changed into sulphurous acid, which is disengaged, and there remains a subsulphate of the peroxide of iron Fe_2O_3,SO_3.

This reaction is represented by the following equation:

$$2(FeO,SO_3)=SO_2+Fe_2O_3,SO_3:$$

Fe_2O_3 is the formula of the peroxide of iron.

If we raise the temperature still higher, the sub-sulphate of the peroxide of iron is, in its turn, decomposed, the sulphuric acid becoming free, and the peroxide of iron remaining. The sulphate of the peroxide of iron still retains a little water at the moment of its decomposition, so that the sulphuric acid which is disengaged is not completely anhydrous.

In the Hartz mountains, where fuming sulphuric acid, called *Nordhausen sulphuric acid* (from the little village where it is deposited for transportation), is chiefly made, the vitriol is heated on a plate exposed to the air, until it loses the greater part of its water. It is then placed in retorts of earthen-ware A (fig. 211) arranged in 3 rows in a galley furnace, each furnace containing 120. It is heated with wood, until the sulphuric acid begins to pass over, which is easily known by the dense vapours it produces in the air. To the vessels A, which act as retorts, are then adapted vessels B nearly resembling them, but smaller, and serving as receivers. Ordinary concentrated sulphuric acid is put in these receivers, being much cheaper than the fuming acid, and is not considered to be changed into Nordhausen acid until it has received the products of four successive distillations. It is then composed of nearly $\frac{1}{6}$ of anhydrous sulphuric acid, and $\frac{5}{6}$ of monohydrated acid.

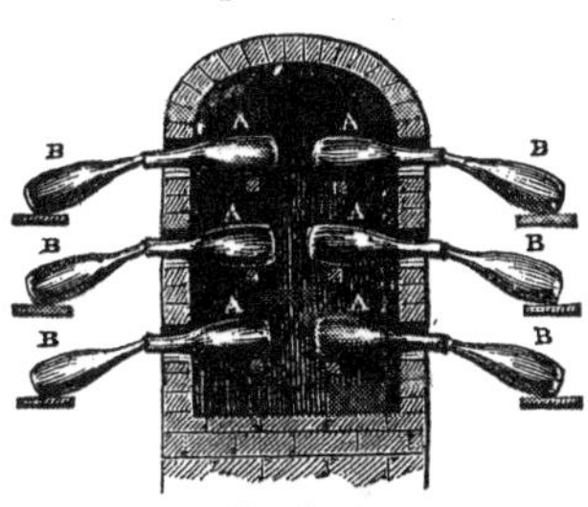

Fig. 211.

A similar acid may be prepared in the laboratory, by introducing into a stone retort, the peroxide of iron of commerce, known under the name of *colcothar*, moistening it with concentrated sulphuric acid, and then distilling. The first products are not collected, as they contain too much water, while the last are very rich in anhydrous sulphuric acid.

§ 139. The preparation of commercial monohydrated sulphuric acid, sometimes called *English sulphuric acid* or *oil of vitriol*, is founded on the following reactions, which we have previously indicated:

1st. The deutoxide of nitrogen NO_2, in contact with an excess of air, is changed into hyponitric acid NO_4;

2d. Hyponitric acid, in contact with a small quantity of water, is changed into monohydrated nitric acid and nitrous acid,

$$2NO_4+HO=NO_5,HO+NO_3.$$

3d. Nitrous acid NO_3, in contact with a large quantity of water, is changed into hydrated nitric acid and deutoxide of nitrogen,

$$3NO_3+nHO=NO_5+nHO+2NO_2.$$

Consequently, hyponitric acid, in contact with a large quantity of water, is changed into hydrated nitric acid and into deutoxide of nitrogen,

$$6NO_4+nHO=4NO_5+nHO+2NO_2:$$

4th. Sulphurous acid SO_2, in contact with hydrated nitric acid NO_5+nHO, is changed into sulphuric acid, while the nitric is transformed into hyponitric acid.

$$SO_2+NO_5+nHO=SO_3+nHO+NO_4.$$

The following experiment explains all the reactions which occur in making oil of vitriol by the English method:

We introduce, at the same time, into a large balloon A (fig. 212)

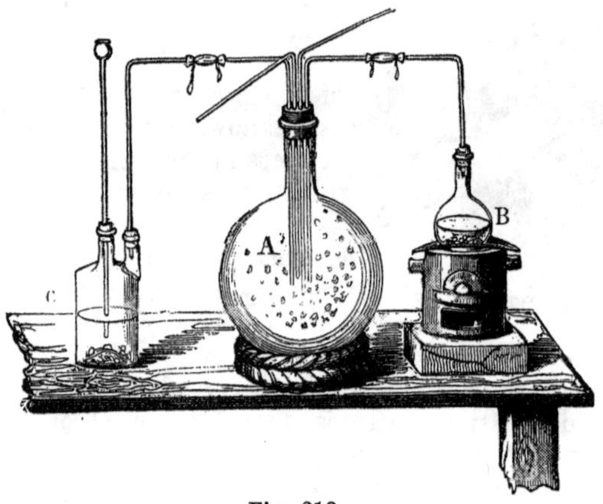

Fig. 212.

filled with air, and the sides of which are moistened, 1st, sulphurous acid gas obtained by heating some copper with concentrated sulphuric acid in a flask, and, 2dly, deutoxide of nitrogen produced in the bottle C, by causing dilute nitric acid to act upon copper.

The deutoxide of nitrogen, mixing with the air of the balloon A, combines with the oxygen, and changes into hyponitric acid NO_4, which, under the influence of the moisture of the balloon, changes, in its turn, into hydrated nitric acid and deutoxide of nitrogen. The nitric acid formed reacts on the sulphurous acid, which it changes into sulphuric, and changes itself into hyponitric acid, which is again decomposed by contact with water into nitric acid and deutoxide of nitrogen. The newly-formed deutoxide of nitrogen, coming into contact with the oxygen of the air, changes into hyponitric acid; and this succession of remarkable reactions continues indefinitely. So that, as long as any oxygen remains in the balloon, the same deutoxide of nitrogen may change an indefinite quantity of sulphurous into sulphuric acid. This result may be obtained by passing into the balloon, through one of its four tubes, a slow current of oxygen, which will replace that disappearing in consequence of the reaction.

The deutoxide of nitrogen may be replaced, in this experiment, by any more oxygenated compound of nitrogen, as hyponitric or nitric acid.

But, in order that all these circumstances may combine, there must be a large proportion of vapour of water in the balloon. That which would be disengaged from the moist sides at the ordinary temperature not being sufficient, it is necessary to heat the bottom of the balloon.

When there is less water, the reaction is indifferent. Let us suppose that there is no water in our balloon; the sulphurous acid and hyponitric gases then act slowly on each other; but we have seen (§ 132) that when the two substances in the liquid state are mixed in a tube, which is then hermetically sealed, they combine after some time, forming a crystallized compound, which is a hydrate of the preceding compound, $NO_3,2SO_3$. This hydrate is constantly formed in the balloon, and deposited on its sides in the form of small crystalline tufts, if the balloon be not heated. The same crystals also frequently form in the manufacture of sulphuric acid on a large scale, and have been called *crystals of the leaden chambers.* They should, however, only be considered as accidental, and their formation avoided; for, if they do not afterward meet with water to decompose them, they dissolve in the sulphuric acid, the purity of which they change, as it thus retains a portion of nitrous acid, which would have served to change an additional quantity of sulphurous into sulphuric acid.

In the manufacture of sulphuric acid on a large scale according to the English method, the balloon of our experiment is replaced by one or more large wooden chambers C (fig. 213) lined with sheet-lead, closely soldered. The sulphurous acid is prepared by burning sulphur in atmospheric air, the combustion taking place in a furnace A, on a large pan of sheet-iron. The furnace is surmounted by a dome and a large flue in mason-work, which conducts the gas into the leaden chamber. The oxygenated compound of nitrogen is the deutoxide of nitrogen, nitrous vapours, or nitric acid. In some manufactories, nitrate of potassa is placed in a small cast-iron pot in the pan containing the burning sulphur. This pot becomes thus highly heated, the sulphurous acid reacts on the nitrate of potassa, transforms it into a sulphate, and deutoxide of nitrogen is disengaged, which enters the leaden chamber, mixed with sulphurous acid and an excess of atmospheric air. In order to produce the reaction which will form sulphuric acid, it is sufficient to inject into the chamber, jets of steam under high pressure from the boiler B. The hydrated

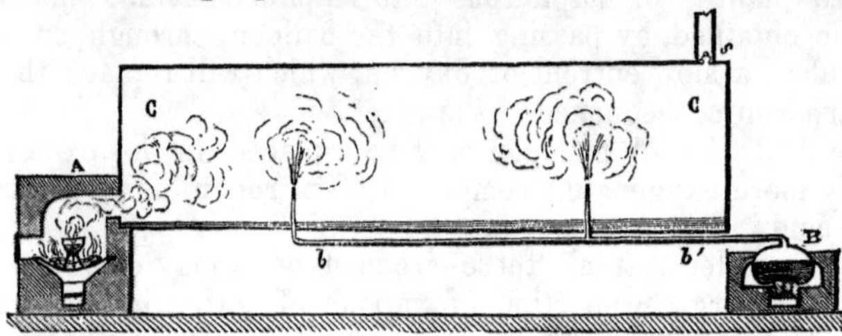

Fig. 213.

sulphuric acid falls in the form of rain upon the floor of the chamber. The quantity of nitrate of potassa used is about $\frac{1}{10}$ that of the sulphur. An opening at the upper part of the chamber, provided with a valve *s*, gives exit to the remaining gases. These gases should be deprived, as completely as possible, of sulphurous acid and oxide of nitrogen, and to do this, several conditions must be fulfilled:

1st. The proportions of nitre and sulphur burned must be properly regulated.

2d. The quantity of steam injected must be proportioned to the quantity of gas on which we operate, for if it be too small, reaction takes place with difficulty, many crystals of the leaden chamber are produced, which cause a loss of the nitrous products, and impair the purity of the sulphuric acid. If the quantity of steam is too great, we obtain a very dilute sulphuric acid, which requires considerable expense to be brought to a proper degree of strength:

3d. The leaden chambers should be made as large as possible: in order that the gases may remain in them for a long time; and they should be so arranged as to effect a perfect mixture of the gases. To do this, they are divided into several compartments, separated by leaden partitions pierced with holes at the bottom; or several chambers are arranged in succession, communicating by leaden pipes. One or several jets of steam are projected into each of the chambers, and regulated by stopcocks. Sulphur is sometimes burned in several chambers, so as to generate sulphuric acid at several points at once. Registers, properly arranged, allow us to graduate the quantity of atmospheric air admitted into the apparatus.

In many manufactories, nitric acid is substituted for the deutoxide of nitrogen. Sulphur alone is burned in the furnaces; the mixture of atmospheric air and sulphurous acid enters the first chamber, which is small, and in which the foreign substances carried over by the current of gas are deposited. A leaden pipe conveys the mixed gases into a second chamber, into which nitric acid is steadily poured. This acid, contained in vessels placed outside, is made to fall on porcelain saucers arranged like a fountain, and immediately beneath the orifice of the pipe which conducts the mixture of sulphurous acid and air. The current of hot gas vapourizes the nitric acid, at the same time that its sulphurous acid decomposes it. The gases, intimately mixed, reach several large leaden chambers successively, where the chief reaction takes place, amid jets of steam projected at various points. Small openings are made in the walls of these rooms, which allow us to inspect them, and ascertain if the gaseous mixture contains a proper quantity of nitrous vapour. The flow of nitric acid is governed by this knowledge.

Iron pyrites is at present substituted in a few manufactories for sulphur, that is to say, a sulphuret of iron FeS_2, found abundantly in many places, and consequently cheaper than sulphur. The pyrites will burn in a furnace previously heated, and its sulphur be converted into sulphurous acid. But the sulphuric acid thus obtained always contains some arsenious acid, arising from the metalline arseniurets which almost always accompany iron pyrites.

The manufacture of sulphuric acid by the English method has greatly advanced in latter years, the apparatus having been improved, the production of the article doubled, and the proportion of the nitre used much diminished. Fig. 214 represents a section of the apparatus now used. (We have supposed its various parts to be arranged in a line, to render the wood-cut more intelligible, though it is not generally the case in large establishments.)

A, A′ are two furnaces coupled together, in which the sulphur is burned, one of them, A′, being seen in section so as to show its internal arrangement. The sulphur burns on a large sheet-iron plate, and the heat produced by the combustion is used to furnish the quantity of steam necessary for reaction in the leaden chambers. For this purpose, a boiler V is placed in each furnace, immediately over the pan on which the sulphur burns, and a pipe *aa′a″* conducts the steam into the different chambers.

The two furnaces communicate with the same chimney *bb′*, which should be at least 6 or 7 metres (20–24 feet) in height, so as to give the gas an ascending force sufficient to drive it through the various parts of the apparatus. The chimney *bb′* conveys the mixture of sulphurous acid gas and atmospheric air into a leaden drum BB, in which are arranged small inclined shelves of lead. A continuous current of oil of vitriol, properly regulated, and strongly charged with nitrous products, is made to fall on the upper shelf, from the vessel R. As the sulphuric acid flows along the shelves, and collects on the bottom of the drum, a portion of

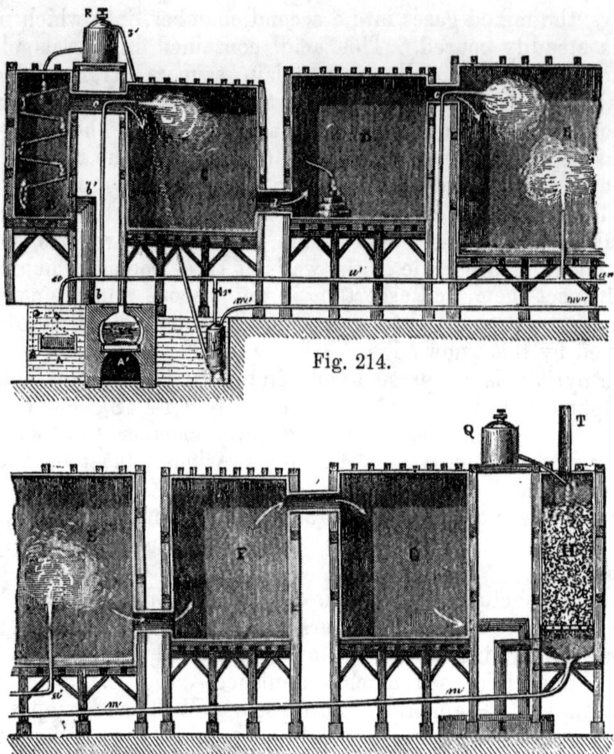

Fig. 214.

the nitrous products reacts on the sulphurous acid, which it converts into sulphuric, while the remainder is disengaged in the state of gas in the gaseous mixture of sulphurous acid and atmospheric air.

From the drum BB, the gases are conveyed by the cast-iron pipe *c*, into a small leaden chamber C, containing about 100 cubic metres (360 cubic feet), and called the *denitrificator*. At the very origin of the pipe *c*, a jet of steam, under high pressure, is driven into the chamber C, to furnish the water necessary for the reaction of the nitrous gas, oxygen and sulphurous acid. The sulphuric acid produced falls on the floor of the chamber C.

The gases are then conveyed, by the pipe *d*, into a second chamber D, of nearly the same size as the first. In front of the orifice of the pipe *d*, an earthen-ware vessel like a cascade-fountain is placed, on the top of which a continuous and properly regulated stream of nitric acid is poured. (This acid is contained in vessels outside of the chamber, and not represented in the figure.) The nitric acid is decomposed; sulphuric acid is formed, and the nitrous gas produced in the reaction mixes with the sulphurous gas and atmospheric air. The sulphuric acid thus obtained is highly charged with nitrous compounds; it falls on the floor of the room D, and thence flows, through a small pipe, into the room C, where it comes into contact with gases containing a large quantity of sulphurous acid, which takes from it its nitrous products. For this purpose, the floor of the chamber D is somewhat higher than that of C.

The gases are then conveyed by the pipe *e* into a large chamber E, where the reaction of the sulphurous, nitrous and oxygen gases chiefly takes place, because the gases remain there for some time. Jets of steam are projected into this chamber at several points. The sulphuric acid produced falls upon the floor. At the same time, the *denitrified* sulphuric acid of the chamber C, of which the floor is somewhat higher than that of E, is brought in. Sometimes, instead of one large chamber E, there are several smaller ones, placed in succession.

The gases, on leaving the room E, are not lost in the air. The temperature of this chamber is very high, and a considerable portion of sulphuric acid still remains there in the form of vapour. Moreover, the gases still contain nitrous products, of which they can be deprived, so as to economize the nitric acid.

The gases, on leaving the chamber E, are passed through two leaden drums, F, G, which act as refrigerators, and in which are arranged shelves which interrupt the gaseous current, and thus assist the deposit of the vapours. The gases then reach a third refrigerator I, cooled externally with water; and, lastly, they reach a last leaden drum H, intended to absorb the nitrous gases, and thence escape into the atmosphere by the pipe T.

The drum H is filled with large fragments of coke, supported by a diaphragm *s*, and on which a continuous current of concentrated sulphuric acid descends from the vessel Q. This acid absorbs the nitrous vapours, and then passes, by the leaden tube $mm'm''$, into a vessel L. This concentrated sulphuric acid, loaded with nitrous products, is then made to ascend into the vessel R, to fall again into the drum BB, where it is denitrified. A very simple arrangement facilitates this transfer: the top of the vessel R communicates with the bottom of the vessel L by the pipe zz'; and the top of the vessel L has a tube, furnished with a stopcock *r*, which joins the general steampipe $aa'a''$. In order to cause the liquid of the vessel L to ascend into the vessel R, we merely open the stopcock *r*: the pressure of the steam in the boiler, always equal to several atmospheres, acting on the surface of the fluid L, causes it to rise to the level R.

By means of the apparatus just described, the quantity of nitric acid necessary to convert 100 kilogrammes of sulphur into sulphuric acid, has been reduced by one half of that formerly used.

§ 140. The solution of sulphuric acid, as it leaves the leaden chambers, has a density varying from 1.35 to 1.50. It is concentrated in leaden pans until its density reaches 1.75. Its boiling point is then between 392° and 410°. Its concentration in leaden vessels cannot be carried farther, as it would attack the lead, and is completed in a large platinum retort, where it is brought to the state of monohydrated sulphuric acid, having a density of 1.85 and a boiling point of 617°.

Hyposulphuric Acid, S_2O_5.

§ 141. If we digest a solution of sulphurous acid, with the peroxide of manganese, in the cold, the acid soon loses its characteristic odour, and the liquid contains the hyposulphate of the protoxide of manganese. Two equivalents of sulphurous acid combine with one equivalent of oxygen, given off by the peroxide of manganese, which passes into the state of protoxide. We have

$$MnO_2+2SO_2=MnO,S_2O_5.$$

If, on the other hand, we pass the current of sulphurous acid through *hot* water, holding finely divided peroxide of manganese in suspension, the gas is likewise absorbed, but the reaction takes place between 1 equivalent of the peroxide and 1 equivalent of the acid, and the sulphate of the protoxide of manganese is formed,

$$MnO_2+2SO_2=MnO.S_2O_5.$$

Thus, the reaction differs according to the temperature.

In order to prepare hyposulphuric acid in the laboratory, finely divided peroxide of manganese is suspended in water, and a current of sulphurous acid gas passed through the liquid. The two reactions first mentioned take place simultaneously, forming at the same time the sulphate and hyposulphate of manganese. The liquid is filtered and decomposed by a solution of caustic baryta, which precipitates the protoxide of manganese, and forms the sulphate and hyposulphate of baryta. The sulphate of baryta is completely insoluble in water, and precipitates along with the oxide of manganese, so that the hyposulphate of baryta alone remains in solution, from which it is crystallized by evaporation.

The hyposulphate of baryta is again dissolved in water, and dilute sulphuric acid carefully added, until the addition of a single drop of this reagent no longer clouds the fluid. The baryta is entirely precipitated in the form of a sulphate, and the liquid only contains hyposulphuric acid. This solution is evaporated under the receiver of an air-pump, until sufficiently concentrated. The evaporation can only be conducted in the cold; for, when the liquid is too highly concentrated, the hyposulphuric acid is decomposed by heat into sulphurous and sulphuric acids.

By double decomposition the various hyposulphates are obtained by means of the hyposulphate of baryta. It is sufficient to pour carefully into the solution of hyposulphate of baryta, a diluted solution of the sulphate of the base we wish to combine with hyposulphuric acid, until no more precipitate is thrown down. The baryta is thus eliminated in the state of a sulphate, and the liquid contains the hyposulphate, which can be crystallized.

§ 142. The composition of hyposulphuric acid may be easily ascertained by the analysis of the hyposulphate of baryta.

By calcining a given weight (5 grammes) of anhydrous hyposulphate of baryta, the salt is decomposed, the sulphurous acid is disengaged, and neutral sulphate of baryta remains, which is exactly weighed. From the known composition of the latter, we infer that 100 parts of hyposulphate of baryta contain

Baryta	51.51
Hyposulphuric acid	48.49
	100.00*

or, if we refer this composition to the weight 76.5 of baryta, which represents the equivalent of this base,

Baryta	76.5
Hyposulphuric acid	72.0
	148.5

If the hyposulphate of baryta be a neutral salt, and if hyposulphuric acid be a monobasic acid, the weight 72 should represent the equivalent of hyposulphuric acid, and should equal the sum of the equivalent of its constituent elements. Now, we obtain the number 72, by the addition of 2 equivalents of sulphur and 5 of oxygen: the composition of hyposulphuric acid is, therefore,

2 eq. sulphur	32.0	44.45
5 " oxygen	40.0	55.55
1 " hyposulphuric acid	72.0	100.0

This composition may be verified by direct analysis. In fact, if we take 5 grammes of dry hyposulphate of baryta, and treat it with concentrated and boiling nitric acid, the hyposulphuric will be converted into sulphuric acid, of which one half only will be saturated by the baryta. But, if we add chloride of barium to the liquid, all the sulphuric acid will be precipitated in the state of sulphate of baryta. We shall find that the weight of sulphate of baryta obtained is precisely double of that formed by the calcination of the hyposulphate.

We hence conclude that 100 of hyposulphate of baryta contain

Sulphur	21.55
Oxygen	26.94
Hyposulphuric acid	48.49

* The numbers given vary a little from the original, from the adoption of the equivalent 68.5 for barium instead of 68.64.—*J. C. B.*

HYPOSULPHUROUS ACID, S_2O_2.

§ 143. This acid has not been hitherto obtained in an isolated state, and is only known combined with bases.

Hyposulphites are obtained in several ways:

By boiling a solution of sulphite of soda, or any other sulphite, with flowers of sulphur in excess, a great quantity of sulphur will be found to dissolve, and the sulphite of soda NaO,SO_2 is changed into hyposulphite NaO,S_2O_2. This salt crystallizes readily.

If chlorohydric acid be poured into a very cold solution of hyposulphite of soda, the liquid is not clouded at first; but a precipitate of sulphur soon forms, and sulphurous acid is disengaged.

Hyposulphites are also otherwise obtained:

A piece of zinc disappears in a solution of sulphurous acid, without any disengagement of hydrogen gas. The oxidation takes place at the expense of a portion of the oxygen of the sulphurous acid, which passes into the state of hyposulphurous acid, and the fluid contains a mixture of sulphite and hyposulphite of zinc. Thus we have

$$2Zn+3SO_2=ZnO,S_2O_2+ZnO,SO_2.$$

The solutions of the alkaline sulphurets, exposed to the air, absorb oxygen rapidly, and are converted into hyposulphites.

When solutions of potassa, baryta, or soda are boiled with an excess of sulphur, hyposulphites are obtained mixed with sulphurets saturated with sulphur. Thus, with potassa, we have the following reaction:

$$3KO+12S=2KS_5+KO,S_2O_2.$$

§ 144. The composition of hyposulphurous acid is ascertained by the analysis of hyposulphite of baryta.

Ten grammes of dry hyposulphite of baryta are treated with concentrated boiling nitric acid, which changes the salt into sulphate of baryta, which is weighed.

We thence deduce that 100 of hyposulphite of baryta contain

Baryta	61.45
Hyposulphurous acid	38.55
	100.00

or in equivalents,

1 eq. baryta	76.5
1 " hyposulphurous acid	48.0
1 " hyposulphite of baryta	124.5

The composition of sulphurous acid is therefore

2 eq. sulphur	32.0	66.67
2 " oxygen	16.0	33.33
1 " hyposulphurous acid	48.0	100.00

This composition may be verified by analysis, as described (§ 142).

Monosulphuretted Hyposulphuric Acid, S_3O_5.

§ 145. Monosulphuretted hyposulphuric (trithionic) acid is obtained under the following circumstances:—A solution of baryta with sulphurous acid is supersaturated to obtain bisulphite of baryta, which is allowed to digest for several days with flowers of sulphur, at a temperature of about 112°. The liquid at first turns yellow, then loses its colour, and on cooling, it deposits a salt crystallized in long white needles, which is the monosulphuretted hyposulphate of baryta. By cautiously pouring sulphuric acid into the solution of this salt, the monosulphuretted hyposulphuric acid is obtained isolated. Its solution may be concentrated under the receiver of an air-pump, but heat readily decomposes it into sulphuric acid and sulphur.

The analysis of monosulphuretted hyposulphuric acid is made in the same way as that of the preceding compounds: we know that its equivalent is 88, and that it contains,

3 eq. sulphur	48	54.54
5 " oxygen	40	45.46
	88	100.00

Bisulphuretted Hyposulphuric Acid, S_4O_5.

§ 146. This compound is obtained by dissolving iodine in a solution of hyposulphite of baryta, when the following reaction takes place:

$$2(BaO,S_2O_2)+I=IBa+BaO,S_4O_5.$$

The liquid contains iodide of barium and the salt of baryta formed by the new acid. This salt, being less soluble than the iodide of barium, separates by crystallization. In order to isolate the acid, the salt of baryta is decomposed by a proper quantity of sulphuric acid. The solution of bisulphuretted hyposulphuric acid (tetrathionic) may be concentrated in vacuo; ebullition decomposes it.

The composition of this substance is ascertained by the analysis of the salt of baryta. We thus find that its equivalent is 104, and its composition as follows:

4 eq. sulphur	64	61.54
5 " oxygen	40	38.46
	104	100.00

Trisulphuretted Hyposulphuric Acid, S_5O_5.

§ 147. Trisulphuretted hyposulphuric acid (pentathionic) is formed when the chlorides of sulphur are decomposed by a solution of sulphurous acid, or even by pure water; but the reaction from which it originates has not been well studied. This acid forms with baryta a crystallizable salt, from the analysis of which the composition of the acid has been deduced.

Trisulphuretted hyposulphuric acid contains

5 eq. sulphur	80	66.67
5 " oxygen	40	33.33
	120	100.00

The composition of trisulphuretted hyposulphuric and hyposulphurous acids are identical. These acids are *isomeric compounds.*

But these salts are very differently compounded, for the quantities of the bases which these acids saturate, are to each other as 5 : 2.

RECAPITULATION OF THE COMBINATIONS OF SULPHUR WITH OXYGEN. EQUIVALENT OF SULPHUR DETERMINED.

§ 148. The seven compounds of sulphur and oxygen, just studied, present the following composition:

Hyposulphurous acid	Sulphur	66.67
	Oxygen	33.33
		100.00
Trisulphuretted hyposulphuric acid	Sulphur	66.67
	Oxygen	33.33
		100.00
Bisulphuretted hyposulphuric acid	Sulphur	61.54
	Oxygen	38.46
		100.00
Monosulphuretted hyposulphuric acid	Sulphur	54.54
	Oxygen	45.46
		100.00
Sulphurous acid	Sulphur	50.00
	Oxygen	50.00
		100.00
Hyposulphuric acid	Sulphur	44.45
	Oxygen	55.55
		100.00
Sulphuric acid	Sulphur	40.00
	Oxygen	60.00
		100.00

If we refer the composition of these various substances to the same quantity, 100 of sulphur, we find

Hyposulphurous acid	Sulphur	100.00
	Oxygen	50.00
		150.00

Trisulphuretted hyposulphuric acid......	Sulphur....	100.00
	Oxygen....	50.00
		150.00
Bisulphuretted hyposulphuric acid........	Sulphur....	100.00
	Oxygen....	62.50
		162.00
Monosulphuretted hyposulphuric acid....	Sulphur....	100.00
	Oxygen....	83.33
		183.33
Sulphurous acid..............................	Sulphur....	100.00
	Oxygen....	100.00
		200.00
Hyposulphuric acid..........................	Sulphur....	100.00
	Oxygen....	125.00
		225.00
Sulphuric acid................................	Sulphur....	100.00
	Oxygen....	150.00
		250.00

If we compare the quantities of oxygen which combines with the same weight of sulphur, we find that they are to each other as the numbers

$$1 : 1 : \tfrac{5}{4} : \tfrac{5}{3} : 2 : \tfrac{5}{2} : 3.$$

Let us suppose that the least oxygenated compound, hyposulphurous acid, be formed of 1 equivalent of sulphur and 1 equivalent of oxygen = 8. It is evident that we shall obtain the equivalent of sulphur by making the proportion,

$$50.00 : 100.00 :: 8 : x, \text{ whence } x = 16.$$

Hyposulphurous acid will therefore be..........	SO
Trisulphuretted hyposulphuric acid.............	SO
Bisulphuretted hyposulphuric acid...............	$SO_{\frac{5}{4}}$
Monosulphuretted hyposulphuric acid...........	$SO_{\frac{5}{3}}$
Sulphurous acid....................................	SO_2
Hyposulphuric acid.................................	$SO_{\frac{5}{2}}$
Sulphuric acid	SO_3

If the above formulæ really represent the equivalents of these various acids, the numerical values of these equivalents, that is, the weights of these acids which combine with an equivalent of a base to form an *anhydrous neutral salt,* will be as follows:

Hyposulphurous acid	24
Trisulphuretted hyposulphuric acid	24
Bisulphuretted hyposulphuric acid	26
Monosulphuretted hyposulphuric acid	$29\frac{1}{3}$
Sulphurous acid	32
Hyposulphuric acid	36
Sulphuric acid	40

Now, we have seen, by direct experiment, that the weights of these various acids which combine with 1 equivalent of a base, with the weight 76.5 of baryta, for example, to form the anhydrous neutral salts, are,

Hyposulphurous acid	48
Trisulphuretted hyposulphuric acid	120
Bisulphuretted hyposulphuric acid	104
Monosulphuretted hyposulphuric acid	88
Sulphurous acid	32
Hyposulphuric acid	72
Sulphuric acid	40

Experiment thus shows us that the equivalents of sulphurous and sulphuric acid are those which we supposed by hypothesis; but that this is not the case with the other acids. The equivalents of hyposulphurous and hyposulphuric acids are twice as great, that of monosulphuretted hyposulphuric acid, thrice, and that of bisulphuretted hyposulphuric acid, four times; and, lastly, that of trisulphuretted hyposulphuric acid five times as great as those we supposed.

The formula of these various combinations will therefore be,

Hyposulphurous acid	S_2O_2
Trisulphuretted hyposulphuric acid	S_5O_5
Bisulphuretted hyposulphuric acid	S_4O_5
Monosulphuretted hyposulphuric acid	S_3O_5
Sulphurous acid	SO_2
Hyposulphuric acid	S_2O_5
Sulphuric acid	SO_3

The number 16, which we will adopt as the *equivalent* of sulphur, possesses, therefore, the property of representing the composition of the numerous compounds of sulphur with oxygen, by entire formulæ, the *most simple possible.* Again, the numerical values of the equivalents of these combinations, calculated from the formulæ, are equal to those obtained by ascertaining experimentally the weights of those compounds necessary to form *anhydrous neutral salts* with 1 equivalent of a base.

We shall subsequently see that this weight 16 of sulphur, chosen as the equivalent, will give, for all the other compounds of sulphur, very simple formulæ, and, when these combinations are acid, their formulæ will also satisfy the second condition just indicated.

In the atomic theory, we suppose 1 atom of sulphurous acid to be composed of 1 atom of sulphur and 2 atoms of oxygen: then 1 atom of sulphuric acid is formed of 1 atom of sulphur and 3 atoms of oxygen.

The atomic formulæ of the compounds of sulphur with oxygen will therefore be the same as their formulæ in equivalents, and the weight of the atom of sulphur will be 16.

COMBINATIONS OF SULPHUR WITH HYDROGEN.

SULFHYDRIC ACID, HS.*

§ 149. Sulphur and hydrogen do not combine directly, even when passed through a porcelain tube heated to redness; but a gaseous combination of the two substances is obtained by decomposing certain metallic sulphides by dilute sulphuric acid. The protosulphuret of iron is the one generally used in the laboratory. The following is the reaction:

$$FeS+SO_3+HO=FeO,SO_3+HS.$$

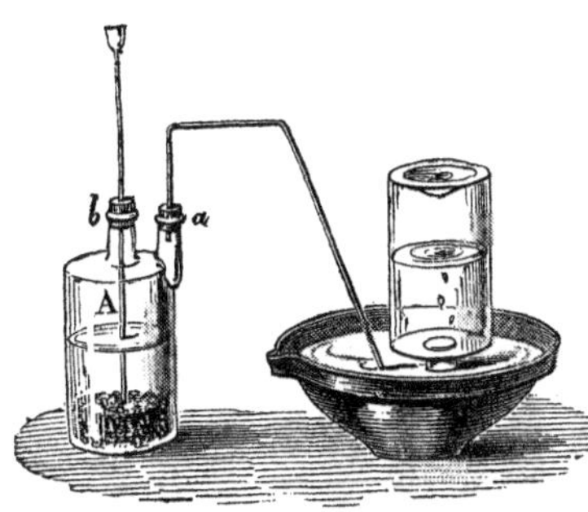

Fig. 215.

The same apparatus is used as for the preparation of hydrogen. The sulphuret of iron, broken into pieces, is introduced into a two-mouthed bottle, a quantity of water poured therein, and sulphuric acid gradually added by the funnel tube (fig. 215).†

Chlorohydric acid may be substituted for the sulphuric, when the reaction is as follows:

Sulphuret of iron....................	{ Sulphur......... Iron..............	Sulfhydric acid.
Chlorohydric acid....................	{ Hydrogen ...... Chlorine........	Chloride of iron.

$$FeS+HCl=FeCl+HS.$$

The sulphuret of iron usually employed in the laboratory to

* This gas was formerly called sulphuretted hydrogen, more recently hydrosulphuric acid, or, better, sulphohydric acid, but I prefer giving the French name, sulfhydric acid.—*J. C. B.*

† A wide-mouthed bottle, with the two tubes passed through the single cork, is as convenient and less costly. Where the gas is to be used in analytic operations, it should be washed by being passed through a small bottle, previous to its entrance into the liquid to be acted on.—*J. C. B.*

obtain sulfhydric acid, is prepared expressly for that purpose, but as it often contains small quantities of metallic iron, which, in contact with dilute sulphuric or chlorohydric acid, gives off hydrogen, the sulfhydric acid gas is mixed with hydrogen. In many experiments, this is of no importance; but, where absolute purity is required, the sulfhydric acid must be prepared by treating sulphuret of antimony with chlorohydric acid. The sulphuret of antimony is a natural product found abundantly in some veins. It can be acted on only by concentrated acids; but sulphuric cannot be used, for, if dilute, it does not attack the antimony, and if concentrated, it destroys the sulfhydric acid as fast as it is generated. In order to prepare the gas with sulphuret of antimony, we place the latter, in fine powder, in a small flask (fig. 216), and add chlorohydric acid gradually by the S-tube. Gentle heat is applied to accelerate the disengagement of the gas.

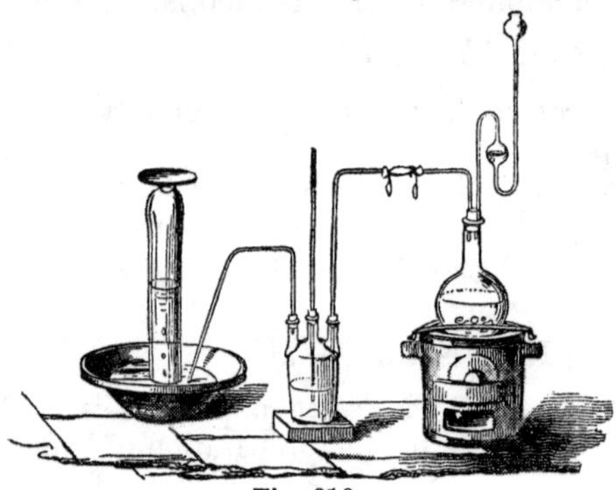

Fig. 216.

§ 150. Sulfhydric acid is a colourless gas, possessing a most fetid odour, resembling that of rotten eggs. Its density is 1.1912. It liquefies under a pressure of 15 or 16 atmospheres at the ordinary temperature, and then forms a very mobile liquid of the density of 0.9.

In order to obtain liquid sulfhydric acid, the apparatus in which it is generated is made to connect with the suction-pipe of a gas pump, which is at the same time a forcing-pump, the second pipe of which connects with a small bulb A (fig. 217) of thick glass, and kept in a refrigerating mixture. By raising the piston of the pump, the gas of the apparatus fills the body of the pump, and by depressing, it is forced into the bulb. The number of strokes of the piston is regulated by the quantity of sulfhydric acid gas the apparatus will furnish. The compressed gas liquefies in the bulb; and when it is three-fourths full, the neck must be sealed hermetically. But as the neck cannot be melted in the flame of a lamp, because the pressure is greater within the apparatus than without, the following plan is adopted. The tube attached to the bulb is composed of a narrow part *ab* and a larger one *bc*: before fitting the tube to the pipe of the pump, a plug of mastic is placed in the latter, so as not to impede the passage of the gas; and, in order to seal the apparatus hermetically, it will suffice to melt it,

Fig. 217.

then to give a stroke with the piston, which will drive the melted mastic into the narrow tube *ab*, where it becomes solid.

Liquid sulfhydric acid may also be obtained by exposing to spontaneous decomposition, in a close vessel, the second combination of sulphur with hydrogen, which we shall soon learn is the *bisulphide of hydrogen*. A certain quantity of this liquid bisulphide is placed in the bottom of a curved tube, as in fig. 218, and the end *b* is sealed in a lamp. The bisulphide decomposes spontaneously into sulphur, which is deposited in the form of crystals, and into sulfhydric acid gas, which accumulates in the empty portion of the tube, where it liquefies by its own pressure. In order to separate the acid from the sulphur which is deposited, it is merely necessary to cool in a refrigerating mixture the curved part *cd* (fig. 219), when the sulfhydric acid passes over and collects at *d*.

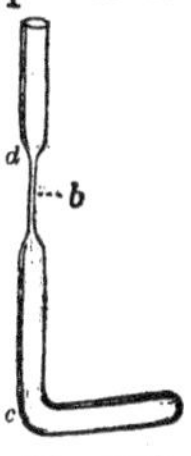

Fig. 218.

Sulfhydric acid is one of the most deleterious gases,* a bird perishing in an atmosphere containing $\frac{1}{1200}$, and a dog $\frac{1}{100}$ of this gas. Labourers who clean sinks are often exposed to asphyxia from this gas. It is remedied by chlorine, which decomposes the sulfhydric acid; but this remedy must be carefully administered. The best plan is to use a napkin soaked in acetic acid, and enclosing some pieces of chloride of lime, through which the patient is made to breathe.† Heat partially decomposes sulfhydric acid into hydrogen and sulphur; but, in order to obtain perfect decomposition, the gas should be repeatedly passed through a highly heated porcelain tube.

Fig. 219.

Sulfhydric acid gas is combustible, burning in the air with a blue flame, and the product is water and sulphurous acid gas. If the gas be inflamed in a test-glass, the sulphur does not burn completely, but is partly deposited on the sides of the glass.

When a mixture of sulfhydric gas and air in a large bottle is in contact with a porous body, especially with lime, at a temperature of 104° to 122°, a considerable quantity of sulphuric acid is gradually formed. The reaction is interesting, because it explains the formation of sulphuric acid and sulphates in localities furnishing sulphuretted hydrogen.

Oxygen, dissolved in water, slowly decomposes sulfhydric acid, water being formed, and finely divided sulphur deposited, rendering the water milky. In order, therefore, to preserve a solution

* This is certainly incorrect, although stated positively in almost all works on chemistry. I have breathed it, and witnessed its effects on others, in large quantity, and cannot say that it is a very deleterious gas. See SULPHUR, in Encyclopedia of Chemistry.—*J. C. B.*

† Spirits of hartshorn (ammonia) may be inhaled with good effect, and, still better, a mixture of ammonia and strong alcohol.—*J. C. B.*

of sulfhydric acid, it should be kept in well-stoppered bottles entirely filled, and inverted.

Sulfhydric acid therefore affords different products of combustion, according to the circumstances under which oxidation takes place; in rapid combustion, it furnishes water and sulphurous acid; when in contact with a porous body, and at a temperature of 104° to 122°, water and sulphuric acid are formed; lastly, dissolved in water, and exposed to the air, it gives water and sulphur, which is precipitated.

Chlorine, bromine, and iodine instantly decompose sulfhydric acid, affording sulphur, and chlorohydric, bromohydric, and iodohydric acids. If the chlorine, bromine, and iodine are in excess, they combine with the isolated sulphur, and form the chloride, bromide, and iodide of sulphur. Advantage is taken of this property to prepare a solution of iodohydric acid.

Sulfhydric gas is a true acid, for it reddens litmus, but, like all feeble acids, it produces a *purplish red;* whilst powerful acids, such as nitric and sulphuric, produce a *light red.* Its acid properties are but feebly developed, and hence it is often called *sulphuretted hydrogen gas* (§ 52).

Water dissolves 2½ to 3 times its volume of sulfhydric acid gas. The solution may be prepared in Woolf's apparatus, by taking care to put into the bottles water recently boiled, and consequently deprived of air. The solution, when heated, parts wholly with the gas. Alcohol dissolves 5 or 6 times its volume of sulfhydric acid gas.

The solution of sulfhydric acid is much used in the laboratory, being employed to precipitate many metals from their saline solutions, in the state of sulphides. These sulphurets, generally insoluble, have frequently characteristic colours, by which the metals contained in them are recognised. Thus, a solution of sulfhydric acid will detect the slightest traces of oxide of lead in a fluid, by the brown or black colour it produces. Reciprocally, the salts of lead discover the presence of the smallest portions of sulfhydric acid. For this purpose, small strips of paper are used, imbued with a solution of sugar of lead. The strips are colourless, but are instantly blackened when dipped into water containing the slightest traces of sulfhydric acid, or when, after having been moistened, they are exposed to an atmosphere containing the slightest traces of the gas.

In nature, many mineral waters are found containing sulfhydric acid, and are used in medicine under the name of *sulphurous waters.*

§ 151. Sulfhydric acid may be analyzed by decomposing it in a curved tube, by means of potassium, as is done in the other combinations of hydrogen with the metalloids (§ 186). Potassium effectually decomposes sulfhydric gas, but the sulphuret which results combines with the undecomposed sulfhydric acid, and forms a *sulfhydrate of the sulphide of potassium;* so that a portion of the gas escapes decomposition. But the analysis may be exactly made (fig. 220) by substituting tin for the potassium. The glass being heated by an alcohol lamp, the tin combines with the sulphur, and the hydrogen is set free. The volume of the gas remaining is found to be exactly the same. We may assure ourselves that the sulfhydric acid has been entirely decomposed by introducing into the glass a fragment of moist potassa, for if sulfhydric acid remain, it is absorbed, and the volume diminished.

Fig. 220.

We infer from the preceding experiment, that 1 volume of sulfhydric acid gas contains 1 volume of hydrogen. Now if, from the density of sulfhydric acid gas.............................. 1.1912
we deduct the density of hydrogen 0.0692

there remains.. 1.1220

which nearly equals the $\frac{1}{6}$ of the density of the vapour of sulphur $=\frac{6.6546}{6}=1.109$.

We therefore conclude that 1 volume of sulfhydric acid gas is composed of 1 volume of hydrogen and $\frac{1}{6}$ volume of vapour of sulphur; or, if we refer the composition to two volumes of hydrogen, its equivalent, we say that 2 volumes of sulfhydric acid gas contain 2 volumes of hydrogen and $\frac{1}{3}$ volume of vapour of sulphur. But as $\frac{1}{3}$ volume of the vapour of sulphur represents the equivalent of gaseous sulphur, sulfhydric acid is therefore formed of 1 equivalent of sulphur and 1 equivalent of hydrogen, and its equivalent is 2 volumes. The volume $\frac{1}{3}$, which we have chosen as the *equivalent of gaseous sulphur*, has, therefore, the advantage of expressing the composition of sulfhydric acid in the simplest manner possible.

§ 152. We shall subsequently see that there is a remarkable analogy between the compounds of sulphur and those of oxygen: hence we ought to expect to find in the compounds of sulphur and hydrogen a constitution similar to that of the compounds of oxygen with this substance. Sulfhydric acid presents, however, in this respect, a very interesting anomaly. In the aggregate of its properties, it ranks with water; and this position is so natural, that chemists, before the density of the vapour of sulphur was known, did not hesitate to attribute to it the same composition. But experiment has proved the supposed analogy to be false, since sulfhydric acid, for 2 volumes of hydrogen, contains only $\frac{1}{3}$ volume of vapour of sulphur, instead of 1 whole volume. This anomaly has been attempted to be explained by saying that the molecule of the vapour of sulphur is a group formed by the union of three chemical molecules.*

We have seen that the weight 1.1912 of sulfhydric acid contained 0.0692 of hydrogen and 1.1220 of sulphur; consequently, 100 parts in weight contain

Hydrogen	5.81
Sulphur	94.19
	100.00

If we refer this composition to the weight 1 of hydrogen, representing its equivalent, we find

Hydrogen	1
Sulphur	16
Sulfhydric acid	17

The formula of the acid in equivalents will therefore be HS; under the atomic theory, it would be H_2S or HS.

Sulfhydric acid is therefore formed of 1 equivalent of sulphur and 1 of hydrogen, and the weight of its equivalent is 17.

Bisulphide of Hydrogen, HS_2.

§ 153. Sulphur forms a second compound with hydrogen, an oleaginous, yellowish liquid, containing a greater quantity of sulphur than sulfhydric acid; but this quantity has not yet been determined with accuracy, because it is difficult to obtain the bisulphuret of hydrogen in a state of purity. It is prepared by pouring a solution of polysulphide of calcium or potassium into chlorohydric acid. The fluid becomes milky, and is poured into a large funnel, the aperture of which has been closed. In a short time, the bisulphide of hydrogen collects in the narrow part of the funnel, in the form of a yellow liquid, and is separated by carefully uncorking the funnel, until the liquid, which is heavy, runs off. Bisulphide of hydrogen is preserved only by contact with moderately concentrated hydrochloric acid, for it decomposes rapidly with pure water or the air; sulfhydric acid gas being disengaged, and sulphur separated. We have seen (§ 150) the use made of this spontaneous decomposition of the bisulphide of hydrogen, to obtain liquid sulfhydric acid.

This substance is supposed to be composed of 1 equivalent of hydrogen and 2 of sulphur, and has been represented by the formula HS_2.

---

* It is probable that the density of the vapour of sulphur at its lowest point of evaporation, a little above the melting point of sulphur, is only 2.22. See Berzelius, Lehrbuch, I. 180, 5th edition.—*J. C. B.*

COMBINATION OF SULPHUR WITH NITROGEN.

SULPHIDE OF NITROGEN, NS_3.

§154. If dry ammoniacal gas be passed through the perchloride of sulphur, we obtain, at first, a brown flaky powder, the formula of which is

$$NH_3,SCl_2.$$

But, if the action of the ammonia be continued, the brown matter absorbs an additional quantity of it, and changes into a yellow substance, the formula of which is

$$2NH_3,SCl_2.$$

If the yellow body be treated with water, it decomposes into the chlorohydrate and hyposulphite of ammonia, which dissolve, and a yellow powder, consisting of free sulphur and sulphide of nitrogen. The powder is rapidly washed with a little water, dried under the receiver of an air-pump, and treated several times with ether, which dissolves the free sulphur, and leaves the sulphide of nitrogen.

Sulphide of nitrogen is a yellow powder, which decomposes slowly into sulphur and nitrogen at a temperature a little above 212°; but when suddenly heated, it decomposes with an explosion. Water decomposes it slowly at the ordinary temperature—much more rapidly at the boiling point.

§155. Sulphide of nitrogen can be exactly analyzed, by carefully and gradually heating a mixture of a known weight of it and metallic copper in the apparatus described (§108). The sulphur combines with the copper, and the nitrogen is disengaged. We have seen how the proportion of this last substance was ascertained, and the peculiar caution necessary in the experiment.

Sulphur may also be directly determined by decomposing the sulphide of nitrogen by nitric acid, which converts the sulphur into sulphuric acid, which is precipitated by the chloride of barium. Sulphide of nitrogen has thus been found to contain

1 eq. nitrogen	14	22.58
3 " sulphur	48	72.42
	62	100.00

The formula NS_3 corresponds to that of nitrous acid NO_3, or that of ammonia NH_3.

SELENIUM.

EQUIVALENT Se = 39.5 (493.75 O = 100.)

§ 156. Selenium,* like sulphur, may be obtained in three states; solid at the ordinary temperature, it becomes liquid at 392°, and gaseous at about 300°. Solid selenium is of a deep brown colour, conchoidal and vitreous, with a fracture. The edges of fracture are often so thin as to be translucent, when it exhibits, by transmitted light, a beautiful red colour. This is also its colour when very finely divided, or when a drop of liquid selenium is pressed between two plates of glass.

Selenium does not pass suddenly, like sulphur, from the liquid to the solid state, but becomes viscid before assuming the latter condition, and may then be drawn out in very fine threads; whence, it has not yet been obtained in crystals by melting. The density of selenium varies according to its molecular condition, being 4.28 in vitreous selenium, and 4.80 in that which is granular and slowly cooled.

Melted selenium is of a very deep brown colour; its vapour of an intense yellow.

Selenium is combustible, burning with a bluish flame, and exhaling a fetid odour of horse-radish, which is characteristic. Selenious acid and oxide of selenium are formed by the combustion, to the latter of which the fetid odour is owing. Selenious acid is soluble in water, and its solution is readily decomposed by substances which have a strong attraction for oxygen: thus sulphurous acid reduces it and passes into the state of sulphuric acid. The selenium, becoming free, is precipitated in the form of a red powder.

The compounds of sulphur and selenium are very analogous, for which reason they are generally studied in connection with each other.

Selenium is found in nature principally in the state of selenide of lead; and in studying this compound, we shall describe the mode of extracting it.

COMBINATIONS OF SELENIUM WITH OXYGEN.

§ 157. Two combinations of selenium with oxygen are known; selenious acid SeO_2 and selenic acid SeO_3, which correspond to sulphurous acid SO_2 and sulphuric acid SO_3. Chemists admit also

* Selenium was discovered in 1817, by Berzelius.

the existence of a third oxide, to which they attribute the fetid odour disengaged by selenium when burning in the air; but its properties are not known.

SELENIOUS ACID, SeO_2.

§ 158. When selenium is burned in oxygen, it is converted into selenious acid. In order to obtain the acid by the combustion of selenium, a fragment of selenium is introduced into a bent tube *abc* (fig. 221), of which the end *a* connects with a small glass retort, containing chlorate of potassa. The chlorate is heated so as to give off oxygen; and the portion *b* of the tube containing the selenium is heated. It burns with a blue flame, and the selenious acid condenses in the upper part of the tube, in the form of white acicular crystals.

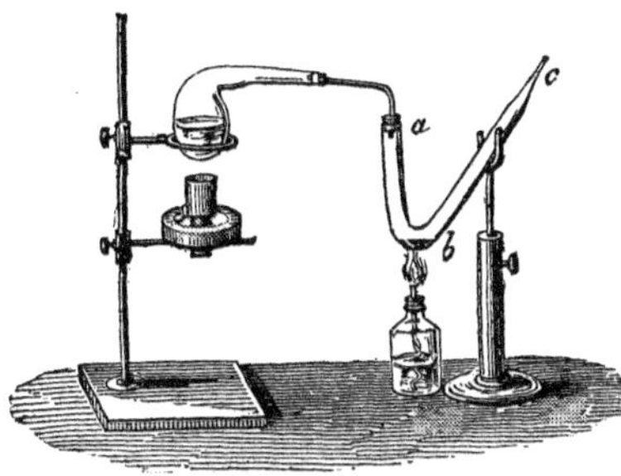

Fig. 221.

Selenious acid may also be obtained by oxidizing selenium by concentrated nitric acid, or, better still, by a mixture of nitric and chlorohydric acids. It dissolves in the state of selenious acid, and if the solution be evaporated, the acid is obtained in the form of a white mass. Under the same circumstances, we have seen sulphur converted into sulphuric acid.

Selenious acid is very soluble in water. It is not very retentive of oxygen; as many substances abstract the gas from it. Iron and zinc decompose dissolved selenious acid, and precipitate the selenium in the form of a red powder. Sulphurous acid effects a similar decomposition.

§ 159. The composition of selenious acid may be ascertained by finding the weight of this acid produced by 1 gramme of selenium treated with nitric acid. It may also be obtained by finding the quantity of selenium afforded by 1 gramme of selenious acid decomposed by sulphurous acid. Lastly, some selenite, that of lead or silver, for example, may be analyzed. Selenious acid has thus been found to contain

Selenium	71.17
Oxygen	28.83
	100.00

SELENIC ACID, SeO_3.

§ 160. By heating together a mixture of nitrate of potassa and selenium or selenide of lead, we obtain the seleniate of potassa, which is purified by successive crystallizations. The seleniate of potassa, dissolved in water, is decomposed by a solution of nitrate of lead, insoluble seleniate of lead being precipitated, which is collected on a filter. The seleniate of lead, well washed, is suspended in water, and subjected to the action of a current of sulfhydric acid gas, whereby sulphuret of lead is precipitated in the form of a black powder, and the hydrated selenic acid is dissolved in the water. We have, in fact,

$$PbO,SeO_3+HS=PbS+SeO_3,HO.$$

The solution of selenic acid may be concentrated by heat, the boiling point of the fluid rising to about 554°. But if we endeavour to concentrate it still further, the selenic acid is decomposed and oxygen disengaged.

Selenic acid is decomposed by chlorohydric acid, disengaging chlorine and forming selenious acid. Sulphuric acid does not act on selenic, whilst it instantly decomposes selenious acid. When we wish to precipitate selenium from selenic acid, the latter must first be converted into selenious acid, by boiling its solution with chlorohydric acid. Sulphurous acid is then added, and the fluid again boiled.

§ 161. Selenic is a very powerful acid, closely resembling sulphuric acid in its properties. Its composition has been determined by the analysis of some seleniate, the seleniate of lead, for example. A known weight p of seleniate of lead is suspended in water, and decomposed by sulphuretted hydrogen, which precipitates the lead in the state of sulphuret of lead. The sulphuret being collected on a small filter, is washed, dried, and calcined with the filter in a platinum crucible.* The sulphuret of lead, thus partly converted into a sulphate, is wholly converted by pouring on it nitric acid and some drops of sulphuric, and then calcining it to redness. The sulphate of lead is weighed, and from its weight we deduce, by calculation, the quantity p' of oxide of lead which exists in the weight p of the seleniate of lead. The quantity of selenic acid is therefore $(p-p')$.

The proportion of selenium in the weight $(p-p')$ of selenic acid, is easily ascertained. It is sufficient to concentrate by evaporation the liquid obtained after the separation of the sulphuret of lead on the filter, and boil this concentrated liquid, first with hydrochloric acid, which converts the selenic into selenious acid, then with sulphurous acid, which decomposes the selenious acid and precipitates the selenium. Let p'' be the weight of selenium obtained, $(p-p'-p'')$ will be the weight of oxygen which constitutes selenic acid with the weight p'' of selenium.

We thus find that selenic acid contains

Selenium	62.20
Oxygen	37.80
	100.00

* This is a dangerous operation except for an experienced chemist, and therefore a porcelain crucible is to be preferred.—*J. C. B.*

§ 162. In short, the two known compounds of selenium contain

Selenious acid	Selenium	71.17
	Oxygen	28.83
		100.00
Selenic acid...	Selenium	62.20
	Oxygen	37.80
		100.00

If we refer the composition of the two acids to the same quantity 100 of selenium, it will be expressed as follows:

Selenious acid	Selenium	100.00
	Oxygen	40.51
		140.51
Selenic acid...	Selenium	100.00
	Oxygen	60.77
		160.77*

Therefore, for the same quantity of selenium, selenic acid contains $1\frac{1}{2}$ times as much oxygen as selenic acid. The most simple manner of expressing the formulæ in equivalents of the composition of these bodies, is to say, that selenious acid is composed of 1 equivalent of selenium and 2 of oxygen, and selenious acid of 1 equivalent of selenium and 3 of oxygen. If we grant this hypothesis, the weight of selenium will evidently be given by one of these proportions:

$$\left.\begin{array}{l} 28.83 : 71.17 :: 16 : x \\ 37.80 : 62.20 :: 24 : x \end{array}\right\} \text{whence } x=39.5.$$

We shall soon see that this same hypothesis represents in the simplest manner possible the composition of selenohydric acid.

§ 163. We must, henceforward, remember that there is a physical law which we have not hitherto applied in fixing the composition of bodies by equivalents, and upon which we shall frequently insist hereafter. We have seen in the introduction (§ 40), that *when two bodies are similarly composed, they generally affect nearly identical crystalline forms;* and reciprocally, *when two compounds have nearly identical crystalline forms, if they are isomorphous, they are generally similarly composed.* Now, the comparative examination of the sulphates and seleniates has shown that the seleniates and sulphates of the same base are isomorphous: they ought, therefore, to have similar formulæ. If, therefore, we write the formula of sulphuric acid SO_3, we should write the formula of selenic acid SeO_3, and, consequently, that of selenious acid SeO_2.

Experiment has shown that the density of the vapour of seleni-

* 40.51 : 60.77 : : 1 : $1\frac{1}{2}$: : 2 : 3.

ous acid is 4.0; consequently, 1 volume of gaseous selenious acid contains 1 volume of oxygen. We have seen that gaseous sulphurous acid also contained its volume of oxygen.

COMBINATION OF SELENIUM WITH HYDROGEN.

SELENOHYDRIC ACID, HSe.

§ 164. Selenium forms a gaseous compound with hydrogen—selenohydric acid, analogous to sulfhydric acid, and is obtained by decomposing the selenide of iron by chlorohydric acid. Selenohydric acid dissolves in water, but its solution decomposes in the air, in the same manner as sulfhydric acid, selenium being deposited in the form of a red powder.

Selenohydric acid is composed of

Hydrogen	1	2.47
Selenium	39.5	95.53
	40.5	100.00

The equivalent of selenohydric acid is therefore 40.5, and its formula HSe.

TELLURIUM.

Equivalent Te = 64.5 (806.5 O = 100).

§ 165. Tellurium* is very rare: it is found in nature, sometimes isolated, but more frequently combined with the metals, principally with gold, silver, bismuth, and lead. We shall subsequently see how it is separated from the bismuth. Tellurium has the physical properties of a metal, and in appearance greatly resembles antimony, but it approximates, on the other hand, in the properties of its compounds, to selenium and sulphur.

Tellurium is of a silvery white colour, and has a bright metallic lustre. It melts at a dull red-heat, and, by careful cooling, crystallizes in large brilliant plates, which are very manifest in its fracture. From the various planes of cleavage, it will be readily seen that the primary form of crystallized tellurium is a rhombohedron. Tellurium may be rendered gaseous, but it requires a very high temperature. It may, indeed, be distilled, but the distillation cannot be performed in the earthen or porcelain retorts used in our laboratories.

The distillation of slightly volatile substances is greatly facilitated by heating them in a current of gas which exerts on them no chemical action. Volatile substances sensibly give off vapours at a temperature far inferior to their boiling point. Thus, water, which boils at 212°, under the ordinary pressure of the atmosphere, disengages, at the ordinary temperature, considerable vapour; and the weight of this vapour cannot exceed, in a limited space, a certain maximum, which depends on the temperature; but it can be conceived that, if these vapours are removed as soon as formed, the maximum will not take place, and new vapour will be constantly generated, until the substance is entirely volatilized.

In order to distil tellurium, it is placed in a small platinum dish, introduced into a porcelain tube arranged in a reverberatory furnace. A current of dry hydrogen gas is passed into one end of the tube, and to the other, which should project somewhat from the furnace, a tube is fitted, to allow the escape of the gas. A current of hydrogen is first passed through the apparatus, so as to expel the atmospheric air completely; the porcelain tube is then

* Tellurium was discovered in 1782, by Müller, of Reichenstein, in the gold-mines of Transylvania; but to Klaproth we are indebted for a knowledge of its principal properties.

heated as highly as possible, still keeping up the current of gas. The sublimed tellurium condenses in the anterior and colder portion of the tube.

The density of tellurium is 6.26, which is very considerable, and in which respect it again resembles the metals properly so called.

Tellurium, heated in the air, burns with a bluish flame, exhaling a peculiar odour difficult to describe.

COMBINATIONS OF TELLURIUM WITH OXYGEN.

§ 166. Tellurium forms two compounds with oxygen, tellurous acid TeO_2, and telluric acid TeO_3, which are obtained in the manner directed for selenious and selenic acid. We shall not stop to describe them.

CHLORINE.

EQUIVALENT Cl = 33.5 (443.75 O = 100).

§ 167. Chlorine* is a gas readily distinguished from all those we have hitherto studied. In fact, all those gases are colourless, whilst chlorine is of a greenish yellow, to which property is due its name (from χλωρος, greenish yellow). If chlorine be compressed, so as to reduce it to a volume 5 times less than it occupies at the ordinary pressure of the atmosphere, it becomes liquid. The density of the liquid, which is of a greenish-yellow hue, is 1.33. It has never yet been congealed by any degree of cold. The density of gaseous chlorine is 2.44: that is, nearly $2\frac{1}{2}$ times that of air.

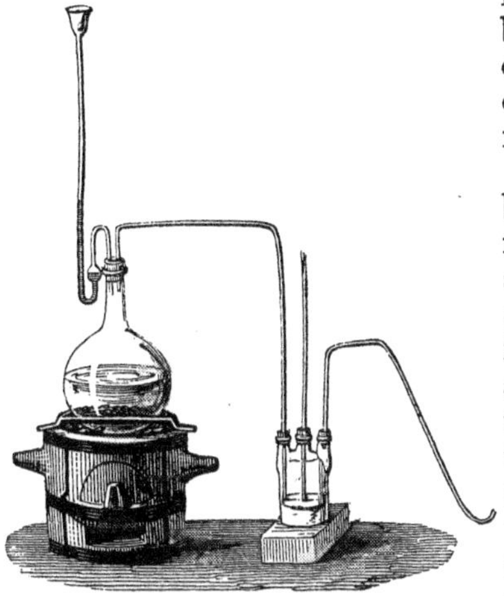

§ 168. Chlorine is obtained by treating the peroxide of manganese by chlorohydric acid. The pulverized peroxide of manganese is placed in a glass flask (fig. 222), and chlorohydric acid poured thereon. A discharging-tube, fitted to the flask, conveys the gas into a bell-glass in the water-cistern. In this reaction, the peroxide of manganese gives off its oxygen to the hydrogen of the chlorohydric acid, one-half of the chlorine disengaged combines with the manganese to form the protochloride of manganese, and the other half is set free.

Fig. 222.

Peroxide of manganese... { Manganese ....
Oxygen............ } Water. } Protochloride of manganese.
Chlorohydric acid.......... { Hydrogen.........
Chlorine. { Chlorine.........
Chlorine.........Is set free.

$$MnO_2+2HCl=MnCl+2HO+Cl.$$

The flask is slightly heated to facilitate the process.

Chlorine may be more steadily generated by substituting a mix-

* Chlorine was discovered in 1774, by Scheele.

ture of sea-salt and sulphuric acid for the chlorohydric acid. We put into a flask 1 part of finely-powdered peroxide of manganese, 4 parts of sea-salt or chloride of sodium, and 2 of the concentrated sulphuric acid of commerce, diluted with its weight of water. The chloride of sodium in contact with the sulphuric acid and water gives rise to sulphate of soda and chlorohydric acid:

Chloride of sodium..	{ Sodium........................		Oxide of Sodium.	Sulphate of soda.
	{ Chlorine...	Chlorohydric acid.........		
Water..................	{ Hydrogen.			
	{ Oxygen........................			
Sulphuric acid..				

$$NaCl+HO+SO_3=NaO,SO_3+HCl.$$

Chlorohydric acid, in contact with the peroxide of manganese, reacts as previously stated, chloride of manganese and sulphate of soda formed, and chlorine disengaged. The sulphuric acid, in excess, acts on the chloride of manganese as on the chloride of sodium, decomposing it with the assistance of the water, so that an additional quantity of chlorohydric acid and sulphate of manganese result; hence the ultimate products of the reaction are the sulphates of soda and manganese, which remain in the flask, and all the chlorine of the chloride of sodium, which is disengaged in the state of gas.

The final reaction is represented by the following equation:

$$NaCl+MnO_2+2SO_3=NaO,SO_3+MnO,SO_3+Cl.$$

Chlorine is more soluble in water than the simple gases we have hitherto studied, 1 volume of water dissolving 2 of chlorine. This great solubility of chlorine in water, prevents us from preserving it over this fluid, and even embarrasses our collecting it there. However, it may be done by working rapidly and causing the discharging-tube to ascend to the upper part of the bell-glass, so that the gas is not obliged to pass through the water in the form of bubbles, and is less exposed to its dissolving power.

Chlorine cannot be collected over mercury, because it combines immediately with this metal, even at the ordinary temperature.

Dry chlorine may be obtained in the following manner:—After having conveyed the gas first into a washing-bottle B (fig. 223), containing a little water, which retains the chlorohydric acid which might have come over, it is made to pass through a tube *ab*, filled with chloride of calcium, or a tube curved like the letter U, containing pumice-stone soaked in concentrated sulphuric acid. These substances rapidly absorb the water, and dry the gas, which is then conveyed by another tube to the bottom of a small-mouthed bottle C. The chlorine, from its great density, occupies the inferior portion, and rises successively in the bottle, driving out the atmo-

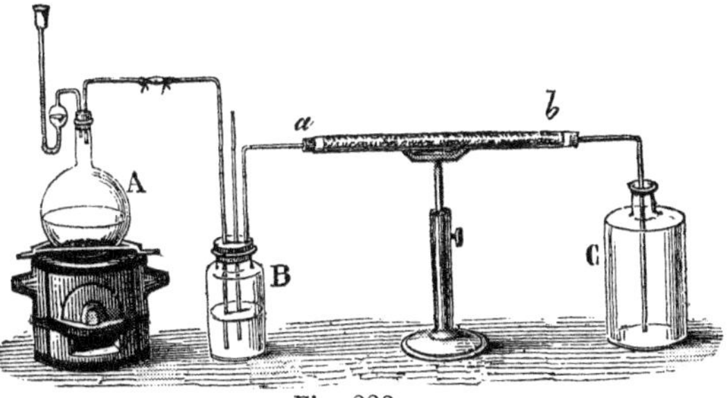

Fig. 223.

spheric air. After some time, the bottle may be supposed to be filled with chlorine, the tube is slowly withdrawn, and the bottle closed with a ground-glass stopper.

The aqueous solution of chlorine is often used in the laboratory and in the arts. For this purpose it is best prepared in a Woolf's apparatus. The gas which does not dissolve in the first bottle, traverses the fluid contained in the second, third, and so on.

The aqueous solution of chlorine and its gas have the same colour. When one of the bottles of the preceding apparatus is surrounded with ice, a flaky crystalline substance is soon formed, of a more intense greenish yellow than the fluid surrounding it. This substance is a combination of chlorine with water, a hydrate of chlorine, containing 28 of chlorine and 72 of water. The crystals may be easily isolated, if the external temperature be sufficiently low. They may be collected in a funnel, allowed to drain completely, and then rapidly compressed between sheets of bibulous paper, previously cooled. They are then introduced into a curved tube *abc* (fig. 224) closed at *a*. The portion *ab* of the tube containing the hydrate is kept cold with ice, while the opposite end *bc* is sealed in a lamp. The hydrate of chlorine decomposes at a few degrees above 32°. If we heat the portion of the tube containing the hydrate of chlorine, by plunging it into water at 95°, the crystalline matter will be seen to separate into two liquid strata, one of which, of a deep-yellow, falls to the bottom of the tube, and is liquid chlorine; the other, of a much lighter hue, is a saturated solution of chlorine in water. If the leg *bc* of the tube be cooled with ice, the liquid chlorine boils in the leg *ab*, and condenses in the coldest part of *bc*: it is thus separated from the aqueous solution.

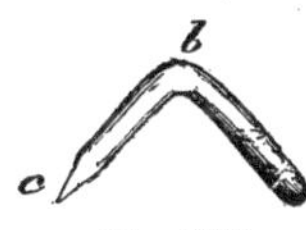

Fig. 224.

Chlorine has powerful affinities. It combines directly with hydrogen, and an explosion always takes place when a lighted taper is plunged into a mixture of the two gases. It combines directly with a majority of the metals. Many substances, amongst them arsenic and antimony, take fire when thrown in a finely-powdered state into a bottle filled with chlorine. If the vapour of water and chlorine are passed through a porcelain tube, the water is decomposed, oxygen being set free, and chlorohydric acid formed.

The aqueous solution of chlorine often acts as a powerful oxidizing agent: thus, it instantly converts sulphurous into sulphuric acid. The water in this case is decomposed, chlorohydric acid being formed, and oxygen in the nascent state added to the sulphurous acid.

$$SO_2+Cl+HO=HCl+SO_3.$$

The solution of chlorine may be preserved unchanged in the dark in a well-stoppered bottle; but, when exposed to solar light, it decomposes the water, chlorohydric and hypochlorous acids being formed.

$$2Cl+HO=ClO+HCl.$$

Chlorine is used in the arts for bleaching linen and cotton fabrics, and, in general, to destroy vegetable colours. Vegetable colouring matters, like all substances of organic origin, are composed of carbon, hydrogen, oxygen, and sometimes of nitrogen. Chlorine acts powerfully on many of them, and decomposes them, by seizing their hydrogen to form chlorohydric acid; the colouring matter bleaches by decomposition. In a similar way, chlorine discolours ordinary writing-ink, the colouring principle of which is a combination of the sesquioxide of iron with an organic substance called *tannin.* If we wish to efface the writing completely, after having removed the characters by chlorine water, we must wash it several times with weak chlorohydric acid, which completely dissolves the sesquioxide of iron. Without this precaution, the characters would reappear on washing the place with a solution of prussiate of potash, which gives, with the sesquioxide of iron, a blue compound. But chlorine will not act on India ink, nor on printing-ink, because the colouring matter of these inks is very finely-divided carbon, which does not combine directly with chlorine.

Chlorine is also used to destroy the putrid miasmata arising from the decomposition of organic matter. These miasmata are owing to the presence of organic substances in the air, so minute, however, that chemical analysis has hitherto been unsuccessful in detecting them. Chlorine destroys these substances by taking away their hydrogen.

Chlorine acts as a poison on the animal economy. Respired in small quantities, it excites coughing, and long exposure to its influence may produce more serious symptoms, bloody expectoration, etc. etc.

COMBINATIONS OF CHLORINE WITH OXYGEN.

§ 169. These combinations are very numerous, five of them being well ascertained, and others more complex exist, which may be regarded as resulting from the union of the former with each other.

The five most important compounds are—

1. Hypochlorous acid........................ ClO
2. Chlorous acid.............................. ClO_3
3. Hypochloric acid......................... ClO_4
4. Chloric acid................................ ClO_5
5. Perchloric acid........................... ClO_7.

We shall begin with chloric acid, which may be considered as the starting point of all the rest.

Chloric Acid, ClO_5.

§ 170. When a concentrated solution of potassa is saturated with chlorine, there separate, after some time, white crystalline spangles of chlorate of potassa, while the fluid contains a large quantity of chloride of potassium, and a small proportion of chlorate of potassa retained in solution. Reaction takes place between 6 equivalents of chlorine and 6 equivalents of potassa; 5 equivalents of chloride of potassium KCl are formed, and 1 equivalent of chlorate of potassa KO,ClO_5; that is, we have the equation

$$6Cl+6KO=5KCl+KO,ClO_5.$$

The chlorate of potassa is purified by solution in boiling water, the greater portion being deposited in the form of crystals during the cooling of the liquid.

Chloric acid, and all the other compounds of chlorine with oxygen, are prepared by means of chlorate of potassa.

In order to obtain chloric acid, we pour into a solution of chlorate of potassa, an excess of hydrofluosilicic acid, whereby a gelatinous precipitate of insoluble silicofluoride of potassium is formed, and the chloric acid remains in the liquid. If only the quantity of hydrofluosilicic acid necessary to exactly precipitate the potassa were poured in, the chloric acid would remain alone in the solution. But, as the silicofluoride of potassum is a transparent gelatinous precipitate, scarcely to be distinguished in the liquid, it is impossible to know when the potassa is completely precipitated, and we are obliged to use an excess of hydrofluosilicic acid. The filtered liquid, containing therefore a mixture of chloric and hydrofluosilicic acids, is saturated with a solution of baryta, until it becomes slightly alkaline. The baryta forms with the hydrofluosilicic acid an insoluble salt, and a soluble chlorate with the chloric acid. The liquid is evaporated after having been again filtered, and crystallized chlorate of baryta is obtained.

The chloric acid is isolated, by dissolving the chlorate of baryta in water, and carefully adding sulphuric acid until no precipitate is formed. The sulphate of baryta is separated on a filter, and the liquid, which contains only chloric acid, is placed under the receiver of an air-pump, where it is brought to the consistence of syrup.

We cannot use heat to concentrate the solution of chloric acid, because it rapidly decomposes at a temperature exceeding 104°. Two acids are formed, one of which, perchloric acid ClO_7, remains in the liquid; and the other, chlorous acid ClO_3, is disengaged in the form of a yellow gas, or decomposes immediately into chlorine and oxygen, according to the temperature.

Litmus paper, dipped into a solution of chloric acid, at first reddens, but is soon as completely bleached as though it were dipped into a solution of chlorine.

If a few drops of a concentrated solution of chloric acid be poured on a piece of linen or paper, and then gently dried, the parts which were moistened take fire and deflagrate.

Chloric acid, mixed with a solution of hydrochloric, gives off chlorine copiously, as may be represented by the following equation:

$$ClO_5+5HCl=6Cl+5HO.$$

Substances easily oxidizable decompose chloric acid by taking its oxygen: thus, by contact with chloric acid, sulphurous is changed into sulphuric acid; phosphorous into phosphoric acid.

§ 171. The composition of chloric acid may be easily deduced from that of chlorate of potassa, which is an anhydrous salt that can be accurately analyzed.

By calcining a weight p of chlorate of potassa in a platinum crucible, oxygen will be disengaged, and there will remain a weight p' of chloride of potassium: $(p-p')$ therefore represents the oxygen which existed in the chloric acid and in the potassa.

If we knew the composition of the chloride of potassium, we could immediately ascertain the quantity c of chlorine and the quantity k of potassium which existed in the weight p' of chloride of potassium. We would then find that a weight p of chlorate of potassa contained a weight

k of potassium.
c of chlorine.
$p-p'$ of oxygen.

But, supposing that the composition of the chloride of potassium is unknown, we can readily ascertain it in the following manner:

By dissolving in water a known weight p' of chloride of potassium, and pouring into the solution an excess of nitrate of silver, the chloride of silver will be precipitated, which is easily collected, and its weight ascertained, after having been previously dried. We thus find that a weight p' of chloride of potassium gives a weight p'' of chloride of silver. Let us admit, for a moment, that the composition of the chloride of silver is known; we then know that, in a weight p'' of this substance, there is a weight c of chlorine.

But, if the composition of chloride of silver were itself unknown, it would suffice, in order to ascertain it, to take 10 grammes of this substance, introduce it into a glass tube, and heat it in a current of hydrogen, when it would be brought to the metallic state, the chlorine separating in the state of chlorohydric acid. By weighing accurately the metallic silver remaining in the tube, we should have the composition of the chloride of silver.

We have first determined the composition of chloride of silver by *analysis;* but it may also be done by *synthesis*. In fact, by dissolving 10 grammes of perfectly pure metallic silver in nitric acid, diluting the fluid with water, and then adding carefully chlorohydric acid, until it ceases to precipitate, the silver will be deposited in the state of a chloride, which can be easily washed by decantation, and then dried. The weight of the chloride obtained, diminished by 10 grammes, will give the weight of chlorine combined with 10 grammes of silver.

Let us admit that potassa is formed by the combination of 1 equivalent of potassium with 1 equivalent of oxygen. Now, the chloride of potassium is obtained by treating 1 equivalent of potassa KO, with 1 equivalent of chlorohydric acid HCl:

$$KO+HCl=KCl+HO.$$

Thus, the composition of chloride of potassium being known, we can thence deduce immediately that of potassa, by making this proportion: the quantity of chlorine combined with a certain quantity of potassium, is to the quantity of oxygen which would form potassa with this same quantity of potassium, as the equivalent of chlorine = 35.5 is to the equivalent of oxygen = 8.

We therefore conclude from all these determinations that 100 parts of chlorate of potassa contain

Potassium	31.95
Chlorine	28.93
Oxygen	39.12
	100.00

Now, since 31.95 of potassium require 6.52 of oxygen to form potassa, there remains, for chloric acid,

T 2

Chlorine	28.93
Oxygen	32.60
	61.53

100 parts of chloric acid are therefore composed of

Chlorine	47.02
Oxygen	52.98
	100.00

The number we shall assume as the equivalent of chlorine, as will soon be seen, is 35.5. We shall thence find that the composition of chloric acid corresponds to

1 eq. chlorine	35.5
5 " oxygen	40
1 " chloric acid	75.5

Perchloric Acid, ClO_7.

§ 172. We have just seen, that by boiling a solution of chloric acid, chlorous or hypochloric acid is disengaged, and perchloric acid, which remains in the fluid, is formed at the same time.

If sulphuric acid be poured upon chlorate of potassa, the mixture assumes a brownish-yellow tinge, a yellow gas, hypochloric acid, is disengaged, and perchlorate and bisulphate of potassa are formed, which remain in the vessel. The reaction must be assisted by gentle heat, by placing the vessel in a water-bath. This experiment requires great caution, for hypochloric acid is a very explosive gas. The perchlorate of potassa is easily separated from the bisulphate by crystallization, being much less soluble than the latter salt.

The perchlorate of potassa is more readily obtained in another way. When chlorate of potassa is heated in a glass retort, in the preparation of oxygen, the substance first melts, and then gives oxygen off for some time; but if the temperature is not continually increased, the fluidity of the substance decreases, and a point arrives at which it assumes a doughy consistence; the evolution of oxygen then ceases, and commences only when the temperature is again raised. The saline mixture remaining in the retort is composed of perchlorate of potassa and chloride of potassium; it is pulverized, and treated with a small quantity of cold water, which dissolves nearly the whole of the chloride of potassium, while it scarcely affects the perchlorate of potassa, which is not very soluble. The residuum is then treated with boiling water, so as to dissolve it wholly. A large portion of the perchlorate of potassa crystallizes on cooling.

Perchloric acid is obtained from the perchlorate of potassa, by exactly following the process indicated for obtaining chloric acid from the chlorate. But, perchloric acid being much more fixed than chloric, the same precautions in concentrating the dilute solution are unnecessary; for the latter may be evaporated by heat, and the concentrated liquid may be distilled in a glass retort. The first portions which pass over are more watery; the temperature in the retort rises to 392°, and an acid is distilled, having a density of 1.65: it is perchloric acid, at its maximum of concentration. This acid is liquid and colourless, and reddens litmus without bleaching it. It is much more fixed than chloric acid, not only when heated, but even in the presence of oxidizable substances. Thus, when cold, it does not act on sulphurous acid.

§ 173. The composition of perchloric acid is deduced from that of perchlorate of potassa, the salt being analyzed in a mode precisely similar to the chlorate of potassa (§ 171). We thus find that perchloric acid contains,

1 eq. chlorine	35.5	38.78
7 " oxygen	56.0	61.22
1 " perchloric acid	91.5	100.00

Hypochlorous Acid, ClO.

§ 174. If we pass a current of chlorine through a dilute solution of potassa, without heat, no chlorate of potassa is formed, as is the case with a concentrated solution and an elevated temperature; but a liquid is obtained, which possesses, in the highest degree, the property of bleaching organic colouring matter, and which contains chloride of potassium and hypochlorite of potassa. The reaction takes place between 2 equivalents of chlorine and 2 of potassa, and is represented by the following equation:

$$2KO+2Cl=KO,ClO+KCl.$$

If whiting be substituted for the potassa, we obtain a corresponding hypochlorite of lime. These products are of vast importance in the arts, as they are used for bleaching, and are often called *bleaching salts*.

A solution of hypochlorous acid is obtained as follows: After pouring into a large bottle filled with chlorine gas, red oxide of mercury, ground and mixed with water, the bottle is corked and shaken. The chlorine is rapidly absorbed, forming an insoluble oxychloride of mercury and hypochlorous acid, which dissolves in the water. The filtered liquid contains hypochlorous acid only.

Hypochlorous acid may also be procured free from water, by passing a current of dry chlorine slowly through a glass tube *ab* (fig. 225) containing oxide of mercury, and preventing the temperature from rising during the reaction. For this purpose, the tube *ab* is

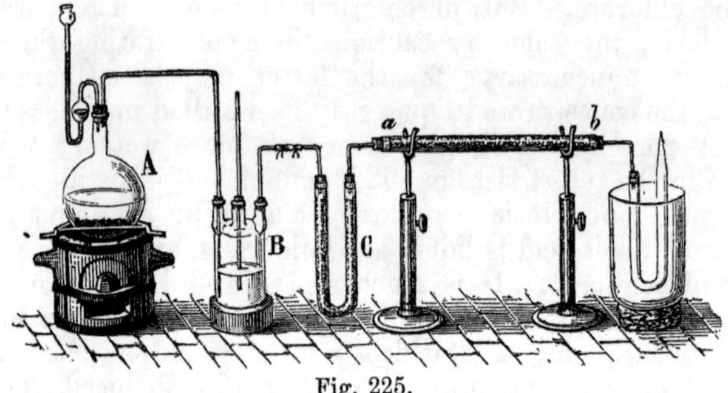

Fig. 225.

surrounded with ice or cold water. Chloride of mercury is again formed, and an orange-yellow gas disengaged, which may be liquefied by conveying it into a tube cooled by a mixture of ice and sea-salt. The temperature should not rise during the reaction; otherwise the hypochlorous acid would entirely decompose, and oxygen alone would be disengaged.

The best oxide of mercury is obtained by decomposing, by an excess of potassa, the nitrate or the chloride of mercury, washing the precipitate, and heating it to a temperature of about 572°.

Hypochlorous acid forms a deep-red liquid, which boils at about 68°, producing an orange-yellow vapour. Water dissolves at least 200 times its volume of the acid, and becomes of a beautiful yellow-colour. The vapour of hypochlorous acid detonates at a very slightly elevated temperature.

The solution of hypochlorous acid exerts powerful oxidizing qualities, decomposing the solutions of protochloride of lead and of manganese, from which it precipitates the binoxide of lead PbO_2 or the sesquioxide of manganese Mn_2O_3. A solution of chlorine does not produce this effect except under the influence of the solar rays.

§ 175. Hypochlorous acid is analyzed as follows:

The gaseous acid is obtained by conveying the chlorine slowly into a tube well cooled and containing the oxide of mercury: to the other end of this tube is fitted a capillary tube, on which several bulbs A, B, C (fig. 226), of a capacity of 20 or 30 cubic centi-

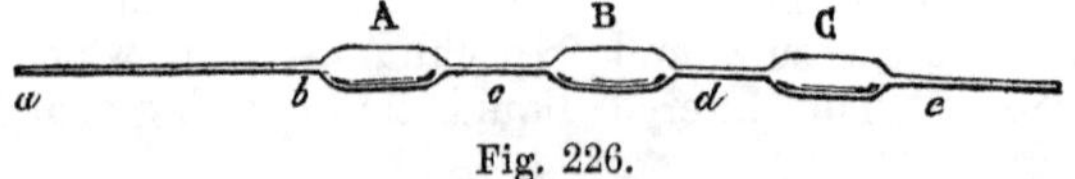

Fig. 226.

metres (1 to 2 cub. in.) have been blown. Heat being applied to the portion *ab* of the tube, the gas decomposes as it reaches this part, and the bulbs are successively filled with a mixture of chlorine and oxygen, in the proportions in which the two gases exist in hypochlorous acid. When we have thus decomposed a sufficient quantity of gas to completely expel the air which originally filled the apparatus, each of the bulbs is closed, by projecting the blowpipe flame upon the points *a*, *b*, *c*, *d* of the capillary tube. Each bulb is then filled with a mixture of oxygen and chlorine in the proportions which form hypochlorous acid, this mixture balancing the pressure of the external atmosphere, at the surrounding temperature. If we open one end of one of the bulbs in a weak solution of potassa, the chlorine is absorbed and the alkaline fluid ascends into the bulb. We sink the bulb so that the level of the fluid shall be the same within and without; then apply the finger to the open end, and remove the tube. Let p' be the weight of the bulb with the fluid it contains. We then fill the bulb completely with the same alkaline fluid, and find its weight p''. Lastly, after having washed and dried the bulb, it is weighed, and found to weigh p. It is evident that the ratio of the weights $\frac{p'-p}{p''-p'}$ is equal to that of the volumes of chlorine and oxygen which enter into the composition of hypochlorous acid. Experiment shows that this ratio is as 2 to 1. We may hence conclude that hypochlorous acid is formed of 2 volumes of chlorine and 1 of oxygen, or 1 equivalent of chlorine, and 1 equivalent of oxygen. We shall therefore have for its composition in weight,

1 eq. chlorine	35.5	81.61
1 " oxygen	8.0	18.39
1 " hypochlorous acid	43.5	100.00

Direct experiment has given, for the density of hypochlorous acid gas, the number 2.977, which shows that it is composed of 2 volumes of chlorine and 1 volume of oxygen condensed into 2 volumes.

In fact, 2 vol. chlorine weighing	4.880
1 " oxygen "	1.105
	5.985

of which the half is 2.9925.

If chlorohydric acid be poured into a concentrated solution of hypochlorous acid, we obtain a copious evolution of chlorine. But, if the two liquids, greatly cooled, are mixed, chlorine is not disengaged; it combines with the water and forms a hydrate of chlorine, which causes the liquid to assume the solid form.

Chlorous Acid, ClO_3.

§ 176. If chlorate of potassa be treated with nitric acid, the chlorate dissolves in the liquid without discoloration, provided the temperature does not exceed 120° to 140°; but, if nitrous acid be poured into the solution, or if the deutoxide of nitrogen be passed through it, reaction instantly ensues, and a yellow gas, which is chlorous acid, is evolved. The easiest way of obtaining this acid consists in heating a mixture of chlorate of potassa, nitric acid, and arsenious acid. The arsenious acid converts the nitric into nitrous acid, which, in its turn, reacts on the chloric acid, depriving it of its oxygen, and reducing it to the state of chlorous acid. The experiment is made in the following manner:

We take...... 3 parts of arsenious acid,
4 " of chlorate of potassa,

and pulverize them together, rub them into a thin paste with water, and add a mixture of

12 parts of ordinary nitric acid,
and...... 4 " of water;

introduce the whole into a flask which is filled to the neck, and heat it carefully in a water-bath.

Chlorous acid is a greenish-yellow gas, which does not liquefy in a refrigerating mixture of ice and sea-salt. Water dissolves about 5 or 6 times its volume of it, and assumes a golden yellow-colour.

§ 177. Chlorous acid cannot be analyzed in the manner pointed out for hypochlorous acid, because, in the decomposition of chlorous acid by heat, a small quantity of perchloric acid is constantly formed, disturbing the results of the analysis.

Chlorous acid combines with bases and forms well-defined compounds, but the combination requires some time to effect it. By pouring into a solution of chlorite of potassa, a solution of nitrate of lead, we obtain a yellowish-white precipitate of chlorite of lead PbO,ClO_3, which may be analyzed by changing it into a sulphate by sulphuric acid. We thus find that 100 parts of chlorite of lead give 88.62 of sulphate of lead, which contain 65.23 of oxide of lead: 100 parts of chlorite of lead are therefore composed of

Oxide of lead	65.25
Chlorous acid	34.75
	100.00

Now, the equivalent of the oxide of lead is 1394.5; the chlorite of lead is therefore composed of

1 eq. oxide of lead	111.7
1 " chlorous acid	59.5
1 " chlorite of lead	171.2

Again, the equivalent 59.5 of chlorous acid corresponds to the following composition of the acid:

1 eq. chlorine	35.5	59.66
3 " oxygen	24.0	40.34
1 " chlorous acid	59.5	100.00

The composition of chlorous acid may also be directly ascertained, by finding the quantity of chlorine contained in 100 parts of chlorite of lead. To do this, we melt in a platinum crucible a known weight of chlorite of lead,* intimately mixed with twice its weight of carbonate of potassa or soda. The oxide of lead is converted into a carbonate, and the chlorous acid affords chloride of potassium. The melted mass is treated with hot water, which dissolves the chloride of potassium and the carbonate of potassa in excess, whilst the carbonate of lead remains in the state of an insoluble residue. The filtered liquid is supersaturated with nitric acid, and an excess of nitrate of silver poured in. The quantity of chlorine contained in the 100 parts of chlorite of lead is inferred from the weight of chloride of silver obtained.

Hypochloric Acid, ClO_4.

§ 178. This compound is obtained by causing concentrated sulphuric acid to act on chlorate of potassa, but the experiment requires great caution, for hypochloric acid detonates with great violence, endangering the apparatus.

Fused chlorate of potassa is preferred. The salt is coarsely broken, placed in a tube closed at one end (fig. 227), sulphuric acid is poured into the tube, and to its open end is fitted a curved tube which is carried to the bottom of a well-dried bottle. The tube is slowly and carefully heated in a water-bath, and it is important not to plunge the tube into the bath as far as the level of the mixture, as the gas might explode. A yellow gas is evolved, which cannot be collected over mercury, because that metal instantly decomposes it, nor over water, which dissolves it in large quantities. If the bottle containing the hypochloric acid be cooled in a refrigerating mixture, it liquefies and forms a red liquid, which boils at 68°. Hypochloric acid detonates with great violence, even in the liquid state. Water dissolves 20 times its volume of it.

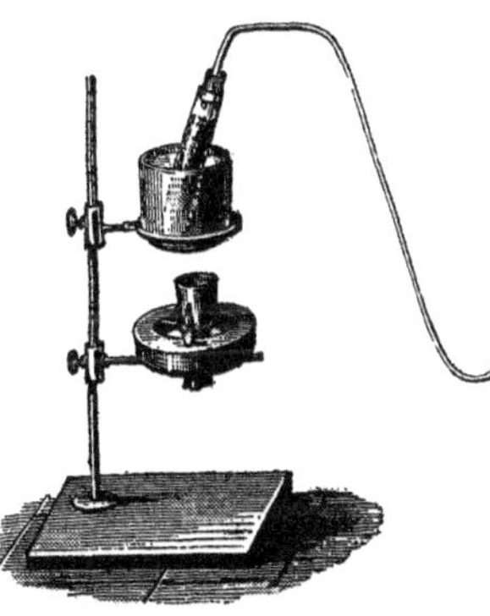
Fig. 227.

Hypochloric acid may be analyzed in the mode described for

* Great care should be used not to employ too high a heat, which would certainly ruin the crucible.—*J. C. B.*

hypochlorous acid, and we thus find it to be composed of 1 volume of chlorine and 2 volumes of oxygen, or of

1 eq. chlorine	35.5	52.59
4 " oxygen	32.0	47.41
1 " hypochloric acid	67.5	100.00

§ 179. Hypochloric is not an acid *per se;* for with bases, it forms a chlorate and chlorite. It is therefore proper to regard it as analogous to hyponitric acid, that is, to suppose it composed of 1 equivalent of chloric and 1 equivalent of chlorous acid: we have, in fact,

$$2ClO_4 = ClO_5 + ClO_3.$$

RECAPITULATION OF THE COMPOUNDS OF CHLORINE AND OXYGEN. EQUIVALENT OF CHLORINE.

§ 180. The five compounds of chlorine and oxygen, which we have studied, present the following composition:

Hypochlorous acid	Chlorine	81.61
	Oxygen	18.39
		100.00
Chlorous acid	Chlorine	59.66
	Oxygen	40.34
		100.00
Hypochloric acid	Chlorine	52.59
	Oxygen	47.41
		100.00
Chloric acid	Chlorine	47.02
	Oxygen	52.98
		100.00
Perchloric acid	Chlorine	38.78
	Oxygen	62.22
		100.00

If we refer these compounds to the same quantity, 100 of chlorine, we shall find:

Hypochlorous acid	Chlorine	100.00
	Oxygen	22.53
		122.53
Chlorous acid	Chlorine	100.00
	Oxygen	67.61
		167.61
Hypochloric acid	Chlorine	100.00
	Oxygen	90.14
		190.14

Chloric acid...................................	Chlorine.....	100.00
	Oxygen......	112.68
		212.68
Perchloric acid..............................	Chlorine.....	100.00
	Oxygen......	157.77
		257.77

The quantities of oxygen which combine with the same quantities of chlorine are to each other as 1 : 3 : 4 : 5 : 7. These numbers are among the most simple of those which can represent similar proportions. Let us therefore suppose that the first compound, hypochlorous acid, be formed of 1 equivalent of chlorine and 1 of oxygen: the numerical value of the equivalent of chlorine will be given by the proportion

$$18.39 : 81.61 :: 8 : x, \text{ whence } x = 35.5.$$

The compounds of chlorine and oxygen will then take the following formulæ and numerical values:

Hypochlorous acid...............	ClO	43.5
Chlorous acid......................	ClO_3.........	59.5
Hypochloric acid..................	ClO_4.........	67.5
Chloric acid........................	ClO_5.........	75.5
Perchloric acid....................	ClO_7.........	91.5

Now, we have found, whilst ascertaining the weight of these various acids which form a neutral anhydrous salt with 1 equivalent of a base, that

The equivalent of chlorous acid is	59.5
" chloric acid	75.5
" perchloric acid......................	91.5

The formulæ of chlorous, chloric, and perchloric acids, as we have just defined them, are therefore verified by the composition of the neutral salts. It is possible that the formulæ of the hypochlorous acid should be Cl_2O_2, and that of hypochloric acid $Cl_2O_8 = ClO_3, ClO_5$. It will be seen, by this splitting of the formula that hypochloric acid may be considered as composed of definite proportions of chlorous and chloric acids.

We shall therefore adopt the number 35.5 as the *equivalent of chlorine*. We shall subsequently see, that this equivalent possesses the property of giving the simplest possible formulæ to the numerous compounds formed by chlorine.

We have seen that, in chloric acid, 1 volume of chlorine was combined with $2\frac{1}{2}$ of oxygen, or 2 volumes of chlorine with 5 of oxygen: that, in perchloric acid, there were 1 volume of chlorine and $3\frac{1}{2}$ of oxygen, or 2 volumes of chlorine and 7 of oxygen. Now, the equivalent in volume of gaseous oxygen being represented by 1 volume, it is evident that the equivalent in volume of chlorine becomes 2 volumes.

§ 181. If we admit the hypothesis (§ 88) that all simple gases contain, for equal volumes, the same number of atoms, we may say that, in chloric acid, 2 atoms of chlorine have combined with 5 atoms of oxygen, and in perchloric acid, 2 atoms of chlorine have combined with 2 atoms of oxygen.

The equivalent of chlorine = 35.5, corresponds therefore to 2 atoms, and the atomic weight of chlorine is 17.75, that is, one-half of the equivalent.

The atomic formulæ of the compounds of chlorine and oxygen would be written as follows:

Hypochlorous acid .... Cl_2O or ꞒlO
Chlorous acid.............................. Cl_2O_3 $ꞒlO_3$
Hypochloric acid........................ Cl_2O_4 $ꞒlO_4$
Chloric acid .... Cl_2O_5 $ꞒlO_5$
Perchloric acid........................... Cl_2O_7 $ꞒlO_7$

COMBINATION OF CHLORINE WITH HYDROGEN.

Chlorohydric Acid, HCl.

§ 182. Chlorine and hydrogen combine directly: if a lighted taper be brought near the mouth of a small bottle containing a mixture of these two gases, they combine with an explosion. Explosion also takes place if a bottle containing the mixture be exposed to the direct rays of the sun. If the bottle be exposed to diffuse light, the two gases still combine, but slowly, and the time required is in proportion to the degree of light. Lastly, in absolute darkness, the two gases appear to have no action on each other. We here see that light produces the same effect as heat.

These gases may be combined so as to ascertain the proportions in which they unite. We select a balloon and a bottle of exactly the same capacity, and grind the neck of each, so that the former exactly fits the latter. The two vessels being perfectly dried, we fill the bottle (fig. 228) with chlorine, and the balloon (fig. 229) with hydrogen, both carefully dried, and then fit the balloon to the bottle: we thus have equal volumes of chlorine and hydrogen. To facilitate the admixture, the balloon is inverted for a few moments (fig. 230): the chlorine, by virtue of its greater density, has a tendency to descend

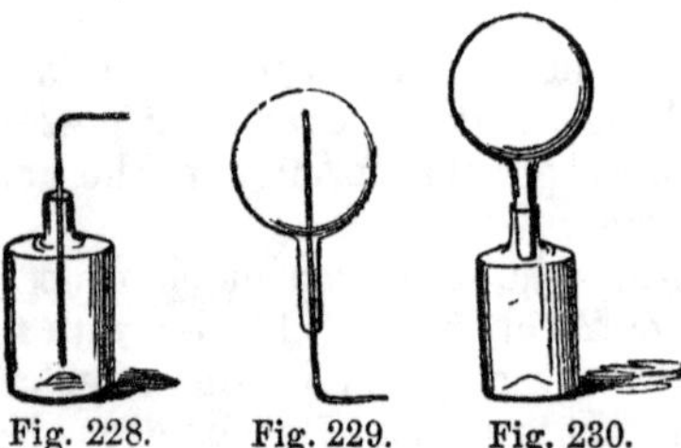

Fig. 228. Fig. 229. Fig. 230.

into the balloon, and the hydrogen, on the contrary, rises into the bottle. The apparatus is left in a well-lighted room, but not exposed to the direct rays of the sun. The green colour of the chlorine fades rapidly, and when no longer perceptible, the apparatus is exposed, for a few moments, to the solar rays, which complete the combination without danger of explosion. The apparatus being taken apart under mercury, we observe that no gas escapes, and that the mercury does not rise in the vessels. Thus, the hydrogen and chlorine, by combining, have produced a gaseous compound which has preserved the same volume under the same pressure. The want of colour of the gas and the non-alteration of the mercury prove that no more free chlorine remains; but an excess of hydrogen may exist. We can prove that there is no more hydrogen, by introducing a small quantity of water into the vessel, when the gas is then entirely absorbed, and the mercury fills the vessel. The water introduced has become strongly acid.

This experiment proves that 1 volume of hydrogen combines with 1 volume of chlorine, and produces 2 volumes of a very acid gas, highly soluble in water. This gas is *chlorohydric* or *hydrochloric acid.*

§183. Chlorohydric acid gas is obtained by treating common salt or chloride of sodium by concentrated sulphuric acid; the water contained in the sulphuric acid taking part in the reaction.

Chloride of sodium......	Chlorine..........................			Chlorohydric acid.
	Sodium....................		Soda	
Concentrated sulphuric acid..................	Water....	Oxygen....		
		Hydrogen..........		Sulphate of soda.
	Sulphuric acid....................			

The reaction is represented by the following equation:

$$NaCl+SO_3,HO=NaO,SO_3+HCl.$$

The chlorohydric acid is collected in a well-dried bell-glass, over mercury.

§184. Chlorohydric acid gas is colourless, gives off copious fumes in the air, which do not form if the atmosphere be perfectly dry. Atmospheric air always contains a certain quantity of vapour of water, with which the chlorohydric acid gas combines, and the compound which results, possessing less tension than that of pure water, is, consequently, precipitated in a form of mist. Chlorohydric acid is very soluble in water, which, at the temperature of 32°, dissolves more than 500 times its volume of it. The solubility diminishes as the temperature rises, so that at 68° water dissolves only 460 times its volume of the gas. The absorption of the gas by water is instantaneous, and is demonstrated as was done in the case of ammonia (§123).

The density of the liquid acid, concentrated in the cold, is

1.21. When heated, it first gives off a considerable quantity of acid gas, which soon ceases, and an acid liquid passes over, presenting an unvarying composition, the boiling point of which is 230°.

A concentrated solution of the acid gives off copious fumes in the air.

If a very dilute solution be distilled, more water than acid passes over at first, and the liquid concentrates in the retort, until it attains the composition of the normal liquid, which boils at 230°.

The solution of chlorohydric acid is one of the most common reagents used in a laboratory. In order to prepare it, we put into a large balloon (fig. 231) equal parts of common salt and oil of vitriol,

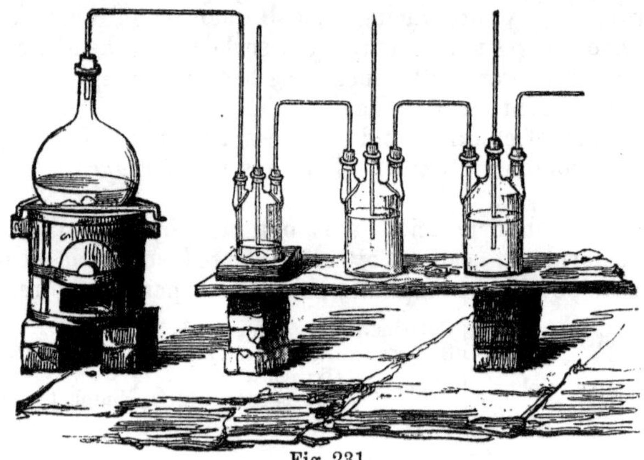

Fig. 231.

to which is added one-third of its weight of water. The balloon connects with a tubulated bottle, which serves as a washing-bottle, and retains the small portion of sulphuric acid brought over by the gas. Succeeding the first bottle, are two others of larger size and three-fourths filled with water. The tubes conveying the gas do not dip deep into the liquid. As the solution becomes more and more dense as it concentrates, the upper strata of the fluid are always less charged, and, consequently, more fitted to dissolve the gas rapidly.

The liquid acid is rarely prepared in the laboratory, being manufactured on a large scale in chemical works, and found at a very cheap rate in commerce. It is obtained by decomposing common salt by sulphuric acid; but, instead of earthen vessels, large cast-iron cylinders, arranged horizontally in a furnace, are used, which send the acid gas into stoneware receivers, having two mouths, and half filled with water, resembling exactly those represented in figs. 181 and 182.

§ 185. The chlorohydric acid* of commerce is rarely pure, almost always showing a yellow tinge, owing to the presence of chloride of iron, and it also contains a small quantity of sulphuric and sometimes of sulphurous acid. It is readily purified by distillation; but it is advisable first to pour into the fluid a small quantity of chloride of barium and shake it, so that the sulphuric acid may be precipitated in the form of sulphate of baryta. If it contains sulphurous acid, some bubbles of chlorine, passed through the liquid, will convert the sulphurous into sulphuric acid.

Fig. 232 represents the apparatus used for the distillation of chlorohydric acid. The retort is heated in a sand-bath. Succeed-

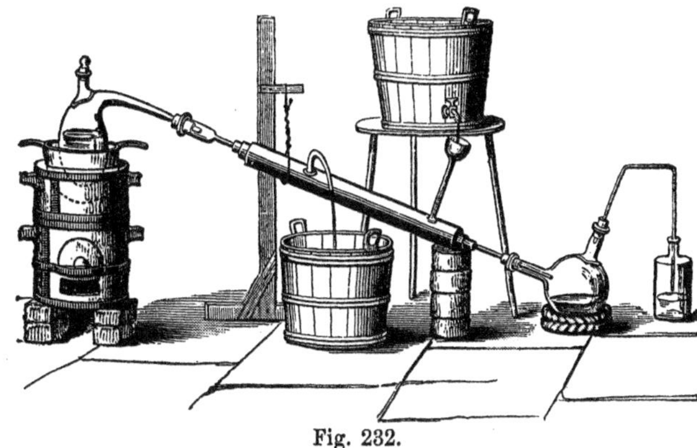

Fig. 232.

ing the balloon-receiver, we arrange a bottle containing a small quantity of water, which retains the greater part of the acid gas driven from the solution by heat.† A solution of the pure acid is perfectly colourless.

§ 186. We have ascertained the composition of pure chlorohydric acid gas by synthesis; but it is more readily done by analysis. In order to do this, a known volume of gas is introduced into a bent tube (fig. 233), over the mercurial trough, and a globule of potassium, passed into this glass by means of a small iron wire, and deposited on the horizontal portion of the tube. An alcohol lamp being applied, the potassium decomposes the chlorohydric acid gas,

Fig. 233.

* Chlorohydric acid is often called *muriatic acid* in commerce: this is the name given to it by the older chemists. They regarded chlorine as a combination of muriatic acid and oxygen, and called it *oxygenated muriatic acid.*

† A very simple and effectual method is to pour oil of vitriol through an S-tube into a flask or retort containing strong and common muriatic acid, whereby the gas is driven over into Woolf's bottles charged with water, without the aid of heat until towards the close of the process. See fig. 195, § 114, for the arrangement, except that a small lamp may be used instead of the furnace.—*J. C. B.*

by seizing upon its chlorine and setting free the hydrogen. The hydrogen is made to pass into the graduated tube in which the chlorohydric gas was measured, and we find its volume to occupy one-half of that previously occupied by the acid.

Now, if from the density of hydrochloric gas... 1.2474
we deduct one-half of the density of hydrogen. 0.0345
there remain.. 1.2129

nearly one-half the density of chlorine: therefore, 1 volume of chlorohydric acid gas contains ½ a volume of chlorine, and ½ a volume of hydrogen, without condensation.

If we wish to know the composition by weight of 100 parts of chlorohydric acid, we make the proportions:

$$1.247 : 0.0345 :: 100 : x = 2.74$$
$$1.247 : 1.2129 :: 100 : y = 97.26.$$

Therefore, 100 parts of chlorohydric acid contain

Hydrogen 2.74
Chlorine 97.26

This composition is expressed in another manner, by referring it to the equivalent 1 of hydrogen: we thus find

Hydrogen 1
Chlorine.. 35.5
36.5

Now, 35.5 is precisely an *equivalent of chlorine.* The acid therefore contains 1 equivalent of hydrogen and 1 of chlorine, and its equivalent weighs 36.5.

1 volume of chlorohydric acid gas contains ½ a volume of hydrogen and ½ a volume of chlorine. If we refer this composition to 2 volumes of hydrogen, we shall say that 4 volumes of the acid gas contain 2 volumes of hydrogen and 2 volumes of chlorine. The equivalent of chlorine in volume will be therefore represented by 2 volumes like that of oxygen, and that of chlorohydric acid by 4 volumes.

We have seen (§ 124) that 1 volume of ammoniacal gas combines with $\frac{2}{2}$ of chlorohydric acid gas, to form the chlorohydrate of ammonia: consequently, 4 volumes or 1 equivalent of ammonia combine with 4 volumes or 1 equivalent of chlorohydric acid. The formula of chlorohydrate of ammonia is therefore

$$NH_3,HCl.$$

We do not know any other compounds of chlorine and hydrogen.

COMBINATIONS OF CHLORINE WITH SULPHUR.

§ 187. Chlorine and sulphur combine in several proportions, but some of these compounds have only been obtained combined with other chlorides. We shall here treat only of the two which have been isolated. The formula of the first is ClS_2, which corresponds to no known compound of chlorine with oxygen in which the chlorine acts as the electropositive element, nor to any compound of sulphur, as the electropositive element, with oxygen.

The formula of the second compound is ClS, which corresponds to hypochlorous acid ClO, or to hyposulphurous acid S_2O_2.

In order to obtain the first compound, chlorine is combined with sulphur, so that the sulphur is in excess: the second is obtained when the chlorine predominates.

The apparatus used is represented in fig. 234.

Fig. 234.

Chlorine is evolved in the balloon A by causing chlorohydric acid to react on the peroxide of manganese; the gas is washed in the bottle B containing water, and then dried by being passed through a tube containing chloride of calcium.

The tubulated retort D containing a certain quantity of sulphur, is connected with a tubulated receiver E, which is kept at a low temperature by a current of cold water from the vessel F. The retort containing the sulphur is heated to a temperature above 212°, while the chlorine is slowly disengaged and brought nearly to the surface of the liquid sulphur; and as it then comes into contact with an excess of vapour of sulphur, the first compound ClS_2 only is formed, which distils over as fast as it is produced. The process is continued until the sulphur in the retort has nearly disappeared. The chloride of sulphur collected in the receiver, contains an excess of sulphur brought over by volatilization; but it is easily removed by redistillation, as the sulphur is much less volatile than the chloride, and remains in the retort.

This chloride of sulphur is a reddish yellow liquid, having a peculiar, disagreeable odour: it boils at 138°. Its density, when liquid, is 1.687. The density of the vapour has been found by experiment to be 4.668.

It decomposes by contact with water; sulphur separating, and chlorohydric, sulphuric, and sulphurous acids being formed. It is composed of

2 eq. sulphur	32
1 " chlorine	35.5
	67.5

1 volume of it, in the gaseous state, is composed of

1 vol. chlorine	2.440
$\frac{1}{3}$ " sulphur $\frac{6.654}{3}$	2.218
theoretical density	4.658

This theoretical density approaches, in fact, very nearly to the density 4.668, which has been found by experiment.

If the solution of the preceding chloride be saturated with chlorine, it absorbs a large quantity of it, and furnishes a deep red fluid, which, for the same quantity of sulphur, contains a double quantity of chlorine. If this substance be subjected to the action of heat, the excess of chlorine which was in solution is at first evolved; but the ebullition soon becomes regular at the temperature of 147°.

The density of this chloride is 1.620. The density of its vapour is 3.549.

Its composition is

1 eq. sulphur	16	31.07
1 " chlorine	35.5	68.93
	51.5	100.00

1 volume of vapour contains

$\frac{1}{6}$ vol. of vapour of sulphur	1.109
1 " chlorine	2.440
	3.549

§188. The chlorides of sulphur are easily analyzed, as follows: We weigh a certain quantity p of it in a closed tube, then insert this tube, previously opened, into a bottle containing 1 litre, half filled with water: the bottle is corked and shaken. The chloride of sulphur is decomposed, forming chlorohydric, sulphuric, and sulphurous acids, and a deposit of sulphur. The latter being separated by filtration, taking care not to lose a drop of the liquid, nitrate of silver is poured into the solution until no precipitate any longer forms, and the precipitated chloride of silver is weighed after desiccation. Let P be its weight: if its composition be known, we know that it contains a weight p' of chlorine, and conclude from the experiment that a weight p of chloride of sulphur contains p' of chlorine, and consequently $(p-p')$ of sulphur.

COMBINATION OF CHLORINE WITH NITROGEN.

Chloride of Nitrogen, NCl_3.

§ 189. This compound is obtained by passing chlorine through a solution of chlorohydrate of ammonia, or any ammoniacal salt. The solution turns yellow, and yellow oleaginous drops soon form, which fall to the bottom of the vessel. Its formation is assisted by a temperature of 77° to 86°. The reaction takes place according to the equation

$$NH_3,HCl+6Cl=4HCl+NCl_3.$$

These oily drops are extremely dangerous to handle, for they often explode spontaneously, and may cause severe accidents. Hence, it is important to understand the circumstances under which this dangerous substance is formed, less when preparing it than to avoid its accidental generation.

Chloride of nitrogen is an orange-yellow fluid, of a density of 1.653. It may be distilled unaltered under a less pressure than that of the atmosphere; but its vapour detonates with extreme violence when it attains the temperature of 212°.

Chloride of nitrogen detonates immediately, at the ordinary temperature, in contact with certain substances, principally with phosphorus, the fixed oils, the essence of turpentine. Its formula is NCl_3, corresponding to ammonia NH_3.

Aqua Regia.

§ 190. A mixture of chlorohydric and nitric acids is called *aqua regia*, a name conferred on it by the alchemists, because it dissolves gold, which they regarded as the *king of the metals*.

When a mixture of chlorohydric and nitric acids is heated, the liquid turns yellow, and if it be boiled, a yellow gas is disengaged, the odour of which recalls at once that of chlorine and of nitrous vapour. This gas is composed of a mixture of chlorine and two peculiar compounds, which we shall call *hypochloronitric* and *chloronitrous* acids. The two compounds are evolved in different proportions, according to the composition of the aqua regia, and as the reaction has more or less progressed. Hypochloronitric acid is obtained by heating, in a bottle A (fig. 235), in a water-bath, an aqua regia made of 1 volume of nitric and 3 of chlorohydric acid. The gaseous product is conveyed into the first bottle B, where some drops of liquid are deposited, then into a tube D filled with pieces of chloride of calcium, which absorbs the moisture; lastly, through a bulb E placed in a refrigerating mixture. In order to judge of the colour of the gas, we generally place an empty bottle C in front of the bulb, and a similar one G after it; and the apparatus is terminated by the tube H, containing a small quantity of water, which allows us to judge of the rapidity of the generation of the gas.

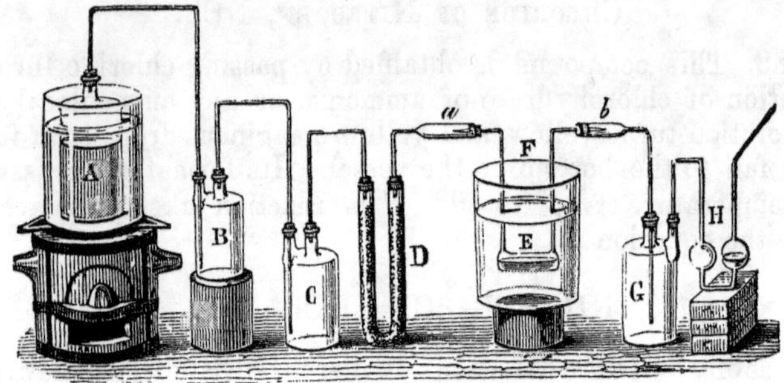

Fig. 235.

The bottle C becomes of a slightly brownish citron-yellow colour, which is the peculiar colour of the gaseous mixture. The greater part of the hypochloronitric and chloronitrous gases condenses in the bulb, in the form of a reddish-brown liquid, and the gas which arrives in the bottle G presents the ordinary colour of chlorine.

When a sufficient quantity of liquid has condensed in the bulb, we seal the points *a* and *b* in a lamp, if we wish to preserve the product. With the proportions of nitric and chlorohydric acids we have supposed, the substance which at first condenses in the bulb is nearly pure hypochloronitric acid; it is a very volatile fluid, which boils at about 44°. Its composition is represented by the formula NO_2Cl_2; and may be regarded as hyponitric acid in which 2 equivalents of oxygen have been replaced by 2 equivalents of chlorine. The reaction from which it arises is represented by the following equation:

$$NO_5+3HCl=NO_2,Cl_2+3HO+Cl.$$

By prolonging the experiment, the condensed product contains proportionally larger quantities of chloronitrous acid. This last compound is slightly less volatile than hypochloronitric acid; its formula is NO_2Cl: it represents nitrous acid of which 1 equivalent of oxygen is replaced by 1 equivalent of chlorine.

Chloronitrous and hypochloronitric acids may be produced by direct combination of chlorine and the deutoxide of nitrogen, by conducting the gaseous products into a bulb cooled by a mixture of ice and crystallized chloride of calcium.

When aqua regia acts on any substance, we may generally suppose that the following reaction takes place between the nitric and chlorohydric acids:

$$NO_5+2HCl=NO_3+2HO+2Cl.$$

If a metal be plunged in this liquid, it dissolves rapidly in the state of a chloride, as in a concentrated solution of chlorine. The metal meets, in fact, in the aqua regia, chlorine in a nascent state, that is, under circumstances in which the combination takes place most easily.

Aqua regia thus acts as a very powerful oxidizing agent; for it converts sulphur into sulphuric acid, much more rapidly than nitric acid alone. This circumstance is owing, on the one hand, to the fact that nitric mixed with nitrous acid oxidizes more powerfully than nitric acid; and, on the other, that chlorine, in contact with water, acts itself as a powerful oxidizing agent, by forming chlorohydric acid and presenting the oxygen in the nascent state.

BROMINE.

EQUIVALENT Br = 80 (100 O = 100).

§ 191. Bromine* is liquid at the ordinary temperature, of a very deep brownish red-colour; almost black when the layer is thick, and of a reddish yellow by transmitted light when the layer is thin. It congeals at −4°, into a crystalline, laminated mass with a grayish tinge. It boils at 116.6°, and at ordinary temperatures the tension of its vapour is considerable. A drop of bromine, in a bottle, volatilizes immediately, filling the vessel with a brownish-red vapour.

The density of liquid bromine is 2.97: that of its vapour is 5.39.

Bromine has a peculiar, very disagreeable odour, whence its name (from βρωμος, a stench). Like chlorine, it acts as a poison on the animal economy, and affects severely the organs of respiration. In all its compounds, it bears a strong analogy to chlorine; its affinities, however, are less active, for chlorine drives it from its combinations. Like chlorine, it destroys organic colouring matter.

Bromine in contact with water at the temperature of 32°, combines with a portion of the water, forming a crystallized hydrate of a brownish red colour, which is more fixed than that of chlorine, and is destroyed only at about 60° or 70°.

Bromine may be procured from bromide of sodium by the

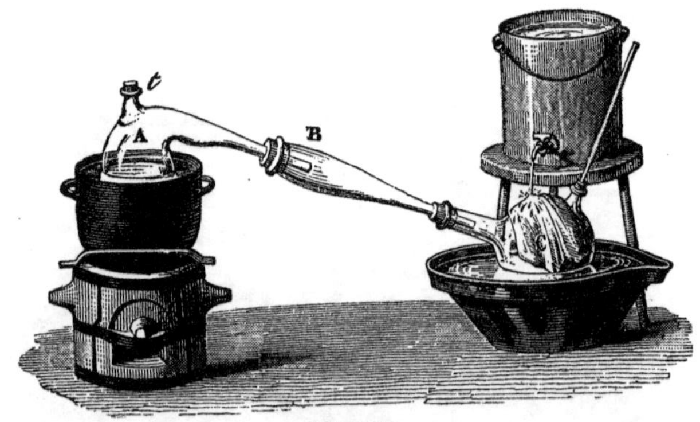

Fig. 236.

* Bromine was discovered in 1826, by Mr. Balard, in the mother waters of the salines of the Mediterranean.

process adopted to procure chlorine from the chloride of sodium, it being only necessary to heat a mixture of bromide of sodium, peroxide of manganese, and sulphuric acid diluted with its weight of water. The mixture is introduced into a tubulated retort (fig. 236) by a funnel in the tubulure *t*. The neck of the retort connects by a cork with the adapter B, communicating with a receiver C, which is cooled by a current of cold water, or by enveloping it in ice. The retort is heated in the water-bath, by placing it in a small kettle filled with water heated over a furnace. The reaction is exactly the same as with chlorine, sulphates of soda and manganese being formed, which remain in the retort, while bromine distils over and condenses in the receiver.

We shall hereafter see how bromine is prepared in manufactories. Its price has hitherto been too great to allow its extensive use in the arts.

COMBINATIONS OF BROMINE WITH OXYGEN.

Bromic Acid, BrO_5.

§ 192. Bromic acid is obtained from the bromate of potassa, which is prepared by dropping bromine into a concentrated solution of potassa, until no more bromine will dissolve in the liquid. The solution is boiled for some time, and, on cooling, deposits small crystals of bromate of potassa. Bromic acid is then extracted from the bromate of potassa, exactly as chloric acid from the chlorate of potassa.

The dilute solution of bromic acid may be evaporated by gentle heat, to the consistence of a syrup; but, if the evaporation be carried further, the bromic acid decomposes.

The composition of the acid is deduced from the analysis of bromate of potassa, in the same way as we deduced from the analysis of the chlorate the composition of chloric acid. We thus find bromic acid to be composed of

Bromine	66.67
Oxygen	33.33
	100.00

Admitting that the formula of bromic acid is BrO_5, similar to that of chloric acid, we find for its composition,

1 eq. bromine	80
5 " oxygen	40
	120

Bromine probably forms several other compounds with oxygen, but they have not been hitherto studied.

COMBINATION OF BROMINE WITH HYDROGEN.

Bromohydric Acid, HBr.

§ 193. Bromine combines with hydrogen, with much more difficulty than chlorine. Thus a mixture of hydrogen and vapour of bromine does not inflame in contact with a lighted taper, and may be exposed to the direct rays of the sun without any combination ensuing; but the combination takes place if the mixture be passed through a porcelain tube heated to redness.

When bromide of sodium is treated with concentrated sulphuric acid, a fuming acid gas is disengaged, which is bromohydric acid; but it is impure, as it contains sulphurous acid and vapour of bromine, owing to the fact that it is decomposed by concentrated sulphuric acid. Water, sulphurous acid and bromine are formed,

Bromohydric acid... { Bromine. / Hydrogen. } Water.
Sulphuric acid....... { Oxygen.... } Water. / Sulphurous acid.

$$HBr+SO_3=SO_2+HO+Br.$$

Pure bromohydric acid gas may be obtained by decomposing bromide of phosphorus, by a small quantity of water.

Bromide of phosphorus. { Bromine .... Bromohydric acid. / Phosphorus.. } Phosphorous acid
Water .... { Oxygen........ } Phosphorous acid / Hydrogen............................ Bromohydric acid.

The reaction is represented by the following equation:

$$PBr_3+3HO=PO_3+3HBr.$$

This experiment is made in the apparatus fig. 237, consisting of a thrice-bent tube *abcde* open at both ends. We place at *d* some bits of phosphorus, and fill the leg *de* with small fragments of moistened glass. By the aperture *a* we pour in the bromine, which falls to *b*. The curve *b* being heated with a live coal, the bromine is volatilized, and meets the phosphorus, with which it combines; but the bromide of phosphorus formed is instantly destroyed by contact with the water, and produces phosphorous acid, which remains in the tube, whilst the bromohydric acid is disengaged, and may be collected over mercury. Very little water should be in the tube, otherwise the bromohydric acid would be entirely dissolved.

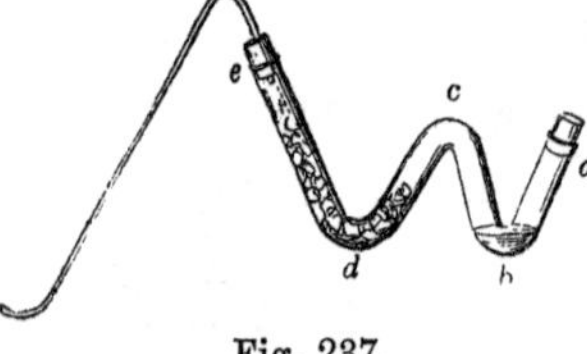

Fig. 237.

Hydrobromic is a colourless acid gas, fuming in the air: its density is 2.731. It is decomposed by chlorine, which seizes its hydrogen to form chlorohydric acid, and frees the bromine, which appears in the form of a brown vapour. If the chlorine be in excess, chloride of bromine is formed. Bromohydric acid is extremely soluble in water, and a concentrated solution gives off copious fumes in the air.

§ 194. It is analyzed in the same way as chlorohydric acid, by decomposing in a bent tube a known volume of bromohydric acid by potassium: we thus find that 1 volume of it contains $\frac{1}{2}$ volume of hydrogen.

Now, if from the density of bromohydric acid ...	2.7310
we subtract half the density of hydrogen............	0.0344
there remains......................................	2.6966

that is, half the density of the vapour of bromine. Bromohydric gas is thus composed similarly to chlorohydric gas, containing a $\frac{1}{2}$ vol. of hydrogen and a $\frac{1}{2}$ vol. of vapour of bromine. Its composition by weight is

1 eq.	hydrogen..........................	1......	1.24
1 "	bromine...........................	80......	98.76
1 "	hydrobromic acid.....	81......	100.00

We shall take as the equivalent of bromine 80, and the equivalent of bromohydric acid will then be 81. The equivalent in volume of the gaseous acid will be represented by 4 volumes.

IODINE.

EQUIVALENT I = 127 (1587.5 O = 100.)

§ 195. Iodine* is solid at the ordinary temperature, presenting the appearance of dark-gray spangles, possessing a high degree of metallic lustre. It melts at 224.6°, forming a brown or nearly black liquid; it boils at about 356°, and gives off a very deep violet-coloured vapour. Iodine gives off very appreciable vapours at the ordinary temperature, which are much more copious toward 120° or 140°, when they are of a beautiful purple-violet hue. From the colour of these vapours it has received its name (from ἰωδης, violet). The vapour of iodine has a peculiar odour, analogous to that of chlorine.

Iodine crystallizes readily. We often find, in the upper part of the bottles which contain it, perfectly regular crystals, deposited there by sublimation. It also crystallizes very readily from solution, which we shall see when treating of iodohydric acid.

Water dissolves but a small proportion of iodine, about $\frac{1}{7000}$, becoming yellow, and it probably exists in this solution in the state of a hydrate. Water dissolves much larger quantities of iodine when it contains certain substances in solution, principally iodides or iodohydric acid, when it assumes a very deep brown colour.

The density of solid iodine is 4.95; that of its vapour 8.716. It greatly resembles chlorine and bromine in its combinations, but its affinities are weaker. It does not destroy the majority of organic substances, and vegetable colours generally resist its action. It combines with several organic substances, imparting to them peculiar colours. It colours the skin brown, but the stain soon disappears.

The most remarkable phenomenon of colouring is that presented by iodine with starch, for an extremely small quantity of it will colour a considerable mass of starch very deeply blue. Advantage is taken of this fact, in the laboratory, to detect the presence of iodine in liquids which are supposed to contain very small quantities of it; and by its means we can ascertain the existence of a millionth part of iodine in solution. The starch is used either in the state of paste, or dissolved in boiling water, and allowed to cool.

---

* Iodine was discovered in 1812, by Courtois: its properties were studied by M. Gay-Lussac.

Iodine is one of the most active poisons, but is used medicinally in goitre and scrofulous diseases.

Iodine is obtained from iodide of sodium, by treating the salt with the peroxide of manganese and sulphuric acid diluted with its weight of water, the same apparatus being used as for bromine (fig. 238). The iodine condenses in the form of crystalline scales

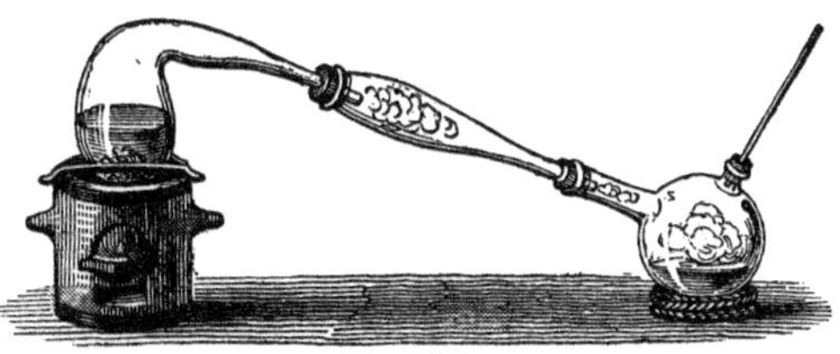

Fig. 238.

in the adapter and receiver. It can be more easily obtained by decomposing a solution of iodide of potassium by a current of chlorine, the iodine being precipitated in the form of a gray powder, which is washed with a little water, and purified by sublimation.

COMBINATIONS OF IODINE WITH OXYGEN.

§ 196. Three of these compounds are known, the first of which will not be described:

1. Hypiodic acid.................................... IO_4
2. Iodic acid.. IO_5
3. Hyperiodic acid .... IO_7.

Iodic Acid, IO_5.

§ 197. Iodic acid is obtained by heating iodine with highly concentrated nitric acid. When the iodine has entirely disappeared, the liquid is allowed to cool, and the greater portion of the iodic acid deposits in the form of crystals.

Iodic acid may also be obtained from the iodate of potassa. This salt is prepared by adding iodine gradually to a boiling solution of potassa until it is saturated. The liquid, on cooling, deposits iodate of potassa, and iodide of potassium remains in solution. The reaction resembles the production of chlorate of potassa in a similar manner. Iodate of potassa is dissolved in hot water, and a concentrated and boiling solution of chloride of barium poured into the still hot liquid, which precipitates iodate of baryta. It is washed, heated, and decomposed by sulphuric acid, forming insoluble sulphate of baryta, while the evaporated liquid deposits crystals of iodic acid.

The best method of preparing iodic acid, in larger quantities, consists in putting equal parts of iodine and chlorate of potassa into a flask with 5 parts of water, to which a few drops of nitric acid have been added. By heating it, chlorine is given off copiously, and the iodine remains in solution in the state of iodic acid. The theory of this operation is very simple: the small quantity of nitric acid added, assisted by heat, decomposes a corresponding quantity of chlorate of potassa, forming a small quantity of nitrate of potassa and chloric acid, which parts with all its oxygen to a corresponding quantity of iodine, while chlorine is disengaged. The iodic acid formed reacts, in its turn, on the chlorate, decomposing an additional quantity of it; whereby chloric acid is set free, and is decomposed in the same manner as before. The iodic acid combines, as fast as it forms, with the potassa of the chlorate, so that, at last, all the chlorate is converted into iodate, the small quantity of nitric acid originally added only serving to commence the reaction.

A solution of chloride of barium in hot water, being poured into that of the iodate of potassa, a copious precipitate of iodate of baryta ensues, which is washed several times, and the iodic acid separated by sulphuric acid.

Crystallized iodic acid contains 1 equivalent of water. If these crystals be heated, they lose at first a small quantity of water, but soon decompose into iodine and oxygen.

The composition of iodic acid is deduced from the analysis of iodate of potassa, the analysis being like that of the chlorate. Iodic acid contains

1 eq. iodine	127	76.05
5 " oxygen	40	23.95
	167	100.00

The formula of the crystallized acid is IO_5+HO.

Periodic Acid, IO_7.

§ 198. A current of chlorine is passed through a solution of iodate of soda, to which carbonate of soda is added, and kept constantly boiling. If the liquid be then allowed to cool, periodate of soda is deposited in silky tufts, which are dissolved in nitric acid, and nitrate of silver is added, which precipitates periodate of silver but slightly soluble. By resolution in boiling nitric acid and cooling, periodate of silver is again deposited. Treated with water, periodate of silver decomposes into basic periodate of silver, which remains, and acid periodate, which dissolves. The solution, when evaporated, yields crystals of periodic acid.

The crystals fuse at about 266°; at a higher temperature, first lose their water of crystallization, and then decompose. They first change into iodic acid, by giving off oxygen, and then, iodic acid itself is decomposed into iodine and oxygen.

The composition of periodic acid corresponds to that of perchloric, and is represented by

1 eq. iodine	127	69.40
1 " oxygen	56	30.60
1 " periodic acid	183	100.00

COMBINATIONS OF IODINE WITH HYDROGEN.

Iodohydric Acid, HI.

§ 199. The affinity of iodine for hydrogen being much more feeble than that of bromine, they do not directly combine, even when a mixture of hydrogen gas and vapour of iodine are passed through a porcelain tube heated to redness. If iodide of sodium be heated with concentrated sulphuric acid, iodohydric acid is not obtained, but only a mixture of sulphurous acid gas and vapour of iodine. There is a mutual decomposition of the sulphuric and iodohydric acids.

Iodohydric acid......	Iodine.	
	Hydrogen.	Water.
Sulphuric acid	Oxygen....	
	Sulphurous acid.	

$$HI+SO_3=SO_2+HO+I.$$

Iodohydric acid is obtained by decomposing iodide of phosphorus by a small quantity of water. Alternate layers of phosphorus, iodine, and broken glass, moistened with water, are introduced into a tube closed at one end (fig. 239), and gently heated. The iodide of phosphorus decomposes as fast as it forms, by contact with water, phosphorous acid being formed, which remains in the tube, and the gaseous iodohydric acid given off. The gas cannot be collected over mercury, which decomposes it by seizing upon the iodine, and liberating the hydrogen, but it must be collected in a dry tincture-bottle, like chlorine (§ 167). The density of iodohydric acid gas is 4.443. It is colourless, fumes copiously in the air, is extremely soluble in water, and generates a strongly acid solution, which fumes when concentrated.

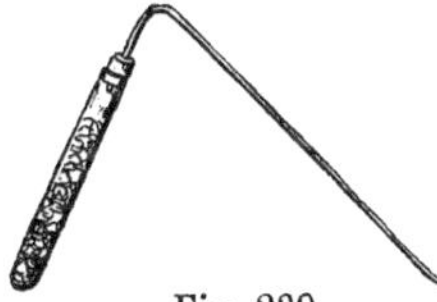
Fig. 239.

Iodohydric acid is not a very stable compound; for bromine and chlorine readily decompose it by seizing upon its hydrogen and liberating its iodine. It is also decomposed, when in solution, by the oxygen of the air, at ordinary temperatures. In fact, its solution soon becomes coloured in the air, a portion of the acid being decomposed by the oxygen of the air, water being formed, and the liberated iodine dissolving in the unchanged iodohydric acid; for a solution of the acid dissolves a large quantity of iodine. As the decomposition of the acid progresses, the colour of the liquid becomes more brown, and there soon remains too little unaltered acid to hold all the iodine in solution, so that it begins to be slowly deposited in very regular and often large crystals.

Iodohydric acid cannot be analyzed in the same manner as chlorohydric and bromohydric acids, that is, by decomposition with potassium in a bent tube over mercury, as this metal itself decomposes it. But it can be readily shown that the acid is composed of 1 volume of hydrogen and 1 volume of vapour of iodine united without condensation. In fact, if we add,

to the density of hydrogen	0.0692
the density of iodine vapour	8.7160
we find	8.7852

nearly the double of 4.443, which has been found by experiment to be the density of iodohydric acid gas.

Its composition in weight is, therefore,

Hydrogen	00.78
Iodine	99.22
	100.00

Or,

Hydrogen	1
Iodine	127
	128

By taking 127 as the equivalent of iodine, that of iodohydric acid gas becomes 128; and the equivalent of the gaseous acid is 4 volumes, like that of chlorohydric and bromohydric acids.

COMBINATION OF IODINE WITH NITROGEN.

Iodide of Nitrogen, NI_3.

§ 200. Iodide of nitrogen is a fulminating compound, like the chloride, but is solid at ordinary temperatures. It is obtained by pouring concentrated ammonia upon small quantities of powdered iodine in watch-glasses. In a quarter of an hour, the compound being formed, is poured upon small filters, and appears as a grayish-black powder, which is rapidly washed. It does not generally detonate while moist, although at times explosion takes place, even in the watch-glasses, when it is touched with a glass rod; but, as soon as it is dry, it detonates on the slightest friction, even that of a feather, and often explodes spontaneously. Its formula, analogous to that of the chloride, is NI_3.

COMBINATIONS OF IODINE WITH SULPHUR.

SULPHURETS OF IODINE.

§ 201. No definite sulphurets have yet been obtained; for when heated together, they combine, but if the temperature be raised, the combination is destroyed and the iodine volatilized.

COMBINATIONS OF IODINE WITH CHLORINE.

CHLORIDES OF IODINE.

§ 202. If a current of chlorine be passed over iodine in a glass tube, the two substances combine, forming at first a brown liquid, but, by continuing the action of chlorine, it forms a yellowish-white crystalline body. These combinations have been hitherto but little studied.

FLUORINE.

EQUIVALENT F = 19 (237.5 O = 100).

§ 203. The properties of isolated fluorine are, as yet, unknown, owing less to the difficulty of separating this substance from its combinations, than to its great affinity for the materials of which our chemical apparatus is generally made; for it instantly attacks glass and all the metals, even platinum. It has only been obtained in vessels cut out of *fluor-spar*, by decomposing fluoride of silver by chlorine, the fluorine being evolved in the form of a colourless* gas.

The compounds of fluorine with oxygen are unknown, but we can readily prepare its compound with hydrogen, fluohydric acid, an acid of great practical importance.

COMBINATION OF FLUORINE WITH HYDROGEN.

FLUOHYDRIC ACID, HF.

§ 204. This acid is obtained by acting with sulphuric acid on fluoride of calcium, or *fluor-spar*, a common mineral. As fluohydric acid attacks glass, porcelain, and the majority of metals, it is prepared in vessels of lead or platinum. The apparatus generally used in the laboratory consists of a leaden retort (fig. 240), made of two pieces which fit into each other, the lower piece, shaped like a cup, containing the mixture, and the upper forming the head and neck of the retort, which conveys the acid vapours into a receiver. The latter is a bent leaden tube, fitted on the neck of the retort, and with a small hole at its end, to give vent to the expanded air, or the excess of vapour: the receiver is surrounded with ice during the operation.

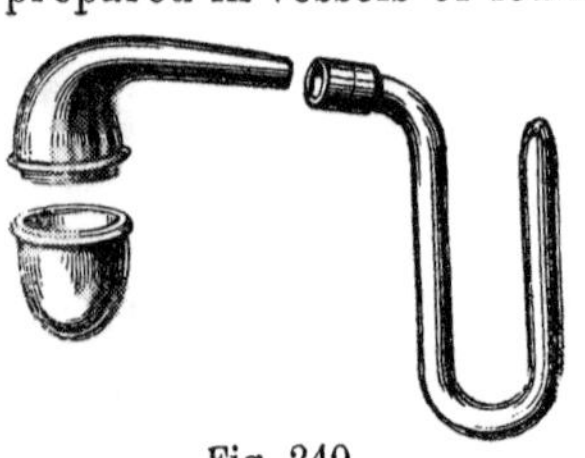
Fig. 240.

The *fluor-spar*, finely powdered, is placed in the cup, and twice its weight of concentrated sulphuric acid poured upon it, and stirred with a platinum or leaden spatula. The apparatus is then fitted together, and the joints covered with an earthy luting, kept in its place by a paper band. The retort is then heated, taking care not to elevate the temperature to the point of fusion of the

* Some say a yellowish gas.—*J. C. B.*

lead. When the operation is terminated, the fluohydric acid which has condensed in the receiver is poured into a silver or leaden vessel, closed with a well-ground stopper of the same.

The fluohydric acid thus obtained is anhydrous, and in order to procure it diluted with water, a certain quantity of water is put into the receiver, and greatly facilitates the condensation of the acid vapours.

The theory of the process is simple, being the same as that for preparing chlorohydric acid (§ 184):

$$CaF+SO_3,HO=CaO,SO_3+HF.$$

Fluohydric acid is very dangerous to handle, a drop of anhydrous acid on the skin producing very acute inflammation—often accompanied with fever. A burn over a large surface might prove fatal. When diluted with water, it is much less corrosive, but, even then, must be handled with caution.

Anhydrous fluohydric acid is a colourless liquid, of the density 1.06, does not congeal at any temperature, and boils at about 86°. It gives off thick, white fumes in the air, from its combination with aqueous vapour, showing a great affinity for water, with which it combines in every proportion; but when sufficiently diluted, it ceases to fume in the air. When the anhydrous acid is poured into water, each drop produces a hissing sound like that of red-hot iron.

Fluohydric acid attacks glass, by a chemical action which will subsequently be explained. It is hence used to engrave on glass, and mark the divisions on thermometer-scales and graduated tubes (§ 83). Engraving can also be executed by gaseous fluohydric acid, whereby still finer divisions are obtained, and more visible, because opaque; while those made by the liquid acid are transparent, and must be deep to be readily seen. To engrave with gas, the body to be marked is exposed to its fumes, arising from a mixture of fluor-spar and concentrated sulphuric acid in a leaden box.

Fluohydric being very analogous to chlorohydric, bromohydric, and iodohydric acids, its composition is probably similar; that is, it is composed of a ½ volume of fluorine and a ½ volume of hydrogen, without condensation. But the composition has not yet been verified by direct experiment, because fluorine has not been isolated so as to determine the proportion, nor has the density of the gaseous acid been determined.

§ 205. The composition by weight of fluohydric acid and the equivalent of fluorine may be ascertained as follows.

A certain weight of fluor-spar, reduced to an impalpable powder, is treated with concentrated sulphuric acid, in a platinum crucible, until it is completely converted into a sulphate, to effect which it must be moistened several times with sulphuric acid, and the excess of acid driven off by heat. The sulphate of lime is at last heated to redness.

It is thus shown that 10 grammes of fluor-spar or fluoride of calcium, CaF, give 17.436gm of sulphate of lime, CaO,SO_3.

Now, the composition of sulphate of lime, or its proportion of lime and sulphuric acid, is easily determined, synthetically, by moistening 10 grammes of pure quicklime, CaO, with sulphuric acid, in a platinum crucible, evaporating off the excess of acid and calcining the sulphate of lime produced.

It is thus found that 10 grammes of lime give 24.286gm of sulphate of lime; and hence we infer that the sulphate of lime contains,

Lime	41.18
Sulphuric acid	58.82
	100.00

Now 58.82 of sulphuric acid contains 35.292 of oxygen, and we have seen (§ 135) that, in neutral sulphates, the quantity of oxygen of the base is $\frac{1}{3}$ of that in the acid; hence 41.18 of lime contains,

Oxygen	11.766
Calcium	29.414
	41.180

Consequently, 100 of lime contain,

Oxygen	28.57	or 1 eq.	oxygen	8
Calcium	71.43	or 1 "	calcium	20
	100.00	or 1 "	lime	28

We may hence calculate, by a simple proportion, that the quantity of calcium in our 17.436gm of sulphate of lime is 5.129.

In the 10 grammes of fluoride of calcium, there are, therefore, 5.129gm of calcium, but as we regard it as formed exclusively of calcium and fluorine, the 10 grammes contain 4.871gm of fluorine, and the composition of fluoride of calcium is

Fluorine	48.72
Calcium	51.28
	100.00

If we admit that the formula of fluoride of calcium is CaF, that is, composed of 1 equivalent of fluorine and 1 of calcium, we can determine the equivalent of fluorine from the following proportion:

$$51.28 : 48.72 :: 20 : x \text{; whence } x = 19.$$

Moreover, the reaction which produces fluohydric acid, and which is represented by the equation

$$CaF + SO_3 + HO = CaO,SO_3 + HF,$$

shows that fluohydric acid is composed of 1 equivalent of fluorine and 1 of hydrogen, and that it therefore contains

1 eq. fluorine	19	95.00
1 " hydrogen	1	5.00
1 " fluohydric acid	20	100.00

This example shows how the composition of bodies which cannot be directly analyzed can be ascertained. But, it is important to observe that our reasoning is based upon this hypothesis, that fluoride of calcium contains only calcium and an element, fluorine, which has not yet been certainly isolated, and, consequently, the foregoing formulæ are inaccurate, if our hypothesis is unfounded.

PHOSPHORUS.

EQUIVALENT P = 32 (400 O = 100).

§ 206. Phosphorus* may be procured in three states; solid, liquid, and gaseous. At the ordinary temperature of summer, it is as soft and yielding as wax; but at the temperature of melting ice, it is hard and friable. Crystallized phosphorus cannot be obtained by fusion, because it passes gradually from the liquid to the solid state, a circumstance always opposed to crystallization; but it can be made to crystallize from its solution. If 2 parts of phosphorus and 1 of sulphur be melted together under water, a compound is obtained containing an excess of phosphorus in solution, from which a portion of it is deposited on cooling, and frequently assumes the form of regular rhombic dodecahedra. (See fig. 22.) Sulphuret of carbon may also be used as a solvent of phosphorus, and when the solution is slowly evaporated, in a current of carbonic acid gas, at the ordinary temperature, it affords beautiful crystals.

The density of phosphorus is about 1.77. It is nearly colourless and translucent when perfectly pure, but it generally has a slightly yellowish tint. It changes colour and becomes red, even in vacuo, when exposed to solar light, which proves that the change is due to molecular modifications, and not to chemical action.

It melts at above 111.5°, and boils at 554°: its vapour is colourless, and has a density of 4.326.

Phosphorus has a powerful affinity for oxygen, and when heated in the air to about 140°, inflames, an effect which may often be produced by simple friction. Exposed to the air, it undergoes a slow combustion, even at ordinary temperatures, so that a stick of phosphorus, in the air, is always surrounded by a light vapour, which is constantly renewed, and is luminous in the dark. From this property it has received its name (from φως, *light*, and φορος, *bearing*). It diminishes considerably by exposure to the air, and at last, if continued sufficiently long, disappears entirely. It is easy to prove that this phenomenon is accompanied by a true combustion of the phosphorus; for if the experiment be made in a bell-glass containing a certain volume of air and placed over the pneumatic cistern, the volume of the gas will be observed to diminish in consequence of the absorption of the oxygen of the air. After

---

* Phosphorus was discovered in 1669, by Brandt, an alchemist in Hamburg, who obtained it by calcining the residue after the evaporation of urine. Brandt kept his process a secret. Kunckel discovered it some years subsequently. But it was only in 1769 that Gahn and Scheele discovered that phosphorus existed in large quantities in the bones of animals, and made known the process for extracting it from them.

some time the light ceases, and with it the diminution of volume; but the phenomenon is repeated, if an additional quantity of pure air be introduced. Air which has been for some time in contact with phosphorus has been deprived of all its oxygen, and can no longer support combustion. If pure oxygen be substituted for air in the bell-glass, the phosphorus is observed to shine only when the temperature is above 68°, while the light would be apparent in atmospheric air at a much lower temperature. We might hence infer that phosphorus burns more readily in atmospheric air than in pure oxygen; and yet we know that its combustion is much more active in oxygen. It has been ascertained that it only combines directly with oxygen, at a low temperature, when this gas is highly expanded, as when it has only the density it possesses in atmospheric air, where $\frac{1}{5}$ of oxygen is mixed with $\frac{4}{5}$ of nitrogen. If a fragment of it be placed in a balloon filled with oxygen, communicating with an air-pump, at a low temperature, it will be observed that the phosphorus is not luminous when the elasticity of the gas is equal to that of the atmosphere; but, upon rarefying the gas by the pump, the phenomenon of light immediately appears.

If marks be made on a wall with a stick of phosphorus, in the dark, they continue luminous for some time, and cease to be so only when the phosphorus which adhered to the wall has disappeared by evaporation and combustion.

Phosphorus, inflamed in oxygen or in the air, produces a white, pulverulent, very deliquescent substance, the *phosphoric acid.* But when it undergoes slow combustion in the air, at ordinary temperatures, it does not form phosphoric acid, but an inferior degree of oxidation, the *phosphorous acid.* We thus find the same substance produce, by its direct combination with oxygen, two different compounds, according to the temperature at which the combination takes place.

Phosphorus is a very dangerous substance to handle, as it so readily inflames; and a burn from it is painful and difficult to heal. It is kept in the laboratory in bottles filled with water. When we wish to use a piece of phosphorus, one of the sticks is taken from the bottle, and a fragment cut off with scissors, while still wet; it is dried with filtering-paper, and handled as little as possible.

It is much more combustible when impure than when perfectly pure. We frequently find use in the laboratory for the phosphorus remaining from divers processes, and in which it is mixed with a small quantity of red oxide of phosphorus. These fragments are more combustible than pure phosphorus, and require to be still more carefully handled, as they often take fire, when dry, in the higher temperatures of the air.

It changes even under water, in corked bottles, when exposed to light, losing its superficial transparency. In this case, it seems to experience only a change in its molecular condition. The change being more slow when protected from light, it should be kept in an opaque vessel, or the bottle containing it should be in a tin or pasteboard case.

By rapid cooling, phosphorus undergoes a modification analogous to that of sulphur under the same circumstances; but it is more difficult to effect it. If melted phosphorus, heated nearly to its boiling point, be poured into very cold water, a dark-brown mass is obtained, the consistence of which is very different from that of ordinary phosphorus. The experiment only succeeds with very pure phosphorus, which has been several times distilled. The presence of a small quantity of foreign matter sensibly changes the physical properties of phosphorus: thus, a thousandth part of sulphur renders it brittle, even at a temperature above 68°.

As phosphorus boils at a low temperature, it may be readily distilled in glass vessels, but the operation demands great caution, on account of its inflammability. In order to distil a small quantity, it is put into a glass retort (fig. 241), the neck of which fits a moderately large tube, *abc*, bent in the form of the letter U, at the bottom of which a layer of water intercepts the communication with the external air and preserves the distilled phosphorus. The retort being heated, the dilated air depresses the water and causes it to rise in the second leg of the tube U, until it can traverse the fluid column in the shape of bubbles. The phosphorus soon distils over, condenses, and falls to the bottom of the bent tube, where it remains fluid, if the temperature of the water be above 104°. If the distillation stops, or even slackens, absorption may take place; but it is not dangerous if the apparatus be properly arranged. The vapour of phosphorus condensing in the retort causes a vacuum, so that the water rises in the leg *a* by the pressure of the atmosphere, and if this leg be not sufficiently large, the water may be driven into the retort, which would burst, and the operator run the risk of a severe burn by phosphorus. But if the leg *a* be large enough to contain all the water, the air enters the retort in the form of bubbles, and no explosion need be feared. The tube *ab* serves, at the same time, as a receiver and a safety-tube.

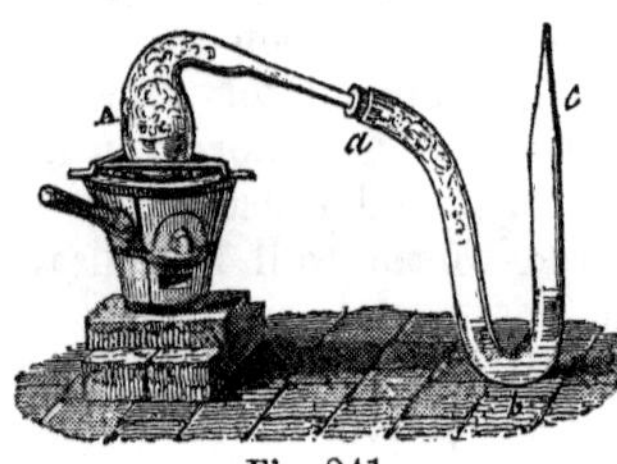

Fig. 241.

We have stated that phosphorus became red when exposed to solar light. It is then converted into a very remarkable isomeric modification, in which it presents properties entirely different from those of ordinary phosphorus. The red modification is obtained in large quantities by keeping phosphorus for several hours at a temperature between 446° and 482°, in a gas on which it exerts no chemical action. The experiment may be made in a retort previously filled with hydrogen or carbonic acid gas. A considerable portion of it distils and condenses as ordinary phosphorus, while another portion is converted into the red modification, the quantity of which increases as the operation is continued. The retort is allowed to cool, and the substance treated several times with sulphuret of carbon, which dissolves the ordinary and leaves the modified phosphorus, in the form of an amorphous powder of a more or less deep red colour.

Red phosphorus differs from the ordinary modification, not less in its chemical than in its physical properties; for while ordinary phosphorus melts at 111°, the red may be heated to 482°, without becoming liquid; but at 500° it passes into the ordinary modification.

Red phosphorus has no sensible odour at ordinary temperatures, but remains unchanged in the air, and is not luminous unless heated to 392°. It does not combine with sulphur, even at the point of fusion of the latter, while ordinary phosphorus, slightly heated with sulphur, combines with it explosively.

These two modifications afford the most remarkable example of isomerism, presenting greater differences in their physical properties and behaviour to reagents than many different simple bodies. The chemical identity of the particles composing the two modifications is only demonstrated by the absolute identity of the compounds which they form.

§ 207. Phosphorus plays an important part in the animal economy, forming a constituent of bones. When bones are burned in the air, their organic matter is completely destroyed, and given off in the form of gaseous products, and the ashes which remain are only a mixture of carbonate and basic phosphate of lime. From these bone-ashes the phosphorus of commerce is extracted. To 3 parts by weight of ashes are added 2 pts. of sulphuric acid, and 15 or 20 pts. of water; the mixture is stirred, and allowed to stand for 24 hours. The sulphuric acid decomposes the carbonate of lime, forming with the lime sulphate of lime, and driving off the carbonic acid. Another portion of the acid acts on the basic phosphate of lime, without entirely decomposing it; for it merely removes a portion of the lime, by forming an additional quantity of sulphate of lime, and leaves the phosphate in the state of an acid phosphate of lime. The latter salt is very soluble in water, while sulphate of lime is but sparingly soluble. The two salts are separated by pouring the whole into a bag of close muslin, which retains the sulphate of lime, and allows the solution of acid phosphate to pass through. The solution being evaporated in a copper vessel to the consistency of syrup, powdered charcoal is gradually added, and the mass completely dried. The mixture, dried at a dull red-heat, is put into an earthenware retort (fig. 242), coated externally with an argillaceous luting, with

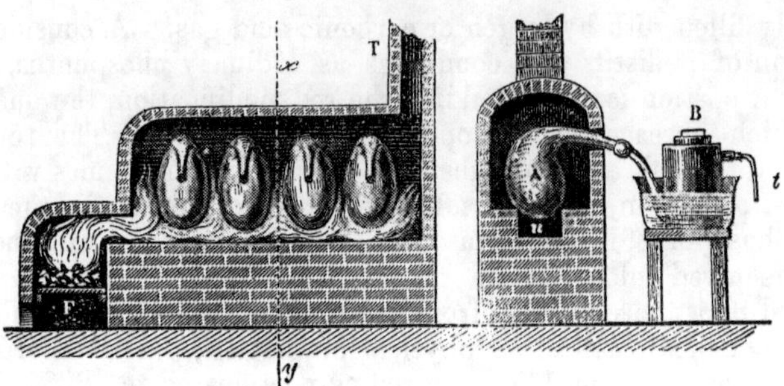

Fig. 242.

its neck fitted into the tube of a copper receiver B, half filled with water, and supplied with a discharging tube *t*. A range of several of these retorts is placed in a reverberatory furnace, communicating with one or two fires, the flame of which passes through the furnace by the horizontal flue *u*, and escapes from the chimney T. The receivers B are placed in the same trough, filled with water, which is kept at a temperature of about 104°, in order that the phosphorus may not become solid and obstruct the tube. A gentle heat being applied at the commencement of the operation, inflammable gases, consisting of hydrogen and oxide of carbon, are disengaged, arising from the water of the acid phosphate of lime, with which it is chemically combined, and retains with force until subjected to a high temperature. As soon as the water becomes free, it is decomposed by the incandescent carbon, producing hydrogen and oxide of carbon,

$$HO+C=CO+H.$$

The acid phosphate of lime is decomposed into a basic phosphate, which is not altered, and phosphoric acid, which, by contact with ignited carbon, gives off phosphorus and oxide of carbon:

Phosphoric acid............ { Phosphorus. / Oxygen...... }
Carbon .... } Oxide of carbon.

$$PO_5+5C=P+5CO.$$

The phosphorus distilling over condenses in a liquid state in the tube and receiver, while basic phosphate of lime remains in the retort, mixed with the excess of charcoal. The phosphorus is filtered by being pressed through a chamois-skin, under hot water, and thus cleansed of its impurities.

Lastly, to give it the usual form of sticks, a slightly conical glass tube is plunged into the phosphorus melted under water, sucked at the other end, and when the column of liquid phosphorus ascends the tube, the opening is suddenly closed with the finger.

and the tube plunged into a bucket of cold water to solidify the the phosphorus. It may then be pushed out by thrusting a rod into the narrower end of the moulding tube.

§ 208. The ready combustibility of phosphorus has led to its application to friction-matches and apparatus for producing instantaneous light, and hence its manufacture has greatly increased within the last few years.

Phosphoric lights consist of small leaden vials, at the bottom of which is a small stick of phosphorus. They must be kept tightly closed, and, in order to use them, an ordinary sulphur match is plunged in, to which some particles of phosphorus adhere. The match does not inflame at once, but must be rubbed on a piece of cork or wood. Such apparatus is dangerous; and, moreover, soon becomes useless, when not kept well corked, for the phosphorus, absorbing oxygen from the air, is converted into phosphorous and phosphoric acids, which attract moisture and destroy the efficiency of the apparatus.

Phosphoric matches, also called *chemical matches*, are ordinary sulphur matches, on the end of which is a small quantity of a hardened combustible paste, which inflames by friction on a hard body. The combustible principle of such pastes is always phosphorus, but other substances yielding oxygen are added, to facilitate the combustion, such as nitrate and chlorate of potassa, and certain metallic oxides, as binoxide of manganese and sesquioxide of lead, or red lead, which readily part with a portion of their oxygen. Chlorate of potassa renders the paste detonating by friction, so that a portion of the burning substance may sometimes be projected to some distance. That made with nitrate of potassa burns tranquilly, but a small quantity of the chlorate seems necessary to render them sufficiently inflammable.

To prepare the paste, phosphorus is melted in a due proportion of water, at 122°, a given quantity of chlorate and nitrate of potassa added, which dissolve in the water; then the metallic oxides, if any be used, and, lastly, mucilage of gum. The whole is stirred until a homogeneous paste is obtained, in which no globule of phosphorus can be seen. The paste is usually coloured with Prussian blue, or red lead.

The ends of sulphur matches are dipped into the paste, and allowed to dry. By rubbing them on a rough hard body, the phosphuretted substance inflames, communicates the same to the sulphur and thence to the wood. To render the friction more effectual, a small quantity of pounded glass is sometimes added to to the paste.*

* There are two classes of phosphoric matches in use; those containing little or no admixture of a body yielding oxygen, which inflame quietly, and those containing such body, and inflaming more or less vigorously, in proportion to its quantity. Those containing Prussian blue as colouring matter are also mixed with

COMBINATIONS OF PHOSPHORUS WITH OXYGEN.

§ 209. Phosphorus affords four compounds with oxygen, three of which are acids, viz.:

1. Phosphoric acid.................................. PO_5
2. Phosphorous acid................................ PO_3
3. Hypophosphorous acid .... PO

The fourth is a neutral compound, an oxide of phosphorus, containing less oxygen than the acids.

PHOSPHORIC ACID, PO_5.

§ 210. Phosphorus, when burned in oxygen or in the air, gives off dense white fumes, which is deposited in the form of a white powder, and rapidly attracts moisture from the air: it is phosphoric acid. In order to obtain any considerable quantity of it, a large dry bell-glass is placed upon an equally well-dried plate (fig. 243), on which a saucer is put containing some pieces of quicklime, and allowed to remain for several hours, in order to dry the enclosed air. The saucer being removed, is replaced by a smaller one, containing a piece of previously ignited phosphorus. Combustion goes on under the bell-glass, as long as it contains sufficient oxygen; phosphoric acid is deposited, in the form of a white powder, on the sides of the glass and on the plate, and after the complete combustion of the phosphorus, there remains in the saucer a reddish substance, the oxide of phosphorus. The pulverulent phosphoric acid is rapidly collected by means of a platinum spatula, and sealed up in a dry bottle.

Fig. 243.

The process may be rendered continuous by means of the apparatus represented in fig. 244, in which the phosphorus is burned in a large three-necked balloon, previously dried. The cork which closes the upper tubulure is traversed by a large tube *ab* of 12 or

clay, chalk, and the like neutral absorbents, whereby the deliquescent acids of phosphorus are either prevented from forming or absorbed. The best matches of rapid ignition contain a mixture of nitrate and binoxide of lead, made by treating red lead with nitric acid, and evaporating to dryness. The pastes with the above ingredients are put on the end of sulphur matches, but some are now made for domestic use without being previously dipped into sulphur. They are made of a very resinous wood, or of soft pine imbued with a little terpentine, and the paste put on their end usually contains, beside nitrate and binoxide of lead, a little chlorate of potassa and sulphur.—*J. C. B.*

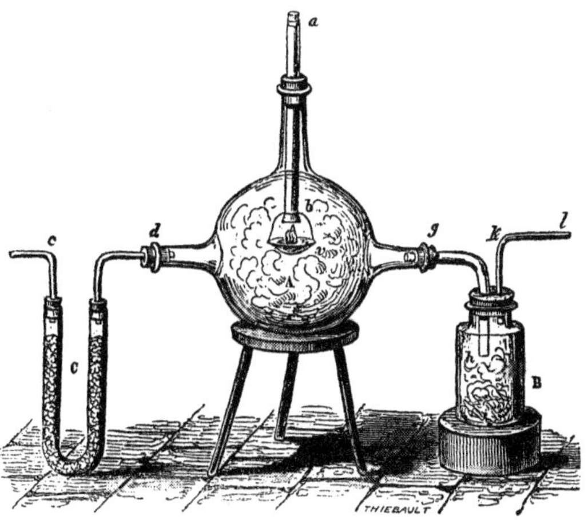

Fig. 244.

14^{mm} diameter, open at both ends, and descending to about the middle of the balloon, where a small porcelain saucer *v* is attached, by a platinum wire. To the second neck *d* a tube C is fitted, filled with some desiccating substance, such as pumice-stone imbued with oil of vitriol. Lastly, to the third neck *g* a large bent tube *gh* is fitted, the other end of which dips into a dry bottle B. This latter is connected by the tube *kl* with a suction apparatus, which may be either a suction bellows or an aspirator, or, lastly, a simple metal tube, of some length, placed either obliquely or vertically, and heated so as to produce a strong draught. A continuous current of air is thus established, which is dried in the tube C, passes through the apparatus, and reaches the aspirator. A piece of phosphorus is dropped through the tube *ab*, kindled by a hot wire, and the upper end *a* then closed with a cork. The phosphorus burns into phosphoric acid, a portion of which is deposited in the balloon A, and the remainder in the bottle B. When the first piece of phosphorus has nearly disappeared, a second may be dropped in, and so on, as long as desirable. It need hardly be said, that the phosphorus should be carefully dried by filtering-paper before being dropped into the saucer.

The phosphoric acid thus obtained is anhydrous, has a great affinity for water, rapidly attracting moisture from the air, and deliquescing; when thrown into water, it produces a sound like that of red-hot iron plunged into this liquid, showing that there is a great deal of heat disengaged in the combination of the anhydrous acid with water.

When the aqueous solution of the acid is evaporated, it yields a syrupy liquid, which deposits crystals of hydrated phosphoric acid, when sufficiently concentrated, but if the solution be still further heated in a platinum capsule, it loses the last portions of water which can be expelled by heat, and fuses, at a red-heat, into a transparent viscid fluid, which solidifies in the form of a vitreous mass. The fused acid gives off sensible vapours, at a red-heat, but even then is still very far from its boiling point at the ordinary pressure of the atmosphere.

Vitreous phosphoric is not anhydrous phosphoric acid, for it still retains 11.2 per cent., or an equivalent of water, which heat alone cannot expel; so that phosphoric acid, once combined with water, can never be restored to the anhydrous state by heat alone.

§ 211. The hydrated acid may be obtained directly by dissolving phosphorus in nitric acid. One part of phosphorus and 13 pts. of nitric acid, diluted to the density of 1.20, are heated in a glass retort (fig. 245), the neck of which connects with a cooled receiver. Reddish fumes are copiously given off, and the phosphorus rapidly disappears. When the nitric acid is more concentrated, the action may become so violent that the vapours and gases, unable to escape by the neck of the retort, may produce a dangerous explosion. If the acid be too dilute, the action is too feeble, and a portion of it distils over without acting on the phosphorus. When the greater part of the liquid has passed into the receiver, the process is arrested, the distillate poured back into the retort, and redistilled. This operation is called *cohobation.*

Fig. 245.

When the phosphorus is completely dissolved, the distillation is continued until the liquid in the retort has assumed a syrupy consistence, when it is poured into a platinum capsule, and the concentration completed, for, in order to drive off the last portions of water and nitric acid, a degree of heat is required at which the phosphoric acid would attack the glass of the retort, and, consequently, become impure. Since fused phosphoric acid contains 11.2 per cent. of water, the quantity of oxygen in this water is to that in the anhydrous acid as 1 : 5; so that the formula of the hydrate is PO_5+HO.

If the vitreous acid be left under a bell-glass, with twice as much water as it already contains, it is converted into a crystalline mass, which is also a definite hydrate, having the formula of PO_5+3HO. The same crystals frequently form in a solution of phosphoric acid sufficiently concentrated.

Lastly, if the vitreous acid come in contact with as much more water only as it already contains, we obtain crystals different from the preceding, and represented by PO_5+2HO.

We are thus acquainted with three well-defined hydrates of phosphoric acid:

1. Monohydrated phosphoric acid........ PO_5+HO
2. Bihydrated " " .... PO_5+2HO
3. Trihydrated " " .... PO_5+3HO

Each of these acids generates a series of peculiar salts, presenting distinct properties, which will be noticed more in detail, when treating of the phosphates:

1. Monobasic phosphates.................... PO_5+RO
2. Bibasic " .... PO_5+2RO
3. Tribasic " .... PO_5+3RO.*

Phosphoric acid is sometimes obtained by calcining phosphate of ammonia, which is procured by decomposing by ammonia the acid phosphate of lime, obtained by treating bone-ashes with sulphuric acid, as in the preparation of phosphorus. The process is economical; but the acid obtained always contains some ammonia.

Phosphoric is a very powerful acid, less energetic, however, at common temperatures, than sulphuric; but, as it is much more fixed, it always expels the latter from its combinations, when the temperature is sufficiently elevated.

§ 212. The composition of phosphoric acid is thus determined: 10 grammes of it are converted into phosphoric acid, by nitric acid in a glass matrass, and the excess of nitric acid, with the greater part of the water, driven off by boiling. 100 grammes of pure oxide of lead being then weighed in a large platinum crucible, the acid contained in the matrass is poured on it, and the matrass several times carefully washed with distilled water, which is added to the liquid in the crucible. After evaporation to dryness, it consists of the oxide of lead and the phosphoric and nitric acids which combined with this oxide; but if the crucible be heated to redness,† the nitric acid is expelled, and the 100 grammes of oxide of lead has increased in weight by the phosphoric acid produced from 10 grammes of phosphorus. We hence conclude, that 10 grammes of phosphorus produce 22.50^{gm} of phosphoric acid; which gives the following composition of phosphoric acid:

Phosphorus..	44.44
Oxygen..	55.56
	100.00

* RO or MO is a general expression for protoxide bases, R signifying radical, and M, metal.—*J. C. B.*

† This would unquestionably endanger the crucible.—*J. C. B.*

The quantity of water contained in hydrated phosphoric acid is ascertained by the process described for sulphuric acid (§ 136).

Phosphorous Acid, PO_3.

§ 213. We have seen that, when phosphorus is burned freely in oxygen or atmospheric air, it is converted into phosphoric acid. But its combustion may be regulated so as to produce an inferior degree of oxidation, (phosphorous acid,) by allowing a slow current of air to pass over the phosphorus gently warmed. In order to perform this experiment, a piece of phosphorus is put into a tube *ab* (fig. 246), drawn out to a very fine opening at one end, the other end being connected with an aspirator filled with water. The phosphorus being warmed, and the water of the aspirator made to flow very slowly, almost drop by drop, air enters by the opening at *a*, and its oxygen burns the phosphorus only into phosphorous acid which condenses, in the form of a pulverulent sublimate, in the anterior portion of the tube *ab*. The sublimate may be volatilized, from one spot to another, in the atmosphere of nitrogen which fills the tube, but it takes fire when heated in contact with the air, and is converted into phosphoric acid.

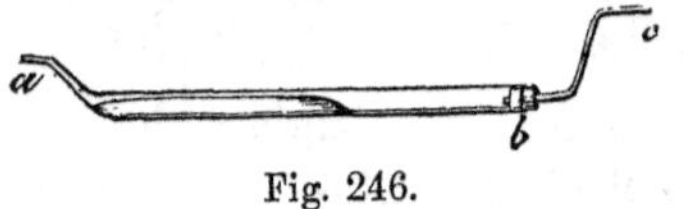

Fig. 246.

Phosphorus, exposed to the air at common temperatures, is always surrounded by a white vapour, which is luminous in the dark, and condenses by contact with water into an acid liquid, which is chiefly composed of phosphorous acid, and in order to obtain any quantity of the acid by this process, a stick of phosphorus is put into each one of a number of glass tubes, as *ab* (fig. 247), terminated at one end by an opening of 1 or 2 millimetres in diameter, and entirely open at the other. Some twenty of them thus charged are placed in a funnel (fig. 248,) in a bottle containing water. The bottle is placed on a plate, and the whole covered by a bell-glass open at top.

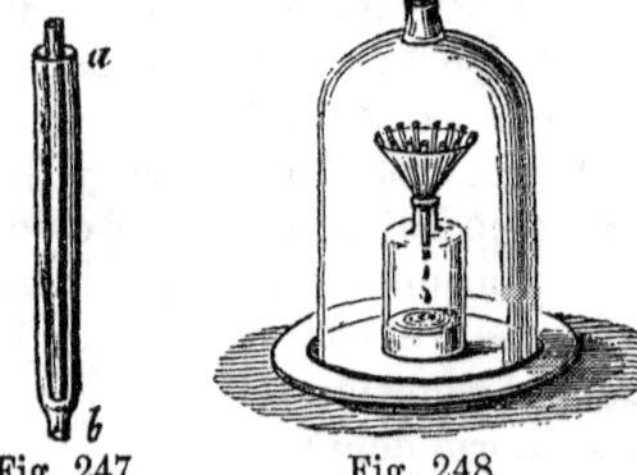

Fig. 247. Fig. 248.

Phosphorus burning slowly in the air, at common temperatures, and the phosphorous acid which results from the combustion, being heavier than the air, descends into the bottle, and dissolves in the water, so that a pretty concentrated solution of this acid may be obtained in a few days.

If the sticks of phosphorus were placed unprotected in the funnel, the heat evolved by their slow combustion would raise the temperature sufficiently to cause their rapid combustion, when phosphoric acid would be the principal product. The glass tubes surrounding the sticks prevent this effect, and the combustion is still less active because the air has not free access to the surface of the combustible.

Nevertheless, the solution thus obtained always contains a portion of phosphoric acid, from the fact that phosphorous acid, by contact with the air, rapidly absorbs oxygen and changes into phosphoric acid. It will therefore be observed that, in the experiment just described, it is difficult to prevent the transformation of a portion of the phosphorous into phosphoric acid.

Phosphorous acid may also be obtained very pure by decomposing protochloride of phosphorus PCl_3 by water; 3 equivalents of chlorohydric and 1 of phosphorous acid being formed. The reaction may be thus represented:

$$PCl_3+3HO=3HCl+PO_3.$$

The phosphorous and chlorohydric acids remain in the liquid, but, by evaporating it to the consistence of a syrup, the former acid is disengaged; and if the concentrated liquid be placed under the receiver of the air-pump, it often becomes a mass of crystals, which are hydrated phosphorous acid, with the formula

$$PO_3+3HO.$$

If the evaporation of hydrated phosphorous acid, by heat, be pushed still farther, the acid will soon begin to decompose, evolving a mixture of hydrogen and phosphuretted hydrogen, which takes fire in the air, and phosphoric acid remains in the liquid. The water and phosphorous acid are simultaneously decomposed; a portion of the hydrogen arising from the decomposition of water being disengaged, while another portion combines with phosphorus of the decomposed phosphorous acid, and the oxygen of this acid, as well as that arising from the decomposition of water, unites with the phosphorous acid remaining, and changes it into phosphoric.

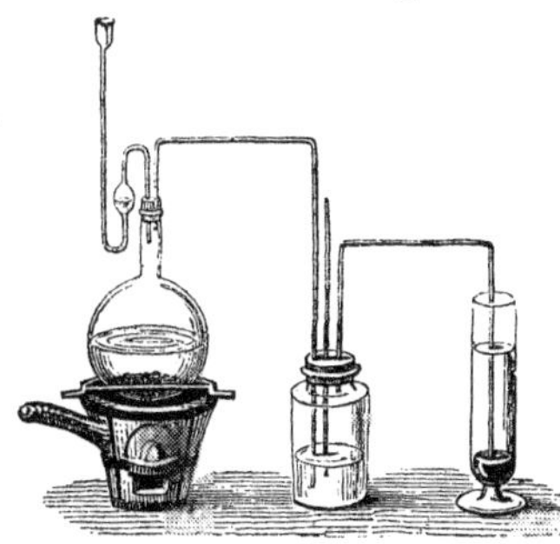

Fig. 249.

§ 214. This acid is further obtained, by causing chlorine to react upon phosphorus in contact with water. A quantity of phosphorus is put under a stratum of water at the bottom of a test-glass (fig. 249), which is kept in a water-bath at 104°–120°, in order that the phosphorus may remain liquid.

Chlorine, being conveyed by a tube to the bottom of the glass, combines with the phosphorus; but the chloride of phosphorus is immediately decomposed, by contact with the water, into phosphorous and chlorohydric acids.

It is difficult, however, to obtain very pure phosphorous acid by this method, because an excess of chlorine rapidly converts the phosphorous into phosphoric acid in contact with water.

§ 215. The composition of phosphorous acid is easily deduced from that of the protochloride of phosphorus; for it appears that, when the protochloride is decomposed by contact with water, its 3 equivalents of chlorine are replaced by 3 equivalents of oxygen. If, therefore, we knew the composition of the protochloride, we could readily calculate the composition of phosphorous acid from the numerical values of the equivalents of chlorine and oxygen.

Now, the elementary composition of protochloride of phosphorus may be exactly determined by decomposing 10 grammes of it by shaking it with water in a ground-stoppered bottle, and then ascertaining the weight of chloride of silver which the solution thus obtained precipitates in a solution of nitrate of silver in excess. It would be found that this weight is 31.085^{gm}, containing 7.686^{gm} of chlorine. The 10 grammes of protochloride consequently contain 7.686^{gm} of chlorine; whence, 100 grammes of protochloride of phosphorus are composed of

Chlorine	76.86
Phosphorus	23.14
	100.00

or,

1 eq. phosphorus	32
3 " chlorine	106.5
1 " protochloride of phosphorus	138.5

Phosphorous acid being formed by means of the protochloride, by replacing the chlorine with an equivalent quantity of oxygen, it must evidently contain,

1 eq. phosphorus	32	57.14
3 " oxygen	24	42.86
1 " phosphorous acid	56	100.00

Hypophosphorous Acid, PO.

§ 216. When phosphorus is boiled with a solution of potassa, soda, baryta, or with whiting, the water is decomposed, phosphuretted hydrogen disengaged, and a hypophosphite of the base is formed, which remains in solution in the liquid. A similar reaction takes place when the phosphuret of lime or baryta is decomposed by water.

Free hypophosphorous acid is easily obtained from the hypophosphite of baryta, by precipitating the baryta with sulphuric acid. The liquid may then be evaporated to the consistence of syrup without decomposition, but it never crystallizes; and when still further heated, the hypophosphorous acid is decomposed; spontaneously inflammable phosphuretted hydrogen gas being evolved, and phosphoric acid remaining.

Hypophosphorous acid exhibits a great affinity for oxygen, by reducing a great number of metallic oxides, and converting those of mercury and copper into their metallic state. Aided by a gentle heat, it decomposes concentrated sulphuric acid, disengaging sulphurous acid, and depositing sulphur.

Hypophosphorous acid forms definite salts with bases, several of which are susceptible of crystallization, and are easily obtained by decomposing the hypophosphite of baryta by soluble sulphates.

The composition of hypophosphorous acid deduced from the analysis of the hypophosphites, has been found to be

1 eq. phosphorus	32	80.00
1 " oxygen	8	20.00
	40	100.00

It is important to remark here, that all the hypophosphites hitherto analyzed contain water, which cannot be removed without decomposing them; and as it is possible that the elements of this water enter into the composition of the acid, its formula would be less simple than that we have assigned to it.

Oxide of Phosphorus.

§ 217. When a piece of phosphorus contained in a small capsule is burned in the air or in oxygen, there always remains after the combustion a red residuum, which is an oxide of phosphorus containing less oxygen than hypophosphorous acid. But the product is impure from admixture with phosphoric acid. It is obtained in a pure form by putting phosphorus in a test-glass (fig. 250), filled with hot water to keep the phosphorus melted, and passing a current of oxygen to the bottom of it. The phosphorus then burns under water, producing phosphoric acid which dissolves, and oxide of phosphorus which floats on the liquid in the form of red flocculi. The flocculi are collected on a filter, rapidly dried on filtering-paper, after being well washed, and then treated with sulphuret of carbon, which dissolves the free phosphorus mixed with the oxide.

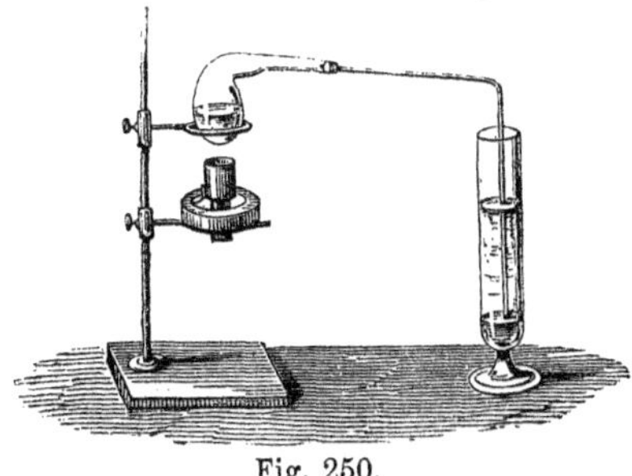

Fig. 250.

Oxide of phosphorus rapidly absorbs the oxygen of the air, and is finally converted into phosphoric acid; but if heated without contact of the air, it is decomposed into phosphorous and phosphoric acids.

When phosphorus is mechanically mixed with a small quantity of oxide of phosphorus, it is much more combustible than when pure. Such mixtures are frequently found in laboratories when old residues of phosphorus kept in badly-stoppered bottles are melted; such impure phosphorus, being more combustible, requires more careful handling than transparent phosphorus.

In order to ascertain the composition of the oxide of phosphorus, a given weight of it (say 1 gramme) is converted into phosphoric acid, by means of nitric acid, and a known weight p of oxide of lead is added to the liquid, more than sufficient to saturate the phosphoric acid formed. It is evaporated to dryness, and the residuum calcined until reddish vapours cease to be given off. If p' be the weight of the residue, it is evident that $(p'-p)$ is the weight of the phosphoric acid formed. As the composition of phosphoric acid is known, we know the weight q of phosphorus contained in $(p'-p)$ of phosphoric acid, and conclude from the experiment that 1 gramme of oxide of phosphorus contains q of phosphorus, and therefore $(1-q)$ of oxygen. The various analyses thus made of the oxide of phosphorus have given different results, and its true formula is yet uncertain.

RECAPITULATION OF THE COMBINATIONS OF PHOSPHORUS WITH OXYGEN.

Equivalent of Phosphorus.

§ 218. The three well-ascertained compounds of phosphorus with oxygen are composed as follows:

Hypophosphorous acid	Phosphorus	80.00
	Oxygen	20.00
		100.00
Phosphorous acid	Phosphorus	57.14
	Oxygen	42.86
		100.00
Phosphoric acid	Phosphorus	44.44
	Oxygen	55.56
		100.00

The composition of these substances, referred to the same quantity 100 of phosphorus, is

Hypophosphorous acid..................	Phosphorus.....	100.00
	Oxygen.........	25.00
		125.00
Phosphorous acid........................	Phosphorus.....	100.00
	Oxygen.........	75.00
		175.00
Phosphoric acid..........................	Phosphorus.....	100.00
	Oxygen.......	125.00
		225.00

The quantities of oxygen which have combined with the same quantity of phosphorus in these three compounds, are to each other as the numbers 1 : 3 : 5. The most simple formulæ which can be assigned to them are, therefore,

Hypophosphorus acid .... PO
Phosphorous acid.................................. PO_3
Phosphoric acid.................................... PO_5

The equivalent of phosphorus is therefore deduced from one of the following proportions :

$$\left.\begin{array}{l} 20.00 : 80.00 :: \ 8 : x \\ 42.86 : 57.14 :: 24 : x \\ 55.56 : 44.44 :: 40 : x \end{array}\right\} \text{whence } x = 32.$$

The numerical value of the equivalents of the three compounds will therefore be,

Hypophosphorous acid...................... PO $= 40$
Phosphorous acid............................ $PO_3 = 56$
Phosphoric acid .... $PO_5 = 72$

Let us compare these theoretical equivalents with the equivalents immediately deduced from the analysis of the salts.

The analysis of the hypophosphite of lead has shown that the equivalent of hypophosphorous acid was equal to 40; so that the formula PO is the one proper to that acid.

The examination of the phosphites has led to a similar conclusion for phosphorous acid, and confirmed the formula PO_3.

We shall hereafter find that phosphoric acid forms several series of salts with the same base, and that we must admit of its forming three classes of salts.

1. Salts in which 1 eq. of acid saturates 3 eq. of base.
2. Salts " 1 eq. of acid " 2 eq. "
3. Salts " 1 eq. of acid " 1 eq. "

The numerical value for the equivalent of phosphoric acid, deduced from the analysis of these various salts, always remembering their various modes of saturation, is constantly 72. Hence, a detailed examination of the phosphates confirms the formula PO_5 for phosphoric acid.

The density of the vapour of phosphorus has been found to be 4.326, by direct experiment. It is easy to calculate the volume of gaseous phosphorus which represents its equivalent in volume. In fact, starting from the composition of phosphorous acid, which we regard as composed of 1 equivalent of phosphorus and 3 equivalents of oxygen, the 3 equivalents of oxygen are represented by 3 volumes, which weigh 3 (1.1056)=3.3168; and from which the proportion is made

$$24 : 32 :: 3.3168 : x.$$

This gives for the weight of the vapour of phosphorus which has combined with 3 volumes of oxygen, x=4.4224, which differs but little from the density 4.326, determined by direct experiment. Phosphorous acid therefore contains 3 volumes of oxygen and 1 volume of vapour of phosphorus, and the equivalent of gaseous phosphorus is represented by 1 volume.

In the atomic theory, the compounds of phosphorus and oxygen are written as follows:

Hypophosphorous acid..................	P_2O or PO
Phosphorous acid.........................	P_2O_3 or PO_3
Phosphoric acid...........................	P_2O_5 or PO_5

Two atoms of phosphorus therefore correspond to our equivalent, so that the atomic weight of phosphorus is 16. This mode of composition has been adopted because it gives formulæ to the compounds of phosphorus with oxygen and hydrogen similar to those of the compounds of nitrogen with the same elements.

Had we started with the hypothesis (§ 88) that all simple gases contain the same number of atoms for equal volumes, we would never arrive at different atomic formulæ. In fact, the composition of phosphoric is different from that of nitric acid, for in the latter, 5 volumes of oxygen are combined with 2 of nitrogen, while, in phosphoric acid, the 5 volumes of oxygen have combined with only 1 volume of vapour of phosphorus. If, therefore, the atomic formula of nitric acid be N_2O_5, conformably to the hypothesis alluded to, that of phosphoric acid must be PO_5. The formulæ of the two acids, and, consequently, of the other combinations of nitrogen and phosphorus, would no longer be similar.

COMBINATIONS OF PHOSPHORUS WITH HYDROGEN.

§ 219. Phosphorus and hydrogen combine in three proportions: 1. A gaseous compound called *phosphuretted hydrogen;* 2. A liquid compound with excess of hydrogen; 3. A solid compound containing the greatest proportion of phosphorus.

Phosphuretted hydrogen gas is obtained by several processes: 1. A small flask (fig. 251) is two-thirds filled with a concentrated solution of caustic potassa, to which a few pieces of phosphorus are added: heat being applied, small bubbles of gas are disengaged, which inflame as soon as they reach the air. A small quantity of gas is allowed to escape before adapting the discharging-tube, in order to expel the air from the flask: an indispensable precaution, for, if the flask were closed immediately, the inflammable gas, coming in contact with the confined air of the flask, might produce an explosion. The gas is evolved under water, and each bubble, as it reaches the air, inflames, producing a curling ring of white vapour, which enlarges as it rises. The circles are very regular when the air is calm. If the bubbles be passed into a bell-glass containing oxygen, the flame is much more brilliant, but the experiment requires great caution, and the bubbles of gas must be very small, or otherwise an explosion would ensue.

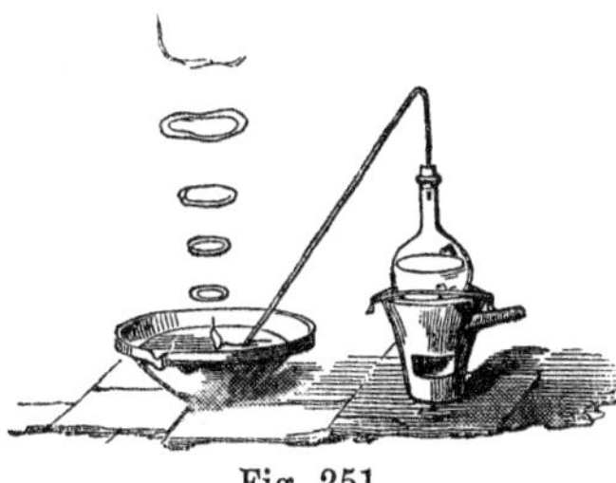

Fig. 251.

The following is the theory of this reaction:—Phosphorus alone does not decompose water, but in contact with potassa, the affinity of the base for hypophosphorous acid, which is one of the products of the reaction, causes the reaction in the same manner as, in the preparation of hydrogen gas, the presence of sulphuric acid causes the decomposition of water by zinc, at ordinary temperatures (§ 69). A portion of phosphorus combines with oxygen to form hypophosphorous acid, which, with the potassa, produces the hypophosphite of potassa, while the hydrogen combines with another portion of phosphorus, and is disengaged in the state of phosphuretted hydrogen.

The gas thus obtained is often mixed with free hydrogen, as may be ascertained by introducing into the bell-glass a solution of sulphate of copper, which absorbs the phosphuretted hydrogen and sets the hydrogen free. The presence of the latter gas is thus explained: if a solution of hypophosphite of potassa be heated with an excess of potassa, water is decomposed, its oxygen changing the hypophosphite into a phosphate of potassa, and its hydrogen being disengaged. This reaction may occur simultaneously with the first, in the process just described.

Hydrated lime may be substituted for the solution of potassa, by making a paste of slacked lime and water, and rolling it into small balls, each of which contains a small piece of phosphorus.

A number of such balls being put into a matrass, and heated, the phosphorus melts and produces a reaction similar to that just described.

But the best process, and that which affords the purest gas, consists in decomposing the phosphuret of calcium by water. The phosphuret is prepared by heating lime in a current of vapour of phosphorus. A strong glass tube, closed at one end, is filled with balls made of the hydrated lime and calcined, and some pieces of phosphorus are placed at the bottom of it. The tube being heated to redness, some hot coals are brought near the end containing the phosphorus, which is volatilized, and its vapour, passing through the tube, combines with the lime.

To procure a large quantity of the phosphuret, a large earthen crucible (fig. 252), having a hole in the bottom, to which is fitted the neck of a small flask containing phosphorus, is filled with balls of lime. The crucible is placed over the grate of a furnace, so that the flask containing the phosphorus shall be below the grate. The crucible being heated to redness, and some coals brought near the flask to vaporize the phosphorus slowly, its vapour passes into the crucible and combines with the lime.

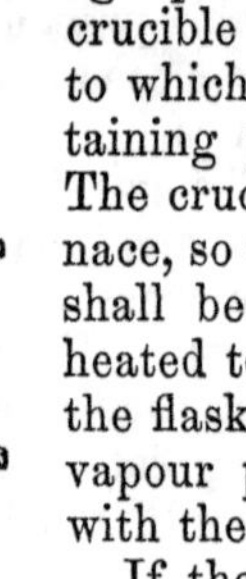
Fig. 252.

If the phosphuret of calcium be thrown into water (fig. 253), reaction immediately takes place, and spontaneously inflammable phosphuretted hydrogen is disengaged.

Fig. 253.

§ 220. Phosphuretted hydrogen is a colourless gas, of an extremely fetid and characteristic odour: its density is 1.185: water dissolves but a small quantity of it. If it be kept for some time over mercury, it undergoes a remarkable change, a brownish deposit takes place on the sides of the glass, and the gas has lost the property of spontaneously inflaming by contact with the air. The volume of the gas has scarcely changed, and, on analysis, its composition is found to be nearly the same.

The gas may be procured immediately, but not spontaneously inflammable, by decomposing the phosphuret of calcium by chlorohydric acid instead of water. It may also be obtained by heating phosphorous and hypophosphorous acids, which are hydrated, and under the influence of heat, the water and acid are both decomposed at once, a portion of the acid gives off its phosphorus, which combines with the hydrogen to form phosphuretttd hydrogen, while its oxygen combines with another portion of the acid and converts it into phosphoric acid.

The difference* in the behaviour of phosphuretted hydrogen prepared by one or other of these processes is due to the presence in the spontaneously inflammable gas of a small quantity of another phosphuretted hydrogen, richer in phosphorus, and which takes fire on contact with the air. In order to separate this liquid, the spontaneously inflammable gas is passed through a tube bent in the form of the letter U and surrounded by a refrigerating mixture. There condense in the tube, at the same time, water which solidifies, and a colourless liquid which may be separated by allowing it to run to that part of the tube unoccupied by water, and then closing it by a flame. The gas which escapes from the U-tube has lost the property of self-inflammability in the air.

Liquid phosphuretted hydrogen is not very fixed, and can be preserved only in the dark, for it decomposes rapidly by light into phosphuretted hydrogen gas and a solid body of an orange-yellow colour, which is a third phosphuret of hydrogen containing still more phosphorus than the liquid phosphuret. It is the same substance that is deposited on the sides of the bell-glass in which spontaneously inflammable hydrogen gas is kept, and which thus loses its inflammability.

Liquid phosphuretted hydrogen is much more easily decomposed by certain acids, as the chlorohydric, etc.; and hence, a non-spontaneously inflammable gas is always obtained when the phosphuret of calcium is decomposed by chlorohydric acid.

Pure phosphuretted hydrogen gas, entirely deprived of liquid phosphuret, is not spontaneously inflammable at ordinary temperatures, but a slight elevation of temperature, as 212°, restores this property. Many substances deprive phosphuretted hydrogen gas of its property of being spontaneously inflammable, such as those which readily decompose the liquid phosphuret. Others, chiefly oxidizing substances, like deutoxide of nitrogen, etc., restore its spontaneous inflammability, by decomposing a small quantity of phosphuretted hydrogen gas, depriving it of a portion of its hydrogen, and thus converting it into the liquid hydruret of phosphorus, which remains in a state of vapour in the undecomposed gas.

A very simple experiment proves that it is the presence of the liquid phosphuret in vapour in the phosphuretted hydrogen gas which communicates to this gas the property of spontaneously inflaming in the air at ordinary temperatures; for the same property may be communicated to all combustible gases, by adding to them a small quantity of the vapour of liquid phosphuret. Thus, if into a bell-glass filled with hydrogen gas a drop of liquid phosphuret of hydrogen be introduced, a gaseous mixture is obtained, which immediately inflames on contact with the air. The vapour of the

* M. Paul Thenard first isolated liquid phosphuretted hydrogen, the vapours of which afford the spontaneously inflammable hydrogen gas, and thus explained the anomalies which had been found in the properties of the gas.

liquid phosphuret takes fire and communicates inflammation to the hydrogen.

§ 221. Phosphuretted hydrogen gas is analyzed by passing it through a tube A (fig. 254), filled with copper heated to redness;

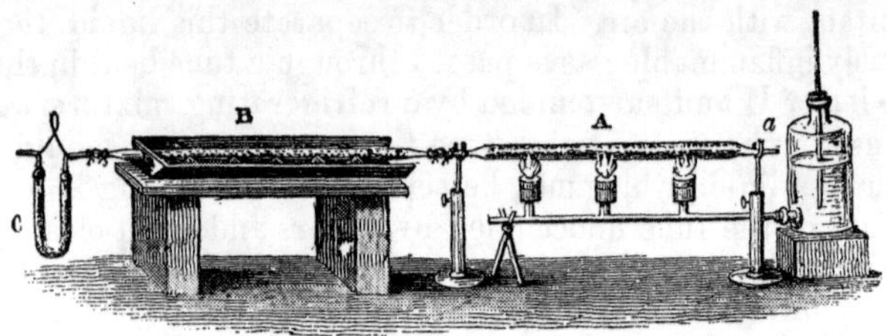

Fig. 254.

the gas is decomposed, the copper seizing on the phosphorus, and hydrogen being set free. The latter gas then traverses a second tube B, heated to redness and filled with oxide of copper, in which it burns, forming water, which condenses in a tube C filled with pumice-stone imbued with sulphuric acid. The first tube A, having been weighed before the experiment, is weighed afterward, and its increase in weight gives the quantity of phosphorus. In order that the tube A may remain unaltered during the experiment, it is heated by alcohol lamps, as represented in the figure. The tubes must also be filled with nitrogen before commencing the experiment, and again washed with it at the close, by connecting a gasometer filled with nitrogen with the end *a* of the tube A. It has thus been found that 100 parts of phosphuretted hydrogen gas contain

Hydrogen	8.57
Phosphorus	91.43
	100.00

This composition corresponds to the following in volumes:

$1\frac{1}{2}$ vol. of hydrogen	0.1032
$\frac{1}{4}$ vol. of vapour of phosphorus	1.0815
	1.1847

nearly agreeing with the density 1.185, as found by experiment.

It has been shown that 1 volume of ammoniacal gas also contains $1\frac{1}{2}$ vol. of hydrogen, but it contains a $\frac{1}{2}$ vol. of nitrogen, while phosphuretted hydrogen only contains $\frac{1}{4}$ vol. of vapour of phosphorus. We have asserted that the compounds of nitrogen and phosphorus corresponded exactly; we have, therefore, between ammonia and phosphuretted hydrogen, an anomaly precisely similar to that already found between sulfhydric acid gas and the vapour of water (§ 152). The anomaly disappears by supposing vapour of phosphorus to be formed by a grouping of two chemical molecules.

Having adopted the number 32 as the equivalent of phosphorus, let us now calculate the composition of phosphuretted hydrogen gas, with reference to this weight of phosphorus, by making the proportion

$$91.43 : 8.57 : : 32 : x, \text{ whence } x=3,$$

which represents 3 equivalents of hydrogen; and phosphuretted hydrogen gas therefore contains

1 eq. phosphorus	32
3 " hydrogen	3
1 " phosphuretted hydrogen	35

The composition of liquid phosphuretted hydrogen has been determined from the quantity of solid and gaseous phosphuretted hydrogen which it gives by decomposition, from which its composition in equivalents is represented by PH_2.

Lastly, the composition of the solid phosphuret is ascertained by finding the volume of hydrogen afforded by a known weight of it, when it is decomposed by metallic copper in a tube heated to redness. The formula of the solid phosphuret is P_2H.

COMBINATION OF PHOSPHORUS WITH NITROGEN.

Phosphuret of Nitrogen, N_2P.

§ 222. If dry ammoniacal gas be passed through liquid protochloride of phosphorus, it is absorbed in large quantities, and a white crystallized body is obtained, the formula of which is

$$PCl_3,4NH_3.$$

By contact with water, it is converted into phosphite and chlorohydrate of ammonia, according to the following reaction:

$$PCl_3,4NH_3+4HO=3(HCl,NH_3)+PO_3(NH_3,HO).$$

If the product be heated in a small retort, different gases are disengaged, and a large quantity of sal ammoniac sublimed, and by continuing the heat until the disengagement ceases, phosphuret of nitrogen remains, as a white residuum, at the bottom of the retort.

Phosphuret of nitrogen bears a red-heat without decomposition, volatilization, or fusion, is insoluble in water and nearly all acids, but is easily analyzed, by heating a known weight of it, mixed with oxide of copper, in the apparatus described (§ 108). It is thus found to be composed of

1 eq. phosphorus........................	32........	53.33
2 " nitrogen............................	28........	46.67
	60	100.00

Its formula is, therefore, N_2P.

COMBINATIONS OF PHOSPHORUS WITH SULPHUR.

§ 223. Sulphur and phosphorus combine in several proportions. When pieces of sulphur and phosphorus are brought into contact, and gently heated to fuse them, they combine with evolution of heat, and sometimes with explosion. The experiment is dangerous, and requires great care; but to perform it with safety, the phosphorus is put under water, in a glass flask, and heated until it fuses, when sulphur is gradually introduced in small pieces. We can thus combine a considerable quantity of sulphur with phosphorus without disturbing the fluidity of the mixture, but, if allowed to cool, a considerable portion of the sulphur separates by crystallization. If, on the other hand, but little sulphur be added, and the phosphorus be in excess, the latter crystallizes during cooling.

By combining 1 equivalent of phosphorus with 1 of sulphur, that is, 1 part by weight of the former with 2 pts. of sulphur, a product is obtained which is still fluid at 41°, but solidifies below that point, without regularly crystallizing.

Phosphorus forms with sulphur a great number of definite compounds which generally correspond to those with oxygen; but as these compounds are often more combustible than isolated phosphorus, manipulation with them requires great caution.

COMBINATIONS OF PHOSPHORUS WITH CHLORINE.

§ 224. Chlorine and phosphorus combine in two proportions, the formulæ of which are PCl_3 and PCl_5, corresponding to phosphorous acid PO_3 and phosphoric acid PO_5.

The apparatus used in their preparation resembles that described (§ 187) for the preparation of the chlorides of sulphur. Phosphorus is put into a tubulated retort D (fig. 255). The combination of phosphorus and chlorine takes place with a great elevation of temperature, and often with flame, so that a piece of phosphorus inflamed in a capsule continues to burn with a greenish flame when plunged into a bottle filled with chlorine.

The high temperature developed during the combination frequently breaks the tubulated retort, but the danger may be obviated by putting at the bottom of the retort a layer of sand, on which the phosphorus rests. In order to prevent the formation of perchloride, the retort must be heated nearly to the boiling point

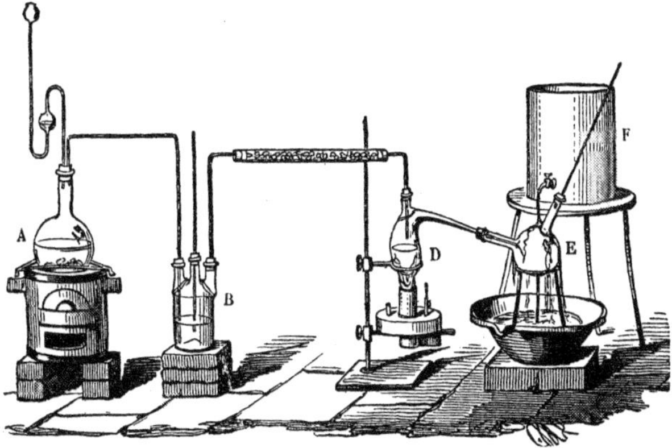

Fig. 255.

of phosphorus, so that the chlorine is constantly in an atmosphere of phosphorus in excess, and the protochloride distils over as fast as it forms. The operation is arrested before all the phosphorus has disappeared. The distilled liquid contains phosphorus in solution, which is separated by redistillation.

Protochloride of phosphorus is a colourless, very limpid liquid, of the density 1.45; it boils at 172.4°, and the density of its vapour is 4.742.

In contact with water, protochloride produces chlorohydric and phosphorous acids, and we have used this property in its analysis, when it was found (§ 214) to be composed of

1 eq. phosphorus	32.0	23.13
3 " chlorine	106.5	76.87
	138.5	100.00

1 volume of the protochloride is composed of

$\frac{1}{4}$ vol. vapour of phosphorus	$\frac{4.326}{4}=1.0845$
$1\frac{1}{2}$ " chlorine	3.6600
	4.7445

The theoretical density of its vapour is therefore 4.744, which is identical with that given by direct experiment.

§ 225. Subjected to the action of chlorine, it absorbs a large quantity of it, and is converted into a white crystalline substance, which is the perchloride of phosphorus. This body boils at about 298°, which is also near its point of fusion, so that at the ordinary pressure of the atmosphere, it passes immediately from the solid to the gaseous state.

In contact with water, the perchloride is thus changed into chlorohydric and phosphoric acids.

$$PCl_5+5HO=PO_5+5HCl.$$

It may be analyzed in the same way as the protochloride; but its composition may also be deduced from that of phosphoric acid, which we have directly ascertained, it being only necessary to substitute 5 equivalents of chlorine for the 5 equivalents of phosphoric acid. We thus have

1 eq. phosphorus	32.0	15.29
5 " chlorine	177.5	84.71
	209.5	100.00

The density of its vapour has been found to be 3.66: 1 volume of the vapour is therefore composed of

$\frac{1}{4}$ vol. of vapour of phosphorus	1.085
1 " chlorine	2.440
	3.525

It may be regarded as formed by the combination of

1 vol. protochloride of phosphorus	4.744
1 " chlorine	2.440
	7.184

of which one-half is equal to 3.59 without condensation.*

COMBINATIONS OF PHOSPHORUS WITH IODINE.

§ 226. Iodine and phosphorus heated together, combine with the evolution of heat, but no definite compounds have been hitherto isolated. The combinations are destroyed by water, producing iodohydric, phosphorous, and phosphoric acids; and it was such a reaction we made use of to obtain iodohydric acid gas (§ 199.)

* Mitscherlich found the specific gravity of the vapour of perchloride of phosphorus to be 4.85, from which it appears to be composed of 1 vol. P + 10 vols. Cl, condensed to 6 vols., i. e. 4.4224 P + (2.453 × 10) = 28.952, and hence one vol. = $\frac{28.952}{6}$ = 4.825, nearly the same as that found, and hence the formula PCl_5. But Regnault gives the result of experiment as 3.66, from which he makes it consist of 1 vol. P + 4 vols. Cl, or 4.422 P + (2.453 × 4) = 14.234, condensed to 4 vols.; thus $\frac{14.234}{4}$ = 3.558. Again, regarding it as composed of $\frac{1}{2}$ vol. protochloride of phosphorus and $\frac{1}{2}$ vol. chlorine uncondensed, its formula becomes PCl_5, and its volume weighs 3.60. Upon the former view, its formula is PCl_2, which is certainly incorrect. The true volume is

$\frac{1}{8}$ vol. of vapour of phosphorus	0.5528
$\frac{5}{4}$ " chlorine	3.0662
	3.619.—*J. C. B.*

ARSENIC.

EQUIVALENT As = 75 (937.5 O = 100).

§ 227. Arsenic closely resembles the metals in its physical properties, but its compounds are so analogous to the corresponding compounds of phosphorus, that it is advisable to study them in conjunction.

Arsenic is of an iron-gray colour, very brittle, possessing a metallic lustre, and a density of about 5.8. Heated to dull redness, it sublimes at once without fusion; so that, at first sight, it would seem capable of assuming only the solid and gaseous states, but the apparent anomaly arises from the fact that its point of fusion very nearly approaches that at which it boils under the pressure of the atmosphere. Volatile substances give off vapour much below their boiling points, a property belonging alike to solid as well as liquid bodies. Arsenic, therefore, gives off vapour copiously at a temperature much below its boiling point, and may wholly sublime without attaining that of fusion.

The distance between the point of fusion and that of ebullition of any body may, however, be increased at pleasure. For *the point of ebullition of a body is the temperature at which the tension of its vapour is equal to the pressure exerted upon it*, and hence, by increasing the pressure, the boiling point is raised without sensibly affecting the point of fusion. We can thus obtain melted arsenic, if, instead of heating it in an open tube, it is heated in a thick glass tube hermetically sealed, so that the increased pressure in the tube opposes the ebullition of the arsenic, which may be fused long before it boils.

Reciprocally, it is evident that a volatile solid body may be always subjected to so slight a pressure that it will boil at a temperature inferior to that at which it melts. Thus, ice at the temperature of 30.2° possesses an elastic force represented by 4.27^{mm} (0.168 inches); in other words, it boils at a temperature of 30.20°, under the pressure of 4.27^{mm}. Ice may therefore be entirely volatilized *by ebullition* under this feeble pressure, without reaching its point of fusion, which is 32°.

The vapour of arsenic is colourless, and has a very well-marked odour, similar to that of garlic, as may be shown by throwing some powdered arsenic on an ignited coal. The density of its vapour is 10.37. The vapour of arsenic is always deposited in the form of crystals, so that crystallized arsenic can be readily obtained by sublimation. For this purpose, a quantity of arsenic is put into an earthen retort, so as to fill about one-third of it, and the retort placed over a furnace, the coals only touching its lower part. To prevent the external air from entering too freely into the retort, the beak is partly closed by inserting a pierced cork into it. The sublimed arsenic condenses in the upper part and neck of the retort, and when the operation is terminated, the retort is allowed to cool completely, and, upon being broken, the dome is found filled with very brilliant crystals. They are rhombohedrons, but, as they are generally grouped in masses, it is often difficult to recognise their forms.

Arsenic oxidizes in the air, even at common temperatures, its surface becoming tarnished and covered with a blackish powder; but the metallic lustre is easily restored by leaving it for a few hours in a solution of chlorine.

It is combustible, burning with a livid flame, and producing *arsenious acid.* This acid is commonly called *arsenic*, or *white arsenic*, and is obtained by roasting metallic arseniurets. The acid is easily decomposed by carbon, which deprives it of its oxygen and restores it to the metallic state.

Metallic arsenic is prepared for the arts by decomposing a natural compound of arsenic, sulphur, and iron, known to mineralogists as *mispickel.* This ore is charged into earthenware pipes of about 1 metre (3½ feet) in length and 0.3 (1 foot) in diameter, together with some pieces of sheet or cast-iron, in order to retain more effectually the sulphur, and the first pipe is covered by a second shorter and larger one, which serves as a receiver. A certain number of these pipes being placed in the same furnace and heated to redness, the arsenio-sulphuret of iron is converted into sulphuret, and arsenic sublimes in the receiver. It is purified by redistillation with carbon.

COMBINATIONS OF ARSENIC WITH OXYGEN.

§ 228. Two combinations of arsenic with oxygen are known, corresponding to phosphorous and phosphoric acids.

Arsenious Acid, AsO_3.

§ 229. When arsenic is heated in a current of atmospheric air or oxygen, it is converted into a white substance which sublimes: it is arsenious acid. It is found in commerce, and is largely used in painting, principally in the form of arsenite of copper, which furnishes a beautiful green-colour.

Arsenious acid is obtained by *roasting* metallic arsenio-sulphurets, such as those of iron, nickel, and cobalt. The principal object of the process usually being the extraction or concentration of the metal combined with the arsenic. The mineral being generally spread on the hearth of a reverberatory furnace, is traversed by a current of hot air which has passed over the grate, and converts sulphur into sulphurous, and arsenic into arsenious acid.

The sulphurous acid escapes by the chimney, whilst the arsenious acid condenses in the recipients arranged between the furnace and the chimney. In order to obtain pure arsenious acid, the crude acid produced by this process is redistilled in sheet-iron tubes.

The freshly prepared acid presents the appearance of perfectly colourless vitreous masses, which, after some time, become opaque and resemble porcelain. The change gradually takes place from the surface to the centre, so that when a piece is broken, which looks externally like porcelain, it is frequently found vitreous inside.

The vitreous and porcellainous acids are two isomeric states of the same body, no change of weight having been observed during the transformation; but the acid, in its two modifications, presents remarkably different properties.

The vitreous is three times as soluble in water as the opaque acid, and dissolves more rapidly.

The opaque is converted into vitreous acid by prolonged ebullition in water, 1 litre ($1\frac{3}{4}$ pints) of which dissolves about 110 grammes (1700 grs.) of the vitreous acid.

Under the influence of water and a low temperature, the vitreous is transformed into the opaque acid, so that a solution of the vitreous acid, after a certain time, falls to the point of saturation proper to the opaque acid.

Mechanical division transforms the vitreous into the opaque acid; so that, if the vitreous acid be very finely pulverized, it possesses only the solubility of the opaque acid.

A solution of arsenious acid reddens the tincture of litmus, but only like a feeble acid. It dissolves more easily and largely in dilute chlorohydric acid than in pure water.

Arsenious acid has no sensible odour at ordinary temperatures; when put on a heated brick, it volatilizes with a white vapour, exhaling a faint odour; but when thrown on an ignited coal, it gives off a very strong odour of garlic. This odour is produced by the vapour of metallic arsenic, to which the carbon has reduced a portion of the acid.

The composition of arsenious acid might be ascertained by finding the increase in weight of a given weight of arsenic, which is converted into arsenious acid by heating it in a current of oxygen; but it is better to deduce its composition from the analysis of the protochloride of arsenic, as the composition of phosphorous acid was deduced from the analysis of protochloride of phosphorus (§ 214).

The chloride of arsenic is decomposed by contact with water into arsenious and chlorohydric acids, which gives for the composition of arsenious acid,

Arsenic	75	75.75
Oxygen	24	24.25
	99	100.00

Arsenic Acid, AsO_5.

§ 230. Arsenic acid is obtained by boiling arsenious acid with aqua regia in excess, and evaporating to dryness to drive off the chlorohydric and nitric acids. The dried residuum dissolves but slowly in water, although arsenic acid is very soluble; but if the solution be evaporated slowly, it deposits large crystals of hydrated arsenic acid, which dissolve readily in water. The solution of the anhydrous acid, i. e. deprived of its water of crystallization, is more slow.

When arsenic acid is heated to a dull red, it decomposes into arsenious acid which sublimes, and oxygen which is evolved. Its composition is readily ascertained by finding the weight of arsenic acid afforded by 1 gramme of arsenious acid. For this purpose, the arsenious acid is heated with concentrated nitric acid, evaporated nearly to dryness, and 10 grammes of oxide of lead added to it. It is perfectly dried, and the residue calcined. The residue is composed of 10 grammes of oxide of lead, increased by the weight p of arsenic acid produced from 1 gramme of the arsenious. 1 gramme of the latter, therefore, absorbs $(p-1)$ gramme of oxygen when converted into arsenic acid. We thus find that arsenic acid is composed of

1 eq. arsenic	75	65.22
5 " oxygen	40	34.78
1 " arsenic acid	115	100.00

When finely powdered metallic arsenic is exposed to a damp atmosphere, it changes into a black substance, considered by some chemists as a peculiar oxide containing less oxygen than arsenious acid. When heated in a closed tube, it is converted into metallic arsenic and arsenious acid.

COMBINATIONS OF ARSENIC WITH HYDROGEN.

§ 231. Two compounds of arsenic and hydrogen are known, the first of which is gaseous, and known as *arsenuretted hydrogen gas;* the second is solid.

Arsenuretted hydrogen gas is obtained by treating arseniuret of tin with concentrated chlorohydric acid. The arseniuret is procured by melting 3 parts of tin with 1 of arsenic in a crucible. The pulverized arseniuret being put into a small flask, and chlorohydric acid poured on it through an S-tube, the evolution of gas commences in the cold, and may be accelerated by a few coals.

The resulting changes are chloride of tin, which remains in the flask, and arsenuretted hydrogen gas, which is disengaged. The gas thus obtained is always mixed with free hydrogen, because all the tin does not combine with the arsenic, and the free metal disengages hydrogen with chlorohydric acid. The presence of hydrogen may be easily ascertained, by introducing into the bell-glass a solution of sulphate of copper, which absorbs the arsenuretted hydrogen.

Arsenuretted hydrogen is a colourless gas, having a peculiar nauseating odour. Its density is 2.69; it liquefies at about −22°, under ordinary pressure. In contact with any burning substance, it inflames in the air, burning with a livid flame, and forming water and arsenious acid, but there is always deposited, on the sides of the glass a brown powder, due to incomplete combustion, which is solid arsenuretted hydrogen.

Heat decomposes arsenuretted hydrogen, for if passed through a tube heated to redness, hydrogen becomes free, and a brilliant ring of metallic arsenic is deposited beyond the heated part of the tube. This behaviour serves to detect the smallest quantities of arsenuretted hydrogen mixed with hydrogen.

Chlorine instantly decomposes arsenuretted hydrogen gas, each bubble of the latter which enters a test-glass filled with chlorine taking fire, and producing chlorohydric acid and chloride of arsenic.

Arsenuretted hydrogen is very poisonous, and great care must be taken not to respire the smallest quantity of it.

The composition of this gas is ascertained exactly in the same manner as that of phosphuretted hydrogen gas (§ 221); by which it is found that 1 vol. of it contains

1½ vol. hydrogen	0.1032
½ " vapour of arsenic	2.5910
	2.6942

Its composition, in equivalents, is AsH_3. Water dissolves a small quantity of it, but also decomposes it, for a bottle filled with it, and left over water for several weeks, is entirely decomposed, forming a brown deposit of solid arsenuretted hydrogen on its sides. The exact composition of the latter is unknown.

COMBINATION OF ARSENIC WITH CHLORINE.

§ 232. Only one compound of arsenic and chlorine is known, and is obtained by passing chlorine over metallic arsenic, in the apparatus represented in fig. 234, the arsenic being put into the tubulated retort D, which is gently heated, to distil the chloride of arsenic as it forms. The affinity of arsenic for chlorine is very strong, for when the powdered metal is thrown into a bottle filled with chlorine, it inflames, and produces dense white fumes of chloride of arsenic. It may also be obtained by distilling in a retort a mixture of 1 part of metallic arsenic and 6 parts of chloride of mercury. When prepared by the action of chlorine gas on arsenic, it has a yellowish tinge, from dissolved chlorine, which is removed by shaking it with a small quantity of finely-powdered arsenic, and redistilling.

Chloride of arsenic is a colourless liquid, which boils at 269.6°; the density of its vapour has been found to be 6.3. In contact with water, it instantly decomposes into arsenious and chlorohydric acids.

$$AsCl_3+3HO=AsO_3+3HCl.$$

It consequently corresponds to arsenious acid, and is composed of

1 eq. arsenic	75.0	41.35
3 " chlorine	106.5	58.65
1 " chloride of arsenic	181.5	100.00

1 vol. of its vapour contains

$\frac{1}{4}$ vol. vapour of arsenic	2.591
$1\frac{1}{2}$ " chlorine	3.660
	6.251

COMBINATIONS OF ARSENIC WITH SULPHUR.

§ 233. Arsenic and sulphur form many compounds, of which we shall mention only the three more important.

A crystallized sulphide is found in nature, the formula of which is AsS_2, corresponding to no known compound of arsenic with oxygen, and is called by mineralogists *realgar*. It can be artificially prepared by fusing together suitable proportions of arsenic and sulphur. It is a vitreous body, of a beautiful orange-red colour, and is used in painting. It fuses and sublimes unaltered.

The second compound, AsS_3, corresponding to arsenious acid, is likewise found crystallized in nature, and is known by the name of *orpiment*. Orpiment, or *sulpharsenious acid*, may be prepared by fusing together proper proportions of arsenic and sulphur, or by passing a current of sulfhydric acid through a solution of arsenious acid, when it forms a bright-yellow, flocculent precipitate.

The third compound, corresponding to arsenic acid, has the formula AsS_5, and has been called *sulpharsenic acid*. It is obtained by pouring a solution of sulfhydric acid into a solution of arsenic acid, when it slowly precipitates, often requiring the lapse of several days.

Sulpharsenic acid is more conveniently prepared by passing a current of sulfhydric gas to saturation, through a solution of arseniate of potassa, $2KO,AsO_5$, converting it into a sulphosalt, $2KS,AsS_5$, in which the monosulphide of potassium acts the part of a base, and the pentasulphide of arsenic that of an acid, the sulpharsenic. Sulpharseniate of the sulphide of potassium remains in solution in the liquid, and is decomposed by chlorohydric acid, which disengages sulfhydric acid, and precipitates sulpharsenic acid in the form of a yellow powder.

The reaction is expressed by the following equation:

$$2KS,AsS_5+2HCl=2KCl+2HS+AsS_5.$$

ON POISONING BY ARSENIOUS ACID.

§ 234. Poisoning by arsenious acid is almost always fatal when the poison has had sufficient time to pass into the circulation, but it may be relieved when recent. The patient should first be made to vomit, in order to force the stomach to reject the greater part of the poisonous matter it retains. We should then administer hydrated peroxide of iron, or, better still, caustic magnesia, suspended in water. These oxides, combining with the arsenious acid, form insoluble arsenites, and destroy the effects of the poison.

Hydrated peroxide of iron is prepared by pouring carbonate of soda into a hot solution of a salt of peroxide of iron, and washing the precipitate.

Caustic magnesia is obtained by calcining, at a moderate heat, the white magnesia of the shops, which is a hydrocarbonate of magnesia. It is sufficiently calcined when it effervesces but feebly with acids; nor should it be too highly heated, for it then combines less readily with arsenious acid.

§ 235. Arsenious acid, by itself, is readily recognised by the characters which distinguish it, and which we now proceed to give more in detail than in § 229.

A pinch of it, thrown on a burning coal, exhales its characteristic garlicky odour.

If a small quantity of the suspected substance in powder be mixed with charcoal, the mixture introduced into a small tube *ad*, closed at one end, (fig. 256), with some splinters of charcoal above it, and then heated by an alcohol lamp, first at that part of the tube containing the charcoal, and progressively from *b* to *a*, that part containing the suspected substance, the arsenious acid will be decomposed by the charcoal, and the volatilized arsenic will condense at *c*, in the form of a brilliant metallic ring, above the heated portion of the tube.

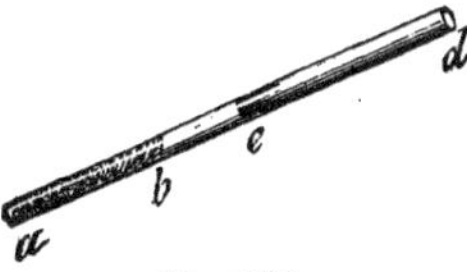

Fig. 256.

All the distinctive characteristics of arsenic may be observed in this ring; thus, it may be sublimed by heat from one part of the tube to another, and may be changed into arsenious acid by combustion in the air. For this purpose, a scratch is made on the tube *ad* (fig. 256), with a file or a diamond, below the deposit of arsenic, and the lower part *od* of the tube detached. Being placed in an inclined position, as in fig. 257, and the ring being heated with an alcohol lamp, it burns in the current of air, and is deposited as arsenious acid, in the form of a white powder, on the uppermost part of the tube. This small quantity may display all the properties which distinguish it. For example, if dissolved in a drop of hydrochloric acid diluted with water, put into a tube closed at one end, and treated with a solution of sulfhydric acid, a clear, yellow, flocculent precipitate of sulpharsenious acid, or orpiment, is formed. The precipitate is insoluble in chlorohydric acid, but dissolves readily in ammonia, producing a colourless solution.

Fig. 257.

The brilliant ring of arsenic, or the deposit of arsenious acid produced by roasting it, may be dissolved in a small quantity of concentrated nitric acid, the solution poured into a porcelain capsule, carefully evaporated to dryness, and then treated with a small quantity of a solution of perfectly neutral nitrate of silver. A *brick-red precipitate* of arseniate of silver is thrown down. It is essential that the solutions be perfectly neutral, for arseniate of silver dissolves in an excess of acid. The arseniate of silver, heated with charcoal in a small tube (fig. 256), affords the brilliant ring of arsenic.

§ 236. Lastly, arsenious acid may be converted into arsenuretted hydrogen, and the properties of the gas ascertained. The operation is extremely important, and requires suitable apparatus; for, it not only furnishes valuable marks for the detection of arsenic, but also allows of the easy separation of a minute quantity of arsenious acid diffused through a large quantity of liquid.

Let us suppose an apparatus (fig. 258) arranged as for the evolution of hydrogen. In the central tubulure of the bottle A is fitted a straight tube *mn*, of 8 or 10 millimetres (0.3—0.4 inches) internal diameter, acting as a safety-tube, and allowing the gradual introduction of liquids into the bottle. A smaller bent tube *ab*, drawn out at its end *b*, is fitted into the second tubulure. Scraps of very pure zinc are put into the bottle, some water added, and, lastly, small quantities of pure sulphuric acid are poured in, so as to produce hydrogen gas. When the air has been entirely driven out of the apparatus, the jet of gas at the end *b* is ignited; and the flame presents the ordinary characters of pure hydrogen when burning, not being brilliant, and, if a cold body, such as a porcelain plate or saucer, be brought near it, small drops of water only are deposited. If a solution of arsenious acid be now introduced through

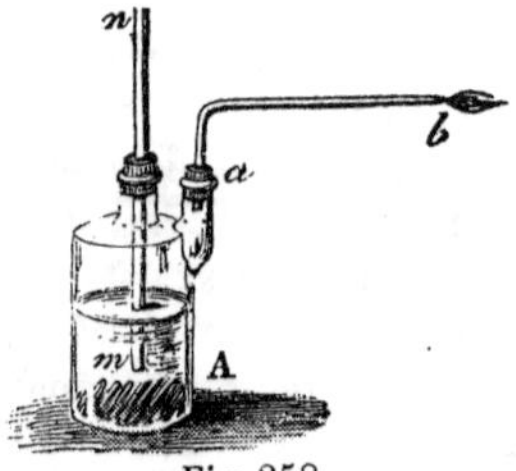

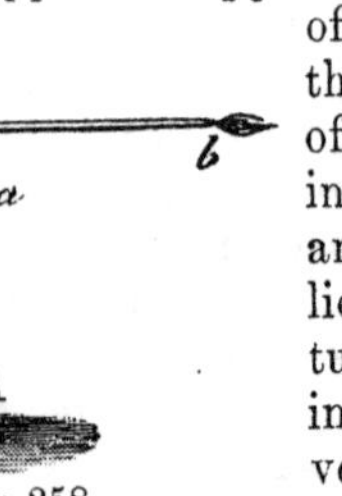

Fig. 258.

the tube, the appearance of the flame is soon changed, assuming a livid tinge, and white fumes of arsenious acid are disengaged. The arsenious acid has been decomposed by contact with the zinc, water, and sulphuric acid, its oxygen having gone to the zinc, and the arsenic, combined with a portion of nascent hydrogen, forming arsenuretted hydrogen. The hydrogen which burns at the end of the tube, therefore, contains arsenuretted hydrogen, which reproduces fumes of arsenious acid by combustion.

When the proportion of arsenious acid introduced into the bottle is not very small, the change in the flame is so evident that the presence of arsenic can be instantly recognised. If the end *b* of the discharging tube *ab* be passed into a larger tube, open at both ends, and inclined, a portion of the arsenious acid resulting from combustion will be deposited on the sides of this tube, and the tests before mentioned may be applied. But if the quantity of arsenious or arsenic acid be very small, the change in the flame is no longer sufficiently evident, and the arsenious acid produced by combustion may be completely carried off by the current of gas. We then have recourse to another character, which enables us to detect and even isolate the smallest quantities of arsenic.

Arsenuretted hydrogen is formed of two elements of very different combustibility, its hydrogen having more affinity for oxygen than arsenic. It therefore follows, that if the gas burns in an insufficient quantity of oxygen, the arsenic will oxidize only when all the hydrogen is consumed, and, since arsenuretted hydrogen is easily decomposed by heat, arsenic, arising both from the decomposition of the gas by heat and from its partial combustion, will be deposited.

These circumstances may be observed in certain parts of the flame at the end of the tube *ab* (fig. 258). If this flame be carefully examined, it will be found closely to resemble fig. 259, being composed of an interior dark portion *a′c′*, and a luminous envelope *oabc*, in which the temperature is very elevated. In the pointed part of the flame, toward the extremity of the interior dark portion, the maximum of temperature exists. These two portions of flame and their respective dimensions can be easily seen, by cutting the flame at different points by a plate of glass, and looking behind it.

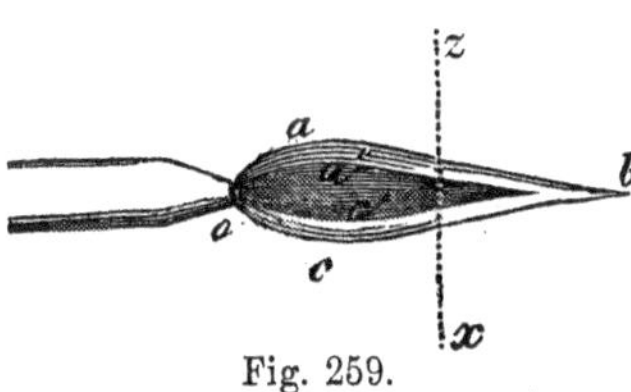

Fig. 259.

On the external surface of the luminous envelope, the combustion is perfect, on account of the excess of atmospheric air; in the strata of the envelope adjacent to the interior dark part, the combustion is imperfect, on account of the want of oxygen; and, lastly, in the dark part there is no combustion, although, in certain parts, toward the plane *xz*, the temperature is sufficiently elevated to decompose the gas into hydrogen and arsenic. If the flame be left free, the arsenic burns toward the end, and is finally disengaged in the form of arsenious acid. But if it be cut at *xz* by a cold body, such as a porcelain saucer, the metallic arsenic is deposited on the saucer, forming a brilliant spot, possessing metallic lustre when the layer is thick enough. By causing the plane to impinge on different points of the saucer, it may be covered with spots of arsenic, and a sufficient amount collected to recognise its characteristics.

The apparatus just described is called *Marsh's apparatus*, from the English chemist who first devised it, to detect the presence of arsenic in medico-legal researches.

It is evident that but a small portion of arsenic is condensed by this process, and, when it is present in very small quantities, the spots are not thick enough to present a metallic lustre, but remain brown; and although a skilful chemist might not be mistaken, particularly if he carefully test the spots, it is to be feared that errors might arise in less experienced hands.

In fact, spots may be produced on porcelain, even when the gas does not contain the least traces of arsenic; but it can always be ascertained whether the spots are arsenical, by subjecting them to the proper chemical tests. Spots are produced on the saucer when the liquid in the bottle is viscous, either because it contains too much sulphate of zinc, or holds organic matter in solution. The disengaged bubbles of gas throw out an infinite number of minute globules of liquid, the lightest of which may be carried into the flame, when the salt of zinc, as well as the organic matters, would be partially decomposed, forming brown spots of oxysulphide of zinc, or only of carbon. This is avoided by passing the gas through a tube filled with cotton or asbestos, before it reaches the small end at which it burns.

It is better, in all cases, to decompose the arsenuretted hydrogen which accompanies the hydrogen in Marsh's apparatus, by passing it through a small tube, heated to redness for about 1 decimetre of its length, so that arsenic may be deposited in the form of a narrow brilliant ring, at a short distance beyond the heat, and thus collected on a small surface.

The best arrangement of the apparatus is that represented in fig. 260. The bottle A, in which the hydrogen gas is evolved, should be rather small, unless large quantities of liquid are to be acted on, and yet should be large enough to hold all the liquid to be tested, and still leave about one-fifth of its capacity empty. The zinc and water being introduced into the bottle, it is closed with a cork pierced with two holes, into one of which is inserted the tube *mn*, of about 1 cm. ($\frac{1}{2}$ inch) in diameter, for pouring in the liquid, and which dips a little way into the water. To the second tube is fitted a bent tube *abc*, having a bulb at *b*, in which the greater part of the water carried over condenses. A glass tube

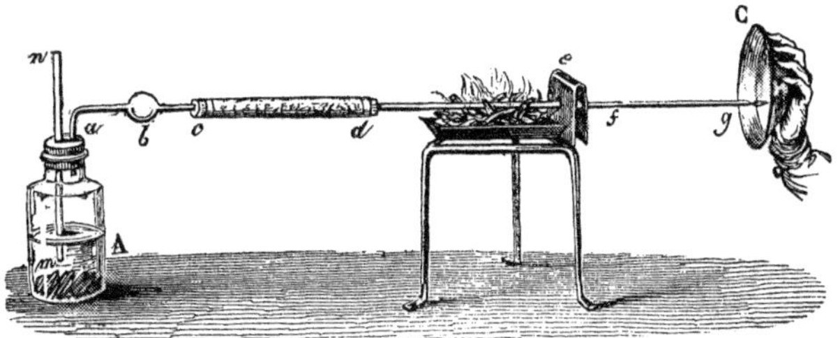

Fig. 260.

cd, filled with asbestos, retains the particles of the solution carried over by the current of gas. Lastly, a narrow tube *efg*, of 3 or 4 dec. (12–16 in.) length, and drawn out to a point *g*, terminates the apparatus.

Hydrogen is first evolved, to expel the air from the apparatus; the tube *dfg* is then heated, for about 1 dec. of its length, by live coals on a chafing-dish. The glass tube should be difficult of fusion, or else surrounded by a sheet of tinsel, to prevent its bending. A screen *e* protects the part *fg* of the tube from the heat. The gas being lighted at the orifice *g*, its disengagement is continued for some time, to observe whether a deposit takes place in the part *fg*, or whether spots can be obtained on a porcelain saucer, in order to ascertain whether the reagents themselves are entirely free from arsenic.

This being done, the suspected liquid is introduced, and a gentle evolution of hydrogen kept up by adding a suitable quantity of sulphuric acid, so that the flame cannot attain a length of more than 5 or 6 mm. ($\frac{1}{5}$ in.) The greater part of the arsenic is deposited at *f*, a short distance beyond the screen, but as there is almost always a small quantity of arsenuretted hydrogen which escapes decomposition and burns in the flame, a portion of it is carefully collected on saucers, and examined for the characteristic reactions of arsenic.

If the liquid contained antimony, a brilliant metallic ring is also obtained, in the tube *fg* (fig. 260); but it is sufficiently distinguished from that produced by arsenic, by its want of volatility, and other characters to be described when treating of antimony.

§ 237. The processes above described are of easy execution, and admit of our detecting, with perfect certainty, the smallest quantities of arsenic, when it exists in the state of arsenious or arsenic acid, or even of a sulphide; for the latter can be readily transformed previously into arsenic acid, by means of nitric acid. But the problem is less simple when it is required to detect the presence of a small quantity of arsenic in large masses of organic matter, as most frequently happens in cases of poisoning. The process to be then pursued will now be succinctly described.

If a portion of the food supposed to have been poisoned still remain, we must examine if there be not, at the bottom of the vessel, a deposit of arsenious acid, as a white powder, which can be immediately recognised by the tests above given. A similar examination should be made of the matters vomited. If these researches are fruitless, the food or matters vomited should be strained through a piece of clean linen, previously washed in distilled water, whereby they are separated into a liquid and a solid portion, which are to be first separately and then conjointly treated. The liquids are evaporated in a porcelain capsule, but as they frequently contain organic matter in solution, they become too viscous to be introduced directly into Marsh's apparatus, where they would produce too much froth, and the experiment could not be accurately conducted. Moreover, since the presence of these organic matters changes remarkably the reactions by which the arsenic might be recognised, they are destroyed by concentrating the liquids highly, and then adding a quantity of oil of vitriol proportioned to the organic matter supposed to exist in the solution. Upon evaporating to drive off the sulphuric acid, organic matter is destroyed, and assumes the form of a spongy charcoal, which is sprinkled with concentrated nitric acid, and again heated to drive off this acid—reddish fumes being copiously given off. The arsenic, if present, is converted into arsenic acid, which dissolves very readily in water. The residue is therefore treated with a small quantity of boiling distilled water, and filtered, and, if the carbonization has been carefully performed, a liquid is generally obtained free from colour, or nearly so, which is easily managed in Marsh's apparatus.

The solid matters remaining in the linen should also be carbonized by sulphuric acid, by sprinkling them with about one-fifth of their weight of concentrated sulphuric acid, and heating them. When the whole mass becomes fluid, the sulphuric acid is driven off by heat, the residue sprinkled with nitric acid, which is also driven off, and, lastly, treated with boiling distilled water. A limpid liquid is obtained by filtration, presenting the same appearance as that resulting from the treatment of the liquid portion. The two liquids are mixed, and treated together in Marsh's apparatus.

When there is a considerable quantity of arsenious acid in the matter subjected to experiment, we may effect its carbonization by sulphuric acid and the successive evaporations in porcelain capsules; but, if the proportion of poison be small, it is always to be feared that some of the arsenious acid may be carried off at the high temperature required for expelling the sulphuric acid. This danger is especially imminent when the substances contain chlorides, because chloride of arsenic, which is very volatile, may be formed. In all cases, it is better to effect the carbonization in a glass retort connected with a cooled receiver, for collecting the distilled liquids, which may afterward be examined for arsenic.

If the chemist be required to investigate a case of poisoning, after the death of the patient, he should examine the contents of the stomach, and the urine in the bladder, in the manner pointed out above.

Lastly, long after the decease of the victim, it may become his duty to examine a corpse in a more or less advanced stage of decomposition. He must then operate on what remains of the stomach, and on the viscera, such as the liver, heart, spleen, etc., which are generally attacked by the poison. They are carbonized in the same way, by sulphuric acid, in a glass retort, after having divided them into small pieces.

Animal matters may also be decomposed by suspending them in water, after having ground them in a mortar, and passing a current of chlorine through the liquid, until the organic matter is deposited in the form of colourless flakes, and the liquid is saturated with chlorine. The bottle is then corked, allowed to stand for 12 hours, when the odour of chlorine should still be distinct, then filtered and concentrated in a retort adapted to a receiver. The small quantity of concentrated liquid remaining in the retort is treated in Marsh's apparatus, and, if necessary, the liquid condensed in the receiver is also examined for arsenic.

It is unnecessary to say that all the chemical reagents used in these processes should be pure, and *previously tested* with the greatest care, to ascertain that they do not contain the slightest trace of arsenic. The chemist may then have entire confidence in the result of his experiments, if they have been properly conducted.

But, as it is essential that the judges should share this confidence, and that no doubt can hang on the result of the experiments, if it show the presence of arsenic, the chemist should be *required* to perform, contemporaneously with the actual experiments, similar operations *without* the suspected matters, with the *same* reagents, in the *same* quantity, and in *exactly similar* apparatus. He should deliver to the judge, on the one hand, the tube *dfg* (fig. 260) of Marsh's apparatus, in which he has finally obtained the result of his experiments of the suspected matters, as well as the saucers on which he has endeavoured to produce spots; and, on the other, the analogous tube of the other Marsh's apparatus, in which he has finally obtained the result of the operations performed on the *reagents alone*, as well as the saucers on which he has endeavoured to produce spots. Such a comparison of the results can leave no doubt on any one's mind.*

* For further details, see the report made to the Académie des Sciences, on arsenic in cases of poisoning.—*Comptes Rendus de l'Académie des Sciences*, tome xii. p. 1076.

BORON.

EQUIVALENT B=10.9 (136.15, O=100).

§ 238. Boron* is found in nature combined with oxygen, in the state of boracic acid; which either exists alone, or in combination with bases. In order to extract boron from boracic acid, the acid is first fused at a red-heat in a platinum crucible, to drive off the water it contains, then reduced to a fine powder, and introduced with potassium or sodium into a glass tube, closed at one end, well dried, and heated by a few coals. A slight detonation takes place at the moment of reaction. The potassium seizes upon the oxygen of a portion of the boracic acid, and is converted into oxide of potassium or potassa, which combines with the undecomposed boracic acid, and forms borate of potassa. By treating the mass when cold with water, borate of potassa is dissolved, and boron floats in the liquid, in the form of a very fine brown powder, which is collected on a small filter, and washed with distilled water until a drop of the wash-water, evaporated on a clean watch-glass, leaves no perceptible residue.

Boron forms a brown powder, which does not fuse when heated to redness in a current of hydrogen, or any other gas which exerts no chemical action on it. Heated in contact with the air, it burns and is converted into boracic acid; but it is difficult to oxidize it completely in this manner, for, as fast as the boracic acid forms, it fuses, and forms a glazed coating, which protects the yet unaltered boron from contact with the air.

COMBINATION OF BORON WITH OXYGEN.

BORACIC ACID, BO_3.

§239. Only one compound of boron with oxygen is known—boracic acid—which is found in nature, either free or in combination with soda, forming a salt known in the arts by the name of *borax*.

In certain volcanic districts of Tuscany, called the *Maremmæ of Tuscany*, jets of gas and vapour constantly exhale from fissures in the soil, which are called *suffioni* (suffumes), and which contain small quantities of boracic acid. Small lakes of water (*lagoni*) have formed around the fissures, through which the jets of vapour and gas escaping, throw up liquid cones, and then pass into the air in whitish clouds.

---

* Boron was discovered simultaneously, by Davy in England, and Gay-Lussac and Thenard in France.

Around these centres of eruption, basins of clay have been built in rough masonry, in which two or more suffioni terminate; and the water of surrounding springs is conducted into the uppermost lagoon A (fig. 261). After 24 hours, during which the waters

Fig. 261.

have been constantly agitated by the current of subterraneous vapours, the liquid in the basin is allowed to run into another, B, where it remains for the same length of time, and becomes charged with an additional quantity of boracic acid. It is then passed successively into the lagoons C and D; the liquid which has run out of a lower basin being immediately replaced by that of an upper one.

The solution in the last basin D is conveyed into reservoirs E, F, where it is allowed to remain for 24 hours, and in which are deposited the greater portion of the earthy substances held in suspension. The supernatant liquid is drawn off and passed successively into a series of shallow leaden pans, or evaporators, G, arranged as in fig. 261, over a flue in mason work, through which the hot vapours of a suffione are constantly passing, and afford sufficient heat to evaporate the liquid.

After remaining 24 hours in the first evaporator, the liquid is diminished by evaporation to one-half, and is then conveyed into the evaporator immediately below, where it remains for the same length of time; thus descending from pan to pan, until, when it reaches the last, it is so concentrated that boracic acid crystallizes on cooling in the crystallizers A (fig. 262). The crystallized acid is collected in baskets C, where it is allowed to drain; and then

Fig. 262. Fig. 263.

dried in an oven (fig. 263) with a double bottom H, through which the vapour of a suffione circulates.

The boracic acid thus obtained is far from being pure, as it contains 18 to 25 per cent. of foreign substances, from which it is purified by solution in boiling water and crystallization.

Boracic acid is often prepared in the laboratory from the borax of commerce, which is very pure, by dissolving 1 part of borax in $2\frac{1}{2}$ pts. of boiling water, and adding chlorohydric acid until the liquid strongly reddens litmus. On cooling, the boracic acid crystallizes in thin plates, which are allowed to drain, and then washed with a little water. If absolutely pure boracic acid be required, it must be again dissolved in boiling water and recrystallized.

Crystallized boracic acid forms colourless scales, containing 43.6 per cent. of water of crystallization. Subjected to heat, it first melts in this water, which is then disengaged, and, if it be heated to redness, it fuses into a colourless liquid, which, on cooling, presents the appearance of a perfectly transparent vitreous mass. Between the states of perfect liquidity and complete solidity, boracic acid passes through all the intermediate stages, and, like all substances possessing this property, it does not crystallize by fusion, so that it remains perfectly transparent after solidification. But its transparency is not permanent, for, even when preserved in hermetically sealed tubes, it ultimately becomes opaque, from its molecules at common temperatures tending to aggregate, according to the laws of crystallization, which govern them at this temperature, so that a multitude of small cleavages result, which soon destroy its transparency. Exposed to the air, the fused acid is soon covered with a pulverulent substance, produced by its absorbing water from the air, and changing into a hydrated acid.

100 parts of water dissolve 2 pts. of the crystallized acid, at the temperature of 50°, and 8 pts. at 212°; so that a solution, saturated at the boiling point, deposits $\frac{3}{4}$ of its acid when it descends to ordinary temperatures.

Its solution is slightly acid, reddening litmus, but, like a feeble acid, it produces a purplish-red colour; and yet, in the cold, it expels carbonic acid from its compounds. In the dry way, it expels the most powerful acids, owing to its great fixedness, for it does not boil even at a white heat. But yet, at this temperature, the tension of its vapour is sufficient to allow the acid to evaporate entirely, in a short time. At a red-heat, it expels sulphuric acid from the sulphate.

The composition of boracic acid has been determined by ascertaining, experimentally, the increase in weight of 1 gramme of boron, when heated in the air so as to convert it into boracic acid. It has been found to consist of

Oxygen	68.78
Boron	31.22
	100.00

It is difficult to give the formula proper to boracic acid, for the number of definite compounds containing boron is still very limited; and the rules we have applied for determining the equivalents of simple bodies are inapplicable to it.

Some chemists adopt for it the formula BO_6; in which case the equivalent of boron is obtained by the proportion

$$68.78 : 31.22 : : 48 : x, \text{ whence } x = 21.8.$$

Others adopt the formula BO_3, whence the equivalent of boron is given by the proportion

$$68.78 : 31.22 : : 24 : x, \text{ whence } x = 10.9.$$

The acid, crystallized by solution, as mentioned above, is combined with 43.6 per cent. of water, which contains a quantity of oxygen equal to that which exists in the anhydrous acid.

The formula of the crystallized acid will then be

According to the first hypothesis	BO_6+6HO
" " second "	BO_3+3HO

COMBINATION OF BORON WITH CHLORINE.

Chloride of Boron, BCl_3.

§ 240. This compound is obtained by heating boron in a current of chlorine, or, more readily, by heating an intimate mixture of boracic acid and carbon in a porcelain tube, while a current of dry chlorine is passed through it.

Chloride of boron is a colourless gas; gives off dense fumes in a moist atmosphere; has a density of 4.035; by contact with water is decomposed into chlorohydric and boracic acids. It formula is, therefore, that of boracic acid in which the oxygen is replaced by an equivalent quantity of chlorine. 1 volume of the gas contains 1½ vols. of chlorine, thus

Boron	0.375	9.28
$1\frac{1}{2}$ vol. chlorine	3.660	90.72
	4.035	100.00

COMBINATION OF BORON WITH FLUORINE.

Fluoride of Boron, BF_3.

§ 241. A gaseous compound of fluorine and boron is obtained by heating, at a very high temperature, in a small porcelain retort, a mixture of 2 parts of fluor-spar and 1 pt. of fused boracic acid. A portion of the acid is decomposed, its oxygen combining with calcium to form lime, which yields borate of lime with the undecomposed boracic acid; while the fluorine and boron combine to form fluoride of boron. The reaction may be represented by the following equation:

$$2BO_3+3CaF=BF_3+BO_3,3CaO.$$

Fluoride of boron is a colourless gas, with a suffocating odour, and a strongly acid taste; its density is 2.37; it is extremely soluble in water, and has so great an affinity for it, that it carbonizes organic substances, like oil of vitriol (§ 134). In consequence of its great affinity for water, it fumes copiously when exposed to the air.

The composition of fluoride of boron corresponds to that of boracic acid, its formula being BF_3.

Water dissolves 700 to 800 times its volume of fluoride of boron, and the solution is easily obtained, in a concentrated form, in the following manner:

Equal parts of fluor-spar and borax are fused together, pulverized, and heated in a glass retort, with concentrated sulphuric acid; an acid liquid distils over, which is a very concentrated solution of fluoride of boron in water. If the solution be diluted with a larger quantity of water, it decomposes into boracic acid, which separates, and a peculiar acid which has been called *borofluohydric acid.* The latter is probably analogous to the silicofluohydric, of which we shall presently treat, and which has been more thoroughly examined.

SILICIUM.

Equivalent Si = 21.3 (266.7 O = 100).

§ 242. Silicium* is one of the most widely diffused bodies in nature; for its combination with oxygen, silicic acid, is one of the most common substances on the surface of the globe.

Silicic acid, heated with potassium, yields silicium and silicate of potassa; but the decomposition is difficult, and does not afford pure silicium. It is preferable to employ the potassium for decomposing a compound of fluoride of silicium and fluoride of potassium, the preparation of which will be given hereafter. The two substances are introduced into a dry glass tube and heated:

Double fluoride of silicium and potassium	Fluoride of potassium.		
	Fluoride of silicium....	Silicium	
		Fluorine	Fluoride of potassium.
Potassium			

$$3KF,2SiF_3+6K=9KF+2Si.$$

The product is treated with cold water, which dissolves the fluoride of potassium; the silicium is collected on a small filter, and washed with distilled water, until the washings leave no perceptible residue on a glass plate.

Silicium is a brown powder, infusible when heated in a close vessel, takes fire when heated in the air, and is converted into silicic acid.

COMBINATION OF SILICIUM WITH OXYGEN.

Silicic Acid, SiO_3.

§ 243. Only one compound of silicium and oxygen is known—the silicic acid—which is generally known by the name of *silex*, and is one of the most common substances in nature. Isolated, it constitutes rock crystal, quartz, quartzose sands, sandstone, etc. Combined with alumina, potassa, or soda, lime, and the oxide of iron, it constitutes many minerals, which are aggregated into granites, slates, etc. In short, all rocks which are not calcareous are silicious.

Colourless rock crystal exhibits crystallized and pure silicic acid. The general form of the crystals is a six-sided prism, terminated by a six-sided pyramid (fig. 58), belonging to the third or hexagonal system of crystallization. Rock crystal is a very hard substance, which scratches glass, and has a density of 2.6.

---

* Silicium was first obtained in a pure state by Berzelius.

The highest temperature of our furnaces does not melt rock crystal; but it fuses into a vitreous globule in the flame of a mixture of oxygen and hydrogen.

At ordinary temperatures, it is not affected by contact with any reagents, except fluohydric acid, which acts upon it rapidly. Caustic potassa has a similar effect at a high temperature.

When silicic acid is obtained in a disaggregated state, it presents more marked characters.

To obtain it in this state, 1 part of finely powdered quartz, and 4 of carbonate of potassa or soda are melted in a platinum crucible, whereby a portion of the carbonic acid is driven off, and silicate of potassa formed. Treated with water, the mass dissolves entirely when subjected sufficiently long to a high temperature. If the liquid be diluted with a large quantity of water, and chlorohydric acid be added until a strongly acid reaction is manifest, the silicic acid is separated from its combination with the potassa, but remains suspended in the liquid, in the state of transparent jelly, and cannot be separated by filtration. If the alkaline matter be dissolved in a small quantity of water, and chlorohydric acid added to the dense solution, the silicic acid forms a gelatinous, flocculent precipitate, which can be filtered.

Nevertheless, its complete separation only takes place by evaporating the liquid supersaturated by the acid to dryness, and treating the residue with boiling water. The silex then separates in the state of a stiff jelly, which is completely arrested by the filter. It is then probably in the state of a hydrate, but soon parts with its water by drying, and assumes the appearance of a light, white, mealy powder, which becomes very hard by calcination.

It is sometimes deposited in the form of a transparent jelly, when certain substances containing it are allowed to decompose spontaneously and slowly. Thus, silicic ether, kept in a badly corked bottle, gradually loses all its ether, while the silica remains in the form of a perfectly transparent jelly, which, in time, becomes very hard, without losing its transparency.

§ 244. The composition of silicic acid is deduced from the analysis of the chloride of silicium, which will soon be described. Chloride of silicium is decomposed, by contact with water, into silicic and chlorohydric acids. Silicic acid is therefore obtained from chloride of silicium, by substituting an equivalent quantity of oxygen for its chlorine. By analyzing chloride of silicium, the composition of the acid may be at once ascertained. By following closely the method described (§ 214) for ascertaining the composition of phosphorous acid, it will be found that silicic acid is composed of

Silicium	47.06
Oxygen	52.94
	100.00

The same difficulty is experienced in establishing the formula of silicic, as that of boracic acid, for silicium, like boron, affords but few definite compounds.

The majority of chemists admit for it the formula SiO_3, analogous to that of sulphuric acid; from which the equivalent of silicium is then given by the proportion

$$52.94 : 47.06 :: 24 : x, \text{ whence } x = 21.3.$$

Others write the formula SiO_2, which gives for the equivalent of silicium,

$$52.94 : 47.06 :: 16 : x, \text{ whence } x = 14.2.$$

Lastly, some adopt the formula SiO, when the equivalent becomes 7.1.

We shall adopt the formula SiO_3; not that it is the most convenient, but simply because it has hitherto been most generally adopted. We therefore take 21.3 as the equivalent of silicium.*

COMBINATION OF SILICIUM WITH CHLORINE.

CHLORIDE OF SILICIUM, $SiCl_3$.

§ 245. If silicium be heated in a current of chlorine, it takes fire, and a colourless volatile liquid is formed, which is the chloride of silicum $SiCl_3$. It may be more easily obtained by passing chlorine over a mixture of silex and carbon heated in a porcelain tube (fig. 264). Chlorine alone will not expel oxygen from silicic acid,

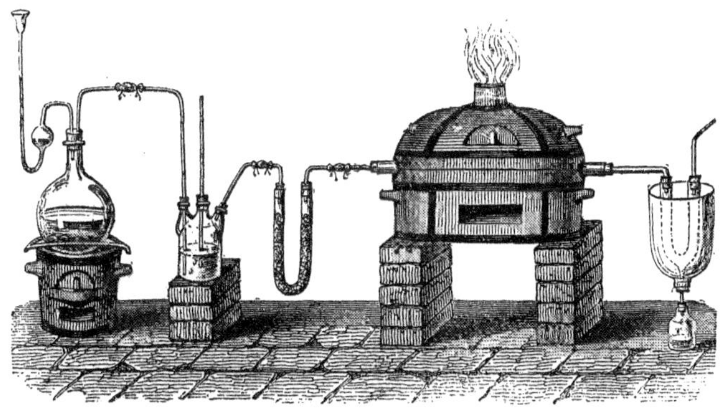

Fig. 264.

even at the highest temperature; but the decomposition is easily effected in presence of carbon, which combines with the oxygen of

* The late investigation of Kopp on the difference of the boiling points between the bromide and chloride of silicium, and that of Pierre on the substitution of sulphur for chlorine in the chloride of silicium, strongly confirm the older view, that silica is SiO_3, and hence that silicium = 21.3.—*J. C. B.*

the silicic acid to form oxide of carbon; the chloride of silicium is collected in a refrigerated receiver. The silica used in this experiment should be the very finely divided, such as that obtained by decomposing silicate of potassa by an acid; for quartz, even when reduced to an impalpable powder, affords only traces of chloride of silicium.

The best method is to mix the silex intimately with an equal weight of lampblack, and sufficient oil to form a paste, and to form it into small balls, which are rolled in powdered charcoal, and calcined in a close crucible. The balls, thus rendered porous, are put into the porcelain tube.

To make a larger quantity of the chloride, the porcelain tube is replaced by a stoneware retort C (fig. 265), holding about a litre

Fig. 265.

(a quart), with a tubulure *a*, to which a smaller porcelain tube *b* is fitted, and carried to the bottom of the retort. The current of dry chlorine is passed through this tube. A tube passing through a condenser is adapted to the neck of the retort, and is succeeded by a U-shaped tube D plunged in a refrigerating mixture contained in an inverted tubulated bell-glass. A straight tube is attached to the lower part of the U-shaped tube, which passes through the tubulure of the bell-glass into a dry bottle, in which the liquid chloride of silicium is collected.

When thus made, it is of a yellow colour, owing to an excess of chlorine, which it holds in solution, and of which it is deprived by shaking it with a small quantity of mercury, and is then obtained perfectly pure by distillation.

Chloride of silicium is a colourless, volatile liquid, of the density 1.52; it boils at 138°, and gives off acid fumes in the air.

By contact with water, it is decomposed into chlorohydric and silicic acids, which proves its correspondence to silicic acid, the oxygen of the acid being replaced by an equivalent quantity of chlorine. Advantage is taken of this reaction to deduce the composition of the acid from the analysis of the chloride, as it presents fewer difficulties than the direct analysis of the acid. We thus find that chloride of silicium is composed of

Silicium	16.71
Chlorine	83.29
	100.00

We may, therefore, express its formula

$SiCl_3$, if we admit SiO_3 for silicic acid.
$SiCl_2$ " " SiO_2 " "
$SiCl$ " " SiO " "

The density of its vapour has been found to be 5.9.

1 volume of the chloride contains 2 volumes of chlorine; for if, to twice the density 2×2.44 of chlorine, we add the corresponding quantity of silicium, which is calculated by the proportion

$$83.29 : 16.71 :: 4.88 : x, \text{ whence } x = 0.98,$$

we find

2 vols. chlorine	4.88
Silicium	0.98
	5.86

which does not differ sensibly from the density of the gaseous chloride found by experiment.

COMBINATION OF SILICIUM WITH FLUORINE.

Fluoride of Silicium, SiF_3.

§ 246. This compound is obtained by heating together, in a glass flask, equal parts of fluor-spar and pounded glass, with 6 or 8 parts of the strongest oil of vitriol. (See fig. 199.) The silicic acid of the glass yields its oxygen to the calcium of the fluor-spar, forming lime, which combines with the sulphuric acid, and the fluorine is united to silicium, to form the gaseous fluoride of silicium. Supposing only the silicic acid of the glass to be present, the reaction may be represented by the following equation:

$$3CaF+SiO_3+3SO_3=3(CaO,SO_3)+SiF_3.$$

The apparatus employed in the experiment should be previously dried with the greatest care, since fluoride of silicium is readily decomposed by contact with water.

Fluoride of silicium is a colourless gas, which must be collected over mercury, as water instantly decomposes it; its density is 3.57; exposed to the air, it gives off very dense acid fumes. Its composition corresponding to that of silicic acid, its formula is SiF_3.

§ 247. When fluoride of silicium is decomposed by water, gelatinous silica is deposited, and the liquid contains a peculiar acid compound, called *silicofluohydric acid.* Reaction takes place between 3 equivalents of fluoride of silicium and 3 equiv. of water. But, of the 3 equiv. of the fluoride, only one is decomposed, producing 3 equiv. of fluohydric acid, which combine with the 2 equiv. of undecomposed fluoride to form silicofluohydric acid. The reaction is therefore represented by the following equation:

$$3SiF_3+3HO=3HF,2SiF_3+SiO_3.$$

The formula of silicofluohydric acid is, therefore,

$$3HF,2SiF_3.$$

When this acid is saturated by a base, the hydrogen of the fluohydric acid is alone replaced by an equivalent quantity of the metal of the base; thus potassa gives the following reaction:

$$3HF,2SiF_3+3KO=3KF,2SiF_3+3HO.$$

The silicofluohydrate of potassa is therefore a double fluoride of potassium and silicium, with the formula

$$3KF,2SiF_3.$$

Fig. 266.

The gelatinous silica which is deposited during the decomposition of the fluoride by water would soon obstruct the orifice of the tube conveying the gas, if it be dipped into water, and might burst the apparatus. The end of the tube is therefore plunged into a stratum of mercury (fig. 266), about an inch thick, at the bottom of the test-glass, before pouring in the water; so that the gas meets with no water to decompose it until after having passed through the stratum of mercury.* The fluoride may likewise be prepared in a glass retort (fig. 267), the neck of which connects with a re-

* Even in this case, the rapid passage of bubbles of gas upward will form tubes of gelatinous silica to the top of the water, through which the gas would then escape into the air. To avoid this inconvenience, it is necessary to break the tubes of silica by stirring with a glass rod.—*J. C. B.*

Fig. 267.

ceiver containing water, without passing through a cork, so that the flask may be easily turned around the neck of the retort, and its sides kept constantly moist. The fluoride, being heavy, falls on the surface of the liquid in the receiver, and a pellicle of gelatinous silex forms, which would soon prevent the action of the water if the flask were not frequently turned.

When a sufficient quantity of fluoride has been decomposed, it is filtered through a cloth, and the residue expressed. To render the liquid more transparent, it should be passed through filtering paper, but even then a small quantity of silica remains in suspension.

Silicofluohydric acid forms a very acid solution, and combines with bases forming double fluorides, the composition of which has been indicated above. Some of these compounds are insoluble; among others, that which it forms with potassa. We have already taken advantage of this property of the acid to precipitate potassa from its solution (§ 170).

If the acid solution be evaporated to dryness with the gelatinous silica deposited during its preparation, the whole substance disappears; water and fluoride of silicium being disengaged. Heat thus produces the inverse reaction of that which takes place in the cold between fluoride of silicium and water; so that now we have,

$$3HF,2SiF_3+SiO_3=3SiF_3+3HO.$$

If the evaporation be performed in a glass vessel, it remains uninjured and retains its transparency; but if, on the other hand, silicofluohydric acid alone, separated by filtration from the deposited silica, be evaporated in a glass vessel, it disappears entirely, and the sides of the vessel are affected, for they must afford sufficient silica to transform the silicofluohydric acid into fluoride of silicium.

CARBON.

EQUIVALENT C = 6 (75 O = 100.)

§ 248. Carbon appears under very different aspects. It is found in nature, perfectly pure and crystallized, in the diamond; which is met with in alluvial formations, resulting from the disintegration of older rocks whose detritus has been carried down by water and has covered extensive valleys and plains. Its principal localities are India, the Island of Borneo, and Brazil. Diamonds are rarely discovered among this detritus, and, in order to find them, it is necessary to wash and sort large quantities of sand. The surface of a crude diamond is generally rough and slightly translucent. Its crystalline form is sometimes well defined, belonging to the regular system of crystallization, and its primitive form the regular octahedron (fig. 20); but the octahedron is most frequently modified by secondary planes, and the crystal presents the appearance of fig. 27. The crystalline faces of the diamond are rarely plane, but more or less convex, so that the edges themselves are curved. The curvature is especially evident in those crystals presenting the general appearance of the regular octahedron; but they are really trisoctahedrons (fig. 27), that is, octahedrons the faces of which have been replaced by low triangular pyramids. The edges of the pyramids being often completely destroyed by the friction the crystal has undergone during transportation with the detritus, it only retains the general aspect of an octahedron with convex faces.

It is generally colourless, but is sometimes found tinged with various hues, the most frequent of which are yellow and a more or less dark brown: blue, rose, and green diamonds have also been found. The density of the diamond varies from 3.50 to 3.55.

The diamond is the hardest of all known substances, scratching all without exception; and its natural facets are harder than those produced by cutting. The latter property is very common among minerals. Glaziers use diamonds to cut glass in any given direction: they select diamond sparks presenting natural curved surfaces, and mount them on a suitable handle, to make the instrument known as a "glazier's diamond." To separate a strip of any width from a pane of glass, they lay a rule along the line to be fractured, and then slide the diamond along the rule, tracing on the glass a very fine line, which renders the glass frangible in this direction; so that, by bending it, it cracks neatly along this line.*

* There is considerable skill required to sever a common glass pane with neatness and confidence. In tracing the line, the diamond should always be held

The diamond can be cut only by its own dust. This operation is begun by rubbing two rough diamonds against each other, and carefully collecting the fine powder which falls down. An outline is thus made of the form the diamond is to receive, and to complete the form and polish it, it is fastened to a copper cup held by steel pincers. It is rubbed on a plate of soft steel, spread with some diamond-dust and olive-oil, and made to revolve very rapidly horizontally around its centre. The various faces to be cut are successively presented to it. The rough diamonds which are rejected are ground in a mortar, and the dust used for diamond cutting.

The diamond being pure crystallized carbon, many attempts have been made to crystallize carbon artificially, in the hope of producing it, but without success. Carbon is completely infusible at the highest temperature which can be generated in our furnaces, so that we cannot hope to crystallize it by means of fusion. And, on the other hand, as we know no solvent for it, it cannot be crystallized by means of solution. Cast-iron may, indeed, at a very high temperature, dissolve a greater portion of carbon than it can retain at a lower temperature; and, on cooling, it parts with a portion, which assumes crystalline forms. But those are very brilliant, black laminæ, frequently quite large, but in no wise resembling the diamond. This crystallized carbon is called *graphite.*

The diamond, placed between the two charcoal cones of a very powerful battery, attains an excessively elevated temperature, and becomes so brilliantly incandescent as to be painful to the eye. But, if observed through a smoked glass, it is seen to swell considerably and separate into several fragments. After cooling, it has entirely changed in appearance, having become of a metallic gray-colour, friable, and precisely similar to the coke arising from bituminous coal. This experiment seems to prove that a high temperature is not favourable to the existence of carbon in the state of the diamond, and that its formation did not take place at a very high temperature.

§ 249. Nature also affords us carbon in a crystalline state entirely different from the diamond, in the state of very fine spangles of a metallic gray-colour, which are often extremely small, and aggregated together, forming shining masses, easily divided by a knife, and leaving a leaden-gray streak on paper. This is the substance known in the arts under the name of *plumbago*, *graphite*, and *blacklead*, of which lead-pencils are made.

Organic bodies are, as we have frequently said, composed of carbon, hydrogen, oxygen, and nitrogen. When subjected to a

in the same position from the beginning to the end of the cut, commencing the cut *near* to one edge, and terminating it lightly at the further edge. The best method of breaking is to hold the pane by both hands, one on each side of the end of the cut, and to bend and pull it slightly apart at the same time.—*J. C. B.*

high temperature, the hydrogen, oxygen, nitrogen, and a portion of the carbon are driven off; and that portion of the carbon which remains presents various appearances, according to the nature of the organic substance. Thus, if a piece of wood be calcined, the coal which remains is black, and exhibits in its fracture the structure of the wood from which it was derived. If sugar or an animal substance be calcined, an extremely light, black, brilliant, swollen coal is obtained, presenting the appearance of fusion. It was not, however, the carbon that fused, but the organic matter which, beginning to melt at the first accession of heat, became more and more doughy as decomposition advanced, and swelled up from the disengagement of gases.

Pit-coal, or bituminous coal, calcined apart from the air, gives a coal, called *coke*, which varies according to the quality of the coal. Fat coal undergoes incipient fusion before being decomposed, and produces a swollen coke of a brilliant metallic gray. The anthracites, which lose but a small quantity of their weight by calcination, afford a coke having the shape, and generally the appearance, of the original piece of anthracite.

Certain organic matters, burning in the air, undergo only an imperfect combustion, emitting a smoky flame, which deposits carbon in the form of an extremely fine black powder. A deposit of this kind is obtained, when a plate of glass is held in the upper part of the flame of a candle. This pulverulent carbon is known in the arts by the name of *lampblack*, and is generally prepared by burning rosin or tar. The apparatus generally used consists of a cylindrical chamber of stone or brick, large enough to allow a sheet-iron cone, having a hole at its apex, and which acts as a chimney, to slide up and down. The walls of the chamber are hung with coarse cloth, which facilitates the deposition of the flakes of lampblack. A cast-iron pot, containing the rosin, is heated by a furnace without, and the entrance of the air is regulated by the working-holes. The incomplete combustion of the combustible vapours produces a considerable quantity of lampblack, which is deposited on the interior of the cone, and chiefly on the walls of the chamber. When the operation is terminated, the cone is allowed to descend: being of a diameter exactly to fill the chamber, it scrapes the sides of it, and throws down all the lampblack on the floor.

Lampblack thus made is always mixed with empyreumatic oils, and, when used as carbon in the laboratory, it must be calcined in a crucible, apart from the air.*

---

* Lampblack is made in Philadelphia by setting fire to rosin or coal-tar contained in a shallow cast-iron vessel, of some 5 feet diameter, which is placed at the outer end of a horizontal semicylindric flue of masonry, of 25 to 40 feet in length. These flues open into a large chamber, with brick or stone walls, and

Carbon, in these various states, presents very different physical properties: its specific gravity ranges over a wide space; thus,

The density of the diamond is	3.50
That of natural graphite	2.20
That of powdered coke varies from ...	1.60 to 2.00

The density of charcoal varies according to its porosity. At first sight, it seems lighter than water, on the surface of which it floats; but it is easy to show that this property depends on its containing cavities into which the water cannot penetrate, for, if pulverized, its powder sinks to the bottom.

Ordinary charcoal is a bad conductor of heat, so that a piece of it, lighted at one end, may be held by the fingers very near the burning portion, without communicating much warmth. It is also a bad conductor of electricity; but becomes a good one, when vividly calcined. Thus the half-burned coals from our fireplaces are used to surround the end of lightning-rods, to facilitate the discharge of the electricity into the earth.

§ 250. The very porous varieties of charcoal possess remarkable powers of absorption, which have been usefully applied in the arts. If a red-hot coal be plunged into mercury, in order to extinguish it, apart from the air, and, without removing it from the mercury, it be then passed into a bell-glass containing any gas, a considerable quantity of the gas will be absorbed, the quantity varying according to the nature of the gas and that of the coal. A measure of charcoal from boxwood absorbs 35 measures of carbonic acid gas, and 90 measures of ammoniacal gas.

If a porous charcoal be left for some time in an atmosphere of sulphuretted hydrogen, so that a large quantity of it is absorbed, and be then passed into a bell-glass filled with oxygen, the coal becomes heated, sulphur separates, and water and sulphurous gas are formed. The combustion is sometimes so sudden that explosion ensues. Similar phenomena takes place with other combustible gases.

Charcoal also absorbs colouring matters dissolved in water. If red wine be shaken for a few moments with certain pulverized porous charcoals, it loses its colour entirely. Charcoal likewise

---

an iron (or sometimes board) roof, and containing 150,000 to 350,000 cubic feet. The whole building is either closed as tightly as practicable, or a portion of smoke is allowed to escape through a chimney or windows covered with coarse wire-gauze. The lampblack deposits on the walls and floor, from the former of which it soon detaches itself, and the whole is collected in a thick layer on the floor. There being two flues, with their separate iron pans, doors, &c., as soon as one is burned out, and a little draft allowed to enter the building, the second is fired; and the operations are thus continued day and night. The quantity made in three establishments, when in active operation, is nearly two tons daily.—*J. C. B.*

absorbs many odorous matters; thus, stagnant waters, exhaling an infectious stench, lose it by contact with charcoal; and it is for this reason that the inside of wooden water-tanks for ships are always slightly charred.

The different kinds of charcoal possess very different powers of absorption. In graphite and the bituminous coals they are null, but are strongly marked in wood charcoal, and powerful in proportion to the number of the pores in the coal. The charcoal derived from the calcination of bones presents this quality in the highest degree. By calcining bones in close vessels, the animal matter they contain is carbonized, and a very porous coal is obtained, mixed with the earthy matter of the bones, which is called in the arts *animal charcoal* or *boneblack*. The bones are calcined in large cast-iron cylinders, arranged horizontally in a furnace, and having a pipe at one end, which communicates with a refrigerating apparatus, in which the ammoniacal products are collected for future use. When the calcination is ended, the coal is withdrawn, extinguished in an extinguisher, and reduced in suitable mills to powder of different fineness.

§ 254. Carbon burns in the air and is converted into carbonic acid gas. Its combustion in oxygen is much more vivid. The charcoal is attached to the extremity of an iron wire, ignited in the blowpipe flame, passed through an alcohol-lamp, and quickly plunged into a vessel filled with oxygen, where it burns with great splendour. The formation of an acid gas by the combustion is easily recognised by pouring into the vessel a little blue infusion of litmus, which is reddened. If lime-water be introduced, it becomes milky, and carbonate of lime is precipitated. The various kinds of charcoals are combustible in an inverse proportion to their density. Thus, wood charcoal burns in the air; compact coke, especially that of anthracite, only burns in a rapid current of air, as that produced by a bellows, or when masses of it are burned together; the diamond and graphite, though heated to ignition, do not continue burning in the air, but their combustion goes on in oxygen. A small diamond being fastened to the end of a pipe-stem, which is attached to a bent wire, it is strongly heated in the blowpipe, (best in the hydroxygen blowpipe,) and when well ignited is quickly plunged into a bottle filled with oxygen, where it continues to burn until it is entirely consumed. It can easily be proved by lime-water that carbonic acid is formed, as in the combustion of ordinary charcoal.

Although carbon has a great affinity for oxygen, it is otherwise a very fixed body. These properties render it a very valuable agent in depriving almost all other substances of their oxygen, and it is hence almost exclusively used in metallurgy for the *reduction* of metallic oxides.

COMBINATIONS OF CARBON WITH OXYGEN.

§ 252. Carbon forms several compounds with oxygen, of which we shall notice only the three most important :

1. Carbonic acid.................................... CO_2
2. Carbonic oxide.................................. CO
3. Oxalic acid .... C_2O_3

The first two are gaseous at ordinary temperatures; and the third has not been isolated, being only known in combination with water or bases.

Carbonic Acid, CO_2.

§ 253. When carbon burns freely in the air or in oxygen, it is converted into carbonic acid. But the simplest method of obtaining this gas in large quantities is to treat carbonate of lime, a mineral widely disseminated through nature, with a strong acid. Our ordinary limestone, chalk, marble, and the shells of shell-fish are essentially composed of carbonate of lime. Statuary marble is very pure carbonate of lime.

To procure carbonic acid, pieces of marble, &c. are introduced into a bottle A, with two tubulures (fig. 268,)* a certain quantity of water poured over it, and the bottle shaken for a few moments, to expel the bubbles of air adhering to the marble. To one of the tubulures *a*, is fitted an exit tube, to collect the gas, and to the other *b* is adapted a larger tube, terminating in a funnel, and descending nearly to the bottom of the bottle. Chlorohydric acid is poured through the tube *b*, and as soon as it reaches the marble, a lively effervescence ensues from the disengagement of carbonic acid gas.

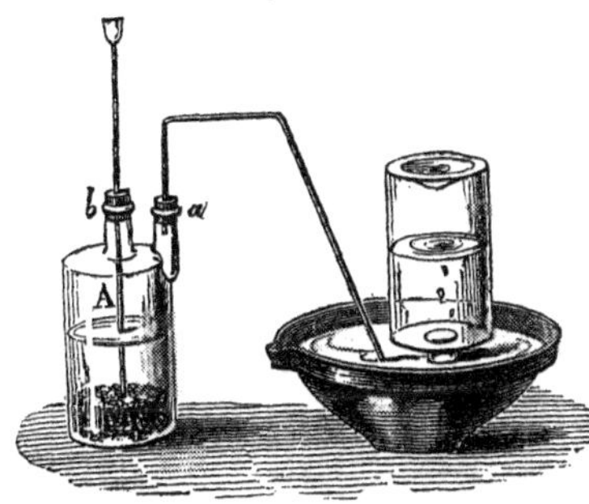

Fig. 268.

The reaction is represented by the following equation :

$$CaO,CO_2+HCl=CaCl+HO+CO_2.$$

The result is therefore carbonic acid, which is disengaged in a gaseous form, and may be collected over water or mercury; chloride of calcium, which dissolves in the water of the bottle; and, lastly, water, which remains mixed with that already contained in

* Or into a wide-mouthed bottle with a cork pierced for the two tubes. —*J. C. B.*

the bottle. In order to obtain pure carbonic acid, a considerable portion of the gas must be allowed to escape before collecting it, for it must expel the air contained in the upper part of the bottle, as well as that lodged in the interstices of the carbonate of lime. The gas is known to be pure when it is completely absorbed by a solution of potassa. The chlorohydric acid is added gradually, through the funnel, and only when the effervescence produced by the preceding portion begins to slacken.

Sulphuric may be substituted for chlorohydric acid; when the reaction is represented by the following formula:

$$CaO,CO_2+SO_3=CaO,SO_3+CO_2.$$

In this case, carbonic acid and sulphate of lime are formed; and, the latter being only slightly soluble in water, the greater part of it is deposited in the form of minute crystalline scales, which eventually prevent the contact of the marble and sulphuric acid, and impede the reaction. This does not occur when chlorohydric acid is employed, because the chloride of calcium is eminently soluble in water, and leaves the pieces of marble freely exposed to the further action of the acid.

§ 253 *bis*. Carbonic acid is a colourless gas, nearly inodorous, having a slightly sourish taste; its density is greater than that of the air, being 1.529 at 32°, under a pressure of $0^m.760$ (29.92 in.) A litre of it, under the same circumstances, weighs $1^{gm}.977$. (100 cub. in. at 32° and 29.92 Bar. weigh 50.03856 grs.)

Carbonic acid gas liquefies at a temperature of 32°, under a pressure of 36 atmospheres. The pressure of 27 atmospheres will suffice at a temperature of 14°, and at that of −22°, which is easily obtained by a mixture of crystallized chloride of calcium and ice, a pressure of 18 atmospheres effects its liquefaction. When the temperature is greater than that of melting ice, a greater pressure is required, so that at the temperature of 86°, the pressure of 73 atmospheres becomes necessary. It forms a very unstable, colourless liquid, remarkable for its great dilatability, for its coefficient of dilatation, which varies greatly with the temperature, is greater than that of atmospheric air, and the coefficient of the latter far surpasses that of all the liquids which we are required to examine at ordinary temperatures.

The spec. grav. of liquid carbonic acid, compared with water at 32°, is 0.98 at 17½°, and 0.72 at 80½°. The acid solidifies at about −94°, when it forms a perfectly transparent vitreous mass.

Carbonic acid is eminently soluble in water, which dissolves about its own volume of gas at ordinary temperatures. Its solubility does not prevent our collecting it over water for ordinary experiments, but, in exact researches, it is better to collect it over mercury.

The quantity of the gas dissolved by water at the same temperature, increases with the pressure to which the gas is subjected. It has been observed that a *volume of water* dissolves its own volume of carbonic acid, whatever be the density of the gas; in other words, whatever the pressure to which it is subjected. Thus, a litre of water dissolves nearly a litre of carbonic acid gas, under the pressure of 1, 2, 3 . . . 10 atmospheres; but, as the densities of the gas are, in this case, nearly as 1 : 2 : 3 : . . . : 10, the weight of carbonic acid dissolved will be in the same proportions of 1 : 2 : 3 : . . . : 10.

A solution of carbonic acid reddens the tincture of litmus, like a feeble acid, producing only a purplish red.

Carbonic acid does not support combustion, and immediately extinguishes a lighted taper plunged into it; nor does it support respiration, for an animal immersed in an atmosphere of it speedily perishes from asphyxia. It does not, however, exert deleterious influence on the organs, for it may exist in considerable proportions in the air, without any inconvenience to animals, provided there be sufficient oxygen to maintain respiration.

As carbonic acid is much heavier than the air, it may be poured, like a liquid, from one vessel into another in the open air, provided it be perfectly tranquil. Of two tubes, A and B (fig. 269), nearly equal, A is filled with carbonic acid over water, the opening closed under water with the hand, and the tube taken out. An assistant handing the glass B, filled with air, the carbonic acid in A is poured into it, as in the figure. It is easy to prove that it has passed from A to B, for a lighted taper continues to burn in A, and is extinguished in B.*

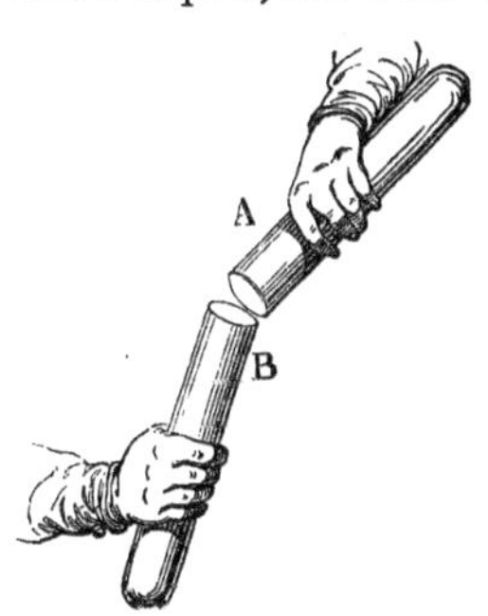

Fig. 269.

Carbonic acid is formed under variety of circumstances; it is constantly produced by combustion in our fireplaces; large quantities of it are given off in respiration; all organic substances exposed to a damp atmosphere are destroyed by fermentation with a copious disengagement of the gas; lastly, burning volcanoes constantly project torrents of it into the air. It is also disengaged from many localities which present no igneous eruptions, but which have formerly been the seat of volcanic activity. In such regions, springs issuing from the earth contain carbonic acid in solution, and their waters effervesce on reaching the surface. They are called *gaseous* or *carbonated mineral waters.*

Gaseous waters are made artificially, by saturating ordinary

* The best method of exhibiting its density, as a class experiment, is to fill a bell-glass with it by displacement (see fig. 223, § 167), and to pour its contents into another, filled with air, and having a burning taper at the bottom. As the dry gas descends, the taper is extinguished.—*J. C. B.*

water with the gas under strong pressure, and immediately transferring it to well-corked jugs or bottles, to prevent the escape of the gas.

If the water has been saturated under a pressure of 10 atmospheres, it contains a quantity of carbonic acid ten times greater than if the saturation had taken place under the pressure of a single atmosphere. A considerable portion of the dissolved gas will therefore escape when the gaseous water is poured into a glass. If the gaseous water be exposed to the air, it will ultimately part with all its carbonic acid, and return to the state of ordinary water. This is a natural consequence of the law of the solution of gases in water—a law developed in § 81. We have seen that water dissolved nearly its own volume of carbonic acid gas, the dissolved gas having the same density as the carbonic acid gas of the atmosphere which presses on this liquid. Now, when the solution is exposed to the air, the density of the carbonic acid which enters into the composition of the atmosphere is exceedingly small, and, as it were, null, so that the carbonic acid of the solution must be disengaged until it acquires an equal density, that is, until this disengagement is nearly complete.

If the gaseous water be poured into a glass, bubbles of gas will be seen to start from its sides, and particularly from the bottom, if it be more rough; and if a very rough body, such as a piece of bread, be thrown into the liquid, a lively effervescence takes place around it. The following is the reason of this phenomenon: Each molecule of carbonic acid in solution is retained by the molecules of the surrounding water, which are uniformly arranged around the molecules of acid, in the interior of the liquid, or even at some distance from the sides. But, immediately in contact with the side, the molecule of acid is only retained in solution by the aqueous molecules on one side, and, on the other, by the surface of the side of the glass. Now, it will be readily perceived that this side will retain the molecule of carbonic acid with much less force than the particles of water whose place it usurps. The molecules of carbonic acid in contact with the glass are therefore the first to assume the gaseous form. But, if a certain number of these molecules have united to form a small gaseous bubble, the latter, passing through the liquid, will necessarily increase by the addition of other molecules of the gas which it meets on its way. For, if we suppose the bubble of gas to be arrested in any one of its positions, it is evident that the molecules of dissolved carbonic acid which are immediately on the periphery of the bubble, being retained only by one-half of the particles of water which keep the molecules of acid dissolved in other parts of the liquid, will escape more rapidly than the latter.

In localities where this gas is exhaled from fissures in the earth, it frequently accumulates in low spots, natural excavations, and grottos, in which the air is not often changed; forming an invisible stratum of variable thickness on the surface of the ground, in which animals perish, if they remain for too long a period. The famous *Grotto del Cane*, near Naples, presents a phenomenon of this character. Men may walk there free from danger, while a dog, with his head nearer to the ground, soon falls asphyxiated.

§ 254. Liquid carbonic acid has been lately used to produce great degrees of cold, in order to liquefy and even solidify many gaseous substances. The apparatus used for this purpose consists of two parts:

1st. The *generator*, in which the liquid acid is produced.

2d. The *receiver*, into which it is transferred by distillation, so as to separate it from the other products of the reaction, and in which the products of several successive operations may be accumulated.

The liquid acid is produced by decomposing bicarbonate of soda by sulphuric acid in the generator. The first portions of acid disengaged assume the gaseous form, but the pressure soon becomes sufficient to liquefy it.

The generator is a vessel closed air-tight, and was formerly made of very thick cast-iron, but the danger of employing cast-iron where great powers of resistance are required, and the occurrence of a terrible accident from an explosion, have proscribed its use.

As now made, it consists of a cylindrical vessel of lead, (fig. 270), covered with copper, and strengthened by rings and bars of wrought iron, and contains 6 or 7 litres (1½–2 gallons). The

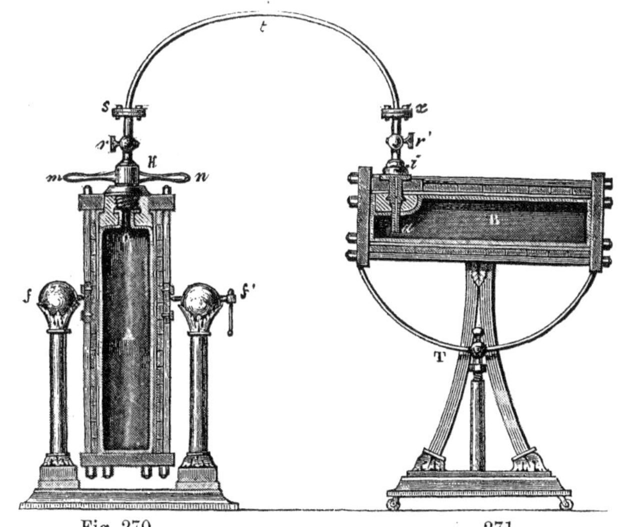

Fig. 270. Fig. 271.

copper cylinder surrounding the vessel is made to fit it exactly, and the ends are further strengthened by iron plates, fastened together by bars of the same metal. The generator is suspended between the two points *f*, *f'*, by a cast-iron stand.

The construction of the receiver (fig. 271) is similar to that of the generator.

The aperture O of the generator is closed by a screw *h'*, having a hole through its axis, and furnished with a stopcock *r*. The screw is worked with a double handle *mn*, and a leaden ring, compressed in a double collar, renders the closure perfect.

There is an aperture *i* on the upper edge of the receiver B, to which is adapted a copper tube, descending nearly to the bottom of the receiver, with a stopcock *r'* on the outside. The receiver and generator can be made to communicate, by means of a fixed copper tube *stx*.

To prepare the liquid acid, the stopper *k* is removed, and there are introduced into the generator 1800 grammes (about 4 lbs.) of bicarbonate of soda, $4\frac{1}{2}$ litres (qts.) of water at 95° to 104°, and a cylindrical copper vessel *uv* (fig. 272) containing 1000^{gm} ($2\frac{1}{5}$ lbs.) of oil of vitriol. This cylinder falls into the axis of the generator, and, while the latter remains vertical, the sulphuric acid cannot come into contact with the bicarbonate of soda.

u

v

Fig. 272.

The stopper *k* being then fixed, and the cock *r* closed, by inclining the generator below the horizontal line, the acid contained in the copper tube is poured out, and the reaction immediately commences. The generator is made to revolve several times around its axis to mix the substances together, and in about ten minutes, the carbonic acid may be passed into the receiver. A connection between the generator and receiver is effected by the tube *stx*, and the cocks *r'* and *r* opened, when the carbonic acid in the generator distils over immediately, and recondenses in the liquid form in the receiver. The distillation occurs by virtue of the difference in temperature between the generator and the receiver. That of the former not being lower than 86°, with a tension of the acid in it equal to about 75 atmospheres. If the temperature of the receiver be 59°, which may be assumed to be that of the laboratory, the maximum tension of the acid being, for that temperature, only 50 atmospheres, distillation must take place by virtue of the difference of pressure of $75-50=25$ atmospheres; that is, it will be extremely rapid; indeed, less than a minute is required to allow the carbonic acid in the generator to pass into the receiver.

The same operation is repeated with 5 or 6 additional quantities of carbonic acid, so as to accumulate about 2 litres (2 qts.) of liquid acid in the receiver.

The cock *r'* being closed, the generator and receiver are disconnected. The latter is then two-thirds full of liquid carbonic acid, surmounted by a gaseous atmosphere exerting a pressure of 50 atmospheres, if the temperature of the laboratory be 59°. It follows, therefore, that if we open the stopcock *r′* of the receiver, the liquid acid will be forcibly expelled from the receiver, and, if projected into the open air, will immediately assume the gaseous form, appearing like a white cloud. A considerable degree of cold necessarily exists in the gaseous current, and, if the jet be directed into a bottle, or, better still, into a very thin metallic box, a large portion of the carbonic acid will volatilize, by abstracting the heat necessary for its change of condition from the sides of the vessel, and from that portion of the carbonic acid which remained liquid. The temperature will fall below −94; and the remaining acid will condense to a solid, in the form of a white cotton-like snow.

Carbonic acid may be preserved in the snowy form much longer than in the liquid state; evaporation being very slow, on account of its bad conducting qualities, and an air thermometer, surrounded by the snow evaporating freely in the air, falls to −110. A flake of snowy carbonic acid may be held on the hand without imparting a feeling of intense cold, because it is constantly kept from immediate contact by a current of gaseous acid; but, if the flake be pressed between the fingers, great pain is felt, like that produced by a heated body, and the skin is disorganized as by a burn.

Figs. 273 and 274 represent the metallic box generally used to collect solid carbonic acid, and is composed of two parts *abcd* and *a′b′c′d′* (fig. 273), which may be readily separated and joined together. The part *abcd* has a tubulure *t*, in which is inserted the small tube *u* (fig. 275), previously fastened to the piece *x* of the receiver (fig. 271). By opening the cock *r′*, a jet of the liquid acid enters the box almost at a tangent to its periphery, and then meeting a tongue *m*, arranged to produce a gyratory movement, a portion of the liquid acid is converted into gas, which, after having passed around the box, escapes through the central tubes *cd* and *c′d′*, while the remainder is solidified in the form of the white snow, which is removed by opening the box. The tubes *cd* and *c′d′* are surrounded by two concentric tubes covered with cloth, so that they can be held in the hand without imparting too great a degree of cold.

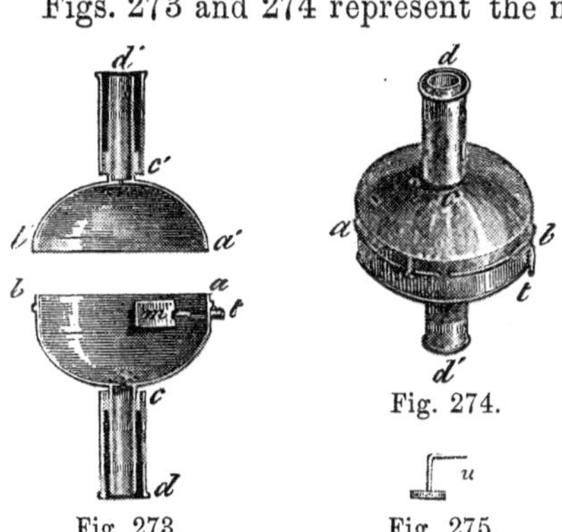

Fig. 273. Fig. 274. Fig. 275.

If upon the solid acid a liquid be poured which does not combine chemically with it, and does not congeal at a very low temperature, the acid evaporates more rapidly, because the interposed liquid considerably increases its conductibility, and a very powerful refrigerating mixture is obtained, which rapidly cools bodies immersed in it, without, however, lowering their temperature much more than solid carbonic acid alone. If such a mixture be placed under the receiver of the air-pump, and the evaporation be accelerated by a vacuum, the temperature falls to $-150°$.

Ether is generally mixed with the snowy acid, and, by means of this frigorific paste, 1 kilogramme (2 lbs.) of mercury can be frozen in a few moments; and, if an hermetically sealed tube, containing the liquid acid, be immersed in it, it congeals to a perfectly transparent vitreous mass.

§ 255. The composition of carbonic acid can be readily determined, approximately, by the following experiment:—A flask holding about 1 litre (1 qt.) is filled with oxygen, over the mercurial trough, and placed in the inverted position represented in fig. 276. A small piece of charcoal fastened to the end of stout platinum wire, being introduced into the flask, is ignited by concentrating the solar rays by a powerful lens, and is converted into carbonic acid. When the combustion is finished, and the gas is allowed to recover its original temperature, it will be found that its volume has not sensibly changed. We hence conclude that carbonic acid gas contains a volume of oxygen equal to itself.

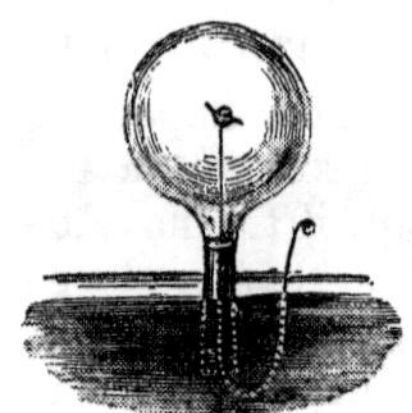
Fig. 276.

Now, 1 vol. of carbonic acid gas weighs..... 1.5290
1 " " oxygen " 1.1056

The weight 1.5290 of carbonic acid contains, therefore, a weight 1.1056 of oxygen, and a weight 0.4234 of carbon; which gives, for the composition of carbonic acid,

Carbon	27.68
Oxygen	72.32
	100.00

But this determination is only an approximation; and it may be ascertained with precision by the following experiment:

A given weight p of pure carbon, as the diamond, contained in a small platinum dish, is introduced into a porcelain tube *ab* (fig. 277), arranged in a reverberatory furnace. One end of the tube *a* is connected with an apparatus which furnishes perfectly dry oxygen gas, and the other end with a series of tubes, as represented in the figure.

The tube A is a U-tube, containing pumice-stone impregnated with oil of vitriol.

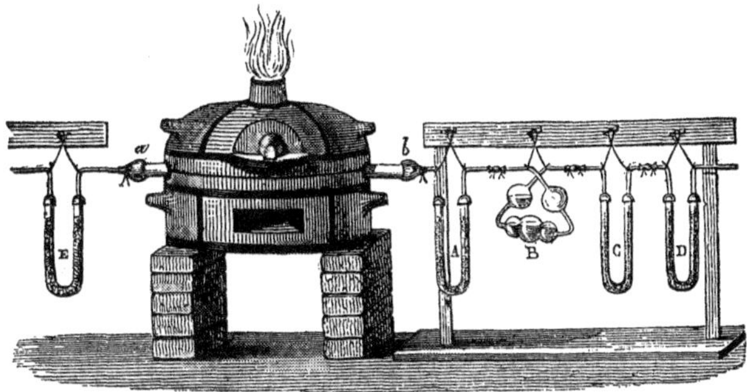

Fig. 277.

The bulbed apparatus B contains a concentrated solution of caustic potassa.

The tube C is filled with large pieces of pumice-stone impregnated with a concentrated solution of caustic potassa.

Lastly, the tube D is filled with large pieces of pumice-stone impregnated with oil of vitriol.

Let P be the exact weight of all the tubes B, C, D. The apparatus is arranged by joining the various tubes together by caoutchouc tubes. The apparatus being filled with oxygen gas, slowly passed through it, the tube *ab*, containing the carbon, is heated to redness, and the gases traverse the series A, B, C, D. The tube A condenses the small quantity of hygroscopic moisture which may be furnished by the interior of the tube *ab*. The carbonic acid formed is almost wholly condensed in the bulbs B; but if it be too rapidly generated, (an occurrence that cannot always be avoided,) a portion of it, which might escape from B without being condensed, is arrested by the tube C.

The gases passing through the bulbs B and the tube C being perfectly dry, and the solution of caustic potassa contained in the apparatus not being sufficiently concentrated to render its tension of vapour insensible, they have a tendency to abstract from this solution a certain quantity of aqueous vapour, which will diminish the weight of the apparatus to that extent. The last tube, D, remedies this defect, by restoring to the gases their condition of absolute dryness which they possessed before passing into the air.

In this combustion of carbon, the formation of a small quantity of oxide of carbon might be feared, which would render the analysis inaccurate; and, to avoid such an error, the anterior part of the tube *ab* is filled with very porous oxide of copper, which is heated to redness during the experiment. The gaseous mixture being obliged to traverse the oxide before reaching the apparatus in which absorption takes place, the small quantities of gaseous oxide of carbon which might be present are necessarily converted into carbonic acid. A plug of asbestos is used to separate that portion of the tube containing oxide of copper from that which contains the small dish holding the carbon.

When the combustion of the carbon is completed, the disengagement of the oxygen is continued for some time, in order to be sure that all the carbonic acid produced has passed through the absorbing apparatus. The apparatus being taken apart, the first step is to ascertain whether the carbon in the dish is completely destroyed. Most frequently, a small residue of incombustible earthy matter is found, which was mechanically mixed with the carbon. The residue, which cannot exceed a few milligrammes, is weighed, and its weight π subtracted from the weight p, in order to obtain the exact weight $(p-\pi)$ of the carbon which has been burned.

Upon finding the weight P' of the apparatus B, C, D, it is evident that $(P'-P)$ will represent the weight of carbonic acid produced. It has therefore been ascertained, that a weight $(p-\pi)$ of carbon produces a weight $(P'-P)$ of carbonic acid.

The apparatus B, C, D should be weighed with special precaution, where precision is required. It displaces a considerable volume of air, and, in order to obtain the absolute weights P, P′, before and after the experiment, the weight of air it displaces under both circumstances must be added. If this air were exactly in the same condition, at the time of both weighings, the additions would be unnecessary, because, being nearly equal in both cases, they would destroy each other in the difference $(P'-P)$. But we can never be sure of establishing this identity of conditions, and it is better to guard against this source of error by the following arrangement, which we have already mentioned (§ 97) for weighing accurately a flask filled with gas.

The dishes of the balance used in the experiment should be furnished with hooks beneath, to one of which the apparatus B, C, D, is attached, by a long piece of wire, to keep it at a great distance from the point of suspension of the dishes to the beam. To the hook of the second dish, and at the same distance, is fastened a system of tubes B′, C′, D′, as similar as possible to the tubes B, C, D, and charged in the same manner. The system B′, C′, D′ should nearly balance the system B, C, D, as weighed before the experiment; and then perfect equilibrium is established by additional weights.

At the second weighing, the system B, C, D has increased by the weight of carbonic acid which it has absorbed which weight will be immediately given by the weights necessary to restore the equilibrium, under the same conditions in which the first weighing was made.

As the two systems B, C, D and B′, C′, D′ displace nearly the same volume of air, it is clear that the result of the weighings, made as directed, will be nearly independent of the small variations which the constitution of the air might undergo between the times of weighing.

It is thus found that carbonic acid contains

1 eq. carbon	6.0	27.27
2 " oxygen	16.0	72.73
1 " carbonic acid	22.0	100.00

If the number 72.73 be divided by the density 1.1056 of oxygen, and the number 100 by the density 1.5290 of carbonic acid gas, the quotients 65.7 and 65.4, which are nearly equal, lead to the conclusion that carbonic acid gas contains a volume of oxygen precisely equal to its own. The difference between 65.7 and 65.4 is owing to the fact that carbonic acid gas departs remarkably from Mariotte's law, even under the ordinary pressure of the atmosphere. These quotients would be much more nearly equal, if, instead of dividing the numbers 72.73 and 100 by the respective densities of oxygen and carbonic acid under the pressure of $0^m.760$, (29.92 in.) we were to divide them by the densities of these same gases under less pressure, as that of $0^m.100$ (3.937 inches).

Carbonic Oxide, CO.

§ 256. Carbonic oxide gas is obtained, by slowly passing a current of carbonic acid through a long porcelain or strong glass tube, containing charcoal, and heated to redness. The carbonic acid combines with a quantity of carbon equal to that which it already contains.

It is, however, easier to heat finely pulverized carbonate of lime intimately mixed with charcoal, in a stoneware retort, in a reverberatory furnace. Carbonate of lime alone is decomposed at a red-heat, giving off its carbonic acid; but the gas at this temperature meets with carbon, and is converted into oxide of carbon. It is necessary to agitate the gas collected in the bell-glasses for a few moments with a solution of caustic potassa, in order to absorb the small proportion of carbonic acid which may have escaped decomposition.

But carbonic oxide gas may be still more readily obtained, by decomposing with oil of vitriol oxalic acid, which is the third combination of carbon with oxygen. The formula of crystallized oxalic acid is C_2O_3+3HO, and it will easily part with 2 equivalents of water without being decomposed, but the third cannot be abstracted without decomposing it into carbonic acid and oxide; for we have $C_2O_3=CO_2+CO$.

The decomposition takes place when the crystallized acid is heated with a substance which powerfully attracts its water, such as an excess of oil of vitriol.

The oxalic acid is introduced into a small flask, and 5 or 6 times its weight of oil of vitriol added. To the flask is fitted an exit tube which carries the gas into a bell-glass over water or mercury.

When first heated, the oxalic acid dissolves in the sulphuric; but an effervescence soon ensues, arising from the decomposition of the oxalic acid into its two gaseous products, carbonic acid and oxide, which are evolved in equal volumes. To the mixed gases collected in a bell-glass are introduced a few cubic centimetres (1 or 2 fl. dr.), of a solution of potassa, which absorbs the carbonic acid, and leaves the carbonic oxide pure. The gaseous mixture, as it is disengaged, may also be passed through a washing-bottle (fig. 278) containing caustic potassa, and the small quantity of carbonic acid which escapes absorption in the bottle may be absorbed in the bell-glass.

Fig. 278.

Carbonic oxide gas is colourless, inodorous, and has not yet been liquefied. It burns in the air with a characteristic bluish flame, and is then converted into carbonic acid. Its specific gravity is 0.967. Water dissolves only about one-sixteenth of its volume of the gas. It does not act upon litmus, nor combine with the acids or bases.

Whenever charcoal is burned in our furnaces, and not supplied with a sufficient quantity of oxygen, a large proportion of carbonic oxide is formed. It thus happens, when a laboratory furnace is filled with ignited coals piled up so as to form a burning heap of several decimetres (a foot or more) in height. The lower strata are at first converted into carbonic acid, from the oxygen of the air passing through the lower bars of the grate, and here the temperature is highest. In the upper strata, combustion being supported only by the highly heated gaseous current which has traversed the lower ones, carbonic acid is converted into oxide of carbon, and the temperature is much lower. Lastly, when the gaseous mixture again comes in contact with the air in the upper part of the furnace, if the temperature is sufficiently high, carbonic oxide is ignited, and burns with a blue flame.

In wind and blast furnaces, employed in metallurgy, and often of considerable elevation, combustion obeys the same laws; but, as the fuel and minerals are thrown in cold at the top of the furnace, the temperature in that part is always low, and the combustion of the oxide of carbon only ensues if designedly inflamed; when it continues indefinitely.

Oxide of carbon is not merely passive in not supporting respiration, but is active as a poison; for an animal perishes if left for some time in an atmosphere containing a few per cent. of this gas. To its presence must be attributed the uneasiness and headache experienced by remaining in a badly ventilated apartment, near a furnace containing burning charcoal, the products of which do not immediately pass up the chimney. If a large proportion of carbonic oxide gas be present in a closely shut room, death ensues from asphyxia.

§ 257. Carbonic oxide is readily analyzed by burning it with oxygen in the eudiometer.

Let us suppose that we have introduced into the eudiometer

100 volumes of carbonic oxide
75 " of oxygen,
175

By passing an electric spark through it, the bulk of gas, after the explosion, is reduced to 125 volumes. If a little potassa be now introduced into the eudiometer and shaken in it, the carbonic acid produced is absorbed, so that the remaining gas will only measure 25 volumes, and prove to be pure oxygen. The bulk of carbonic acid gas produced contains, therefore, 100 volumes; that is, it is equal to that of the carbonic oxide operated on, and the volume of oxygen consumed is $75-25=50$.

One volume of carbonic oxide therefore consumes a $\frac{1}{2}$ volume of oxygen, and produces 1 volume of carbonic acid. Now, 1 volume of carbonic acid gas contains 1 volume of oxygen; and, consequently, 1 volume of carbonic oxide gas only contains a $\frac{1}{2}$ volume. If, therefore, we subtract from the density of

Carbonic oxide	0.9674
$\frac{1}{2}$ the density of oxygen	0.5528
We have	0.4146

which is the weight of carbon combined with a weight 0.5528 of oxygen, to form a weight 0.9674 of oxide of carbon. Oxide of carbon is therefore composed of

1 eq. of carbon	6.0	42.86
1 " oxygen	8.0	57.14
1 " oxide of carbon	14.0	100.00

Chloroxicarbonic Gas, CO,Cl.

§ 258. Chlorine and carbonic oxide combine under the influence of solar light; and, in order to obtain the compound, a dry flask is exhausted of air as completely as possible, and filled with dry carbonic oxide until the pressure of the gas is equal to one-half the pressure of the atmosphere. The flask being closed, chlorine gas is introduced until the internal pressure is exactly equal to that of the atmosphere, so that the flask contains equal volumes of chlorine and carbonic oxide. The gases are merely mixed if the chlorine has been introduced in a room illuminated only by diffused light, or, better still, by the light of a candle; but, if the flask be exposed to the direct rays of the sun, combination immediately ensues, and the greenish colour of chlorine entirely disappears. Combination will also ensue in the diffused light of day, but after a greater lapse of time. Under all circumstances, however, after combination has been effected, if the flask be made to communicate with the manometer which measured the internal pressure, the latter will be found to be only one-half of that of the atmosphere. We hence conclude that 1 volume of chlorine has combined with 1 volume of carbonic oxide to form 1 volume of the new gas, which is called *chloroxicarbonic*, (also chlorocarbonic acid, phosgen gas.) The density of the gas is obtained by adding to

the density of chlorine	2.440
" " carbonic oxide	0.967
Density of chloroxicarbonic gas	3.407

and its formula is COCl. It may be regarded as carbonic acid CO_2, or CO,O, in which one of the equivalents of oxygen is replaced by an equivalent of chlorine.

Chloroxicarbonic gas is colourless, and has a peculiar, suffocating odour. It is decomposed by contact with water, an equivalent of each body producing chlorohydric and carbonic acids. Thus,

$$CO,Cl+HO=CO_2,HCl.$$

Oxalic Acid, C_2O_3.

§ 259. Oxalic acid exists in a great number of vegetables. It is prepared artificially by boiling sugar with slightly dilute nitric acid, which, by yielding a portion of its oxygen, evolves deutoxide of nitrogen and carbonic acid, while oxalic acid remains in the liquid, from which it crystallizes on cooling. Six parts of nitric acid, of the density 1.2, are employed for 1 part of sugar, and about $\frac{1}{4}$ oxalic acid is obtained.

The crystals deposited in the liquid always retain some nitric acid, from which they are purified by redissolving in boiling water, and again crystallizing them. Nine parts of water, at the ordinary temperature, are required to dissolve 1 part of oxalic acid; but a much smaller quantity of boiling water will suffice.

The formula of the crystallized acid is C_2O_3+3HO. If it be heated to 212° in a current of dry air, or if exposed for a long time to a dry atmosphere, it loses about 28 per cent. of its weight, corresponding to 2 equivalents of water. But the last equivalent of water cannot be abstracted except by combining the acid with a base. The endeavour to deprive it in any other way of the last equivalent of water decomposes it into carbonic acid and carbonic oxide. Advantage was taken of this reaction to obtain carbonic oxide.

Oxalic is a powerful acid, combining with bases, and producing well-defined salts. It readily expels carbonic acid from all its compounds.

§ 260. Oxalic acid is analyzed in the following manner:—Let us first suppose that it is required to analyze crystallized acid containing 3 equivalents of water, according to the formula C_2O_3+3HO. One gramme of the acid reduced to powder is accurately weighed, and mixed with 20 or 30 times its weight of recently calcined and perfectly dry oxide of copper, and the mixture introduced into a strong glass tube, 5 or 6 decimetres (18–22 in.) in length, open at one end *a*, and drawn out to a fine point at the other end *b*. Pure oxide of copper being poured upon the mixture, so as to fill the tube to within 3 or 4 centimetres ($1\frac{1}{4}$–$1\frac{1}{2}$ in.) of its opening *a*, the tube is arranged in a sheet-iron furnace, made as represented in fig. 279. The series of tubes A, B, C, arranged as

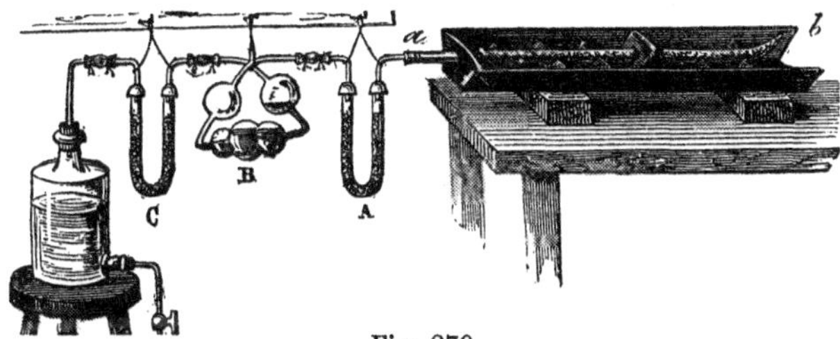

Fig. 279.

directed for the analysis of carbonic acid (§ 255), are connected with the tube in the furnace by a cock. Lastly, the end of the tube C is connected with an aspirator furnished with a tube containing sulphuric pumice (not represented in the figure), the object of which is to prevent the entrance of moisture into the tube C, from the external air. The tube A having been weighed alone, let P be that weight. The tubes B and C having also been weighed together, let P′ be their joint weight.

When the apparatus is arranged, that portion of the tube *ab* containing oxide of copper alone is first heated to redness, and when it appears red for the length of 1 or 2 decimetres (4–7 in.), live coals are carefully approximated to that part of the tube containing the mixture of oxide of copper and oxalic acid. The decomposition of this acid soon commences, and the oxide of copper yielding sufficient oxygen to burn the carbon into carbonic acid, water becomes free, and the mixture of carbonic acid gas and aqueous vapour passes successively through the tubes A, B, C. The tube A retains all the vapour of water, while the carbonic acid is dissolved in the bulbs B and the tube C. The operation is continued until the fire entirely covers the tube, when the combustion of the oxalic acid is terminated. The evolution of gas ceases, and as the absorbing action of the solution of potassa continues in the bulbed apparatus B, the pressure in the interior becomes less than that of the atmosphere, and the solution in the bulbs ascends toward the tube A. It might even be projected into this tube, unless the precaution were taken to give the bulbs the position represented in fig. 281, instead of that in fig. 280, which last it maintains during the combustion. There is then nothing to fear from absorption; for the potassa can only half fill the bulb *e*, and, if the rarefaction of the interior gas continues, atmospheric air enters the apparatus by the tube C, traversing the bulbs B in the form of bubbles.

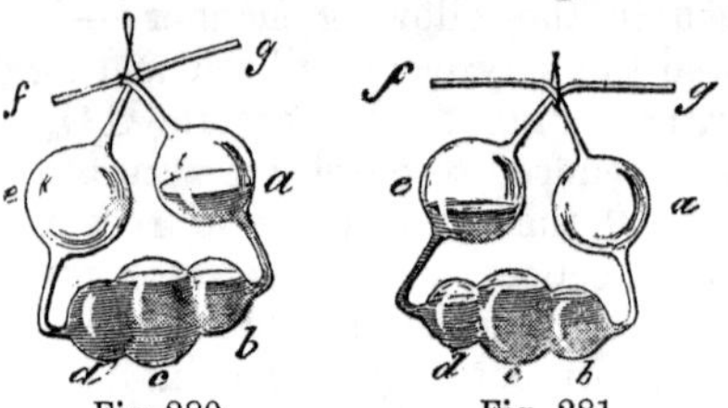

Fig. 280. Fig. 281.

The carbonic acid and water arising from the combustion of the acid are not, however, entirely absorbed, for a portion of them remains in the combustion tube, and must also be passed through the absorbing tubes. In order to effect this, the coals surrounding the end *b* of the combustion tube are withdrawn, and when this part is cooled, the fine point *b* is broken, and a tube immediately fitted to it, by a caoutchouc connecter, containing pieces of caustic potassa. Water being run out of the aspirator at the same time, the external air is drawn into the apparatus, being first deprived of its moisture and its small content of carbonic acid, by traversing the tube containing potassa, just appended to the apparatus. As it traverses the combustion tube and the absorbing tubes A, B, C, it deposits in the latter the water and carbonic acid still remaining in the combustion tube. When 1 litre (1 qt.) of water has been drawn off, we may be certain that all the products of the combustion of oxalic acid have been concentrated in the absorbing tubes. The escape of water is stopped, the tubes detached and separately weighed.

Let Q be the weight of the tube A, containing sulphuric acid, which has condensed the water, and Q′ the joint weight of the tubes B and C which have condensed the carbonic acid.

It is evident that the water produced by the combustion of 1^{gm} of oxalic acid weighs (Q—P), and the carbonic acid from the same (Q′—P′).

If the experiment has been accurately performed, then will

$$(Q-P)=0^{gm}.249$$
$$(Q'-P')=0^{gm}.698.$$

Now $0^{gm}.429$ of water contain $0^{gm}.0476$ of hydrogen, while $0^{gm}.698$ of carbonic acid contain $0^{gm}.1905$ of carbon. Now, since oxalic acid contains only carbon, hydrogen, and oxygen, the composition of 1^{gm} is

Hydrogen	0.0476
Carbon	0.1905
Oxygen	0.7619
	1.0000

and, consequently, of 100 parts,

Hydrogen	4.76
Carbon	19.05
Oxygen	76.19
	100.00

In order to ascertain the ratio of the equivalents of the three elements in oxalic acid, it is only necessary to divide the proportional weight of each by its chemical equivalent; which gives

$$H=\frac{4.76}{1}=4.760$$
$$C=\frac{19.05}{6}=3.175$$
$$O=\frac{76.19}{8}=9.524$$

These numbers being to each other as 3 : 2 : 6, the formula of the crystallized acid is either $C_2H_3O_6$, or its multiple.

Now, the formula $C_2H_3O_6$ gives

3	eq. of hydrogen	3.0
2	" carbon	12.0
6	" oxygen	48.0
1	" crystallized oxalic acid	63.0

§ 261. Having observed that oxalic acid, heated to 212° in dry air, lost a certain quantity of water, it is necessary to ascertain this proportion exactly by experiment. An accurately weighed quantity of oxalic acid is introduced into a glass tube having the form represented in fig. 282. The tube is first weighed empty, the pulverized acid poured in, taking care that none remains in the vertical leg *ab*, and again weighed. The increase in weight represents exactly the quantity of matter introduced, which suppose to be = $1^{gm}.000$. The apparatus *abcd* is connected by the end *d* with an aspirator, filled with water (fig. 283), and, by the end *a*, with a U-tube filled with

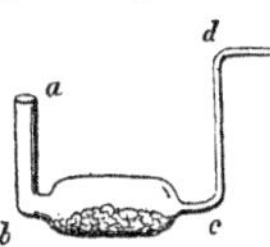

Fig. 282.

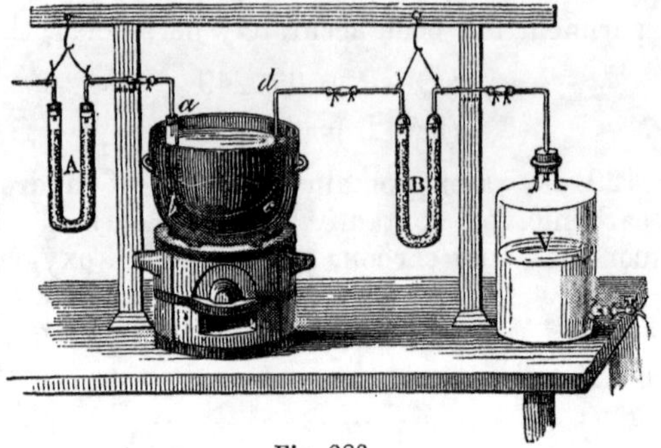

Fig. 283.

sulphuric pumice-stone. The apparatus *abcd* is placed in a vessel of boiling water, if the substance is to be heated to 212°; or in a saturated solution of salt, if a temperature of 230° is required; or, again, in an oil-bath, if the heat is to rise to 390°. A mercurial thermometer indicates the temperature, which may be maintained nearly uniform by a proper management of the fire. In the present case, the temperature of boiling water is sufficient.

By drawing off water from the aspirator, the external air traverses the apparatus, being first dried in the tube A, containing sulphuric acid, and then passing over the heated matter, which loses its water. When the aspirator is emptied, the tube *abcd* is accurately weighed again, and the difference between the two weights of the tube shows the quantity of water lost. But it is necessary to ascertain whether the substance, if subjected for a longer time to the heat of 212°, might not lose an additional quantity of water; and, in order to determine this, the tube *abcd* is replaced in the apparatus, the aspirator again filled and drawn off, and the tube *abcd* weighed once more. If the same weight be found as before, it is a proof that the substance had parted with all the water it could lose at 212°; but if the weight be less, the heated substance must be again subjected to a current of dry air, until consecutive weighings evince no discrepancy.

By operating on 1^{gm} of the crystallized acid, the loss of weight amounts to 0.826^{gm}, corresponding to 2 equivalents of water. We have, in fact,

1 eq.	hydrogen....................	1.0	
2 "	carbon......................	12.0	
4 "	oxygen......................	32.0	
1 "	desiccated oxalic acid....	45.0.........	71.43
2 "	" water	18.0.........	28.57
1 "	crystallized oxalic acid...	63.0.........	100.00

The formula of the desiccated acid is C_2O_4H, which may be written C_2O_3,HO; for 1 equivalent of water may still be eliminated, if replaced by 1 equivalent of base.

If nitrate of lead be poured into a soluble oxalate, as the neutral oxalate of potassa, a white precipitate of oxalate of lead is formed, the formula of which is PbO,C_2O_3, as may be demonstrated by a direct analysis of the salt.

The proportion of oxide of lead is first determined by weighing accurately a certain quantity of oxalate of lead in a platinum crucible, and heating it with an alcohol lamp, when the oxalate is decomposed, and oxide of lead remains.* One gramme of oxalate of lead gives 0.742^{gm} of oxide of lead.

$1^{gm}.000$ of the oxalate is also burned in a tube with oxide of copper, like the crystallized acid (§ 260). Water is not obtained, but only 0.315 of carbonic acid, representing 0.086 of carbon.

Oxalate of lead is therefore composed of

Carbon	0.086
Oxygen	0.172
Oxide of lead	0.742
	1.000

Whence we deduce the following composition:

2 eq. carbon	12.0	8.60
3 " oxygen	24.0	17.19
1 " oxide of lead	111.5	74.21
1 " oxalate of lead	147.5	100.00

The above experiments therefore show that the formula of oxalic acid in the salts is C_2O_3; that of the crystallized acid from an aqueous solution is C_2O_3+3HO; and, lastly, that of the desiccated acid is C_2O_3+HO.

RECAPITULATION OF THE COMPOUNDS OF CARBON AND OXYGEN.

Determination of the Equivalent of Carbon.

§ 262. The three compounds of carbon with oxygen, which we have studied, are composed as follows:

Carbonic oxide	Carbon	42.86
	Oxygen	57.14
		100.00

* A porcelain crucible or piece of glass tube is preferable, as platinum would be very liable to injury from the reduction of the oxide. The decomposition may, however, be effected safely in platinum, at a low temperature, and with free access of air, which is also necessary to prevent the formation of suboxide.—*J. C. B.*

Carbonic acid..................	Carbon..........	27.27
	Oxygen.........	72.73
		100.00
Oxalic acid.....................	Carbon..........	33.33
	Oxygen.........	66.67
		100.00

By calculating their composition with reference to the same quantity, 100, of carbon, we have

Carbonic oxide................	Carbon..........	100.0
	Oxygen.........	133.3
		233.3
Carbonic acid.................	Carbon..........	100.0
	Oxygen.........	266.7
		366.7
Oxalic acid.....................	Carbon..........	100.0
	Oxygen.........	200.0
		300.0

The proportions of oxygen combined with the same quantity of carbon are, therefore, as $1 : 2 : \frac{3}{2}$.

The most simple formulæ which can be assigned to the compounds are

Carbonic oxide..................	CO	equivalent=14.0
Carbonic acid...................	CO_2	" =22.0
Oxalic acid......................	$CO_{\frac{3}{2}}$	" =18.0

The oxalic is a powerful acid, completely saturating bases, and affording neutral salts, which can be obtained in an anhydrous state. Their analysis has shown that an equivalent of a base (for example, the weight 111.5 of oxide of lead) combines with 36 of oxalic acid, so that the number 36 represents its true equivalent. Now, as this number is precisely double of that obtained when the formula $CO_{\frac{3}{2}}$ is given to oxalic acid, its true formula is C_2O_3.

Carbonic is likewise an acid, but a feeble one, incapable of neutralizing bases completely. Moreover, with powerful bases, such as potassa and soda, it forms several carbonates; so that it is doubtful which one should be selected as the neutral salt. But, with less powerful bases, as baryta, strontia, lime, and the metallic oxides, it forms but a single series of carbonates; and these are generally regarded by chemists as the neutral carbonates. The analysis of any one of these proves that an equivalent of the base is combined with a weight 22 of carbonic acid. The number

22 is therefore its equivalent, and its formula is, consequently, CO_2.

As carbonic oxide is an indifferent compound, whose reactions are not well defined, its formula is undetermined; and, although we write it CO, we may, on almost equally good grounds, write it C_2O_2.

The formulæ of the compounds of oxygen and carbon being fixed, it is evident that the equivalent of carbon can be immediately deduced from them, from any one of these three proportions:

$$\left.\begin{array}{l} 57.14 : 42.86 :: 8 : x \\ 72.73 : 27.27 :: 16 : x \\ 66.67 : 33.33 :: 24 : 2x \end{array}\right\} \text{whence, } x=6.0$$

§ 263. It has been shown that 1 volume of carbonic oxide contains a $\frac{1}{2}$ volume of oxygen, and that 1 volume of carbonic acid gas contains 1 volume of oxygen. But we cannot say what is the volume of gaseous carbon or vapour of carbon found in 1 volume of carbonic oxide, or of carbonic acid, as carbon has not yet been vaporized. It is, however, conceivable that its vaporization is possible, at higher temperatures than those hitherto produced.

If the laws laid down (§ 121) were perfectly demonstrated, it is evident that it would be most frequently possible, the volume of a gaseous binary compound being known, as well as the gaseous volume of one of its elements, to determine, by means of these laws, the gaseous volume of the second element, without finding it directly by experiment, or even without knowing the density of its vapour. This case will particularly occur when the two components form several gaseous compounds. Let us admit that these laws are exact, and apply them to the composition of carbonic oxide and acid.

One volume of carbonic oxide containing a $\frac{1}{2}$ volume of oxygen, it should contain, from the laws laid down, either a $\frac{1}{2}$ volume of vapour of carbon without condensation, or else, 1 volume of vapour of carbon, condensed to a $\frac{1}{2}$ volume; that is, that a $\frac{1}{2}$ volume of oxygen, by combining with 1 volume of vapour of carbon, should form 1 volume of carbonic oxide.

One volume of carbonic acid gas containing 1 volume of oxygen should contain a $\frac{1}{2}$ volume of vapour of carbon; making the condensation in this case also equal to a $\frac{1}{2}$ volume.

But, if 1 volume of carbonic acid gas, with the density of 1.5290
contain 1 volume of oxygen with the density........ 1.1056
we have for the weight of a $\frac{1}{2}$ vol. of vapour of carbon.... 0.4234

And for the density of one volume of this vapour, 0.8468.

It is evident, that only the first of the two modes of composition assumed for carbonic oxide gas is possible, for it is the only one which, with the density of the vapour of carbon just deduced from the composition of carbonic acid, will give the density 0.967 for carbonic oxide gas. Thus,

$\frac{1}{2}$ vol. of vapour of carbon....................	0.4234
$\frac{1}{2}$ " oxygen................................	0.5528
	0.9762

The density 0.8468 for the vapour of carbon can only be considered as an approximative value, because it has been deduced from the density of carbonic acid gas, which, at ordinary temperature and pressure, is too great. A more exact value is obtained, by starting from the composition which synthetic analysis, founded on weight, has given for carbonic acid, and admitting only the observed density of oxygen gas. It is given by the proportion

$$72.73 : 27.27 :: 1.1056 : \frac{x}{2}$$

$$\text{whence } x = 0.8290.$$

Since the atomic theory admits that carbonic acid is composed of 1 atom of carbon and 2 of oxygen, the atomic formulæ of the compounds of carbon and oxygen are the same as their formulæ in equivalents, and the atomic weight of carbon is 6.0.

COMBINATIONS OF CARBON WITH HYDROGEN.

§ 264. The compounds of carbon and hydrogen are very numerous. Two of them are gaseous at ordinary temperatures, the others liquid or solid. Several of them will be described when treating of organic bodies, and our attention will now be confined to the principal properties of the two gaseous combinations.

PROTOCARBURETTED HYDROGEN, C_2H_4.

§ 265. It is also called light carburetted hydrogen, in distinction from the next compound, and *marsh-gas*, because it is evolved in large quantities from the waters of stagnant pools. When the muddy bottom of such waters is stirred with a stick, bubbles of gas are observed to arise, which are easily collected in an inverted bottle, filled with water (fig. 284), and a funnel inserted in its mouth. The gas thus obtained is impure, from the admixture of nitrogen and carbonic acid.

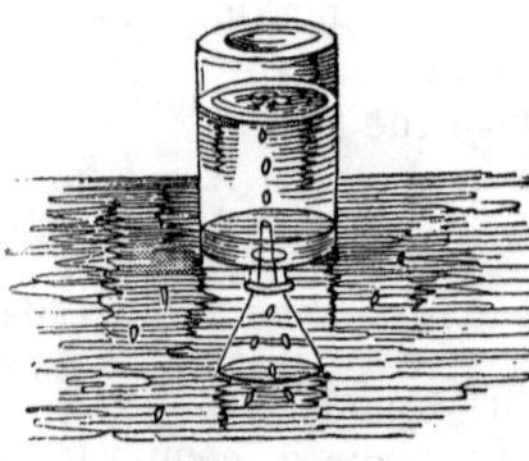

Fig. 284.

Pure protocarburetted hydrogen is obtained, by heating a mixture of acetate of soda and an energetic base, such as caustic potassa or lime, in a glass retort or flask. A mixture of the two bases is generally preferred, and is made by dissolving the potassa in a small quantity of water, and adding powdered lime, so as to form a paste. We will explain hereafter the reaction which, in this experiment, produces the protocarburetted hydrogen.

Protocarburetted hydrogen is a colourless, inodorous gas, of the density 0.5590; burning in the air with a bluish flame, and producing water and carbonic acid: water dissolves but a very small quantity of it.

This gas is abundantly produced in certain mines, and being lighter than the air, it accumulates in the upper part of the shafts, and causes terrific explosions, attended with a great loss of life. Hence, miners call it the *fire-damp.*

It is analyzed by the eudiometer, into which suppose we have introduced 100 volumes of protocarburetted hydrogen and 300 of oxygen. After the passage of the electric spark, the gaseous volume will be reduced to 200, and if a piece of moist potassa be passed into the mixture, the carbonic acid produced by the combustion will be absorbed, leaving 100 volumes of oxygen. The 100 volumes of carbonic acid contain 50 of vapour of carbon and 100 of oxygen, and therefore 100 volumes of oxygen have disappeared, by forming water with the hydrogen of the gas. The latter gas containing 200 of hydrogen, 100 volumes of the carbohydrogen are composed of

200 of hydrogen,
50 of vapour of carbon;

which proportion is confirmed by the value of the density of the gas:

2 vol. of hydrogen weigh........	0.1382......	25.00
$\frac{1}{2}$ " vapour of carbon..........	0.4145......	75.00
	0.5527......	100.00

The formula of protocarburetted hydrogen is C_2H_4.

Bicarburetted Hydrogen, C_4H_4.

§ 266. It is frequently called *olefiant gas*, and heavy carburetted hydrogen, and is prepared by heating together 1 part, by weight, of alcohol, and 5 or 6 parts of oil of vitriol. The reaction is too complicated to be explained at present; the gaseous products being bicarburetted hydrogen, and carbonic and sulphurous acids. The mixture of sulphuric acid and alcohol is introduced into a capacious glass retort (fig. 285), because it puffs greatly toward the close of the operation, and the gases are passed first through a washing-bottle containing water, and then through a second bottle con-

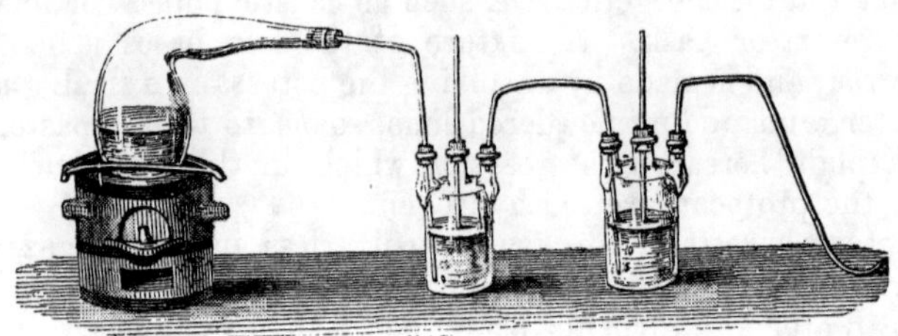

Fig. 285.

taining a solution of potassa, to absorb the carbonic and sulphurous acids.

Bicarburetted hydrogen is a colourless gas, of the density 0.9784; burns in the air with a brilliant flame; is partially decomposed when passed through a porcelain tube heated to redness, carbon being deposited on the sides of the tube.

It burns in chlorine, its hydrogen forming chlorohydric acid, and its carbon being deposited. Bicarburetted hydrogen and chlorine also combine in the cold, when the two gases are mixed over water, an oily volatile liquid being formed, of an agreeable, ethereal odour.

Its analysis is conducted in the same manner as that of the light carburetted hydrogen.

Bicarburetted hydrogen	100
Oxygen	400

being introduced into the eudiometer, 300 remain after the passage of the spark, of which caustic potassa absorbs 200, which is carbonic acid, containing 100 of vapour of carbon and 200 of oxygen, and the gas remaining in the eudiometer is oxygen. 100 volumes of oxygen have therefore been burned by the hydrogen of the olefiant gas, which gives for the composition of 100 volumes of the gas,

200 of hydrogen,
100 " vapour of carbon.

Now,	2 vol. of hydrogen weigh	0.1382	14.29
	1 " vapour of carbon	0.8290	85.71
		0.9672	100.00

which approaches very nearly to the density 0.9784 found by experiment.

The formula assigned to bicarburetted hydrogen is C_4H_4.

The gas used for lighting buildings is principally composed of carburetted hydrogen gas, and will be treated of under organic chemistry.

COMBINATION OF CARBON WITH SULPHUR.

Sulphide of Carbon, or Sulphocarbonic Acid, CS_2.

§ 267. Sulphur and carbon do not combine when mixed together and heated under the ordinary pressure of the atmosphere, for the sulphur distils over before the temperature is sufficiently elevated to cause their combination. But if the carbon be heated to redness in a porcelain tube, and vapour of sulphur be passed over it, the carbon burns in this vapour as in oxygen. Now, when carbon burns in oxygen, it is changed into carbonic acid, CO_2; and when it burns in the vapour of sulphur, it is changed into sulphuret of carbon, or sulphocarbonic acid, CS_2. When burned in oxygen, the latter must be in excess, or, otherwise, carbonic oxide alone is formed; but this result is not to be feared in the combustion of carbon in vapour of sulphur, for nothing is ever formed but sulphocarbonic acid, and no less sulphuretted compound of carbon has yet been obtained.

To obtain sulphuret of carbon, a porcelain tube is filled with small pieces of coal, and arranged in a reverberatory furnace (fig. 286). The end *a* of the tube is closed with a cork, and should project far enough from the furnace so as not to burn the cork. To the other end *b*, a curved adapter is filled, the beak of which descends into a very small quantity of water in a receiving-bottle. When the porcelain tube is heated to redness, a piece of sulphur is introduced at *a*, and the cork immediately replaced. The sulphur fuses, and the tube being slightly inclined from *a* to *b*, it flows toward the hottest part of the tube, where it is vaporized, passes in this state over the ignited carbon, combines with it, forming sulphide of carbon, which is deposited in the adapter, and falls in oily drops to the bottom of the water in the receiver. When the vapour has ceased to pass over, another piece of sulphur is introduced, and so on, until the greater part of the carbon in the tube has disappeared.

Fig. 286.

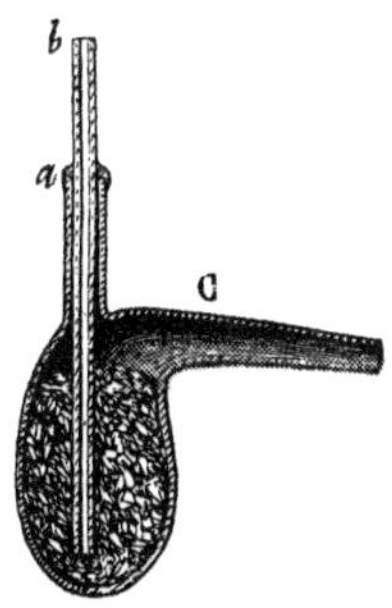

Fig. 287.

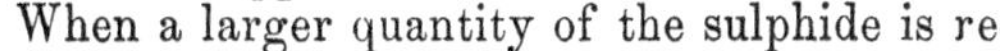

When a larger quantity of the sulphide is required, the porcelain tube is replaced by a tubulated stoneware retort (fig. 287), into the tubulure of which is fitted a porcelain tube *ab*, descending nearly to the bottom of the retort, and luted with clay at the tubulure *a*. The retort being then filled entirely with coals, and placed in a furnace (fig. 288), to its neck is

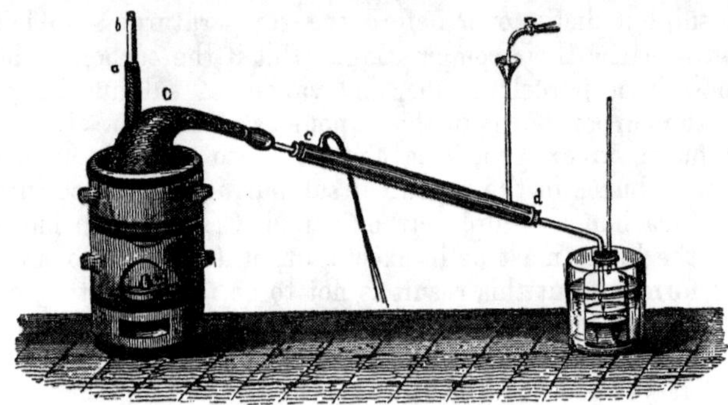

Fig. 288.

adapted a long tube, which passes through a condenser *cd* filled with cold water, and communicates with a receiver, as in the preceding operation.

The retort being brought to a strong red-heat, pieces of sulphur are successively dropped into the porcelain tube, which is immediately closed by a cork. The sulphur, in its descent to the bottom of the retort, is converted into vapour, and traverses the mass of ignited carbon, producing sulphide of carbon, which condenses in the refrigerator and flows into the receiver. In a few hours, several hundred grammes (a lb., more or less) of the sulphide may thus be obtained.

The sulphide forms a yellow oily stratum under the water of the receiver, but is not pure, and always contains more or less sulphur in solution. To purify it, it is distilled from a glass retort in a water-bath, the sulphur remaining in the retort, and the sulphide of carbon distilling under the form of a colourless liquid. The distilled liquid, being kept in contact, for some time, with chloride of calcium, is deprived of its water, and again distilled in a dry apparatus.

§ 268. Sulphide of carbon is a colourless, very volatile liquid, possessing a peculiar and extremely disagreeable odour; its density is at 32°.. 1.293
and at 59°.. 1.271

It boils at 118½°, under the ordinary pressure of the atmosphere, so that, at common temperatures, its vapour has already a considerable tension, and the liquid evaporates rapidly, producing a great degree of cold.

Although it does not dissolve appreciably in water, yet water which has been for some time in contact with it becomes impregnated with its peculiar odour. Absolute alcohol and ether dissolve and mix with it in every proportion, whether singly or together. It burns in the air with a blue flame, producing carbonic and sulphurous acids.

It dissolves sulphur and phosphorus in large quantities, and if the solutions be allowed to evaporate slowly, they are deposited in regular crystals. It was observed that crystallized sulphur could be obtained in this way, in the form of octahedrons of the fourth system, resembling those found in the solfaterræ.

§ 269. Sulphide of carbon is analyzed, by burning it with the oxide of copper, so as to transform the carbon into carbonic, and the sulphur into sulphuric acid.

It is necessary, in the first place, to weigh a certain quantity of it accurately, and under such circumstances that, notwithstanding its great volatility, it cannot lose by evaporation. To do this, a bulb A (fig. 289), blown between two points *a*, *b*, finely drawn out, is weighed, and then filled with the sulphide of carbon, by inserting one of the points *a* into the liquid, and sucking at the other point *b*, until the bulb is nearly filled. The open end *b* being closed with the finger, the end *a* is inserted in the flame of an alcohol lamp, and closed hermetically by fusion. The same process is repeated with the end *b*, so that the sulphide of carbon is hermetically closed in the globe. By again finding the weight of the bulb when filled, its increase in weight necessarily represents the quantity of sulphide introduced.

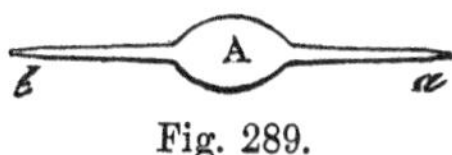

Fig. 289.

On the other hand, a glass tube is prepared of similar size with that in § 260, drawn out to a point at one end *b*, and freely open at its end *a* (fig. 290). Some oxide of copper has been previously

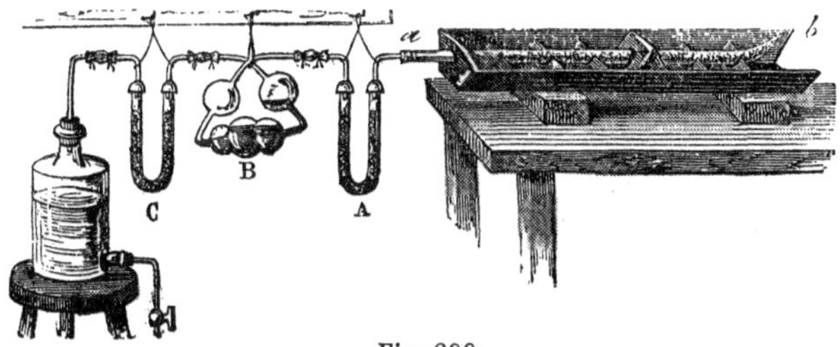

Fig. 290.

calcined in an earthen crucible, and allowed to cool where it could not attract the moisture of the air. The tube having been perfectly dried, a scratch is made with a file on one of the ends of the bulb, which is then broken off, and the liquid exposed. The bulb and detached piece of glass being allowed to fall to the bottom of the tube, a depth of 2 or 3 dec. (8 in.) of oxide of copper is immediately poured on it, and the balance filled with oxide of lead or litharge, which should occupy at least 3 dec. (10 in.) of the tube. The tube is placed on a long sheet-iron furnace, and its open end *a* fitted to the apparatus A, B, C, described in § 260. The tube A, containing sulphuric pumice-stone, has been accurately weighed alone, and the potassa bulbs B, with the tube C, containing fragments of potassa, have been weighed together.

It is important to arrange the apparatus with the least possible delay, since the sulphide of carbon contained in the open bulb might give off its vapours through the tube, and escape combustion at the commencement of the experiment. When all is thus prepared, the anterior portion of the tube containing the oxide of lead is heated rapidly with ignited coals; then progressively that portion containing oxide of copper; and, lastly, a coal is placed, with great care, near the bulb, so as to effect a gentle distillation of the sulphide. Its vapour passing over the oxide of copper, its carbon is burned to carbonic acid, and the greater portion of its sulphur remains combined with the oxide of copper, in the state of a sub-sulphate of the protoxide. A portion, however, being disengaged in the state of sulphurous acid, would accompany the carbonic acid, if it were not entirely absorbed by the heated oxide of lead which is in the anterior part of the tube. Carbonic acid alone is therefore absorbed in the tubes B and C. When the evolution of gas has ceased, the experiment is concluded in the manner described in § 260. On again weighing the tube A, it will be found not to have appreciably increased in weight, which proves that the substance contained no hydrogen. The increase of weight of the tubes B and C gives the weight of carbonic acid produced, and, consequently, that of the carbon contained in the sulphide of carbon subjected to analysis.

As this body contains only carbon and sulphur, it is evident that the difference will give the quantity of sulphur; but the latter can also be directly determined, and thus a complete analysis of the substance executed.

To do this, an additional quantity of the sulphide is weighed in a closed bulb (fig. 289), and, after having opened one end of it, it is placed at the bottom of a glass tube, resembling that used in the preceding experiment, but not so long. It is filled entirely with a mixture of oxide of copper and carbonate of soda, and the open end closed with a perforated cork. The mixture of oxide of copper and carbonate of soda is gradually heated, and when this portion of the tube is heated to a dull red, coals are approached near the end containing the bulb. The vapour of the sulphide burns, carbonic acid is evolved, and the sulphur is converted into sulphuric acid, which combines with the soda.

When the operation is terminated, and the tube entirely cooled, the mixture is withdrawn from the tube, and thrown into a capsule; the tube rinsed several times with hot water, which is poured into the same capsule, taking care not to lose a single drop; and, lastly, the dish, capsule, and its contents, heated for some time. The excess of carbonate of soda and the sulphate of soda having dissolved, the liquid is filtered, and the residue washed with hot water, until it no longer shows traces of soluble matter. All the sulphuric acid produced by the combustion is then found in the liquid, together with a large excess of carbonate of soda: chlorohydric acid is poured into the solution until it becomes highly acid, whereby carbonate is changed into chloride of sodium; and if a solution of chloride of barium be now poured into the liquid, the sulphuric acid will be precipitated in the state of sulphate of baryta. From the weight of the sulphate obtained, we can infer the quantity of sulphur contained in the sulphide of carbon.

By combining the results of the two analyses, it is ascertained that the substance analyzed contains only sulphur and carbon in the ratio of

1 eq. carbon	6.0	15.79
2 " sulphur	32.0	84.21
	38.0	100.00

1 vol. of its vapour contains

$\frac{1}{3}$ vol. vapour of sulphur	2.2180
$\frac{1}{2}$ " " carbon	0.4145
	2.6325

The density of the vapour, as found by direct experiment, is 2.67.

Sulphide of carbon presents the same formula in equivalents as carbonic acid. As carbonic acid combines with the metallic protoxides RO, forming carbonates RO,CO_2, so, sulphide of carbon combines with the metallic protosulphides RS to form true salts RS,CS_2, which are often isomorphous with the corresponding compounds RO,CO_2.

The name of *sulphocarbonic acid* has therefore been properly given to sulphide of carbon, and the name of *sulphocarbonates* to its compounds with the monosulphides.

COMBINATION OF CARBON WITH NITROGEN.

Bicarburet of Nitrogen, or Cyanogen, C_2N, or Cy.

§ 270. Carbon and nitrogen form a very important compound—cyanogen*—the detailed study of which will be more appropriate

* The discovery of cyanogen, due to M. Gay-Lussac, has been of great importance in chemical science, because it furnished the first example of a compound body performing the functions of an element in its combinations.

among the products derived from the animal kingdom; but as its compounds with the metals present a complete analogy with the corresponding chlorides, and are frequently used as reagents to characterize metallic solutions, and distinguish them from each other, we shall detail at present its principal properties, as well as those of its compound with hydrogen, or *cyanohydric acid*, which closely resembles chlorohydric acid.

Nitrogen and carbon do not combine directly; but, if a mixture of carbonate of potassa and carbon be heated together in a porcelain tube, while a current of nitrogen is passed through it, carbonic oxide is disengaged; and if the residue be treated with water, a considerable proportion of cyanide of potassium is dissolved. Cyanide of potassium is prepared, on a large scale, by heating in iron vessels mixtures of carbonate of potassa and the carbonaceous residues from the incomplete calcination of animal matters, such as flesh, bones, horn, etc. It will be described more fully when treating of cyanide of potassium.

If a hot solution of nitrate of mercury be poured into a hot and concentrated solution of cyanide of potassium, and the mixture be allowed to cool, crystallized cyanide of mercury is separated, which may be purified by recrystallization. By means of the cyanide of mercury, cyanogen and cyanohydric acid are readily obtained.

Cyanogen is obtained by heating cyanide of mercury in a small retort, or in a tube closed at one end, and furnished with an exit tube (see fig. 239, § 199), which conveys the gas into a bell-glass over water, or, better still, over mercury (fig. 291). The cyanide

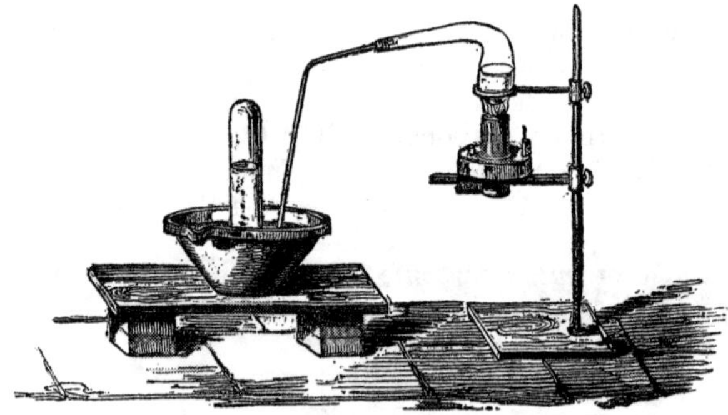

Fig. 291.

is decomposed into free cyanogen and metallic mercury, the latter condensing in the upper part of the retort. By continuing the heat until the disengagement of gas ceases, it will be observed that the cyanide does not entirely undergo the simple decomposition just mentioned; for a brown substance remains, presenting exactly the same composition as cyanogen, and which has therefore been called *paracyanogen*. The proportion of cyanogen passing into this isomeric condition varies according to the manner in which the cyanide is heated; but hitherto it has never been so decomposed as entirely to avoid its formation.

Cyanogen is a colourless gas, with a sharp, peculiar smell, resembling that of wild-cherry water; its density is 1.86; it is liquefied at common temperatures, under a pressure of 4 or 5 atmospheres, or when cooled to —4°, without an increase of pressure, and is then a colourless, very volatile liquid, of the density 0.9.

It burns with a very characteristic purple flame, giving off carbonic acid, and setting the nitrogen free.

Water dissolves 4 or 5 times its volume of the gas, but readily parts with it when the temperature is raised. The aqueous solution, left to itself, even in a well-corked bottle, becomes at last of a brown colour, and deposits, after some time, a brown powder. The decomposition in this case is too complicated to be introduced here; and has not, moreover, been sufficiently explained. Alcohol dissolves 20 to 25 times its volume of the gas.

§ 271. Cyanogen being a combustible gas, and affording, by its combustion, gaseous products easily separated, it might be supposed that it could be readily analyzed by the eudiometer; but if a mixture of cyanogen and oxygen be exploded in the eudiometer, the combustion is always observed to be imperfect. A more perfect combustion will be obtained by adding to the mixture of oxygen and cyanogen a certain proportion of a detonating mixture of oxygen and hydrogen in the proportions constituting water. Such a detonating mixture is easily prepared by decomposing water by a galvanic battery, and collecting the gases disengaged at both poles in the same vessel.

Suppose that

	100	of oxygen gas,
	250	" cyanogen "
Total............	350	

are introduced into the eudiometer, and, in addition, an indeterminate volume of the detonating mixture, which need not be measured, since combustion will convert it wholly into water: after waiting a few moments, to allow the gases to mix freely, an electric spark is passed through. The detonating mixture is converted into water, and the cyanogen gives off carbonic acid and free nitrogen. The volume of gas is measured, composed of carbonic acid, nitrogen, and the excess of oxygen, and found to be 350.

If the gaseous mixture be shaken with a small quantity of a solution of caustic potassa, the carbonic acid is absorbed, and nitrogen and oxygen alone remain, whose volume is found to be 150.

The 100 of cyanogen have therefore afforded 200 of carbonic acid, containing 100 of vapour of carbon.

It being still requisite to analyze the mixture, 150 of nitrogen and oxygen, a certain quantity of hydrogen, say 150 volumes, is introduced into the eudiometer, making the total volume 300, and the electric spark passed through it. After the explosion, the volume of gas remaining is found to measure 150, so that 150 volumes have disappeared by combustion; and they are evidently composed of oxygen and hydrogen in the proportions forming water, that is, 100 of hydrogen, and 50 of oxygen. Therefore, in the 150 of the mixture of nitrogen and oxygen which remained after the absorption of carbonic acid by potassa, there were 50 of oxygen, and, consequently, 100 of nitrogen.

It follows, therefore, that 100 volumes of cyanogen contain

100 of vapour of carbon,
100 of nitrogen.

1 volume of cyanogen gas, therefore, contains 1 volume of vapour of carbon, and 1 volume of nitrogen, condensed into 1 volume. The analysis is confirmed by the density of cyanogen gas, which has been ascertained by direct experiment.

1 vol. of vapour of carbon weighs............	0.8290
1 " nitrogen................................	0.9713
The sum weighs..................................	1.8003

which does not differ materially from the number 1.86 given by the direct determination. The difference between the two numbers is, however, too great to attribute it to error of observation, and is rather due to the fact that, at ordinary temperatures, the molecules of cyanogen gas are already closer than they should be, if it could be assimilated to the more perfect gases, as nitrogen, hydrogen, etc.

The eudiometric analysis just described does not furnish very exact results; because, 1st. The cyanogen gas is measured in a state of anomalous condensation, as just stated, and consequently its observed volume is too small; 2d. In the combustion of cyanogen with oxygen, in the presence of mercury, a small quantity of protonitrate of mercury is frequently formed, which causes a certain quantity of nitrogen and oxygen to disappear.

The composition of cyanogen can be ascertained more accurately by burning it with oxide of copper, and collecting the gaseous products of combustion. A glass tube being filled half with oxide of copper, and half with metallic copper, to one end of it is fitted an exit tube for conveying the gases over a mercurial trough, and to the other end, by means of a cork, a small glass retort containing cyanide of mercury. When the tube is heated to redness, the cyanide is slowly decomposed by heat. Cyanogen first passes over the oxide of copper, where it is resolved into carbonic acid and nitrogen, and the mixture of the two gases then passing through the anterior part of the tube containing metallic copper, the latter decomposes any oxides of nitrogen which might have formed by the combustion of cyanogen. After having allowed a small quantity of gas to escape, so as to be sure that the apparatus no longer contains the smallest proportion of air which previously filled it, a portion of it is collected in a graduated tube or bell-glass, and measured accurately. A small quantity of solution of potassa is then introduced, and absorbs the carbonic acid; whereby the gaseous volume is reduced to $\frac{1}{3}$.

The experiment proves that, by burning cyanogen with oxygen, it yields a volume of carbonic acid, double that of the nitrogen which is set free, and by combining the result with the known densities of cyanogen and nitrogen, and with the composition of carbonic acid, it gives the composition of cyanogen.

For, 2 volumes of carbonic acid contain 1 volume of vapour of carbon, which weighs.................................. 0.8290
1 vol. of nitrogen weighs............................. 0.9713

1.8003

Since a weight 1.8003 of cyanogen contains
0.8290 of carbon,
0.9713 of nitrogen,

then 100 of cyanogen contain

Carbon	46.15
Nitrogen	53.85
	100.00

Since the number 1.800 differs so little from the 1.86 found by experiment for the density of cyanogen that it may be attributed to the want of normal elasticity of the gas at ordinary temperatures, it may be inferred from the above numbers that 1 vol. of cyanogen contains 1 vol. of vapour of carbon, and 1 vol. of nitrogen.

Cyanogen may also be analyzed by another method, still more exact than those hitherto described, which simply consists in burning with oxide of copper a metallic cyanide, the composition of which is easily ascertained, such as the cyanide of mercury.

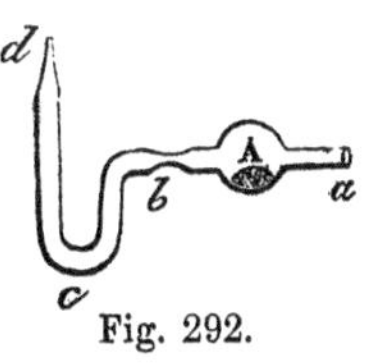

Fig. 292.

The quantity of mercury contained in 1^{gm} of the cyanide is first ascertained by putting a given weight of it into the bulb A of a curved tube *abcd* (fig. 292), the end *a* being made to communicate with an apparatus which slowly disengages hydrogen, the end *d* is drawn to a point. The bulb A being heated by an alcohol lamp, the cyanide is decomposed, and mercury being set free, is carried by the current of gas into the part *bcd*, where it is condensed. When the operation is terminated, which can be ascertained by the mercurial vapour ceasing to condense, the tube is broken off at *b*. The weight of the portion *bcd*, with the contained mercury, having been determined, the mercury is removed entirely, and the tube *bcd* replaced in the balance. The weight necessary to restore the equilibrium is exactly that of the mercury obtained.

It will thus be found that 100 parts of cyanide of mercury contain

	79.36 of mercury
and consequently......	20.64 of cyanogen
	100.00

The composition of the cyanide being known, to determine that of cyanogen, a known weight of the cyanide is burned with oxide of copper, and the weight of the resulting carbonic acid and nitrogen determined.

The carbonic acid is determined exactly as in the analysis of oxalic acid (§ 260), except that, as the substance contains nitrogen, and the production of a little oxide of nitrogen is to be feared, a longer tube is employed, and about 2 decimetres (8 in.) of its anterior part filled with metallic copper. The mercury condenses in the tube A, which has been filled with pieces of chloride of calcium, and the increase in weight of the tubes B, C gives the weight of carbonic acid produced.

In order to determine the quantity of nitrogen contained in the cyanide of mercury, the apparatus employed to determine the nitrogen in the nitrate of lead is used (§ 108).

A quantity of bicarbonate of soda is put at the bottom of the tube *ab*; above it, a column of 4 or 5 centimetres (1½ to 2 in.) of oxide of copper, then a mixture of a given weight of cyanide of mercury and oxide of copper, followed by an additional quantity of pure oxide of copper, and, lastly, a length of 2 decimetres (8 in.) of metallic copper. The operation is conducted exactly as prescribed in § 108, and, when concluded, the vol. of nitrogen which alone remains in the bell-glass is determined, and from it the weight of nitrogen contained in the given weight of cyanide operated on.

Cyanohydric Acid, H,C_2N, or HCy.

§ 272. Cyanogen and hydrogen do not combine directly, and the cyanohydric acid is obtained by decomposing the metallic cyanides by chlorohydric acid. It may be procured in the anhydrous state, or in solution.

To obtain the anhydrous acid, cyanide of mercury is decomposed

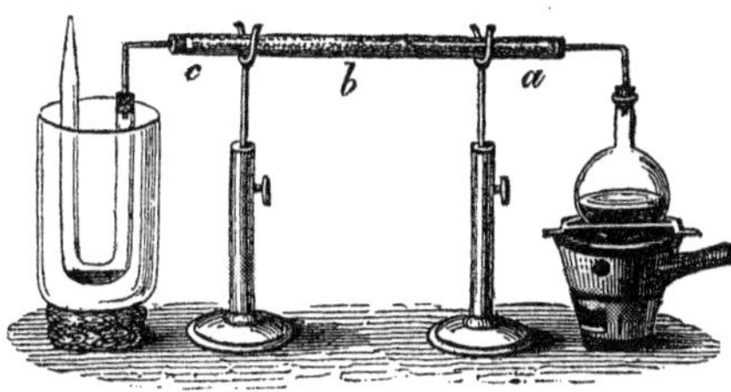

Fig. 293.

by concentrated chlorohydric acid in a flask (fig. 293), connected with a tube *abc*, the first half of which, *ab*, is filled with pieces of marble, and the second half, *bc*, with pieces of fused chloride of calcium. Following the tube *abc* is a U-tube, surrounded by a frigorific mixture. The chlorohydric acid decomposes the cyanide of mercury,

$$HgCy+HCl=HgCl+HCy,$$

disengaging gaseous cyanohydric acid, which carries over chlorohydric acid and aqueous vapour, when the mixture passes through the tube *abc*. The chlorohydric, being a powerful acid, decomposes the marble, forming chloride of calcium, water, and free carbonic acid,

$$CaO,CO_2+HCl=CaCl+HO+CO_2.$$

But cyanohydric being, on the contrary, a very feeble acid, does not react upon carbonate of lime. We have, therefore, a mixture of cyanohydric and carbonic acids and aqueous vapour, which penetrates the second half *bc* of the tube, filled with chloride of calcium, where aqueous vapour alone is absorbed, and the mixed acids pass into the refrigerated tube. Cyanohydric acid is condensed into the liquid state, while the carbonic acid maintains its gaseous condition; but the former acid necessarily contains all the carbonic acid it can absorb under the circumstances.

The anhydrous acid is better prepared by decomposing cyanide of mercury by gaseous sulfhydric acid, in a long glass tube *ab*, to

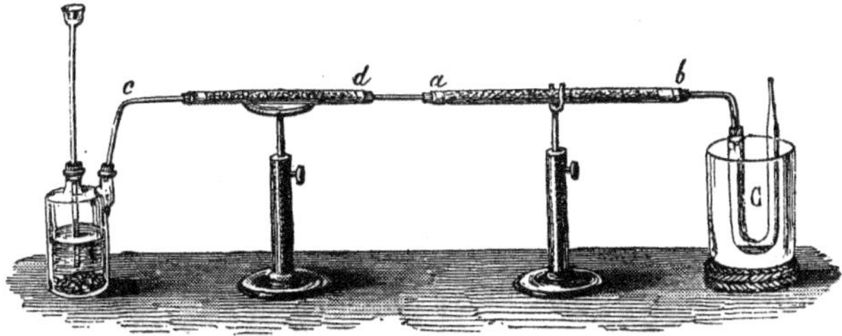

Fig. 294.

which is fitted a U-tube cooled by a refrigerating mixture. The end *a* is connected with an apparatus for disengaging dry sulfhydric acid, which is prepared by decomposing fused protosulphide of iron by cold dilute sulphuric acid in a tubulated bottle. A slow current of sulfhydric gas, which can be regulated at will, is produced, and dried by being passed through a tube *cd*, filled with pieces of chloride of calcium. The cyanide is decomposed by the sulfhydric acid, forming sulphide of mercury and anhydrous cyanohydric acid, which remains gaseous in the tube *ab*, if kept at a temperature above 77°, but condenses in the refrigerated receiver. The decomposition takes place progressively from the extremity *a*, if the sulfhydric current be slow, and as the white cyanide is converted into a black sulphide, the progress of the operation may be easily followed. If, therefore, the experiment be stopped before the whole of the cyanide is decomposed, perfectly pure cyanohydric acid is obtained in the receiver.

Cyanohydric acid is a colourless, very volatile liquid, solidifying at 5°, and boiling at 79.7°. The degree of cold produced by its evaporation is generally sufficient to congeal the portion remaining liquid. The density of the acid is 0.697; that of its vapour, 0.947. Its odour is very penetrating, resembling that of bitter almonds.

§ 273. This acid can be accurately analyzed by determining the hydrogen and carbon simultaneously, and then the nitrogen. To perform both operations, the liquid acid is introduced into a small bulb drawn out at both ends, closed, and accurately weighed.

To determine the hydrogen and carbon, a strong glass tube is prepared, about 60 centimetres (2 ft.) in length, open at one end, and drawn out at the other into the form of an open tubulure. It is partly filled with oxide of copper, and the remainder with metallic copper, which should occupy at least 2 decimetres (8 in.) of its length. The open end is fitted to the apparatus intended to collect the water and carbonic acid, as described in § 260, and represented in fig. 279.

The bulb containing the given weight of acid is fixed, by means of caoutchouc, to the tubulure which terminates the tube, so that the pointed part, which is closed, may enter the tubulure to the distance of about 1 centimetre ($\frac{1}{2}$ in.). When the combustion-tube is heated to redness, by pressing the point of the bulb against the side of the tubulure, it is broken, and the bulb opened. The acid immediately distils over, and its vapour is burned by the oxide of copper into water, carbonic acid, nitrogen, and deutoxide of nitrogen, which last is decomposed by the heated metallic copper filling the anterior part of the tube, and converted into nitrogen. The water and carbonic acid are condensed in the apparatus A, B, C (fig. 279). The distillation of the acid may be easily regulated by cooling the bulb.

The nitrogen is determined exactly as in the analysis of hyponitric acid (§ 120), except, that two-thirds of the combustion tube is filled with oxide of copper, and the remaining third, with metallic copper, as in the preceding experiment. It is thus proved, that 1^{gm} of the acid yields

0.333^{gm} of water,
1.629^{gm} of carbonic acid,
412.1^{cc} of dry nitrogen gas at 32°, and under a pressure of 0^{m}.760 (29.92 in.), corresponding to the weight 0.518^{gm} of nitrogen.

We infer, from these experimental data, that cyanohydric acid is composed of

1 eq. of	hydrogen	1.0	3.70
2 "	carbon	12.0	44.44
1 "	nitrogen	14.0	51.86
1 "	cyanohydric acid	27.0	100.00

Its formula is therefore H, C_2N or HCy. Cyanogen and hydrogen are combined in it in the same manner as chlorine and hydrogen in chlorohydric acid. 1 volume of cyanohydric acid contains a ½ volume of hydrogen, and a ½ volume of cyanogen without condensation, for we have

½ the density of hydrogen	0.0346
½ " cyanogen	0.9300
	0.9646

and direct experiment has given 0.947 for its density.

§ 274. Cyanohydric acid should be preserved in hermetically sealed tubes, filled in the manner described for sulphurous acid (§ 129); but it does not long remain unaltered, for in a few days the liquid turns brown, and deposits a brown powder. The chemical reaction occurring in this imperfect decomposition appears to be very complex, and has not yet been thoroughly investigated.

Cyanohydric, commonly called *prussic acid*, is one of the most violent poisons known. A drop, placed on a dog's tongue, kills him instantly. We should therefore handle it with great caution, and be particularly careful not to inhale its fumes.

It is soluble in every proportion in water; and its aqueous solutions are used in medicine.

To prepare solutions of the acid, into a flask A, heated by a water-bath (fig. 295), are introduced 1 part of ferrocyanide of potassium, or yellow prussiate of potash (the double cyanide of potassium and iron, 2KCy+FeCy), and 1½ parts of oil of vitriol, diluted with 2 pts. of water. A long glass tube *abc* is adapted to the flask, passes through a condenser DE, through which a current of cold water circulates, and enters the water of the refrigerated bottle B. By introducing into the bottle more or less water, a more or less concentrated solution of prussic acid is obtained. In all cases, it is necessary to ascertain the quantity of acid dissolved in the liquid, which is easily done by pouring into a given quantity of it a solution of nitrate of silver, whereby a precipitate of

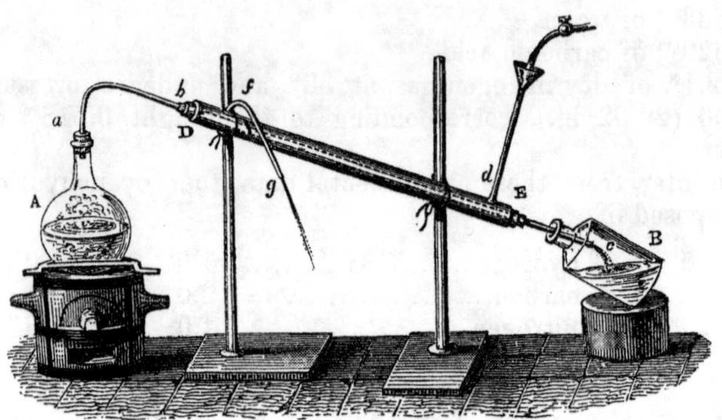

Fig. 295.

cyanide of silver is formed, from the weight of which the quantity of acid can be inferred.

We can also obtain a standard solution of this acid, by dissolving a given quantity of cyanide of mercury in water, and passing a current of sulphuretted hydrogen through the liquid; and removing the excess of sulfhydric acid by shaking the liquid for some minutes with carbonate of lead.

A solution of prussic acid is liable to alteration, and should therefore be made only as it is required.

REMARKS ON THE EQUIVALENTS OF THE METALLOIDAL ELEMENTS.

§ 275. We have referred the equivalents of the elements to the equivalent of hydrogen, assumed to be 1.0; but any other element might have been selected as a term of comparison, as oxygen, chlorine, etc., and would have given rise to other series of numbers, differing greatly in their absolute values from those adopted. They would, however, have always presented the same proportions to each other.

Let us assume the equivalent 8 of oxygen as unity or 100, and calculate the numerical value of three of the other metalloidal elements. It is evident that, in order to obtain the equivalent of hydrogen, according to this hypothesis, we must make the proportion

$$8 : 1 :: 100 : x, \text{ whence, } x = 12.5.$$

The equivalents of the other elements can be calculated in the same way; and the following series will result:

	O=100	H=1
Equivalent of oxygen	100.00	8.0
" hydrogen	12.50	1.0
" nitrogen	175.00	14.0
" sulphur	200.00	16.0
" selenium	494.25	39.5
" tellurium	802.50	64.2
" chlorine	443.75	35.5
" bromine	1000.00	80.0
" iodine	1575.00	125.0
" fluorine	237.50	19.0
" phosphorus	400.00	32.0
" arsenic	937.50	75.0
" boron	137.50	10.9
" silicium	266.75	21.3
" carbon	75.00	6.0

A glance at the second column of figures shows that, of fifteen elements, the equivalents of ten, or two-thirds, of them are represented by whole numbers, that is they are exact multiples of that of hydrogen, the lightest of them all. They are:

Hydrogen	Equivalent =	1.0
Oxygen	"	8.0
Nitrogen	"	14.0
Sulphur	"	16.0
Bromine	"	80.0
Iodine	"	125.0
Fluorine	"	19.0
Phosphorus	"	32.0
Arsenic	"	75.0
Carbon	"	6.0

If only these ten were known to us, the law would immediately be assumed that *the equivalents of the metalloidal elements are exact multiples of the equivalent of hydrogen.** But the other five metalloids form an exception to the law.

It must, however, be observed, that great uncertainty still exists as to the true value of the equivalents of these last substances; for many of them are rare, we are not sure of having obtained them in a state of purity, and the numbers found by various experi-

* An English chemist, Dr. Prout, first announced this law, about twenty-five years since. His confidence in the precision of this law was such, that he did not hesitate to change, arbitrarily, the numerical values which direct experiment had assigned as the equivalents of the elements, in order to render them exact multiples of that of hydrogen. Prout's ideas were not generally adopted by chemists on the continent, but M. Dumas, by his accurate determination of the equivalents of hydrogen, carbon, and some metallic elements, has again drawn attention to the point, and shown the only manner in which the question can be decided.

menters differ often more widely than the corrections which might be required for the equivalents we have adopted, in order to include them in the law advanced. Whereas ten elements which satisfy the law are those of which the equivalents are known with most certainty, and which have been recently determined, by a great number of experiments perfectly corroborating each other.

Among the elements which form the exception, there is only one, chlorine, which has been, and quite recently, the object of many experiments, the special design of which was to ascertain if its equivalent could be considered as a multiple of that of hydrogen. Those of the experiments to which chemists attach most confidence have given the number 443.2, that of oxygen being represented by 100. According to the hypothesis of hydrogen being equal to 1.00, that of chlorine, from these experiments, is 35.45: it is, therefore, not an exact multiple of the equivalent of hydrogen.

It will be subsequently seen, that the equivalents of a certain number of simple metallic bodies, carefully determined within the last few years, are exact multiples of that of hydrogen, while others do not present equally simple relations.

We shall, therefore, not decide whether the foregoing law be admitted for all the elements, or whether it be applicable to only a certain number of them. There may possibly be a group of elements whose equivalents are multiples of hydrogen, and, as regards the others, their equivalents may be multiples of the equivalent of some other element, or even they may be represented by a sum of which one of the components may be a multiple of the equivalent of hydrogen, and the remainder multiples of the equivalents of one or several other elements.

The attention of chemists is now directed to this important question, and its solution may be soon expected from their united researches.*

---

* Having adopted the hydrogen scale (H=1) in this translation, because of its more general adoption by English chemists, we have also preferred the equivalent numbers given in the Annual Report of Liebig and Kopp. Hence, the slight deviations observable in the equivalents of some of the metalloids, which, however, have no material influence on the science at present. Hence, also, the remarks in § 275 of the original work, which were applied to the hydrogen scale, starting from that of oxygen, have been modified in the translation, to apply them from the hydrogen to the oxygen scale.—*J. C. B.*

PART II.

THE METALS.

§ 276. It was stated (§ 55) that the metals are simple bodies, good conductors of heat and electricity, and possessing a peculiar brilliancy, called the *metallic lustre.* They exhibit great diversity in their physical and chemical properties, and are therefore susceptible of the most varied applications.

Some of them possess great malleability and tenacity, and are the only ones used in an isolated state; the others are only valuable in combination.

Some of them have a feeble affinity for oxygen, being scarcely affected by atmospheric air, in which they remain unaltered for an almost indefinite period, provided the air be not saturated with moisture. Others again readily combine with the oxygen of the air, even in the cold, and are converted into oxides. It is evident that the latter, in their metallic state, cannot be ordinarily used.

The metals are hence divided into two great classes, according to their applications.

First Class.—Metals which, on account of their great affinity for oxygen, are rapidly oxidized in the air, and cannot be used in the arts in their metallic state. They are:

Potassium,	Zirconium,
Sodium,	Thorium,
Lithium,	Yttrium,
Barium,	Cerium,
Strontium,	Lanthanum,
Calcium,	Didymium,
Magnesium,	Erbium,
Glucinum,	Terbium.
Aluminum,	

The metalloidal compounds of these metals are used in the arts when they abound in nature, and their separation from their natural combinations is not too expensive. It will be shown that potassium, sodium, barium, calcium, magnesium, and aluminum furnish a host of products of the highest practical value. The other metals comprised in the foregoing list have as yet received no useful application, and possess only a purely scientific interest.

Second Class.—Metals whose affinity for oxygen is so feeble as to render them but slightly alterable in our atmosphere at ordinary temperatures. They are:

Manganese,	Titanium,
Iron,	Tantalum or columbium,
Cobalt,	Niobium,
Nickel,	Ilmenium,
Chromium or chrome,	Pelopium,
Tungsten,	Antimony,
Molybdenum,	Uranium,
Vanadium,	Silver,
Zinc,	Gold,
Cadmium,	Platinum,
Copper,	Palladium,
Lead,	Rhodium,
Bismuth,	Iridium,
Mercury,	Ruthenium,
Tin,	Osmium.

This is the more numerous class of metals, but in order that they may be really useful in the arts, they must satisfy several conditions which singularly reduces their number. Thus, two essential conditions are a certain degree of malleability and tenacity, without which they cannot be worked into a convenient form; and they should possess these properties in such a degree as to render their working not too expensive. Again, the substances in nature from which they are extracted should not be too rare, nor difficult to manage, as otherwise the metal acquires too great a commercial value, and is used only when a cheaper substitute cannot be found. Iron, manganese, nickel, and cobalt, in their metallic state, present nearly similar properties; but iron is much more abundant in nature, more easily extracted from its ores, and is naturally preferred to the other three when it can subserve the same ends. Manganese is more oxidizable than iron, and changes more rapidly in the air; thus affording another reason for preferring iron. Nickel and cobalt, on the other hand, are less oxidizable, possess a ductility and tenacity comparable in this respect to iron, and would certainly take its place in many of its applications, were they less expensive.

The brittle metals are not employed in the metallic state, but are frequently combined with the malleable metals, forming alloys which present peculiar physical properties.

The metals which possess sufficient malleability to be used in the metallic state, are:

Manganese,	Nickel,
Iron,	Zinc,
Cobalt,	Cadmium,

Copper,	Gold,
Lead,	Platinum,
Mercury,	Palladium,
Tin,	Iridium.
Silver,	

Several of them, however, have not yet been applied in the arts, because their ores are too rare, and difficult to manage, or because their properties resemble those of other metals more readily and cheaply obtained.

§ 277. *State of the Metals in Nature.*—Metals exist in various states in nature. Some are found isolated, and are then called *native.* Those which, having a very feeble affinity for oxygen, do not change under atmospheric influence, belong to this class: such are, gold, platinum, rhodium, iridium, palladium, silver, mercury, and bismuth. Many others are found in combination with oxygen, sulphur, or arsenic; such as manganese, iron, cobalt, nickel, chrome, tungsten, molybdenum, vanadium, zinc, cadmium, copper, lead, bismuth, mercury, tin, titanium, antimony, uranium, and silver. Some of this division are found in the state of insoluble salts, chiefly in that of carbonates or silicates. The metals of the first class which, as will be remembered, have a great affinity for oxygen, are formed in the state of salts, especially in that of insoluble silicates or carbonates; they are, however, sometimes met with as soluble salts, dissolved in the waters of the ocean or of salt-springs.

A knowledge of the *natural situation* of the different metals is highly important to the chemist and metallurgist; and we shall be careful to indicate it, when describing each particular metal. But, in order to give our indication some value, it is necessary to premise a few elementary remarks on geology, or the science which treats of the nature and mode of aggregation of the various materials which compose our globe.

GENERAL REMARKS ON THE CONSTITUTION OF THE EXTERIOR CRUST OF THE GLOBE.

§ 278. That portion of the crust of the globe which is accessible to us is composed of mineral substances of various character, which when aggregated in masses are called *rocks.* Rocks differ from each other, either in the *chemical nature* of the minerals which compose them, or only in the manner in which these minerals are united, whereby they receive a different structure.

In some rocks, minerals are distributed with a certain degree of regularity, being *stratified* in parallel layers, which may be traced to a great extent. The stratification is often evinced by parallel fissures in the rocks, separating them into *layers* or *courses* analogous to those seen in edifices constructed of hewn stone. At other times, the stratification is recognised by the tendency of the rock to divide in parallel layers, as in the slates. These are called *stratified rocks.* Others do not present this characteristic, for the fissures which traverse them are irregular, and their fracture shows that the minerals are indiscriminately arranged, without any appearance of symmetry. To distinguish these from the former, they are called *compact*, or *non-stratified rocks.*

Non-stratified rocks are composed of crystalline minerals, and their appearance is that of a mass of heterogeneous mineral substances, which, after having been fused, are allowed slowly to cool. The chemical elements composing the mass are then grouped according to their reciprocal affinities, and different compounds result, which segregate by crystallization. The mass, after cooling, presents the appearance of an agglomeration of different crystals, arbitrarily scattered, and without any appearance of regular arrangement. Non-stratified rocks are, therefore, often called *Plutonic rocks*, or *rocks of igneous origin*, which tacitly admits that they were originally fluid, and assumed their present form by solidifying during a slow process of cooling.

§ 279. Stratified rocks, on the contrary, present an appearance similar to that of deposits still forming at the bottom of seas and rivers, and the large quantity of remains of aquatic animals contained in the majority of them renders the analogy still more striking. Geologists admit that these rocks have been formed under water, and therefore call them *Neptunian*, or *sedimentary rocks.*

The deposits which form at the bottom of seas and rivers naturally take the form of nearly horizontal layers, and the inferior layers are, evidently, first deposited. The same must have taken place with the sedimentary rocks found on the surface of the globe; so that the order in which these rocks have been superimposed on each other gives a certain index of the periods of their formation and their relative age. We may thus establish a *chronological scale* of their formation.

In level countries, stratified rocks are nearly horizontal (fig. 296), but in mountainous regions they are generally observed to be inclined (fig. 297), often assuming a vertical direction, and are

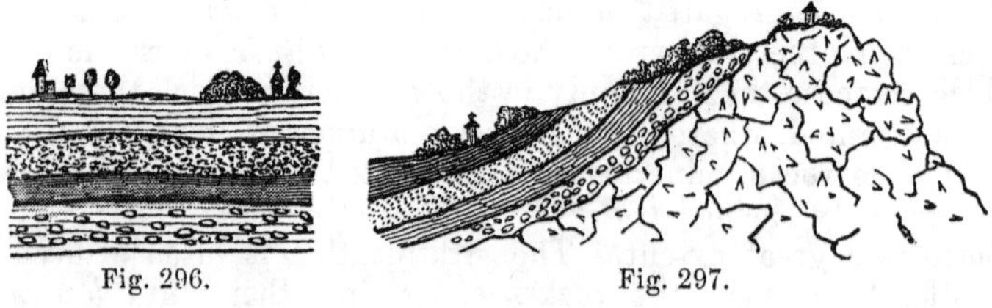

Fig. 296. Fig. 297.

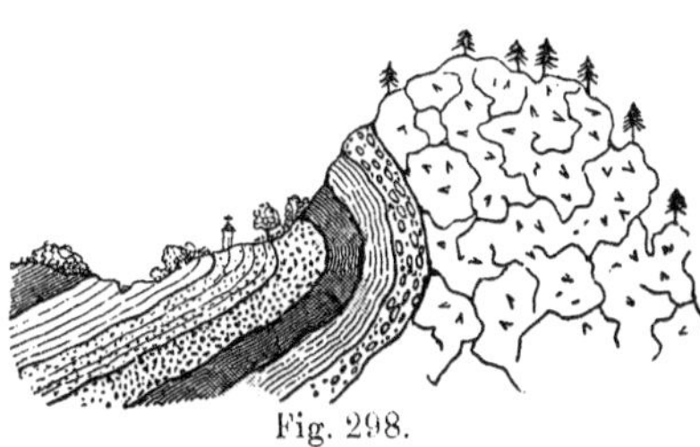

Fig. 298.

sometimes even overturned, and lean in a contrary direction, as in fig. 298.

It frequently happens that inclined strata are covered with horizontal layers, with a different direction of stratification from the former; in which case the latter are said to be *unconformable* (fig. 299). It is evident that, between the deposit of the two series of strata, some great revolution has taken

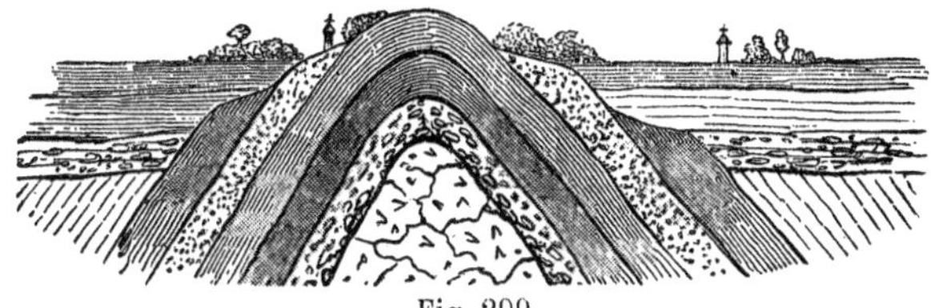

Fig. 299.

place on the surface of the globe, which has remarkably altered its original aspect. An attentive study of the constitution of the globe has shown that this effect upon the strata has been produced by the *upheaval* of a more or less considerable mass of non-stratified rocks. The latter does not always force its way to the surface, and the stratified rocks have been merely upheaved, as in fig. 299. But the non-stratified rock has frequently pierced the sedimentary rocks, and formed the projecting spire of a range of mountains, both sides of which are covered by the edges of sedimentary strata (fig. 300).

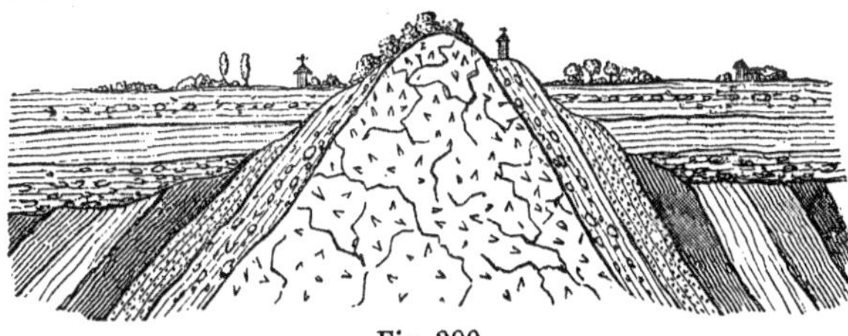

Fig. 300.

When sedimentary rocks are in immediate contact with igneous masses upheaved from the interior, they are frequently and deeply modified. Their texture becomes crystalline, as if the materials composing them had undergone fusion, or, at least, as if they had been sufficiently softened to allow their molecules to aggregate in the form of crystals. Rocks thus modified are called *metamorphic*.

The upheaval of rocks must have remarkably changed the relative size and shape of the continents and seas which existed at the time of its occurrence. It may have entirely changed the direction of the marine currents which transported the sedimentary matter; and the new strata deposited horizontally on the old, more or less altered from their original position, are often composed of materials of a very different nature.

The upheaval of older strata is well defined only in the vicinity of the upheaving igneous matter. At a short distance, the same strata may be horizontal, and present, consequently, a stratification more conformable to the newer strata.

Every sudden change in the composition and nature of the two superimposed layers, even in conformable stratification, must have coincided with some revolution occurring on the surface of the globe, which changed the direction of the marine currents. But this revolution may have taken place at a great distance from the location of these strata, and, in that case, exercised no influence over their direction.

It is equally conceivable that, in submerged localities where, at a certain period, the waters were sufficiently calm to deposit the substances they held in suspension, these waters might, in consequence of one of these revolutions, become greatly agitated, and, far from forming new deposits, carry away even those already formed, and transport them to other localities where the current was more feeble. In this way, excavations in older rocks have been formed (fig. 301). Sometimes, the waters becoming more tranquil,

Fig. 301.

these cavities have received new deposits, and horizontal strata have formed, filling the basins existing in the former (fig. 302).

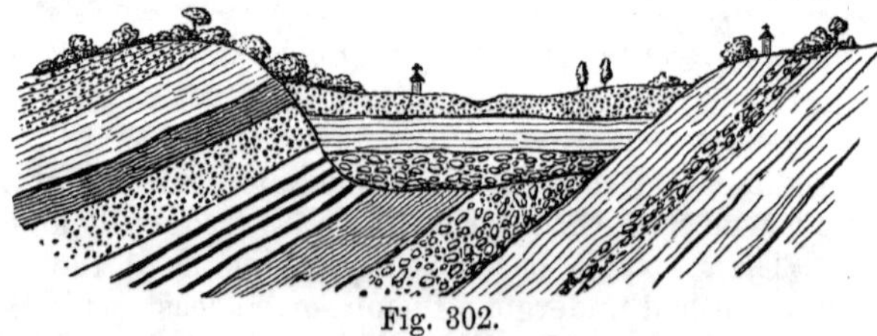

Fig. 302.

It is therefore clear that the order in which the strata are deposited enables us to judge of the period at which they were formed, and establishes, as it were, their geological age.

§ 280. The geologist is guided by a character of another order in determining the periods of formation of the strata on which he founds their classification. The majority of the sedimentary rocks contain the remains or bear the imprint of animals and vegetables which lived on the surface of the globe when these rocks were formed. Now, animals and vegetables have undergone, at these various geological epochs, frequent and often well-marked changes; so that the comparative study of animal fossils, known by the name of *paleontology*, furnishes valuable data to the geologist.

§ 281. The series of stratified rocks is rarely complete in the same locality, one or more terms being often wanting, and groups, widely separated in the geological scale, being in immediate contact. Such gaps, repeated at various stages of the sedimentary formation, prove that the strata are only deposited locally in the parts at that time covered by the waters, and that continents have undergone, at different periods, partial submersions and emersions, before reaching the condition in which we now behold them.

When two systems of strata are observed, in any locality, resting on each other unconformably, it may be asserted that an upheaval has taken place between the deposit of the two systems. If the two unconformable systems follow each other immediately in the geological scale, the epoch of upheaval is clearly defined; but if they are widely separated in the scale, in consequence of the absence of intermediate strata, the epoch of upheaval becomes more uncertain. An attentive study of the same upheaval, wherever it has exerted its influence, generally points out a portion, at least, of the missing strata in other localities, and the uncertainty as to the epoch of the upheaval is confined to narrower limits.

The successive upheavals which have modified the primitive form of the globe have produced the various chains of mountains which now exist, so that the epochs of their formation may be referred to the chronological scale furnished by the succession of stratified rocks. In this way their relative age may be determined. Reciprocally, the entire series of sedimentary strata may be subdivided into several groups, each of which is separated from that which precedes and that which follows it by the phenomena of two mountain chains, which have upheaved the strata existing at the time of their formation; so that our principal mountain chains form very valuable landmarks accurately dividing the sedimentary strata.

§ 282. What were the physical causes which produced these successive upheavals, and thus changed the form of continents and seas? Imagination here finds a vast field over which to wander; and hence there is no lack of theories. Without attempting to unfold the various hypotheses which have been proposed, we shall be content to indicate one physical cause which has certainly exerted a great influence over all these revolutions, if it alone did not produce them all.

Geodetic measurements have shown the earth to be a spheroid, flattened in the direction of its axis of rotation. This is precisely the form assumed by a fluid globe subjected to a rotary motion; and it is easy to conceive in this fluid a density varying with the distance from the centre, such that, when influenced by the same rotary movement, the heterogeneous liquid globe would become flattened like the terrestrial globe. This circumstance renders it very probable that our globe was originally in a state of fusion, caused by a very high temperature; that the temperature fell gradually, in consequence of the radiation of heat into space; that the surface naturally cooled more rapidly than the interior, and, at any point of time, the different solidified strata have presented a temperature decreasing from the centre to the circumference. If our hypothesis be correct, this condition of things must exist at the present day. And, in fact, all observations hitherto made in mines, or in boring Artesian wells, have shown that, at a certain distance from the surface, the temperature remains constant throughout the year, uninfluenced by the variation of the seasons; and that, in starting from this stratum of invariable temperature, the temperature increases regularly as we descend. The most accurate observations have shown that the increase of temperature is about 1° centigrade for 30 metres, (98½ ft. for 1° C., or 55¼ ft. for 1° Fahr.) Now, if this increase of temperature continue in the same manner below the strata hitherto accessible to us, the temperature ought to be 1000° C. (1800° F.), at a depth of 30,000 metres (98,430 ft. = 18⅝ miles), and 2000° C. (3600° F.) at a depth of 60,000 metres, (37 miles); and as the earth's radius is at least 6,366,200 metres in length, at a depth less than $\frac{1}{100}$ of the earth's radius, the temperature ought to be 2000° C. (3600° F.)—sufficient completely to fuse all the substances composing the superficial crust of the earth. The internal mass, being fluid, may present nearly everywhere the same temperature. We shall not attach to the numbers just given a value they do not deserve, but regard them as only a probable approximation, sufficient to give great probability to the hypothesis advanced.

While the temperature of the surface of the earth was very high, the sea-water, and a portion of the substances composing the secondary formations, were diffused through the atmosphere in a gaseous state. But when the surface had cooled sufficiently to allow the water of the atmosphere to remain on it, seas were formed, whose agitated waters broke down the primitive rocks, and drifted their detritus to a greater or less distance, to deposit them, in the form of stratified layers, in localities where the current was less rapid. This was the origin of the first stratified rocks, which were necessarily deposited in nearly horizontal layers.

The earth continuing to cool, and consequently to contract, the external solid crust which was formed while the whole mass occupied a larger space, being no longer supported on all sides, split in directions where it found the least resistance. The fluid matter of the interior, escaping through the fissures, produced in their vicinity linear upheavals of the layers already formed, and, by following the direction of the fissures, formed the mountain chains, the sides of which are flanked by the edges of the strata, and through the apices of which the fluid matters of the interior frequently escape. If the sides of the chain are still under water, new sedimentary deposits will form, but their horizontal layers will not be parallel to those previously deposited, at least where the latter have been affected by the upheavals. At such points, the stratification of the two systems of strata will therefore be unconformable.

Subsequently to the deposition of the newer strata, the globe has again split, most frequently in another direction, and has effected an arrangement of the first two systems of strata in a direction differing from their former; and, if still newer strata were superimposed, we should again have unconformable stratification in the vicinity of the new upheaval.

We know not how animals and vegetables were developed on the surface of the globe; but it is evident that no living being existed on the earth, except when the temperature was sufficiently low, and it cannot, therefore, be surprising that their remains are not found in the first sedimentary deposits. They appear only at a later period. It may also be imagined that the great revolutions in the surface of the globe occasioned by the upheaval of a chain of mountains must have instantaneously destroyed the beings existing upon them, and buried their debris among the sedimentary deposits. Equilibrium being restored after some time, a new reign of tranquillity began; life reappeared, but under other influences; new species peopled the continents and the seas, and new sediments were again deposited on the line of new shores. This reign of tranquillity was closed by a new catastrophe, which was itself followed by a new period of calm. But, as new animal or vegetable species replaced those which disappeared in these great revolutions, their forms became modified, their organization developed and perfected, and creation, generally more simple in the older rocks, ascended gradually to man, of whom no remains are found in any sedimentary strata properly so called, and who, placed on earth at a comparatively recent period, when things were nearly in the state we now behold them, appears to have witnessed only local and more limited revolutions, the traces of which are still visible on the surface of the earth, and the remembrance of which lives in the annals of all nations.

§ 283. Geologists give the name of *rock* to every agglomeration of mineral substances, whether it be hard and firm, as the granites, sandstones, and limestones, or loose, as the sands. The name of *formation* is given to every system of superimposed rocks in which a certain analogy of structure is recognised, and is chiefly applied to a collection of rocks forming one of the great geological subdivisions.

The different rocks constituting the external crust of the earth were first divided into two great classes, *primary* and *secondary;* the primary composed of the non-stratified rocks, the secondary comprising all the sedimentary rocks. The last were then subdivided into the *transition*, the *secondary, properly so called*, and the *tertiary*. The name *transition rocks* was given to the lower stratified layers, which often contain crystalline minerals; the more modern stratified layers were called *tertiary rocks*, and the appellation of *secondary rocks* was assigned to the intermediate layers. But the limits separating the various formations not being accurately defined, each one fixed them at pleasure, and great confusion ensued.

Geologists now divide stratified rocks into a certain number of groups, the formations of which are separated by the upheavals which gave birth to our principal mountain chains, and which are distinguished from each other by the unconformable stratification of their layers in the vicinity of the upheavals. They have thus made 14 groups of strata, which will be presently enumerated.

PRINCIPAL KINDS OF ROCK.

§ 284. Primary rocks are formed by the agglomeration of different crystallized minerals, the most abundant of which are, quartz, feldspar, mica, hornblende, augite, and chrysolite. Quartz is silicic acid. Feldspar is composed of the silicates of alumina, lime, potassa, or soda; mica of the silicates of alumina, potassa, lime, and the oxide of iron. Hornblende, augite, and chrysolite are formed by the silicates of alumina, lime, and the protoxide of iron.

Granite, which constitutes the greater portion of the primary formation, is formed by the aggregation of three minerals, feldspar, mica, and quartz. It presents various shades of colour, owing to the presence of a small quantity of oxide of iron or manganese. The proportion of these three minerals varies in every granite. When the feldspar greatly predominates, the rock is called *porphyroidal granite*.

The *porphyrys* are granites in which the quartz and mica are entirely wanting, and are composed of a feldspathic paste, with imbedded crystals of feldspar.

The plates of mica scattered through the granite sometimes lie parallel to the same plane, giving the rock a slaty or band-like appearance, when it is called *gneiss*.

The *trachytes* are volcanic products, of ancient date, and which do not appear to have been always fluid, for they frequently arise from the bosom of the earth in a pasty condition, and form rounded mountains. At other times, they are extended over a horizontal plane, in the form of thick layers. The paste of the trachytes is feldspar, containing many crystals of feldspar, often of large size, and presenting well-marked crystalline faces.

The *basalts* are the result of volcanic eruptions of more modern date than the trachytes. They are composed of augite (silicate of lime, magnesia, and iron), and of labradorite (a species of feldspar, with a base of alumina, lime, and soda). These crystals, being extremely delicate, give the rock a compact appearance.

Basalt sometimes pierces the sedimentary strata, spreading over their surface in horizontal layers, as shown in fig. 303, which repre-

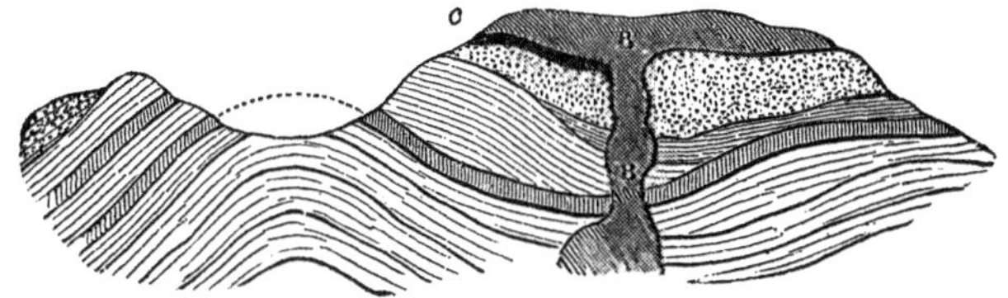

Fig. 303.

sents a section of Mount Meissner, in Hessia. Having pierced the secondary strata, in the form of a nearly vertical column BB, it has spread itself over the top of the mountain. Secondary rocks are deeply modified by the contact, or in the vicinity of basalt. Thus, in the stratum *c*, formed of a tertiary combustible, brown coal, the latter is changed into coke in the neighbourhood of the basalt.

Basalts ordinarily form gigantic prisms, joined together, and presenting an appearance of regularity, which is owing to their splitting during the process of cooling. This arrangement in prismatic columns gives to basalt, where it is exposed to view, a peculiar appearance, such as the columns (fig. 304) of the famous cave of Fingal, in the island of Staffa, north of Scotland.

The term *lava* has been applied to the fluid mineral substances ejected by our modern volcanoes, and spreading in thin layers over their sides.

The name *slate*, or *schist*, has been assigned to rocks presenting a foliated texture.

Pudding-stones are rocks formed by an aggregation of rounded pebbles, imbedded in siliceous cement; they are often of extreme firmness and hardness.

Sands are formed by small particles of disaggregated quartz.

Fig. 304.

When the grains of sand are united together by a quartzose cement, the rock takes the name of *sandstone*. Sandstones, sometimes colourless, are often tinged red or gray by the presence of certain metallic oxides.

Calcareous rocks, or *limestones*, are composed of carbonate of lime, and vary according to the state of aggregation of the substance; being crystallized in marble, compact and often very hard in the Jura limestone, and friable in chalk.

Clay is principally composed of silicate of alumina, almost always associated, however, with a small quantity of silicate of potassa. Argillaceous rocks are characterized by being impervious to water, and retain all the waters which pass through superincumbent rocks, forming large aqueous reservoirs on their surface.

Clays are often mixed with considerable proportions of carbonate of lime, and are then called *marls*.

Anhydrous sulphate of lime, or *anhydrite*, and the *hydrated sulphate of lime*, or *gypsum*, sometimes form actual strata in secondary formations, while at other times they only form a kind of flattened lenses in the midst of other formations.

§ 285. Secondary rocks are sometimes formed at the expense of the primary, which have been broken down and drifted by water; but, at the same time, the substances composing them have been chemically altered by the joint action of water and air. Thus, feldspar becomes changed into clay and into alkaline salts; mica produces clay and calcareous salts; quartz furnishes sands and sandstone. The presence of organized beings, vegetable or animal, must necessarily have exerted a great influence over these chemical changes. The carbon which we find in combustible minerals, in the bosom of the earth, probably existed in the atmosphere, in the state of carbonic acid, which vegetables decomposed, as they now do, assimilating to themselves the carbon, and disengaging the oxygen. Through animals, calcareous salts have been principally changed into carbonate of lime; and such is probably the origin of the calcareous layers which abound in various formations. They have been formed by the detritus of shells, often entirely disaggregated; while at other times the shells have preserved their original forms, so that certain calcareous rocks are actual collections of shells, the species of which can be determined at this day with perfect accuracy.

In modern times, several silicious rocks have been ascertained to be entirely formed of the silicious skeletons of certain microscopic insects.

GEOLOGICAL DIVISION OF THE FORMATIONS.

§ 286. The following table exhibits the series of divisions of the formations now admitted by geologists, with the principal rocks which compose them, and the system of upheaval which characterizes them. They are arranged in the descending order, that is, commencing with the most modern.

<table>
<tr><td colspan="4">FIRST GROUP.—Contemporaneous or Recent Formation.</td></tr>
<tr><td>RECENT FORMATIONS.</td><td>........................</td><td>Alluvial deposits filling the valleys of rivers.
Modern volcanoes, both extinct and burning. The great volcanoes of the Andes arose during this epoch.</td><td></td></tr>
<tr><td colspan="4">SECOND GROUP.—Upper Tertiary. (Pliocene and Miocene.)</td></tr>
<tr><td rowspan="5">TERTIARY FORMATIONS.</td><td>System of the principal chain of the Alps..............</td><td>Strata of ancient sand and alluvium; boulders, drift; tufa, (breccia,) containing fossil bones. The eruption of the majority of trachytes and basalts correspond to this epoch.</td><td></td></tr>
<tr><td colspan="3">THIRD GROUP.—Middle Tertiary.</td></tr>
<tr><td>System of the Western Alps ....</td><td>Fresh-water limestone with burrstones; sometimes containing lignite.........
Sandstone of Fontainebleau</td><td>Upper Eocene.</td></tr>
<tr><td colspan="3">FOURTH GROUP.—Lower Tertiary.</td></tr>
<tr><td>System of the islands of Corsica and Sardinia.................</td><td>Marls with gypsum; fossil remains of the mammiferæ.
Coarse limestone.
Plastic clay with lignite.</td><td>Middle Eocene.

Lower Eocene.</td></tr>
</table>

SECONDARY FORMATIONS.

FIFTH GROUP.—*Upper Cretaceous.*

System of the chains of the Pyrenees and Apennines..........	Extensive limestone stratum, called *chalk*, with layers of silex interposed.

SIXTH GROUP.—*Lower Cretaceous.*

System of Mount Viso.	Tufaceous chalk of Touraine. Sand, or sandstone, generally green, and hence called *green sand.* Ferruginous sands.

SEVENTH GROUP.—*Oolitic or Jurassic.*

System of the Côte d'Or.................	Calcareous strata, more or less compact and marly, alternating with layers of clay. They are divided into several sub-groups, the upper bearing the name of *oolite*, and the lower being called *lias.* Sandstone below the lias.

EIGHTH GROUP.—*Trias.*

System of the Thuringerwald.............	Marls of various colours, called *variegated marls*, (Keuper,) often containing masses of gypsum and rock salt. Limestone, very fossiliferous, and hence called *muschelkalk.* Variously coloured sandstone, termed *variegated sandstone*, (Buntersandstein, grès bigarré.)

NINTH GROUP.—*Sandstone of the Vosges.*

System of the Rhine.	Conglomerate and sandstone.

TENTH GROUP.—*Permian.*

System of the Low Countries and of Wales...............	Stratum of limestone mixed with slate and called *zechstein.* Stratum of conglomerate and sandstone, termed *new red sandstone*, (Rothtodtliegendes.)

Class	Group	System	Rocks
TRANSITION EARTHS.	ELEVENTH GROUP.—*Carboniferous.*	System of the North of England..........	Sandstone, slates with seams of coal and carbonated iron, (clay-ironstone.) Carboniferous or mountain limestone with seams of coal.
	TWELFTH GROUP.—*Devonian.*	System of the balloons of the Vosges, and the hills of the forest of Normandy...	Heavy beds of sandstone, called *old red sandstone*, containing small seams of anthracite.
	THIRTEENTH GROUP.—*Silurian.*	....	Limestone, roofing-slate, coarse-grained sandstone, called *gray-wack.*
	FOURTEENTH GROUP.—*Cambrian.*	System of Westmoreland and Hundsruck in Scotland..........	Compact limestone, argillaceous shale or slate. These rocks have often a crystalline texture.
PRIMITIVE EARTHS.	FIFTEENTH GROUP.—*Primary Rocks.*	....	Granite and gneiss forming the principal base of the interior of the globe, accessible to our means of observation.

METALLIC VEINS.

§ 287. It has been shown that the gradual cooling of the globe must have produced a great number of fissures in the solidified crust, which were not always sufficiently large to allow the contained fluids to reach the surface. The strata have frequently only been split in different directions, and the rents subsequently filled with very different substances, which have reached them either in the state of vapour arising from the interior, or in solution in water coming from the surface or the interior.

These fissures have received the names of *veins*, *feeders*, or *lodes*. They often contain only earthy matters, as carbonate of lime, sulphate of baryta, quartz; and these possess but little interest. They are, however, frequently filled, either wholly or in part, with metallic substances, when they become of great importance. Metallic veins are generally found in primary rocks, or the most ancient stratified formations, of which the transition contains the principal veins which have been worked.

A metallic lode is rarely found isolated; several being most frequently observed in the same locality, when they present a nearly parallel direction. Fig. 305 exhibits a transverse section of one of these systems of metallic veins. The similarity of the mineral contents of the lodes in the same system demonstrate their common origin. One system is often traversed by another (fig. 305), affording very different mineral matter from the former; the latter are called *intersecting lodes.*

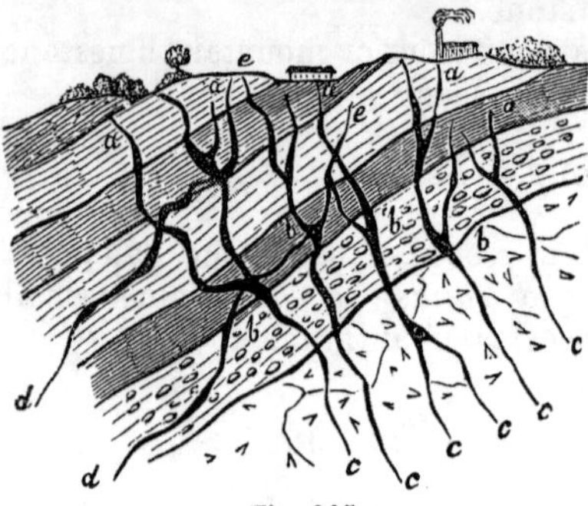

Fig. 305.

A lode is rarely found filled with metalliferous minerals, which most frequently form a network *abcdefg*, more or less irregular, amidst a stony crystalline substance, filling the vein (fig. 306). The thickness of a metalliferous filament varies at different points of the lode, being sometimes considerable, at others very small, and sometimes entirely disappearing. The stony minerals which separate the metalliferous substance from the sides of the rock constitute the gangue or matrix of the ore.

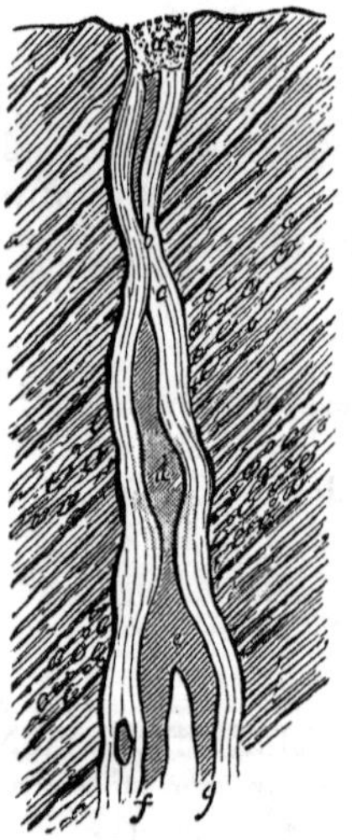

Fig. 306.

When a metallic vein reaches the surface, it manifests itself either by a line of bold relief, when the substance which forms it is harder than the adjoining rock; or by a line of depression, in the contrary case. The *head* or *levels* of a metallic vein are often modified by the chemical changes which have affected the substances composing it.

§ 288. Numerous cavities have been formed in certain stratified formations, probably by the dissolving action of subterranean waters. They are found in all parts of the formation, and have been generally filled at a later period with new substances very different from the surrounding rock. They are called *deposits.*

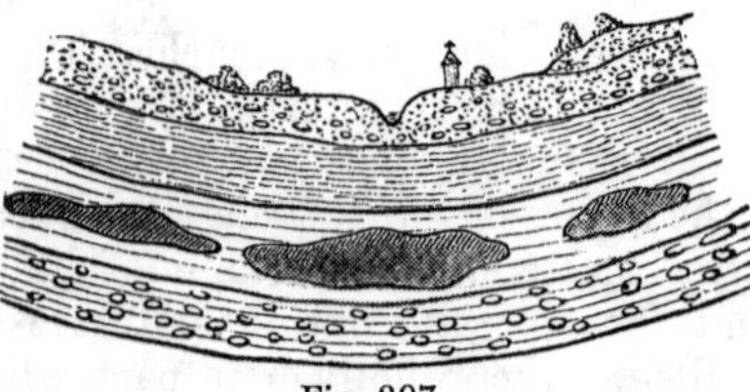

Fig. 307.

Thus deposits of rock salt are found in the muschelkalk and the variegated marls (fig. 307).

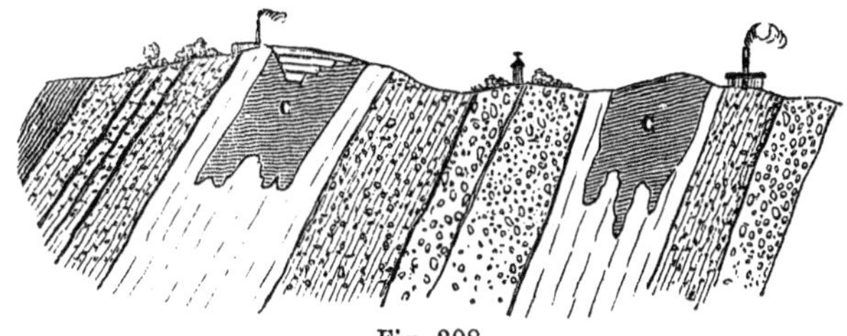

Fig. 308.

Fig. 308 represents deposits C, C of carbonate of zinc which have been formed at the upper part of a stratum of transition limestone.

---

§ 289. Before entering upon the study of each particular metal, we shall succinctly define the general physical and chemical properties of the metals and of their chief compounds. This will facilitate our progress when we arrive at the special history of each metal.

PHYSICAL PROPERTIES OF THE METALS.

§ 290. The physical properties of the metals most deserving of study are, their opacity, lustre, colour, crystallization, malleability and ductility, tenacity, their power of conduction and capacity for heat.

§ 291. *Opacity.*—Metals are very opaque, and do not allow the transmission of light even when reduced to exceedingly thin laminæ. Gold, however, in the form of gold-leaf, as produced by the goldbeater, admits of the passage of a considerable quantity of light of a beautiful green colour. The peculiar physical qualities of this light show that it has really passed through the metal, and not merely through the small fissures made in the leaf by beating.

§ 292. *Lustre.*—Metals aggregated by hammering or fusion, present a peculiar lustre, familiar to every one, but very difficult of definition. When reduced to very fine powder, or in the condition of chemical precipitates, their lustre disappears, but it immediately reappears if the substance be rubbed with a burnisher, or any hard and polished body.

§ 293. *Colour.*—The majority of metals are of a more or less gray colour, in the form of powder, and become whiter when in masses and polished. Some, however, possess well-marked colours: thus, copper and titanium are red; gold is yellow. The alloys formed by white or gray metals are themselves white or gray. Those composed of a coloured metal are tinged by its hue, when it exists in any quantity. Thus, an alloy of $\frac{2}{3}$ of copper and $\frac{1}{3}$ of zinc, called brass, is of a beautiful yellow colour; and an alloy of 90 parts of copper, and 10 parts of tin, called bronze, is also yellow. The metal of the reflectors of a telescope is made of 67 parts of copper, and 33 of tin, and are white.

The white metals reflect the various simple rays of the spectrum in proportions which are nearly the same as those in which these rays compose white light. But, as these proportions are not exactly the same, except in white light, and vary with the incidence of the luminous rays, such metals present a peculiar tinge, which may be ascertained by delicate experiment.

Coloured metals reflect certain simple rays of the spectrum more copiously than the others, and the proportion of simple rays reflected varying with the angle of incidence, it follows that the shades of these metals change, according as they are seen more or less obliquely.

All the metals reflect in the same proportion the various simple rays which fall on their surface at very small angles of incidence, so that they all appear white when sighted along their surface; but, as their reflecting power for different simple rays varies more and more as the angle of incidence increases, they then become evidently coloured. Their discoloration will be more marked, if, instead of causing the ray of light to be reflected once from their surface, it be reflected several times; in which case, those which generally appear colourless become very sensibly tinged. In order to make this experiment, two mirrors, formed of the metal, are set parallel to each other, and a ray of light observed, which is reflected several times successively from their surfaces, at an angle approaching 90°.

After a single normal reflection, copper presents an orange-red colour, but $\frac{9}{10}$ of the reflected light is white light, so that the hue appears very faint. After 10 successive reflections, the copper assumes an intense red colour, which is mixed with only $\frac{2}{10}$ of white light.

Bell-metal has a pale orange-yellow tinge, but after 10 successive reflections, the light is of an intense red, and only contains $\frac{2}{10}$ of white light.

The light reflected once from the surface of polished brass is evidently yellow, but after 10 reflections, it becomes orange, but is still mixed with $\frac{6}{10}$ of white light.

Silver appears perfectly white when the light is reflected only once from its surface; but, after 10 reflections the light assumes a marked red tinge, although feeble, because it is mixed with $\frac{9}{10}$ of white: its hue nearly resembles that of bell-metal after a single normal reflection.

Zinc is white after one reflection, but it becomes indigo-blue after 10: the hue is, however, always feeble, because $\frac{8}{10}$ of white light remain.

Steel, after 10 reflections, becomes of a violet hue, but always feeble, because it is mixed with 0.97 of white light.

The metal of mirrors is white after one reflection, but becomes evidently red after 10.

It is important to be acquainted with the modifications of hue, experienced by light when reflected several times from the surface of metals, inasmuch as they explain the various shades of colour seen on the inside of a polished and shallow metallic vessel.

The hue assumed by white light when reflected several times from the surface of polished metals, also enables us to assume with a good deal of certainty the colour which they would present by transmitted light, if they could be made sufficiently thin to become transparent. This colour would necessarily be the complement of that which would prevail in the light when reflected a number of times from their surface. Thus, light reflected 10 times from the surface of polished gold, is of a beautiful red colour. The complemental colour of red is green; and, in fact, very thin gold-leaf exhibits a bright green colour by transmitted light.

§ 294. *Crystallization of metals.*—All the metals are susceptible of crystallization, but it is not easy to place them always under conditions in which they will assume regular forms. Those found in the native state are often well crystallized; thus, gold, silver, and copper are frequently met with in this form.

Some metals crystallize when allowed to cool slowly after fusion. The crystals may be isolated by the process described for sulphur (§ 125). Bismuth, in this way, affords very regular crystals. Antimony, lead, and tin also crystallize in this manner, but not so readily.

The crystallization of the metal sometimes occurs in the midst of a solid mass, when the latter is maintained for some time at a high temperature. Thus, we frequently find crystals in the interior of the large masses of iron which enter into the construction of our metallurgic furnaces.

Many metals crystallize when slowly separated from a solution, principally under the influence of feeble electro-chemical forces. If we plunge, for instance, into a solution of sulphate of copper, two plates of copper communicating with the two poles of a battery, the plates of the negative pole become covered with crystals of metallic copper, whilst that of the positive pole gradually dissolves. Sometimes the crystals are so small as only to be discernible by the microscope; at others, they are larger.

The tenacity of metals is greatly influenced by their crystalline structure; for when it is strongly marked, their tenacity is generally very feeble, and they are, most frequently, brittle.

Almost all metals which have cooled slowly after fusion exhibit, either in their interior or on their surface, marks of crystallization; but their texture is much modified by the manipulations they have undergone. When forged or rolled, their molecules are made to assume forced positions, whereby their physical properties are remarkably modified, and often to great advantage in mechanical applications.

The most common crystalline form of the metals is the regular octahedron or cube; but antimony crystallizes in a rhombohedron. We shall indicate the crystalline form of each metal under its appropriate head.

§ 295. *Malleability and ductility.*—When metals are subjected to blows with the hammer, some flatten out into sheets, and others fly into fragments; the former are called *malleable*, the latter *brittle metals.*

Metals are reduced into sheets, either by beating with a hammer, or by passing them through rollers.

The rollers consist of two metallic cylinders, placed horizontally, one above the other, and are made to revolve with equal rapidity, in the directions indicated by the arrows in fig. 309. The cylinders may be set at various distances apart from each other, but, once fixed, they maintain a uniform distance, which must be somewhat less than the thickness of the metallic plate to be rolled. The plate, after being bevelled on one of its edges, is inserted between the cylinders, and being obliged to follow their motion, is extended so as to be enabled to pass through. It is again passed through cylinders now more closely set, and thus reduced to any given degree of thinness.

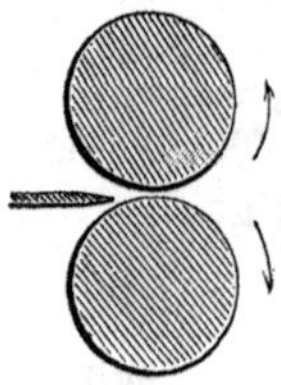

Fig. 309.

Some metals can be rolled when cold; others require a high degree of temperature.

During this forced flattening of the sheet, the metal undergoes a remarkable change in its molecular arrangement, which frequently alters greatly its physical properties, and especially its malleability. It becomes more hard and brittle, and if the rolling be continued, the sheets would inevitably tear. The metal is then said to be hammer-hardened, but its original ductility is restored by annealing it, which consists in heating it, and allowing it to cool slowly. Under the influence of heat, the molecules assume their respective normal positions, and the sheets may again be passed through the rollers.

The malleability and ductility of only such metals have been determined which have been obtained in a state of compactness and purity; for the presence of any foreign body, even in the smallest quantity, singularly alters their malleability.

The following are those whose malleability and ductility have been well determined:—

Silver,	Gold,
Cadmium,	Palladium,
Cobalt,	Platinum,
Copper,	Lead,
Tin,	Potassium,
Iron,	Sodium,
Mercury,	Zinc.
Nickel,	

Gold and silver are exceedingly malleable, as is shown by the extremely thin leaves manufactured by the goldbeater, which are so thin as to require more than 10,000 to form the thickness of a millimetre, (250,000 to 1 inch.)

§ 296. *Wire-drawing.*—Certain metals may be drawn out into very fine wire. The malleable metals are the only ones which possess this property; but they must have, in addition, a certain *tenacity*, in order to prevent them from breaking.

The wire-plate consists of a steel plate pierced with circular holes of various diameters, the edges of which are sharpened. The metallic rod intended to be drawn is made rather larger than the hole, No. 1 of the plate, and one of its ends is pointed so as to allow it to pass through hole No. 1, when this end is seized with a pincers, and the whole rod drawn forcibly through the hole. It is necessarily elongated and lessened in size. It is then passed successively through holes No. 2, 3, 4, etc., the diameters of which gradually decrease.

Metals become hardened in this operation, as in rolling, and it is necessary to anneal them from time to time, to restore their original ductility.

Pure metals and certain alloys can thus be drawn out into very fine wire, but not of extreme tenuity; for at a certain point they no longer possess sufficient tenacity, and break under the traction necessary to draw them through the wire-plate. Much finer threads, however, can be obtained, by resorting to different contrivances, a single example of which will be given, by describing a process whereby platinum wire has been made as fine as a spider's web.

A cylinder of silver is bored in the direction of its axis, with a hole 1 or 2 millimetres ($\frac{1}{25}$ or $\frac{1}{12}$ inch) in diameter, into which a platinum wire is inserted, of the same diameter, and then the cylinder drawn through the wire-plate. A very fine silver wire is thus obtained, in the centre of which there is a platinum thread still more delicate. The compound wire is then treated with dilute nitric acid, which dissolves the silver, and leaves the platinum thread untouched.

The following table exhibits the order in which metals pass with greatest facility through

The rollers.	The wire-plate.
1. Gold.	1. Gold.
2. Silver.	2. Silver.
3. Copper.	3. Platinum.
4. Tin.	4. Iron.
5. Platinum.	5. Nickel.
6. Lead.	6. Copper.
7. Zinc.	7. Zinc.
8. Iron.	8. Tin.
9. Nickel.	9. Lead.

The two series will be seen to differ remarkably from each other.

§ 297. *Tenacity.*—The tenacity of metals is that property by virtue of which they resist attempts to break them, and varies greatly in different metals. In order to test their tenacity, wire of the different metals is made of the same diameter, by passing them through the same hole in a wire-plate. Equal lengths of these wires are attached to a fixed point, and to the other end is suspended a dish to receive weights, by which the smallest weight which will effect the breakage of the wire, can be ascertained. This weight may then be considered as a measure of their resistance to rupture, or their *tenacity.*

Metals are thus proved to possess very different degrees of tenacity. The following table exhibits the smallest weights which have broken a wire of 2 millimetres (0.079, or $\frac{1}{12}$ inch) in diameter. It contains only the malleable metals, which are ranged in the order of decreasing tenacity:

	Kilogr.		Lbs. avoir.		Kilogr.		Lbs. avoir.
Iron	250	=	551	Zinc	50	=	110¼
Copper	137	=	302	Nickel	48	=	99¼
Platinum	125	=	275½	Tin	16	=	35¼
Silver	85	=	187½	Lead	12	=	26½
Gold	68	=	150				

The tenacity of metals has a great influence upon their application in the arts; and it frequently varies considerably in the same metal, according to its purity and mode of preparation.

When a metallic wire has been extended by the addition of successive weights, it is elongated in proportion to the weight it supports; and if the weights are gradually removed, the wire recovers the length which it formerly had under the same load. But this proposition is true for each wire only to a certain amount of weight, beyond which the wire retains a permanent elongation after the removal of the load. It is then said to have exceeded the *limit of its normal elasticity.* This maximum weight is often much less than that which breaks the wire. In building, therefore, a wire, or a metallic beam, should never be loaded to this point; for it would soon change under the prolonged effort of traction, and shortly break under a lighter load than it originally would have easily supported.

§ 298. *Conduction of Heat.*—Metals conduct heat more or less readily; and the study of this property is important in some of their applications, as, for example, in the construction of evaporators and steam-boilers. The quantity of liquid evaporated in a given time, depends necessarily on the conducting power of the metal of which the vessel is made; for, with equal thickness, similar vessels, formed of different metals, will transmit, in the same time, quantities of heat in proportion to their powers of conduction.

The following table contains the metals arranged in the order of their decreasing conduction:

Gold	200	Zinc	73
Silver	195	Tin	61
Copper	180	Lead	36
Iron	75		

§ 299. *Capacity of Heat.*—Very different degrees of heat are required to heat equal weights of different metals to the same number of degrees. Thus, the quantity of heat necessary to heat 1 kilogramme of water from 32° to 212°, being represented by 1.000, that which will effect the same elevation of temperature in 1 kilogramme of the various metals, is represented by the following numbers:

Iron	0.1138	Cadmium	0.0567
Nickel	0.1086	Tin	0.0562
Cobalt	0.1070	Antimony	0.0506
Zinc	0.0955	Platinum	0.0324
Copper	0.0952	Gold	0.0324
Palladium	0.0593	Lead	0.0314
Silver	0.0570	Bismuth	0.0308

CHEMICAL PROPERTIES OF THE METALS.

§ 300. We shall now make some remarks on the manner in which the metals behave with the metalloids, and on the general properties of the compounds which they form with those bodies.

Action of Oxygen on the Metals.

§ 301. Although all the metals have been obtained combined with oxygen, their affinities for it are very different. Some, such as potassium and sodium, combine with it directly, even at the lowest temperatures; others, as gold and platinum, have so feeble an affinity for it, that they do not combine directly with it under any circumstances, and their oxides are obtained only by indirect methods. The former retain oxygen at the highest temperatures, while the latter part with it readily when their oxides are heated.

The affinity of the metals for oxygen may be ascertained,

1st. From the manner of their behaviour to oxygen gas at various temperatures.

2dly. From the greater or less facility with which their oxides are restored to the metallic state.

3dly. From the decomposing action which they exert upon the same oxide under various circumstances; water being the oxide usually made use of. Certain metals decompose water, even at the temperature of 32°; others decompose it only at a temperature greater than 122° or 140°; some require a temperature of 212°; others react on the vapour of water only at a red-heat, or at a still higher temperature; and, lastly, some do not decompose water at any degree of heat attainable by our laboratory furnaces.

4thly. From their decomposing influence upon water in the presence of powerful acids. Many metals decompose water, in the cold, in the presence of sulphuric acid; while others do not even when the temperature is elevated. This property does not depend alone upon the greater or less affinity of the metals for oxygen; but depends especially on the basic affinity of the metallic oxide for the acid (§ 69).

The metals have, therefore, been divided into six sections, based upon the above properties.

Section 1.—Those which absorb oxygen at all temperatures, even at the highest, and decompose water even at the lowest temperatures, producing a copious evolution of hydrogen gas. They are—

Potassium,	Barium,
Sodium,	Strontium,
Lithium,	Calcium.

The first three are called *alkaline metals;* the last three, *alkalino-earthy metals.*

Section 2.—Those which absorb oxygen at the highest temperatures, and whose oxides are indecomposible by heat alone: they do not sensibly decompose water at very low temperatures, but readily above 122°. They are—

Magnesium,	Aluminum;
Manganese,	

to which may, probably, be added the following metals, whose decomposing action on water has not been yet studied with sufficient care:

Glucinum,	Lanthanium,
Zirconium,	Didymium,
Yttrium,	Erbium,
Thorium,	Terbium.
Cerium,	

Section 3.—Those which absorb oxygen at a red-heat, but do not yield it up again by heat alone, which decompose water only at a temperature superior to 212°, but below a red-heat, and decompose cold water in the presence of powerful acids. They are—

Iron,	Vanadium,
Nickel,	Zinc,
Cobalt,	Cadmium,
Chromium,	Uranium.

The temperature at which these metals combine with oxygen, and that at which they decompose water, depends greatly on their state of division. Aggregated iron, even in the state of filings, combines with dry oxygen only at a dull red-heat; while the same metal very finely divided, which can be done by reducing the oxides of iron by hydrogen gas at the lowest temperature possible, takes fire when thrown into the air, and oxidizes, consequently, at ordinary temperatures. Aggregated iron decomposes the vapour of water only at a red-heat, while pulverulent iron decomposes it at a temperature of about 392°.

Section 4.—Those which absorb oxygen at a red-heat, and whose oxides are irreducible by heat alone. They readily decompose the vapour of water at a red-heat, but do not decompose water in the presence of powerful acids. This is owing to the fact that their oxides are but feeble bases; while they form, on the contrary, with oxygen, bodies which exhibit strong acid properties with reference to energetic bases. Hence, the greater part of them decompose water in the presence of potassa with an evolution of hydrogen gas. This 4th section comprises—

Tungsten,	Titanium,
Molybdenum,	Tin,
Osmium,	Antimony;
Tantalum,	

to which we may probably add—

Niobium,	Pelopium.
Ilmenium,	

Section 5.—Those which absorb oxygen at a red-heat, whose oxides are not decomposed by heat alone; which decompose water only at a very elevated temperature, and then very feebly. They do not decompose water either in the presence of strong acids or of powerful bases. They are—

Copper,	Bismuth.
Lead,	

Section 6.—Those whose oxides are reducible by heat alone, at a more or less elevated temperature, and which do not decompose water under any circumstances. They are—

Mercury,	Palladium,
Silver,	Platinum,
Rhodium,	Ruthenium,
Iridium,	Gold.

§ 302. It is useful to remark, that all the metals whose oxides are irreducible by heat alone, can decompose water at a higher or lower temperature; which is due to the fact that water itself is separated into its two elements at an extremely elevated temperature. If a small ball of platinum, affixed to the end of a wire of the same metal be heated to whiteness by the hydro-oxygen blowpipe, and plunged rapidly into water, small bubbles of gas, formed of a mixture of hydrogen and oxygen, are disengaged. The water has been therefore decomposed by heat alone, for the metal has seized on neither of its constituent gases. A similar decomposition takes place when a platinum wire immersed in water is heated intensely by passing through it the electric current of a powerful battery.

Action of dry Oxygen on the Metals.

§ 303. The direct combination of metal with oxygen is a true combustion with disengagement of heat; and when the combination is rapidly effected, the temperature rises sufficiently high to render the substance incandescent. The combustion is more active when the metal is finely divided, because it then presents a greater surface to the action of oxygen; but if the metal be in mass, and the oxide do not fuse at the temperature at which oxidation takes place, the combustion is suddenly arrested, because the metal becomes covered with a coating of oxide, which defends it from further contact with the oxygen. Thus, finely divided copper previously heated to dull redness, burns readily in oxygen, and is wholly changed into an oxide, while a sheet of copper, under similar circumstances, is only covered with a coating of oxide. Iron, heated to redness, burns freely in oxygen, even when the metal is in the shape of large wire, because the resulting oxide fuses at the temperature of combustion, and keeps the surface of the metal exposed.

When the metal is volatile, it may also burn with great energy, and even with flame, if it has been previously heated to a proper degree. Thus, zinc heated to redness in a crucible, burns with a very brilliant white flame. In this case, it is the vapour of zinc which burns; and as the oxide of zinc is fixed, its solid particles, suspended in the flame, become luminous, and add great brilliancy to it.

Action of moist Oxygen on the Metals.

§ 304. Metals which do not combine when cold with dry oxygen, frequently oxidize rapidly when exposed to a damp air. Iron preserves its brilliancy in dry oxygen for an indefinite time, while it changes rapidly in moist air, and becomes covered with an ochreous coat, which is the hydrated sesquioxide of iron. Many other metals belong to the same category; but, in some, the change is only superficial, while in others it continues until the whole of the metal is converted into an oxide. An iron bar exposed to a damp air is completely destroyed by rust, while a sheet of zinc soon becomes covered by a pellicle of oxide which preserves it from further change.

The presence of acid vapours in the air greatly facilitates the oxidation of metals. Iron, which remains unaltered in dry oxygen, and even in water deprived of its air by boiling, soon changes when in contact with oxygen and water at the same time; for it then meets with oxygen dissolved in the water, that is, under the most favourable conditions for its combination. Moreover, iron has a certain basic affinity for water, which again facilitates the formation of this oxide, according to the principle laid down (§ 69). For the same reason, iron and zinc, which alone do not decompose cold water, decompose it readily in presence of powerful acids, as if the presence of the acid had increased their affinity for oxygen. The presence of acid vapours in the air greatly facilitates the oxidation of a metal, for they increase its affinity for oxygen to a greater degree than water, which only acts the part of a feeble acid.

Those metals some of whose oxides play the part of acids with reference to energetic bases, oxidize more rapidly in the air when moistened with an alkaline solution, or in the midst of a moist atmosphere containing ammoniacal vapours.

§ 305. It is frequently observed that when a certain quantity of oxide has formed on the surface of a metal, its oxidation becomes much more rapid, as if the presence of the oxide increased the affinity of the metal for oxygen. This peculiarity is very evident in iron, and the following experiment demonstrates it clearly.

If moistened iron filings be exposed to the air, oxidation goes on very slowly at first, but is soon accelerated, and the iron rusts rapidly. At the same time the fetid odour of hydrogen gas is observed, which occurs when ordinary iron is dissolved in dilute sulphuric acid. In fact, a sufficient quantity of hydrogen is disengaged to allow of its collection after some time, if the experiment be made in a suitable apparatus.

The oxidation of the metal is, at first, effected by the absorption of the oxygen of the air dissolved by the water which moistens the filings; but the coat of oxide which covers the metal soon forms a voltaic circle, in which iron is the electropositive element. Iron itself is electropositive as regards oxygen; and if it forms the electropositive element of a pile, it becomes still more electropositive than it naturally is, its affinity for oxygen is increased, and experiment proves that this affinity may be sufficiently great to decompose water at the ordinary temperature.

If, on the contrary, a body which becomes the electropositive element of a voltaic circle be brought into contact with iron, the latter, becoming less electropositive than in its isolated state, loses some of its affinity for oxygen: it has become less oxidizable, and may be preserved from oxidation under circumstances in which this would inevitably have ensued had it been isolated. Advantage has been taken of this property, in the arts, to render objects made of iron less changeable in the air, by covering them with a thin coating of zinc, which becomes the electropositive element of the circle, and preserves the iron from oxidation. The zinc, on the contrary, oxidizes rapidly; but its oxidation is only superficial, for the small pellicle of oxide developed on the surface forms an impervious varnish which preserves the inner layers. Iron, thus protected by a coating of zinc, is called *galvanized iron*.

The same principle has been applied to prevent the oxidation of other metals, such as the copper used in sheathing ships. Unfortunately, it has been found that shells will then adhere in greater numbers to the ship's bottom, and her sailing powers are lessened in consequence of the increased friction.

Action of Sulphur on the Metals.

§ 306. All the metals combine directly with sulphur, when heated with it, or when it is passed in the state of vapour over the heated metal.

Some, such as copper, burn in the vapour of sulphur with brilliancy. Others combine with it, even at ordinary temperatures, if water be present. A mixture of iron-filings and flowers of sulphur slightly moistened, soon disengages a considerable degree of heat, owing to the combination of the iron with the sulphur.

Action of Chlorine on the Metals.

§ 307. Chlorine acts on the metals still more powerfully than oxygen, and converts them readily and entirely into chlorides.

The majority of them combine with chlorine even in the cold. In some, the combination is so energetic that the temperature rises to ignition, and many of them, when pulverized, take fire when thrown into a bottle containing gaseous chlorine.

Action of Bromine and Iodine on the Metals.

§ 308. The action of bromine and iodine on the metals generally resembles that of chlorine; but the affinities are more feeble.

Action of Phosphorus on the Metals.

§ 309. The metals of the first section combine easily with phosphorus when heated with it; but those of the other sections do not, because the phosphorus volatilizes before the temperature is sufficiently elevated for reaction to take place. Some metals of the third and fifth sections may combine with a certain quantity of phosphorus, when heated to a very high temperature in its vapour.

Action of Arsenic on the Metals.

§ 310. Arsenic combines with the metals much more readily than phosphorus, and several arseniurets are directly obtained by heating a powdered mixture of the metal and arsenic.

Action of Boron, Silicium, and Carbon on the Metals.

§ 311. Some of the metals can combine directly with boron, silicium, and carbon: we shall, as we proceed, point out several of these compounds.

COMBINATIONS OF THE METALS WITH EACH OTHER, OR ALLOYS.

§ 312. The majority of the metals can combine with each other, forming alloys endued with metallic properties which partake at once of the nature of both combined metals. By alloying metals with each other, we create, so to speak, new metals, possessing special properties, and more suitable for certain purposes in the arts than the pure metals.

The metals used in a pure state in the arts are,

Iron,	Silver,
Copper,	Gold,
Zinc,	Platinum,
Lead,	Mercury.
Tin,	

Of these, platinum and iron are the only ones exclusively employed in a state of purity. The others are often used alone, but are more frequently alloyed with each other, or with some other metals, such as antimony and bismuth, which last are never used alone, on account of their brittleness.

Copper is a very valuable metal, easily worked by the hammer, but destitute of a great degree of hardness. This quality can be much increased, without greatly diminishing its ductility, by alloying $\frac{2}{3}$ of copper with $\frac{1}{3}$ of zinc. An alloy called *brass* is thus obtained, of an agreeable yellow colour, and admitting a large number of applications. But brass thus made is not easily filed, as it sticks to the file and *clogs* it; but the inconvenience is remedied by adding to the alloy 2 or 3 per cent. of lead or tin.

§ 313. For artillery, a metal is required which is hard without being brittle, and which can be cast, and worked in a turning-lathe. Pure copper partly fulfils this condition, but it is too soft, and before the ball leaves the cannon it rebounds several times in the chamber of the piece, soon forming cavities which impair the accuracy of the aim. An alloy of 90 parts of copper and 10 parts of tin presents more hardness and possesses sufficient tenacity. This alloy, called *bronze*, is used for cannon and many ornamental objects, such as statues, candelabras, etc. By increasing the proportion of tin, we obtain alloys still harder, but also more brittle. The alloy of 20 parts of tin and 80 of copper is extremely hard and sonorous, and is used in the manufacture of clocks, cymbals, and tomtoms. The alloy of 67 of copper and 33 of tin, is of a slightly-yellowish white colour, susceptible of a most brilliant polish, and is used for the reflectors of telescopes.

Thus, by alloying two metals in different proportions, alloys are obtained differing greatly from each metal in their physical properties, and capable of very various uses.

§ 314. For printing-types, a metal is required which must satisfy many conditions. It should be very fusible, for the types are cast; it must take the exact impress of the mould, in order that the characters be well defined; and, lastly, it must possess a certain hardness, without being too brittle, for, if the metal is too soft, the types are crushed in the press, and if too hard and brittle, they break.

Iron and copper are not sufficiently fusible. Silver, gold, and platinum melt only at a very high temperature, and are, moreover, too expensive. Zinc, antimony, and bismuth are too brittle. Lead and tin are too soft. But a perfectly suitable alloy is obtained by mixing 80 parts of lead and 20 of antimony.

§ 315. Many metals seem to possess the power of combining with each other in indefinite proportions. But when melted alloys are allowed to cool slowly, they generally separate into several others, presenting a definite composition, and often a crystalline structure. This decomposition of the same homogeneous alloy, and several others which separate more or less perfectly, takes place sometimes when the alloy is exposed for a long time to a high temperature, although less than that producing its fusion. Examples of this will hereafter be adduced.

These separations may be easily recognised in alloys fusible at a low temperature, by observing the fall of a thermometer, the bulb of which dips into a certain quantity of fused alloy which is cooling in the air. If the experiment be made upon melted tin, heated to 120° or 140° above its melting point, it will be observed that the temperature falls at first rapidly, but with a decreasing celerity, because the rapidity of cooling of a substance in the air is nearly in proportion to the excess of its temperature over the surrounding medium. But when the temperature reaches 437°, the thermometer stops suddenly, and remains stationary for a longer or shorter time, according to the mass of metal on which we are operating, and then begins again to fall. The point at which the thermometer stops corresponds to the solidification of the tin. The metal, by solidifying, gives off its latent heat of fusion, which compensates at every instant for the loss of heat effected by radiation and the contact of cold air; and the cooling recommences only after the metal is entirely solidified. The same phenomenon is evinced in all homogeneous bodies, whether simple or compound, the constitution of which does not change while cooling slowly after fusion. But, if the same experiment be made on certain very fusible alloys, and principally on the ternary alloys of lead, tin, and bismuth, which, melting at low temperatures, are very suitable for this kind of observation, several points of stoppage are generally observed during their cooling; sometimes as many as three or four. Each of these stoppages corresponds to the solidification of a particular alloy with definite proportions, which is formed at the expense of the elements of the primary homogeneous alloy, and separates in the form of a crystalline powder. After the separation of one or several of these compounds, the substance presents the consistence of a *sandy paste;* and only becomes completely solid after the crystallization of the alloy which remains fluid last.

Thus, although we may fuse the three metals together in indefinite proportions, and obtain apparently homogeneous alloys by rapid solidification, the metals have a tendency to combine in definite proportions, like all other substances in nature; and definite compounds are formed whenever, during slow cooling, the molecules have time to obey their elective affinities.

§ 316. The point of fusion of an alloy is often less than that of the most fusible metal which enters into its composition.

Thus, lead melts at.......................... 617°
bismuth, " .... 509°
tin, " .... 442°

The alloy formed of 5 parts of lead, 3 of tin, and 8 of bismuth, melts at 203°, that is, at a temperature much lower than that of its most fusible component.

OF THE METALLIC OXIDES.

§ 317. The metallic oxides present the most diversified properties. Some are more or less powerful bases, which combine with acids forming well marked salts; others, on the contrary, play the part of acids, and combine with the powerful bases; lastly, some of them combine neither with acids nor bases.

In this point of view, the oxides are generally divided into five classes:

1st. *Basic oxides*, that is, those which combine readily with the acids, and produce definite, crystallizable salts. The protoxides of potassium, sodium, calcium, iron, lead, etc. etc. are basic oxides.

2dly. *Acid oxides*, which do not combine, or at least very rarely, with the acids, and which form, on the contrary, well defined salts with powerful bases. Chromic acid CrO_3, manganic acid MnO_3, stannic acid SnO_2, plumbic acid PbO_2, antimonic acid SbO_5, are true metallic acids, which form crystallizable salts with several powerful bases, particularly with potassa.

3dly. *Neutral oxides*, which at the same time play the part of acids with powerful bases, and that of bases with energetic acids. Alumina Al_2O_3 is an oxide of this kind.

4thly. *Simple oxides*. These oxides combine neither with the acids nor with the bases. Under the influence of acids, they part with a portion of their oxygen, or of their metal, and are converted into protoxides, which combine with the acid. The peroxide of manganese MnO_2 is an oxide of this class. When heated with sulphuric acid, it parts with one-half of its oxygen and forms the sulphate of the protoxide of manganese. The suboxide of lead Pb_2O is changed, by contact with acids, into metallic lead Pb, and protoxide of lead PbO, which combines with the acid. These oxides frequently undergo decompositions analogous to the bases. Thus, the binoxide of manganese MnO_2, melted with caustic potassa, is changed into the sesquioxide of manganese Mn_2O_3, and into manganic acid MnO_3, which combines with the potassa:

$$3MnO_2+KO=Mn_2O_3+KO,MnO_3.$$

5thly. *Saline oxides*. These oxides result from the combination of a basic metallic oxide with a higher oxide of the same metal. They are true salts, in which the electropositive elements of the acid and the base are formed by the same metal. The oxides of iron Fe_3O_4, of manganese Mn_3O_4, of chromium Cr_3O_4, belong to this class, and their formulæ should be written FeO, Fe_2O_3; MnO,Mn_2O_3; CrO,Cr_2O_3. The brown oxide of chromium

CrO_2, belongs to the same class: it should be written $Cr_2O_3,CrO_3=3CrO_2$. The same is true as regards antimonious acid SbO_4, the formula of which should be $SbO_3,SbO_5=2SbO_4$.

§ 318. Certain metals form a great number of compounds with oxygen, which are included in the five classes just defined, and of which manganese furnishes a remarkable example.

The protoxide of manganese MnO is a powerful base. The sesquioxide Mn_2O_3 is a very feeble base, but we know as yet of no compounds in which it plays the part of an acid: it forms the limit of the neutral oxides. The binoxide MnO_2 is a simple oxide. The oxide Mn_3O_4 is a saline oxide, the true formula of which is MnO,Mn_2O_3. Manganic acid, MnO_3 and hypermanganic Mn_2O_7 are powerful metallic acids.

§ 319. In general, the oxide of the formula RO is the most powerful base among those which can be formed of the same metal. The oxides R_2O_3 are very feeble bases, and frequently play the part of acids with powerful bases; in which latter case, they are ranked with the neutral oxides. The oxides RO_2 are often metallic acids, such as the peroxides of lead PbO_2, and of tin SnO_2: they are sometimes simple oxides, as the binoxide of manganese MnO_2; and sometimes they should be regarded as saline oxides, such as the brown oxide of chromium, $CrO_2=\frac{1}{3}(Cr_2O_3,CrO_3)$. Lastly, the oxides which have more complex formulæ, such as Fe_3O_4, Mn_3O_4, are saline oxides, which should be written FeO, Fe_2O_3 and MnO,Mn_2O_3.

§ 320. The metallic oxides are obtained by the following processes:—1. By heating the metal in the air or in oxygen, the various steps of which oxidation have been explained (§ 303). The lower are also changed into higher oxides by calcination. Protoxide of manganese MnO heated in the air is converted into the sesquioxide. When protoxide of barium or baryta BaO is heated to 750° in a current of oxygen, it absorbs the gas, and is changed into the binoxide of barium BaO_2. A red-heat, on the contrary, decomposes the binoxide of barium, and restores it to the state of a protoxide.

2. The metal may be oxidized by calcining it with a substance which parts readily with its oxygen. By heating antimony with nitrate of potassa, antimoniate of potassa is obtained; and by treating this salt with an acid, antimonic acid is isolated. This process is often adopted to change lower into higher oxides, especially into metallic acids. Thus, by fusing oxide of chrome Cr_2O_3 with the nitrate of potassa, this oxide is changed into chromic acid CrO_3, and chromate of potassa obtained.

3. The metal, or one of its inferior oxides, may be oxidized by acting on it with nitric acid, and evaporating off the excess of acid. Some metals are thus changed into higher oxides, which remain uncombined; as tin and antimony, which become stannic

acid, SnO_2, and antimonic acid SbO_5. Most frequently, nitrates are formed, which are decomposed by calcination, and that oxide remains which is formed when the metal is heated in oxygen at the temperature at which the decomposition of the nitrate takes place.

4. Some peroxides are obtained by acting on the lower oxides by the binoxide of hydrogen (§ 90). In this way, binoxide of calcium and several metallic peroxides are prepared, which cannot be obtained in any other mode.

5. Heat alone converts some higher into lower oxides. The sesquioxides of cobalt and nickel Co_2O_3 and Ni_2O_3 change at a red-heat into protoxides CoO and NiO. Binoxide of lead PbO_2 is changed into the protoxide PbO. The binoxide of manganese MnO_2 passes into the state of a saline oxide MnO,Mn_2O_3:

$$3MnO_2 = MnO,Mn_2O_3 + 2O.$$

6. Hydrogen, at a red-heat, reduces a great number of oxides to the metallic state, but reduces some higher oxides only to the state of protoxides. The sesquioxide of manganese Mn_2O_3, heated in a current of hydrogen, is converted into the protoxide MnO.

7. The solution of a metallic salt, or of the corresponding chloride, is precipitated by an alkaline base or by ammonia. By pouring a solution of potassa or ammonia into a solution of the sulphate of the protoxide of iron, or of the protochloride of iron, a precipitate is obtained of the hydrated protoxide of iron:

$$FeO,SO_3 + KO + HO = KO,SO_3 + FeO,HO;$$

$$FeCl + KO + HO = KCl + FeO,HO.$$

The same alkaline liquid gives, with solutions of the sulphate of the sesquioxide or sesquichloride of iron, a precipitate of hydrated sesquioxide of iron:

$$Fe_2O_3,3SO_3 + 3KO + HO = 3(KO,SO_3) + Fe_2O_3,HO;$$

$$Fe_2Cl_3 + 3KO + HO = 3KCl + Fe_2O_3,HO.$$

Potassa is often replaced by ammonia, and sometimes even by carbonate of potassa, when the oxide of the salt does not combine with carbonic acid.

The oxides thus prepared in the humid way, generally precipitate in the state of hydrates, but heat suffices to transform the majority of them into anhydrous oxides. The hydrates of the oxides formed by the metals of the first section are alone undecomposable by heat.

8. All the carbonates, except those of the metals of the first section, are decomposed by heat, setting their oxides at liberty. Thus, by calcining the carbonates of baryta, strontia, and lime, at

a high temperature, baryta, strontia, and lime are obtained. The carbonate of lead PbO,CO_2 gives off its carbonic acid at a lower temperature than the preceding carbonates, and the protoxide of lead PbO, remains.

When the protoxide which forms the base of the salt has a great affinity for oxygen, it frequently happens that it decomposes the carbonic acid and seizes upon part of its oxygen. Thus, when the native carbonate of the protoxide of iron FeO,CO_2, which mineralogists call *sparry iron*, is heated, it gives the saline oxide FeO, Fe_2O_3, and a mixture of carbonic acid and carbonic oxide is disengaged:

$$3(FeO,CO_2)=FeO,Fe_2O_3+2CO_2+CO.$$

Action of the Metalloids on the Oxides.

§ 321. *Action of Oxygen.*—Oxides which have not reached their maximum of oxidation can sometimes combine directly with a new proportion of oxygen. The combination is sometimes effected in the cold by exposure to the air; but it takes place more readily if water be present, as when the oxide is combined or only moistened with water. The hydrates of the protoxide of iron and manganese promptly absorb oxygen from the air, and are converted into hydrated sesquioxides. Other oxides combine with oxygen only when moderately heated in the air: thus, protoxide of lead, heated to a temperature of about 750°, absorbs oxygen from the air, and is converted into a new oxide, *minium.* A higher temperature, on the contrary, decomposes the minium and restores it to the state of protoxide.

§ 322. *Action of Hydrogen.*—Many oxides are decomposed by hydrogen, which seizes upon their oxygen to form water, but the reaction generally requires a certain elevation of temperature.

The oxides of the metals in the first two sections are not decomposed by hydrogen at any temperature. Those of the metals in the other sections are all reduced to the metallic state by hydrogen, at higher or lower temperatures. Those of the sixth section are all decomposed by hydrogen, at a temperature slightly above that of boiling water; the others require a red-heat.

Hydrogen reduces the oxides of iron at a red-heat, and vapour of water is formed. On the other hand, it was shown (§ 68) that iron, when heated to redness in a current of steam, is oxidized by decomposing the water, and disengaging hydrogen gas. Two entirely opposite effects are here produced under circumstances apparently identical. We might infer, from the decomposition of the oxides of iron by hydrogen, that, at a red-heat, the hydrogen has more affinity for oxygen than the iron, while, from the decomposition of steam effected by iron at a red-heat, we would conclude, on the contrary, that the iron had more affinity for oxygen than the hydrogen. We shall subsequently meet with several analogous phenomena. Chemists explain these apparent contradictions, by saying that substances act not only by virtue of the electric affinities, but also according to the respective quantities which are present. So that if two substances are in contact with a third, for which they have slightly different affinities, that which predominates in the sphere of action expels the other. In the two experiments just described, we have had in contact at a red-heat, iron, oxide of iron, vapour of water, and hydrogen. In that in which the vapour of water is passed over heated iron, the iron may be considered as predominating with reference to the hydrogen, because this gas, as fast as it is produced, is carried off by the current of steam, of which it constitutes only a small proportion, so that the iron will consequently oxidize. In the experiment in which oxide of iron is heated in a current of hydrogen, each molecule of the oxide is in the sphere of action of a great number of molecules of hydrogen, and the latter, consequently, seizes on the oxygen.

From this it is evident that, for a given temperature, there exists a certain proportion of hydrogen and vapour of water, which exerts no reducing action on oxide of iron, nor oxidizing action on metallic iron. If the proportion of vapour of water is greater, the metal will oxidize; if less, the oxide will be reduced. These proportions in which hydrogen and oxygen should exist, so as to exert no action either on metallic iron or on the oxide of iron, probably vary with the temperature.

§ 323. *Action of Carbon.*—Carbon reduces all the metallic oxides which are decomposed by hydrogen; and at a very high temperature, some oxides are reduced which resist the action of hydrogen. Thus, the oxides of potassium and sodium are entirely decomposed by carbon at a white-heat, and their metals set free.

When the reduction of the oxide takes place at a low temperature, carbonic acid is disengaged: if it occur only at a high temperature, carbonic oxide is given off. Many metals, in fact, decompose carbonic acid at a red-heat, and convert it into carbonic oxide. Charcoal produces a similar decomposition.

§ 324. *Action of Sulphur.*—At a high temperature, sulphur acts on the majority of metallic oxides. When heated with metals of the first section, a mixture of sulphate and sulphide is formed; but if charcoal be added, a sulphide alone is produced.

The oxides of the metals of the second section are not changed when heated with sulphur; but several of them produce sulphides when their oxides mixed with charcoal are heated intensely in a current of vapour of sulphur.

The oxides of the metals of the last four sections are changed into sulphides by sulphur, with the disengagement of sulphurous acid; but it is often necessary, for this purpose, to pass the vapour of sulphur over the highly heated oxide, and sometimes even to mix the latter previously with charcoal.

§ 325. *Action of Chlorine.*—Chlorine acts variously on the oxides, according to its dryness, moisture, and temperature.

When cold, or influenced by heat, dry chlorine changes nearly all the oxides into chlorides. We must except, however, the oxides of some metals of the second section, which resist the action of chlorine, even at the highest temperatures. But by taking care to mix the oxide previously with charcoal, and to heat the mixture in a current of dry chlorine, the affinity of carbon for oxygen, combined with that of chlorine for the metal, always effects the decomposition of the oxide; carbonic oxide being given off, and a metallic chloride formed.

When the oxides are dissolved or suspended in water, the action of chlorine is, generally, very different from that first mentioned.

If a current of chlorine be passed through a solution of potassa, the reaction varies with the state of dilution or concentration of the liquid, and the temperature. If the solution be dilute, and the temperature not allowed to rise, a reaction takes place between 2 equivalents of potassa and 2 of chlorine, forming hypochlorite of potassa and chloride of potassium, as expressed by the following equation:

$$2KO+2Cl=KCl+KO,ClO.$$

If the solution be concentrated, and the temperature allowed to rise, reaction takes place between 6 equivalents of potassa and 6 of chlorine, and a mixture of chlorate of potassa and chloride of potassium is obtained; thus,

$$6KO+6Cl=KO,ClO_5+5KCl.$$

If the concentrated alkaline solution be kept constantly boiling, chloride of potassium and chlorate of potassa are again formed; but the proportion of chlorate is less, and oxygen gas is given off.

The oxides of all the metals of the first section behave in the same manner.

The oxides of a majority of the metals of the second section are not changed by chlorine under the influence of water, even at the temperature of 212°, except magnesia and protoxide of manganese. The oxide of magnesium is changed, in this case, into chloride of magnesium and hypochlorite of magnesia: the protoxide of manganese behaves, under the influence of moist chlorine, like the protoxides of the metals of the third section.

The protoxides of the metals of the third section, suspended in water, are changed by chlorine into chlorides and sesquioxides. With the protoxide of iron, we have,

$$3FeO+Cl=FeCl+Fe_2O_3.$$

If the oxide be suspended in an alkaline liquid, the protoxide is completely transformed into a sesquioxide, and the chloride of potassium is produced:

$$2FeO+KO+Cl=Fe_2O_3+KCl.$$

Chlorine does not act on the sesquioxides of the metals of the third section suspended in water, unless the liquid contains a large quantity of potassa. In this case, the oxide of iron may pass into the state of a compound containing more oxygen than the sesquioxide, ferric acid, which forms, with potassa in excess, the ferrate of potassa. Thus,

$$Fe_2O_3+5KO+3Cl=2(KO,FeO_3)+3KCl.$$

The oxides of the metals of the last three sections are changed into chlorides by the action of chlorine in presence of water.

The action of bromine and iodine on the metallic oxides is in general analogous to that of chlorine.

§ 326. *Action of the Metals on the Metallic Oxides.*—The action of the metals on the metallic oxides may often be foreseen, when we have a very clear idea of the affinity of the metals for oxygen. But it is difficult to generalize upon this action, for the relative affinity of the metals for oxygen varies greatly with temperature. Thus potassium decomposes oxide of iron at a red-heat, whilst at a higher temperature, as a strong white-heat, iron, on the contrary, decomposes oxide of potassium.

METALLIC CHLORIDES.

§ 327. Many of the metals combine directly with chlorine, especially if heated in a current of the gas, when they are rapidly and entirely transformed into chlorides. This property must be attributed, partly to their great affinity for chlorine, partly to the physical properties of the chlorides. The chlorides are, in fact, all very fusible, and many of them volatile; so that when a metal is heated in a current of chlorine, its surface is always exposed freely to the action of the gas, either because the melted chloride runs off or volatilizes as it is formed.

The metallic chlorides are, in general, undecomposable by heat alone, excepting the chlorides of gold, platinum, and, probably, those of several other metals of the sixth section, which are reduced to the metallic state by an elevated temperature.

Many metallic chlorides are obtained by dissolving their metals in chlorohydric acid; the protochlorides of metals of the third section being thus readily obtained. The chlorohydric acid is decomposed, chloride formed, and hydrogen disengaged.

$$Fe+HCl=FeCl+H.$$

The metals of the fifth section do not decompose chlorohydric acid, even at the boiling point; but a chloride is formed when nitric acid is added, that is, when the metal is treated with aqua regia. The metals of the third section are changed, in this case, into perchlorides.

Action of the Metalloides on the Metallic Chlorides.

§ 328. *Action of Oxygen.*—Oxygen does not act on the chlorides of metals of the first section; but readily oxidizes those metals in the second, third, fourth, and fifth sections, when their chlorides are heated in a current of oxygen. The chlorides of the sixth section, which are not decomposed by heat, are not changed when heated in oxygen; while those, on the contrary, which are decomposed by heat alone, give off their chlorine without combining with the oxygen.

§ 329. *Action of Hydrogen.*—The chlorides from metals of the first two sections are not decomposed at any temperature by hydrogen; but those from the last four sections are decomposed by it at various temperatures. This behaviour offers a convenient method for obtaining several metals in a state of purity, but is difficult of application to others, because decomposition takes place only at the highest temperature. An inverted action is, moreover, observed here, exactly resembling that pointed out (§ 322) when speaking of the action of hydrogen on the oxides. Thus, chloride of iron is decomposed by hydrogen at a red-heat, chlorohydric acid being disengaged and metallic iron remaining. On the other hand, metallic iron decomposes chlorohydric gas at the same temperature, forming chloride of iron and setting hydrogen free. The anomaly was explained (§ 322).

§ 330. *Action of Carbon.*—Carbon exerts no sensible action on the metallic chlorides.

METALLIC BROMIDES AND IODIDES.

§ 331. Metallic bromides and iodides are prepared like the corresponding chlorides, and their reaction with the metalloids is analogous to that of the chlorides.

METALLIC SULPHIDES OR SULPHURETS.

§ 332. It was stated (§ 306) that all metals can combine with sulphur when heated with it, or still better, when heated to a high temperature in the vapour of sulphur. A great number of metallic sulphides can also be obtained by heating the oxides with sulphur, or by calcining in a crucible covered with damp charcoal, a mixture of metallic oxide, carbonate of potassa or soda, and sulphur. The alkaline carbonate is then changed into a polysulphide, which itself converts the metallic oxide into a sulphide, while oxygen is disengaged in the state of carbonic oxide. If the metal can form an electronegative sulphide, as happens with the metals of the fourth section, this sulphide combines with a portion of the alkaline sulphide which has become a monosulphide, and a sulphosalt is formed, in which the alkaline monosulphide plays the part of a base.

A great number of metallic sulphides can also be prepared by passing a current of sulphuretted hydrogen through a solution of the metallic salts, especially insoluble sulphides from metals of the fifth and sixth sections.

Sulphides from metals of the third section may also be prepared in the humid way, by pouring a solution of alkaline sulphide into a saline solution of the metal. Thus, with sulphate of the protoxide of iron and monosulphide of potassium, the reaction is

$$FeO,SO_3+KS=KO,SO_3+FeS.$$

If an excess of alkaline sulphide be poured into the solution of a salt formed by a metal of the fourth section, there is formed, at first, a precipitate of the metallic sulphide, but it is subsequently dissolved in the excess of alkaline sulphide, by producing a sulphosalt, in which it plays the part of an acid.

The sulphides of the third and fifth sections have a well-marked metallic lustre.

Metallic sulphides resist powerfully the action of heat, there being only a few sulphides of the sixth section which are decomposed at a very elevated temperature.

Action of the Metalloids on Metallic Sulphides.

§ 333. *Action of Oxygen.*—Oxygen acts energetically on all metallic sulphides, at a higher or lower temperature.

The sulphides of the metals of the first section, heated in contact with oxygen, are changed into sulphates; the metal and sulphur both combine with oxygen, and the products of combustion remain combined. The sulphide of magnesium, which belongs to the second section, presents a similar reaction. Those of the third and fifth sections, and the sulphides of manganese belonging to the second, are decomposed by oxygen; but the products of decomposition vary according to the temperature. When the latter is very elevated, sulphurous acid is disengaged, and the metal remains in the state of an oxide. At a lower temperature, at a dull red-heat, for instance, a certain quantity of sulphate is always formed, so that we obtain a mixture of oxide and sulphate.

Metallic sulphides of the fourth section are changed into oxides, and the sulphur disengaged in the state of sulphurous acid. Lastly, sulphides from the sixth section, heated in a current of oxygen, are reduced to the metallic state, and the sulphur disengaged in the state of sulphurous acid.

Oxygen can also act when cold on the majority of sulphides, principally under the influence of water, whereby many of them are finally changed into sulphates.

METALLIC PHOSPHURETS.

§ 334. The metals of the first section are the only ones which combine easily with phosphorus. Phosphurets of several other metals are obtained by passing a current of phosphuretted hydrogen through saline solutions, by which an insoluble phosphuret is precipitated. In this way, the phosphurets of copper, lead, and tin can be prepared. But the best mode of obtaining the phosphurets consists in heating the phosphates mixed with charcoal.

The phosphurets of metals of the first section are decomposed by water, and disengage phosphuretted hydrogen, thus readily evincing their nature.

METALLIC ARSENIURETS.

§ 335. A great number of metallic arseniurets may be prepared by heating together the metal and arsenic, both finely powdered. They are also obtained by decomposing the arseniates by charcoal, at a high temperature. The arseniurets, in general, possess a metallic lustre; and when heated with chlorohydric acid, they disengage arseniuretted hydrogen.

GENERAL CONSIDERATIONS ON THE SALTS.

§ 336. I give the name of *salt* to every combination of two binary compounds, one of which acts the part of an electropositive element, or base, and the other that of an electronegative element, or acid.

The bases, or electropositive binary compounds, always result from the combination of a metal with a metalloid, such as the protoxide and protosulphide of potassium. The acids, or electronegative binary compounds, are most frequently combinations of two metalloids, as sulphuric, nitric, phosphoric, etc. acids; sulphocarbonic and sulpharsenious acids. But they sometimes result from the combination of a metal with a metalloid, as chromic, manganic, stannic, etc. acids, the sulphides of antimony and tin.

The majority of known bases are compounds of a metal with oxygen; the majority of the known acids, compounds of oxygen with a metalloid, or metal. Thus, the most numerous, and by far the most important salts, are the *oxysalts*.

We are now, however, acquainted with a considerable number

of *sulphosalts*, formed by the combination of an electropositive metallic sulphide or *sulphobase*, with an electronegative metalloidal or metallic sulphide, or *sulphacid*.

We also know some double chlorides, which may be considered as resulting from the combination of an electropositive metallic chloride, or *chlorobase*, with an electronegative metalloidal or metallic chloride, or *chloracid*. These compounds, called *chlorosalts*, are not yet very numerous; but others will undoubtedly be found, when the attention of chemists is directed to this point.

An oxyacid may possibly combine with a sulphobase or with a chlorobase, and a sulphacid or a chloracid with an oxybase, so as to form a salt; but hitherto, no compound of this kind is certainly known.

337. The oxysalts are, therefore, by far the most important, and the only ones which have hitherto been carefully studied. All our general remarks on the salts, in this chapter, will relate principally to the oxysalts. We should probably make similar remarks on the other classes of salts, were they as well known to us.

The oxysalts are divided into *neutral*, *acid*, and *basic salts*. The characters on which this distinction is founded are easily defined as regards salts formed by the combination of powerful bases with energetic acids; but they become less clear in salts formed by powerful bases with feeble acids, or by feeble bases with powerful acids, or, lastly, by feeble bases and acids. The difficulty is still greater when the acid, or base, or resulting salt are insoluble in water.

The nature of neutral, acid, or basic salts is generally recognised by the changes of colour they produce on certain vegetable colouring matters, called *coloured reagents* or *tests*, the most important of which is the *tincture of litmus*.

338. The blue tincture of litmus is a true salt, resulting from the combination of a mineral base with a vegetable acid, which is red. When the tincture is treated with a strong acid, its base is removed and the vegetable acid set free, which then shows its true colour, a bright red. But, if it be treated with a feeble acid, only a portion of its base is removed, and there remains a salt with an excess of vegetable matter, having a purplish tint. A soluble base, on the contrary, changes the reddened tincture of litmus to blue, because it combines with the acid and forms a blue salt. In order that the blue tincture may be as sensitive as possible to the action of acids, it necessarily should not be mixed with an excess of free base; for, in this case, the first portions of acid added would simply combine with the free base, and there would be no reaction on the tincture after the complete saturation of the free base. Again, in order that the red tincture of litmus may possess its maximum of sensitiveness to the action of bases, the blue tincture should have been decomposed by a quantity of acid exactly sufficient to

isolate the red vegetable acid, and no other free acid should be formed in the liquid.

Sulphate of potassa does not react with tincture of litmus, because the sulphuric acid and potassa are combined with so great an affinity that they cannot combine separately, either with the acid or with the base of the coloured tincture, so that the latter remains intact and preserves its colour. But, if a colouring matter existed, the acid of which was powerful enough to remove the potassa from the sulphate of potassa, it is clear that this matter would manifest an alkaline reaction in the presence of the sulphate of potassa.

The indications of the coloured reagents are, therefore, not absolute, but merely relative. It might even happen that the same substance would evince an acid reaction with one colouring matter and alkaline reaction with another. In this way, boracic acid produces a purplish colour with the blue tincture of litmus, thus manifesting the reaction of a feeble acid, while it turns hematin blue, and presents, as regards this colouring matter, a basic reaction. In the same manner, the nitrate and acetate of lead redden the tincture of litmus and turn hematin blue. The base of the tincture of litmus removes the acids from the two salts of lead, and the coloured acid being set free, the blue tincture is reddened. The red acid of the hematin, on the contrary, abstracts the oxide of lead from the nitrate and acetate, and a blue salt is produced.

339. Let us now examine the salts which sulphuric acid forms with various bases.

Sulphuric acid reddens strongly the blue tincture of litmus, and the reaction is so delicate that $\frac{1}{10000}$ part of sulphuric acid thrown into water evinces it in a very marked manner. Potassa, on the contrary, blues the tincture of litmus previously reddened by an acid, and the reaction is as evident as that exerted by the acid on the blue tincture, provided the litmus has been reddened only by the smallest possible quantity of acid.

If a dilute solution of sulphuric acid be carefully poured into a solution of potassa, testing with the greatest accuracy the reaction of the liquid with the tincture of litmus, a liquid is obtained which no longer manifests an alkaline reaction on the tincture, without presenting, however, the acid reaction; and yet the liquid is such that the addition of a single drop of the acid would immediately show an acid reaction. We then say that the alkaline properties of the potassa have been exactly neutralized by the acid properties of the sulphuric acid, that there has been a *saturation* or *neutralization* of the acid by the base in their action on the tincture of litmus. If the liquid be evaporated to dryness, a crystalline salt, the sulphate of potassa, remains.

The analysis of this salt shows that it contains quantities of potassa and sulphuric acid, such that the acid contains three times as much oxygen as the base; and, as we have agreed to call the *equivalent of potassium* the quantity of this metal which combines with 8 of oxygen, the formula of the sulphate of potassa should evidently be written KO,SO_3.

If soda or lithia be saturated in the same manner with sulphuric acid, and the liquid neutral to tincture of litmus be evaporated, a salt is obtained, the sulphate of soda or lithia. In these two salts, *the quantity of oxygen contained in the sulphuric acid is again exactly triple of that contained in the base.*

If the same experiment be made in solutions of baryta and strontia, which powerfully blue the reddened tincture of litmus, it will be observed that the first drops of acid added cloud the liquid, and a white precipitate is formed. This insoluble compound will continue to be deposited until the liquid begins to exert a slight acid reaction, when the filtered solution will leave no residue upon evaporation. The insoluble sulphate thus formed does not react on the tincture of litmus; but it cannot hence be concluded that the product is really neutral. For, in order that a substance may act on the tincture of litmus, it must be soluble in water, so that the molecules of the salt may come into contact with those of the tincture.

The analysis, however, of the sulphates of baryta and strontia thus produced, again shows that *the oxygen in the acid is equal to three times that in the base.* Chemists have agreed to consider these sulphates as neutral salts, although their neutrality with coloured reagents cannot be directly verified.

All the basic oxides of the metals of the other sections being insoluble in water, it is impossible to ascertain their peculiar action on coloured reagents. By combining them with sulphuric acid, sulphates are still obtained, and, when soluble, they generally redden the tincture of litmus. Nevertheless, in all these sulphates, *the oxygen in the sulphuric acid is treble of that in the base,* as in the neutral sulphates of potassa, soda, and lithia.

Chemists have agreed to consider as neutral sulphates all the sulphates in which the quantity of oxygen in the acid is treble of that in the base, whatever may be, otherwise, their reaction on vegetable colours.

Potassa, soda, and lithia may form salts with sulphuric acid, which contain more acid than the neutral sulphates. If the bases be dissolved in an excess of sulphuric acid, and the solution be evaporated, crystallized sulphates are obtained, in which the oxygen in the acid is six times that in the base. These salts will therefore be *acid sulphates,* or *bisulphates.*

340. A solution of potassa, exactly saturated with nitric acid, affords when evaporated a crystallized salt, in which the oxygen of the acid is quintuple that of the base. In the same way, if solutions of the metallic oxides of the first section be saturated with nitric acid, soluble salts are obtained perfectly neutral to coloured

tinctures, and which crystallize after the evaporation of the liquid. In all these nitrates, the oxygen of the acid is quintuple that of the base.

But, if the metallic oxides of the other sections be dissolved in nitric acid, nitrates are obtained which crystallize after the evaporation of the liquid, and which present the same proportion of 5 : 1, between the quantity of oxygen in the acid and the base, but their solutions exhibit a strongly acid reaction.

We regard as a neutral nitrate every nitrate in which the oxygen in the acid is quintuple of that in the base, whatever may be its reaction on tincture of litmus.

341. Water plays the part of a base with reference to powerful acids. Monohydrated sulphuric acid may therefore be regarded as a true salt, and even as a neutral sulphate, for the proportion between the oxygen of the acid and that of water is as 3 : 1. For the same reason, monohydrated nitric acid will be a neutral nitrate of water. It may therefore be said that when nitric or sulphuric acid is combined with bases, these bases are made to react on salts already formed, on nitrate or sulphate of water, and that the base is only substituted in place of the basic water, by virtue of its greater affinity.

342. In the two examples first selected, the composition of the neutral salts was determined by finding the quantities of potassa, soda, and lithia which exactly saturate, with regard to coloured reagents, the same weight of sulphuric or nitric acid. Now, these quantities are found to be such that they contain precisely the same weight of oxygen. The same relation is observed in the crystallized salts which the same acids form with other metallic oxides. This very remarkable law may therefore be advanced: *The ponderable quantities of the various bases which form neutral salts with the same weight of nitric or sulphuric acid, contain exactly the same quantity of oxygen.* If these quantities of the various bases be referred to the weight of sulphuric and nitric acid chosen to represent their equivalents, and be designated by *a*, *b*, *c*, *d*..., it may be said: *If the equivalent* A *of sulphuric acid form neutral salts with the weights* a, b, c, d..., *of potassa, soda, baryta, lime, etc., the equivalent* B *of nitric acid will also form neutral salts with the same weights* a, b, c, d..., *of these bases;* so that these weights *a*, *b*, *c*, *d*..., which *are equivalent to each other* as regards the weight A of sulphuric acid, *are also equivalent to each other* as regards the weight B of nitric acid.

343. Let us now examine the compounds which weak acids form with these bases, and ascertain how chemists proceed in determining the composition of their neutral salts.

With weak acids, such as sulphurous, carbonic, boracic, etc., the saturation of the alkaline properties of potassa, as regards coloured reagents, is never completely effected, whatever may be the quantity of acid added. The liquid always retains an alkaline reaction, and the character of saturation evinced by coloured reagents cannot be invoked to define the neutral salts.

344. If a current of sulphurous acid gas be passed through a concentrated solution of potassa, until the latter can no longer dissolve it, a crystallized salt is deposited after some time, in which the oxygen of the acid is quadruple that of the base. If this salt be redissolved in water, and a quantity of potassa added equal to that it already contains, a new crystallizable salt is obtained by evaporating the liquid, in which the oxygen of the acid is double that of the base.

Which of these salts shall be assumed as the neutral salt? Chemists are governed in their choice by the following considerations.

By endeavouring to form sulphites with the various metallic oxides, two series of salts are obtained with the metals of the first section, which correspond to the two sulphites formed by potassa; but, with the metals of the other sections, only a single series of salts is obtained, viz. that in which the oxygen of the acid is double of that of the base. *Chemists have agreed to regard those as neutral sulphites which exist in the greater part of the metallic oxides.* Consequently, the neutral sulphite of potassa takes the formula

$$KO,SO_2,$$

and the sulphite containing a double quantity of sulphurous acid is considered as an *acid sulphite*, or a *bisulphite*, and its formula becomes

$$KO,2SO_2.$$

§ 345. A precisely similar circumstance occurs in the carbonates. If a concentrated solution of potassa be saturated with carbonic acid, a crystallized salt is deposited, after some time, the acid of which contains four times more oxygen than the base. If this salt be redissolved in water, and a quantity of potassa added equal to that it already contains, a new crystallized carbonate can be obtained by evaporating the liquid, in which the acid only contains a quantity of oxygen double that of the base. Moreover, both salts exhibit an alkaline reaction to coloured tinctures. Soda and lithia afford two similar carbonates. Baryta, strontia, lime, and magnesia form carbonates frequently found in beautiful crystals in a native state. In all these carbonates, the relation between the oxygen of the acid and that of the base is as 2 : 1. They are insoluble in water, but dissolve slightly in water charged with carbonic acid. The latter solution may be regarded as containing carbonates in which the oxygen of the carbonic acid is equal to four times that of the base; but these have not yet been obtained in a crystalline form. The liquid, when evaporated, always deposits carbonates, in which the oxygen of the acid is double that of the base. The metals of the other sections also afford only the first series of carbonates.

This consideration has induced the majority of chemists to regard those as neutral carbonates in which the oxygen of the acid is double that of the base. The formula of the neutral carbonate of potassa is therefore KO,CO_2, and the second salt becomes a bicarbonate, the formula of which is written $KO,2CO_2$.

Some chemists, however, even now regard this last salt as a neutral carbonate, because it approaches the neutrality shown by coloured reagents more than the first. They write its formula KO,C_2O_4; and the first salt becomes a *subcarbonate*, or a *bibasic carbonate*, of which the formula is written $2\,KO,C_2O_4$. In this point of view, the formula of carbonic acid is C_2O_4, and the weight of its equivalent is twice as great as we have admitted it (§ 262).

§ 346. Boracic acid forms two salts with alkalies, both of which have an alkaline reaction. If boracic acid be dissolved in a solution of soda and the liquid be evaporated, a salt is obtained in which the boracic acid contains six times more oxygen than the base. If this salt be melted in a platinum crucible with as much more soda as it already contains, a new salt is obtained which dissolves in water and crystallizes upon evaporating the liquid. In this salt, the boracic acid contains only three times more oxygen than the soda. Which of them shall we choose as the *neutral salt?* The difficulty is here greater than with the sulphites and carbonates, which have been more minutely studied than the borates, so that chemists are not agreed upon this point. Some regard the first borate above mentioned as the neutral salt, and give it the formula NaO,BO_6; in this case, the second borate becomes a bibasic salt, and its formula is written $2NaO,BO_6$. Others, on the contrary, consider the second borate as the neutral salt, and write its formula NaO,BO_3: the first salt then becomes a biborate, the formula of which is $NaO,2BO_3$.

§ 347. The definition of a neutral salt presents peculiar difficulties with some acids, even very powerful ones, which chemists regard as *polybasic*, that is, as possessing the property of forming neutral salts, not with one, but with several basic equivalents. We shall give an idea of these difficulties by taking phosphoric acid for an example. It was stated (§ 211) that phosphoric acid can be obtained in three states. That which is obtained by dissolving phosphorus in nitric acid, differs remarkably in its properties from the acid obtained by the combustion of phosphorus in oxygen; for the two modifications produce perfectly distinct classes of salts. We are acquainted with even a third modification of the acid, which afford a third series of phosphates, differing from the first two. These facts will be developed more in detail when treating of the phosphates of soda, and it will now be sufficient to consider the salts formed by phosphoric acid, obtained by the solution of phosphorus in nitric acid.

If a great excess of a solution of phosphoric acid be poured into a solution of soda, and the liquid be evaporated, a crystallized salt is obtained in which the phosphoric acid contains five times more oxygen than the soda.

If this salt be redissolved in water, and as much more soda added as it already contains, a new crystallized salt is obtained by evaporating the liquid, in which the oxygen of the acid is to that of the base as 5 is to 2. Lastly, if the last salt be dissolved in water, and an excess of soda be added, a third crystallized phosphate of soda is obtained by evaporation, in which the oxygen of the acid is to that of the base as 5 to 3.

The first of these three phosphates has an acid reaction on litmus; the other two, on the contrary, have an alkaline reaction.

The same modification of phosphoric acid gives therefore three very different phosphates. How shall we decide which of them shall be considered as the neutral phosphate? Chemists have been induced, by a mass of facts which will be developed when treating of the phosphates of soda, to admit that the three phosphates have the same mode of constitution; as all those formed of 1 equivalent of the acid combine with 3 equivalents of base. In the third phosphate, the 3 equivalents of base are 3 equivalents of soda; in the second, there are 2 equivalents of soda and 1 equivalent of basic water; and, lastly, in the first phosphate, the 3 equivalents of base are formed of 1 equivalent of soda and 2 equivalents of basic water. Thus, the three phosphates, although one has an acid, and the other two an alkaline reaction, are all considered as having the same composition; and, if one of them be regarded as a neutral salt, the others are equally so.

§ 348. The consideration of the water which may act the part of a base in salts has greatly modified the views of chemists on the classification of these salts. The majority of acid salts may be regarded as neutral, the excess of acid being considered as combined with the basic water. Thus, the crystallized bisulphate of potassa contains 1 equivalent of water, which it does not abandon, by the sole action of heat, without decomposition. We have, therefore, some reason for regarding this salt as resulting from the combination of the neutral sulphates, the sulphate of potassa and sulphate of water, and writing its formula KO,SO_3+HO,SO_3. This reasoning is applicable to the majority of other acid salts. By generalizing it, we are led to regard the same acid as forming only a single series of salts, all presenting the same mode of constitution, and differing only in the nature of the bases combined with the acid.

§ 349. We thought it proper to insist on the definition of the neutrality of salts and their division into neutral, acid, and basic salts, because this division is now generally adopted. The somewhat prolix discussion in which we have indulged shows these definitions to be vague and full of contradictions; and it would be desirable for chemists to abandon them entirely.

§ 350. If an oxybase and a hydracid be brought together, there is not a simple combination of the two bodies, but a reciprocal decomposition, the hydrogen of the hydracid combining with the oxygen of the base to form water, and the electropositive element of the base, the metal, combining with the electronegative element of the hydracid, to form another binary compound which corresponds in its composition to the oxybase used. Thus, potassa and chlorohydric acid produce water and the chloride of potassium:

$$KO+HCl=HO+KCl.$$

With sesquioxide of iron and chlorohydric acid, water and sesquichloride of iron are formed:

$$Fe_2O_3+3HCl=3HO+Fe_2Cl_3.$$

The saturation of the hydracid by the base, ascertained by means of coloured reagents, is often as complete as those of a powerful oxacid by the same base. Thus, the solution of chlorohydric acid, which strongly reddens the tincture of litmus, may be rendered perfectly neutral to the tincture by adding the proper quantity of potassa; and if the liquid be then evaporated, only water and chloride of potassium are obtained.

§ 351. Several chemists assume that, in solution, the hydracid and oxybase are simply combined, and that the reciprocal decomposition takes place only at the moment of crystallization. Many reasons are advanced in favour of and in opposition to this view, which we shall not stop to consider, but admit, with the majority of chemists, that the reciprocal decomposition of the hydracid and oxybase takes place at the very moment when the two bodies are brought into contact.

The binary compounds of the metals with those metalloids capable of forming hydracids with hydrogen, present physical properties analogous to those of the salts; and, in a great number of chemical reactions effected in water, they behave like simple compounds of the oxybase with the hydracid. Thus, when chloride of potassium is heated with hydrated sulphuric acid, sulphate of potassa is formed and chlorohydric acid disengaged. The reaction is therefore precisely similar to that which would take place if the sulphuric acid decomposed a salt formed by the direct combination of the hydracid with the oxybase, and simply expelled the latter in order to combine with the base. But, in reality, the reaction is more complex; for the water combined with the sulphuric acid is decomposed, its oxygen uniting with the metal of the binary compound, its hydrogen with the electronegative element, and, lastly, the newly-formed oxybase forming a salt with the oxacids:

$$KCl+SO_3,HO=KO,SO_3+HCl.$$

On account of the great resemblance between this class of binary compounds and the salts properly so called, in their physical properties, and even in a great number of chemical reactions, many chemists consider them as a peculiar class of salts, which they term *haloid salts;* and call *halogen bodies*, or *halogens*, those bodies, simple or compound, which form hydracids with hydrogen, and, consequently, haloid salts with the metals. We shall not adopt this view, for it is incompatible with the definition we have given of the word salt, a definition we think proper to preserve with precision. Moreover, the binary compounds we are now considering present no analogy with the salts, except when they are soluble in water, and subjected to chemical reaction in this liquid.

§ 352. The salts are nearly all solid at the ordinary temperature. Those resulting from the combination of a colourless acid with a colourless base are themselves colourless; those formed of a coloured base with various colourless acids are coloured, and present nearly the same colour when crystallized in water. Salts formed by colourless bases with the same coloured acid, generally approximate to the colour of the free acid.

The taste of soluble salts depends most frequently on the base; thus, the salts of soda have a decided saline flavour, resembling that of common salt; the salts of potassa have a slightly bitter, saline taste; those of magnesia are insufferably bitter; those of alumina are sweet and astringent, etc. Sometimes, however, the flavour of the salt is strongly affected by the nature of the acid, as in the sulphites, those formed by metallic acids, sulphosalts, etc.

§ 353. Many salts may be obtained either in the anhydrous state or combined with a certain quantity of water. A great number of soluble salts, when deposited from solution, retain water in combination, called *water of crystallization*, the quantity of which is always the same in the same salt, when crystallized *at the same temperature* and in an *identical* solution, and presents a simple ratio in equivalents with the equivalents of the acid and base which enter into the composition of the salt. Thus, *the water of crystallization of salts follows the laws of combination in definite proportions, which we have observed in all other chemical compounds.*

§ 354. The same salt frequently combines with very different quantities of water, when deposited from the same solution, but at different temperatures. Thus, sulphate of soda takes 10 equivalents of water, when crystallized in an aqueous solution, at a temperature below 91°; but is deposited in an anhydrous state if the temperature of the liquid be above 91°. Protosulphate of manganese, crystallized in an aqueous solution, at a temperature below 43°, has for its formula MnO,SO_3+7HO; when crystallized between 43° and 68°, its formula is MnO,SO_3+6HO; and, lastly, when crystallized between 68° and 86°, it has only four equivalents of water, and its formula is MnO,SO_3+4HO. In these different states of hydration, the crystals of the sulphate of manganese present very different and incompatible crystalline forms, showing that water of crystallization influences the crystalline form in the same way as the other elements of the salt. The sulphate of manganese MnO,SO_3+7HO soon loses its transparency, and at the temperature of 50°, effloresces and falls into powder. In a short time, it contains only six equivalents of water. Thus, even in the solid state, the salt has assumed the composition peculiar to it at this temperature, and with which it would have been deposited had it crystallized in a solution at the temperature of 50°. So also, the sulphate MnO,SO_3+6HO, exposed for a long time to the temperature of 86°, falls to pieces, and assumes the composition MnO,SO_3+4HO. If this last salt be heated to a temperature of about 212°, it again loses three equivalents of water; but it retains the last equivalent, which can be abstracted only by heating it above 392°. Thus, the same sulphate of manganese has hitherto been obtained with the following compositions:

MnO,SO_3	anhydrous sulphate; crystallized salt heated to 572°,
MnO,SO_3+HO	crystallized sulphate, heated to 248°,
MnO,SO_3+4HO	crystallized between 68° and 86°,
MnO,SO_3+6HO	crystallized between 43° and 68°,
MnO,SO_3+7HO	crystallized below + 43°.

§ 355. The hydrated salts can therefore abandon successively their water of crystallization as the temperature rises. It is natural to suppose that the water which is disengaged at the lowest temperature is retained in the compound by a more feeble affinity than that which resists. It is hence evident that it is interesting to study carefully these successive dehydrations of various salts, in order to assign to each portion of water the part which actually belongs to it. We shall even have occasion, subsequently, to remark that a hydrated salt cannot always completely lose its water without an entire modification of its composition and chemical qualities. Thus, the formula of common phosphate of soda crystallized at a low temperature is $(2NaO),PO_5+25HO$. It effloresces in the air, losing a portion of its water; and if crystallized at about 86°, it combines with less water, and the crystals, no longer efflorescent in the air, present the formula $(2NaO)PO_5+17HO$. If the same salt be heated to about 300°, a phosphate is obtained, $(2NaO)PO_5+HO$, with only 1 equivalent of water. But, if these variously hydrated salts be dissolved in water, and again crystallized at a low temperature, the same primitive salt $(2NaO)PO + 25HO$ is obtained. Thus, the successive dehydrations which the salt has undergone do not prevent it from assuming its original composition when brought into contact with water. But if the phosphate of soda be heated to a dull red-heat, it loses its last equivalent of water, and its composition is entirely changed; for, upon solution in water and recrystallization, the ordinary hydrated phosphates are not obtained, but salts entirely different in their forms and chemical reactions. The last equivalent of water in this salt, therefore, plays a much more important part than the others, since it cannot be driven off without entirely changing the nature of the salt. This last equivalent of water is called the *water of constitution*, and all the others *water of crystallization.*

§ 356. Many salts lose a portion of their crystal-water when exposed to the air at ordinary temperatures, if this air is not saturated with moisture, and part with it more readily when the air is perfectly dry. The dehydration of a salt may often be pushed very far by keeping it in vacuo under a bell-glass, near a dish containing oil of vitriol. If we wish to ascertain exactly the quantity of water lost by the salt under these circumstances, a certain quantity of the finely powdered salt is weighed in a small capsule, and placed under the receiver of an air-pump, over a larger capsule containing oil of vitriol. After remaining 24 hours in vacuo, the capsule is again weighed, and the difference expresses the water lost. Upon replacing it in the vacuum, and weighing it at the end of 12 hours, if it has not experienced an additional loss of weight, it is certain that the salt has parted with all the water it can lose under the circumstances. But if there has been a diminution of weight, the capsule must be replaced a third time, and so on, until no change of weight between two consecutive weighings can be observed.

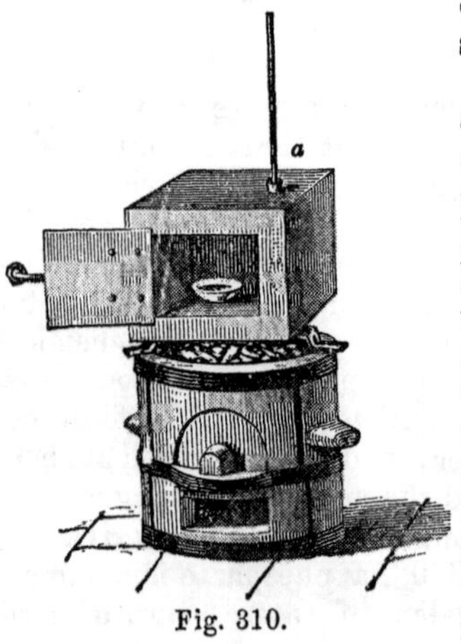

Fig. 310.

§ 357. In order to ascertain the quantity of water which a salt gives off successively, at different temperatures, a small oil-stove or bath (fig. 310) is frequently used in the laboratory, and consists of a double upper box, with a door on one side, and the space between the sides filled with a fixed oil. The stem of a thermometer, passing through the tubulure *a*, has its bulb in the oil-bath, to indicate the temperature. The stove is heated by a small furnace until the thermometer marks the temperature required, which is kept nearly stationary by regulating the furnace. The dish, containing an exact weight of the salt to be dried, is placed in the small chamber of the stove, and the door closed.

It is difficult to ascertain in this manner the precise temperature at which the desiccation of the salt takes place, since it may differ essentially from that indicated by the thermometer; and, in order to operate with greater precision, the process detailed in § 261, for oxalic acid, must be adopted.

§ 358. Salts containing a great deal of crystal-water often fuse when heated, experiencing what is called the *aqueous fusion;* and the fused substance may be considered as a solution of the anhydrous salt in the crystal-water of the salt. By continuing the heat, the water of crystallization gradually escapes; the substance dries, and may in its turn fuse, if the temperature be sufficiently high and the salt can support it without decomposition. The anhydrous salt is then said to undergo the *igneous fusion.*

§ 359. Certain anhydrous salts, such as common salt, exhibit slight detonations when thrown on burning coals, and are then said to *decrepitate.* The decrepitation of crystals is often occasioned by a small quantity of water, interposed between the crystalline laminæ, being suddenly converted into vapour by the heat, producing a series of small detonations. Decrepitation is often owing, also, to the bad conducting power of the salt for heat, which results in a host of small fractures in each individual crystal, accompanied by explosion.

§ 360. *Action of Electricity.*—The electric battery readily decomposes salts, particularly when dissolved in water. If the battery be powerful, the decomposition may be very complex, effecting a separation even of the elements; but if it be feeble, the acid merely separates from the base, seeking the positive pole, while the base repairs to the negative. The decomposition is evident, if the experiment be conducted as follows: A solution of a neutral salt, as the sulphate of potassa, is poured into the curved tube *abc* (fig. 311), and coloured with a small quantity of syrup of violets. The colouring matter of the syrup is reddened by acids and greened by alkalies. The two poles of the battery, terminating in platinum wire, are inserted into the open ends of the U-tube. The liquid becomes red in the leg *ab*, at the positive pole, and green in the leg *bc*, or the negative pole. In a short time the separation is well marked, and continues while the battery is acting; but if the wires be removed, the liquids in the two legs mix slowly, reproducing sulphate of potassa, and the colouring matter assumes its original violet hue. The same effect would ensue immediately if the tube were shaken so as to mix the liquid in the two legs more rapidly.

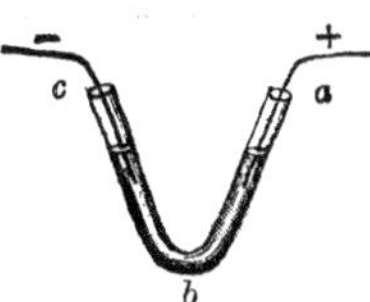

Fig. 311.

SOLUBILITY OF SALTS.

§ 361. The study of the solubility of salts in various liquids is one of the most important in chemistry. In fact, on the difference of their solubility are founded the processes by which they are separated when mixed together, as well as various modes of preparing them.

Water is the most usual and important solvent of salts, as it dissolves a great number of them, and often in considerable quantity. Some salts likewise dissolve in alcohol and wood-spirit, and they are generally such as are very soluble in water.

The solubility of salts in liquids varying with the temperature, it is necessary to determine it for the different degrees of the thermometric scale, from the lowest temperature to that at which the saturated solution boils under the ordinary pressure of the atmosphere. It would even be very interesting to study the solubility of salts at more elevated temperatures, by operating in close vessels, in which the pressure could be increased at pleasure, and consequently the boiling point of the liquid raised; but this has never yet been done. The solubility of salts generally increases with the temperature; but we shall have occasion to point out some exceptions to the rule.

§ 362. A saturated solution of a salt at a given temperature may be obtained in two ways. The solvent may be poured on a great excess of salt, so that fragments of the latter may rise above the level of the liquid, and the whole kept for several hours at the temperature required. The decanted liquid then contains all the salt it can dissolve at that temperature, and is said to be *saturated.*

The solution of a salt may also be effected at a temperature higher than that at which we wish to ascertain its solubility, and the liquid allowed to cool slowly until it reaches this temperature, when it is kept stationary for 15 minutes. A portion of the salt is deposited during the cooling of the liquid, and that quantity only which it can dissolve at the desired temperature remains in solution. Experience has shown that the same coefficient of solubility is obtained for the same salt by adopting either of these processes. The second, however, requires some precaution. It has been observed that a liquid, when not in contact with perfectly formed crystals of the salt which it contains, may retain a much larger portion of the salt than corresponds to its normal solubility at that temperature. The saturated solution of certain salts, more soluble in hot than in cold, may be cooled several degrees without depositing crystals; but if a small crystal of the supersaturating salt be dropped into the solution, the excess of the salt crystallizes immediately, and in a few moments the liquid contains only the normal quantity of the salt it dissolves at that temperature. Such abnormal solubilities are therefore never observed when the liquid is allowed to remain in contact with an excess of the salt.

Agitation of the supersaturated liquid, or the introduction of a foreign body, particularly if the latter present projecting points, frequently effects the separation of the excess of dissolved salt. The phenomenon is analogous to that observed in the congelation of liquids, and may be attributed to the same cause, namely, a certain difficulty experienced by the saline molecules of moving in the liquid and assuming an arrangement suitable to crystalline aggregation. In this way water may be cooled several degrees below the ordinary temperature of its congelation without becoming solid, when the vessel containing it is in a state of absolute rest; but if a small piece of ice or of pointed glass be thrown in, congelation immediately ensues.

§ 363. Sulphate of soda presents a remarkable instance of the inertia of saline molecules in solution. Its solubility increases rapidly with the temperature from 32° to 91½, but from 91½ it diminishes with the increasing temperature, although more slowly than it had increased from 32° to 91½; and, at the boiling point, the liquid contains a much more considerable proportion of salt than at ordinary temperatures. If a thin stratum of oil, or spirit of turpentine, be poured over a hot saturated solution of sulphate of soda, and the liquid be allowed to cool slowly and quietly, it will not deposit crystals, even at temperature at which the liquid could have originally contained only one-half of the salt, by virtue of its nominal solubility. But if a pointed piece of glass be plunged through the stratum of oil into the saline solution, crystallization commences immediately.

A still more striking experiment may be made on the same salt. A solution of it, saturated when hot, is poured into a funnel-shaped glass tube (fig. 312) so as to fill about ⅞ of *ab*. Being made to boil for a few moments to expel the air, and a feeble ebullition still maintained, the narrow part *e* is rapidly closed by the blowpipe. The tube being allowed to cool, the solution may then be cooled to 32° without crystallizing; and yet it contains ten times more salt than it could dissolve by its normal solvent power. The tube may even be shaken without crystallization taking place; but if the narrow portion be suddenly broken, the salt instantly crystallizes, and the liquid becomes solid. At the same

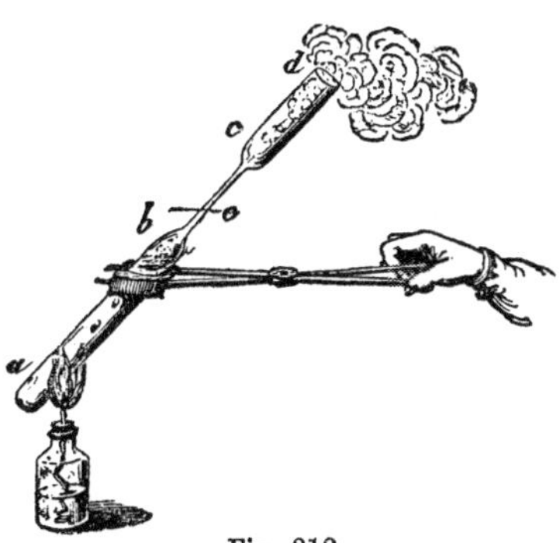

Fig. 312.

time the tube becomes sensibly warm to the hand. The disengagement of heat is due to the fact that all substances give off heat in passing from the liquid to the solid state. Now, the dissolved sulphate of soda was liquid; and by solidifying into crystals, heat was disengaged. A similar effect ensues whenever a salt crystallizes from solution; but is only appreciable when the crystallization is copious and rapid. If crystallization take place slowly, such as during the gradual cooling of a liquid, the heat disengaged by the solidification of the salt only retards the rapidity of cooling. If crystallization take place by spontaneous evaporation, it is still slower, because the evaporation of the liquid carries off heat, and that given off by the crystals in solidifying cannot be appreciated but by most delicate experiments.

§ 364. To determine the solubility of a salt in water at a given temperature, we always endeavour to find the quantity of salt contained in a saturated solution at that temperature. The solution is prepared by one of the processes indicated above, taking care to keep it for at least half an hour in the presence of an excess of crystallized salt, at the temperature required. About 50 grammes of the liquid are poured into a flask (fig. 313), the neck of which may be about 2 decimetres in length, and its exact weight rapidly ascertained. The liquid is evaporated over a small furnace by boiling, taking care to keep the neck of the flask inclined at an angle of 45°, in order to avoid loss of the salt. When the liquid

Fig. 313.

is evaporated, the flask is still heated until the salt has lost, not only the water which dissolved it, but also its water of crystallization. To drive off the last traces of moisture, a glass tube attached to the nozzle of a bellows is introduced into the flask, and air gently blown into it, the current of which completely removes the moisture. The flask being weighed after cooling, gives the weight of the anhydrous salt contained in the solution.

Let P be the weight of the solution subjected to evaporation, p the weight of the anhydrous salt obtained; $(P-p)$ will be the weight of the water. A weight $(P-p)$ of water dissolves a weight p of anhydrous salt; consequently, 100 parts of water dissolve $100 \cdot \frac{p}{P-p}$ of anhydrous salt, at a known temperature T.

If the crystallized salt contains crystal-water, we may inquire what is the smallest quantity of water which can dissolve a given weight of it at the temperature T. Let π be the weight of crystal-water required by a weight p of anhydrous salt to form $(p+\pi)$ of hydrated salt: the quantity of water which dissolves the weight $(p+\pi)$ of hydrated salt is evidently $(P-p-\pi)$. Therefore, a weight $(P-p-\pi)$ of water dissolves a weight $(p+\pi)$ of hydrated salt to form a liquid saturated at the temperature T. One hundred parts of water will therefore form a liquid saturated at the temperature T with a weight $100 \cdot \frac{p+\pi}{P-p-\pi}$ of crystallized hydrated salt: or, again, 100 parts of crystallized hydrated salt will dissolve in a weight $100 \cdot \frac{P-p-\pi}{p+\pi}$ of water.

§ 365. The solubility, at various temperatures, of a salt containing water of crystallization may be expressed in two ways; either by the quantity of water contained in a solution of the salt, saturated at those temperatures; or by the quantity of water required to dissolve a certain weight of hydrated salt, and to obtain a saturated solution at the temperature T. In the former case, the solubility is referred to the anhydrous salt, and the water of crystallization is considered as co-operating in the solution. In the latter case, it is confidently assumed that the salt still exists in the solution in the hydrated state, and that the water added acts only as a solvent.

Many hydrated salts fuse in their crystal-water, at a higher or lower temperature, undergoing what is called the *aqueous fusion.* At the temperature which effects the fusion, it is evident that a weight π of water dissolves a weight p of anhydrous salt; but the solubility of the crystallized salt is *infinite* at this temperature; for a gramme of water would dissolve at this temperature an indefinite quantity of crystallized salt, because the salt dissolves in its own water of crystallization.

§ 366. It is frequently more easy and more accurate, instead of evaporating a saline solution to determine the proportion of anhydrous salt it contains, to treat the salt chemically, by forcing one of its constituents into an insoluble combination. Thus, to determine the quantity of sulphate of soda which a liquid contains, a few grammes of this solution may be weighed, diluted with an indefinite quantity of water, and treated with an excess of chloride of barium. The precipitated sulphate of baryta being collected on a filter, washed, and weighed after calcination, we can infer, from its weight, the weight of anhydrous sulphate of soda from which it was produced. For let p be the weight of the sulphate of baryta, the composition of which is

1 eq. baryta	76·5
1 " sulphuric acid	40·0
1 " sulphate of baryta	116·5

A weight p of sulphate of baryta, therefore, corresponds to $p \cdot \frac{40}{116 \cdot 5}$ of sulphuric acid.

The sulphate of soda contains

1 eq. of soda	31
1 " sulphuric acid	40
1 " anhydrous sulphate of soda	71

The weight of sulphate of soda, which corresponds to the weight $p \cdot \frac{40}{116 \cdot 5}$ of sulphuric acid, and consequently to the weight p of sulphate of baryta, is given by the proportion

$$40 : 71 :: p \cdot \frac{46}{116.5} : x, \text{ whence } x = p \cdot \frac{71}{116.5}.$$

The same mode of treatment will serve to ascertain the solubility of any sulphate whatever.

Reciprocally, the solubility of a salt of baryta may be determined by precipitating the baryta by a soluble sulphate, and calculating the proportion of the salt of baryta, of which the composition is known, from the weight of sulphate of baryta obtained.

The solubility of a chloride may be ascertained by precipitating the chlorine in the state of chloride of silver. There are even salts in which this is the only plan that can be used; such as those which are decomposed by heat before reaching the anhydrous state, and which oxidize readily by contact with the air. For example, chloride of magnesium, dissolved in water, cannot be brought to the anhydrous state without partial decomposition, so that its solubility cannot be accurately determined by the general method, founded on evaporation, and explained in (§ 364).

§ 367. Let us suppose that we have thus determined the solubility of the same salt in water at all temperatures, from the lowest unto that at which its saturated solution boils under the ordinary pressure of the atmosphere: we may represent the ratio of solubility to the temperature, by a mathematical curve, counting the temperature on the line of the abscissas, and marking on the corresponding ordinates lengths proportional to the quantity of salts dissolved by the same weight of water. This curve may be constructed with sufficient precision, when a certain number of direct determinations of solubility (8 or 10) have been made at sufficient distances apart in the scale of temperatures, and the curve can afterward be used to ascertain the solubilities at all intermediate temperatures.

The annexed plate represents the curves of solubility of a great number of salts. The horizontal line AX is divided into 110 equal

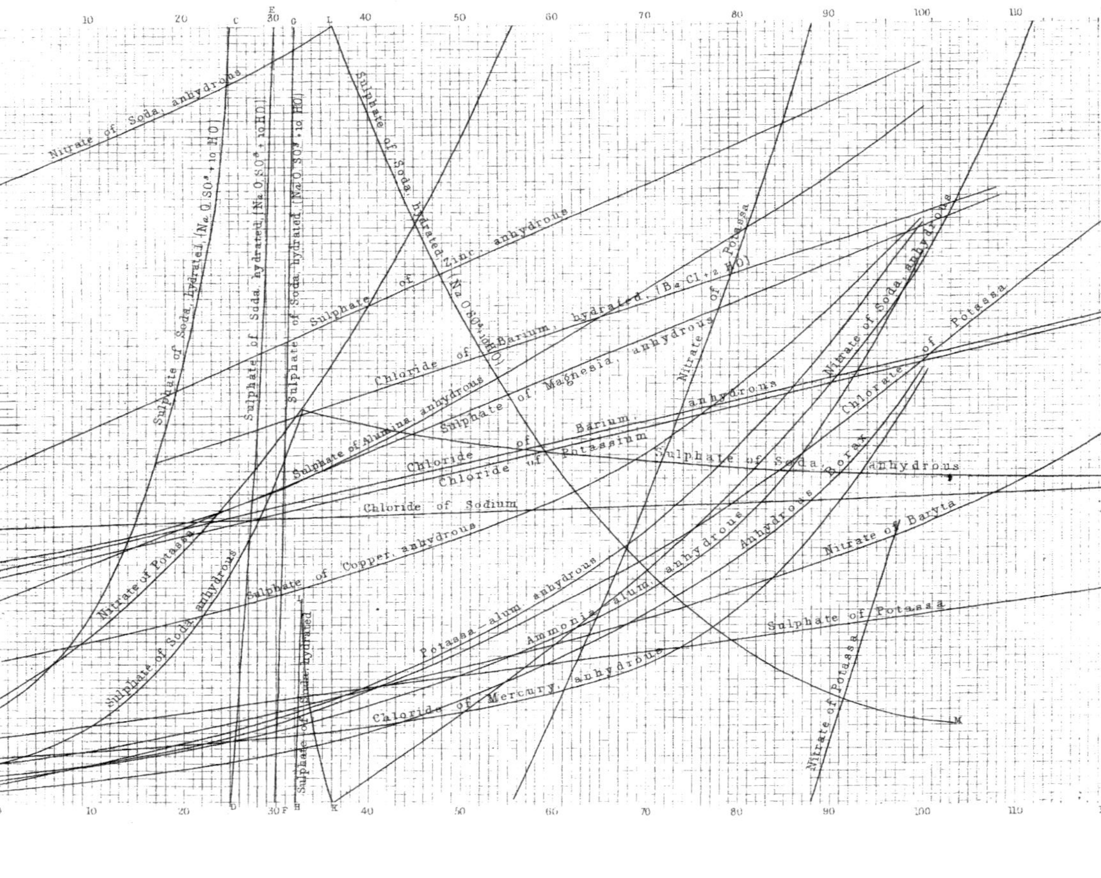

Nitrate of Soda, anhydrous
Sulphate of Soda, hydrated (Na O SO³ + 10 HO)
Sulphate of Soda, hydrated (Na O SO³ + 10 HO)
Sulphate of Soda, hydrated (Na O SO³ + 10 HO)
Sulphate of Soda, hydrated (Na O SO³ + 10 HO)
Sulphate of Zinc, anhydrous
Chloride of Barium, hydrated (Ba Cl + 2 HO)
Sulphate of Alumina, anhydrous
Sulphate of Magnesia, anhydrous
Nitrate of Potassa
Nitrate of Soda, anhydrous
Chlorate of Potassa
Chloride of Barium, anhydrous
Chloride of Potassium
Sulphate of Soda, anhydrous
Borax, anhydrous
Chloride of Sodium
Nitrate of Potassa
Sulphate of Copper, anhydrous
Sulphate of Soda, anhydrous
Sulphate of Soda, hydrated
Potassa-alum anhydrous
Ammonia-alum anhydrous
Nitrate of Baryta
Sulphate of Potassa
Chloride of Mercury, anhydrous
Nitrate of Potassa

parts, each of which represents one degree of the centigrade thermometer; the temperature of melting ice corresponding to the zero of the division. 100 equal divisions are marked on the vertical line AY, but are not necessarily equal to those of the horizontal line AX.

Let us suppose that it is required to construct the curve of solubility of sulphate of soda in water. Direct experiments have given us the following numbers:

Temperature. Centig. Therm.	Anhydrous salt dissolved in 100 pts. of water.	Crystallized salt dissolved in 100 pts. of water.
0.00°	5.02	12.17
11.67	10.12	26.38
13.30	11.74	31.33
17.91	16.73	48.28
25.05	28.11	99.48
28.76	37.35	161.53
30.75	43.05	215.77
31.84	47.37	270.22
32.73	50.65	322.12
33.88	50.04	312.11
40.15	48.78	291.44
45.04	47.81	276.91
50.40	46.82	262.35
59.79	45.42	244.30
70.61	44.35	229.70
84.42	42.96	217.30
103.17	42.65	210.20

The temperatures inscribed in the first column of the table are marked on the line of abscissas, and on the corresponding ordinates a number of divisions are taken, equal to that which represents the number of grammes of salt dissolved by 100 grammes of water. These numbers are contained in the second column, for the solubility of the anhydrous salt; and in the third column, for the solubility of the crystallized, hydrated salt.

The numbers in the second column are obtained directly by experiment. Those in the third are thence deduced, as follows:

The equivalent of the anhydrous sulphate of soda is 71, and the composition of crystallized sulphate is,

1 eq.	of anhydrous sulphate of soda	71
10 "	of water of crystallization	90
1 "	of crystallized sulphate of soda	161

Let us suppose, that at the temperature T, 100 grammes of water dissolve p grammes of anhydrous sulphate of soda. Then p grammes of anhydrous salt correspond to $p \cdot \frac{161}{71}$ of crystallized salt, and require $p \cdot \frac{90}{71}$ grammes of water to be changed into the crystallized salt; we may therefore say that $p \cdot \frac{161}{71}$ of crystallized sulphate of soda are dissolved in $(100 - p \cdot \frac{90}{71})$ grammes of water. Consequently, we can find the weight of crystallized salt dissolved by 100 grammes of water, by making the proportion:

$$100 - p \cdot \tfrac{90}{71} : p \cdot \tfrac{161}{71} :: 100 : x,$$

$$\text{whence } x = 100\, p \cdot \tfrac{161}{71} \cdot \frac{1}{100 - p \cdot \frac{90}{71}}.$$

§ 368. The curve of solubility of sulphate of soda may be constructed on our plate in the ordinary manner, between the temperatures of 0° C. (32° F.) and 25° C. (77° F.), and is represented by the curve line BC, between these extremes of temperature. But, for temperatures above 24° C. (77° F.), 100 parts of water dissolving more than 100 parts of crystallized salt, the ordinates become greater than 100, and can no longer be marked on our plate. Nevertheless, if we suppose a second plate, similar to the first, placed above it, we shall have in all 200 vertical divisions, and the construction of the curve may be continued. Above 30° C. (86° F.), the ordinates become greater than 200, and, if we wish to continue the curve, we must superpose a third plate on the second, and so on. Now, let us suppose that the second, third, and fourth plates, after having been placed end to end above the first, are subsequently superposed on it; the branch of the curve of which the ordinates are comprised between 100 and 200 will then assume the direction DE; the branch with its ordinates comprised between 200 and 300 will have the direction FG; the branch with its ordinates greater than 300 will be at HIK; lastly, the branch of which the ordinates are comprised between 300 and 200, and corresponding to the temperatures between 36° C. (96.8° F.) and 111° C. (231.8° F.) will be at LM. In order to obtain the real ordinates of the branch DE, we must add 100 to the ordinates measured immediately on the plate. The real ordinates of the branches FG and LM will be obtained by adding 200 to the apparent ordinates measured on the plate. Lastly, we obtain the ordinates of the branch HIK, by adding 300 to the ordinates measured on the plate. The same mode of construction has been used for the curves of solution of salts whose solubility is greater than 100, beyond a certain temperature, such as nitrate of potassa.

§ 369. The solubility of a considerable number of salts increases nearly in proportion to the temperature, so that their curve of solubility scarcely differs from a right line. Sometimes this right line is only slightly inclined to the line of abscissas; as is the case with chloride of sodium, the solubility of which does not sensibly increase with the temperature. The right lines representing the solubility of sulphate of potassa, chloride of potassium, chloride of barium, and sulphate of magnesia, are more inclined to the line of abscissas. The curves of solubility of nitrate of potassa, nitrate of baryta, and chlorate of potassa, turn their convexity toward the axis of the abscissas: the curve of the nitrate of potassa rises very rapidly, in proportion as the abscissas increase.

The curve of solubility of sulphate of soda presents a very remarkable form, rising rapidly between 0° C. (32° F.) and 33° C. (91° F.), and at about 33° C. presenting a point of retrogression from which the curve descends towards the axis of the abscissas, always turning its convexity towards this axis. The singular point presented by the curve of solubility of the sulphate of soda for the abscissa of 33° C. (91° F.) corresponds with a remarkable change which takes place at this temperature in the constitution of the salt. In fact, if it be crystallized by evaporation from a liquid maintained at a temperature below 33° C. (91° F.), the salt always crystallizes in the hydrated state NaO,SO_3+10HO. But, if the same solution be crystallized above 33° C., the salt is always deposited in the anhydrous state NaO,SO_3. Thus, the discontinuity which we observe in the curve of solubility for the abscissa of 33° C., coincides with a change of the constitution of the salt at this temperature. The first branch comprised between the abscissas 0° C. and 33° C. relates to the hydrated salt NaO,SO_3+10HO; the second branch between 33° C. and the abscissa corresponding to the boiling point of the saturated liquid, refers to another salt, the anhydrous sulphate of soda NaO,SO_3.

§ 370. A knowledge of the relative solubility of the various salts, at different temperatures, is of deep interest, because it enables us to foretell the order in which these salts crystallize at a given temperature when their solutions are evaporated. Let us suppose a mixture of only two salts, the nitrate of potassa and chloride of sodium. These two salts present equal solubilities at the temperature of 23.6° C. (74.48° F.), which is the abscissa corresponding to the crossing of their curves. Below 23.6° C. the solubility of the nitrate of potassa is less than that of the chloride of sodium, whilst above this temperature it is more soluble. It therefore follows that, if a solution containing equal proportions of the two salts be evaporated at a temperature below 23.6° C., nitrate of potassa will crystallize first; and, on the contrary, if the solution be evaporated by heat, chloride of sodium will be first deposited.

The inversion, in the order of solubility of salts with the temperature, frequently determines the double decompositions employed in the arts, of which chloride of sodium and sulphate of magnesia afford a remarkable example. If a liquid containing chloride of sodium and sulphate of magnesia be evaporated at a temperature above 53½°, the chloride of sodium is deposited in crystals, and the sulphate of magnesia remains in solution. If, on the contrary, the evaporation takes place below 45°, or better still, if the liquid saturated at 59° be cooled to about 32°, crystals of sulphate of soda are deposited, and chloride of magnesium remains in solution. There is, in this last case, a double decomposition.

§ 371. It is, however, important to remark, that what has just been said of the solubility of salts refers only to their solution in pure water, and that their solubility may be very different in water already containing other salts. Thus, a solution of nitrate of potassa, saturated at a given temperature, cannot dissolve an additional quantity of nitrate at this temperature ; but it will dissolve a considerable quantity if a certain proportion of common salt has been previously added. So that the solubility of nitrate of potassa is greater in salt water than in fresh. The solubility of the nitrate of potassa is, on the contrary, less in a solution of chloride of potassium than in pure water, for in dissolving the latter in a liquid saturated with nitrate of potassa, it precipitates a portion of the nitrate in small crystals.

Experience has shown that when two salts differ both in their acid and their base, and that a double decomposition can take place, the presence of one of these salts may favour the solubility of the other. In this way, the presence of chloride of sodium favours the solubility of nitrate of potassa, because nitrate of soda and chloride of potassium are formed, which are respectively more soluble than nitrate of potassa and chloride of sodium, at least at temperatures above 77°. When, on the contrary, the two salts contain the same base or the same acid, there can be no double decomposition, and the presence of one of the salts in the solution diminishes the solubility of the other. For this reason, a solution of chloride of potassium dissolves less nitrate of potassa than pure water. We must, however, except the case in which the two salts combine to form a double salt possessing peculiar solubility.

§ 372. Saline solutions boil at higher temperatures than pure water; the difference, with the same salt, is in proportion to the quantity of it in solution. The boiling point of a saline solution should be measured by a thermometer with its bulb kept in the boiling liquid; for if it were placed only in the vapour, at some distance above the liquid, it would indicate a temperature very little above 212°.

The following table contains the boiling point of several saturated saline solutions:

Names of the salts.	Proportion of salt in 100 of water.	Boiling point.
Chlorate of potassa	61.5	219.56°
Chloride of barium	60.1	219.92°
Carbonate of soda	48.5	220.28°
Chloride of potassium	49.4	226.94°
Chloride of sodium	41.2	227.12°
Chlorohydrate of ammonia	88.9	237.56°

Names of the salts.	Proportion of salt in 100 of water.	Boiling point.
Nitrate of potassa	335.1	240.62°
Chloride of strontium	117.5	244.04°
Nitrate of soda	224.8	249.8°
Carbonate of potassa	205.0	275.0°
Nitrate of lime	362.0	303.8°
Chloride of calcium	325.0	355.1°

§ 373. The solution of salts, or of any other substances in water, is accompanied sometimes by depression, sometimes by elevation of temperature. A substance which has crystallized from an aqueous solution at a low temperature, and which contains, consequently, all the combined water it can assume at this temperature, produces cold by resolution in water, at the same or higher temperatures. The production of cold is owing to an absorption of heat from the disaggregation of the salt which, by dissolving, passes from the solid to the liquid state. The heat may be regarded as a species of latent heat of fusion of the salt, but is probably very different from the latent heat of fusion properly so called, that is, the heat which the substance absorbs when it undergoes the igneous fusion. We shall give it the name of *latent heat of solution of a salt.*

Sulphate of soda, crystallized at a low temperature, according to the formula NaO,SO_3+10HO, produces cold by dissolving in water; and the same takes place with crystallized chloride of calcium $CaCl+6HO$. The salts which crystallize when cold without any water of crystallization, as the chlorides of potassium and sodium, produce likewise a depression of temperature by solution.

The quantity of heat which equal weights of various substances absorb by dissolving in water, is often very different, even when they are analogous in the aggregate of their properties. Thus, 50 grammes of common salt, dissolved in 200 centimetres of water, produce a depression of temperature of 3.42°, while 50 grammes of chloride of potassium depress the temperature 24.52° when dissolved in the same quantity of water.

Anhydrous salts, which combine with water of crystallization when separating from an aqueous solution at a low temperature, generally produce heat, when dissolved in water in their anhydrous state. Thus, anhydrous sulphate of soda and anhydrous chloride of calcium produce a considerable elevation of temperature by solution in water. There is, in that case, a superposition of two effects: 1st. A disengagement of heat due to the combination of the anhydrous substance with water; 2dly. An absorption of heat produced by the solution of the hydrated body in the same liquid. Accordingly, as one of these effects predominates over the other, there is absorption or disengagement of heat.

§ 374. Advantage is often taken of the absorption of heat produced by the solution of certain substances in water, to obtain *refrigerating mixtures.* By effecting the solution in the coldest water we can procure, we can lower its temperature to several degrees below 32°. Thus, by dissolving 1 part of chloride of potassium in 4 parts of water at 50°, a solution is obtained at the temperature of 29½°. If the solvent water is at 32°, the liquid marks 11½° after solution.

The depression of temperature is often greater and more rapid when, instead of dissolving the salt in pure water, it is dissolved in an acid liquid. Thus, by dissolving crystallized sulphate of soda in a solution of chlorohydric acid, a depression is obtained of 45° or 55°. On this property a process has been founded for procuring ice at all seasons. The apparatus used, and known by the name of *the family ice-box,* is represented in figs. 314 and 315.

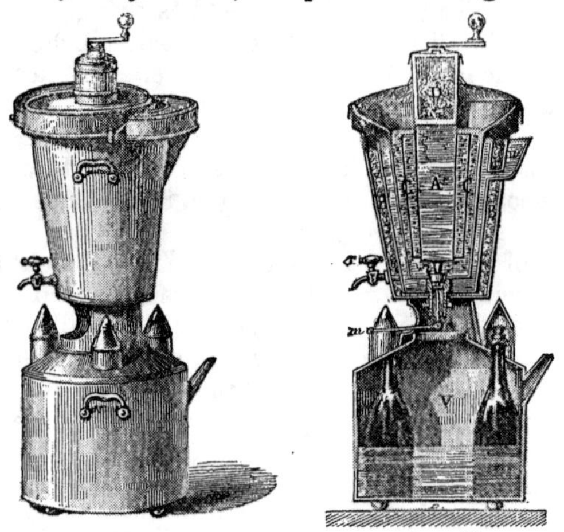

Fig. 314. Fig. 315.

It is composed of a hollow cylinder C, destined to receive the refrigerating cylinder I, for containing water, which becomes a hollow cylinder of ice from the effect of the internal refrigerant. Into the refrigerating mixture itself is inserted another cylindrical vessel A, closed at bottom, and turned by a winch, and which, by means of suitable projections, agitates the mixture, and renews the points of contact of the refrigerating body with the inner and outer vessels. If the hollow vessel be filled with water, the latter freezes like the surrounding water. In order to prevent its being warmed by the circumambient air, the space I is surrounded by an envelope of some bad conductor, as cotton or tow. The cover D of the inner cylinder A is likewise stuffed. In order to obtain the maximum effect, it is advisable to cause the whole refrigerating mixture to act gradually. 1500^{gm} (3⅓ lb.) of sulphate of soda and 1200^{gm} (2⅔ lb.) of chlorohydric acid are first introduced into the cylinder C, when the temperature of the water to be frozen will fall, in 5 or 6 minutes, from +77° to 32°. The liquid mixture is then allowed to flow into the lower vessel V, by opening the stopper *s* by means of the lever *mn*. Another quantity of the mixture, equal to the first, is then introduced into the cylinder C, allowed to act for 15 minutes, and again run off into the vessel V. The third and fourth quantities of the mixture should likewise act for 15 minutes. Thus, we have used altogether 6 kil. (13 lb.) of sulphate of soda, and about 5 kil. (11 lb.) of chlorohydric acid; the operation has lasted an hour, and 5 or 6 kil. (11–13 lb.) of ice have been obtained. The cold liquid collected in the lower vessel V may be used for cooling bottles of wine.

Many bodies soluble in water, when brought into contact with ice, melt it rapidly, and dissolve in the water thus produced. A considerable depression of temperature is thus obtained, depending at the same time on the latent heat of solution of the salt and the latent heat of fusion of the ice. By mixing pulverized sea-salt and pounded ice, a mixture is obtained which reduces the temperature to 6°. By mixing finely powdered chloride of calcium with snow or pounded ice, the temperature falls to —49°.

A considerable depression of temperature can also be produced by adding ice to a cold and concentrated solution of chloride of calcium, in which it melts rapidly, and the temperature may fall to —22°.

OF THE DECOMPOSING POWER EXERTED BY ACIDS ON SALTS, AND THE BINARY COMPOUNDS RESULTING FROM THE UNION OF METALS WITH METALLOIDS.

§ 375. The reactions which the various acids exert on salts, and the binary compounds resulting from the reaction of hydracids on oxybases, may be foreseen from certain general laws which observation has proved, and which will now be explained.

If the reacting acid is identical with that already in the salt, it often happens that the salt combines with a new quantity of acid, and a salt is formed with an excess of acid. If sulphuric acid be added to sulphate of potassa KO,SO_3, the bisulphate of potassa $KO,2SO_3$ is formed. So, also, if a current of carbonic acid gas be passed through a solution of neutral carbonate of potassa KO,CO_2, the bicarbonate of potassa $KO,2CO_2$ is produced.

If the base of the salt does not combine with a greater quantity of acid, the salt often dissolves in the acid added, especially if the latter be mixed with a large quantity of water. Thus, the nitrate of potassa dissolves in a dilute solution of nitric acid; but if the liquid be evaporated, the nitrate crystallizes unchanged.

§ 376. If the reacting acid differs from that existing in the salt, decomposition will ensue under several circumstances.

Decomposition will ensue when, the salt being soluble in water, the reacting acid can form an insoluble compound with its base.

By pouring sulphuric acid into a solution of nitrate of baryta, sulphate of baryta is immediately precipitated, and nitric acid set free in the liquid. If the base of the salt forms a soluble salt with the new acid, and the reaction takes place in sufficient water to dissolve one or the other salt, it cannot, in general, be decided whether a new salt has formed or the first has remained unchanged in the liquid. But, if the new salt is less soluble than the original salt, the decomposition can always be effected by evaporating the liquid to a point when the new salt can no longer remain in solution. The new salt is then deposited by virtue of the principle announced; for it is actually insoluble in the liquid at the degree of concentration given to it.

If sulphuric acid be poured into a dilute solution of nitrate of potassa, no signs of decomposition are apparent; but, if the liquid be properly evaporated, sulphate of potassa is deposited, because it is less soluble than the nitrate, especially at an elevated temperature. Nitric acid may, on the contrary, decompose sulphate of potassa, if the evaporation takes place at a very low temperature; for at 32° the nitrate is less soluble than the sulphate.

Similar reactions take place between hydracids and salts, or between oxacids and the binary compounds of metals with the metalloids which form hydracids with hydrogen; and they are determined by the same circumstance of insolubility. By pouring chlorohydric acid into a solution of sulphate of silver, chloride of silver is precipitated, and the liquid contains free sulphuric acid:

$$AgO,SO_3+HCl+nHO=AgCl+SO_3+(n+1)HO.$$

Again, if chlorohydric acid be poured into a solution of nitrate of lead, chloride of lead is deposited in small crystalline scales; but if the liquid is much diluted, there is still water enough to dissolve the chloride of lead, and nothing evinces the occurrence of decomposition; it soon, however, becomes apparent, if the liquid be evaporated to the proper degree.

§ 377. Sometimes *decomposition is determined by the insolubility of the acid which exists in the salt.* If sulphuric or nitric acid be poured into a concentrated solution of borate of soda, sulphate or nitrate of soda is produced, and boracic acid is precipitated in small crystalline scales. When the liquid is sufficiently dilute to dissolve boracic acid, the decomposition does not manifest itself immediately by visible signs: it is easily seen, however, that decomposition has taken place, even in the dilute liquid. It will be sufficient to remember that boracic acid acts on litmus only like a feeble acid, producing a purplish red, while sulphuric and nitric acids produce a bright red colour. If, therefore, the first drops of sulphuric or nitric acid added have remained free, the liquid should produce with litmus the bright red colour; but if they have decomposed a corresponding quantity of borate of soda, by liberating boracic acid, the liquid should assume a purplish red hue. Now, it is observed that the tincture becomes vinous red on the addition of the first drops of acid, and preserves this colour until the borate is entirely changed into sulphate. The addition of the least drop of sulphuric acid then changes the tincture to a bright red. Here the reaction has not been produced by the insolubility of the boracic acid, but by the fact that *sulphuric and nitric are much more powerful than boracic acid.*

§ 378. *A salt can always be decomposed by an acid less volatile than that which it contains.*

Carbonic acid is gaseous at ordinary temperatures, and is but slightly soluble in water. Nitric acid dissolved in water has its boiling point above 212°; so that it will readily expel carbonic acid, even in the cold. All the carbonates are, in fact, decomposed by nitric acid. A similar decomposition of the carbonates is effected by the hydracids, such as chlorohydric acid, which is gaseous at ordinary temperatures; but as it is very soluble in water, and its solution boils above 212°, it must drive off carbonic acid.

Since aqueous nitric acid boils at some degrees above 212°, and concentrated sulphuric acid above 600°, the latter, under the influence of heat, will readily expel nitric acid from all its compounds.

Sulphuric and phosphoric are two powerful acids; but as the latter is still less volatile than oil of vitriol, it readily expels sulphuric acid, by the assistance of heat.

It was observed that sulphuric acid decomposes the borates in solution in the cold; but boracic, being a much more fixed acid, decomposes all the sulphates at a high temperature.

Silica behaves like a very feeble acid in solutions; for the soluble alkaline silicates are decomposed by the most feeble acids, even by carbonic. On the other hand, with the assistance of heat, silicic acid expels all other acids.

The reactions exerted by the various acids on a salt depend on the nature of the liquid in which this salt is dissolved; for, the order of solubility may be entirely inverted in passing from one solvent to another. If acetic acid be poured into an aqueous solution of carbonate of soda, carbonic acid is disengaged with effervescence. This decomposition may be attributed to two causes: the acetic is a stronger acid than the carbonic, and the latter is gaseous at ordinary temperatures, and at the same time is but slightly soluble in water. On the other hand, acetate of potassa dissolved in alcohol is decomposed by carbonic acid, owing to the insolubility of carbonate of potassa in strong alcohol. The decomposition is therefore caused by insolubility.

The state of concentration of an acid and the temperature exert a powerful influence over these reactions. If a solution of sulfhydric acid be poured into a dilute solution of chloride of antimony, a precipitate of sulphide of antimony is formed. But, if sulphide of antimony be heated with a concentrated solution of chlorohydric acid, chloride of antimony is formed, and sulfhydric acid disengaged.

§ 379. *When the acid of a salt, and that employed to react on it, are both gaseous, and at the same time but slightly soluble in water, and when, moreover, their affinities for the bases are nearly equal, the acid which is present in excess will expel the other.* Thus, by passing a current of carbonic acid gas for some time through the solution of an alkaline sulphide, the latter is entirely converted into a carbonate, and sulfhydric acid driven off. Reciprocally, by passing sulfhydric acid for some time through a solution of an alkaline carbonate, it is entirely converted into sulphide of potassium.

The vapour of water, at a high temperature, expels carbonic acid from alkaline carbonates, when the latter are heated in platinum tubes in a current of steam, and hydrate of potassa is formed. Reciprocally, the hydrate of potassa, heated to the same temperature in a current of carbonic acid, is converted into carbonate of potassa.

These facts exhibit the influence of mass, analogous to that already mentioned in § 322.

ACTION OF BASES ON SALTS, AND ON THE BINARY COMPOUNDS OF HYDRACIDS ON OXYBASES.

§ 380. When a salt is brought in contact with an additional quantity of the same base which it already contains, it frequently happens that no reaction ensues, and never occurs when the acid cannot form a salt more basic than the original. If potassa be added to a solution of sulphate of potassa, and the liquid evaporated, the original sulphate crystallizes anew. At other times, combination ensues; thus, potassa added to a solution of bisulphate of potassa produces the neutral sulphate. A solution of neutral acetate of lead can dissolve an additional quantity of oxide of lead and form a basic acetate.

If the base added to a saline solution is different from that existing in the salt, the original salt is frequently decomposed, and a new one formed; and the decomposition is determined by circumstances analogous to those which cause the reaction of acids on salts.

§ 381. *Generally speaking, a soluble salt is decomposed, when the reacting base can form an insoluble salt with the acid of the salt.* If baryta be added to a solution of sulphate of potassa, sulphate of baryta is precipitated, and caustic potassa remains in the liquid. Baryta also decomposes carbonate of potassa in a dilute solution, and carbonate of baryta is precipitated. The state of concentration of the liquid exerts great influence over these decompositions; for, if carbonate of baryta be boiled with a concentrated solution of caustic potassa, a considerable quantity of carbonic acid is abstracted from it, and carbonate of potassa formed.

§ 382. *The decomposition is often determined by the insolubility of the base which exists in the salt.* Thus, potassa decomposes nitrate of lead, and hydrated oxide of lead is precipitated. The same is true for all the salts formed by the insoluble metallic oxides. In this case, nevertheless, it is proper to attribute the decomposition partly to the preponderating affinity of the potassa for the acid, for potassa is a much more powerful base than such metallic oxides.

§ 383. *An insoluble metallic oxide sometimes decomposes a salt formed by a base equally insoluble.* Thus, oxide of silver decomposes nitrate of copper in solution, precipitating oxide of copper; and the decomposition is determined, in this case, only by the preponderating affinity of oxide of silver for nitric acid.

§ 384. *When the base of a salt is volatile, it is generally expelled by a more fixed base*, particularly when assisted by heat. Thus, lime readily expels ammonia from its compounds. The same decomposition is effected with the assistance of heat, by the insoluble metallic oxides, whose salts, when in solution, are, on the contrary, decomposed by ammonia. Thus, oxide of lead, heated dry with hydrochlorate of ammonia, disengages ammonia, and chloride of lead is formed. Ammonia, on the other hand, decomposes chloride of lead in solution, and precipitates oxide of lead.

RECIPROCAL ACTION OF SALTS ON EACH OTHER, AND OF BINARY COMPOUNDS ON EACH OTHER AND ON SALTS.

§ 385. When two salts are mixed together, several phenomena may ensue:

The two salts sometimes combine to form a double salt. Sulphate of alumina combines with sulphate of potassa, forming a double salt known by the name of *alum.* Chloride of potassium combines with perchloride of platinum, and produces a double chloride of platinum and potassium.

At other times, there is no apparent reaction of the two salts upon each other, and evaporation reproduces the two salts which have been mixed.

Frequently, however, the two salts suffer mutual decomposition, which is determined by certain general circumstances,* demanding

* The laws which govern the double decomposition of salts, and the reaction of the acids and bases on the salts, are called *Berthollet's laws.*

a careful analysis, for they generally enable us to foretell the reactions which will ensue. We shall distinguish the case in which the two salts are heated without the contact of water, or the *dry* way, and that in which they are brought into contact in solution, or by the *humid* way.

Mutual Action of Salts in the dry way.

§ 386. When two salts of the same acid, but of different bases, are heated together, the two salts frequently combine in definite proportions, producing double salts which crystallize on cooling. In this manner a great number of double silicates may be produced which, from their beautiful crystallization, present the characters of definite compounds. In the same manner, we may obtain, in the dry way, double chlorides and several other double salts; but the combination is often destroyed upon dissolving the compound in water, the two original salts crystallizing separately.

§ 387. *When two salts of different acids and bases are heated together, and when, by the mutual interchange of acids and bases, a new salt more volatile than the first two can be formed, its formation is generally determined by this circumstance.*

If chlorohydrate of ammonia be heated with carbonate of lime, chloride of calcium and carbonate of ammonia are formed, the latter of which is much more volatile than either of the original salts. For the same reason, sulphate of ammonia, heated with the chloride of calcium, produces chlorohydrate of ammonia which volatilizes, and sulphate of lime which remains. It frequently happens that the reactions thus produced in the dry way between two salts, are precisely the inverse of those which take place in an aqueous solution. Thus, we have just seen that, by heating a mixture of chlorohydrate of ammonia and carbonate of lime, carbonate of ammonia and chloride of calcium are formed; but if carbonate of ammonia be poured into a solution of chloride of calcium, carbonate of lime is produced, and chlorohydrate of ammonia remains in solution. In the first case, the reaction is determined by the volatility of carbonate of ammonia, and in the second by the insolubility of carbonate of lime.

Mutual Action of Salts in the humid way.

§ 388. *When solutions of two salts are mixed together, capable of producing an insoluble salt by the interchange of their acids and bases, decomposition always ensues, and the insoluble salt is precipitated.*

If a solution of sulphate of soda be poured into a solution of nitrate of baryta, sulphate of baryta is precipitated, and nitrate of soda remains in solution:

$$NaO,SO_3+BaO,NO_5=BaO,SO_3+NaO,NO_5.$$

So, also, if a solution of carbonate of soda be added to a solution of chloride of calcium, carbonate of lime is precipitated, and chloride of sodium is formed, which remains in solution:

$$CaCl+NaO,CO_2=CaO,CO_2+NaCl.$$

It is not necessary for such reaction between the two salts that a salt insoluble in water should be formed from their elements, but it is sufficient that a salt less soluble than the two original salts can be produced under circumstances realizable at will.

Thus, if solutions of chloride of potassium and nitrate of soda be mixed, and the liquid evaporated at a low temperature, the two salts originally mixed separate, chloride of potassium crystallizing first, and nitrate of soda remaining in the liquid. If, on the contrary, the solution be evaporated at the boiling point, a double decomposition takes place, chloride of sodium being deposited, which, at the given temperature, is the least soluble of all the compounds which can be formed by the acids and bases present, and nitrate of potassa remains in the liquid. The decanted liquid deposits crystallized nitrate of potassa on cooling.

§ 389. By crystallizing liquid at different temperatures, inverse decompositions may frequently be obtained. Supposing sulphuric and chlorohydric acids, soda, and magnesia to exist in solution at the same time, in such proportions that acids and bases exactly saturate each other, it may be presumed that the liquid contains:

Either chloride of sodium
and sulphate of magnesia,
Or chloride of magnesium
and sulphate of soda,
Or both chlorides of sodium and magnesium
and sulphates of soda and magnesia.

It is impossible to decide in what order the acids and bases have combined in the liquid. If the solution be evaporated at a temperature above 59°, chloride of sodium crystallizes, being the least soluble of all the possible products at the given temperature. The greater part of the chloride of sodium may be thus separated; and if the evaporation be continued, sulphate of magnesia is obtained mixed with a small quantity of chloride of sodium.

If, on the contrary, the liquid be evaporated at a low temperature, as at 32°, sulphate of soda becomes the least soluble of all possible compounds, and is first deposited, while chloride of magnesium remains in the liquid.

Thus, with the same solution, we may obtain at will, according to the temperature of evaporation, chloride of sodium or sulphate of magnesia; or, sulphate of soda and chloride of magnesium; and we can always foretell, by consulting the plate of solubilities, page

407, what salts will be formed at a certain temperature, and in what order they will be deposited. It is, therefore, conceivable that an exact knowledge of the curves of solubility of the different salts is of great importance; but, unfortunately, they are only known for a small number.

The deposition of one of the salts can be frequently determined without evaporating the liquid, by merely modifying the nature of the solvent. If solutions of acetate of potassa and of chloride of calcium be mixed, there is no apparent reaction, if the liquids are not highly concentrated. But, by adding a sufficient quantity of alcohol to the solution, chloride of potassium is deposited, and acetate of lime remains in the liquid.

§ 390. When acids and bases exist simultaneously in solution, it is generally impossible to decide in what manner they are combined, and to draw conclusions as to the order in which they will be successively deposited by crystallization; for the order is determined solely by inferior solubility at the operating temperature, and it may be admitted that the less soluble salt is formed at the very moment of its crystallization.

Bases, however, exist, in which a probable decision can be given as to the nature of the salts existing in a solution, as in a mixture of two groups of acids and bases, when, one of the bases forming colourless salts with the two acids, the other base forms coloured salts with them, but of different shades of colour. If solutions of the protosulphate of iron and acetate of soda be mixed together, the brown shade of the liquid proves that it contains acetate of iron and sulphate of soda immediately after mixture; because sulphate of iron forms a light green, and acetate of iron a brown solution. Again, a current of sulfhydric acid gas exerts no action on a solution of protosulphate of iron, while it decomposes proto-acetate of iron, producing a deposit of black sulphide of iron. Now, the same precipitate is formed when sulfhydric acid is passed through a liquid in which acetate of soda and protosulphate of iron have been dissolved at the same time. This latter character is, however, less decisive than the colour; for it might be said that the reciprocal decomposition of the two salts takes place only by virtue of the sulfhydric acid, and is determined by the insolubility of the sulphide of iron, which may be formed in the case of reciprocal decomposition, but would not form if no reaction took place in the mixture of the two salts.

§ 391. *An insoluble salt may sometimes be decomposed by boiling it for a long time with a soluble salt.* This occurs whenever the base of the original insoluble salt can form an insoluble salt with the acid of the reacting soluble salt. Thus, the insoluble salts of baryta, strontia, and lime, as the sulphates of baryta and strontia, the phosphates or arseniates of all three bases, are decomposed when they are boiled with a solution of carbonate of potassa or soda. Carbonates of baryta, strontia, and lime are formed, and the liquid contains the alkaline base combined with the acid of the original insoluble salt. But, to render the decomposition complete, a large excess of alkaline carbonate must be used. The same decomposition is much more readily effected, by operating by the dry way; and frequent use will hereafter be made of it to recognise the nature of an insoluble salt. For the acid of such a salt forms a soluble alkaline salt, the acid of which may be recognised by characters soon to be developed. The base remains in the state of an insoluble carbonate; but by treating the carbonate with an acid which forms a soluble salt with the base, such as nitric acid, a solution of the base is obtained, in which the chemical reactions characteristic of the base may be ascertained.

DISTINCTIVE CHARACTERS FOR RECOGNISING THE ELECTRONEGATIVE ELEMENT OF BINARY COMPOUNDS FORMED BY THE METALS, AND THE NATURE OF THE ELECTRONEGATIVE ELEMENT, OR ACID, ENTERING INTO THE COMPOSITION OF A SALT.

§ 392. A binary compound, formed by a metal and a metalloid, or a salt formed by a metallic oxide, being given, how can the nature of the binary compound, or that of the salt, be ascertained? The solution of this important question is generally divided into two parts: 1st. The determination of the electronegative element; that is, the metalloid of a binary compound, or the acid of a salt. 2dly. The determination of the electropositive element; that is, the metal of the binary compound, or the base of the salt.

At present, we shall consider only the first part of the question, and treat the second part fully in detail under each particular metal.

Determination of the Electronegative Element, that is, of the kind of Binary Compounds formed by the Metals with the Metalloids.

§ 393. *Oxides.*—The characters employed for deciding whether a binary metallic compound is an oxide are often reduced to the physical characters of these oxides, characters which will be indicated with precision when describing each metal. At other times we rely on their property of dissolving in strong acids, such as oil of vitriol, without disengaging any gas or acid vapour, and on our inability to detect in the solution any other acid than the one employed to effect solution.

The majority of the metallic oxides are reduced by hydrogen when heated, the metal remaining free, and the vapour of water alone being disengaged. By taking the precaution to use dry hydrogen, the appearance of non-acid drops of water condensing in the anterior and cold portion of the tube in which the substance is heated, is a sure indication that an oxide is operated on.

Certain metallic oxides, however, are not reduced by hydrogen, such as the oxides of potassium, sodium, lithium, barium, strontium, calcium, magnesium, aluminum, and of all the earthy metals. But the oxides of potassium, sodium, lithium, barium, strontium, calcium, and magnesium, are more or less soluble in water, and exhibit a decided reaction on the tincture of litmus, a property they share only with the corresponding sulphides. Now, sulphides are easily distinguished from oxides, from the manner of their behaviour to acids which disengage sulfhydric acid abundantly, easily recognisable by its odour.

The oxides of aluminum and of all the other earthy metals are not decomposed by hydrogen, nor do they dissolve in water, nor, consequently, exert any action on the tincture of litmus. They are known, both by their insolubility in water, and, when treated with sulphuric acid, by their dissolving without disengaging acid vapours, and by the impossibility of ascertaining in the liquid the presence of any other acid than the sulphuric.

§ 394. *Sulphides.*—Sulphur, like oxygen, frequently forms several compounds with the same metal, so that we may have monosulphides, bisulphides, trisulphides, etc. The monosulphides of potassium, sodium, and lithium are alone soluble in water; all other monosulphides are insoluble, or, at least, very slightly soluble. The polysulphides of potassium, sodium, lithium, barium, strontium, and calcium, are equally soluble.

A monosulphide, heated with dilute sulphuric, or with chlorohydric acid, disengages sulfhydric acid gas, easily recognised by its odour, and no sulphur is deposited:

$$RS+SO_3+HO=RO,SO_3+HS, \text{ or } RS+HCl=RCl+HS.$$

If it be a bisulphide, or, in general, a polysulphide, sulphuretted hydrogen is also disengaged, but, in addition, a deposit of sulphur is formed.

$$RS_2+SO_3+HO=RO,SO_3+HS+S$$

or

$$RS_2+HCl=RCl+HS+S.$$

Many of the metallic sulphides, are attacked with difficulty by aqueous chlorohydric acid, even at the boiling point, but are always decomposed by nitric acid, or aqua regia. The sulphur is then changed into sulphuric acid, the presence of which may be always recognised by the characteristic properties of the sulphates, to be hereafter explained.

When sulphides are heated with a mixture of carbonate and nitrate of potassa, they produce alkaline sulphates soluble in water and easily recognised.

The metallic monosulphides act the part of bases to other sulphides, forming sulphosalts, which we shall subsequently learn to recognise.

§ 395. *Selenides.*—The seleniurets, treated with chlorohydric acid, disengage selenohydric acid gas. Heated with nitric acid, or aqua regia, they produce selenious acid, the presence of which is recognised by sulphurous acid, which precipitates selenium in the form of a characteristic red powder. When heated in the dry way with a mixture of carbonate and nitrate of potassa, they give seleniate of potassa; but if the resulting alkaline salt be boiled with an excess of chlorohydric acid, the selenic is changed into selenious acid, from which selenium may be then precipitated by sulphurous acid.

§ 396. *Phosphurets.*—The phosphurets of the alkaline and alkalino-earthy metals disengage phosphuretted hydrogen gas in contact with water, and the gas is instantly recognised by its odour. The phosphurets of the other metals, heated with potassium, yield their phosphorus to it, and it then disengages phosphuretted hydrogen when moistened with water.

§ 397. *Arseniurets.*—The metallic arseniurets possess metallic lustre. Treated with nitric acid or aqua regia, they are converted into arseniates, recognisable by characters we shall afterward explain. Heated with nitrate of potassa, they produce a soluble alkaline arseniate.

§ 398. *Chlorides.*—The metallic chlorides are nearly all soluble in water, that of silver and protochloride of mercury being the only exceptions.

A metallic chloride, treated with oil of vitriol, disengages chlorohydric acid. Heated with a mixture of peroxide of manganese and sulphuric acid, chlorine is given off, which is easily recognised by its odour and other physical properties.

The chlorides, dissolved in water, give with nitrate of silver a white precipitate, which collects into flakes by shaking the liquid. The precipitate is blackened by sunlight, assuming first a violet tinge. The rapidity of the change of colour is proportioned to the intensity of light, and rapidly ensues when exposed to the direct rays of the sun. The precipitate of chloride of silver is insoluble in acids, but readily dissolves in ammonia.

§ 399. *Bromides.*—A bromide, treated with oil of vitriol, disengages chlorohydric acid; but vapours of bromine are constantly disengaged, at the same time imparting a brown colour to the gas. If the bromide be treated with a mixture of sulphuric acid and peroxide of manganese, bromine only is disengaged. A solution of a bromide gives, with nitrate of silver, a light yellowish-white precipitate of bromide of silver, which is insoluble in an excess of acid, and readily dissolves in ammonia. The precipitated bromide is coloured by light like the chloride, but is immediately tinged brown, while the chloride assumes at first a violet hue. The bromides, in solution, are decomposed by chlorine, and bromine being set free, colours the liquid brown.

§ 400. *Iodides.*—The iodides, treated with oil of vitriol, instantly produce a considerable deposit of iodine; and if the mixture be heated, intense violet vapours are disengaged. The reaction is due to the decomposition of oil of vitriol by iodohydric acid, water and sulphurous acid being formed, and iodine set free. The iodides in solution are decomposed by chlorine, iodine being precipitated, the smallest quantity of which in solution is instantly detected by its imparting to starch an intensely blue colour.

A certain quantity of the solution is mixed with a solution of starch, effected in boiling water and cooled, or with ordinary starch-paste, and then a few drops of chlorine-water are added to decompose the iodide and liberate iodine. The mixture immediately assumes a decided blue colour. It is important not to add an excess of chlorine, which would destroy the blue colour by decomposing water, and generating chlorohydric and iodic acids.

§ 401. *Fluorides.*—A fluoride, treated with oil of vitriol, disengages vapours of fluohydric acid, which may be immediately recognised by its property of attacking glass. If silicic acid or pounded glass be added, and the mixture heated, gaseous fluoride of silicium is disengaged, which is decomposed by contact with water, affording a deposit of gelatinous silica. Solutions of fluorides are not precipitated by nitrate of silver.

§ 402. *Cyanides.*—The cyanides, treated with sulphuric or chlorohydric acid, disengage cyanohydric (prussic) acid, easily recognised by its odour. The most feeble acids, such as the carbonic, give off the same odour with soluble cyanides, and even the alkaline cyanides manifest it in a damp atmosphere.

The cyanides, with salts of protoxide of iron, give a white precipitate which rapidly turns blue in the air.

Determination of the Oxacid which enters into the constitution of an Oxysalt.

§ 403. *Nitrates.*—Nearly all nitrates are soluble in water, a few sub-nitrates alone being insoluble. Heat decomposes them, affording products which are rich in oxygen and powerfully assist combustion. In consequence of this property, the nitrates deflagrate on hot coals, and often detonate when heated with powdered charcoal. The alkaline nitrates, subjected to a gradually increasing temperature, disengage at first pure oxygen, and are changed into nitrites. Heated still further, they are entirely decomposed, evolving nitrogen and oxygen. The other nitrates disengage oxygen and deutoxide of nitrogen, or oxygen and hyponitric acid. When those formed by soluble bases are decomposed by heat, they leave a strongly alkaline residue.

Heated with sulphuric acid, they disengage vapours of nitric acid; and if a small quantity of metallic copper be added to the mixture, deutoxide of nitrogen is immediately disengaged, recognised by the reddish vapours it forms in the air.

The presence of a very small quantity of nitric acid in a liquid may be ascertained by pouring a small quantity of the liquid into a solution of the protosulphate of iron, acidified by sulphuric acid, and then plunging into it a strip of iron. If the liquid contains nitric acid, it turns red or brown after some time. Influenced by the sulphuric acid, the metallic iron decomposes the nitric acid, and deutoxide of nitrogen is disengaged, which dissolves in the protosulphate of iron and colours the liquid (§ 114).

§ 404. *Nitrites.*—The nitrites are decomposed by heat, like the nitrates, fusing on coals, and deflagrate when heated with powdered charcoal. With sulphuric acid, they immediately disengage reddish vapour, which suffices to distinguish them from the nitrates.

§ 405. *Chlorates.*—The chlorates are all decomposed by heat. Those of the alkalies and alkaline earths disengage oxygen, yielding a residue of chloride which is *neutral* to coloured tests, while the corresponding nitrates, under the same circumstances, leave a strongly *alkaline* residue. The chlorates of the other metallic oxides disengage by heat a mixture of oxygen and chlorine, leaving an oxide or oxychloride.

The chlorates are energetic supporters of combustion, deflagrate on heated coals, and produce violent detonations when heated with very combustible bodies, such as charcoal, sulphur, and phosphorus.

Treated with sulphuric or chlorohydric acid, they disengage a yellow gas, chlorous acid, recognisable by its colour, peculiar odour, and property of readily detonating on a slight elevation of temperature.

The chlorates do not precipitate salts of silver, because chlorate of silver is soluble in water; but the residue left after calcining the alkaline and alkalino-earthy chlorates being a chloride, gives, with a solution of nitrate of silver, a precipitate of chloride of silver, which may be recognised by its characteristic properties (§ 398).

§ 406. *Perchlorates.*—The perchlorates behave like the chlorates when subjected to the action of heat, or when heated with combustibles, but are easily distinguished from them, because they do not disengage chlorous acid by the action of oil of vitriol, and, consequently, are not coloured, for perchloric acid is merely isolated, without decomposition.

Perchlorate of potassa is but slightly soluble in water, and hence the salts of potassa give, with the perchlorates, a granular crystalline precipitate when the liquids are not too dilute.

§ 407. *Hypochlorites.*—The hypochlorites disengage the peculiar and characteristic odour of hypochlorous acid, which they give off copiously when treated with an acid. Their solutions bleach vegetable colours. Only the hypochlorites of potassa, soda, and lime, have been studied. They behave like energetic oxidizing agents, immediately changing sulphurous into sulphuric acid, and peroxidizing metallic protoxides.

§ 408. *Bromates.*—The bromates are decomposed by heat like the chlorates. Those of the alkalies and alkaline earths leave a residue of bromide, which may be recognised by the characters designated in § 399. When heated with sulphuric acid, bromic acid is isolated and decomposed into oxygen and bromine, the latter tinging the gas brown.

§ 409. *Iodates.*—The iodates are decomposed by heat. The alkaline salts alone leave a residue of iodide. The alkalino-earthy iodates, and those of all other metallic oxides, leave an oxide or an oxiodide, violet vapours of iodine mixed with oxygen being copiously given off. Sulphuric acid precipitates iodic acid from the iodates in a concentrated solution; and if some reducing body, as sulphurous acid, be added to the liquid, iodic acid is decomposed, and iodine precipitated.

§ 410. *Periodates.*—The periodates behave, when heated, like the iodates, but are distinguished from the latter by the slight solubility of periodate of soda, even in the presence of an excess of alkali, and the slight solubility of periodate of silver.

§ 411. *Sulphates.*—Nearly all the sulphates are soluble in water; those of baryta, strontia, and lead are nearly insoluble; that of lime is slightly soluble. The sulphates of the alkalies, alkaline earths, and of lead are indecomposable by heat alone: the other sulphates are decomposed, and generally yield a gaseous mixture of sulphurous acid and oxygen. Some sulphates, however, are decomposed at so low a temperature that the sulphurous acid and the oxygen remain united, and are disengaged in the state of sulphuric acid (§ 138).

All the sulphates are decomposed by carbon, assisted by heat; the products of the composition vary with the nature of the base and the temperature. The alkaline sulphates, heated rapidly with carbon, at a high temperature leave a residue of monosulphide; at a lower temperature they afford a mixture of polysulphide and carbonate. Those of the alkaline earths, with the exception of magnesia, give similar products. Those of the other metallic oxides, heated with carbon, yield a residue either of sulphide, or oxide, or even of metal, if the temperature be sufficiently elevated. But the experiment can always be performed with any sulphate, so as to obtain a sulphide, if a certain quantity of carbonate of potassa be added to the mixture. The alkaline sulphide remaining after calcination is easily recognised, as it gives off sulphuretted hydrogen with acids. The same character evidently belongs to the salts formed by all the oxacids of sulphur, as well as to the sulphates, but we shall soon learn how to distinguish them from each other.

As sulphuric acid does not act on the sulphates, this fact immediately distinguishes the sulphates from all salts which, under similar treatment, disengage acid vapours.

The sulphates soluble in water give, with the soluble salts of baryta, a white precipitate which is insoluble in an excess of acid; a property entirely characteristic of the sulphates.

§ 412. *Sulphites.*—The alkaline and alkalino-earthy sulphites, heated in a close vessel, are changed into sulphates and sulphides:

$$4(KO,SO_2)=3(KO,SO_3)+KS.$$

The other metallic sulphites disengage sulphurous acid, and the oxide remains as a residue. Heated with carbon, they give products similar to those of the sulphates.

Sulphuric acid, poured upon a sulphite, disengages sulphurous acid gas, easily recognised by its odour, and no deposit of sulphur takes place.

Concentrated boiling nitric acid changes the sulphites into sulphates. Chlorine produces the same change on the sulphites in solution. The soluble sulphites also absorb oxygen from the air, and are changed into sulphates.

§ 413. *Hyposulphates.*—The hyposulphates are all soluble in water. Those of the alkalies, alkaline earths, and of oxide of lead disengage sulphurous acid when subjected to the action of heat, leaving sulphates. Those of the other metallic oxides are more completely decomposed, and an oxide generally remains.

The hyposulphates, treated with cold sulphuric acid, manifest no apparent decomposition; but, when heated with the acid, they give off sulphurous acid.

They do not precipitate the salts of baryta, for hyposulphate of baryta is soluble in water. They are readily converted into sulphates by nitric acid, or by an aqueous solution of chlorine, and are then precipitated by salts of baryta.

§ 414. *Hyposulphites.*—Nearly all the hyposulphites are soluble, those of silver and lead alone being nearly insoluble. Heat decomposes the alkaline salts into sulphates or sulphides. Chlorohydric and sulphuric acids, poured into a solution of a hyposulphite, evolve sulphurous acid gas, and cause a deposit of sulphur; but the reaction does not always take place immediately, and often does not ensue for some time, unless the liquid be slightly heated.

Highly concentrated nitric acid, chlorine, and solutions of the hypochlorites, cause all the sulphur of the hyposulphites to pass into the state of sulphuric acid.

The hyposulphites give, with the salts of silver, a white precipitate, which, however, soon blackens from its conversion into a sulphide:

$$KO,S_2O_2+AgO,NO_5=KO,SO_3+AgS+NO_5.$$

The alkaline hyposulphites readily dissolve chloride, bromide, and iodide of silver in large quantities.

The majority of characters enumerated as distinguishing the hyposulphites, also belong to the monosulphuretted hyposulphates KO,S_3O_5, to the bisulphuretted hyposulphates KO,S_4O_5, and to the trisulphuretted hyposulphates KO,S_5O_5. These last salts have, hitherto, been too little studied to allow us to assign to them any distinctive characteristics, and we are obliged to resort to chemical analysis.

§ 415. Recapitulation.—All the salts formed by the oxacids of sulphur give sulphides when heated with a mixture of alkaline, carbonate, and charcoal, so that the product of calcination disengages sulphuretted hydrogen with chlorohydric acid. This character distinguishes the salts formed by the oxacids of sulphur from all others. They might, indeed, be confounded with the sulphides and the sulphosalts; but these bodies immediately disengage sulphuretted hydrogen with the acids.

The salts formed by the oxacids of sulphur are easily distinguished from each other by the following characters, if they are treated with sulphuric acid:

No reaction ensues with the sulphates;

With the hyposulphates, there is no apparent reaction when cold, but, assisted by heat, sulphurous acid is evolved;

With the sulphites, sulphurous acid is disengaged, without any deposit of sulphur;

With the hyposulphites, and with the mono, bi, and trisulphuretted hyposulphates, sulphurous acid is disengaged, and a more or less copious deposit of sulphur formed. This reaction frequently does not follow unless the temperature be elevated.

§ 416. *Phosphates.*—The alkaline phosphates alone are soluble in water: all the others are insoluble in it, but readily dissolve in an acid liquid. The soluble phosphates afford a precipitate with salts of baryta; but it is dissolved if the liquid be acidified with nitric or chlorohydric acid.

The phosphates evince no apparent reaction with oil of vitriol, and are thus instantly distinguished from all salts, which disengage acid vapours under the same circumstances.

All the phosphates, heated to a high temperature with a mixture of carbon and boracic or silicic acid, give off free phosphorus. A dry phosphate, heated with potassium, gives off phosphorus, which, by contact with water, disengages phosphuretted hydrogen. These two reactions are equally manifest with the salts formed by the other oxacids of phosphorus.

An insoluble phosphate may be readily converted into a soluble alkaline phosphate, by simply boiling it with a solution of an alkaline carbonate. The presence of phosphoric acid may be, subsequently, recognised in the liquid, by supersaturating it with chlorohydric acid, and ascertaining that it is not precipitated by the salts of baryta. But, if the acid be neutralized by ammonia, a precipitate of phosphate of baryta is immediately formed. The neutral liquid also affords a white precipitate with salts of lead; and phosphate of lead is easily known, because it is fused by the blowpipe into a globule which, on becoming solid, assumes crystalline facets.

§ 417. *Phosphites.*—The alkaline phosphites alone are soluble. All phosphites are decomposed by heat, giving a residue of phosphate, and disengaging a mixture of hydrogen and phosphuretted hydrogen. Nitric acid and chlorine transform them into phosphates.

The phosphites reduce a certain number of metallic oxides, —among others, those of silver and mercury, and the reaction is more rapid if the liquid be acidified. The red oxide of mercury, heated with the solution of a phosphite, to which a small quantity of chlorohydric acid has been added, is converted into a black powder of metallic mercury.

§ 418. *Hypophosphites.*—The reactions of the hypophosphites closely resemble those of the phosphites. They are decomposed by heat, affording phosphates, and evolving phosphuretted hydrogen. Nitric acid and chlorine transform them into phosphates.

They are distinguished from the phosphites, because they never precipitate the salts of baryta, while the phosphites do precipitate them when perfectly neutral.

§ 419. *Arseniates.*—The alkaline arseniates alone are soluble; those of all the other metallic oxides are insoluble, but they readily dissolve in an excess of acid.

Any arseniate, heated with boracic acid and charcoal in a small tube, closed at one end, gives a sublimate of arsenic, which forms a metallic ring in the upper part of the tube.

The solutions of the arseniates, treated in Marsh's apparatus (§ 236), afford copious arsenical spots. With the nitrate of silver, they give a brick-red precipitate, which dissolves readily in an excess of acid; so that the precipitate is only formed when the liquids are perfectly neutral.

The soluble arseniates give a yellow precipitate with sulphuretted hydrogen, but a long time is frequently required for its appearance.

§ 420. *Arsenites.*—The arsenites, heated with charcoal and boracic acid, give a sublimate of arsenic. In Marsh's apparatus they produce arsenical spots.

If an acid be poured into the concentrated solution of an alkaline arsenite, a crystalline precipitate of arsenious acid is formed. The arsenites in solution precipitate the salts of silver yellow, and those of copper, green; but the liquids must be perfectly neutral, for the insoluble arsenites are readily dissolved in an excess of acid.

Sulphuretted hydrogen affords, with the arsenites in solution, a copious yellow precipitate, insoluble in an excess of acid, but which readily dissolves in ammonia. This precipitate is formed immediately, while, with the arseniates, some lapse of time is necessary.

The arsenites, heated with nitric acid, are converted into arseniates, with the evolution of reddish vapours. The arseniates have no similar properties, not being altered by oxidizing substances.

§ 421. *Carbonates.*—The alkaline carbonates are the only soluble carbonates. They are also the only ones which cannot be decomposed by heat. All the other carbonates part with all their carbonic acid at a higher or lower temperature. All the carbonates, without exception, are decomposed when heated to a very high temperature, with charcoal, carbonic oxide being disengaged.

When vapour of phosphorus is passed over an alkaline carbonate heated to redness, the carbonic acid is completely decomposed, and carbon separated, colouring the substance black.

The carbonates, treated with an acid, produce a lively effervescence, owing to the evolution of carbonic acid, and this reaction characterizes them; for carbonic acid is easily recognised by being inodorous and tasteless, and precipitating limewater. This reaction alone suffices to distinguish the carbonates from all other salts.

§ 422. *Borates.*—The alkaline borates alone are soluble; all the others are insoluble. At a high temperature, they fuse and form colourless glass, when the metallic oxides combined with the boracic acid are themselves colourless; otherwise they form coloured glass.

Charcoal acts with difficulty on the borates; only a few of which are decomposed by it at a very high temperature, and produce metallic borides.

Sulphuric, nitric, and chlorohydric acids decompose the borates in the wet way, liberating boracic acid. If the solution of borate be concentrated, the boracic acid is precipitated in the form of small crystalline scales, in which the characteristic properties of the acid are easily detected. Boracic acid, on the contrary, expels these acids in the dry way.

If a mixture of any borate and fluor-spar be heated with oil of vitriol, fluoride of boron is disengaged, recognised by the dense white fumes it gives off in the air, and its mode of decomposition by contact with water (§ 241).

§ 423. *Silicates.*—The majority of the silicates are insoluble, the alkaline, with a great excess of base, being alone soluble in water. The silicates, decomposable by sulphuric and chlorohydric acids, are easily recognised; for when heated with the acid, silicic acid separates in the state of a colourless, transparent jelly, which aggregates into an insoluble white powder, and when collected on a filter, its characteristic properties are easily shown. The silicates which are not decomposed by the acids, may be readily converted into the former by fusing them in a platinum crucible with three or four times their weight of carbonate of soda. A more basic silicate is thus obtained, containing a large quantity of alkali, and it is easily and entirely decomposed by the acids, leaving a residue of gelatinous silica.

The silicates generally fuse when subjected to heat; but some, as the silicates of alumina and lime, require the very highest temperatures. Charcoal reduces some of the silicates at a high temperature, only a portion of the metal separating, and the remaining silicate containing a large excess of acid. Those partially decomposed by charcoal are such as contain easily reducible metallic oxides.

The silicates, heated in a vessel of lead or platina with fluorspar and oil of vitriol, disengage gaseous fluoride of silicium, which fumes in the air, and is decomposed by contact with water, precipitating gelatinous silica.

§ 424. *Sulphosalts.*—The sulphosalts, treated with powerful but not oxidizing acids, as dilute sulphuric or chlorohydric, disengage sulphuretted hydrogen, and the sulphacid separates. The majority of sulphacids being insoluble in water, the properties characterizing them may be recognised in their precipitates.

Thus, with the sulphocarbonate of the monosulphide of potassium, sulfhydric acid is disengaged, and liquid sulphide of carbon is precipitated:

$$KS,CS_2+HCl=KCl+HS+CS_2.$$

With the sulpharseniate of the monosulphide of potassium, sulfhydric acid is disengaged, and sulphide of arsenic is precipitated in the form of a yellow powder:

$$KS,AsS_5+HCl=KCl+HS+AsS_5.$$

With the sulfhydrate of the monosulphide of potassium, there is an analogous reaction, but sulfhydric acid only is disengaged, one-half of which proceeds from the monosulphide of potassium, and the other half from the sulphacid which separates. Since the reaction does not distinguish this sulphosalt from monosulphide of potassium, the following process is adopted:—The monosulphides of the alkaline and alkalino-earthy metals are the only ones which act the part of bases with sulfhydric acid; if, therefore, a metallic salt, such as the sulphate of copper, be poured into a solution of sulfhydrate of monosulphide of potassium, a double decomposition ensues, sulphate of potassa and monosulphide of copper being formed. But, as the latter sulphide does not play the part of a base with the sulphacid HS, this sulphide becomes free, and, consequently, sulfhydric acid is disengaged:

$$KS,HS+CuO,SO_3=KO,SO_3+CuS+HS.$$

If, on the contrary, a solution of sulphate of copper be poured into a solution of a monosulphide, a precipitate of metallic sulphide is formed, but no sulphuretted hydrogen is disengaged:

$$KS+CuO,SO_3=KO,SO_3+CuS.$$

In order that this last proposition may be true, the metallic solution should not contain an excess of acid, which would decompose a portion of the monosulphide and disengage sulphuretted hydrogen.

The monosulphides and sulfhydrates of sulphides are, moreover, distinguished from the polysulphides, inasmuch as they do not afford, like the latter, a deposit of sulphur when decomposed by the acids.

OF THE METALS INDIVIDUALLY.

§ 425. In the following investigation of the most important metals, we shall preserve the classification indicated in § 276, viz. metals which are too oxidizable to be used in the metallic state, and those which remain unchanged in the air for so long a time that their alterability is no obstacle to their use.

The first class will be thrown into three subdivisions:

1. The alkaline metals, comprising

Potassium,	Lithium.
Sodium,	

The term *alkaline metals* has been given to them, because their oxides have, for a long time, borne the name of *alkalies*.

2. The alkalino-earthy metals, whose oxides partake, at once, of the properties of the alkalies and of the earths. They are,

Barium,	Magnesium,
Strontium,	Glucinum.
Calcium,	

3. The earthy metals, so called, because their oxides have for a long time borne the name of *earths*. They are,

Aluminum,	Cerium,
Zirconium,	Lanthanum,
Thorium,	Didymium,
Yttrium,	Erbium.
Terbium,	

I. ALKALINE METALS.

POTASSIUM.

EQUIVALENT = 490.0.

§ 426. POTASSIUM is a metal pretty extensively spread over the earth, but it exists only in combination with other bodies. A great majority of the minerals which compose the crystalline rocks, as the feldspars, micas, etc., contain silicate of potassa. The debris of these rocks, altered by water, constitute the sedimentary rocks, which have lost a large portion of their potassa, but still retain a sufficient quantity to be found by chemical analysis. The salts of potassa are indispensable to the growth of plants, which gradually abstract them from the soil and manure; and their ashes furnish the greater portion of the salts of potassa used in the arts.

The consistence of potassium varies with the temperature. Below 32° it is slightly friable, and its fracture presents indications of crystallization. At 59° it is soft, and may be kneaded, and easily cut with a knife. When recently divided, it affects the colour and lustre of silver, but the lustre is evanescent, for as the metal rapidly combines with the oxygen of the air, its surface becomes tarnished. At 131° it becomes perfectly liquid, and then resembles mercury. Lastly, it distils at a red-heat, as a beautiful emerald-green vapour.

Its density has been found to be 0.865 at about 59°, and is consequently lighter than water.

It oxidizes rapidly in the air, even at ordinary temperatures, its surface becoming covered with the hydrated oxide of potassium or potassa; but some time is necessary, for the change to penetrate the centre of a globule of any considerable size. If it be heated in the air, it takes fire and burns with a violet flame.

Potassium decomposes water at ordinary temperatures, disengaging hydrogen. If a fragment of it be thrown on water, it is observed to glide over its surface in the form of a brilliant little sphere, the size of which rapidly diminishes, and to be accompanied by a violet-coloured flame. When the combustion ceases, the little globule bursts, and its fragments are thrown in every direction. In making this experiment, care must be taken to use a deep bell-glass (fig. 316), lest the eyes or person of the operator be injured by the explosion. After the experiment, the water in the bell-glass will be found to be alkaline, and to blue the reddened tincture of litmus.

Fig. 316.

The various circumstances of this phenomenon are

easily explained. The fragment of potassium swims on the water, because of its greater levity. Water being decomposed, the heat developed fuses the metal, which takes the form of a glittering globule; the hydrogen gas evolved raises up the metal, preventing it from remaining constantly in contact with the water, and drives it over the surface. The temperature of the globule of potassium being sufficiently high to inflame the hydrogen, it burns, as fast as it is formed, with a violet flame, the colour of which is due to the admixture of a small quantity of vapour of potassium arising from the heated metal. Whenever the globule falls back on the surface of the liquid, the small quantity of oxide of potassium formed is dissolved in the water. Lastly, when the combustion ceases, there remains a small globule of very hot potassa, which falls on the liquid, where it bursts, in consequence of sudden cooling; and as a large quantity of steam is instantly developed at this spot, its expansive force throws small fragments of potassa in every direction.

The great liability of potassium to alteration, requiring peculiar care in its preservation, it is generally kept in ground-stoppered bottles, nearly filled with naphtha, which is a compound of carbon and hydrogen unalterable by the metal.

Potassium, being one of the substances possessing the greatest affinity for oxygen, is constantly used to abstract the oxygen from oxidized bodies. Boron was prepared (§ 238) by decomposing boracic acid by potassium. The protoxide and deutoxide of nitrogen (§ 111 and 115) were analyzed by decomposing them by potassium. Some bodies can, however, remove oxygen from the oxide of potassium at a high temperature, and set potassium free, such as iron, at a white-heat. At a dull red-heat, potassium decomposes carbonic acid; but, at a white-heat, carbon deprives the potassa of its oxygen. Advantage is taken of this property in the preparation of potassium.

§ 427. Potassium was at first isolated by decomposing the hydrate of potassa by a powerful voltaic pile. To effect it, a certain quantity of mercury was placed in a platinum crucible, and, above it, a concentrated solution of potassa, containing fragments of solid potassa. The negative pole of the pile being brought in contact with the platinum crucible, and the positive pole, terminating in a strong platinum wire, being plunged into the solution of potassa, the decomposition of the hydrated oxide of potassium commenced immediately. Water and oxide of potassium being decomposed at the same time, hydrogen and potassium were found at the negative, and oxygen at the positive pole. The hydrogen and oxygen were evolved in the gaseous state, the potassium was dissolved in the mercury, which assumed, after some time, a pasty consistence. The pasty metal being quickly introduced into a small glass retort, heated by an alcohol lamp, the mercury was driven off, and a globule of potassium remained in the retort. Very small quantities of potassium were obtained in this way, sufficient, however, to verify its principal properties.*

§ 428. Soon after, larger quantities of potassium were obtained by decomposing potassa in vapour by iron at a white-heat. Fig. 317 represents the apparatus employed for the operation.†

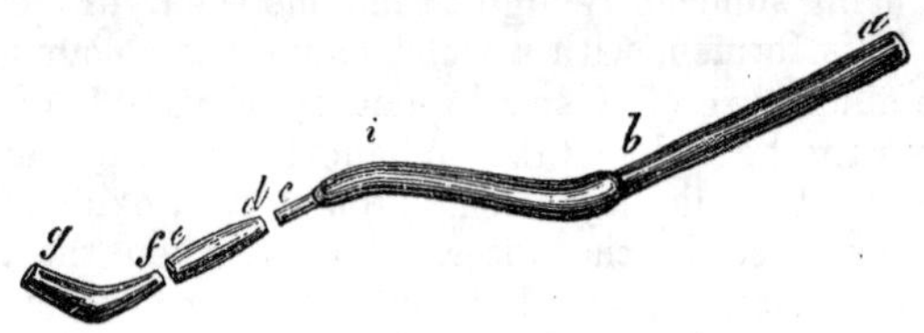

Fig. 317.

A gun-barrel *abc* is bent at *b* and *i*, so as to give it the shape represented in fig. 317; and as this portion *bi* is to be intensely ignited, its surface would soon oxidize and the barrel be rendered useless, if its surface were not protected by an unalterable lute which covered it completely. This lute is composed of 4 or 5 parts of sand and 1 part of potter's clay, and being spread to a thickness of 1 or 2 centim. ($\frac{1}{2}-\frac{3}{4}$ in.), is first dried slowly in the air, and then before the fire. The cracks made in drying are filled with clay. The gun-barrel being filled with bright iron turnings, or small bundles of clean iron wire, and the part *ab* with pieces of potassa, it is placed in a reverberatory furnace (fig. 318). The end *a* of the iron tube is closed with a cork, fur-

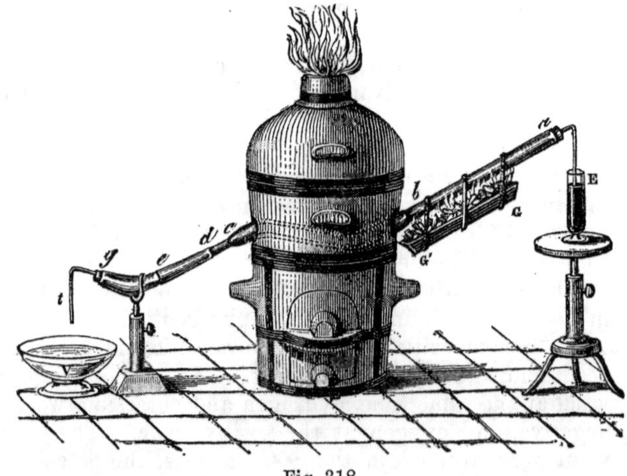

Fig. 318.

* Davy, in 1807, first isolated potassium in this way.

† The credit of this process is due to Messrs. Gay-Lussac and Thenard.

nished with a tube, entering the test-glass E, filled with mercury. A chaffer GG′ of wire or sheet-iron is suspended below the part *ab*.

The extremity *c* is passed into a copper receiver *deg*, made of two pieces *de* and *fg* (fig. 317 and 318), fitted together by grinding, and the naphtha is introduced into the lower part *ge*, in order to collect the potassium. A tube *t* allows the escape of the gas formed during the experiment.

The apparatus being arranged, the furnace is filled with charcoal, and as the natural draught would not afford sufficient heat, the combustion is assisted by a large bellows, the nozzle of which enters the door of the furnace, the surrounding apertures being closed with pieces of brick and clay.

When the tube *bc* has reached a strong white-heat, hot coals are introduced into the chaffer GG′, so as to slowly fuse the fragments of potassa contained in the tube *ab*. The fused potassa flowing into the heated tube *bc*, where it meets the iron intensely ignited, the decomposition of water and oxide of potassium takes place at the same time; the iron is converted into oxide of iron; the potassium in vapour is carried forward by the current of hydrogen gas, and condenses in the receiver *ge*.

As it sometimes happens that the end *c* becomes closed during the experiment, so that the gases cannot readily escape, they would issue through the joints of the various parts of the apparatus, and render it useless. The disengagement tube *a*E remedies the inconvenience, and immediately indicates when the aperture *c* is obstructed, by gases escaping through the mercury in the test-glass E.

§ 429. Potassium is now* prepared by decomposing carbonate of potassa by charcoal at intense ignition, whereby much larger quantities of potassium can be procured than by the older processes. It is essential that the carbonate of potassa be intimately mixed with the charcoal. Only an imperfect mixture is obtained by mechanically mixing the carbonate with charcoal; and as this carbonate melts long before its decomposition by the charcoal can take place, the latter, being lighter, floats on the surface, and the mixture is destroyed. On the other hand, a very intimate mixture of potassa and charcoal can be obtained by decomposing certain salts of potassa with organic acids by heat. The bitartrate of potassa is well adapted to the purpose, as it leaves a great deal of charcoal, and is not expensive, if procured in the state of impure bitartrate or *crude tartar* or *argol*.

The crude tartar being placed in a large clay crucible, closed by a cover, and luted to prevent the admission of air, is heated to redness in a furnace, until no more gas is disengaged. When the crucible is cooled, the black substance is pulverized in a mortar,

* This process was contrived by Brunner.

mixed with coarsely broken charcoal, and introduced into a wrought-iron bottle. The iron flasks ordinarily used in commerce for mercury are well adapted to the object. They have only one opening at *o* (fig. 319), which is closed with an iron screw for the transportation of mercury; but, for our purpose, a thread is cut on an iron tube, so as to fit the aperture *o*. The joint is closed as tightly as practicable by clay. In order to prevent the alteration of the bottle during the operation, its surface is covered with an argillaceous luting, carefully applied. The bottle, three-fourths filled with the mixture, is arranged, as represented in fig. 319, in a furnace in which intense ignition can be obtained.

Fig. 319.

This furnace is built of a rectangular form, with its walls of fire-brick, for ordinary bricks would fuse at the high temperature necessarily required. It is generally open at the top, to facilitate the arrangement of the iron bottle, or of crucibles when the furnace is used for other purposes, as well as to supply the fuel. The opening is closed with a cover M, made of bricks, bound in an iron frame. The furnace communicates with a high chimney U, by the *flue* O, and a damper R serves to regulate the draught. The ash-pit C has an aperture in front, by which air enters the furnace. One of the side-walls of the furnace has a rectangular opening, which is closed with fire-brick when the furnace is used for heating crucibles; but when employed for the preparation of potassium, it is closed by a cast-iron door *rn*, having a hole through which an iron tube *uo* passes.

The bottle V is placed in the furnace on two stout iron bars, or, better still, on two fire-bricks projecting from the sides, and the iron tube *uo* enters a copper receiver A, of peculiar construction. It is composed of two parts B and C, which fit into each other, represented in section in fig. 320, where they are separated. The lower part is a cylindrical copper vessel, with an oval base. The upper part, which serves as a cover, enters the former as far as the height *mn*, and is divided into two compartments by a vertical partition *cd*, which descends to within a short distance of the bottom of the vessel C, when the two parts are together. Two tubulures *a*, *b* are placed exactly opposite to each other, and the vertical wall *cd* has an opening in the direction *ab*. A third tubulure *f* is placed on the anterior face of the cover, as seen in fig. 319.

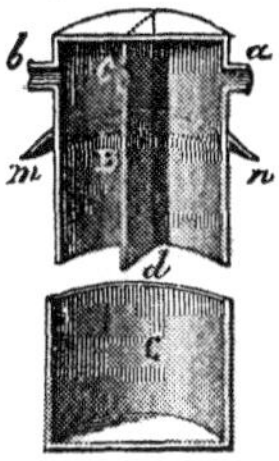

Fig. 320.

Naphtha is poured into the vessel C to a depth of 5 or 6 centimetres (2–2½ in.), the two pieces fitted together, and the tube *uo* adjusted in the tubulure *a*, by closing the interstices tightly with an argillaceous lute. Into the tubulure *f* a glass tube *g* is fitted, which gives exit to the gas; and, lastly, the tubulure *b* is closed with a cork.

The receiver rests on a support S (fig. 319), covered with a sheet-iron plate, having a drain at T.

The apparatus being arranged, live coals are first introduced into the furnace, then common charcoal, and when the fire is well kindled, it is fed with a mixture of equal parts of charcoal and coke. At each time of charging with fuel, a poker should be passed into the furnace to prevent cavities from forming under the retort.

The reaction of charcoal on the carbonate of potassa soon commencing, carbonic oxide gas is copiously disengaged from the tube *fg*; and the potassium set free volatilizes, condenses in the receiver, and sinks under the naphtha. As the receiver would soon become heated by radiation from the furnace and the passage of heated gases, it is kept cool by allowing a constant current of cold water to flow over the top. The ledge *mn* prevents the water from entering into the lower compartment, and it finally runs off by the drain T. It frequently happens in the operation that the iron tube *uo* is obstructed by substances carried over mechanically, or by those arising from a peculiar reaction which will soon be explained. This is known by the cessation of the current of gas in the tube *fg*, and is remedied by introducing through the tubulure *b*, an iron wire (fig. 321) fastened to a wooden handle, and turning it around until it has pierced the deposit formed in the tube *uo*, and made a free passage for the gas.

Fig. 321.

The operation is terminated, when no more gas passes through the tube *fg*, although the tube *uo* be not obstructed. The receiver being removed, the potassium is found in the form of irregular globules, mixed with various accidental substances, which are separated by filtering through cloth. The impure potassium, being placed in a cloth tied like a bag, is plunged into a cup filled with naphtha at 120° to 140°. The bag being compressed with pincers, the potassium filters in the form of metallic globules through the cloth, and falls to the bottom of the capsule, where it collects into larger globules. The foreign matter remains in the bag.

It has been stated that potassium decomposes carbonic oxide at a dull red-heat; and hence, it is difficult to prevent the occurrence of an inverse reaction in our apparatus, and the loss of a portion of the isolated potassium during the first reaction. The carbonic oxide gas and vapour of potassium, when leaving the retort, enter into the iron tube *uo*, where they meet a much lower temperature, and the inverse reaction ensues. A portion of the potassium decomposes carbonic oxide, forming peculiar products, to which the names of *croconate* and *rhodizonate of potassa* have been assigned. They are deposited in the tube *uo* with free carbon, and tend to obstruct it. A portion of them is carried as far as the receiver, in the form of black flakes, which may be used to extract the two salts of potassa just named. To diminish, as much as possible, the loss of potassium occasioned by this inverse reaction, it is necessary to shorten the tube *uo* as far as practicable.

§ 430. To obtain absolutely pure potassium, it is redistilled in a wrought iron vessel A (fig. 322), to which is screwed the curved iron tube *abc*. Potassium, and a portion of naphtha are introduced into the vessel, which is then heated in a furnace, and the extremity of the tube *abc* plunged into a bottle containing naphtha. From time to time, a gentle blow should be given to the tube *abc*, in order to cause the melted potassium to flow into the receiver.

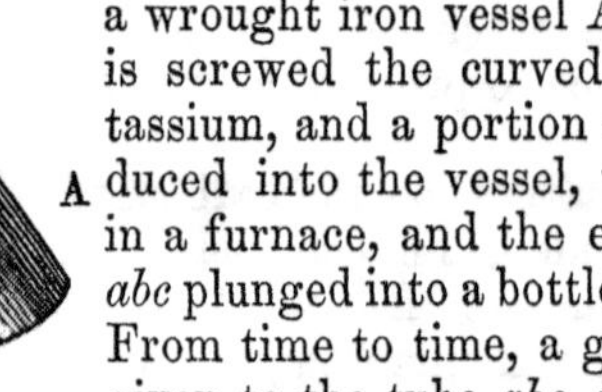

Fig. 322.

COMBINATIONS OF POTASSIUM WITH OXYGEN.

§ 431. Potassium forms two compounds with oxygen; a protoxide to which has been assigned the formula KO, and a peroxide which contains three times as much oxygen, and, consequently, takes the formula KO_3.

When a globule of potassium is heated in a small silver tray put in a glass tube, and traversed by a current of dry oxygen, the metal takes fire, and is changed into a yellow fusible substance, which is peroxide of potassium. It readily dissolves in water, but is decomposed, two-thirds of its oxygen being set free, and protoxide of potassium dissolved. If the solution be evaporated to dryness, the hydrated protoxide of potassium is obtained, which fuses at a dull red-heat, but cannot be deprived of its water of combination.

The preparation of the protoxide is accompanied by great difficulties. In order to obtain it, a known weight of potassium is converted into peroxide by heating it in a silver tray, in a current of oxygen; twice the weight of potassium in the peroxide is put with the latter in the same tray, which is heated in the same tube, in a current of nitrogen gas:

$$KO_3+2K=3KO.$$

It may also be obtained by heating a known weight of the hydrated protoxide of potassium KO+HO, or *potassa*, with a weight of potassium equal to that which exists in the potassa, in which case the hydrogen of the water is set free, and 2 equivalents of protoxide formed:

$$KO,HO+K=2KO+H.$$

The protoxi e cannot be obtained by decomposing nitrate of potassa by heat, a process by which many anhydrous protoxides are prepared, as those of barium, strontium, calcium, etc. Nitrate of potassa, heated in a glass or porcelain retort, decomposes at a dull red-heat into oxygen, which is set free, and a nitrite, which remains in the retort:

$$KO,NO_5=KO,NO_3+2O.$$

If the heat be raised still higher, the nitrite itself is decomposed, and oxygen and nitrogen evolved; but the protoxide of potassium seizes on a portion of the oxygen, and passes partly into the state of peroxide. A complete decomposition of the nitrite cannot be effected in glass or earthenware vessels; for the silicates constituting the body of these vessels are attacked by the oxides of potassium, and the vessels soon destroyed. There is no better success in a vessel of platinum; for it is soon corroded by the oxides of potassium, especially in the presence of oxygen. Silver resists the action of these oxides much better, but it is too fusible to allow the complete decomposition of the nitrite.

It will soon be shown that the hydrate of potassa may be readily obtained in large quantities, and that it is one of the most useful substances in the laboratory.

Of the two compounds which potassium forms with oxygen, only the protoxide plays the part of a base, and it is the most powerful base of our laboratories. No compound formed by the peroxide being yet known, it possesses but little interest. It is immediately decomposed by contact with water and the acids, disengaging oxygen, and forming a salt of the protoxide of potassium.

SALTS FORMED BY THE PROTOXIDE OF POTASSIUM, OR POTASSA.

Combinations of the Protoxide of Potassium with Water.

§ 432. The protoxide of potassium, or potassa, forms, with water, two definite compounds or *hydrates*, a monohydrate $KO+HO$ or KO,HO, and a pentahydrate $KO+5HO$.

When potassium decomposes water, the hydrate of potassa KO,HO is formed, and remains in solution in the water. The same hydrate is produced by decomposing a salt of potassa by a base which forms an insoluble compound with the acid of the salt. The last process is the one always used in the laboratory for the preparation of the hydrates of potassa, which are very important reagents. For this purpose, carbonate of potassa is decomposed by lime, an insoluble carbonate of lime being formed, and the potassa remaining in the liquid in the state of hydrate.

One part of carbonate of potassa is dissolved in 10 of water. If the carbonate does not dissolve without residue, on account of its impurity, the liquid is allowed to stand, and then decanted into a clean cast-iron kettle, in which it is boiled. Slacked lime diffused in water is then added by small quantities to the boiling liquid. A small quantity of the liquid being taken up with a pipette and poured into a glass, is allowed to repose for a few moments, until the suspended matter is deposited, when a portion of the clear liquid is transferred to a test-glass, and an excess of chlorohydric acid added. If all the carbonate of potassa has been converted into hydrate, no effervescence will ensue. If effervescence takes place, the ebullition is continued for some time, small quantities of lime being added, if necessary, until no effervescence occur in another experiment performed in the same way. The kettle being removed from the fire, the liquid is allowed to clarify by repose, keeping the kettle covered, to prevent the potassa from absorbing carbonic acid from the air. If the potassa is to be preserved in solution, the liquid is drawn off with a siphon, and collected in a ground-stoppered bottle. Bottles made of hard green glass are most suitable, inasmuch as those of flint-glass contain more or less oxide of lead, which is attacked by the solution of potassa, so that the latter will be impregnated, after a time, with an appreciable quantity of the oxide, and its efficiency as a test injured.

If solid potassa is to be made, the solution is evaporated rapidly in a copper, or still better, in a silver vessel. The ebullition should be very active, in order that the constant evolution of vapour may prevent the contact of the air with the potassa, and the consequent abstraction of carbonic acid. The temperature being at length elevated to dull redness, the hydrate of potassa KO,HO, which alone remains, fuses into a liquid of an oily consistence. If a small quantity of carbonate of potassa has been formed during the operation, as it fuses only at a much higher temperature, it swims on the surface of the hydrate, and may be skimmed off. The melted hydrate is then poured upon a copper plate, on which it instantly congeals. The potassa is broken into pieces, and preserved in well-closed bottles.

The hydrate of potassa, thus prepared, is the *caustic potash* of commerce. When purified carbonate of potassa has been used, and the operation carefully conducted, the hydrate of potassa is nearly pure. This is, however, rarely the case with the caustic potash of commerce, for beside the carbonate of potassa used in its manufacture generally containing sulphate and silicate of potassa and chloride of potassium, the decomposition of the carbonate is rarely complete.

§ 433. To purify crude caustic potash, it is introduced, broken in small pieces, into a large flask filled with very strong alcohol. The liquid is frequently shaken, and even moderately warmed, to hasten the solution, and then allowed to repose. A crystalline deposit, chiefly composed of sulphate of potassa and chloride of potassium, is formed at the bottom of the flask, above which is a sirupy liquid, formed chiefly of a solution of carbonate of potassa in the water, abstracted from the alcohol. The rest of the liquid is a solution of the monohydrate of potassa in nearly absolute alcohol. The supernatant liquid is drawn off by a syphon, poured into a retort or other suitable apparatus for distilling, and after distilling off about two-thirds of the alcohol, which is absolute, the remaining liquid is poured into a silver dish and evaporated as rapidly as possible. It is lastly heated to dull redness, in order to fuse the hydrate of potassa, which is then formed on the silver plate. The alcoholic solution is generally coloured brown during the evaporation, owing to the alteration of a small portion of alcohol by potassa and the oxygen of the air, forming a brown organic acid, which remains combined with the potassa. But, when the potassa melts, the substance loses its colour entirely, the organic acid being destroyed, and affording carbonic acid, which remains combined with the potassa.

The potassa, thus purified, and called alcoholic potassa, always contains a certain quantity of carbonate, but is entirely freed from chlorides and sulphates. If we wish to deprive it entirely of carbonic acid, it is redissolved and boiled with a small quantity of milk of lime, allowed to cool, and kept in a well-closed bottle. The liquid then contains a small quantity of lime in solution, which may be precipitated by the addition of a few drops of carbonate of potassa.

§ 434. The decomposition of carbonate of potassa by lime is only effected with ease when the liquid is diluted, so that a very weak solution of potassa is the necessary result, and a great deal of water must be evaporated in order to obtain solid potassa.

When the carbonate is dissolved in a small quantity of water, it cannot be reduced to the caustic state, even by prolonged ebullition with a great excess of lime. Moreover, when a concentrated solution of caustic potassa is boiled with carbonate of lime, the potassa abstracts nearly all the carbonic acid from the lime. It is evident, therefore, that with a solution of carbonate in a certain state of concentration, its decomposition by lime must stop at a given point, which cannot be exceeded by prolonging the operation. We may even retrograde, that is to say, may form again a new quantity of carbonate of potassa, if the liquid becomes too concentrated by boiling.

Theoretically, 1 equivalent of lime $CaO=28$ will decompose 1 equivalent of carbonate of potassa $KO,CO_2=69.2$; but experience shows that, in order to obtain a rapid decomposition, at least double the quantity of lime just mentioned should be employed. And so much the more lime must be used, as the solution of potash is concentrated.

Caustic potassa (hydrated potassa) presents the form of opaque white masses, with a crystalline fracture. Its density is about 2.1. It melts at a dull red-heat, and volatilizes without alteration at a white-heat. It parts with its water only when in contact with a more powerful acid with which the oxide of potassium can combine.

§ 435. In order to determine experimentally the quantity of water contained in the hydrate of potassa, a certain quantity of the hydrate is weighed rapidly in a platinum crucible, covered by its lid to prevent its absorbing water during weighing. A small quantity of water is added to dissolve the potassa, and a slight excess of sulphuric acid carefully poured in to form sulphate of potassa. It is then evaporated to dryness with care, to avoid loss by projection during the evaporation. The dried substance is calcined at a strong red-heat, to drive off the excess of sulphuric acid and reduce the residue to the state of neutral sulphate of potassa KO,SO_3. The crucible is again weighed, and gives a weight P of sulphate of potassa, produced by the weight p of hydrate of potassa. If we knew the composition of the sulphate of potassa, we should immediately know the weight q of anhydrous potassa KO contained in the weight P of sulphate of potassa, and should thence conclude that a weight p of hydrate of potassa contains a weight q of anhydrous potassa, and consequently a weight $(p-q)$ of water.

Let us suppose that we did not know the composition of the sulphate of potassa. The weight P of sulphate of potassa is dissolved in distilled water, washing the crucible several times, so as not to lose the smallest portion of the substance. An excess of a solution of chloride of barium is poured into the collected waters, slightly acidulated by the addition of a few drops of chlorohydric acid, and heated to the boiling point. The sulphuric acid will be completely precipitated in the state of insoluble sulphate of baryta, which is readily deposited in hot liquids. The precipitate being collected on a small filter, washed with distilled water, and then dried, is calcined in contact with the air to burn off the filter, when a weight Q of sulphate of baryta is obtained. Now, we may grant that the composition of this sulphate is known; for, if it were not, it might be determined by the experiment described § 135.

It will thus be found that 100 parts of hydrate of potassa KO,HO contain 16 parts of water, corresponding to the following composition in equivalents:

1 eq. of protoxide of potassium......	47.2......	83.99
1 " " water...........................	9.0......	16.01
1 " " hydrate of potassa...........	56.2.....	100.00

§ 436. The monohydrate of potassa dissolves in water with disengagement of heat, proving that it is not a simple solution, which always cools the liquid, but that it combines with an additional quantity of water, and the heat evolved by this combination exceeds that which is absorbed in the act of solution. If the monohydrate be dissolved in a very small quantity of hot water, and the solution allowed to cool in a close bottle, crystals are formed belonging to a second hydrate of potassa, containing 5 times as much water as the first, and with the formula KO+5HO. This hydrate dissolves in water, producing a depression of temperature.

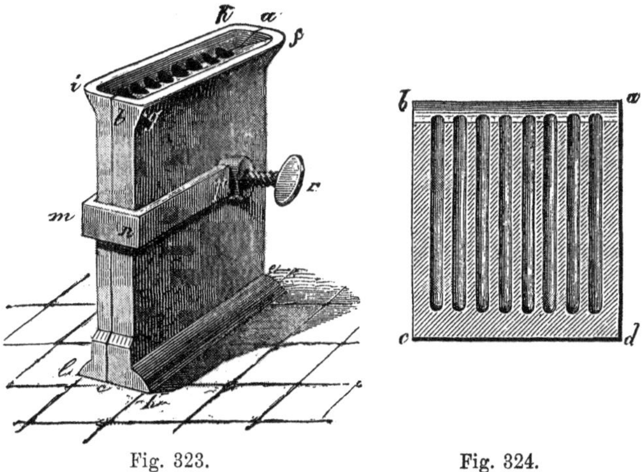

Fig. 323. Fig. 324.

Hydrate of potassa is deliquescent, a fragment of it exposed to the air in a porcelain capsule being soon converted into a sirupy liquid. It absorbs carbonic acid from the air at the same time, and the product remains liquid, because the neutral carbonate itself is deliquescent; but, at length, bicarbonate of potassa is formed and crystallizes.

§ 437. Potassa attacks and dissolves animal substances; it is used by surgeons as a cautery, known by the name of *caustic potassa*, (formerly *causticum commune acerrimum*.) For this purpose it is cast into small cylindrical sticks in a bronze or bell-metal mould, made of two pieces *abcdefgh* and *abcdikl*, which are separated to remove the cylinders of caustic. Fig. 323 represents these two halves united, and fig. 324 shows them when separated.

Carbonates of Potassa.

§ 438. Potassa forms three compounds with carbonic acid: a neutral carbonate KO,CO_2, a sesquicarbonate $KO,\frac{3}{2}CO_2$, and a bicarbonate $KO,2CO_2$.

Neutral Carbonate of Potassa KO,CO_2.—The neutral carbonate is usually extracted from the ashes of plants whose juices contain several soluble salts, and chiefly those formed by potassa and soda combined with organic acids. Since these acids are compounds of carbon, hydrogen, and oxygen, they are destroyed, when the plants are burned, and the potassa and soda remain in the ashes as carbonates. But the ashes of plants contain also several other salts, particularly the chlorides of potassium and sodium, the sulphates of potassa and soda, the carbonates and phosphates of lime and magnesia, and the silicate of alumina.* Plants growing on the seacoast contain principally soda, whilst those of more inland origin abound chiefly in potassa. From the ashes of the latter, carbonate of potassa is for the greater part procured.

Upon treating ashes with water, the soluble salts are dissolved, that is, the carbonates of potassa and soda, with the chlorides and sulphates. An insoluble residue remains, formed principally of silicate of alumina, carbonate, and phosphate of lime. The solution, commonly called *lye*, is evaporated to dryness, and the crude mass sold in commerce under the name of *crude potash*, and after resolution, evaporation, and calcination, is termed *pearlash*.

The weight of ashes furnished by the various plants varies with their nature and the character of the soil on which they grow. The herbaceous afford more than ligneous plants. The various parts of the same plant produce also very different proportions of ashes. The leaves furnish more than the branches, and the bark more than the trunk.

Crude potash can be manufactured to advantage on a large scale only in countries in which fuel is not expensive, and whose plants

* It is doubtful whether alumina is an essential constituent of plants, and its presence in ash is usually attributed to adhering soil. A considerable proportion of the insoluble silicate in ash is an alkaline silicate.—*J. C. B.*

are burned expressly to obtain their ashes for the purpose. Ashes are used in all countries, either as manure, or to form solutions of impure carbonate of potassa, or lye, for bleaching linen. Almost all the crude potash consumed in the arts comes from Russia and America; and since its composition is very variable, and its value depends chiefly on the proportion of alkaline carbonate it contains, it is important that the dealer should be able to ascertain readily, and exactly, the value of the article he is purchasing. The method of ascertaining this will be explained hereafter.

Crude potash contains 60 or 80 per cent. of the carbonates of potassa and soda, and the rest of it is made up of the sulphate and chloride, and of a small quantity of silicate of potassa. It may be purified by solution, and a carbonate of potassa obtained containing only 2 or 3 per cent. of foreign matter. To do this, crude potash or pearlash is treated with its weight of cold water, and allowed to digest for several days, shaking it from time to time. The greater part of the foreign salts, as the sulphate (and silicate) of potassa and chloride of sodium, being less soluble, remains as a residue. The liquid, being decanted, is subjected to rapid evaporation, until it begins to be clouded by a deposit of small crystals, when the fire is withdrawn and the liquid allowed to cool. During the crystallization, the liquid is stirred, in order that small crystals alone may form. The cold liquids are then poured through a strainer, which retains the crystals of carbonate of potassa. These crystals are washed with a small quantity of a solution of pure carbonate of potassa.

The purest carbonate of potassa is obtained by decomposing, by heat, in an iron crucible, purified bitartrate of potassa, called in commerce *cream of tartar.* A mixture of carbonate of potassa and carbon remains, which is sometimes used in the laboratory under the name of *black flux.* It is again treated with water, which dissolves carbonate of potassa and leaves carbon, and the liquid is evaporated to dryness. Carbonate of potassa is sometimes prepared by projecting gradually, in small quantities, into a cast-iron kettle heated to redness, a mixture of 1 part of bitartrate of potassa and 2 parts of nitrate of potassa. The carbon of the tartaric acid is entirely consumed by the oxygen of the nitric acid, and a white substance remains, which is called *white flux,* and is almost wholly composed of carbonate of potassa. But as it always contains a small quantity of nitrite of potassa, the defect is remedied by employing a smaller proportion of nitrate. The carbonate no longer contains nitrite, but always a little cyanide of potassium.

The most certain method of obtaining a pure carbonate consists in preparing the binoxalate of potassa, by combining pure hydrate of potassa with an excess of oxalic acid, and after purifying the salt by several crystallizations, it is decomposed, by heat, in a platinum crucible.

Carbonate of potassa is very soluble in water, yielding a strongly alkaline solution. A heated and highly concentrated solution of it deposits, on cooling, crystals containing 20 per cent. of water, with the formula KO,CO_2+2HO.

§ 439. *Bicarbonate of potassa* $KO,2CO_2$.—This salt is obtained by passing carbonic acid through a concentrated solution of the neutral carbonate, when bicarbonate of potassa is deposited in the form of crystals. In this operation, we use the carbonic acid which is copiously evolved during the fermentation of sweet wine or other sweet liquids; or, again, the carbonic acid which issues from the earth in various localities.*

Bicarbonate of potassa dissolves in 4 parts of cold water. Its crystals contain 9 per cent. of water, and their formula is $KO, 2CO_2+HO$. When heated, they lose their water and one-half of the carbonic acid, becoming the neutral carbonate.

Alkalimetry.

§ 440. The composition of the crude commercial potashes being very variable, and their value necessarily depending on the quantity of pure carbonate they contain, it is of importance to the purchaser to ascertain the value of the article offered for sale, expeditiously and accurately.

The examination is founded on the alkaline reaction exerted by carbonate of potassa on tincture of litmus, which becomes of a light yellowish-red, in presence of the smallest quantity of a powerful acid; whilst any quantity of carbonic acid will communicate to it only a purplish red.†

---

* Carbonic acid, generated from limestone by sulphuric acid, is frequently employed, as well as the gas arising from the combustion of coal.—*J. C. B.*

† Although the plan and numbers here given agree exactly with the original of Regnault, (except that we use the hydrogen scale, H=1,) the details of the method, as pursued in England and the United States, are believed to be superior. It is difficult to weigh pure carbonate of potassa, on account of its deliquescence, and hence, carbonate of soda is employed to determine the strength of the acid, and the alkalimeter is graduated altogether for testing soda. When potash is to be tested, its strength is calculated from the observed per cent. on the alkalimeter, by a proportion between the equivalents of soda and potassa, 31 : 47.2; or a larger quantity of the crude potash to be tested is weighed out agreeably to the same equivalent proportion. As we generally use 100 grs. of a crude soda, we should, in the latter case, weigh 152¼ grs. of a crude potash; so that the number of measures used from the alkalimeter will express, in both cases, the per cent. of real alkali.

As it is well to prepare a quantity of normal acid at once, the best method is to weigh out one more pounds of common oil of vitriol, distilled acid being wholly unnecessary, and dilute it with 10 parts of water, pouring the acid into the water, and allowing it to cool. It is poured into the alkalimeter to the division 0°. Having next weighed out 170.97 grs. of pure and semifused carbonate of soda, and dissolved it in a few ounces of pure water, the acid is poured in from the alkalimeter as rapidly as the effervescence will allow, until some 10 or 15 measures

The number of kilogrammes of real alkali contained in a quintal is called the *ponderal standard* of crude alkali. To determine this, a certain quantity of acid is taken, which is divided into 100 parts, and also a quantity of alkali, such, that if it were pure, it would exactly neutralize the 100 parts of acid. The number of parts of acid used for neutralizing an impure alkali expresses its ponderal standard, (or the per cent. of real alkali.)

Sulphuric is the acid selected. We assume as unity, 5 grammes of this acid at its maximum concentration, that is, in the state of a simple hydrate SO_3+HO, and dilute them with water until the mixture occupies 100 cubic demi-centimetres. In order to saturate 1 eq. of hydrated sulphuric acid, or 49, 1 eq. of pure anhydrous potassa $KO=47.2$ is required: consequently, to saturate the 100 hundredths of our aqueous mixture, or 5 grammes of monohydrated acid, we must take a quantity of pure anhydrous potassa, given by the proportion,

$$49 : 47.2 : : 5.000 : x;$$

$$\text{whence, } x=4^{\text{gm.}}.816.$$

If, therefore, the number of hundredths of acid saturated by $4^{\text{gm.}}.816$ of any potassa be required, this number will evidently represent the number of kilogrammes of pure potassa contained in 100 kilogrammes of crude potash, that is, the ponderal standard of alkali.

The preparation of the solution of sulphuric acid used for this purpose, and which is called the *normal acid*, requires peculiar care. The concentrated sulphuric acid of commerce is never at its maximum of concentration, and is frequently impure. That sold as *pure distilled acid*, may be considered as free from foreign

remain, when it is poured in drop by drop, up to exact neutralization, as described in the text. The number of measures used have exactly neutralized one hundred grains of real alkali, or oxide of sodium; so that if diluted with as many measures of water as remained unused, then the whole hundred measures would have neutralized the 170.97 gm. of carbonate, containing 100 gm. of alkali. The whole of the dilute acid is therefore measured, and diluted with x measures of water in the following proportion—measures used : meas. remaining : : meas. of all the acid : x. As a condensation takes place in mixing acid and water together, a fresh quantity of 170.97 gm. of pure carbonate of soda should be retested by 100 measures of the acid as just diluted, and as much more water added as there are measures unused. In testing carbonated alkali, containing the solution of litmus, the purplish-red tint is a good sign of approaching neutralization; but the character of the froth can also be relied on after a little experience, for the bubbles of froth break and subside rapidly at first, but towards the close are very persistent and finer. Instead of agitating the vessel E, it is better to stir the liquid with a rod, and towards the close to sprit down the solution spattered on the side, to avoid apparent loss of alkali. After putting a drop on the litmus paper, or touching the end of a small strip to the liquor, the paper should be suffered to dry, for the red color produced by carbonic acid is evanescent, and the paper may reassume a bluish tint, showing that the neutralization is not yet complete. A permanent red, after drying, indicates that the point of neutrality is passed.—*J. C. B.*

substances, but it contains a little more water than the monohydrated acid. For greater safety, the acid of commerce may be distilled in the apparatus described (§134), separating the first fourth which passes over, because it is too dilute, and retaining only the two intermediate fourths for preparing the normal acid. A small quantity of the sulphate of the protoxide of iron should be thrown into the retort, to destroy the nitrous products which the acid may contain.

100 grammes of this acid are accurately weighed in a small flask. Again, a vessel A (fig. 325), holding 1 litre of cold water when filled to the mark *a*, engraved on the neck, is half-filled with water, and the weighed acid poured slowly into it. The flask is rinsed several times with cold water, which is added each time to that in the vessel A; and lastly, this vessel is filled to the mark *a*, shaking it to render the liquid homogeneous. As the liquid is heated by the mixture of the acid and water, it must be allowed to fall to the surrounding temperature, and then exactly levelled to *a* by adding water with a pipette. The normal acid liquor thus prepared is preserved in a well-stoppered bottle.

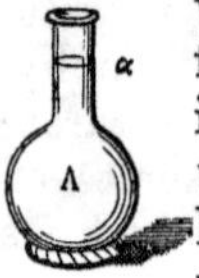

Fig. 325.

A blue solution of tincture of litmus, and paper coloured by it, are further required to test potash. Litmus is found, in commerce, in small cones or cubes, two or three of which are dissolved in a decilitre of boiling water, and filtered to procure the blue solution. To prepare litmus paper, a sheet of sized, fine letter-paper is painted on one side with the blue solution. The dried paper should be of a clear blue colour, but not too deep a blue, as might occur by too frequent application of the solution, because it would not be a sufficiently delicate tint.

In order to test a potash, several pieces are taken out from various parts of the samples, so as to obtain, as nearly as possible, an average specimen of the whole. These being broken up and intimately mixed, $48^{gm.}16$ are accurately weighed and dissolved in such a quantity of water that the volume of the solution shall be exactly a $\frac{1}{2}$ litre.

In order to make this solution conveniently, the $48^{gm.}.16$ of potash is put into a cylindrical vessel B (fig. 326). A test-glass C (fig. 327) being provided, containing a $\frac{1}{2}$ litre, as far as the circular mark *b*, is half-filled with water, which is then poured into the vessel B. To facilitate the solution of the potash, it is stirred with a glass rod. When the solution is complete, if a considerable insoluble residuum remains, the liquid is filtered through a small filter immediately over the test-glass C. The vessel B is washed several times with small quantities of water, which are passed through the same filter. Lastly, when the filter has been well washed, water is added by

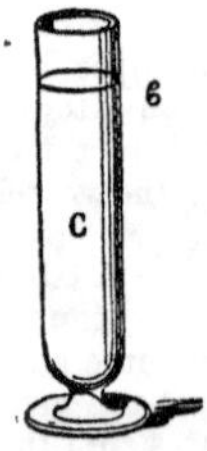

Fig. 326.

Fig. 327.

a pipette to the test-glass C, in order to level the liquid exactly to the mark δ. This glass should necessarily stand on a perfectly horizontal table, to insure exactness of the level.

The $48^{gm.}.16$ of crude potash being thus dissolved in a $\frac{1}{2}$ litre of liquid, if $\frac{1}{10}$ of this volume be taken, that is 50 cubic centimetres, we shall have a quantity of liquid containing $4^{gm.}.816$ of potassa. A pipette D (fig. 328) is used for this purpose, containing 50 centimetres of liquid, when filled to the mark γ. To fill it, its point a is dipped into the liquid, and the mouth being applied to the other end, a quantity of liquid is sucked up, so as to rise above the mark γ. The upper orifice being then closed with the forefinger, by afterwards opening it suddenly, the liquid is allowed to flow very gently, until it falls exactly to the level γ. The drop adhering to a is removed by touching it against the side of the test-glass C.

Fig. 328.

The liquid in the pipette is then poured into a cylindrical glass vessel E (fig. 329). When the pipette is empty, the last drop is expelled by blowing through it. The liquid is coloured with solution of litmus, until it has a decided blue colour, and then saturated with the normal acid.*

Fig. 329.

To measure the normal acid liquor, a peculiar glass apparatus is employed, called an *alkalimeter*, consisting of a glass tube *ab* (fig. 330), of the diameter of 12 or 14 millimetres, ($\frac{1}{2}$ inch,) to the lower part of which a much narrower tube *cd* has been attached, bent so as to be parallel to the former, and again bent at its upper extremity, so as to form a spout. The alkalimeter is divided into cubic demi-centimetres, and the divisions marked on the larger tube *ab*, but in inverse order, that is, the zero is put at the topmost division, and increases to 100 as it descends to the bottom. This arrangement of the scale is convenient, since it enables us to read immediately the number of divisions which have been poured out. A film of tallow or wax is put below the opening of the spout *d* to prevent the liquid from flowing down on the outside.

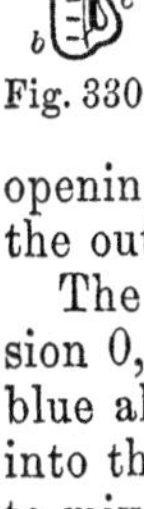

Fig. 330.

The alkalimeter, being filled with normal acid as far as the division 0, is held in the right hand, and the vessel E, containing the blue alkaline liquid, in the left. The acid liquor is poured slowly into the alkaline solution, constantly shaking the vessel E, so as to mix the liquids more rapidly. In order to observe any change of colour the more readily, a sheet of white paper is kept below the vessel E.

The first portions of acid poured in do not produce any sensible

* After blowing through the pipette, a little pure water should be drawn up into it, shaken around, and run out, to remove the last traces of the solution of potash.—*J. C. B.*

change in the liquid. When a quantity of acid has been added somewhat greater than one-half of that which would produce saturation, the liquid assumes a purplish-red tinge. Having reached this point, the acid must be added dropwise until a yellowish-red tinge is visible. The division at which the acid liquor is arrested is then read on the alkalimeter. Supposing this division to be 55, we conclude that 55 hundredths of acid have been poured in, and consequently, then the quintal contains 55 kilog. of pure potassa.

The first test should only be regarded as an approximation, because much greater precision can be attained by repeating the experiment. 50 cubic centimetres of the alkaline solution are again taken with the pipette D and poured into the jar E. We add immediately 50 or 52 measures of acid liquor, and, after having shaken the mixture, pour in the quantity of solution of litmus necessary to produce the proper colour. The normal acid is then added with great care, in order to determine the precise moment of saturation. The spout of the alkalimeter being small, the liquid can be easily dropped, and it will be found that nearly the same number of drops are required to form each measure of the alkalimeter. Let us suppose, for example, that 5 drops form a division: each division may be subdivided into fifths by counting the number of drops. The acid liquor is therefore dropped into the jar E, and after the addition of each drop the liquid is stirred with a glass rod, which is then drawn out and its wet extremity touched to a piece of litmus paper. The process is continued until the paper assumes a yellowish-red colour, (after drying,) when the number of measures and drops is noted.

Let us suppose that 53 measures and 3 drops have been poured out, that is $53+\frac{3}{5}$. This quantity of acid exceeds by a certain number of drops that absolutely necessary to effect saturation; because the first drops of acid, added in excess, do not immediately change the colour of the litmus, some time being required for the alteration. But as, after the addition of each drop, the liquid is applied to a strip of litmus paper after some time, all the strips on which the acid is in excess turn red, so that it is easy to find the number of drops in excess. Supposing that the last four strips have become red, it proves that 4 drops of acid liquor have been added in excess, and that these 4 drops, that is $\frac{4}{5}$ of a division, must be subtracted from the number first found. The true ponderal standard (per cent.) of the substance is therefore $52\frac{4}{5}$ or 52.8.

§ 441. If the potash to be tested were wholly caustic potassa, the colour would change immediately from blue to that of yellowish red, as soon as the acid predominated.

If the alkali be in the state of a simple carbonate, or if dissolved in a sufficient quantity of water, or lastly, if the liquid is constantly agitated, no carbonic acid is disengaged during the addition of the first half of the acid; because the carbonic acid which is set free combines with the undecomposed carbonate, transforming it into a bicarbonate, and the liquid until then preserves its blue colour. A new addition of acid changes the colour to a purplish red, because it decomposes a portion of the bicarbonate and disengages carbonic acid; and this colour continues until the bicarbonate is entirely decomposed and sulphuric acid predominates.

Lastly, if the alkali is wholly in the state of a bicarbonate, the first drops of acid added produce a purplish red, because they liberate carbonic acid.

§ 442. In the same way, the quantity of real alkali contained in a litre of a solution of potassa can be accurately determined. 50 cubic centimetres of the solution are taken with the pipette and saturated with the normal acid. Supposing that 42 measures of the alkalimeter have been used, then 50 cubic centimetres of the solution of potassa contain $4^{gm.}.816 \times 0.42 = 2^{gm.}02$ of alkaline matter, and consequently each litre contains $40^{gm.}.4$.

Nitrate of potassa.

§ 443. Nitrate of potassa, commonly known in commerce by the name of *nitre* or *saltpetre*, is found as a natural production. It may be obtained directly by combining nitric acid with potassa, or by decomposing the carbonate of potassa by the same acid. The liquid, when evaporated, deposits prismatic crystals, which generally present a grooved appearance, because they are formed by the agglomeration of many small crystals. As they contain no water, their formula is KO,NO_5.

Nitrate of potassa has a cool, slightly bitter taste; its density is 1.933. Subjected to the action of heat, it melts at about 662°, forming a mobile liquid, which congeals on cooling, with a vitreous appearance. It is decomposed at a higher temperature, evolving pure oxygen, while the nitrate KO,NO_5 is converted into a nitrite KO,NO_3. Heated still further, the nitrite itself is resolved into a mixture of oxygen and nitrogen gases, and a residue of caustic potassa KO; but this potassa always contains a certain proportion of peroxide of potassium KO_3. It cannot be perfectly decomposed either in glass or porcelain vessels, because the potassa acts powerfully on and soon destroys them.

The solubility of nitrate of potassa increases rapidly with the temperature:

100 parts of water	at	32°	dissolve	13.32	of nitrate of potassa,
"	"	64.4°	"	29.00	"
"	"	113°	"	74.60	"
"	"	206.6°	"	236.00	"

Hence, a hot saturated solution, on cooling, deposits the greater portion of the salt which had dissolved.

Nitrate of potassa is an energetic oxidizing agent. Thrown on ignited coals, it *fuses*, increasing the combustion of the coal at the point of contact. A mixture of it with sulphur, thrown into a heated crucible, produces a vivid combustion, with great evolution of light, and forms sulphate of potassa. On account of this property, it is frequently used in the laboratory to oxidize substances: thus, we have seen (§ 160), that selenium, heated with it, gives seleniate of potassa; and that arsenious acid, under the same circumstances, produces arseniate of potassa. Nitrate of potassa is also one of the components of gunpowder.

§ 444. We have said that nitre was found in nature. In many hot countries, principally in India and in Egypt, a copious saline efflorescence is observed on the surface of the earth after the rainy season. The earth is removed to a certain depth, and treated with water, which dissolves the soluble salts. The solution, being transferred to large reservoirs, where it soon evaporates by solar heat, deposits large crystals of nitrate of potassa. This is the salt known in commerce by the name of *crude nitre*. The mother waters are rejected; but as they contain a large quantity of the nitrates of lime and magnesia, they might still afford some nitre if they were mixed with salts of potassa.

A considerable quantity of nitre is likewise collected in certain natural caverns. In the Island of Ceylon, there are several caverns the walls of which are covered with nitrous efflorescence. The exterior layer of the rocks is annually picked off, and treated with water, which, on evaporation, affords nitrate of potassa.

§ 445. Saltpetre is also obtained artificially, by imitating the conditions which probably cause its production in nature. The manufacture consists in mixing nitrogenous animal matter with carbonates, generally the native carbonates of lime and magnesia, as finely divided as possible. When practicable, alkaline carbonates are added. The mixture, exposed to the air for some years, determines the formation of the nitrates, principally those of lime and potassa, which are afterward completely changed into nitrate of potassa by a suitable addition of the salts of potassa. These heaps of matter are called *artificial nitre-beds*.

The calcareous earths usually mixed with vegetable mould and manure are collected on a water-tight floor made of clay, and covered by a roof. From time to time, the mass is moistened with dung-water or urine, and frequently turned. Ashes, or even spent ashes, or disintegrated rocks containing potassa, such as decomposed feldspar, are often added to the heap, which is made in various shapes in different countries. One of the best forms is that of a wall, having one perpendicular side, and the opposite surface sloping by terraces, on each of which is placed a little canal, intended to contain the liquid with which they are to be watered. The vertical face is exposed to the wind which usually prevails in that part of the country, or by which evaporation is rendered most active. The liquids which moisten the earthy mass seek, from capillary attraction, this surface; and as evaporation is very rapid there, the waters deposit the substances they contain in solution, and the wall is soon covered by a nitrous efflorescence. When sufficient nitrous matter has collected on the wall, a layer of several inches thickness of the earth is removed, and lixiviated. The insoluble residue is added to the heap, and distributed over the terraces, so that the wall retains nearly the same shape. The process is repeated so long as may be deemed necessary.

Sometimes, the earths are previously prepared in stables, principally in sheep-stables. The floor, being made of impervious clay, is covered to the depth of nearly a foot with the calcareous earth to be nitrified, and the earth again by the ordinary litter of the animals. After remaining four months in the stable, the dung is removed, the earth completely turned, a new layer of earth of about eight inches thickness superimposed, and again fresh litter added. This process is again repeated in four months; and, at the end of the year, the earths are considered to be prepared.

The earths being then removed, are heaped to the height of about a yard, under a shed, and additional permeability given to the heap by the interposition of straw or small twigs. Lastly, they are turned, every month or two, with forks, and in about two years they are fit for lixiviation.

§ 446. Chemists are not yet agreed upon an explanation of the formation of native saltpetre. The majority admit that its formation is influenced by animal matters in a state of decomposition, as in artificial nitre-beds, and that the nitrogen is exclusively furnished by these matters. Others suppose that the nitrogen and oxygen of the air may combine directly, under certain circumstances, as, for instance, in the presence of porous substances and the carbonates of powerful bases; but hitherto no direct experiment has demonstrated this possibility. The latter hypothesis admits that the spontaneous decomposition of the animal matters produces carbonate of ammonia, which would dissolve in water, and there meet with oxygen and nitrogen, which water always dissolves when exposed to the air. Influenced by the carbonate of ammonia, which has a strong alkaline reaction, the oxygen and nitrogen would combine to form nitric acid, which would produce nitrate of ammonia. This nitrate reacting on the carbonates of lime and magnesia, nitrates of lime and magnesia would be formed, and carbonate of ammonia be regenerated, thus indefinitely producing nitrates. The double decomposition would be determined by the great volatility of the carbonate of ammonia (§ 387). Moreover, carbonate of ammonia might also generate nitrates in another way, by undergoing itself a slow combustion by the oxygen dissolved in the water, during which combustion its nitrogen would change into nitric acid. On the other hand, we know that rain-water always contains traces of nitrate of ammonia, which probably results from a combination of the gases by atmospheric electricity, that is, under circumstances analogous to those of the experiment described § 104, in which we have seen nitrogen and oxygen combining under the influence of the electric spark and forming nitric acid. It is not impossible that a portion of the native nitre may be produced by this combustion.*

§ 447. The lixiviation of nitrified substances requires skill and experience. For, on the one hand, we must endeavour to obtain as large a quantity of nitre as possible; and, on the other, use no more water than is essential, so as to require the least amount of evaporation, and to obtain the salt at the least cost. For this purpose, a systematic lixiviation is followed, the principles of which we shall rapidly run over.

Let us suppose that we have put into a vat 1 cubic metre of nitrified matter containing 40 kilogrammes of saltpetre, and that we have poured upon it 500 litres of water, the quantity of liquid necessary to saturate the mass completely, and more than sufficient to dissolve the soluble matter. After 12 hours, the water is allowed to run off by small holes in the bottom of the vat. About 250 litres are collected, the remainder being absorbed by the matter. We have therefore separated 250 litres of a liquid A containing 20 kilog. of saltpetre, and there remain in the earths 250 litres of water containing 20 kilog. of saltpetre. 250 litres of fresh water are added, which are drawn off in 12 hours. We thus collect 250 litres of liquid B containing 10 kilog. of saltpetre, and there remain 250 litres of water also containing 10 kilog. Another addition of 250 litres of water will afford 250 litres of liquid C containing 5 kilog. of saltpetre, and so on. Thus we have,

In the	1st	washing,	250	litres of liquid	A	containing	20	kilog.
"	2d	"	250	"	B	"	10	"
"	3d	"	250	"	C	"	5	"
"	4th	"	250	"	D	"	2.50	"
"	5th	"	250	"	E	"	1.25	"
"	6th	"	250	"	F	"	.63	"

Supposing that the washings are carried no further, there have been removed 39.37 kilog. of saltpetre, dissolved in 1500 litres of water. Had the 1750 litres of water been poured directly on the earths, 1500 litres of liquid would have been collected, containing only 34.3 kilog. of soluble matter, and 5.7 kilog. would have remained in the mass.

Upon pouring into a second vat, filled with fresh materials, the

* The experiments of Mulder on the formation of ammonia in vegetable mould, and of Kuhlmann on nitrification, have thrown some light upon the subject, but are not yet decisive as to the formation of nitre.—*J. C. B.*

liquids A and B from the first and second washings of the first vat, that is, 500 litres of water containing 30 kilog. of soluble matter, and allowing the water to run off in 12 hours, 250 litres of a liquid A′ are obtained containing 35 kilog. of saltpetre. This solution is sufficiently rich to be immediately evaporated. Since the earths retain an equal quantity of saltpetre, we pour upon them 250 litres of the liquid C containing 5 kilog. of saltpetre. We draw off in 12 hours 250 litres of a liquid B′ containing 20 kilog. of saltpetre, and consequently identical with the liquid A arising from the first washing of the first vat. If we now pour over the substance 250 litres of the liquid D containing 2.50 kilog. of saltpetre, we will obtain 250 litres of a liquid C′ containing 11.25 kilog. of saltpetre, and consequently somewhat richer than the liquid B of the first vat. The 250 litres of the liquid E containing 1.25 of soluble matter, having been poured in their turn on the earth, we draw off in 12 hours 250 litres of a liquid D′ containing 6.25 kilog. of saltpetre, and which resembles the liquid C of the first vat. Lastly, the 250 litres of the liquid F containing .63 of saltpetre, passed through the earths, give a quantity equal to a solution E′ containing 3.44 of saltpetre. In the last place, by passing pure water twice successively over the materials, we obtain a liquid F′ containing 1.72 kilog., and a second liquid G′ containing .86 kilog.

We operate with the liquids A′, B′, C′, D′, E′, F′, G′, precisely as has been described for the liquids A, B, C, D, E, F, G. They are passed over a new quantity of fresh materials in the first vat; and no liquid containing less than 35 kilog. of saltpetre in 250 litres should be evaporated.

§ 448. The lye of nitrified substances contains nitrate of potassa, but especially nitrates of lime and magnesia, and also chlorides of sodium and calcium. All the nitrates are to be converted into nitrate of potassa. To effect this, a suitable quantity of carbonate or sulphate of potassa is added to the lye, whereby carbonate or sulphate of lime is deposited; and when the liquids are clear, they are drawn off into evaporators. The lye is sometimes filtered through wood-ashes, which furnish carbonate and sulphate of potassa to decompose the nitrates of lime and magnesia, so that the clear liquor which passes through may be immediately evaporated.

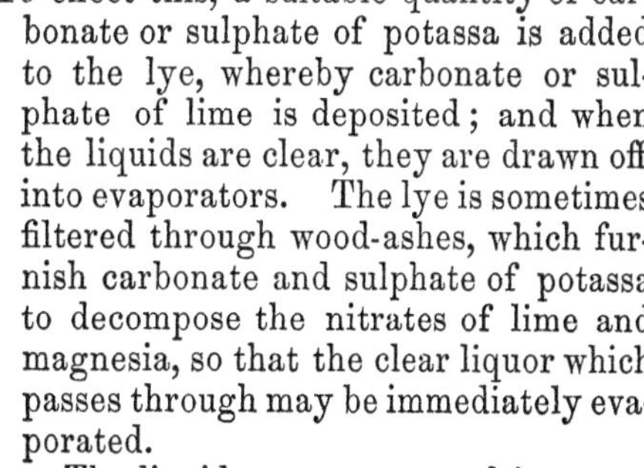

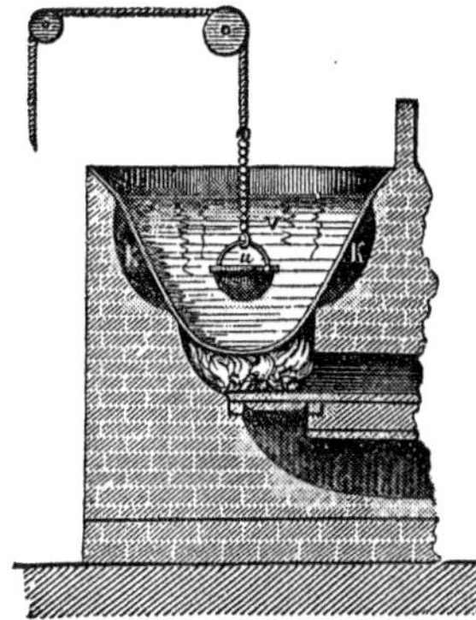

Fig. 331.

The liquids are evaporated in a copper kettle at the boiling point (fig. 331). As the water evaporates, an additional quantity of lye is added, which keeps the kettle always full. A great deal of froth is formed on the surface, which is skimmed off and put in baskets so arranged near the kettle that their drippings may fall back into it. Deposits of earthy matters also take place in the kettle, and are collected by an ingenious contrivance, in a smaller kettle suspended from a chain in the centre of the larger one. As the liquid ascends the sides of the kettle, when it becomes heated, and descends in the centre, and as, moreover, the liquid currents are more feeble in the centre, it follows that the earthy matters, being raised by the ascending currents along the sides, and carried by the descending currents toward the centre, will be deposited in the smaller kettle. The smaller one is removed from time to time, the earthy deposit in it removed, and the kettle replaced. The liquid soon becomes sufficiently concentrated to enable common salt to deposit, as it is scarcely more soluble when hot than cold. The smaller kettle is then removed, and the common marine salt deposited at the bottom of the larger one is withdrawn with a scoop. The liquid is known to be sufficiently concentrated, when a drop, thrown on a cold body, immediately crystallizes. It is then poured into large receivers and left to cool completely, when the greater part of the saltpetre is deposited in crystals. The mother waters, when they still contain a considerable quantity of nitrates, are mixed with the concentrated lye in the kettle, or else added to other strong lye.

§ 449. Manufacturers of saltpetre now find it more advantageous to first convert the calcareous and magnesian nitrates into nitrate of soda by means of sulphate of soda, and then, by chloride of potassium, to convert the nitrate of soda into nitrate of potassa.

They break the nitrified substances into pieces of the size of a filbert, by crushing them between grooved cast-iron cylinders, and then lixiviate them as described § 447. The waters of lixiviation are collected in a vat placed above the kettle; to which vat the sulphate of soda intended to decompose the calcareous nitrates has been added. The sulphate of soda is obtained either from the manufacture of nitric acid, where the nitrate of soda is decomposed by sulphuric acid, or from the salt-cake of the soda manufacture, in which sea-salt is decomposed by sulphuric acid. This sulphate of soda always contains an excess of sulphuric acid, which is neutralized by the addition of lime to the vat. A copious precipitate of sulphate of lime is formed, and allowed to fall to the bottom. The clear liquor is run into the kettle, and the mud left in the bottom of the vat is added to the nitrified mass and lixiviated with it.

The liquor being boiled briskly in the kettle, a great deal of froth is produced, which is removed as it forms; and when the solution is sufficiently concentrated, chloride of potassium, obtained from vareck, is added gradually, so as not to arrest ebullition, as its solution produces a great degree of cold. The liquid being still further concentrated, sea salt is soon deposited, which is removed and allowed to drain somewhere near the kettle.

When the solution has acquired a proper degree of concentration, it is allowed to rest for two hours, when it is run into the crystallizers, where the saltpetre crystallizes on cooling.

The salt thus obtained is called *crude saltpetre*, and contains about 15 or 25 per cent. of foreign matter, consisting principally of chlorides of sodium and potassium. These are separated by the process of *refining*.

§ 450. The refining of saltpetre is founded on its rapidly increasing solubility with the elevation of temperature, while the solubility of the chlorides of sodium and potassium is nearly uniform.

Six hundred litres of water and 1200 kilogrammes of crude saltpetre are introduced into a large copper boiler (fig. 332), which is heated gently to effect solution, and additional quantities of saltpetre successively thrown in until the amount introduced equals 3000 kilogrm. The solution is constantly agitated, and the froth removed. The water in the boiler can dissolve, when hot, 3000 kilog. of saltpetre; but as it cannot dissolve all the foreign salts, especially chloride of sodium, which is mixed with it, the greater portion of this salt remains at the bottom of the boiler, and may be withdrawn by means of rakes.

Fig. 332.

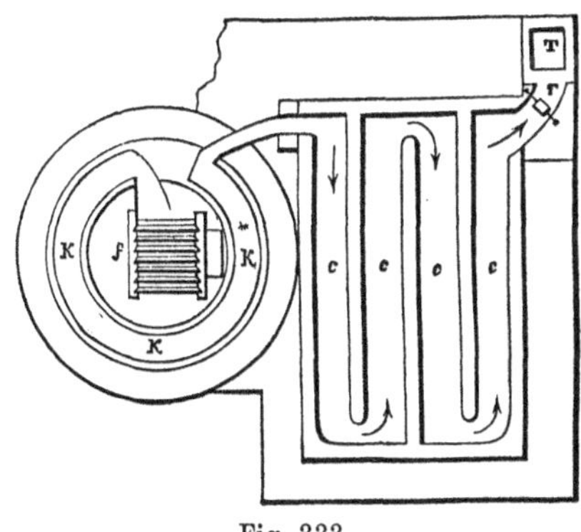

Fig. 333.

400 litres of water being then added gradually, so as not to cool the solution too rapidly, 1 kilog. of glue dissolved in hot water is poured in, and the whole well stirred. The glue, mixing with the liquid, seizes upon the organic matter which renders the solution viscous, coagulates, and rises to the surface in the form of froth. This is carefully removed, and after boiling for some time, the liquid be-

comes perfectly clear. The fire is then removed, and the solution allowed to cool to about 194°. The hot liquor is then carefully ladled out and carried to the crystallizer. During this operation, the liquor in the kettle should be agitated as little as possible, to avoid disturbing and raising the crystals of sea-salt deposited at the bottom.

The crystallizer is a large shallow vat, the bottom of which is formed by two inclined planes terminating in a trough in the middle. Fig. 334 represents a ground-plan of the vat, fig. 335 a transverse section of it.

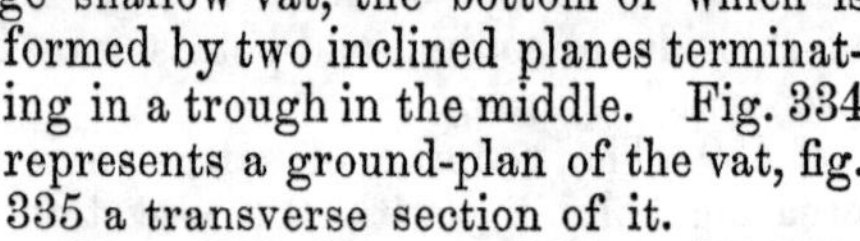

Fig. 334.

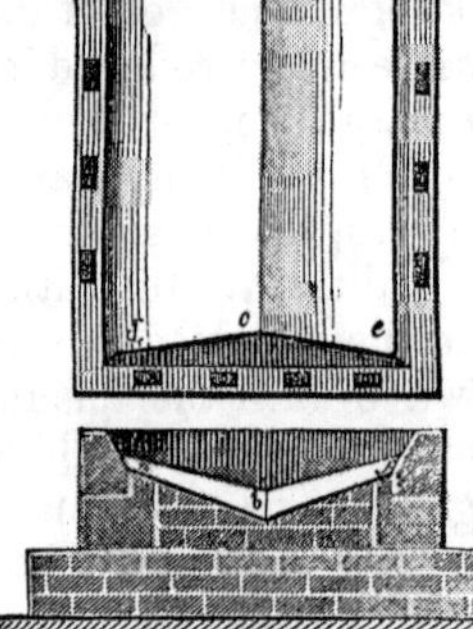

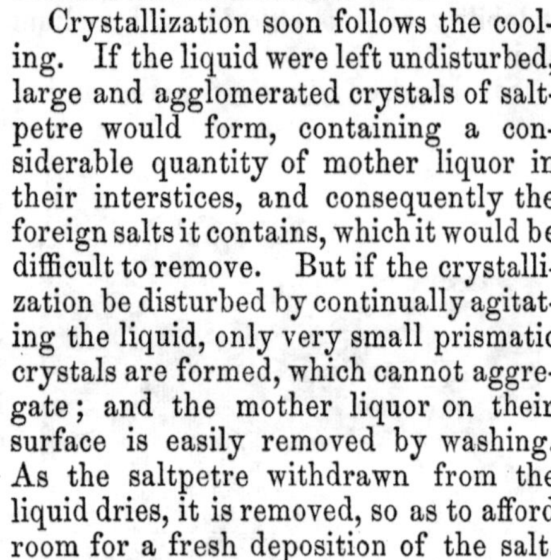

Fig. 335.

Crystallization soon follows the cooling. If the liquid were left undisturbed, large and agglomerated crystals of saltpetre would form, containing a considerable quantity of mother liquor in their interstices, and consequently the foreign salts it contains, which it would be difficult to remove. But if the crystallization be disturbed by continually agitating the liquid, only very small prismatic crystals are formed, which cannot aggregate; and the mother liquor on their surface is easily removed by washing. As the saltpetre withdrawn from the liquid dries, it is removed, so as to afford room for a fresh deposition of the salt. This process is continued until the temperature of the liquid scarcely exceeds that of the surrounding medium, when it is easily ladled out by raising one end of the crystallizer.

Fig. 336.

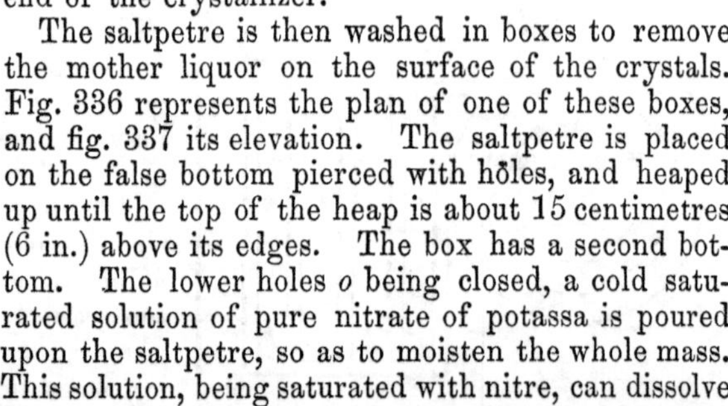

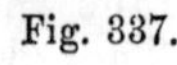

Fig. 337.

The saltpetre is then washed in boxes to remove the mother liquor on the surface of the crystals. Fig. 336 represents the plan of one of these boxes, and fig. 337 its elevation. The saltpetre is placed on the false bottom pierced with hōles, and heaped up until the top of the heap is about 15 centimetres (6 in.) above its edges. The box has a second bottom. The lower holes *o* being closed, a cold saturated solution of pure nitrate of potassa is poured upon the saltpetre, so as to moisten the whole mass. This solution, being saturated with nitre, can dissolve no more of it, but it can dissolve the chlorides. In a few hours the aperture *o* is opened and the liquid drawn off. After complete draining, the salt is washed with pure water, which is allowed to act for 2 hours, and then flows off saturated with nitrate of potassa, but still contains some traces of chlorides.

The saltpetre, being thus refined, is dried by placing it in the pans *ab* (fig. 332), which are arranged near the furnace in which the crude saltpetre is refined, and are heated by the waste heat of the furnace which circulates beneath through the flues *c*, *c*, *c* (figs. 332 and 333). The salt should be continually stirred during desiccation to prevent its agglomeration.

§ 451. *Analysis of Saltpetre.*—Since crude saltpetre, as delivered to the refiners, may present various degrees of purity, it should be previously analyzed, which may be performed in two different modes.

The first method, which has been in use for a long time, is founded on the fact that a solution of nitrate of potassa, saturated at a certain temperature, may be left in contact with an additional quantity of saltpetre at the same temperature, without sensibly dissolving any of it; while, under the same circumstances, it can dissolve sea-salt and many other soluble salts.*

400 grammes of pulverized crude saltpetre are accurately weighed in a beaker, and treated with a demilitre of water, saturated with pure nitre, at the surrounding temperature. After agitation for fifteen minutes with a glass rod, the liquid is poured upon a filter. 300 cubic centimetres of the same solution are then poured upon the salt, and allowed to act for ten minutes, with frequent shaking. The whole is then poured upon a filter, and the saltpetre detached as completely as possible from the sides of the beaker. The filter, being well drained, is removed, put on several thicknesses of bibulous paper, and the salt spread over the whole filter. When the bibulous paper has absorbed all the water it can, the salt is removed with a silver spatula and replaced in the beaker, taking care not to leave any of it on the filter, and is dried by heating the beaker in a sand-bath. It is then stirred with a glass rod until perfectly dry, when it is weighed in the beaker, and the loss it has suffered represents the weight of foreign matter mixed with the nitrate of potassa.

This process was, however, found to occasion a serious error, to the advantage of the refiner and the detriment of the manufacturer, so that it made the standard of saltpetre too low. This source of error is owing to the fact that a saturated solution of nitre does not dissolve a new quantity of the salt when brought in contact with pure nitre; but when it has dissolved a certain quantity of sea-salt, it has acquired the property of being able to dissolve an additional quantity of nitre (§ 371), and the quantity of it which it dissolves is in proportion to that of the sea-salt it contains. Thus, the more sea-salt there is in the saltpetre to be analyzed, the

* This is a simple example of the general law, that a saturated solution of one salt can dissolve a considerable quantity of another, and when saturated with these two, can still dissolve a portion of a third, fourth, and so on.—*J. C. B.*

greater will be our error as to its standard. It was therefore necessary to make direct experiments to appreciate this cause of error in the analyses, and make the proper correction in each case. 5, 10, 15, 20 per cent. of sea-salt have been successively dissolved in water saturated with saltpetre, and then the proportion of saltpetre dissolved under these different conditions has been sought. The result is seen in the following table:

Quantity of solution of Nitre used.	Sea-salt added.	Saltpetre dissolved by means of Sea-salt.	Saltpetre originally dissolved.	Total of Saltpetre dissolved.
gm.	gm.	gm.	gm.	gm.
100	5	0.746	21.63	22.376
100	10	1.267	21.63	22.897
100	15	1.658	21.63	23.288
100	20	1.827	21.63	23.457
100	25	2.583	21.63	24.213
100	26.85	3.220	21.63	24.850

The temperature at which the operation was conducted was 64.4°, but the results would be very different at a different temperature.

It will be seen from this table, that if a saltpetre is analyzed containing 20 per cent. of sea-salt, by treating 400 grammes of it with 400 cubic centimetres of water saturated with nitre, about 2 per cent. of nitre will be dissolved, and the standard of the saltpetre be lowered by about 2 hundredths. From the waste suffered by the crude saltpetre, we can calculate, with sufficient accuracy, the correction necessary to be made in the standard.

But this mode of correction is adapted only to the case in which the saltpetre contains sea-salt alone. Now, saltpetre frequently contains a considerable proportion of chloride of potassium, which is always the case when ashes, or potash residues from various chemical operations, have been added to the lye. The analysis is also inaccurate in this case, but the error is reversed and in favour of the manufacturer, but a loss to the refiner. When a solution of pure nitre is digested with chloride of potassium, this latter salt is dissolved, but a corresponding quantity of nitre is deposited from the liquid (§ 371). So that if a crude saltpetre is analyzed, containing much chloride of potassium, its standard will be too high, because the proportion of nitre which the saturated solution of nitre deposited by dissolving the chloride of potassium contained in the saltpetre, is reckoned as pure nitre.

The following table shows the errors which are made in the analysis of a crude saltpetre, composed of 70 parts of saltpetre and 30 of a mixture of various proportions of sea-salt and chloride of potassium:

Sea-salt.	Chloride of Potassium.	Nitre.	Waste.	Error of Test.
0	30	70	17.8	−12.2
10	20	70	23.6	− 6.4
20	10	70	28.1	− 1.9
30	0	70	36.85	+ 6.5

If, therefore, we were to analyze a crude saltpetre containing no sea-salt, but composed of 70 of pure nitre and 30 of chloride of potassium, the analysis would indicate 82.2 of pure nitre. If, on the contrary, it were composed of 70 of nitre and 30 of chloride of sodium, the analysis would indicate a richness of 63.5 of nitre. From this may be seen the defects of this mode of analysis, and the danger of trusting too entirely to it.

§ 452. The second and more certain method is founded on the principle, that if a mixture of nitrate of potassa and the chlorides be heated with charcoal, the nitrate is changed into a carbonate, with a strong alkaline reaction, while the chlorides remain unchanged, and preserve their neutrality with coloured infusions. Let us suppose that we have mixed with charcoal 5 grammes of crude saltpetre, and effected a reaction by means of heat. The product, being treated with water, the liquid is filtered, and sufficient water added to make the whole volume equal to 50 cubic centimetres. The alkalimetric analysis of this liquid is made (§ 440), and from the standard found, the quantity of pure nitre contained in the 5 grammes of saltpetre is easily calculated.

The performance of this experiment requires great care. If a mixture of saltpetre and charcoal were to be subjected immediately to the action of heat, the reaction would be so great that a portion of the substance might be thrown out of the crucible. It is necessary to add to the mixture 3 or 4 times its weight of some inert matter, which considerably weakens the reaction. It is generally executed in the following manner:—Having weighed exactly 20 grammes of crude saltpetre, it is mixed with 5 grammes of charcoal and about 80 grammes of sea-salt. The mixture is gradually projected into a crucible heated red-hot, when the reaction ensues quietly without any loss of substance. When all the mixture is in the crucible, it is allowed to cool, and then dissolved in water. The liquid is filtered, and sufficient water added to make the whole volume equal to 200 cubic centimetres. This liquid is subjected to alkalimetric analysis.

The analysis of crude nitre, however, done in this way, is liable to objection, if the nitre contains nitrate of soda, which would then be estimated as nitrate of potassa.

The analysis would likewise be inaccurate if the crude nitre contained sulphates; for they would be converted by deflagration with charcoal into sulphurets, which exert, like the carbonates, an alkaline reaction on litmus. This source of error would, however, be rendered apparent by the odour of sulphuretted hydrogen, which would be disengaged while saturating the liquid with the normal acid.

We shall hereafter detail another process, which affords a very exact analysis of the nitrates, particularly when they contain only a single nitrate, as the nitrate of potassa.

Sulphates of Potassa.

§ 453. Potassa and sulphuric acid form two crystallizable compounds. A solution of potassa or its carbonate, neutralized by sulphuric acid, gives, upon evaporation, anhydrous crystals of sulphate of potassa KO,SO_3. These crystals are characterized among soluble salts by their great hardness; they decrepitate when heated, and fuse at a red-heat without decomposition.

100 parts of water at	32°	dissolve	8.5	of sulphate of potassa.
"	50	"	10.2	"
"	77	"	12.7	"
"	122	"	16.8	"
"	212	"	25.3	"

From this it will be seen that the solubility of sulphate of potassa increases in proportion to the temperature; or, in other words, it is represented by a right line. (See plate at page 407.) It is insoluble in absolute alcohol.

If the preceding sulphate be dissolved in an excess of sulphuric acid, a liquid is obtained which gives, on evaporation, another crystallizable sulphate, termed the *bisulphate of potassa*, but is more correctly called a *double sulphate of potassa and water*. Its formula is KO,SO_3+HO,SO_3. Heated to 392°, it fuses without decomposition and without parting with its water. At a higher temperature, it gives off monohydrated sulphuric acid, and the simple sulphate KO,SO_3 remains. Concentrated alcohol also removes the sulphate of water, and leaves the sulphate KO,SO_3.

The double sulphate of potassa and water may also combine in other proportions. If to the simple sulphate of potassa KO,SO_3, a quantity of sulphuric acid be added equal to one-half of that which the salt contains, a crystallized salt is obtained with the formula $4(KO,SO_3)+HO,SO_3$. By treating this salt with a small quantity of water, it is decomposed into the simple sulphate, which remains, and the double sulphate KO,SO_3+HO,SO_3, which is dissolved:

$$4(KO,SO_3)+HO,SO_3=3(KO,SO_3)+(KO,SO_3+HO,SO_3).$$

Chlorate of Potassa.

§ 454. Chlorate of potassa KO,ClO_5 is an anhydrous salt, which crystallizes in the form of small spangles. They are, however, larger when crystallization is effected slowly. It is much more soluble in hot than in cold water:

100 parts of water	at 32°	dissolve	3.33	pts. of chlorate of potassa.
"	56°	"	5.60	"
"	27⅔°	"	6.03	"
"	76°	"	8.44	"
"	95°	"	12.05	"
"	120⅓°	"	18.96	"
"	166¾°	"	35.40	"
"	220⅔°	"	60.24	"

Its solubility, therefore, increases rapidly with the temperature, and is represented by a curve, the convexity of which is turned toward the axis of temperature. (See plate at page 407.) Alcohol does not appreciably dissolve it.

Chlorate of potassa fuses at about 750°. At a higher heat, it parts with its oxygen, and is ultimately reduced to chloride of potassium. It deflagrates vividly on ignited coals. It is one of the most active oxidizing agents, and forms explosive mixtures with the majority of combustible substances. Thus, an intimate mixture of it and sulphur produces a violent detonation when placed on an anvil and struck with a hammer. These mixtures should be made with great care and in small quantities, to avoid accidents.

The detonating mixtures formed of chlorate of potassa are much more powerful than the corresponding mixtures made with nitre. Gunpowder, much superior to that in ordinary use, has been made with chlorate of potassa; but it was excessively *explosive*, and burst the firearms in which it was used. Its preparation and preservation being very dangerous, its manufacture has been abandoned.

A mixture of chlorate of potassa and sulphur has also been used in the fabrication of percussion caps for guns, but *fulminating mercury* is now preferred.

If a drop of concentrated sulphuric acid be thrown on a mixture of sulphur and chlorate of potassa, the sulphur takes fire. Advantage was taken of this property for producing fire, and the process was generally followed until it was superseded by the phosphoric matches described § 208.

A paste was made with 30 parts of chlorate of potassa and gum-water, and 10 parts of flowers of sulphur added, with a little cinnabar to colour it. The end of each match, previously covered with sulphur, was dipped into the mixture, and allowed to dry. On the other hand, a small glass bottle was prepared, containing asbestus imbued with oil of vitriol. On plunging the match into this bottle, the paste of sulphur and chlorate became moistened by the sulphuric acid; it took fire, and the combustion extended to the sulphur, and thence to the match. The bottles were kept well stopped; otherwise the sulphuric acid would have attracted moisture from the air, and its action on the mixture of chlorate and sulphur would not have been sufficiently powerful to excite combustion.*

§455. Chlorate of potassa is obtained by acting with chlorine upon a concentrated solution of potassa, the reaction taking place between 6 equivs. of chlorine and 6 equivs. of potassa:

$$6KO+6Cl=5KCl+KO,ClO_5.$$

Chlorate of potassa, being much less soluble in cold water than chloride of potassium, separates in the form of crystalline spangles, while the chloride remains in solution. To prepare a large quantity of the chlorate, the apparatus is arranged in a peculiar way. As the tube, conveying chlorine into the solution of potassa, might be obstructed by crystals of chlorate, it is better to select a large tube, or better still, to arrange the apparatus as in fig. 338.

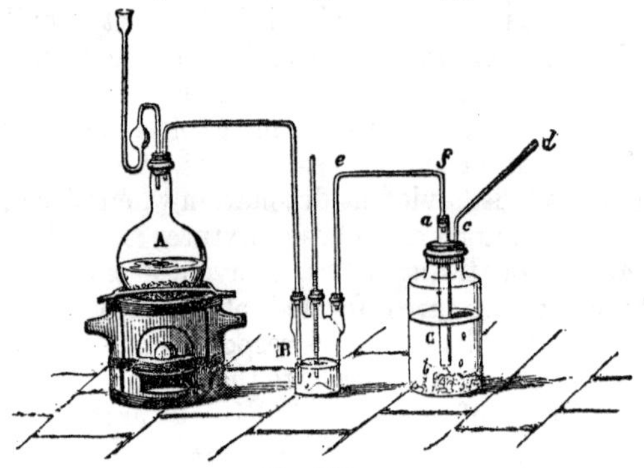

Fig. 338.

Chlorine gas is generated in the flask A, and washed in the bottle B, containing water. The bottle C contains the solution of potassa, or, preferably, of carbonate of potassa, as this salt is less expensive. Two tubes pass through the cork of the bottle C; a narrow one *cd*, which allows the escape of gas, and a straight tube *ab*, 15 mm. ($\frac{1}{2}$ inch) in diameter, open at both ends, and descending nearly to the bottom of the bottle. The tube *ef* of the washing-bottle, is inserted into the tube *ab* by means of a cork *a*. If the end *b* of the large tube be closed by the deposition of crystals, it can readily be cleared by a glass rod introduced through the opening *a*.

During the first stage of the operation, bicarbonate of potassa,

---

* The paste for these matches was generally made of a mixture of the above substances, with a quantity of sugar. They were superseded by the lucifer match, which was a flat splint of wood tipped by a mixture of chlorate, sulphur, and gum, and was drawn rapidly between sand-paper to inflame it. These again gave place to the locofoco or phosphoric match.—*J. C. B.*

chloride of potassium, and hypochlorite of potassa are formed, and very little chlorate. The greater part of the chloride being deposited in crystals, it is better, at this period, to interrupt the process, in order to allow as much as possible of the chloride to deposit. The supernatant liquid is decanted, and again subjected to the action of the chlorine until it is supersaturated, when a crystalline deposit of chlorate is formed, which is more copious if the liquid be allowed to cool completely. The mother liquor affords, by evaporation, an additional quantity of chlorate. The chlorate thus obtained always contains some chloride, to remove which it is first treated with a small quantity of cold water, which dissolves the greater part of the chloride, and the remaining crystals are dissolved in boiling water. The liquid, on cooling, deposits chlorate of potassa nearly pure.

Hypochlorite of Potassa.

§456. By passing chlorine through a cold and dilute solution of carbonate of potassa, a liquid is obtained which contains chloride of potassium and hypochlorite of potassa.

$$2KO+2Cl=KCl+KO,ClO.$$

This solution destroys vegetable colours rapidly, and is therefore used in bleaching; but, on a large scale, the cheaper hypochlorite of lime is preferred. In commerce, this bleaching liquid is called *Javelle water*, because it was first prepared at Javelle, near Paris.*

Oxalates of Potassa.

§457. Oxalic acid forms three compounds with potassa. By neutralizing a solution of potassa with oxalic acid, a solution is obtained which crystallizes on evaporation, in the state of a *neutral oxalate*, with the formula KO,C_2O_3+HO. It is soluble in 3 parts of cold water.

If oxalic acid be added to a solution of the neutral oxalate, a second crystallizable oxalate is obtained, the *binoxalate*, with the formula KO,C_2O_3+HO,C_2O_3+2HO. It may be regarded as a double oxalate, composed of the neutral oxalate of potassa and monohydrated oxalic acid. It requires 6 parts of boiling and 40 parts of cold water for its solution, so that it is easily separated from the neutral oxalate by crystallization. The binoxalate exists in the juice of many plants, and the acidity of sorrel is chiefly due to it. A large quantity is extracted from these juices, and is commercially known as *salt of sorrel.*

If to the binoxalate of potassa a quantity of oxalic acid be added

* It is usually prepared from carbonate of soda in England and the U. S., and termed *bleaching soda.—J. C. B.*

equal to that which it already contains, and the whole be dissolved in a small quantity of boiling water, there is deposited, on cooling, a *quadroxalate* with the formula $KO,4C_2O_3+7HO$. It should probably be regarded as a double oxalate, formed by the combination of 1 equiv. of the simple oxalate KO,C_2O_3 and 3 equivs. of monohydrated oxalic acid HO,C_2O_3, and its formula should be written

$$KO,C_2O_3+3(HO,C_2O_3)+4HO.$$

COMPOUNDS OF POTASSIUM AND SULPHUR.

§458. Many compounds of sulphur and potassium are known, of which chemists admit five, viz:

Monosulphide of potassium KS, corresponding to the protoxide KO,
Bisulphide " KS_2,
Trisulphide " KS_3, corresponding to the peroxide KO_3,
Quadrisulphide " KS_4,
Pentasulphide " KS_5.

The *monosulphide* is obtained by heating in a crucible a mixture of sulphate of potassa and charcoal:

$$KO,SO_3+4C=KS+4CO.$$

The sulphide fuses into a reddish mass. If a mixture of 2 parts of sulphate of potassa and 1 part of lampblack be heated, a very divided sulphide is obtained, the particles of which cannot unite together, on account of the particles of carbon with which they are intimately mixed. This sulphide is so inflammable, that it takes fire on being projected into the air, and is hence called *pyrophorus.*

The monosulphide, as prepared above, is never pure, but always contains a small quantity of polysulphide, which is readily detected by pouring into its solution an excess of acid, when a slight deposit of sulphur always ensues: it would not occur if the solution contained only monosulphide (§ 394).

The best mode of preparing the monosulphide consists in dividing a solution of potassa into two equal parts, saturating one of them with sulphuretted hydrogen, and then mixing it with the other, which is in the state of caustic potassa. The solution of potassa, saturated with sulphydric acid, is converted into a sulpho-salt, the sulphydrate of monosulphide of potassium KS,HS. When this salt is mixed with a quantity of potassa equal to that which produced it, it gives a simple monosulphide:

$$KS,HS+KO,HO=2KS+2HO.$$

By evaporating the liquid, the monosulphide is deposited as a colourless, crystalline mass.

The other sulphides are readily prepared from the monosulphide by heating 1 equiv. of it with 1, 2, 3, or 4 equivs. of sulphur. The pentasulphide KS is most easily obtained, it being sufficient to heat the monosulphide with an excess of sulphur, and raise the temperature so high that the sulphur, which cannot enter into combination, is volatilized. The temperature should not, however, be raised to bright redness, for the pentasulphide would then give off a portion of its sulphur, and pass into the state of trisulphide.

Pentasulphide is produced under many other circumstances. If a mixture of carbonate of potassa and sulphur be heated, the reaction begins at the fusing point of sulphur, and carbonic acid is disengaged. If the sulphur be in excess, and the temperature be not elevated above 480°, pentasulphide of potassium and hyposulphite of potassa are formed, and remain mixed with the excess of sulphur:

$$3KO+12S=2KS_5+KO,S_2O_2.$$

But, if the mixture be heated to redness, the hyposulphite is destroyed, and the excess of sulphur distils over, so that the pentasulphide of potassium and sulphate of potassa are obtained. In fact, at a red-heat, the hyposulphite is converted into pentasulphide and sulphate:

$$12(KO,S_2O_2)=9(KO,SO_3)+3KS_5.$$

Pentasulphide may be separated from sulphate by treating the mixture with alcohol, which dissolves only the sulphide.

If charcoal be added to the mixture of carbonate of potassa and sulphur, at a dull red-heat, pentasulphide of potassium alone is formed.

This compound may also be obtained in the humid way, by boiling a solution of caustic potassa with an excess of sulphur. A large proportion of the sulphur is dissolved, and a liquid of a deep orange-yellow colour is formed, containing pentasulphide and hyposulphite.

The pentasulphide obtained by any of these processes is called *liver of sulphur*, and is used in cutaneous diseases.

SULPHOSALTS FORMED BY THE MONOSULPHIDE OF POTASSIUM.

§ 459. Monosulphide of potassium combines with a great number of electronegative sulphides, with which it forms true salts; but the majority of them have not yet been studied with sufficient care. The most important are the sulfhydrate and sulphocarbonate of sulphide of potassium.

*Sulfhydrate of potassium** is obtained by passing, to saturation,

* As we say, in English, arseniate of iron, meaning thereby oxyarseniate of oxide of iron, so we may say, for brevity, sulpharseniate of iron, instead of the long name sulpharseniate of sulphide of iron. In like manner, we prefer the abbreviated expression sulfhydrate of potassium, for sulfhydrate of sulphide of potassium.—*J. C. B.*

a current of sulfhydric acid through a solution of potassa. The concentrated liquid deposits crystals, of which the formula is KS+HS or KS,HS. It will be seen to correspond exactly to the hydrate of potassa KO+HO, in which an equivalent quantity of oxygen takes the place of sulphur.

The *sulphocarbonate of potassium* is obtained by pouring bisulphide of carbon into an alcoholic solution of monosulphide of potassium. An orange-coloured crystalline deposit is formed, the sulphocarbonate of sulphide of potassium KS,CS_2, which may be redissolved in water or boiling alcohol and crystallized.

COMPOUND OF POTASSIUM AND CHLORINE.

§ 460. Only one compound of potassium and chlorine is known, and is obtained by neutralizing a solution of potassa or carbonate of potassa with chlorohydric acid. The liquid on evaporation deposits cubic anhydrous crystals of chloride of potassium, KCl. The density of this chloride is about 1.84; it fuses at a red-heat, without decomposition, and, at a higher temperature, gives off a considerable quantity of vapour.

In France, chloride of potassium is extracted from varec, derived from certain plants growing on the rocks covered by the waters of the ocean. After being gathered on the shore, where they are thrown by the waves, they are dried, and reduced to ashes in small pits made in the ground. A half-melted ash remains, which is termed *varec-soda*. It is lixiviated hot, and the various salts it contains extracted by successive crystallizations. It generally furnishes 30 per cent. of chloride of potassium.

Chloride of potassium is obtained, as a secondary product, in many of the arts. A considerable quantity is formed in refining crude potash furnished by the lixiviation of ashes. It is also extracted from the mother liquor remaining from the refining of nitre. We have seen (§ 455) that it is obtained in the manufacture of chlorate of potassa. Lastly, the ashes of the leaves and stems of tobacco contain a considerable quantity of it. It is a valuable salt, because it is readily converted into other salts of potassa, by double decomposition. It may be used to convert the nitrate of lime into nitrate of potassa, in the extraction of nitre from nitrified substances. It is also used in the preparation of alum.

As chloride of potassium produces a considerable depression of temperature by solution in water, advantage is taken of this property, as will be shown hereafter, to ascertain the proportions of chlorides of potassium and sodium contained in a mixture of the two salts.

COMPOUND OF POTASSIUM AND IODINE.

§ 461. *Iodide of potassium* is obtained by dissolving iodine in a concentrated solution of potassa until the liquid is coloured by an excess of iodine. A crystalline deposit of iodate of potassa is formed, and the liquid contains, at the same time, iodide of potassium and some iodate. If the iodide only is to be prepared, the liquid is evaporated to dryness, and the residue calcined in a platinum crucible. The iodate is decomposed, and nothing remains but the iodide, which is redissolved in water and crystallized. Iodide of potassium forms anhydrous cubic crystals.

A considerable quantity of iodide of potassium may be extracted from the mother waters of varec by crystallization, when they have deposited chlorides of potassium and sodium, as well as the sulphates which they hold in solution.

COMPOUND OF POTASSIUM AND CYANOGEN.

§ 462. *Cyanide of potassium* is most readily obtained by decomposing, at a red-heat, the double cyanide of potassium and iron $2KCy+FeCy$, commonly called *prussiate of potash.* The cyanide of iron alone decomposes, forming an insoluble compound of iron and carbon. The residue, treated with water, yields cyanide of potassium, which is crystallized by evaporation in anhydrous cubes. The manufacture of the impure cyanide of potassium, from which the double cyanide of iron and potassium is made, will be described under the compounds of iron.

DISTINCTIVE CHARACTERS OF THE SALTS OF POTASSA.

§ 463. Alkaline salts are distinguished from all other metallic salts, by affording no precipitate with a solution of alkaline carbonates.

The salts of potassa are recognised by the following properties:

1. By their physical properties, chiefly by those of the sulphate of potassa, an anhydrous, easily crystallizable salt, having a certain degree of hardness.

2. By forming with the sulphate of alumina a double salt, alum, which crystallizes in regular octahedrons. It is sufficient to pour into a concentrated solution of a salt of potassa, a concentrated solution of sulphate of alumina, and shake the liquid, to have a precipitate of alum, composed of small regular octahedrons, easily recognised by the microscope.

3. By forming with tartaric acid a bitartrate of potassa, slightly soluble in water, so that if a solution of tartaric acid be poured in excess into a slightly concentrated solution of a salt of potassa, a precipitate is formed.

4. By affording, with the bichloride of platinum, a yellow precipitate of the double chloride of potassium and platinum, when the solution is not very dilute; and which is more copious if a certain quantity of alcohol be added to the solution. The precipitate

of this double salt is destroyed by a red-heat; bichloride of platinum being decomposed and metallic platinum remaining, and the chloride of potassium being set free. By treating the residue with water, chloride of potassium alone is dissolved.

5. The salts of potassa give, with a solution of silicofluohydric acid, a translucent, gelatinous precipitate of the double fluoride of potassium and silicium, at first scarcely visible in the liquid, but depositing, after some time, in the form of a colourless, nearly transparent jelly.

SODIUM.

Equivalent = 23.

§ 464. Sodium exists, in the state of silicate of soda, in certain minerals constituting primary rocks. Combined with chlorine, it forms chloride of sodium, or sea-salt, which is in solution in sea-water, and forms, in many countries, considerable masses among strata of the trias group. Plants growing on the borders of the ocean absorb a considerable quantity of the salts of soda, which are found in their ashes.

Sodium closely resembles potassium in its physical properties. It is brittle at a low temperature, and then presents a crystalline fracture; at the ordinary temperatures of 60° or 68°, it is so soft as to be easily cut with a knife; about 140°, it may be moulded like wax, and at about 194° becomes liquid. It boils at a red-heat, and distils at a lower temperature than potassium.

Sodium, when freshly cut, has a brilliant metallic lustre resembling silver; but the brilliancy is of short duration in the air, as the metal rapidly combines with oxygen. It should therefore be preserved in naphtha. Its density is greater than that of potassium, being about 0.97 at ordinary temperatures.

Sodium decomposes water at the lowest temperatures. A piece of it thrown on water, fuses into a brilliant globule, from the heat disengaged by its oxidation, and runs over the surface of the liquid, but without the inflammation exhibited by potassium. The gas, however, may be inflamed by keeping the globule stationary on the surface of the liquid, whereby there is less loss of heat, and the temperature rises sufficiently high to inflame the hydrogen. Combustion likewise ensues if the metal be thrown on water thickened by gum or starch. The liquid becomes strongly alkaline from the hydrate of protoxide of sodium or *soda*, which is dissolved.

§ 465. Sodium is obtained by the same processes as potassium. It was first procured, in small quantities, by the decomposition of soda by the voltaic pile (§ 427), and subsequently by decomposing the hydrate of soda by incandescent iron (§ 428). It is now prepared by decomposing carbonate of soda by charcoal at a high temperature, in a wrought-iron vessel, in the same manner as prescribed for potassium (§ 429). To obtain an intimate mixture of carbonate of soda and charcoal, a given amount of pure carbonate of soda is dissolved in the smallest quantity of hot water possible, and about one-third as much powdered charcoal added to the liquid. A homogeneous paste is made, which is completely dried, and a certain quantity of charcoal, in small pieces, is added, to render the mass more porous. This mixture is placed in the iron bottle. The preparation of sodium is easier than that of potassium, in consequence of the lower temperature at which it distils.

COMPOUNDS OF SODIUM AND OXYGEN.

§ 466. Sodium forms two compounds with oxygen, which resemble those of potassium, and are prepared in the same manner.

Sodium heated in dry oxygen burns, and is converted into a peroxide NaO_3. When the peroxide is heated with twice as much sodium as it already contains, it gives the anhydrous protoxide of sodium. When sodium is oxidized by decomposing water, the protoxide is still formed, but it combines immediately with the water, producing a hydrate which cannot be decomposed by heat.

The composition of protoxide of sodium is deduced from the analysis of chloride of sodium, like that of protoxide of potassium from its chloride (§ 435). It has been found to contain

Sodium	74.19
Oxygen	25.81
	100.00

The equivalent of sodium is then given by the proportion:

$$25.81 : 74.19 : : 8 : x; \text{ whence } x=23.$$

SALTS FORMED BY THE PROTOXIDE OF SODIUM OR SODA.

§ 467. The protoxide is the only oxide of sodium which plays the part of a salifiable base, and affords a great number of salts, of the highest importance.

Hydrate of soda.

§ 468. This compound is formed when sodium is oxidized by contact with water. It is prepared in the laboratory by decomposing carbonate of soda in solution by hydrate of lime, precisely according to the process for preparing the hydrate of potassa (§ 432), and demanding like precautions. To decompose

1 eq. of dry carbonate of soda	53
1 " of anhydrous lime	28

is required; but in order to make the reaction complete and rapid, it is better to use twice as much lime, so that nearly equal weights of carbonate of soda and lime are employed. The caustic solution, separated from the sediment by decantation, is rapidly evaporated to dryness, and the fused *caustic soda* poured upon a copper plate, where it solidifies on cooling. It may be purified by dissolving it in alcohol, as was done with potassa (§ 433).

Hydrate of soda resembles perfectly, in appearance, hydrate of potassa, and, like the latter, contains 1 equiv. of water:

1 eq. of	protoxide of sodium.........	31	......	77.5
1 "	water..........................	9	......	22.5
1 "	hydrate of soda..............	40	......	100.0

It does not part with its water at any temperature, and distils, without change, at a strong red-heat. It may be used for the same purposes as caustic potassa, and is preferable to the latter, being cheaper and more readily obtained in a state of purity; because very pure carbonate of soda is found in commerce.

A solution of hydrate of soda, concentrated when hot, deposits, on cooling, crystals more hydrated, but their exact composition has not yet been ascertained. The solid hydrate, exposed to the air, soon deliquesces by combining with the water of the atmosphere; but if the sirupy liquid be left indefinitely exposed, crystals of carbonate of soda form, presenting an appearance of efflorescence. Hydrate of potassa does not exhibit similar phenomena, because its carbonate is deliquescent.

Sulphate of Soda.

§ 469. Soda and sulphuric acid combine in several proportions; the most important compounds being the neutral sulphate and the bisulphate.

Neutral sulphate of soda was formerly called *Glauber's salt*, and is found, in commerce, in large crystals, containing more than one-half of their weight of water, and with the formula NaO,SO_3+10HO.

1 eq. of	anhydrous sulphate of soda	71	......	44.1
10 "	water..........................	90	......	55.9
1 "	crystallized sulphate of soda	161	......	100.0

The crystallized salt fuses in its own water of crystallization, at a slightly elevated temperature. If the heat be continued, a portion of the water is driven off in vapour, and a crystallized deposit is formed of anhydrous sulphate of soda. The same anhydrous sulphate is deposited when the aqueous solutions are crystallized, at a temperature above 91½°. The sulphate with 10 equivs. of water, is only formed when crystallization takes place at a temperature below 68°. It effloresces in the air, and its crystals soon fall to powder. If the crystallization takes place between 68° and 86°, there is still formed a hydrated sulphate, which contains, however, less water than the preceding. The crystals of this hydrate are unalterable in the air.

The crystals of anhydrous sulphate likewise fall to powder in the air, but this efflorescence is due to an opposite cause from that of the sulphate with 10 equivs. of water, and is owing to the fact that the anhydrous sulphate takes water from the atmosphere, and disaggregates by changing into the second hydrate.

The solubility of this salt presents a remarkable anomaly, of which we have already spoken (§ 369). Below 32° its solubility is but feeble, for 100 parts of water at 32° only dissolve 5; but it increases rapidly with the temperature to 91.4, which is its maximum. 100 parts of water then dissolve 322 parts of the sulphate with 10 equivs. of water. Its solubility after this diminishes with the temperature. We have graphically represented, on the plate annexed to page 407, the curve of solubility of the sulphate, supposed to be *anhydrous*. We have also described (§ 363) a remarkable peculiarity in the crystallization of this salt.

Sulphate of soda exists in small quantities in the waters of the ocean and of many saline springs; and a large quantity may be extracted from the mother liquors after making salt, by merely reducing them to a very low temperature, in order to diminish as much as possible the solubility of the sulphate of soda. Large quantities are thus collected in the vicinity of Montpellier, during winter, from the mother waters of the salines. We shall hereafter treat of this manufacture.

§ 470. The greater portion of the sulphate of soda consumed in France is prepared by decomposing sea-salt by sulphuric acid. This process was explained in § 184, where chlorohydric acid is obtained at the same time. In localities where this acid is not sold, the decomposition is effected in a reverberatory furnace; but as the acid fumes cannot be allowed to escape into the air, to the injury of the surrounding vegetation, the manufacturers are obliged to condense them by passing the gas from the furnace through brick flues, in which water flows constantly, and which communicate with a chimney the draught of which is increased by a special fire. The acid waters are carried off by wells, as much as practicable.

§ 471. Sulphate of soda may be fused at a red-heat, without decomposition. By adding to a solution of it a quantity of sulphuric acid equal to that which it already contains, an acid liquid is obtained, which gives, after proper evaporation, crystals of the *bisulphate of soda*, with the formula $NaO,2SO_3+3HO$. The formula may also be written NaO,SO_3+HO,SO_3+2HO; in which case it is regarded as a double sulphate of soda and water. This salt, heated with caution, first fuses in its crystal water, and then readily parts with the two equivalents; but if the heat be continued, its third equivalent of water may be driven off, and an anhydrous salt obtained which is a true *bisulphate*. The anhydrous bisulphate, heated in a retort, gives off one-half of its acid in the state of anhydrous sulphuric acid (§ 138).

By adding to the solution of the neutral sulphate smaller quantities of sulphuric acid, another double sulphate of soda and water may be obtained, with the formula

$$3(NaO,SO_3)+HO,SO_3+2HO.$$

Carbonates of Soda.

§ 472. *Neutral carbonate of soda* is a salt of vast importance, on account of its uses in the arts, and may be prepared in various ways. For a long time it was only obtained from the lixiviation of the ashes arising from the combustion of plants growing on the shores of the sea. Plants growing inland afford ashes highly charged with the salts of potassa, while marine plants contain principally salts of soda. The various marine plants furnish very different proportions of soda; those which are richest being the *salsola soda* and the *salicornia europœa.* The *sea-wrack*, or varec, contains but little carbonate of soda, but a considerable quantity of sulphate and chloride. Spain formerly furnished the greater part of the carbonate used in Europe, and it was called *Alicant*, or *Malaga soda*, or barilla.* A certain quantity was also collected on the shores of the Mediterranean in France, and called *Narbonne soda.* During the wars of the Revolution and the Empire, as the supply of Spanish soda was very limited, it rose to a very high price. Chemists, encouraged by the government, made many attempts to manufacture the article, from materials indigenous to the country. After many experiments, which answered more or less perfectly, one was found which furnished soda in any quantity and at a reasonable price. This process, still in use, is called the *process of Leblanc*, from the French physician who discovered it.

The process of Leblanc consists first in converting chloride of sodium into sulphate of soda by sulphuric acid; then in decomposing the sulphate by heat, with a mixture of carbonate of lime and charcoal. Carbonate of soda and oxysulphide of calcium are the result, and are easily separated.

If a mixture of 1 equiv. of sulphate of soda and 1 equiv. of carbonate of lime be fused together, there is a double decomposition, sulphate of lime and carbonate of soda being formed; but, if it be now treated with water, the greater part of the carbonate of soda passes again into the state of sulphate. This inverse reaction, effected by water, is owing to the fact that carbonate of lime is much more insoluble than the sulphate. If 4 equivs. of charcoal be added to the mixture of 1 equiv. of sulphate of lime, and 1 equiv. of carbonate of lime, the sulphate of lime is changed into a sulphide by the action of heat; and, as this sulphide is but slightly soluble in water, we may hope to separate carbonate of soda by water. The separation is, however, imperfect, for a certain quantity of carbonate of lime is always formed, and sulphide of sodium dissolves at the same time with carbonate of soda. But if we heat together

* It was also largely prepared on the coast of Scotland, and termed *kelp.*

2 eq. of	sulphate of soda	142
3 "	carbonate of lime	150
9 "	carbon	54
		346

the reaction takes place in the following manner:—

$$2(NaO,SO_3)+3(CaO,CO_2)+9C=2(NaO,CO_2)+2(CaS,CaO)+10CO,$$

the 2 equivs. of sulphide of calcium combining with 1 equiv. of lime to form an oxysulphide of calcium 2CaS,CaO, perfectly insoluble in water. Water dissolves out from this substance only the carbonate of soda.

The best proportions which have been found by experience, and which do not differ essentially from those found by theory, are

1000 of anhydrous sulphate of soda,
1040 of carbonate of lime,
530 of charcoal.

The reaction takes place on the brick hearth of a reverberatory furnace, where the mixture is heated to the point of fusion and constantly stirred. Carbonic oxide gas is evolved, and burns with small jets of bluish flame. When the evolution of this gas has ceased, the workman withdraws a small quantity of the mass from the furnace, in order to judge, by its homogeneous appearance, if the reaction is perfected. He then rakes out the doughy substance, which, being cooled, is pulverized in a vertical mill, and then lixiviated in boxes, as described §447. The liquids are evaporated in kettles to the crystallizing point, and then run into the crystallizers, where the salt is deposited. To obtain pure carbonate of soda, the crystallization must be disturbed by continually stirring the liquid, whereby small granular crystals are deposited, which are gradually removed, and then washed with pure water.

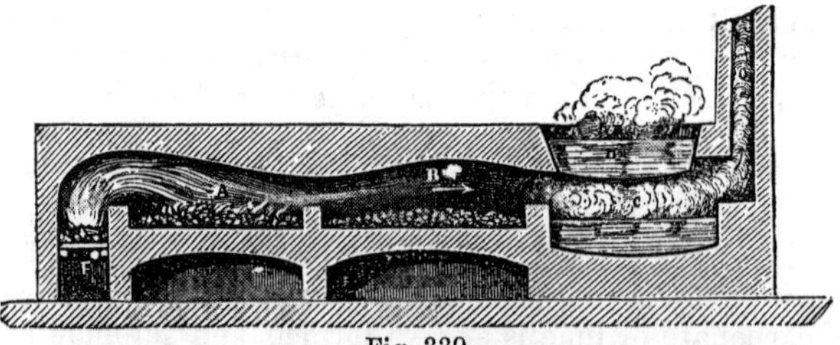

Fig. 339.

Fig. 339 represents a vertical section of a soda-furnace of recent construction, in which the heat of the fuel is greatly economized. The flame of the fuel, which burns on the grate F, traverses the compartment A, where the highest temperature prevails; passes into the compartment B, which is only separated from A by a low brick-wall; traverses the compartment C, and escapes by the chimney O. The hearth of the compartments A and B is of brick; that of C is made like a water-tight kettle. The roof of C is formed by a sheet-iron kettle D. The mixture of sulphate of soda, carbonate of lime, and charcoal, is first heated in the compartment B, and then conveyed into A, where the chemical reaction takes place. The liquors from lixiviation of the crude soda being concentrated by heat in the kettle D, are conveyed into the kettle C, where the evaporation is finished. The carbonate of soda is withdrawn perfectly dry from the furnace.

The soda furnaces at Marseilles are usually composed only of the compartments A and B. The former, A, is destined for the fabrication of carbonate of soda, while in B the sulphate is prepared by the reaction of sulphuric acid on chloride of sodium. The chlorohydric acid gas which is evolved traverses the condensing tubes, where the greater portion of it is dissolved.

§473. Carbonate of soda crystallizes when cold, in large crystals, containing 62.9 per cent. of water, with the formula NaO,CO_2+10HO. They soon effloresce in the air, and are more soluble in hot water than in cold. Boiling water dissolves nearly its own weight of them, while cold water only dissolves one-half. It may also crystallize with a smaller proportion of water when formed in a hot solution; for the small granular crystals deposited from a liquid concentrated by boiling contain only about 18 per cent. of water. Carbonate of soda, when heated, soon parts with its water, and, at a red-heat, fuses into a very fluid liquid, which crystallizes on cooling.

§474. *Bicarbonate of Soda.*—The bicarbonate is obtained by passing a current of carbonic acid gas through a concentrated solution of the neutral carbonate, and, not being very soluble in water, is deposited in the form of crystals. Its composition is

$$NaO,2CO_2+HO \text{ or } NaO,CO_2+HO,CO_2.$$

100 parts of water, at ordinary temperatures, dissolve about 8 parts of this salt.

The bicarbonate is easily decomposed by the action of heat, and parts with one-half of its carbonic acid, leaving a neutral carbonate. Its solution is also decomposed by heat, and prolonged ebullition changes it into the neutral carbonate.

The bicarbonate is extensively used in medicine as an antacid. Small pastilles, made by mixing it with some sweetened vehicle, are called *Darcet's digestive pastilles.*

Bicarbonate of soda is manufactured by exposing, in wooden boxes, the crystallized neutral carbonate to a current of carbonic acid gas, which changes it entirely into bicarbonate. The carbonic acid employed is sometimes derived from natural sources.

§ 475. *Sesquicarbonate of Soda.*—A crystallized sesquicarbonate, with the formula $2NaO,3CO_2+4HO$, is found in nature, and known by the name of *natron*, or *sal trona.* In certain hot countries, as Egypt, Mexico, and India, during the rainy season, small lakes or ponds are formed in low spots, the waters of which evaporate during the hot season, and develop efflorescences or crystalline masses of natron. This salt does not effloresce in the air, and often presents a considerable degree of hardness.

It appears to be formed by the reaction of carbonate of lime on sea-salt; at least, a considerable quantity of sesquicarbonate of soda is always produced, when a mixture of these two salts is left undisturbed for a long time, the natron appearing on the surface.

§ 476. *Analysis of the crude Sodas of commerce.*—This analysis resembles precisely that of potassa (§ 440), except that to saturate 5 gm. of monohydrated sulphuric acid, only 3.61 gm. of pure anhydrous soda are necessary. We therefore operate upon 31.61 grammes.*

Nitrate of Soda.

§ 477. Nitric acid and soda form only one compound, the *nitrate of soda;* which may be obtained by decomposing carbonate of soda by nitric acid. It crystallizes in rhombohedrons differing but little from the cube, from which the salt has been called *cubic nitre.* In Peru, it forms a stratum of variable thickness, extending over more than 100 square leagues, and is covered only by a layer of clay. The salt is sent to Europe in the state in which it is extracted from the earth, and readily refined by solution in water and evaporation.

It may be advantageously employed, on account of its low price, to manufacture nitric acid, where sulphate of soda, the secondary product of the process, finds a ready sale. For equal weights, it affords more nitric acid than nitrate of potassa, because the equivalent of soda is lower than that of potassa. It has also been used in the manufacture of gunpowder; but, as the powder thus made attracts moisture from the atmosphere more powerfully than common powder, it has been abandoned. The use of this salt in making nitrate of potassa with nitrified matter was pointed out in § 449.

It can also be converted directly, by double decomposition, into nitrate of potassa, by treating it with carbonate of potassa. The liquid being evaporated, and allowed to crystallize at a low temperature, deposits nitrate of potassa. The same decomposition may also be effected with chloride of potassium, by concentrating the liquid by boiling, when it deposits a large quantity of sea-salt, which is removed; and, on allowing the liquid to cool, it deposits nitrate of potassa.

Phosphates of Soda.

§ 478. The compounds of soda with phosphoric acid are nume-

* See note to § 440, for the alkalimetric test of soda.

rous, and their study very interesting. Chemists now divide them into *tribasic* or *ordinary phosphates*, *bibasic* or *pyrophosphates*, and *monobasic* or *metaphosphates*.

Tribasic Phosphates, or Ordinary Phosphates.

§479. The ordinary phosphate of soda of commerce is prepared by adding carbonate of soda to a solution of the acid phosphate of lime, (which is obtained by treating bone-ashes with sulphuric acid,) until no effervescence or deposit ensues. The lime separates in the state of an insoluble sub-phosphate, and the liquid contains phosphate of soda in solution. The evaporated liquid deposits, on cooling, beautiful transparent crystals, which are purified by re-crystallization. Its formula is $2NaO,PO_5+25HO$, but it should be written $(2NaO+HO)PO_5+24HO$, which indicates that the phosphoric acid has combined with 3 equivalents of base, viz. 2 equivs. of soda, and 1 equiv. of basic water. The salt has a decided alkaline reaction on coloured tests. It effloresces in the air; and dissolves in 2 parts of boiling and 4 parts of cold water. Subjected to heat, it first fuses in its own crystal-water, which it gradually parts with, and if the temperature be not raised too high, it remains in the state of the anhydrous tribasic salt $(2NaO+HO)PO_5$. By redissolving it in water and again crystallizing it, it reappears as the original salt; but if the heat be carried still higher, so as to make it undergo igneous fusion, it loses its equivalent of basic water and becomes $2NaO,PO_5$. Its nature has then entirely changed; for by resolution and recrystallization, the original salt is no longer obtained, but an entirely different salt, which will be described under the name of *pyrophosphate of soda*.

If a solution of nitrate of silver, *neutral* to coloured tests, be poured into a solution of ordinary phosphate of soda $(2NaO+HO)PO_5+24HO$, which has an alkaline reaction, a yellow precipitate is obtained of phosphate of silver $3AgO,PO_5$, and the liquid possesses, after complete precipitation, an *acid* reaction. Double decomposition takes place between 1 equiv. of tribasic phosphate of soda and 3 equivs. of nitrate of silver, as represented by the following equation:

$$(2NaO+HO)PO_5+3(AgO,NO_5)=3AgO,PO_5+2(NaO,NO_5)+HO,NO_5.$$

Since the liquid, therefore, contains 2 equivs. of nitrate of soda, which are *neutral* to tincture of litmus, and 1 equiv. of nitrate of water with a strong *acid* reaction, it must redden tincture of litmus.

2. *Tribasic Phosphate of Soda*, $3NaO,PO_5+24HO$.—If an excess of carbonate of soda be added to a solution of the preceding phosphate, and the concentrated liquid be crystallized, a salt is obtained with a strong alkaline reaction, and composed according to the for-

mula $3NaO,PO_5+24HO$. It readily parts with its water by heat, and then presents the composition $3NaO,PO_5$. It may be fused without changing its state of *tribasic phosphate;* and by resolution in water, it crystallizes again as the original phosphate $3NaO,PO_5+24HO$.

A *neutral* solution of nitrate of silver, poured into the solution of this phosphate, with its strong *alkaline* reaction, gives a yellow precipitate of phosphate of silver $3AgO,PO_5$, and the liquid, after precipitation, is *neutral* to coloured reagents, as represented by the following equation:

$$3NaO,PO_5+3(AgO,NO_5)=3AgO,PO_5+3(NaO,NO_5).$$

The liquid therefore contains, after precipitation, 3 equivs. of nitrate of soda, and must be neutral to coloured tests.

3. *Tribasic Phosphate of Soda*, $(NaO+2HO)PO_5+2HO$.—If an excess of phosphoric acid be added to the first tribasic phosphate $(2NaO+HO)PO_5+24HO$, and the liquid concentrated, a third phosphate NaO,PO_5+4HO is obtained, and should be written $(NaO+2HO)PO_5+2HO$, for the phosphoric acid in it is always saturated by 3 equivs. of base; but only one of them is soda—the two others are water. This salt has a strong acid reaction. By heating it moderately, its 2 equivs. of water of crystallization can be driven off, and the salt reduced to the state $(NaO+2HO)PO_5$. The salt still preserves its 3 equivs. of base, for if it be dissolved in water, and again crystallized, the original salt $(NaO+2HO)PO_5+2HO$ is obtained. But if the temperature be raised still higher, we can abstract from it successively, first one, and then two equivalents of basic water. In the first case, the phosphoric acid is only saturated by 2 equivs. of base $(NaO+HO)PO_5$, and the salt has become *bibasic* phosphate, or a *pyrophosphate.* In the second case, it contains only 1 equiv. of base NaO,PO_5, and has become a *monobasic phosphate* or *metaphosphate.* By redissolving these new salts in water, they preserve the modification imparted to them by the heat, and no longer reproduce crystals of the original salt $(NaO+2HO)PO_5+2HO$.

A *neutral* solution of nitrate of silver, poured into the solution of the third tribasic phosphate $(NaO+2HO)PO_5+2HO$, which has a strong *acid* reaction, gives a yellow precipitate of phosphate of silver $3AgO,PO_5$, and the liquid then exhibits an *acid* reaction, as may thus be shown:

$$(NaO+2HO)PO_5+3(AgO,NO_5)=3AgO,PO_5+NaO,NO_5+2(HO,NO_5).$$

Thus, the liquid contains, after precipitation, 1 equiv. of nitrate of soda, and 2 equivs. of nitrate of water, so that its reaction must be strongly acid.

Bibasic Phosphates of Soda, or Pyrophosphates.

§480. It was shown (§479) that by calcining the first tribasic phosphate of soda $(2NaO+HO)PO_5+24HO$, so as to expel, not only its water of crystallization, but also its basic water, a salt is obtained which, when redissolved in water, no longer reproduced the original salt. In fact, if the ordinary phosphate be subjected to igneous fusion, and crystallized a second time in water, a new salt is obtained, the formula of which is $2NaO,PO_5+10HO$, and its properties are very different from those of the phosphate from which it originated. It is generally called the *pyrophosphate of soda*, and does not effloresce in the air.

A *neutral* solution of nitrate of silver, poured into the solution of this salt, which has an alkaline reaction, gives a *white* precipitate of phosphate of silver $2AgO,PO_5$, which presents, consequently, a different composition from the yellow precipitate afforded by the tribasic phosphates; moreover, the liquid is *neutral* after precipitation. The reaction now takes place between 1 equiv. of bibasic phosphate and 2 equivs. of nitrate of silver,

$$2NaO,PO_5+2(AgO,NO_5)=2AgO,PO_5+2(NaO,NO_5);$$

so that the liquid contains, after precipitation, only 2 equivs. of nitrate of soda, and is consequently neutral to coloured reagents.

Second Bibasic Phosphate of Soda.—If an excess of phosphoric acid be added to a solution of the preceding salt, a crystallized salt NaO,PO_5+HO is obtained; but its formula should be written $(NaO+HO)PO_5$, for the phosphoric acid is always combined in it with 2 equivs. of base, 1 equiv. of soda, and 1 equiv. of water. This salt has a strong acid reaction. If it be heated only so far as to drive off its crystal-water, and not its basic water, (which last requires a higher temperature,) the salt is not changed; for by resolution in water the original salt is reproduced. But if it be heated so as to drive off its basic water, the phosphoric acid remains combined with only 1 equiv. of base, and the salt is entirely changed, for it no longer reproduces the original compound when redissolved in water. It has then become a *monobasic phosphate* or a *metaphosphate*.

The bibasic phosphate of soda $(NaO+HO)PO_5$ gives, with nitrate of silver, the white precipitate $2AgO,PO_5$ of phosphate of silver, and the liquid becomes acid, as shown by the equation,

$$(NaO+HO)PO_5+2(AgO,NO_5)=2AgO,PO_5+NaO,NO_5+HO,NO_5.$$

The same bibasic phosphate $(NaO+HO)PO_5$ is obtained by heating the third tribasic phosphate $(NaO+2HO)PO_5+2HO$, so as to expel, not only its water of crystallization, but also 1 equiv. of its basic water.

Monobasic Phosphate of Soda, or Metaphosphate.

§481. If the third tribasic phosphate $(NaO+2HO)PO_5+2HO$,

or the second bibasic phosphate $(NaO+HO)PO_5$, be heated to fusion, both the basic and crystal-water are entirely driven off, the phosphoric acid remains combined with a single equivalent of base, and a salt is obtained the properties of which are very different from those of the substances from which it originated. In fact, this *monobasic phosphate*, also called *metaphosphate*, is a deliquescent salt, which does not crystallize when dissolved in water. With nitrate of silver it gives a white precipitate, but which differs greatly from the white precipitate of the bibasic phosphates; for its composition is AgO,PO_5. Double decomposition takes place between 1 equiv. of metaphosphate of soda and 1 equiv. of nitrate of silver, and the liquid is neutral after precipitation:

$$NaO,PO_5+AgO,NO_5=AgO,PO_5+NaO,NO_5.$$

The metaphosphates are also distinguished from the ordinary phosphates and pyrophosphates, by coagulating the white of egg, while the latter do not produce this effect.

§ 482. These three series of phosphates, which we have just described under the phosphates of soda, are also formed with the majority of other bases; but they have not hitherto been sufficiently studied. They are even found in the phosphates of water, or hydrated phosphoric acids. It was stated (§ 211) that phosphoric acid afforded three definite hydrates: the hydrates $3HO,PO_5$ and $2HO,PO_5$, which have been obtained in a crystalline form, and the hydrate HO,PO_5, which remains when either of the preceding hydrates is heated to redness. The hydrate $3HO,PO_5$, or tribasic phosphate of water, is most easily prepared, being formed in solution whenever phosphorus is oxidized in the humid way, such as by treating it with nitric acid. This hydrate, saturated with bases, affords only tribasic phosphates. The monohydrate HO,PO_5 or monobasic phosphate of water, gives with bases principally monobasic phosphates or metaphosphates; but a certain quantity of bibasic, and even of tribasic phosphate, is nearly always found in the liquid. The crystallized bihydrate $2HO,PO_5$ or bibasic phosphate of water, furnishes a mixture of bibasic and tribasic phosphate. This circumstance is owing to the fact that the monobasic and bibasic phosphates of water are much less fixed than the corresponding phosphates of soda, so that when dissolved in water, they are readily converted into the tribasic acid.

The majority of chemists* consider these three series of phosphates as formed by three different modifications, or three isomeric states of phosphoric acid, in which the acid presents the same elementary composition, but has different properties. The most striking differences, or rather those which are best ascertained, are

* To Mr. Graham, an English chemist, is due the thorough investigation of the various phosphates; previous to which it was impossible to explain the various and anomalous properties observed in the phosphates of soda.

that in the three states the power of saturation of phosphoric acid differs as regards the bases. Thus, the tribasic phosphates contain an acid, called *ordinary phosphoric acid*, possessing the property of combining with 3 equivs. of base. The bibasic phosphates, or pyrophosphates, contain an acid isomeric with the former, and called *pyrophosphoric*, but it combines with only 2 equivs. of base. Lastly, in the monobasic or metaphosphates, a third isomeric state of phosphoric acid is found, *metaphosphoric acid*, which combines with only 1 equiv. of base.

§ 483. These peculiarities of phosphoric acid can, however, be explained, without supposing the acid to exist in three different isomeric states, by admitting a principle in perfect conformity with the laws of mechanical equilibrium, and which appears to be established by a great number of experiments. I shall call it the *principle of preservation of molecular grouping.*

The molecules of ordinary phosphoric acid and of the tribasic phosphates consist of groups formed of 1 equiv. of phosphoric acid and 3 equivs. of the base. These groups, or molecular systems, possess a certain degree of stability, and a great tendency to remain permanent. In all double decompositions, the three equivalents of the original base are totally or partially replaced by equivalent quantities of other bases, but the tribasic grouping is always maintained. Nevertheless, if the tribasic phosphate contains volatile bases, as water or ammonia, heat may drive them off; the tribasic grouping will be destroyed, and a bibasic or monobasic grouping be formed. If only one equivalent of the base be disengaged, a bibasic grouping will be formed, and this grouping, once formed, will have a *tendency to permanence* equal to that of the tribasic grouping. In reactions effected in water, the grouping is only modified by double decomposition, by means of substitution. Its basic equivalents are replaced by equivalents of other bases, but the bibasic grouping is preserved.

If the tribasic phosphate contain 2 equivs. of a volatile base, then 2 equivs. may be disengaged by heat, and a third grouping, the *monobasic*, be formed, which has an equal tendency to permanence, and is only modified by substitution when subjected to feeble reactions, like those of double decomposition effected in the humid way.

Thus, while the three groupings will remain permanent in all feeble reactions, they may pass from one to the other in powerful reactions. As it was shown that heat could transform the tribasic into the bibasic and monobasic groups, so the inverse is practicable, and the latter groups may be transformed into the tribasic by merely fusing them with an excess of a powerful base, such as potassa or soda. Influenced by these bases, which have a great affinity for acids, phosphoric acid combines with the greatest quantity of base possible, and constitutes the tribasic group. The transformation does not ensue, however, in the humid way, at ordinary temperatures, because it is opposed by the tendency of the molecular system to stability, which requires a high temperature to destroy it.

This tendency of molecular grouping to permanence appears to play an important part in chemical phenomena, and explains at once the different actions frequently observed between anhydrous and hydrated acids. Hydrated acids are ready-formed *saline groupings*, which, when brought into contact with bases, merely substitute a more powerful base for their water. Anhydrous acids, on the contrary, present entirely different groups; and frequently only combine with bases by transforming their original grouping into a saline grouping, through the intervention of a high temperature, so that at ordinary temperatures they do not behave like true acids, which do not combine directly with bases.

So also hydrated bases, such as the hydrate of potassa, present a saline group, in which the water plays the part of an acid. Such bases will immediately form salts, even with an anhydrous acid, because the saline grouping is already *perfectly established*, and the acid merely takes the place of the water.

Chlorate of Soda.

§ 484. The chlorate of soda may be prepared, like the chlorate of potassa, by the reaction of chlorine on a concentrated solution of soda. The liquid contains, after the operation, chlorate of soda and chloride of sodium, but they are separated with difficulty from each other by crystallization. Chlorate of soda is easily obtained pure by decomposing a concentrated hot solution of chlorate of potassa by a solution of bitartrate of soda. The bitartrate of potassa, being slightly soluble, almost immediately separates from the liquid, and the solution contains chlorate of soda, which can be crystallized by evaporation.

Borates of Soda.

§ 485. The neutral borate of soda is called, in the arts, *borax.* It is found, in commerce, in two states, *common borax* and *octohedral borax*, which differ from each other only in the proportion of their water of crystallization. The formula of ordinary borax is $NaO,2BO_3+10HO$, containing 42.7 per cent. of water; that of octohedral borax is $NaO,2BO_3+5HO$, containing only 30.8 per cent. of water.

Common borax effloresces slightly in the air; dissolves in 2 parts of boiling and 12 parts of cold water, and the solution has a strong alkaline reaction. When heated, it first fuses in its water of crystallization, then swells up, and becomes a spongy mass of anhydrous borax. At a more elevated temperature, the anhydrous salt undergoes igneous fusion, producing a viscous liquid, which does not crystallize on solidifying, but presents a vitreous appearance. Fused borax is so tenacious that it may be drawn out into long delicate threads. When hot, the glass of borax dissolves the majority of the metallic oxides, assuming peculiar colours, which enables us to distinguish the various metals from each other. This property is very valuable in qualitative analysis, and may be proved on very small quantities of matter. For this purpose, a platinum wire (fig. 340) is generally employed, one end of it being twisted into a ring. The moistened ring being dipped into powdered anhydrous borax, a few particles of the metal to be examined are added to it. The mixture is then fused by the blowpipe (fig. 341) into a globule or bead, in which the metallic oxide is dissolved, and which, on cooling, presents the peculiar colour characteristic of the metallic oxide.*

Fig. 340.

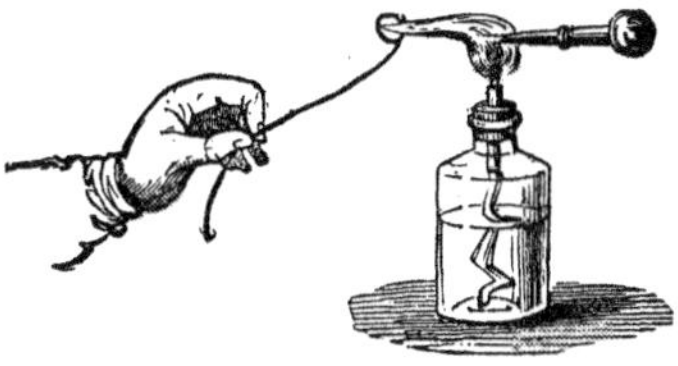

Fig. 341.

The flame used to effect the fusion may be that of an alcohol or oil lamp, or of a wax candle. When the metal has several degrees of oxidation, it frequently happens that it imparts two very different colours to the borax; and as these colours may be produced at pleasure, they are both used to ascertain the nature of the metal. In the brilliant part *b* of the flame (fig. 342) which is immediately beyond the interior dark cone *aa′* the gas acts reducingly, because its combustible parts are not yet entirely burned, especially if the aperture of the blowpipe be very small. At *c*, beyond the brilliant part *b*, the flame has, on the contrary, an oxidizing action, because it is mixed with an excess of atmospheric air. The borax is therefore heated at *b* to obtain the colour belonging to the protoxide, and at *c* for the colour of the peroxide.†

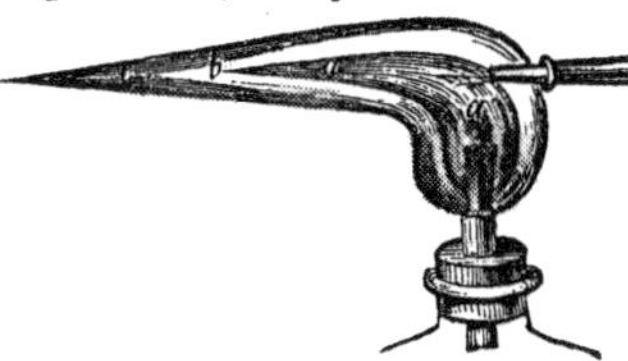

Fig. 342.

* The platinum wire may be simply crooked ſ at the end, instead of being bent into a complete circle. After taking up a little powdered borax on the end of the wire, it is advisable to fuse it, to be certain that the borax will yield a clear and colourless bead, and then to add a particle of the substance to be tested, either by touching the red-hot bead to it, or by moistening the cooled bead on one side, and then attaching the particle. If the first plunge into the borax does not yield a bead of sufficient size, the still heated bead may be dipped into the borax, when a larger quantity will adhere. The fusion of borax by the blowpipe may likewise be effected on clean charcoal, and the metallic colouring be rendered apparent, the only inconvenience being the tendency of the bead at first to spread while cooling.—*J. C. B.*

† In order to understand how the same flame will produce one or the other of these colours in borax, it is necessary to make a few remarks on the constitution of flame.

Let us first examine the flame of a burning gas. If a moderate jet of hydrogen

§ 486. Borax is generally used in the arts for soldering metals. Two pieces of metal are soldered together by interposing another metal, or a metallic alloy, more fusible than the piece to be joined, and heating the point of junction to a temperature sufficiently high to fuse the interposed metal, called the solder, but not to fuse the

---

Fig. 343.

be inflamed at the end A of a tube drawn out (fig. 343), it will be observed that the flame, though not very brilliant, is composed of three distinct parts: 1st. An internal dark portion *aa'*, in which the hydrogen is pure; 2d. A luminous envelope *feg* in which the combustion of the hydrogen is effected by the oxygen of the surrounding air, but to which, nevertheless, sufficient air has not access to complete the combustion of the hydrogen; 3d. An external envelope *bcd* barely visible, in which the combustion of the gas is completed, and where the air is in excess. The maximum of temperature is between *e* and *c* toward the point *e*, because combustion is there more intense, and the chief current of gas, raised to a high temperature, passes through that point. Near the point *c* of the external envelope there is also a high temperature; but there is, at the same time, an excess of oxygen, so that the flame has an oxidizing power. If, on the contrary, we approach the point *a* of the internal dark space, we find an excess of hydrogen, because this gas has not yet met with oxygen sufficient to burn it. At that point the flame will be reducing. If borax, mixed with the metallic oxide, be heated toward the point *c* of the luminous envelope, the colour will be produced by that metallic oxide which forms at this temperature in the presence of an excess of oxygen; thus, in the case of iron, it will be the colour of the sesquioxide. If, on the contrary, the mixture be heated toward the point *a* of the internal dark space, we shall have the colour given by the oxide, at this lower temperature, in the presence of an excess of hydrogen; such as that produced by the protoxide of iron. Sometimes the oxide may be completely reduced to the metallic state, but it is always difficult to effect it with borax, on account of the affinity of boracic acid for metallic oxides, an affinity which gives them a greater stability than when they are isolated.

Let us now suppose the flame to be produced by a combustible gas, decomposable by heat, such as carburetted hydrogen. In this case we can also distinguish three parts in the flame: 1st. An internal dark part, formed by the unaltered gas; 2d. A very brilliant luminous envelope, in which the gas undergoes only partial combustion, because there is not yet a sufficient supply of oxygen in that part, and in which the hydrogen burning first a large portion of the carbon is set free, and its incandescent particles render that part extremely brilliant; 3d. An external envelope of much less brilliancy, in which the combustion is completed. The maximum of heat is found near the point *e* of the internal brilliant envelope; between *e* and *c* the flame is oxidizing; and between *a* and *e* it is reducing, because that part contains an excess of combustible material at a high temperature.

The flame around a wick imbued with alcohol, oil, or any melted combustible, is of exactly the same nature.

The liquid ascends by capillary attraction in the wick, where it is heated, by the radiation of the flame, to a point sufficient to volatilize it, when, like alcohol, it can distil without decomposition, or to decompose it into volatile products, as occurs with oil and other fat substances. The volatile substances form the internal dark space, which surrounds and rises above the wick. The rest of the flame then resembles that produced by bicarburetted hydrogen gas.

In a wax or other candle, the combustible material is solid at ordinary temperatures, and surrounds a cotton wick (fig. 344). In this case the material melts by the radiation of the flame, so that the wick is constantly bathed by the melted substance which rises up its capillary tubes. The wick, though formed itself of a combustible material, cannot burn, because it is in a region of flame where there is no oxygen.

Fig. 344.

metal which is to be soldered. In order that the operation may succeed, the two metallic surfaces to be joined must be perfectly clean, and well *scraped*, so that the fused solder may come into immediate contact with the metal. Now, the metal often oxidizes at the fusing temperature of the solder, and the interposed oxide

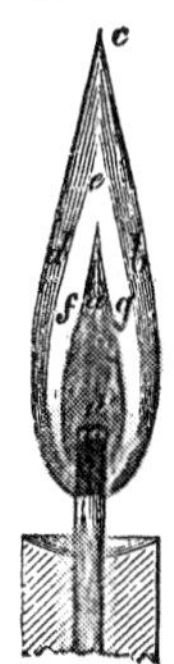

Fig. 345.

At its lower part, where it is constantly moistened by the ascending liquid, it does not even decompose, but it is carbonized above, because the liquid does not reach it in sufficient quantity to prevent it from burning. As the fatty matter is consumed a larger portion of the wick is exposed, until the upper part of it rises above the dark space, and, by reaching that part of the flame in which oxygen exists, is incinerated. But that portion of the wick in which the liquid no longer rises on account of the destruction of the capillary tubes, is an inert body, which attracts a great deal of heat and embarrasses the regular combustion. As it lowers the temperature, a portion of the carbon does not burn and the flame becomes smoky, so that its illuminating power is considerably diminished. In order to restore the original brilliancy of the flame, the upper portion of the wick must be removed by *snuffing the candle.* In wax candles (fig. 345) this is unnecessary, because, if the wick, which is much smaller, be properly twisted, it assumes a horizontal direction as soon as it has acquired a certain length. The wick then stands no longer vertically in the flame, but bends over as it elongates, and its end constantly burns off in the lateral portion of the luminous envelope.

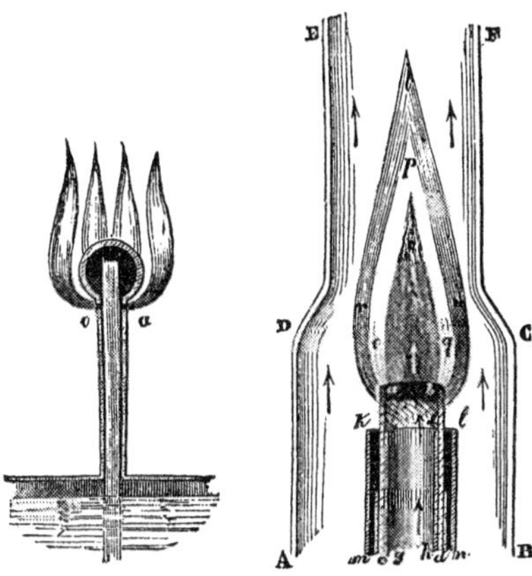

Fig. 346. Fig. 347.

In latter years lamps have been constructed to burn liquid carbohydrogens, which are volatile without decomposition, such as spirits of turpentine, and the volatile oils obtained by the distillation of pit-coal or certain bituminous shales. The wick of these lamps is not combustible, being made of asbestus, the lower part of which enters the burning-fluid (fig. 346), and the upper part terminates in a closed metallic tube, which has several lateral openings *o*, *o*. In order to light such a lamp, a metallic ring, imbued with burning alcohol, is passed over the tube. The heat communicated to the tube vapourizes the fluid, moistening the asbestus, and the vapour, passing through the apertures *o*, takes fire. The ring being then removed, the heat produced by the combustion of the fluid is sufficient to continue the distillation. The fluid should be entirely consumed, for the escape of a very small portion gives out a disagreeable odour. A mixture of spirits of turpentine and alcohol is chiefly used in these lamps.* The combustion is ingeniously regulated. The tube (fig. 346) containing the wick terminates in a hollow metallic ball of larger diameter and of some thickness. When the jets of combustible vapour which escape through the orifices *o* are feeble, the flame rises vertically and heats the ball. This heat is conducted along the tube, and produces a more copious distillation of the fluid which moistens the wick. If, on the contrary, the vapour escapes too freely through the orifices, the flame radiates from the axis and the ball is less heated, so that the temperature of the tube falls, and the distillation of combustible vapours diminishes.

* It is known in the United States as burning-fluid and spirit-gas, and consists of a solution of camphine or spirit of turpentine in alcohol.—*J. C. B.*

prevents the union of the metallic particles. But the inconvenience is remedied by adding a small quantity of borax to the solder, which, by undergoing igneous fusion, forms a coating to protect the metal from oxidation, and, by combining with any oxide on the surface of the pieces to be united, cleans them perfectly. By

---

A large extent of flame cannot be obtained in an oil-lamp by means of a cotton wick which simply descends into the oil. The atmospheric air having access only to the periphery of the flame, the latter cannot be made very large, and is generally smoky, because the carbon is imperfectly burned. On the other hand, flames of any required size can be obtained by using circular cotton wicks *abcd* (fig. 347), contained in the annular space *kmgefhln*, which communicates with the reservoir of oil. The flame is then circular, and the air has free access to it internally and externally. The current of air is increased by surrounding the flame by a glass chimney AEFB which rises to the distance of some decimetres above it, and produces a strong draught of air along the interior and exterior of the flame. This kind of lamp* has therefore been called *a lamp with a double current of air*. The shape and arrangement of the chimney exert a material influence on the length of flame and intensity of light. In a well-made lamp, the chimney can be raised or lowered at will, until it is brought to the position in which the flame has the greatest brilliancy and the combustion of the carbon is perfect. If the draught be too great, the flame is very brilliant, but it does not acquire sufficient development, because the combustion is effected in too small a space. If the draught is too feeble, the flame becomes very long, because the combustible gases rise very high before meeting with the quantity of oxygen necessary for their complete combustion. The flame is then less luminous, and smokes, and the lamp is said *to flare*.

The ordinary shape of glass lamp-chimneys is that of two cylinders of different diameters; the larger one below, and their junction CD at the height of the flame. The object of this arrangement is to deflect the external current of air, and direct it against the flame, so as to render combustion more intense.

In certain lamps, the intensity of the light has been greatly increased by giving the chimney a diameter nearly equal throughout, and making a contraction *aa''* (fig. 348), which is brought on a level with the flame. The great diameter of the chimney affords considerable draught, while the contraction turns against the flame a very rapid current of hot air.

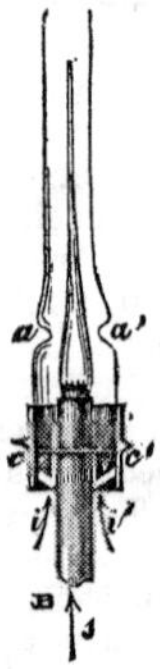

In order that the wick of an oil-lamp may not become carbonized, it should always be moistened to the top with a sufficient quantity of oil. But this condition is imperfectly satisfied in common lamps; for when the reservoir is full of oil, the wick is properly moistened, but when the greater part of the oil is burned, the wick is less completely imbued with oil, and it carbonizes. Its capillary tubes being thus destroyed, the combustible material does not reach the upper portion, and the illuminating power of the lamp is much diminished. The same inconvenience does not exist in the *Carcel lamp*, in which small forcing-pumps are moved by clockwork, and continually project to the top of the wick a quantity of oil greater than that which is consumed: the surplus falls back into the reservoir.

Fig. 348.

Old cotton wicks frequently burn with difficulty in an oil-lamp, and are said to be *dead*, (*eventée*.) The ligneous substance composing the wicks has undergone a spontaneous alteration, which has more or less completely destroyed its capillary tubes. As the oil ascends with difficulty, the wick soon carbonizes, and the lamp gives but little light.

When we blow with the blowpipe through the flame of an alcohol-lamp or of a wax candle, the constitution of the flame nearly resembles that of a lamp with a double current of air; for the inner current is produced in this case by the

---

* Such lamps are usually termed Argand lamps; and a burner for oil, gas, camphine, or other illuminating fluid, constructed of a circular form, and employed with interior and exterior draft, is termed an Argand-burner.—*J. C. B.*

pressing the pieces to be soldered upon each other, the excess of solder, as well as the borax interposed, is squeezed out.

Borax is chiefly used in the soldering of gold and silver. For brass or copper, resin or sal-ammoniac is generally employed, and exerts a reducing action on the metallic oxides which may exist on the surface of the metals.

Ordinary borax NaO,BoO_3+10HO is inconvenient for soldering, because it swells greatly before undergoing igneous fusion, and suffers loss by projection. Octohedral borax, containing less water, is therefore preferred.

§ 487. All the borax used in the arts formerly came from India, China, Persia, and Peru, and was obtained from the evaporation of saline ponds. Such impure borax was imported into Europe under the name of *crude borax* or *tincal*, and was afterward purified by *refining*. The greater part of the borax now used in France is prepared from the boracic acid of Tuscany and artificial soda.

Crude boracic acid, such as is procured by evaporating the waters of the suffioni, contains only about 74 to 83 per cent. of crystallized acid, but, if purified by recrystallization, only contains a small proportion of foreign matter. For 1000 kilog. of boracic acid, 1200 kilog. of crystallized carbonate of soda, and about 2000 kilog. of water are used. A portion of the water is furnished by the mother waters of a preceding operation, or by the condensation of the vapour used in heating.

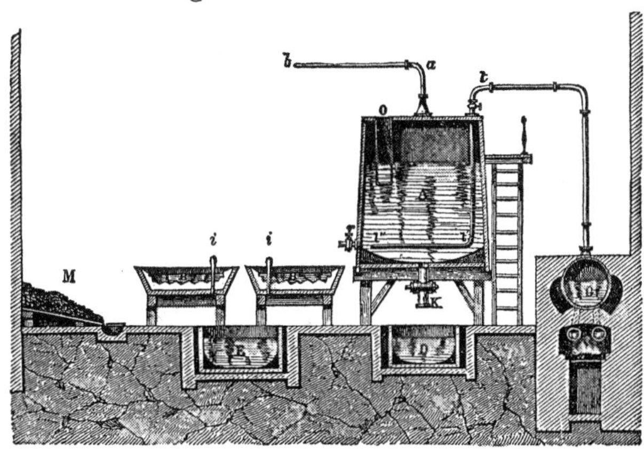

Fig. 349.

A solution of carbonate of soda is first made in a vat A (fig. 349), lined with lead, to the bottom of which is conveyed steam from a

---

blast from the blowpipe. The oxidizing portion of the flame is found toward the point *c* (fig. 342), and the deoxidizing portion between *a* and *b*. In order to obtain a deoxidizing effect, a very small opening is given to the blowpipe, in order not to project a great deal of air into the interior of the flame.

high pressure boiler G, a stopcock t being used to regulate the quantity admitted. The tube conveying the steam to the bottom of the vat is formed into a horizontal circle t', t'', and pierced with a great number of small holes to allow the escape of the steam. When the solution of the carbonate is effected, and the temperature has reached about 212°, the boracic acid is gradually added in small quantities, so that the effervescence produced by the evolution of carbonic acid gas may not cause the liquid to overflow. The vat is kept almost entirely covered, to diminish the loss of heat. When all the boracic acid has been added the liquid is again heated to about 219° or 221°, the steam stopped off, and the liquid allowed to repose for 12 hours. A deposit of insoluble matter is formed at the bottom of the vat. The clear liquid is run off by the cock r, into wooden crystallizers B, lined with lead.

When the crystallization is finished, the mother water is conveyed into cast-iron reservoirs E, by the opening i. The crystals are removed, and drained on an inclined plane M, from which the mother waters flow into a special reservoir.

The deposits formed in the vat A are run through a large cock K into a cast-iron reservoir D, from which they are withdrawn to be washed.*

§ 488. The borax thus obtained is still unfit for the market, not so much from its want of purity as from the want of solidity of its crystals. To remove this defect, they are refined by solution and very slow crystallization.

For this purpose, the borax is redissolved in a large vat A (fig. 350), lined with lead, holding 9000 kilog. of borax, with the water necessary for its solution. It is heated by steam conveyed from the boiler through t, t', t'' to the bottom of the vat. The salt is placed in a sheet-iron basket C suspended to a chain, and the basket only partly immersed in the liquid, so that the solution of the salt, being more dense than the water, falls to the bottom of the vat. The basket is refilled as the salt it contained is dissolved. For each quintal of borax, 8 kilog. of crystallized carbonate of soda are added, and the liquid is brought to 21° of Baumé, at the temperature of about 212°, at which solution is effected. The boiling liquid is then conveyed into a large crystallizer B, which should be kept perfectly still, in order that the crystallization may be undisturbed. It is cooled as slowly as possible, by keeping the vat covered, and even by surrounding by boards or straw-mats. In 25 or 30 days the crystallization is completed; the liquid still showing a temperature of 77° to 86°. It is withdrawn by a siphon, and the crystals removed by the chisel and hammer.

* The vapours arising from the ebullition of the solution in the vat A are passed off through a b, and condensed, in order to obtain salts originally in the crude boracic acid. The first crystallization is finished at 92°, the refining crystallization at 80°; but for octohedral borax, the temperature should not fall below 140°.—*J. C. B.*

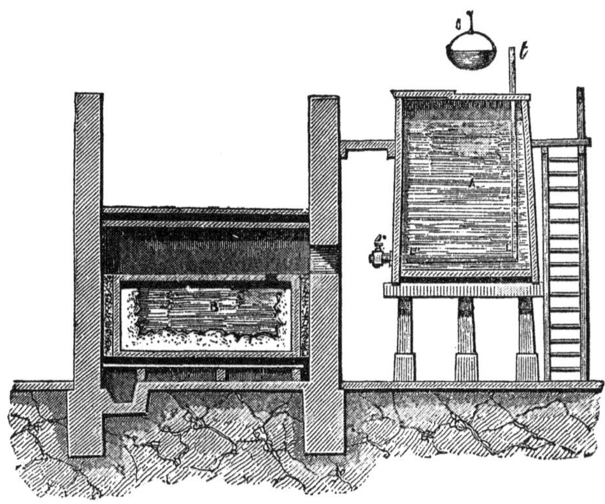

Fig. 350.

§ 489. To prepare octohedral borax, crude borax is dissolved in the same way, and in the same vat; but the solution is concentrated up to 30° Baumé, at the temperature of 212°, and in that state is conveyed into the crystallizer. The crystallization commences when the liquid has reached 174°, and continues until the temperature falls to 138°. The mother water is immediately withdrawn by a siphon, to avoid the superposition of common or prismatic borax on the former, and, being conveyed into large basins, deposits a copious crop of prismatic borax.

§ 490. In refining crude India borax, it is very important first to ascertain its richness, which is readily effected by the alkalimeter process (§ 440). The process is based upon the fact, that whatever may be the quantity of boracic acid, it only produces a purplish red with the blue tincture of litmus, while the smallest quantity of free sulphuric acid, develops a light-red colour. If, therefore, sulphuric acid be added gradually to a solution of borax, coloured by litmus, only the purplish colour appears so long as any borate of soda remains undecomposed; but as soon as the last particles of the borate have been converted into sulphate of soda, the smallest excess of sulphuric acid will change the purple into a light-red color.

The process is performed as follows:—15 grammes of borax being dissolved in 50 cubic centimetres of hot water, and coloured with some litmus, the normal acid liquor (§ 440) contained in the alkalimeter is gradually added until the colour becomes light-red, when the number of measures used is noted. The operation requires some care; for as long as the solution is hot, the great quantity of boracic acid which it contains renders the change of colour less perceptible; but upon approaching complete decomposition, the liquid should be allowed to cool, in order that the greater part of the boracic acid may be deposited in crystals. The addition of acid liquor is then continued until the colour changes.

The sulphate of soda and boracic acid in fact mask slightly the reaction of sulphuric acid on litmus; but direct experiments have shown that about a $\frac{1}{2}$ division of the alkalimeter overcomes this inertia. Thus, at the moment of passing from the purplish colour to the light-red, an excess of a $\frac{1}{2}$ measure of acid has been added; but, by subtracting the $\frac{1}{2}$ measure from the number of measures poured out, the exact number which has effected the decomposition is obtained.

An equivalent of anhydrous borate of soda weighs 100.6, and requires, to be converted into sulphate of soda, 49, that is 1 equiv., of monohydrated sulphuric acid. The volume of normal sulphuric acid which fills 100 divisions of the alkalimeter, contains 5 gm. of monohydrated sulphuric acid, and decomposes 10.282 gm. of pure anhydrous borax.

We should, therefore, always operate on about 10.282 gm. of borax, dissolved in about 50 cubic centimetres of water. If the borax is pure and anhydrous, 100 measures of normal acid must be added, and the salt is said to contain 100 hundredths of real borax. If the borax is pure prismatic borate of soda, the decomposition is effected by 50.2 measures, and the salt contains $\frac{50.2}{100.0}$ of real borax.

To obtain great exactness, the operation must necessarily be repeated several times, in which cases 4 times 10.282 gm., or 41.128 gm. of borax, are dissolved in 200 cubic centimetres of water, and each fourth of the solution tested.

§ 491. A second compound of soda and boracic acid is known, and is obtained by fusing together 1 equiv. of borax with 1 equiv. of carbonate of soda. The fused mass, being dissolved in boiling water, deposits, on cooling, crystals with the formula NaO,BoO_3+8HO.

Hyposulphite of Soda.

§ 492. This salt has acquired some importance from its application to the daguerreotype. It is used to dissolve the sensitive salt of silver which remains unchanged after its exposure in the dark chamber of the camera. It possesses, in fact, the property of readily dissolving the chloride, bromide, and iodide of silver.

Hyposulphite of soda is prepared by dissolving sulphur in a concentrated hot solution of sulphite of soda until the latter is saturated. The liquid, subjected to crystallization, deposits the hyposulphite in the form of large transparent crystals, with the formula NaO,S_2O_2+5HO. When heated, it first fuses in its water of crystallization, and, by properly regulating the heat, the whole of its water may be driven off without decomposition; but, if it be further heated, it is decomposed into a sulphate and sulphide.

COMBINATION OF SODIUM WITH CHLORINE.

§493. Sodium forms only one compound with chlorine, the chloride of sodium, or common table salt. It exists in large quantities in the water of the ocean, from which a large portion of that which is consumed in domestic economy and the arts is derived. On this account, the chloride of sodium is also called *sea-salt*, *marine-salt*. It likewise forms large masses in the earth, called *rock-salt*.

It is nearly equally soluble in hot and cold water, and its curve of solubility (see plate at page 407) is a right line, very slightly inclined toward the axis of temperatures. 100 parts of water dissolve 37 parts of it, so that a saturated solution contains 27 per cent.

Chloride of sodium crystallizes in cubes. When the crystallization is rapidly effected, the crystals are very small, usually adhering to each other, so as to form four-sided pyramids, hollow internally, the walls of which have the appearance of steps, because the rows of small cubic crystals retreat from each other. This particular grouping of crystals (fig. 351) has received the name of *hopper-shaped*. The manner of their formation may be explained as follows:—Let us suppose that a small cubical crystal has formed on the surface of the solution. From its greater density the crystal has a tendency to fall to the bottom of the liquid, but capillary action keeps it on the surface (fig. 352). New crystals soon form, which are joined to the former at its four upper horizontal edges, and constitute a

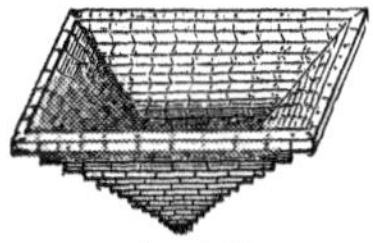

Fig. 351.

Fig. 352. Fig. 353.

Fig. 354. Fig. 355.

frame above the first little cube. As the whole descends into the fluid (fig. 353), new crystals are grouped around the first frame, constituting a second; so that the group of crystals assumes the shape of fig. 354. After the deposit of the third frame, the system has assumed the shape of fig. 355, and so on. We can understand, moreover, why the crystals must form principally on the surface of the liquid; for the salt, being equally soluble, whether cold or hot, has no tendency to deposition on cooling except by the evaporation of the water, which occurs only on the surface.

We have supposed that only a single row of small cubical crystals forms around the horizontal edges of the previous frame; but two, three, or four rows may form, comprised in the same horizontal plane, when the crystalline group does not descend into the liquid immediately after the formation of a first row. It is, therefore, conceivable that the elevation of the hollow pyramids may vary greatly in relation to the area of their base, according as the liquid is more or less tranquil, or in proportion to the power of capillary action.

Chloride of sodium, crystallized in cubes, contains no combined water. In damp weather it abstracts water from the atmosphere, and becomes moist, but parts with it again when the weather is dry. The larger crystals usually contain a small quantity of mother water interposed between the crystalline layers, and to the presence of this water is generally attributed the property which salt possesses of decrepitating when thrown on burning coals.

When a solution of sea-salt is crystallized at a very low temperature, at 50°, for example, crystals are deposited which do not belong to the regular system. They are hydrated, and their formula is $NaCl+4HO$. They lose their water of crystallization, even in water, when the temperature rises above 14°.

§ 494. Rock-salt is generally found in large masses in the strata of muschelkalk, belonging to the trias system. The masses are generally interpolated in the strata, or rather in lenticular masses of gypsum. It is sometimes white and perfectly pure, with a decided cubical cleavage; at other times is tinged yellow or red by oxide of iron.

When rock-salt is pure, it is extracted immediately from the earth, either by an open quarry, when it is near the surface, or by regular mining operations with shafts, etc., as in coal mines. The salt extracted is ground in a mill. The principal mines are those of Vieliczka in Poland, and Cardona in Spain.

Some varieties of rock-salt possess the remarkable property of producing slight decrepitations by solution in water, from the evolution of a quantity of nearly pure hydrogen. The gas, having been confined in the salt by a high pressure, bursts the walls of the cavities when they have been sufficiently thinned by solution.

When rock-salt is impure, it is purified by solution in water and crystallization, the solution being generally made in the mine itself. A boring is made from the surface of the ground to the centre of the mass of salt, about 15 centimetres (6 in.) diameter, for the first 30 or 40 metres (33 to 43 yds.), and then diminished to 10 centimetres (4 in.) for the rest of its length. Copper pipes, screwed together, are inserted into the bore, their lower end being closed, and perforated by small holes, through which the water can enter, at a distance of 2 or 3 metres (yds.) from the bottom. The pipes are suspended above to a very strong beam

AB (fig. 356), firmly fixed in mason-work. The part *cdef* serves as the trunk of a pump, and has a flange *ef* corresponding to the narrowing point of the pipe, so that it rests upon the rock. The valve *s*, or *fixed clapper*, is at this part of the pipe.

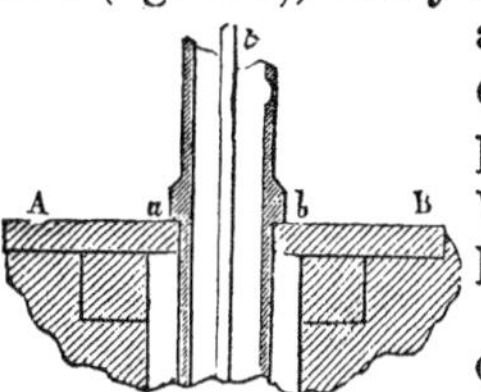

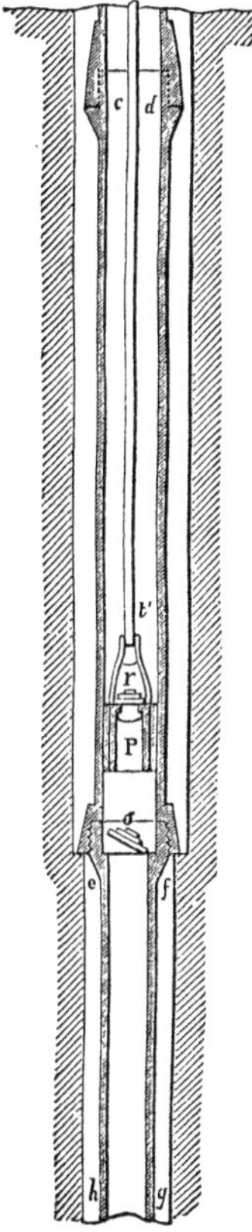

Fig. 356.

Fresh water, being run between the walls of the bore and the pipe, descends to the rock-salt, dissolves it, and the solution or brine, being more dense, falls to the bottom of the bore, and enters the lower end of the pipe. The pipe is therefore filled with brine, which does not rise to the surface, but stops at a distance below it which will equipoise the annular column of fresh water. The density of the latter being 1.00, that of water saturated with salt is about 1.20. If, therefore, the bore is 200 metres high, the column of salt water will rise in the tube to $\frac{1.00}{1.20}$. $200^{m}=166$ metres. The salt column will therefore stop at 34 metres below the surface, and must be raised by means of the pump.

Upon first opening such a salt-well, the water raised by the pump is not saturated, because it does not remain long enough in contact with the rock-salt; but, after a few months, vast excavations are formed in the mass of salt, where the water remains for a long time; and as the pump raises only the lower strata of liquid, that is the most dense, it throws out a saturated solution containing 27 per cent. of salt.

The fresh water which enters the bore is spring-water, conveyed from a reservoir in the vicinity, situated higher than the bore, so as to keep it constantly filled. The upper part of the pipe passes through this reservoir, and empties the water into a trough which carries it into another covered basin. The salt water thus obtained is generally very pure, usually containing only a small quantity of sulphate of soda, some chloride of calcium and magnesium. It is also saturated with sulphate of lime; but this salt is but sparingly soluble in water. In order to extract the sea-salt, the brine is merely evaporated by heat, when the salt separates by crystallization. But as the quantities of water to be evaporated are considerable, the evaporating apparatus should be so contrived as to economize fuel as much as possible. Figs. 357 and 358 represent a portion of the evaporating arrangements of the saline at Rottenmünster, in Wirtemberg. Fig. 358, represents a ground-plan of the building; fig. 357, a vertical section of the same, in the direction of the line XY of the ground-plan.

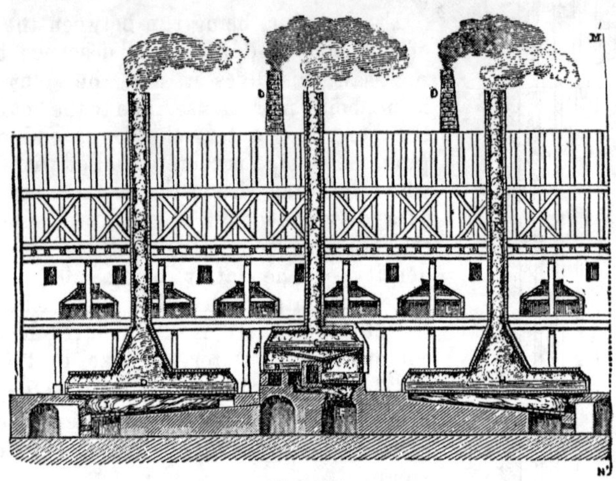

Fig. 357.

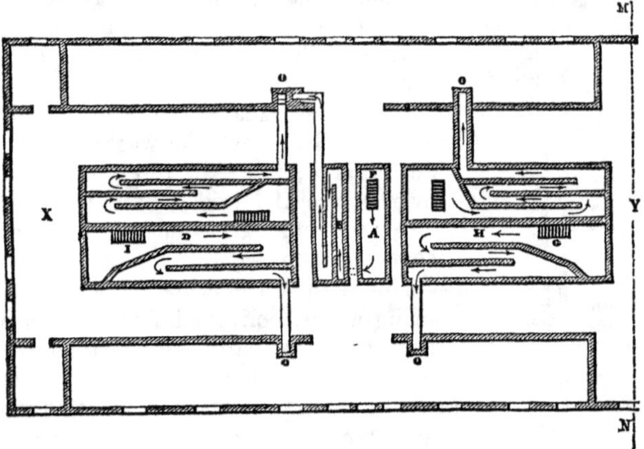

Fig. 358.

The brine of the reservoir is first conveyed into a large sheet-iron kettle or pan C, with a flat bottom, and heated to about 212° by the steam which rises from the kettles A and B. From C it is allowed to flow into the two evaporating-pans A and B, of which A is directly heated by a furnace beneath it, and B by the waste heat of this furnace, which circulates several times beneath it before escaping from the chimney O. The waters are rapidly concentrated by boiling, and, as fast as they evaporate, are replaced by additional quantities drawn from the pan C. The evaporation is pushed until a crystalline pellicle forms on the surface of the liquid. A large portion of the foreign salts, principally the sulphates of lime and soda, separates in the state of a double salt, which attaches itself as a solid crust to the sides of the pan, (hence called pan-stone.) As the pan C is heated only by the steam arising from the concentrating-pans A and B, it is necessary to prevent the water, arising from the condensation of this steam on the bottom of C, from falling back into the lower pans. This is effected by covering A and B by two roofs *de*, *df*, made of slats of wood, arranged with intervals between them, but overhanging each other. The condensed water, falling on these roofs, is carried off by a gutter.

The concentrated brine of the pans A and B is conveyed into other larger pans H, D, heated by furnaces, and under which the smoke is made to circulate several times, in order to economize the heat as much as possible. The salt is crystallized in these pans. The workman disturbs the crystallization constantly, and with a rake draws the crystallized salt toward the edges of the pan upon small inclined planes, from which the drainage flows back into the pans. As the level of the liquid falls in the crystallizing-pans, additional brine is introduced from the pans A and B. The evaporation is not arrested until a considerable incrustation of the double sulphate of lime and soda (pan-stone) has formed on the pans, because the strong coating produced by this salt on the bottom of the pans impedes the transmission of heat. The mother waters, now containing the deliquescent salts, are then drawn off, because they would yield an impure salt by continuing the evaporation.

The pans are covered by large hoods, made of plank and surmounted by wooden chimneys, through which the steam escapes. Gutters are arranged along the sides of the chimneys to collect the condensing waters and carry them off.

The salt, when withdrawn from the crystallizing-pans, is dried in a series of parallel wooden closets (L, fig. 357), arranged in an upper story, and across the building. Fig. 359 represents a transverse section of one of these closets. The damp salt is placed on a floor AB, made of a great number of small wooden slats, arranged with spaces between them. This floor divides all the closets into two compartments, through the upper one of which hot air passing, traverses the damp salt, abstracts its moisture, and then escapes through a chimney. The upper lid EF of the closet opens like a desk, to allow the introduction and removal of the salt.

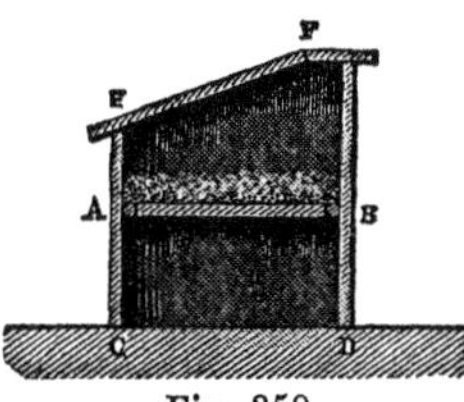

Fig. 359.

The air intended for drying is heated by the evaporating furnaces, where it is conveyed by cast-iron tubes several times under the grate, which the tubes support, (fig. 360,) and thence passes into the drying compartments. Another portion of air is heated by traversing the compartments *o* made in the cast-iron boxes which line the walls of the ash-pit C.

Fig. 360.

The salt, being taken from the drying-room perfectly dry, is put into bags and exported.

§ 495. Where considerable masses of rock-salt exist in the earth, salt springs or salines are usually found in the vicinity, the waters of which sometimes furnish large quantities of chloride of sodium. They are usually dilute solutions or weak brines, because they necessarily pass through various strata of earth, and become mixed with more or less fresh water.*

The waters of salines are rarely sufficiently concentrated to admit of their direct evaporation by heat, and are therefore previously concentrated by evaporation by the air. The composition of the water of two salines which are worked is given below. One of them, that of Schönebeck, near Magdeburg in Prussia, is a strong brine; the other at Moutiers in Savoy, is much feebler.

The composition has reference to 100 parts of water.

	Schönebeck.	Moutiers.
Chloride of sodium	9.623	1.058
Sulphate of soda	0.249	0.100
" magnesia	0.012	0.055
" lime	0.339	0.251
" potassa	0.014	—
Chloride of magnesium	0.083	0.030
" potassium	0.007	—
" iron	—	0.010
Carbonate of lime	0.026	0.076
iron	0.001	0.012
Free carbonic acid	—	0.075
	10.354	1.667

The waters of the salines, being conveyed into large reservoirs,

* Salines are not uncommon where rock-salt has never been found, although eagerly sought by boring. It appears as if fresh water, passing through the strata, may take up, in its lengthened course, small quantities of salt disseminated in sandstones and slates, and issue again at the surface as feeble salines. Such are the springs in Western New York and Pennsylvania. Even very feeble salines, in the latter State, are worked profitably, because the waters issuing among strata of bituminous coal can be directly submitted to evaporation without the use of a graduation-shed.—*J. C. B.*

are pumped into peculiar buildings, called *graduation-houses*, and thence allowed to flow slowly over large surfaces exposed to the action of the wind, which evaporates a great portion of the water. The graduation-houses (fig. 361) are long frame buildings, the longest side of which is exposed to the prevailing wind of the locality, or rather that which produces the greatest amount of evaporation. The floor of the building is made of a large clay

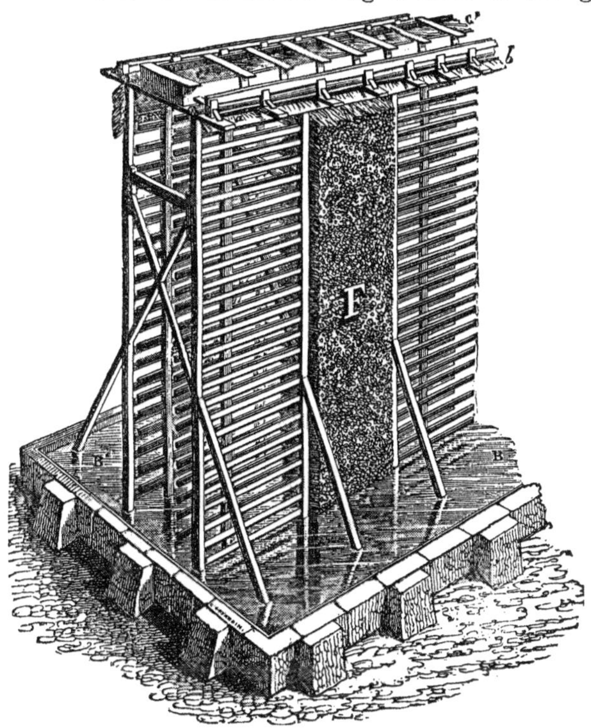

Fig. 361.

basin BB′, intended to collect the waters which have been concentrated by evaporation. The frame is placed on pillars of masonwork. The spaces between the frame are filled with bundles of fagots, as seen at F, so that the building looks like a vast wall of fagots, 10 or 15 metres (yds.) in height, and 400 or 500 metres in length. The spring-water is pumped into a trough CC running along the top of the building, from which it flows over and among the fagots, through small holes in the sides of the trough, partly closed. By thus descending slowly in thin sheets over the branches, a great portion is evaporated, if the air be dry and the wind favourable. It is generally allowed to flow over only one side of the building, that which is exposed to the wind. As it is important, however, to have the wall of fagots sufficiently thick to retain as perfectly as possible the particles of salt-water, which a strong wind would otherwise carry off from the dripping water, the wall is made about 3 metres (10 ft.) thick at its base, and 2 at its upper part. After having traversed the wall of fagots, the water collected in the lower basin is again elevated by pumps into the trough of a second graduation-house, similar to the first, where it is again concentrated by a *second graduation.* The water is usually passed four or five times successively through the graduation-houses, until it has become sufficiently concentrated to be evaporated by heat. The amount of evaporation depends chiefly on atmospheric conditions, especially on temperature, the state of dryness of the air, and the force and direction of the wind.

The waters, being brought by graduation to contain 16 or 20 per cent. of salt, are collected in reservoirs, to be afterwards evaporated in pans.

Salines readily abandon their carbonic acid to the air, in the reservoirs in which they were collected previously to passing through the graduation-houses, so that the carbonates of lime and iron, which were dissolved only by this free carbonic acid, are there deposited. The same takes place with the sulphate of lime, which incrusts the fagots during the evaporation of the waters in the graduation-houses.

§496. The waters concentrated by graduation are evaporated in pans in the same manner as the saturated waters previously mentioned (§494). But, as they are much less pure, it is necessary to divide the operation into two periods; the first, which is called *sludging*, (schlotage,) is intended to separate a large portion of the foreign salts, principally the double sulphate of lime and soda. The salt crystallizes during the second stage of the operation, which is called *salining*, or *soccage.*

About 30 cubic metres of salt-water being introduced in the pan, it is made to boil briskly, and as it evaporates, an additional quantity is run in, until from 46 to 50 cubic metres of water are introduced. The surface of the liquid soon becoming covered with scum, from the organic substances which are coagulated by heat, it is skimmed off. A copious deposit of sulphate of lime, combined with the greater portion of sulphate of soda, is then formed, called *sludge*, (schlot,) which is raked out and put into a hole near the pan. After some time the fire is slackened, and the sludge again removed. At Moutiers, the sludging continues for 20 to 36 hours; at the end of which time the salt begins to appear. The temperature of the liquid is then maintained at about 170°, and as the salt crystallizes, it is brought to the edge of the pan to drain. The salining lasts for 70 to 75 hours, when it is stopped, on account of the impurity of the salt deposited from the mother waters, being highly charged with deliquescent salts. These mother waters being allowed to flow off, the operation is again commenced.

The sludge, as well as the incrustation, on the sides of the pan, is subjected to a peculiar process, which yields a quantity of sulphate of soda. They are placed in a close wooden box, into which steam is passed, in order that the hot water, condensing, may dissolve the sulphate of soda. The solution being conveyed into crystallizers and allowed to cool as much as possible, sulphate of soda is deposited in crystals.

§ 497. Salt is extracted from sea-water in two different ways:—1st. By the spontaneous evaporation of the water in large, shallow vessels. 2d. By reducing the sea-water to a very low temperature, when a portion of the water separates in the form of ice, which is removed, and the remainder contains near all the salt, dissolved in a smaller quantity of water. This latter process is adopted only in northern countries, as on the shores of the White Sea, and affords water sufficiently concentrated to be evaporated advantageously by heat. The former is used in hot, and even in temperate regions. In France, it is adopted on the shores of the ocean and of the Mediterranean. We shall describe this manufacture in detail, not only on account of its importance, but also because it furnishes a great number of applications of the principles we have established on the solubility and mutual decomposition of salts.

A salt-marsh, sometimes also called a *saline*, consists essentially of an extended surface, intended for the spontaneous evaporation of sea-water, and is divided into a series of compartments, through which the water flows successively in a slow current, which can be regulated at pleasure. When the water has reached the end of its course and remained for some time in the last compartments, it has always deposited the greater portion of the salt it held in solution.

The saline is constructed near the sea or a salt lake, and, if possible, below their level, so that the water naturally flows into the saline, and its quantity can be regulated by means of a floodgate. It is usually, however, above the level of the sea, so that the water must be elevated by hydraulic machines.

Fig. 362 represents a saline in the environs of Montpellier.

The water is conveyed from the sea A into a vast irregularly shaped basin C, serving as a reservoir, in which the waters undergo a first evaporation. It should, therefore, be very large and shallow, so as to present as great a surface as possible for evaporation. From this the water flows gradually and slowly, by means of a properly arranged shoot, into a series of rectangular basins *d*, *d*, *d*..., more shallow than the large reservoir C; and, after having traversed these basins, where it is again evaporated, is conveyed by a canal E, E, E into large wells F, called the *wells of weak brine*, (*puits des eaux vertes*.) By suction or other pumps the water is lifted into a gutter G, G, which conveys it into other

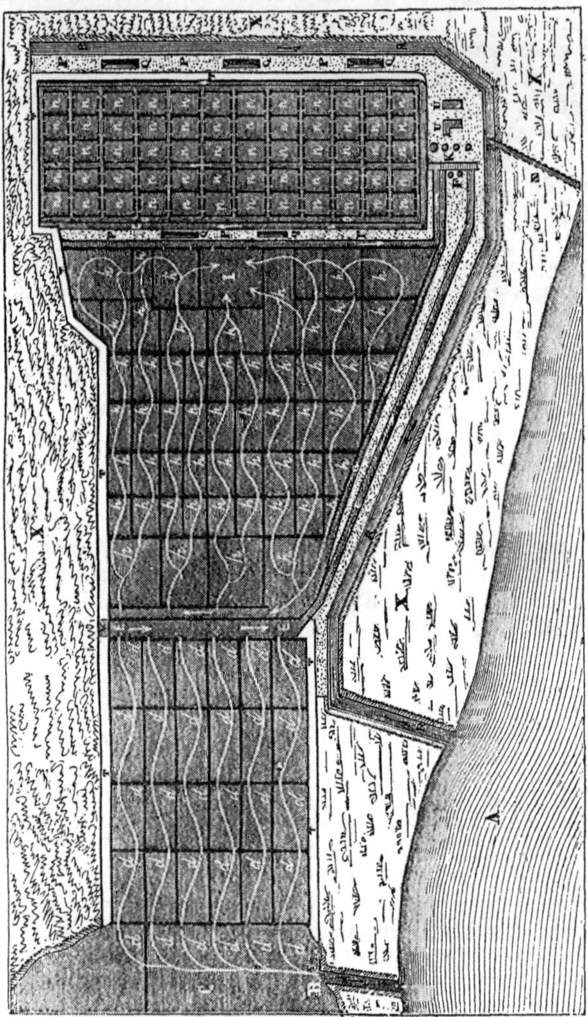

Fig. 362.

evaporating basins *h*, *h*, *h*, *h*, more carefully constructed than the former, and in which the evaporation is continued. The flow of water is so arranged that when it reaches the last basin I, called the *principal compartment*, (*pièce maîtresse*,) it has attained the degree of concentration at which it begins to deposit salt. It is thence conveyed, by the gutter J, J, J, into other wells K, called *wells of strong brine*, (*puits de l'eau en sel.*) The evaporating basins *h*, *h*, *h* are called the *interior warming-place*.

The strong brine is pumped from the wells K into new evaporating basins *n*, *n*, *n*, smaller and very carefully made, and called *salt-tables*. A gutter L, L, L, surrounding them, receives the water of the pumps, and distributes it over the tables by means of smaller gutters called *needles*. These also serve to convey the waters, which have deposited the greater portion of their salt on the tables, into a surrounding canal O, O, O, whence they can again flow into the sea.

The layer of water covering the tables should not exceed 5 or 6 centimetres (2–2½ in.) in depth, and is renewed daily, or every two days, according to the evaporation. The salt forms a compact layer, which gradually increases. The operation is continued for five or six months, from April to September, or during the fine weather.

The salt, being collected by allowing the tables to dry and removing it with shovels, is piled into long heaps Q, Q, called *camelles*.

§ 498. Let us now examine the chemical operation of salt-making.

Sea-water presents, on an average, the following composition:

Water	96.470
Chloride of sodium	2.700
Chloride of potassium	0.070
Chloride of magnesium	0.360
Sulphate of magnesia	0.230
Sulphate of lime	0.140
Carbonate of lime	0.003
Bromide of magnesium	0.002
Loss	0.025
	100.000

The water, when evaporated, first deposits its carbonate of lime, which is often tinged yellow by the hydrated peroxide of iron; but as the presence of iron has not yet been detected in sea-water, the oxide found in this first deposit probably arises from the soil on which the evaporation is effected. The peroxide is converted into protoxide by the spontaneous putrefaction of organic matter developed in the salt-water; and forms carbonate of the protoxide of iron, which at first dissolves on account of the excess of carbonic acid, but is afterward decomposed by contact with the oxygen of the air, and deposits the hydrated sesquioxide of iron. In fact, as long as the salt-water does not exceed a density of 5° or 6° of the hydrometer by concentration, numerous confervæ are developed, which perish when the water is further concentrated.

§ 499. The water, by passing from one table to another, becomes more and more concentrated, and, when it marks 15° or 18° of the hydrometer, deposits a considerable quantity of sulphate of lime, which is hydrated, and has the same composition and crystalline form as gypsum. In this case, therefore, it does not combine with sulphate of soda, to form the double sulphate of soda and lime called *sludge*, which is deposited during the evaporation of sea-water by heat, because the latter is never formed in the cold, when the sulphate of soda exists in the hydrated state in solution; and is formed only in hot solutions, in which the sulphate is found in the anhydrous state.

The whole of the sulphate of lime is deposited when the water marks 25° hydrometer, because, although it is quite soluble in pure water, it is completely insoluble in a saturated solution of sulphate of magnesia, which the concentrated waters contain in quantity.

Having reached this degree of concentration, the water begins to deposit sea-salt, the stratum of which becomes thicker as the evaporation continues. The crystals are at first transparent, and increase in size, without augmenting in number, so long as the water is not very concentrated. But when concentration renders it richer in chloride of magnesium, which interferes with the solubility of sea-salt, the latter is deposited in smaller crystals, of a dead-white colour.

The mother waters must then be removed before they have deposited all the sea-salt they contain, because the latter portions of it would be injured by the salts of magnesia. The concentration is rarely carried beyond 30°, when the water is drawn off, and replaced by new portions from the well of strong brine. The mother waters are emptied 3 or 4 times during the season. The salt is collected in heaps, and, when sufficiently drained, is generally very pure.

§ 500. The mother waters from the drainage and evaporation, are generally rejected, but, as they contain many useful products, they might be worked if their manufacture were not too expensive. Of late years, the solution of this question* has received much attention at the salt-works on the Mediterranean, and the extraction of secondary products has become quite important. When the mother waters mark 30° hydrometer, they contain, in 100 parts,

Chloride of magnesium	16.6
Chloride of sodium	4.6
Sulphate of magnesia	2.0

This composition differs greatly from that of the mother waters which remain after the extraction of salt from salt-springs. Thus the mother waters of the salines of Moutiers contain—

Chloride of magnesium	4.8
Chloride of sodium	20.8
Sulphate of magnesia	9.5

* The details of working the mother waters of salines have been furnished us by Mr. Balard, who has made the subject his peculiar study.

The mother waters of the Mediterranean salt-works are about four times richer in chloride of magnesium than those of Moutiers. The presence of this chloride, diminishing considerably the solubility of sea-salt, explains the poverty of the former in chloride of sodium.

§ 501. The concentration of the mother waters yields nearly pure sea-salt by evaporation during the day; but, by cooling during the night, sulphate of magnesia is deposited. As the deposits generally take place in the same table, a coherent saline stratum is obtained, composed of crystals of sea-salt, cemented together by sulphate of magnesia. The sulphate being less soluble in water containing chloride of magnesium than in pure water, the increasing quantity of the latter in the mother water contributes greatly to the deposition of the sulphate of magnesia.

If the temperature of the air falls suddenly to 50°, as sometimes happens in September after a storm, the waters, spread over an empty table, may yield considerable quantities of pure sulphate of magnesia.

§ 502. When the waters, by proper concentration, have been reduced to a density of about 34° hydrometer, they begin to deposit sulphate of potassa, not in a pure state, but in that of a double magnesian salt KO,SO_3+MgO,SO_3+6HO. At this degree of concentration, they deposit scarcely any sea-salt, but almost exclusively the double sulphate just alluded to, and which is produced at the same time, either by evaporation or by cooling. The crude double salt collected on the tables is easily purified by resolution and recrystallization.

§ 503. When the waters have been reduced by concentration to about 36°, they deposit, especially on cooling, a new product, a double chloride of potassium and magnesium, $KCl+MgCl$. It is, however, difficult to evaporate them, on account of the deliquescence of the chloride of magnesium, of which they contain a large proportion. The evaporation is more effectually performed by the direct application of heat. If the mother water be evaporated by fire, after it has been subjected for some time to a low temperature, as 35° or 37°, when it parts with nearly all its sulphate of magnesia, almost the whole of the potassa may be obtained in the state of a double chloride of potassium and magnesium.

When the mother water has been concentrated to 40°, it then contains only chloride of magnesium, which it deposits in large crystals at a temperature approaching to 32°.

§ 504. In these successive evaporations, the quantity of the water has greatly diminished. As it deposits, in the course of concentration, a considerable quantity of saline matter, which increases its density, the increase of degrees noted by the hydrometer is far from being in the inverse ratio of the diminution of volume. The following example exhibits this fact:

10 litres of sea-water, marking 25° hydrometer, occupy only a volume of 935 cubic centimetres, which is reduced to 200 cubic centim., when the water marks 30°. The water only marks 31° when evaporation has reduced it to 50 cubic centim. Lastly, the mother water marking 34° occupies a volume of only 30 cubic centim.

In conclusion, it appears, that besides sea-salt, the evaporation of the mother waters yields three series of saline products:

1st. A mixture of sulphate of magnesia and sea-salt;

2dly. A saline mixture rich in the double sulphate of potassa and magnesia;

3dly. A salt containing chiefly the double chloride of potassium and magnesium.

§505. We shall now see how these various products may be treated, in order to extract from them the useful substances which they contain.

1st. If we wish to extract the sulphate of magnesia from the first mixture, we might do it by dissolving it in water at a temperature of about 86°, and allowing the solution to cool. But this temperature must not be exceeded, for a double decomposition would ensue, producing a true *magnesian sludge*, the double sulphate of soda and magnesia. The last double salt, redissolved in water and crystallized at a low temperature, would divide into sulphate of magnesia, which would remain in the mother waters, and sulphate of soda, which would crystallize.

The best method of utilizing the saline mixture consists in dissolving it in water charged with sea-salt, so that the liquid may contain, for 1 equiv. of sulphate of magnesia, 2 equivs. of sea-salt, and dissolving it at the lowest temperature possible. A double decomposition takes place, producing sulphate of soda, which crystallizes in the hydrated state, and chloride of magnesium, which remains in the mother waters.

At 28°, four-fifths of the sulphate of magnesia are converted into sulphate of soda, which is deposited on the ground, in a state of great purity. It is collected perfectly free from earthy matter, if the ground on which it was deposited has been previously covered with a coating of sea-salt. The mother water, rich in chloride of magnesium, contains only about one-fifth of the sulphate which previously entered into its composition. It must be removed immediately, because, if the temperature rises, the water redissolves, by an inverse decomposition, the sulphate of soda deposited during the night. Water charged with chloride of magnesium dissolves, in fact, much more sulphate of soda than pure water. That, on the contrary, which contains chloride of sodium, dissolves much less than pure water; and for this reason, it is proper that the solution should contain more than 1 equiv. of sea-salt for 1 equiv. of sulphate of magnesia.

The sulphate of soda thus collected is dried in a reverberatory furnace, and employed either in the manufacture of soda or of glass.

It is not only from a solution composed solely of sulphate of magnesia and chloride of sodium, that the sulphate of soda can be obtained. The mother water of the salines itself deposits a certain quantity of this salt, when it is reduced to a low temperature. The same is true of sea-water concentrated to 25°, before it has depoted sea-salt; but the proportion of sulphate of soda obtained in this case is small, and requires a much lower temperature. In fact, in the latter case, the solution is but slightly concentrated, and is especially poor in sulphate of magnesia. In the other case, the mother water, although concentrated, contains a great deal of chloride of magnesium, which interferes with the solubility both of chloride of sodium and of sulphate of magnesia. The chloride of magnesium here acts as a cause preventing the two salts, between which decomposition is to take place, from coming into each other's presence in a state of solution. It is then as if the complicated solution which is to yield the sulphate were less concentrated. The same presence of chloride of magnesium increasing the solubility of the sulphate of soda, the solution in which it exists is in the same situation as if its temperature were less depressed. This double cause acts in the same way, and must greatly diminish the quantity of sulphate of soda produced. In order to obtain a large quantity of sulphate of soda, we must eliminate as much chloride of magnesium as possible and operate, on the contrary, with a great excess of sea-salt.

2d. The saline mixture, composed principally of the double sulphate of potassa and magnesia, need only be redissolved hot and again crystallized in order to deposit, on cooling, this double salt in a state of great purity, and leave the foreign salts in the mother waters. The operation may even be performed on the ground, on tables arranged by stages, so that the waters flowing toward sunset, from an upper on to a lower table, may deposit sea-salt, in the former, *by evaporation during the day;* and in the latter, *by cooling during the night*, the double sulphate of magnesia and potassa, nearly in a state of purity.

The division of this product into sulphate of potassa and sulphate of magnesia is not readily effected on a large scale, but the double salt itself may be used in the manufacture of alum. Carbonate of potassa may also be prepared from it by Leblanc's method of making artificial soda (§ 472), for which purpose 100 parts of the hydrated double sulphate are heated in a reverberatory furnace with 46 of carbonate of lime and 26 of charcoal. Proceeding as in the fabrication of artificial soda, a crude potash is obtained which marks 24 per cent. alkali on the alkalimeter. By treating it with water and evaporating the liquid, a richer product is obtained, containing 55 to 60 per cent. of potassa, which is about the richness of the crude potash of commerce. In this operation the sulphate of magnesia is destroyed, and magnesia remains in the insoluble residue with the oxysulphide of calcium.

3d. The transformation of the double chloride of magnesium and potassium into two single chlorides presents fewer difficulties than that of the double sulphate, it being only necessary to expose the double chloride to the action of a slightly moist atmosphere, which liquifies the chloride of magnesium and separates it from the alkaline chloride. It is still better to dissolve this double chloride in boiling water and evaporate the hot liquor, during which nearly pure chloride of potassium precipitates. At last, however, the double chloride is also deposited; when the liquor being allowed to cool, the greater part of the double chloride crystallizes. It is separated and operated on in the same way as the original double chloride. The mother waters, when well cooled, contain scarcely any potassa, but only chloride of magnesium.

Use may also be made of these last mother waters, for chloride of magnesium is decomposable by steam at a high temperature, with the production of magnesia and chlorohydric acid. It is therefore conceivable that these mother waters, as well as those which had furnished the saline product by evaporation on the ground, might be used, by merely arranging an apparatus for collecting large quantities of chlorohydric acid. Moreover, the bromides being concentrated in the last mother waters, they will yield a large quantity of bromine by distilling them with proper quantities of sulphuric acid and binoxide of manganese; for it was shown (§ 504) that in this state of great concentration, they result from a considerable quantity of sea-water.

COMPOUNDS OF SODIUM WITH SULPHUR.

§ 506. Sodium forms a great number of compounds with sulphur, corresponding exactly to those of potassium, and prepared in the same manner. The protosulphide of sodium crystallizes more readily than that of potassium, and it may be obtained in the form of large octohedrons. A great number of sulphosalts are formed, of which the majority are susceptible of crystallization. The hydrate of soda and carbonate behave also, with sulphur, both in the dry and humid way, like the hydrate and carbonate of potassa (§ 458).

DISTINCTIVE CHARACTERS OF THE SALTS OF SODA.

§ 507. We shall here present only the characters which distinguish the salts of soda from those formed by the other alkalies; for we have seen (§ 463) that the alkaline salts can readily be distinguished from all others.

The distinctive characters of the salts of soda are based principally on the physical properties of a few of them, which are instantly distinguished from the corresponding salts of potassa. Sulphate of soda, crystallized when cold, contains a great deal of water of crystallization, effloresces in the air, and readily undergoes aqueous fusion. Sulphate of potassa is anhydrous, does not change in the air, and fuses only at a high temperature. Equally marked differences distinguish the two carbonates, that of soda being efflorescent, while that of potassa is deliquescent.

Chloride of sodium forms, with bichloride of platinum, a double chloride, analagous to that formed by chloride of potassium; but the double salt is very soluble in water, and even in alcohol, while the double chloride of platinum and potassium is but slightly soluble. It follows thence that the solutions of salts of potassa yield a yellow crystalline precipitate when a solution of bichloride of platinum is poured into them, while the salts of soda yield none.

In like manner, the salts of soda yield no precipitate, either with tartaric or perchloric acid, even when their solutions are concentrated.

LITHIUM.

EQUIVALENT = 6.43 (O = 80.37.)

§ 508. Lithium* has hitherto been obtained only in small quantities by decomposing oxide of lithium by the voltaic pile, in the same manner as potassium; but it might probably be obtained by the processes of reduction now employed in the preparation of large quantities of potassium and sodium. In its physical properties it is very analagous to potassium and sodium, and decomposes water at ordinary temperatures.

Lithium exists in several minerals, the most important of which are *petalite*, and a species of mica called *lepidolite*. Lithia is generally extracted from lepidolite, which contains 3 or 4 per cent. of it, besides potassa, soda, alumina, oxide of iron, silicic acid, and a small quantity of chlorine. The lepidolite, finely powdered and mixed with double its weight of quicklime, is calcined in a strong forge-fire, pulverized, and then boiled for some time with water, to which slaked lime is added. The liquid is decanted, saturated with chlorohydric acid, and evaporated, when a quantity of chloride of potassium is deposited. By pouring an excess of carbonate of ammonia into the mother waters, a small quantity of alumina and lime is precipitated. The solution being evaporated to dryness, and the residue calcined to drive off ammoniacal salts, there remain only the chlorides of potassium, sodium, and lithium. The chlorides are finely powdered, and treated by concentrated alcohol, which dissolves only the chloride of lithium.

Chloride of lithium is a deliquescent salt. By heating it with concentrated sulphuric acid, sulphate of lithia is obtained. By pouring acetate of baryta into the solution of sulphate of lithia, a precipitate of sulphate of baryta is formed and the acetate of lithia remains in solution. The acetate by calcination yields carbonate of lithia.

Carbonate of lithia is but partially soluble in water, so that somewhat concentrated solutions of the salts of lithia yield a precipitate with the carbonates of potassa and soda.

Lithia itself is prepared by decomposing a solution of carbonate of lithia by hydrate of lime, which yields a hydrate of lithia with the formula $LiO+HO$, even after calcination; for the hydrate is not decomposed by heat. Lithia attacks platinum energetically, a globule of it melted on a plate of platinum leaving a black spot, and if the fused alkali be kept for some time in a platinum crucible, it may corrode through the metal.

---

* Lithia was discovered in 1817, by Mr. Arfwedson, a Swedish chemist.

Only one oxide of lithium is as yet known, and is composed of

Lithium	44.56
Oxygen	55.44
	100.00

from which the equivalent of lithium may be deduced = 6.43.

CHARACTERS OF THE SALTS OF LITHIA.

§ 509. The salts of lithia are distinguished from those formed by other metals, except the alkaline, by the property of not being precipitated by alkaline carbonates when their solutions are dilute. If the solutions were concentrated a precipitate might form, because carbonate of lithia is but partially soluble in water.

Lithia is distinguished from potassa and soda,

1st. By the feeble solubility of its carbonate in cold liquids;

2dly. By chloride of lithium being deliquescent and dissolving in alcohol, while the chlorides of potassium and sodium do not change in an atmosphere which is not saturated with moisture, and do not dissolve sensibly in concentrated alcohol;

3dly. By the slight solubility of phosphate of lithia; for when a solution of an alkaline phosphate is gradually poured into a solution of a salt of lithia, a precipitate is formed, which is generally a double phosphate.

AMMONIACAL COMPOUNDS.

§ 510. It was shown (§ 122 and follow.) that ammonia is a compound of nitrogen and hydrogen, having a strong alkaline reaction on coloured reagents, and combining with acids, which it saturates as perfectly as the most powerful bases. As it is derived from organic matter, the study of it and its compounds would seem more appropriate to the last part of this work, devoted to the compounds extracted from organized beings. But as ammoniacal salts present such a perfect analogy with the corresponding salts of potassa and soda, and are, moreover, used in the laboratory as frequently as the alkaline salts, it would be embarrassing to delay further their consideration; to which we therefore now proceed.

§ 511. Ammonia has not as yet been combined with elementary substances. The metalloids either do not act on ammonia, or they decompose it. Thus, oxygen exerts no action in the cold on ammonia, and decomposes it by heat, combining with hydrogen to form water, and setting nitrogen free. Chlorine and iodine decompose it even in the cold, as was shown in § 92.

§ 512. Ammoniacal gas combines directly with the anhydrous hydracids. One volume of the gas combines with 1 volume of chlorohydric acid gas, affording a white crystalline compound, which should be considered as a chlorohydrate of ammonia, with the formula NH_3,HCl. The same compound is formed when a solution of chlorohydric acid is mixed with a solution of ammonia, the liquid yielding, after evaporation, crystals having the same formula NH_3,HCl.

§ 513. Ammonia also combines with the oxacids, forming true salts, which are frequently neutral with coloured reagents. By saturating a solution of sulphuric acid with ammonia, a salt is obtained, after evaporating the liquid, with the formula NH_3,SO_3+HO, and presenting the same crystalline form as the sulphate of potassa KO,SO_3. The equivalent of water which this salt contains cannot be abstracted from it by heat without decomposition; a circumstance which always obtains in the ammoniacal salts formed by the oxacids. They all contain 1 equivalent of water, necessary to their existence, and we are authorized to say that the ammonia NH_3 does not play the part of a base with the oxacids, but that ammonia combined with 1 equivalent of water does. Basic ammonia will, therefore, always be represented by the formula NH_3,HO.

By comparing sulphate of ammonia with sulphate of potassa, with which it is isomorphous, it appears that hydrated ammonia NH_3,HO performs the functions of potassa KO. In consequence of this correspondence, some chemists write the formula of hydrated ammonia NH_4,O; that is to say, they regard it as the oxide of a peculiar radical NH_4, to which they give the name of *ammonium*, and assimilate it to a metal, such as potassium. The chlorohydrate of ammonia NH_3,HCl, may then be considered as a chloride of ammonium NH_4,Cl, exactly corresponding to the chloride of potassium KCl.

§ 514. Dry ammoniacal gas, however, can combine with the anhydrous acids, but the resulting compounds are not true salts. Thus, anhydrous sulphuric acid absorbs ammoniacal gas rapidly; but a compound NH_3,SO_3 is formed, very different from the ordinary sulphate of ammonia $(NH_3,HO)SO_3$, and to which the name of *sulphamide* has been given. For if an excess of chloride of barium be poured into a solution of ordinary sulphate of ammonia, all the sulphuric acid is at once obtained in the state of sulphate of baryta; and such is the behaviour of all the sulphates formed by the oxacids. But if the same experiment be made on a solution of sulphamide, a very small portion only of the sulphuric acid is precipitated, and the whole of the acid can only be precipitated by boiling the liquid for a long time with an excess of chloride of barium.

By acting with dry ammoniacal gas on chlorosulphuric liquid SO_2Cl, (the preparation of which was given in § 132,) a compound is obtained which, after solution in water, behaves like a mixture of chlorohydrate of ammonia and sulphamide:

$$SO_2Cl+2NH_3+HO=NH_3,HCl+NH_3,SO_3.$$

The chlorohydrate of ammonia in this solution presents the usual reaction of metallic chlorides. Thus, nitrate of silver completely precipitates the chlorine in the state of chloride of silver, and ammonia may be precipitated by the bichloride of platinum, with which the chlorohydrate of ammonia forms a compound $(NH_3,HCl+PtCl_2)$ of slight solubility and corresponding to the double chloride of platinum and potassium, (mentioned in § 463.) On the other hand, the anhydrous sulphate of ammonia, or sulphamide NH_3,SO_3, which is found in the same liquid, behaves in a very different manner from the ordinary sulphate of ammonia $(NH_3,HO)SO_3$, for it yields no precipitate, either with the salts of baryta or with the bichloride of platinum.

If dry ammoniacal and sulphurous gases be mixed together, they combine in equal volumes, and form a yellow crystalline compound. Since the equivalent of ammoniacal gas is represented by 4 volumes, and that of sulphurous acid by 2 volumes, 1 equivalent of ammonia has combined with 2 equivalents of sulphurous acid, and the formula of the compound is $NH_3,2SO_2$. This substance dissolves in water, but is soon decomposed into sulphate and hyposulphate of ammonia, the decomposition taking place much more rapidly in the presence of strong acids or bases. The bisulphite of ammonia $(NH_3,HO)2SO_2$, presents no similar properties.

Thus, by the side of ordinary ammoniacal salts, we have a parallel series of products, which only differ from the corresponding ammoniacal salts in not containing the equivalent of water of composition which is found in all the ordinary ammoniacal salts. These products, to which the generic name of *amides** is given, are readily converted into the ordinary ammoniacal salts, usually by merely boiling them for some time with water. The amide, by taking 1 equivalent of water, is converted into an ordinary ammoniacal salt.

Chlorohydrate of Ammonia.

§ 515. It was stated (§ 124) that chlorohydric and ammoniacal gases combine directly to form a solid compound, the chlorohydrate of ammonia NH_3,HCl. The same compound is obtained by mixing solutions of the two gases, when the salt crystallizes upon evaporating the liquid. Hydrochlorate of ammonia is the most important of all the ammoniacal compounds, being exclusively used in the laboratory in the preparation of ammonia (§ 122); and has various applications in the arts, where it is known by the name of *sal ammoniac.* It dissolves in 2.7 parts of cold, and in its own weight of boiling water, so that a hot concentrated solution deposits, on cooling, the greater portion of the salt dissolved, crystallizing in long needles, the true form of which it is, at first, difficult to ascertain. By means of a powerful lens or microscope, the needles will be found to consist of small regular octohedrons aggregated at their angles. The elementary form of sal ammoniac belongs, therefore, to the regular crystalline system, like those of the chlorides of potassium and sodium. The same grouping of octohedral crystals is observed in the substance formed by the direct combination of ammoniacal and chlorohydric gas, as well as in sublimed sal ammoniac. This tendency of the crystals to collect in threads, gives the salt great elasticity and a certain degree of flexibility, which renders it a difficult matter to reduce it to a very fine powder.

Chlorohydrate of ammonia is soluble in alcohol. Heated to redness, it volatilizes without fusing; and, to obtain it in a liquid form, it must be heated under a pressure greater than that of the atmosphere. Its density is about 1.5.

§ 516. Chlorohydrate of ammonia is manufactured in various ways. For a long time, all the sal ammoniac used in the arts came from Egypt, where the inhabitants, from the scarcity of wood, use camel's dung as fuel, made into balls, which are dried in

---

* Oxamide $NH_3C_2O_3$ (or NH_2,C_2O_2), the first substance of this group of bodies which arrested the attention of chemists, was discovered by M. Dumas.

Fig. 363.

the sun. The soot deposited in the chimneys where this fuel is burned, containing a great deal of sal ammoniac, is carefully collected and sold to the manufacturers of sal ammoniac, who sublime it in large glass vessels (fig. 363). The sal ammoniac volatilizes and condenses on the upper part of the vessels, which are then broken, and the salt removed. It is generally coloured brown by the empyreumatic oils which are evolved during the calcination.

Sal ammoniac is now prepared in Europe, being an incidental product of several processes. When bituminous coal is distilled for the purpose of making gas, a great deal of carbonate of ammonia is disengaged, which is condensed in water or in a solution of chlorohydric acid. A large quantity of carbonate of ammonia is also obtained in calcining animal matters for the preparation of nitrogenous charcoal, intended for the manufacture of cyanide of potassium. The calcination is effected in large sheet-iron cylinders communicating with a series of casks, through which the gases must pass before escaping into the air, and in which the empyreumatic products, with a large quantity of carbonate of ammonia, are condensed. After the first operation the charcoal is withdrawn, and an additional quantity of the substance introduced. The ammoniacal liquids are drawn off from time to time, by spigots in the lower part of the casks, and run into large reservoirs where they are allowed to settle. The oily matters collecting on the surface are skimmed off. Solid carbonate of ammonia is also deposited in the upper part of the casks. This carbonate is either dissolved in the ammoniacal liquid, or immediately purified by sublimation, in order to obtain solid carbonate of ammonia. The ammoniacal liquid is then saturated with chlorohydric acid, and evaporated, when it yields crystals of impure sal ammoniac. In order to purify them, they are heated in an oven to a temperature approaching that at which the salt volatilizes, whereby the organic matter they contain is destroyed. By treating them with water, sal ammoniac is dissolved, and a carbonaceous residue remains. The solution, boiled with animal charcoal to bleach it, yields perfectly white crystals after evaporation. It must, however, be sublimed, in order to give it the appearance to which we are accustomed, before it is marketable. The sublimation is effected in large earthenware flasks, which are filled three-fourths full, and heated from below to the temperature at which the salt sublimes. It is necessary to guard against a stoppage of the mouth of the flasks to prevent their bursting, and this is effected by passing an iron rod through the opening and piercing the crust of sublimed matter, if the neck be obstructed. The flasks are then broken and the cake of sublimed sal ammoniac withdrawn.

A certain quantity of chlorohydrate of ammonia is also extracted from the carbonate of ammonia contained in putrefied urine. The urine is distilled in an alembic, until about one-third of the liquor passes over; which third contains all the carbonate of ammonia. It is saturated with chlorohydric acid, the hydrochlorate crystallized, and purified by sublimation. The preparation of sulphate of ammonia frequently precedes that of the chlorohydrate, by filtering the ammoniacal waters arising from the distillation through a dense stratum of plaster, whereby an insoluble carbonate of lime is formed, and sulphate of ammonia remains in solution. The liquid being concentrated, and sufficient sea-salt added to convert the sulphate into chlorohydrate, it is evaporated to dryness and the dried residue sublimed. Chlorohydrate of ammonia sublimes, while the sulphate of soda remains at the bottom of the vessel. At other times, the solution of the two salts is rapidly evaporated at the boiling temperature; the sulphate of soda, which crystallizes, is raked out as fast as it forms, and when a large proportion of the sulphate has been thus removed, the liquid is allowed to cool. The solubility of sulphate of soda increasing as the temperature falls from the boiling point of the solution to 92°, none of it will be deposited during cooling, while the solubility of sal ammoniac diminishing rapidly with the temperature, the greater portion of this salt crystallizes. The crystals are collected, allowed to drain, and purified by sublimation.

Ammonia and Sulfhydric Acid.

§ 517. Ammoniacal and sulphuretted hydrogen gases combine volume for volume, yielding a very volatile yellow compound. The equivalent of ammoniacal gas being 4 volumes, and that of sulfhydric acid gas 2 volumes, the compound is a sulfhydrate, the formula of which is $NH_3,2HS$. A simple sulfhydrate NH_3, HS may, however, be obtained by the direct combination of the two gases, but a great excess of ammonia is required, and the vessel must be very cold. The compound is destroyed and parts with one-half of its ammonia, when the temperature rises.

Sulfhydrates of ammonia, in different degrees of sulphuration, are obtained by distilling sal ammoniac with various alkaline sulphides, or with mixtures of quicklime and sulphur. Fetid, fuming liquid products are evolved, which were formerly called *Boyle's fuming liquid.*

Bisulfhydrate of ammonia in solution is often used in the laboratory as a test, and is prepared by passing hydrosulphuric acid gas through a solution of ammonia to saturation.

The simple sulfhydrate plays the part of a sulphobase with electronegative sulphides, forming a great number of sulphosalts. It combines with sulphide of carbon, the sulphides of arsenic, sulphide of antimony, etc. When these sulphacids are digested with the bisulfhydrate of ammonia $NH_3,2HS$, they expel one-half of its sulfhydric acid, and yield the sulphosalts $(NH_3,HS)CS_2$; $(NH_3,HS)AsS_3$; $(NH_3,HS)AsS_5$; $(NH_3,HS)S6_2S_3$, etc.

Sulphate of Ammonia.

§ 518. Neutral sulphate of ammonia $(NH_3,HO)SO_3$ is obtained by saturating a solution of ammonia by sulphuric acid. In manufactories, the impure ammoniacal liquid arising from the distillation of animal substances is used; but it is frequently decomposed by sulphate of lime. The salt is crystallized by evaporation, and purified by a gentle calcination so as to decompose the organic substances which adulterate it. It is then redissolved and crystallized. The sulphate $(NH_3,HO)SO_3$ contains no water of crystallization, and is isomorphous with sulphate of potassa KO,SO_3. It dissolves in 2 parts of cold, and in only 1 part of boiling water. It is decomposed by heat, water and nitrogen being disengaged, and sulphite of ammonia $(NH_3,HO)SO_2$ subliming.

By adding sulphuric acid to the preceding sulphate, a bisulphate is obtained, which can be crystallized, and of which the formula is

$$3[(NH_3,HO)SO_3+HO,SO_3]+HO.$$

Nitrate of Ammonia.

§ 519. This salt is obtained by saturating a solution of ammonia or of carbonate of ammonia by nitric acid, evaporating the solution, and allowing it to cool, when crystals of nitrate of ammonia will be deposited, with the formula $(NH_3,HO)NO_5+HO$. They fuse at a low temperature, and, if further heated, decompose into water and protoxide of nitrogen. By means of this reaction, the protoxide of nitrogen is prepared (§ 109). Nitrate of ammonia deflagrates vividly on burning coals, a reddish flame being produced by the combustion of hydrogen by the oxygen of the nitric acid. From this property it has been called *nitrum flamans.*

Phosphates of Ammonia.

§ 520. Ammonia forms several compounds with phosphoric acid, the most important of which is that corresponding to the ordinary phosphate of soda $(2NaO+HO)PO_5$, and is obtained by decomposing biphosphate of lime by a solution of carbonate of ammonia. The liquid, which ought to manifest a slight alkaline reaction, is evaporated, and deposits crystals, with the formula $[2(NH_3,HO)+HO]PO_5$.

By adding to a solution of this salt as much more phosphoric acid as it already contains, and evaporating the liquid, a new salt is obtained, with the formula $(NH_3HO+2HO)PO_5$.

The phosphates of ammonia, subjected to heat, part with the

greater portion of their ammonia, leaving vitreous phosphoric acid, which always retains a certain quantity of ammonia.

Carbonates of Ammonia.

§ 521. Ammonia and carbonic acid combine in several proportions, but the compounds are not very stable, and are readily converted into each other. The two dry gases combine, in the proportion of 2 volumes of ammoniacal gas and 1 volume of carbonic acid gas, if an excess of ammonia be found in the mixture. These proportions correspond to the formula NH_3,CO_2. The substance dissolves readily in water, and presents the characters of the carbonates; so that on dissolving it in water, the compound NH_3CO_2 immediately takes the equivalent of water which is necessary for its transformation into the carbonate of ammonia $(NH_3,HO)CO_2$.

A great deal of carbonate of ammonia is produced in the distillation of animal substances, but its composition varies, because it generally results from a mixture of several carbonates in different degrees of saturation. In order to purify the crude carbonate, it is merely distilled with animal charcoal, when the carbonate sublimes perfectly white. The formula $2(NH_3,HO)3CO_2$ represents the most frequent carbonate. When exposed to the air, ammonia is disengaged, and the bicarbonate of ammonia $(NH_3,HO)CO_2+HO,CO_2$ remains. Its solution in water likewise changes finally into the bicarbonate, when exposed for a long time to the air.

The bicarbonate in solution, subjected to heat, parts with its carbonic acid more readily than with its ammonia, and has a tendency to be converted into a neutral carbonate; but prolonged ebullition completely drives off the whole salt.

The bicarbonate is also obtained by passing a current of carbonic acid gas through a solution of ammonia, until the gas ceases to be dissolved. If a very concentrated solution has been used, a portion of the bicarbonate is deposited in crystals.

Action of Potassium and Sodium on Ammonia.

§ 522. Potassium and sodium, heated in ammoniacal gas, are converted into a crystalline substance of an olive-green colour, which melts at about 212°, and at the same time a volume of hydrogen gas, equal to that which the metal would evolve on contact with water, is disengaged. The olive-green substance is decomposed by heat; ammonia and a mixture of hydrogen and nitrogen being disengaged in the proportions constituting ammonia, while an infusible graphitic substance remains.

The olive-green compound, treated with water, yields potassa and ammonia. We have no precise information as to the composition of this substance, but the foregoing reactions are explained by supposing that the formula of the graphitic body is NK_3, and that of the olive-green compound NK_3+2NH_3.

Action of the Voltaic Pile on Ammonia in solution.

§ 523. Having put at the bottom of a glass, a stratum of mercury which is connected with the negative pole of a battery, a concentrated solution of ammonia is poured over it, into which the positive pole is plunged, carrying the end of the platinum wire to the distance of about 2 millimetres from the surface of the mercury. Bubbles of gas are immediately evolved at the negative pole, and, after some time, are also formed at the positive pole; at the same time, the mercury loses its fluidity, and increases considerably in volume, still preserving its metallic lustre.

The same metallic compound may be obtained by dissolving a small quantity of potassium or sodium in mercury, and pouring on the amalgam a concentrated solution of chlorohydrate of ammonia. If the experiment be made in a glass tube, filled to only one-third by the amalgam, the substance swells so much as to escape from the tube.

This remarkable compound has been but imperfectly studied: it is very unstable, decomposing with the evolution of heat by contact with pure water. That portion of the substance combined with mercury is, moreover, very small, scarcely constituting $\frac{1}{2000}$ of the whole mass. When the amalgam is decomposed, a mixture of 2 volumes of ammonia and 1 volume of hydrogen is disengaged, which leads to the presumption that there exists, in combination with the mercury, a compound NH_4, presenting the composition of ammonia of which we have spoken above. The experiment is, in fact, adduced, as demonstrating the existence of a compound NH_4, acting the part of a true metal, analogous to potassium. For the metals are the only substances which combine with mercury, without detroying its metallic appearance.

DISTINCTIVE CHARACTERS OF THE AMMONIACAL SALTS.

§ 524. The ammoniacal salts are distinguished from all the other metallic salts, except the alkaline salts, by not being precipitated by the alkaline carbonates.

The ammoniacal salts, heated with an alkaline hydrate, or with the hydrate of lime, disengage ammoniacal gas, easily recognised by its characteristic odour, which is evident even in very small quantities of gas. When the ammoniacal salt exists in a very small quantity in a mixture, and when the feeble quantity of ammoniacal gas disengaged in the reaction is no longer perceptible from its odour, the presence of this gas may still be ascertained by bringing a glass rod dipped in chlorohydric acid near the opening of the tube in which the substance is heated with the alkaline hydrate: ammonia, even in a quantity inappreciable by its odour, is disengaged, and a thick white vapour forms around the rod.

A solution of perchloride of platinum, poured into the solution of an ammoniacal salt, produces a yellow crystalline precipitate, resembling that formed with the salts of potassa. But the two precipitates are easily distinguished from each other; for the ammoniacal precipitate evolves ammonia when heated with an alkaline hydrate. They are also readily recognised by heating them to redness in a platinum crucible. The two double chlorides are thereby decomposed, that of potassium being converted into chloride of potassium and metallic platinum, from which the chloride of potassium is removed by water; while the double ammoniacal chloride is decomposed into metallic platinum, and chlorohydrate of ammonia, which volatilizes in white fumes; so that if the residue be treated with water, no chloride is dissolved.

ANALYTIC DETERMINATION OF THE ALKALIS AND AMMONIA.

§ 525. The best mode of determining potassa, soda, or lithia when one of them is isolated in a liquid, consists in transforming the base into a sulphate, and weighing the ignited alkaline sulphate. To do this, it is necessary that all the other bases shall have been previously precipitated, and that no acid more fixed than sulphuric exists in the liquid. The solution is then evaporated in a thin platinum dish, a small excess of sulphuric acid added to the concentrated liquid, and the whole evaporated to dryness. The residue being ignited, consists of the neutral alkaline sulphate which is weighed.

If the liquid contained acids less volatile than the sulphuric, they must first be precipitated. If the less volatile acid were silicic, it would suffice to evaporate to dryness the solution supersaturated by sulphuric acid, and to treat it again with water, when the silicic acid would remain as an insoluble residue. If the solution contained phosphoric or boracic acid, a solution of baryta should be added, until the liquid has acquired a strong alkaline reaction, when phosphate or borate of baryta would be precipitated; and the excess of baryta may then be separated by sulphuric acid.

An alkali is sometimes determined as a chloride, in which case the solution should contain only chlorohydric acid or such acids as may be easily driven off or decomposed by the latter. The solution is evaporated to dryness, and the residue ignited; but this method is less accurate than that of the sulphates, because the alkaline chlorides are somewhat volatile at a red-heat.

Ammonia is often determined from the quantity of nitrogen gas yielded by the ammoniacal substance when decomposed by metallic copper, and the operation is exactly like that employed in determining the nitrogen of nitrates (§ 108). An ammoniacal salt is usually decomposed by lime, or by a mixture of lime and soda, which is obtained by imbuing quicklime with a concentrated solution of caustic soda and drying the mixture in a crucible. The decomposition of the ammoniacal salt is effected in a glass tube *abc*, drawn out and closed at *c*, and the ammoniacal gas is collected in strong chlorohydric acid. The ammoniacal salt should not be mixed with the lime out of the tube; for even when cold, a small quantity of ammoniacal gas would be evolved and lost. Fig. 364 represents the apparatus used in this experiment. A small quantity of lime being poured to the bottom of the tube *abc*, the ammoniacal salt, exactly weighed, is placed above it, and the tube filled with lime. The bulbed apparatus A, containing a small quantity of concentrated chlorohydric acid, is fitted to the tube. The tube *abc*, being arranged on a long sheet-iron furnace, is gradually heated throughout its whole length. The ammoniacal salt being decomposed by the lime, the ammonia is disengaged and dissolved in the chlorohydric acid. When the decomposition is completed, the point *c* is broken off, and by sucking through the apparatus A, the ammonia remaining in the tube is drawn through the acid. The acid liquor being poured into a porcelain capsule, and the apparatus A washed several times with distilled water, which is added to the liquid in the capsule, an excess of a solution of bichloride of platinum is poured into the same liquid, and the whole evaporated at a gentle heat. The residue is treated by a mixture of alcohol and ether, which dissolves the excess of bichloride of platinum, and leaves the double chloride of platinum and ammonia in the form of a crystalline precipitate. The precipitate is washed with the mixture of alcohol and ether, and weighed after careful desiccation. 1 gramme of ammoniacal chloride of platinum contains 0.0771 of ammonia. We shall detail this subject more fully in the fourth part of the work (§ 1217).

Fig. 364.

DETERMINATION OF THE PROPORTIONS OF POTASSA AND SODA WHICH EXIST IN A MIXTURE OF THE SALTS FORMED BY THESE TWO BASES WITH THE SAME ACID.

§ 525 *bis*. The salts of potassa and soda are frequently mixed together, and it is often necessary to determine the proportions of the two bases contained in the mixture. The question presents itself, not only in experimental chemistry, but also in commercial operations.

If we suppose the two bases to be in the state of sulphates, their proportions may be determined by the following analysis:—The mixture is heated to fusion in a platinum crucible, by which the sulphates become neutral and are deprived of water. A certain weight P of the mixture, being accurately weighed, is dissolved in water, and the sulphuric acid precipitated by chloride of barium. From the weight of sulphate of baryta obtained, the weight p of sulphuric acid is calculated, which had combined with the two bases. From this datum alone the proportions of the two sulphates may be calculated. Let x be the weight of the sulphate of potassa; $(P-x)$ will be that of the sulphate of soda. Now, a weight x of sulphate of potassa contains a weight $x.\frac{40}{87.2}$ of sulphuric acid, and a weight $(P-x)$ of sulphate of soda contains $(P-x.)\frac{40}{71}$ of sulphuric acid. The whole of the sulphuric acid combined with the two bases, is therefore represented by

$$x.\frac{40}{87.2}+(P-x).\frac{40}{71};$$

but direct experiment has shown that this weight was p; we have therefore,

$$x.\frac{40}{87.2}+(P-x)\frac{40}{71}=p, \text{ or}$$

$$x.\frac{1}{2.18}+(P-x).\frac{1}{1.775}=p, \text{ whence}$$

$$x=\frac{P\times 2.18-p\times 3.869}{0.405}.$$

Instead of weighing the precipitate of sulphate of baryta which the solution of the saline mixture yields with an excess of chloride of barium, the volume of a solution of chloride of barium may be determined, which exactly precipitates the sulphuric acid from the sulphates to be analyzed. To effect this, a solution of chloride of barium is prepared, so that a volume of 50 cubic centimetres will exactly precipitate 5 gm. of real sulphuric acid. It is evident that the number of cubic centimetres necessary to produce the complete precipitation will represent the number of decigrammes of sulphuric acid which existed in the solution subjected to analysis.

The principal objection to this process is that the sulphate of baryta is not deposited rapidly in a cold liquid, and it is necessary to filter, from time to time, a small quantity of the liquid, in order to ascertain that no more sulphuric acid remains to be precipitated.

§ 526. The proportions of two chlorides of sodium and potassium mixed together may be determined in the same way. A given weight of the mixture is dissolved in water, and the chlorine precipitated by nitrate of silver. The weight of chlorine combined with the two bases is calculated from that of the chloride of silver obtained, and the proportions of the two chlorides determined by a calculation similar to that just made of the sulphates.

A standard solution of nitrate of silver can also be employed, and the exact volume measured which is required to precipitate the whole of the chlorine contained in a given weight of the substance.

These methods of analysis afford considerable accuracy when the two bases have very different equivalents and exist in nearly equal proportions in the mixture. But the result would be very uncertain if the numerical value of the equivalents differed but slightly, or if one of the bases predominated much over the other.

§ 527. When the two alkaline metals are in the state of chlorides, a given weight of the mixture is dissolved in a small quantity of water, and a concentrated solution of perchloride of platinum poured into it, until the liquid assumes a very decided yellow colour. Chloride of potassium is precipitated in the state of a double chloride of potassium and platinum, but as a small quantity of it remains in solution, it may be easily separated by evaporating the liquid to dryness and treating it with alcohol, which dissolves the double chloride of platinum and sodium, and leaves all the double chloride of platinum and potassium. The precipitate is collected on a filter, washed with alcohol, and weighed after desiccation. The composition of the double chloride being known, the quantity of chloride of potassium it contains can be immediately deduced from it.

The two processes just described are those generally used in scientific inquiries to determine the proportions of potassa and soda in a mixture. They are, however, too delicate to be applied to the arts. We shall mention some practical methods, which may be of service to manufacturers in special cases.

§ 528. Chloride of potassium is used by the makers of saltpetre; but the commercial chloride is always mixed with chloride of sodium, which is valueless in the fabrication of saltpetre. The proportions of the two chlorides may be ascertained in a very simple way, and with sufficient exactness for all commercial purposes.

This method is founded on the very unequal decrease of temperature produced by the chlorides of potassium and sodium on the water in which they are dissolved. We have seen (§ 373) that 50 gm. of chloride of potassium, dissolving in 200 gm. of water, produce a decrease of temperature of 24.5°, while 50 gm. of chloride of sodium only produce a decrease of 3.4°. 50 gm. of the mixture is put into a bottle containing 200 cubic centimetres of water at the surrounding temperature, which is exactly measured by a delicate thermometer plunged into the liquid. In order to hasten the solution, it is stirred with the thermometer, and, after complete solution, the temperature is again observed. Let us suppose that it indicates a depression of temperature of $t°$, produced by the act of dissolving. This datum alone will allow us to calculate the proportion of the two chlorides, if no other salt be present in the mixture. If x be the number of grammes of chloride of potassium in the 50 gm. of the mixture, the decrease of temperature θ produced by the x gm. of chloride of potassium, by dissolving in 200 cubic centimetres of water, will be given by the proportion

$$50 : 24.5° :: x : \theta, \text{ whence } \theta = \frac{24.5}{50} \cdot x.$$

So again, the decrease of temperature θ' produced by the solution of the $(50-x)$ gm. of chloride of sodium, by dissolving in 200 cubic centimetres of water, will be given by the proportion

$$50:3.4^\circ::50-x:\theta', \text{ whence } \theta'=\tfrac{3.4}{50}.(50=x).$$

The decrease of temperature produced by the 50 gm. of the mixture will therefore be expressed by

$$\tfrac{24.5}{50}.x+\tfrac{3.4}{50}.(50-x).$$

But the decrease of temperature observed is t; we have, therefore,

$$\tfrac{24.5}{50}.x+\tfrac{3.4}{50}.(50-x)=t, \text{ whence}$$

$$x=\tfrac{50\,(t-3.4)}{21.1}.$$

§ 529. When the two salts are in the state of sulphates, we can determine pretty exactly their respective proportions, by a process founded on the increased density occasioned by sulphate of soda dissolving in a saturated solution of pure sulphate of potassa. The increase is moreover the more sensible, as the solubility of sulphate of potassa is remarkably increased by the presence of sulphate of soda.

Let us take 50 gm. of a mixture of known proportions of sulphate of soda and sulphate of potassa, and treat them with 300 cubic centimetres of a solution of sulphate of potassa saturated at a constant temperature of 68°. This quantity of water would be sufficient to dissolve entirely the sulphate of soda of the mixture, even if the latter were wholly composed of it. If no residue remains, which only happens in mixtures very poor in sulphate of potassa, we will add an excess of this salt, in order that the liquid may be saturated with it. A hydrometer is plunged into the liquid. It is evident that the instrument can be graduated so that its degrees shall mark precisely the percentage of soda existing in the mixture. Thus, when the hydrometer is plunged into a solution of pure sulphate of potassa, 0° is marked at its level. When plunged into a solution obtained by digesting a mixture of 50 gm. of dry sulphate of soda and an excess of sulphate of potassa with a saturated solution of sulphate of potassa at 68°, the number of degrees is marked at this level equal to the percentage of soda existing in the dry sulphate of soda.

Lastly, some intermediate points of the scale are determined in the same way. The instrument, thus graduated, is called a *natrometer*, and may be used to determine the proportion of soda contained in any saline mixture composed of potassa and soda alone, provided that the two bases are combined with an acid which can be easily driven off by sulphuric acid. To do this, 50 gm. of the mixture are put into a porcelain capsule, decomposed by sulphuric acid, and evaporated to dryness to drive off the other volatile acids.

It is treated with a small quantity of hot water, and the excess of acid neutralized with carbonate of potassa. The liquid being cooled to 68°, when a great deal of sulphate of potassa usually separates, is filtered into a test-glass which has been marked at a point corresponding to 300 cubic centimetres by volume. The precipitated sulphate of potassa is washed with a solution of the same sulphate saturated at 68° until the level of the liquid reaches the mark on the test-glass. The natrometer being plunged into the liquid, the number of degrees indicated is observed, and is equal to the number of hundredths (per cent.) of soda contained in the mixture.

In the experiment just described, the same temperature is employed: the instrument may be graduated so as to determine the proportion of soda at any temperature. In that case, two scales are marked on the stem of the hydrometer; one indicating, for each degree of the centigrade thermometer, the level of a saturated solution of pure sulphate of potassa, which may be called the *scale of temperature;* the divisions of the second, representing the hundredths of soda, may be termed the *soda-scale.* The zeros of the two scales coincide, so that, if operating at 32°, the soda will be directly determined by the soda-scale. But if operating at 77°, the instrument is plunged into a solution of pure sulphate of potassa saturated at that degree to a level that would indicate 8 hundredths of soda. At this point, therefore, the zero of the soda-scale should commence for this temperature.

Experience shows that the divisions of the soda-scale are the smaller as they correspond to a greater proportion of soda; while the divisions of the scale of temperature which mark the densities of the solution of sulphate of potassa saturated at different temperatures are remarkably equal. When a test is made with the natrometer at a temperature t, this number t, representing the temperature of the liquid, is subtracted from the observed level m on the scale of temperature, and the number of divisions n noted on the soda-scale corresponding to the number $(m-t)$ of divisions on the scale of temperature. This number expresses the hundredths of soda with sufficient accuracy for all commercial purposes.

II. ALKALINO-EARTHY METALS.

BARIUM.

EQUIVALENT = 68.64 (858, O = 100).

§530. Barium* may be obtained by decomposing its protoxide by the galvanic battery. Some mercury being placed in a platinum capsule communicating with the negative pole of a battery, a solution of baryta mixed with crystals of hydrated baryta is poured upon it, and the positive pole plunged into the paste. The decomposition of the baryta and water are simultaneous; and as barium is set free, it combines with the mercury, which soon loses its fluidity. When the mercury is charged with an appreciable quantity of barium, it is removed, dried rapidly, and distilled in a glass retort, through which a current of nitrogen or hydrogen is passed to prevent all oxidizing action. The mercury volatilizes, leaving barium in the form of a metallic globule, if the heat has been carried to redness; but as barium attacks glass at this temperature, it is better not to raise the heat so high.

Barium may also be obtained by decomposing anhydrous baryta by the vapour of potassium at a red-heat. For this purpose, an iron tube is used, open at both ends, in the middle of which is placed a platinum cup containing the anhydrous baryta, and, at a certain distance from one end of it, some pieces of potassium. A current of hydrogen gas being passed in through the same end, that part containing the baryta is highly heated, and communicates its heat to the potassium, which is vapourized. The vapour of potassium decomposes the baryta, oxide of potassium being formed and barium set free. The tube is allowed to cool perfectly in the current of hydrogen gas, the cup removed, and the substance treated by mercury, which dissolves the barium. The amalgam, distilled in a current of hydrogen gas, leaves metallic barium.

Barium exhibits the colour and lustre of silver; possesses a certain degree of malleability; melts at a red-heat, but is not sufficiently volatile to be distilled; and is heavier than oil of vitriol, for a globule of the metal sinks to the bottom of the acid.

Barium has a powerful affinity for oxygen, so that it oxidizes rapidly in the air and decomposes water immediately in the cold.

The great density of the compounds of barium distinguishes them from the compounds of the alkaline, alkalino-earthy, and earthy

---

* Baryta was discovered in 1774, by Scheele. Davy isolated barium in 1807, by decomposing baryta by the galvanic battery. He obtained strontium and calcium in the same way.

metals; and it was from this property the metal received its name, (from βαύρς, heavy.)

COMPOUNDS OF BARIUM AND OXYGEN.

§ 531. Barium forms two compounds with oxygen: the protoxide BaO, or *baryta*, and the binoxide BaO_2.

Protoxide of Barium and Baryta.—Two insoluble salts of baryta are found in nature; the carbonate and the sulphate, from each of which baryta may be obtained. The carbonate calcined in a strong forge-fire loses all its carbonic acid, and baryta remains; but a lower temperature will suffice if the carbonate be previously mixed with charcoal, because the carbon has a tendency to abstract a portion of oxygen from the carbonic acid. Carbonic oxide is disengaged, and the baryta is mixed with charcoal; which is not objectionable, if the base is to be dissolved in water.

Baryta is generally made by dissolving the carbonate in nitric acid, and evaporating the liquid to form the nitrate of baryta in anhydrous crystals. The nitrate is put into a porcelain retort (fig. 365), the mouth of which is closed with a bored cork, and the retort heated gradually in a reverberatory furnace until no more gas is evolved. Baryta remains in the form of a grayish-white porous mass which appears to have been fused; but baryta itself is infusible at a furnace-heat, and it is the nitrate which fused on the first impression of heat: as it decomposed, its fluidity diminished and the substance became doughy, until it at last remained puffed up by the bubbles of gas which traversed it. Anhydrous baryta fuses only at the highest temperatures, such as are produced by the oxy-hydrogen blowpipe.

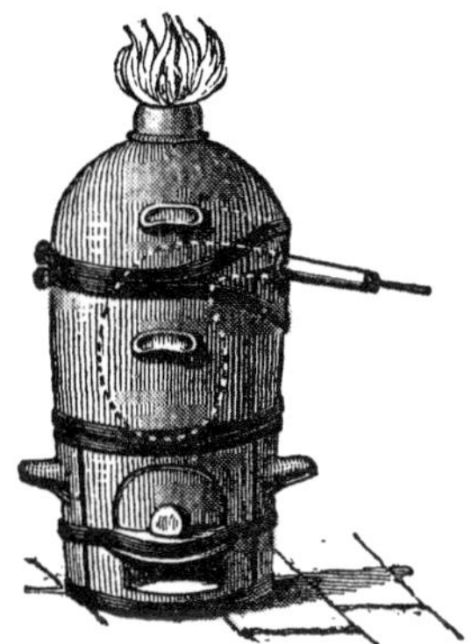

Fig. 365.

§ 532. In order to obtain baryta from the natural sulphate, it is first transformed into a sulphide by calcination with charcoal. The sulphate, finely powdered, is mixed with one-tenth of its weight of charcoal, and sufficient oil added to form a consistent paste, which is heated to redness in a clay crucible. The oil is intended to bring every particle of sulphate in contact with the charcoal, and is decomposed by heat, leaving a residue of carbon intimately mixed with the substance.

Organic matters may be substituted for the charcoal and oil, such as sugar, starch, and resin, for they leave a copious residue of carbon when decomposed by heat, and, moreover, melt before decomposition. The calcined matter is treated with boiling water, which dissolves the sulphide of barium. Nitric acid, gradually poured into the filtered liquid, converts the sulphide of barium into nitrate of baryta with disengagement of sulphohydric acid. The nitrate of baryta obtained by evaporating the liquid yields by calcination caustic anhydrous baryta, the density of which is about four times that of water.

§ 533. Baryta has a great affinity for water, for upon pouring a small quantity of water upon it, there is a considerable elevation of temperature, and a portion of the water is disengaged as steam. The baryta is converted into a hydrate, which falls to dust if the quantity of water added be not too great. When once combined with water, it can no longer be restored to the anhydrous state by heat alone.

Hydrate of baryta is frequently used in the laboratory, and may be prepared by treating anhydrous baryta with water; or it may also be obtained immediately from the solution of sulphide of barium above mentioned by merely boiling it with oxide of copper. Copper seizes on the sulphur, forming an insoluble sulphide of copper, and hydrate of baryta remains in the liquid:

$$BaS + CuO = BaO + CuS.$$

It is easy to ascertain the moment at which the sulphide of barium is entirely changed into oxide, by pouring a small quantity of the liquid into a test-glass and adding a solution of acetate of lead. If no more sulphide remains, a white precipitate of the hydrated protoxide of lead is formed; but if any sulphide remain, the precipitate is more or less dark, from the admixture of black sulphide of lead with the white hydrate. If the solution of barium subjected to the experiment be concentrated, it is sufficient to allow the liquid to cool, when a large portion of the hydrate of baryta crystallizes; but if it be dilute, it must be rapidly concentrated by heat.

Hydrate of baryta crystallizes in the form of laminæ, or in large prismatic crystals if the crystallization is slow. It contains 10 equivalents of water, so that its formula is $BaO + 10HO$. The crystals, when heated, readily part with 9 equivalents of water, and are restored to the state of a monohydrate $BaO + HO$, which is no longer decomposed by heat. The monohydrate melts at a red-heat, and is not sensibly volatile. It dissolves in 2 parts of boiling, and 20 parts of cold water. Its solution is strongly alkaline; and it quickly attracts the carbonic acid of the air, becoming cloudy from the formation of insoluble carbonate of baryta.

The hydrate of baryta and all the soluble compounds of barium are energetic poisons.

§ 534. The composition of baryta, BaO, is deduced from the analysis of the chloride $BaCl$, which, when crystallized, contains water in combination, but soon loses it by the action of heat. Ten grammes of anhydrous chloride being dissolved in water and boiled, nitrate of silver in excess is poured in, when an insoluble chloride of silver is precipitated, collected, and weighed after desiccation. The weight of the chloride of silver will be 13.773 gm., containing 3.406 gm. of chlorine, so that in 10 gm. of chloride of barium, there are

Chlorine	3.406 gm.
Barium	6.594
	10.000

In order to find the quantity of oxygen which forms baryta with the same quantity of barium, it is sufficient to make the proportion

35.5 : 8 : : 3.406 gm. : x, whence x =0.768.

Thus, baryta is formed of

Barium	6.594 gm.
Oxygen	0.768
Baryta	7.362

The equivalent of barium will be given by the proportions,

$$\left.\begin{array}{r} 0.768 : 6.594 :: 8 : x \\ \text{or } 3.406 : 6.594 :: 35.5 : x \end{array}\right\} \text{whence } x{=}68.64$$

Thus, the oxide of barium is composed of

1 eq. of barium	68.64	...	89.57
1 " oxygen	8.00	...	10.43
1 " baryta	76.64	...	100.00

and the chloride of barium of

1 eq. of barium.....................	68.64	...	65.94
1 " chlorine	35.50	...	34.06
1 " chloride of barium	104.14	...	100.00

The quantity of water existing in the hydrate is ascertained by the process described for hydrate of potassa (§ 435).

§ 535. *Binoxide of Barium.*—The protoxide is converted into the binoxide when heated in a current of oxygen at a temperature of 550° to 750°. The baryta, broken into fragments, being put into a green glass retort, to the bottom of which the current of oxygen is passed, absorbs the latter without changing its form, its colour only becoming slightly more gray. The binoxide readily combines with water, forming a white hydrate slightly soluble in water. Boiled with water, the hydrated binoxide is decomposed, oxygen being evolved, and baryta dissolved. The binoxide is employed in the preparation of oxygenated water (§ 89).

SALTS FORMED BY PROTOXIDE OF BARIUM OR BARYTA.

Sulphate of Baryta.

§ 536. This salt is found crystallized in nature, forming considerable veins in the older rocks, and being remarkable among earthy minerals for its great weight, has been called by mineralogists *heavy spar*. Its density is 4.4. The sulphate is insoluble in water, and scarcely soluble even in water acidulated by nitric or chlorohydric acid. It may therefore be readily obtained by double decomposition, by pouring a solution of an alkaline sulphate, or even sulphuric acid, into a solution of nitrate of baryta or of chloride of barium. We have seen frequent use made of the insolubility of the sulphate of baryta to precipitate the sulphuric acid existing in a solution. To avoid the introduction of another acid into the liquid, the precipitation is effected by a solution of hydrate of baryta. In order that the precipitated sulphate may collect in the form of a heavy powder and readily sink to the bottom of the vessel, the liquid should first be heated to boiling; except where heat would decompose the acid to be isolated.

Sulphate of baryta, on precipitating, generally carries with it a portion of the soluble salts existing in the solution, on which account the precipitate requires careful washing. The alkaline nitrates particularly are carried down in quantities. Time should be allowed the precipitate to deposit, after which the clear liquid is decanted and the precipitate boiled with water acidulated by chlorohydric acid.

The sulphate of baryta dissolves in oil of vitriol, but is again deposited when the liquid is diluted.

Sulphate of baryta contains,

1 eq. of baryta	76.64 ...	65.71
1 " sulphuric acid	40.00 ...	34.29
1 " sulphate of baryta	116.64 ...	100.00

Nitrate of Baryta.

§ 537. We have seen (§ 531) how nitrate of baryta is obtained from the native carbonate and sulphate. The nitrate crystallizes in regular anhydrous octahedrons, which are soluble in 8 parts of cold and 3 parts of boiling water. It is much less soluble in an acid liquid, for upon pouring into its solution a large quantity of nitric acid, it precipitates in the form of a crystalline powder.

Carbonate of Baryta.

§ 538. Crystallized carbonate of baryta is found in nature, and called *witherite* by mineralogists. It is obtained by double decomposition, by pouring an alkaline carbonate into a solution of nitrate of baryta or of chloride of barium. The carbonate fuses at a white heat, and is then decomposed, parting with its carbonic acid. It is very slightly soluble in water, which dissolves scarcely $\frac{1}{4000}$ of it; but rather more when it contains free carbonic acid.

COMPOUNDS OF BARIUM WITH SULPHUR.

§ 539. We have already seen the mode of preparing monosulphide of barium by calcining the sulphate with charcoal. The residue, treated with boiling water, yields a yellow liquid which deposits white laminated crystals of the monosulphide. The crystals produce a colourless solution in water, and the original yellow colour of the liquid is due to its always containing a small quantity of polysulphide of barium.

Polysulphides of barium may be obtained by boiling the solution of the monosulphide with sulphur. If the sulphur is in great excess, a pentasulphide BaS_5 is formed. The polysulphides may likewise be obtained by heating to redness a mixture of baryta and sulphur.

The monosulphide acts the part of a base with the sulphides, furnishing a great number of sulphosalts.

COMPOUND OF BARIUM WITH CHLORINE.

§ 540. Only one compound of barium with chlorine is known, and is easily prepared by dissolving the native carbonate in chlorohydric acid. It may also be obtained from the sulphate, by first converting it into a sulphide by calcination with charcoal, and then decomposing the solution of the sulphide by chlorohydric acid. The evaporated solution yields a crystallized chloride, with the formula $BaCl+2HO$. The salt readily parts with its water on the application of heat, and the anhydrous chloride fuses at a red-heat.*

Chloride of barium dissolves in 2–3 parts of water at 61°, and in 1–3 at the boiling point.

On a large scale, it is prepared by calcining, in a reverberatory furnace, powdered sulphate of baryta with half its weight of chloride of calcium arising from the manufacture of ammonia. The

* The chloride being frequently employed as an agent, it is important to obtain it in a pure state. The processes recommended for this purpose are to crystallize it repeatedly or to boil its solution with some carbonate of baryta, whereby iron is precipitated. Both of these methods are tedious and imperfect, and I have found it the shortest and best process to make a chloride from the sulphide, by using an ordinary muriatic acid, (not containing much sulphuric acid,) drawing off the liquids from the residue 2 or 3 times, evaporating to dryness, and fusing the dry chloride in a crucible. It may then be dissolved and crystallized. The fusion most effectually renders the iron insoluble.—*J. C. B.*

mass, when withdrawn from the furnace, is reduced to a fine powder and briskly stirred with cold water, which dissolves chloride of barium and leaves sulphate of lime. The liquid is rapidly drawn off and evaporated. It is essential that the operation should be done quickly and at a low temperature; for, otherwise, an inverse decomposition would take place, by the regeneration of chloride of calcium and sulphate of baryta, because the latter compound is the most insoluble of them all. We should probably obtain a larger product by adding charcoal to the mixture, so as to form, as in the fabrication of artificial soda, an insoluble oxysulphide of calcium ($2CaS+CaO$), which would allow the chloride of barium to be wholly separated.

DISTINCTIVE CHARACTERS OF THE SALTS OF BARYTA.

§ 541. The salts of baryta are not precipitated by ammonia, provided the latter base be perfectly pure, that is, free from carbonate or sulphate.

Carbonate of ammonia and the alkaline carbonates precipitate baryta in the state of an insoluble carbonate.

Sulphuric acid and the sulphates yield, with solutions of the compounds of barium, a white precipitate entirely insoluble in water and in dilute chlorohydric and nitric acids. The latter generally enables us to ascertain the presence of a compound of barium in a solution. However, the salts of strontium and lead present a similar reaction; but the salts of strontium are distinguished from those of baryta by different characters, to be soon described; and as to the salts of lead, they are distinguished by being blackened by sulphuretted hydrogen, while those of barium remain uncoloured.

STRONTIUM.

EQUIVALENT = 44.

§ 542. Strontium* is very analogous to barium in all its combinations, which are obtained by processes resembling those for obtaining the corresponding compounds of barium.

Strontium, like barium, is found in nature in the state of a carbonate and sulphate. The carbonate is called by mineralogists *strontianite*, from its having been found at Cape Strontian, in Scotland, whence was derived the name *strontium*, given to the metal. The sulphate is called *celestine*, and is found in several localities. The gypseous rocks of Montmartre contain flattened nodules composed of small crystals of sulphate of strontia, carbonate of lime, and gypsum.

Strontium is extracted from strontia, precisely as barium from baryta.

COMPOUNDS OF STRONTIUM WITH OXYGEN.

§ 543. Strontium forms two compounds with oxygen, a protoxide SrO, and a binoxide SrO_2.

The *protoxide of strontium, or strontia*, being procured, like baryta, from the native carbonate or sulphate, we shall not stop to consider it. The strontia prepared by the calcination of the nitrate, appears in the form of porous masses, of a grayish white, resembling those of baryta.

Strontia combines with water with the evolution of considerable heat. The hydrate dissolves in water, and as it is much more soluble in hot than in cold water, a greater part of it crystallizes on cooling. The formula of the crystallized hydrate is $Sr_2O+10HO$. Subjected to heat it soon loses 9 equivalents of water, but retains the last equivalent, even at the highest temperature of our furnaces.

The *binoxide*, obtained by pouring oxygenated water into a solution of hydrate of strontia, is deposited in the form of small crystalline spangles.

SALTS FORMED BY THE PROTOXIDE OF STRONTIUM, OR STRONTIA.

Nitrate of Strontia.

§ 544. The nitrate of strontia, like that of baryta, is prepared from the native carbonate or sulphate, and crystallizes at ordinary temperatures in large regular octahedrons, which are anhydrous. If it be crystallized at a low temperature, it is deposited in another form and in a hydrated state, its formula being SrO,NO_5+5HO.

Nitrate of strontia is used by the makers of fireworks, from its communicating a beautiful crimson colour to the flame of burning

* Strontia was discovered in 1793, by Klaproth and Hope.

substances, a property possessed by all the compounds of strontia. Red fire is made by burning a mixture of 40 parts of nitrate of strontia, 13 of flowers of sulphur, 10 of chlorate of potassa, and 4 of oxysulphide of antimony.

Carbonate of Strontia.

§ 545. Carbonate of strontia is found in nature, and is easily obtained by double decomposition, by pouring a solution of an alkaline carbonate into a solution of nitrate of strontia. Carbonate of strontia is wholly decomposed at a white-heat, and does not fuse, like carbonate of baryta, before decomposing.

Sulphate of Strontia.

§ 546. The sulphate is the most common state in which strontium is found; it may be obtained by double decomposition, by pouring a solution of an alkaline sulphate into a solution of nitrate of strontia. It is very slightly soluble in water, but much less insoluble than sulphate of baryta; for water in which the sulphate of strontia has been digested, is perceptibly clouded when mixed with a solution of a salt of baryta.

COMPOUNDS OF STRONTIUM WITH SULPHUR.

§ 547. Strontium forms several sulphides, which correspond exactly to those of barium, and are obtained in the same way. The monosulphide is a powerful base, forming a great number of sulphosalts.

COMPOUND OF STRONTIUM WITH CHLORINE.

§ 548. The chloride is prepared by decomposing the native carbonate, or the sulphide derived from the native sulphate, by chlorohydric acid. It is very soluble, and even deliquescent; and dissolves remarkably in concentrated alcohol, which does not dissolve chloride of barium. Advantage is sometimes taken of this property to separate the two chlorides when mixed. The formula of crystallized chloride of strontium is

$$SrCl+6HO.$$

DISTINCTIVE CHARACTERS OF THE SALTS OF STRONTIA.

§ 549. The salts of strontia are not precipitated by pure ammonia. The alkaline carbonates precipitate the strontia in the state of a carbonate.

Sulphuric acid and the sulphates produce in a solution of a compound of strontium a precipitate of sulphate of strontia, which resembles that produced by the compounds of barium. But the salts of strontium are easily distinguished from the salts of barium in not being precipitated by a solution of chromate of potassa, which gives a yellow precipitate with the compounds of barium. Silicofluohydric acid precipitates the salts of baryta, and not those of strontia.

CALCIUM.

EQUIVALENT = 20.

§ 550. Calcium is a metal very widely diffused throughout nature. Combined with oxygen and carbonic acid, it forms carbonate of protoxide of calcium, or *carbonate of lime*, which is found in immense strata in all sedimentary groups of strata. Sulphate of lime, called *gypsum*, or *plaster*, also forms considerable masses, interwoven with secondary and tertiary strata. Lastly, oxide of calcium, combined with silicic acid, enters into the composition of a great number of minerals which form the primary rocks. Lime likewise exists abundantly in organized bodies. The shells of the molluscæ are composed of nearly pure carbonate of lime, and the bones of all animals contain a large proportion of phosphate and carbonate of lime.

Calcium is extracted from lime, precisely as barium from baryta. It is a white brilliant metal, resembling silver; melts only at a high temperature; rapidly absorbs oxygen from the air, and is converted into an oxide; decomposes water energetically at ordinary temperatures, with the evolution of hydrogen, and is converted into hydrated lime.

COMPOUNDS OF CALCIUM WITH OXYGEN.

§ 551. Two compounds of calcium with oxygen are known: a protoxide CaO, called *lime*, and a binoxide CaO_2.

Lime is of daily use, not only in the laboratory, but also in the arts, and is the essential principle of the mortar used in building.

Lime is obtained by calcining the native carbonate of lime. When only a small quantity is required, Iceland spar, or white statuary marble is chosen, and calcined in a clay crucible in a strong forge-fire. If it be necessary to have the lime absolutely pure, it is preferable to dissolve the carbonate in nitric acid, which is digested cold with the powdered carbonate until effervescence ceases. By boiling the liquid for a short time with a little lime, the foreign metallic oxides are precipitated, such as alumina, or oxide of iron, if any be present. It is then evaporated to dryness, and the nitrate of lime which remains calcined to redness.

Lime is a white amorphous substance, presenting the external form of the calcareous stone which produced it, with a density of about 2–3. It has a caustic taste, and blues the tincture of litmus reddened by an acid. It does not fuse at the highest temperature we have ever been able to produce in furnaces, but undergoes a sort of fusion in the hydroxygen blowpipe.

Lime combines with water, evolving a great deal of heat, so that a portion of the water escapes in the form of vapour, and the elevation of temperature is frequently sufficient to inflame gunpowder. The maximum of temperature is produced by adding to lime about one-half of its weight of water. The operation by which water is combined with lime is called *slaking*, and hydrated lime is said to be *slaked*, to distinguish it from anhydrous lime, which is called *quicklime*. Lime, on hydrating, increases considerably in volume. If not too great a quantity of water be added, a monohydrate of lime $CaO+HO$ is formed, which assumes the form of a light, white, soft powder. By adding a greater quantity of water, a milky paste, called *milk of lime*, is produced.

Water which has remained on lime contains a certain quantity of the base in solution, exerts a strongly alkaline reaction, and is called *lime-water*. The quantity dissolved is very small; for 1000 parts of water dissolve only 1 of lime. Lime-water, which is frequently used in the laboratory, is made by keeping a certain quantity of slaked lime in a well-corked bottle, filled with distilled water, and shaking it from time to time, in order to saturate the water. The hydrated lime in excess falls to the bottom, and the supernatant liquid can be drawn off by a siphon. Lime-water rapidly attracts carbonic acid from the air, and a white pellicle of the carbonate forms on the surface of the liquid. Lime-water, evaporated slowly under the receiver of the air-pump, deposits small crystals of hydrate of lime CaO,HO. Lime is less soluble in hot than in cold water; for lime-water, saturated cold, becomes cloudy when its temperature is raised.

Quicklime, exposed to the air, attracts its water and carbonic acid, falls into dust, and no longer evolves heat when moistened with water. It is then said *to fall* in the air. There ensues, in this case, a definite combination of carbonate and hydrate of lime, CaO,CO_2+CaO,HO; but as the atmosphere always contains more vapour of water than carbonic acid, much more of the hydrate than of the carbonate is formed in the same time; so that the preceding compound remains mixed with a considerable proportion of hydrate of lime. It is only after a long while, the absorption of the carbonic acid continuing incessantly, that the mass approaches the definite composition of which we have given the formula.

§ 552. The composition of lime may be deduced from the analysis of chloride of calcium in the same way as that of baryta was deduced from the analysis of the chloride of barium (§ 532); but it may also be inferred from the analysis of carbonate of lime. For this purpose, a very pure native carbonate is selected, such as Iceland spar, broken into small fragments, and an exact weight P determined in a platinum crucible. The crucible, covered by its lid, is placed in a second crucible of clay, the cover of which is luted with clay, and which is heated for at least two hours in a strong forge-fire, in order to be sure that the decomposition of the carbonate of lime is completed. After cooling, the platinum crucible, with the quicklime it contains, is weighed. Let p be the weight of the lime; $(P-p)$ will be that of the carbonic acid disengaged. Now, as carbonate of lime is formed of 1 equiv. of lime and 1 equiv. of carbonic acid = 22, the equivalent of lime is determined by the proportion,

$$(P-p) : p :: 22 : x.$$

Whence x is equal to 28. But, by hypothesis, 1 equiv. of lime is composed of 1 equiv. of calcium and 1 equiv. of oxygen = 8. The equivalent of calcium is therefore 20. Consequently, the following is the composition of lime:

1 eq. calcium	20	71.43
1 " oxygen	8	28.57
1 " lime	28	100.00

It is necessary to be certain that the carbonate of lime has been wholly converted into caustic lime by calcination. This is easy; for the lime should dissolve in acids, without disengaging carbonic acid: therefore, if a portion of undecomposed carbonate of lime remain, effervescence will take place during the solution of the substance in the acid.

The foregoing analysis may be verified by converting the lime into a sulphate, which is effected by slaking the lime in a small quantity of water, and adding an excess of sulphuric acid to transform it into a sulphate. It is heated gently to drive off the water, and the crucible ignited to drive off the excess of sulphuric acid. Anhydrous sulphate of lime CaO,SO_3 remains, which is weighed. Let Q be its weight; $(Q-p)$ will be the weight of sulphuric acid which has combined with the weight p of lime, to form sulphate of lime. Now, the equivalent of sulphuric acid weighs 40, which gives the equivalent of lime, by making the proportion,

$$(Q-p) : p :: 40 : x.$$

The value of x, obtained by this proportion, ought to be the same as in the preceding proportion, based on the analysis of the carbonate of lime.

§ 553. Lime is used in making mortar, of which it is an essential ingredient, and is prepared on a large scale by calcining carbonate of lime, or limestone, in furnaces, technically called *limekilns*. Calcareous rocks are rarely pure carbonate of lime, and almost always contain more or less magnesia, oxide of iron, quartz, clay, etc. The quality of the lime depends greatly on the degree of purity of the limestone which yields it and the nature of the foreign matters it contains. When the limestone contains any considerable quantity of these substances, it yields a lime which differs greatly from the pure lime described in (§ 549). Thus, with water, it evolves but little heat, does not swell much, nor form a soft paste. It is then said to be *poor*. The lime furnished by a limestone containing but a small quantity of foreign matter, nearly approaches, in its properties, lime chemically pure. It swells considerably when moistened, evolves a good deal of heat, and is then called *fat lime*. We shall see, when discussing the theory of mortars, that these two kinds of lime have special uses. For the present, we shall confine ourselves to the manufacture of fat lime.

§ 554. Limestone parts with its carbonic acid, at a much lower temperature in an open furnace than in a crucible, owing to the fact that gases are more readily disengaged from their combinations in an atmosphere composed of other gases. Thus, a hydrated salt loses readily, and often entirely, its water of hydration when it is kept at a certain temperature in a current of dry air: while it does not perceptibly lose it at the same temperature in an atmosphere of aqueous vapour. Carbonate of lime, calcined in a covered crucible, is constantly in an atmosphere of carbonic acid gas; while, in an open furnace, it is in an atmosphere in which the air, more or less vitiated by combustion, predominates greatly over the carbonic acid. Decomposition is necessarily more rapid in the latter than in the former case.*

The various limestones are not decomposed with equal facility, even when composed of carbonate of lime in the same degree of purity, for the degree of cohesion of the stone exerts a powerful influence over the decomposition. Chalk, which is very feebly aggregated carbonate of lime, is much more easily decomposed than marble or Iceland spar, in which the carbonate of lime is aggregated by crystallization.

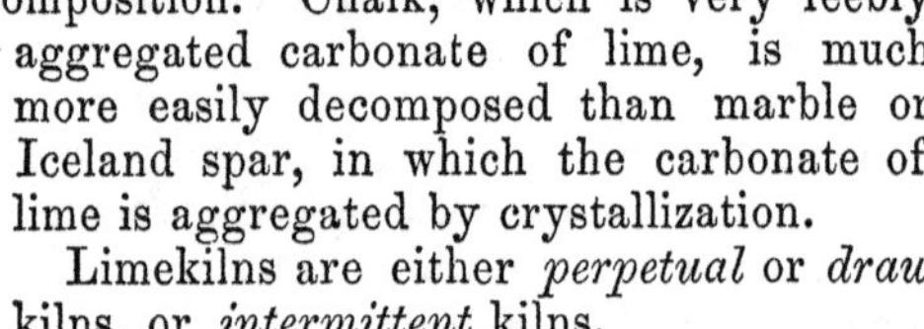

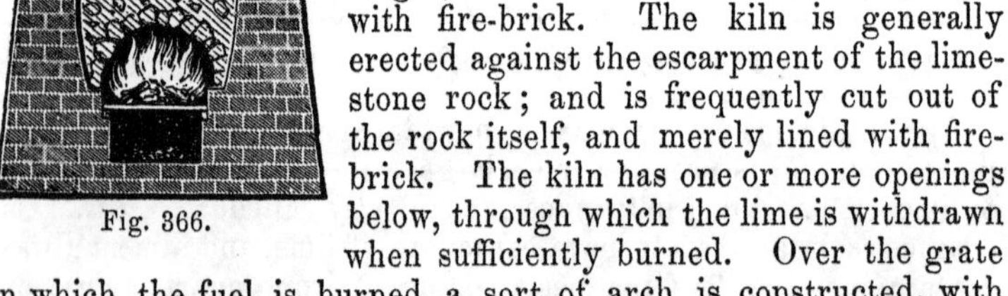

Fig. 366.

Limekilns are either *perpetual* or *draw* kilns, or *intermittent* kilns.

Fig. 366 represents an ordinary limekiln. It is about 3 metres (10 feet) in height, and built of common brick, lined with fire-brick. The kiln is generally erected against the escarpment of the limestone rock; and is frequently cut out of the rock itself, and merely lined with fire-brick. The kiln has one or more openings below, through which the lime is withdrawn when sufficiently burned. Over the grate on which the fuel is burned, a sort of arch is constructed, with large pieces of limestone supporting the mass of calcareous stone

* Doubtless, the *current* of air passing through the furnace also facilitates the liberation of the carbonic acid.—*J. C. B.*

which fills the kiln. The wood, fagots, brushwood, or peat on the grate being kindled, the fire is so regulated at first as simply to heat the whole mass. In 12 hours, the heat is increased, and the process continued until all the limestone is properly burned. It is then allowed to cool, and the lime is withdrawn.

Lime-burning in perpetual kilns is much more profitable, as it economizes the heat, to a greater degree, and is exclusively used in localities where lime has a steady sale. It is effected in two ways:

1st. In kilns which are charged with alternate layers of limestone and pit-coal. As they gradually descend in the kiln, the lime is withdrawn by the lower openings as fast as it is burned, and replaced by fresh charges of limestone introduced by the upper opening.

2dly. In kilns which are filled entirely with limestone and heated by lateral fires. Figs. 367 and 368 represent one of these furnaces; fig. 367 being a vertical section through the axis of the kiln, and fig. 368 a horizontal section, made at the height of the lateral fires g, g', g'', of fig. 367. The cavity of the kiln is about 8 or 10 metres (25–33 feet) in height, and lined with fire-brick. The kiln is built against a steep hillside, in order to afford greater facility for feeding it. Three openings o, o', o'', slightly inclined outward, are made at the base of the kiln, and used for withdrawing the lime. Three other openings c, c', c'', made at a distance of about 2 metres from the ground, communicate with the grates g, g', g'', on which the fuel is burned. The air necessary for combustion penetrates by the side-openings e, and is regulated by dampers. The openings o, o', o'' and i, i', i'' are closed by sheet-iron doors. Working-arches B, in the body of the stack, allow the workmen to draw the lime from the openings for that purpose. Vertical chimneys l leading from the arches carry off the heated air while drawing, which would otherwise be insupportable.

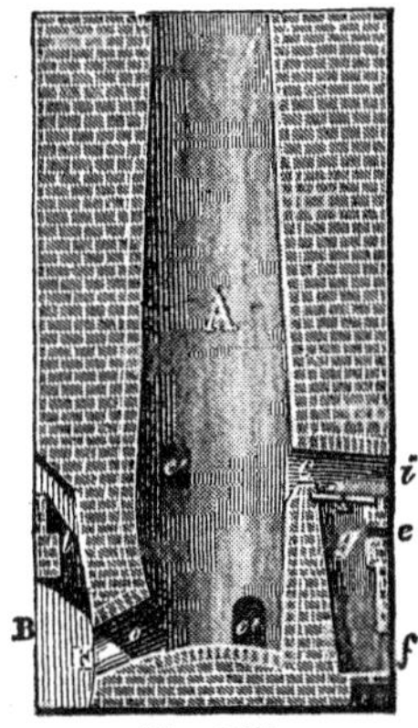

Fig. 367.

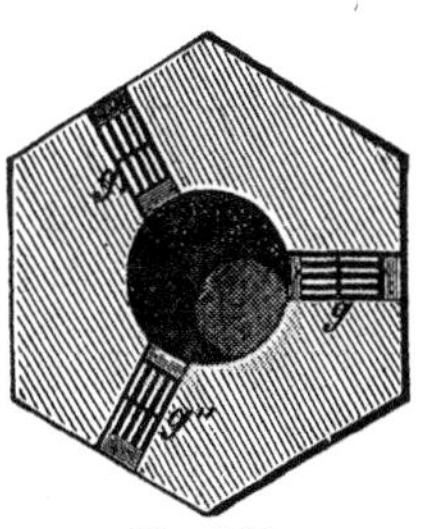

Fig. 368.

When beginning a firing, the lower part of the kiln is filled with fagots, as high as the grates g, g', g''; limestone is charged from above so as to fill the kiln, and the fagots are set on fire. The limestone immediately above the fire is soon burned, and falls down as the fuel is consumed. Fire is then kindled on the grates, the fuel being peat, or pit-coal of an inferior quality. The heat evolved burns the limestone in the upper portions of the kiln. Every 12 hours, the lime is drawn from the bottom of the kiln, which is kept filled by charges of fresh limestone through the upper opening. This is continued until the kiln becomes so damaged as to be useless.

§ 555. Common quicklime is frequently used in the laboratory, but is generally mixed with the ashes of the fuel with which it was burned, and the lumps coated by alkaline chlorides and sulphates, which might injuriously affect chemical investigations. These can be easily removed by slaking quicklime with a small quantity of water, so as to cause it to fall into a pulverulent hydrate, putting the hydrate on a filter, and washing it with water, until the washings manifest no cloudiness with a solution of nitrate of silver. The hydrate is then calcined in a clay crucible. Quicklime thus treated is very finely divided, and sufficiently pure for most of the uses of the laboratory.

Binoxide of calcium CaO_2 is obtained by pouring oxygenated water into lime-water, when the binoxide is deposited in the form of small crystalline plates. This compound is not very fixed, and readily parts with one-half of its oxygen when heated.

SALTS FORMED BY PROTOXIDE OF CALCIUM, OR LIME.

Sulphate of Lime.

§ 556. Sulphate of lime is found in nature in two states; in that of anhydrous sulphate of lime CaO,SO_3, termed by mineralogists *anhydrite ;* and in that of hydrated sulphate of lime CaO,SO_3+2HO, called *gypsum, plaster of Paris.* These two minerals frequently form considerable lenticular masses in the strata of trias, where they are generally associated with rock-salt. Similar collections of gypsum are found in the inferior tertiary rocks. It is in this geological formation that the plaster in the environs of Paris is found, where it is interposed in strata of marl, above the waste limestone (*calcaire grossier*) which constitutes the building-stone of Paris. The gypsum belonging to this geological epoch is a fresh-water formation, as is proved by the fresh-water shells, the remains of which are found in the adjacent strata.

The density of the anhydrous sulphate, or anhydrite, is 2.9. It forms compact masses, of a crystalline texture and some degree of hardness, and is sometimes found in well-formed crystals belonging to the fourth system of crystallization. Anhydrous sulphate of lime fuses at a red-heat, and, if allowed to cool slowly, assumes a crystalline texture, the cleavages of which lead to the form of the native crystal.

The hydrated sulphate CaO,SO_3+2HO is sometimes found, in

nature, in the state of well-terminated crystals, recognisable, as a mineral, by their want of hardness, so that they can be scratched with the nail. They are generally hemitropes, or twinned crystals, and their form, that of fig. 119, belongs to the fifth system of crystallization (§ 38). Similar, and frequently well-defined crystals, are deposited in the graduation-houses, on the twigs on which the waters of salt-springs are concentrated. Another hemitropic form exhibits flattened lenticular masses, the outer faces of which are slightly curved. The masses are easily cleaved in a direction parallel to the two oblique axes, and the result of cleavage assumes the shape of a spear-head (fig. 369), from which it has been called *spear-headed gypsum.* It may be divided by a pen-knife into extremely thin laminæ, perfectly transparent and colourless, which break readily in the fingers, in two other directions of cleavage, giving them a rhomboidal shape.

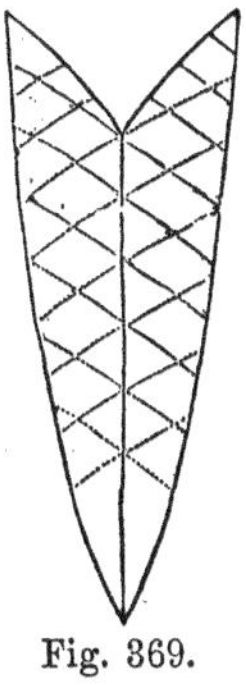

Fig. 369.

Crystals of hydrated sulphate of lime, differing from those of gypsum, are often formed in the boilers of high-pressure engines, in which water charged with plaster, and called *selenitic water*, is used. The formula of this hydrate is $2(CaO,SO_3)+HO$.*

The crystals of gypsum are frequently irregularly interwoven with each other, sometimes forming white masses, at others masses coloured by hydrated oxide of iron. Such gypsum constitutes *alabaster*, which is used for ornamental purposes, such as the manufacture of vases, clock-cases, etc. Common plaster is also composed of an aggregation of crystals of gypsum; but foreign substances are generally mixed with it, such as carbonate of lime, clay, or sand.

The plaster in the environs of Paris contains,

Sulphate of lime	70.39
Water	18.77
Carbonate of lime	7.63
Clay	3.21
	100.00

§ 557. Sulphate of lime is but slightly soluble in water; 1000 parts of the latter, at ordinary temperatures, dissolving about 2 parts of it. Its solubility diminishes with the temperature, so that a solution saturated in the cold is visibly clouded when heated to

* Similar deposites are formed in boilers by sea-water and by waters which cannot be termed selenitic, because sulphate of lime is not their prevailing constituent. The deposite is mostly anhydrous, for its very small percentage of water is easily driven off, and is not sufficient to make the formula given in the text. The deposite in the boilers of ocean-steamers usually contains sulphate of magnesia, beside that of lime, or, where a high heat has been employed, caustic magnesia.—*J. C. B.*

212°. Its solubility even exhibits an anomaly similar to that of sulphate of soda, its greatest solubility corresponding to 95°. The same anomaly has been observed in the seleniate of soda, which is isomorphous with the sulphate of soda. The following numbers express the solubility of sulphate of lime at various temperatures:

100 parts of water at	32°	dissolve	0.205	of sulphate of lime.
"	41	....	0.219	"
"	53.6	....	0.233	"
"	68	....	0.241	"
"	86	....	0.249	"
"	95	....	0.254	"
"	105	....	0.252	"
"	122	....	0.251	"
"	148	....	0.248	"
"	158	....	0.244	"
"	176	....	0.239	"
"	194	....	0.231	"
"	212	....	0.217	"

A solution of the sulphate, evaporated slowly, deposits small brilliant crystals, presenting the same form as the native hydrated sulphate.

§ 558. Gypsum, heated to 248° or 266°, parts wholly with its water, and is converted into anhydrous sulphate of lime; but, in this state, it soon recovers the water it has lost, and becomes perceptibly warm. This latter property, however, is observed only when the gypsum has not been too highly heated, for if the temperature be raised to only 320°, the anhydrous substance recovers its water very slowly. Native anhydrous sulphate of lime, or anhydrite, does not combine with water, and behaves like gypsum which has been calcined to redness. Sulphate of lime fuses at a red-heat, and solidifies, on cooling, into a crystalline mass, the cleavages of which are the same as those of anhydrite.

The use of plaster in building-mortar and in making casts is founded on its property of parting with its water of crystallization at a low temperature, and of recovering it when again mixed with this liquid. By mixing finely powdered dehydrated plaster with water, a liquid paste is formed, in which, at first, the particles of anhydrous sulphate of lime are mechanically mixed with the water, but it soon combines with the water and is changed into a hydrated sulphate. A portion of the water disappears in the combination; and the particles which were disaggregated in the liquid paste, aggregate in small crystals at the moment of combining with the water. These small crystals *dovetail*, as it were, with each other, and the whole substance becomes a solid mass. A paste of plaster, poured into a mould, fills accurately all its cavities, but soon solidifies into a single compact mass, when it is said to *set*, in consequence of the combination of the anhydrous sulphate with water. If, after some time, the mould be removed, a piece of solid plaster can be taken from it, presenting in relief all the cavities of the mould. So, also, by spreading over a wall of rough stone a coat of boiled plaster mixed with water, so as to fill all the irregularities of the wall, a perfectly plane surface is obtained, on which all kinds of moulding can be fashioned, so long as the plaster does not set. A large quantity of plaster is thus used to cover the walls, partitions, and ceilings of houses.

§ 559. Plaster for building is calcined in a heap, under a shed (fig. 370). A series of small arches are first made with large pieces of the plaster, on which the material to be calcined is heaped, placing the largest pieces at the bottom. Brushwood or fagots are burned in the arches, and the flame permeates the whole mass. The combustion is conducted slowly, in order that the temperature may not rise too high at the lower part, for it was stated that plaster, when too strongly burned, no longer sets with water. When the calcination is completed, which the workman knows by the appearance of the material, he demolishes the heap, separates the pieces which appear to be too much calcined, or *burned*, and those which are not sufficiently calcined. The remainder, being reduced to a fine powder by stamping or grinding, and then sifted, is packed in small bags and sent to market.

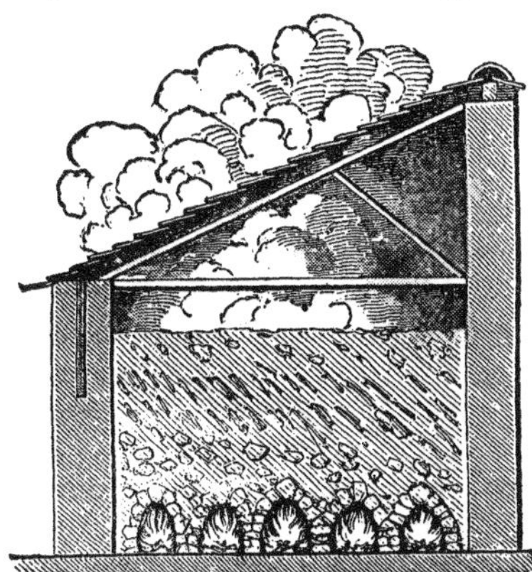

Fig. 370.

§ 560. Plaster is usually employed to obtain impressions of objects of which several copies are required; the impressions in basso, which serve as a mould, being used to obtain new impressions in relief.

In order to mould a medal, it is surrounded with a border of pasteboard or wax. The medal is then coated with oil, to render the separation of the plaster more easy; then painted with a brush dipped in a thin mixture of very fine plaster, so as to fill the most delicate cavities of the medal and prevent the admission of air between the medal and the plaster. A thicker coat of plaster is then spread over the medal as high as the border. When the plaster has become solid, the medal is inverted, and a few gentle blows on its reverse will separate the plaster.

In order to take the impression of a spherical embossed object, the mould must be made of several pieces which can be easily separated. To give an idea of this process, let us suppose we are required to mould a hand. The hand, first covered with a very thin coat of oil, is laid upon a napkin, and a strong silk thread extended over it. With a brush, a thin coating of plaster is applied, which penetrates into all the folds of the skin; and before it has time to set, a thicker coat is poured on, which is gradually increased by successive additions of the same material, until it is several centimetres thick. After waiting a few moments until the plaster has assumed some consistency, the silk thread is raised by one end, thus dividing the plaster into two equal parts. After waiting a little longer, until it is still harder, the two halves of the plaster are separated, and the hand withdrawn. The two halves, again united, are lubricated with oil, and make a mould of tempered plaster, which will reproduce the hand as often as required.

In a similar way, moulds are constructed for making statues and other ornamental objects; but the mould must be composed of a greater number of pieces, which are held together by an outer framework, or *shell*. The joints of the various pieces are reproduced on the cast in the shape of small projecting threads, which are easily scraped off.

Plaster intended for moulding delicate objects should be purer than that used in building: it should be carefully calcined, and not come in contact with the fuel. In Paris, the spear-headed gypsum, which forms the fine layers of the gypseous rocks of Montmartre, is used for this purpose. This gypsum is broken into pieces about as large as a walnut, and calcined in ovens, the heat of which is most carefully regulated.

§ 561. *Stucco*, which is used to cover walls, and columns, and in making various ornamental objects in imitation of marble, is made by tempering the best plaster with a solution of gelatine or strong glue. The plaster, baked in an oven, is ground, sifted, and then tempered with a solution of strong glue; but it sets much more slowly than when tempered with pure water. For white stucco, a colourless glue is employed, such as fish-glue; for coloured stucco, metallic oxides are added, such as the hydrated sesquioxide of iron, of manganese, copper, etc., hydrocarbonates of copper, etc. For marble stucco, different plasters are mixed, tempered with glue, and coloured with the various metallic oxides. The skilful workman makes the pattern at will, by properly regulating the mixture. The plaster, thus tempered, is applied in layers over the object to be covered. When it has become sufficiently hard, its moistened surface is rubbed with pumice-stone to render it perfectly smooth. A very thin coat of plaster, tempered with a stronger solution of gelatine than that originally used, is then spread uniformly over it. When the surface is dry, it is polished with tripoli on a fine cloth. From time to time, its surface is moistened with olive-oil, and the polishing is continued until it is completed.

§ 562. Of late years, a plaster calcined with alum, called *alumed plaster*, has been used in the arts. It becomes harder than ordinary plaster, and is more beautiful, being less dead, and possessing a certain degree of translucency. In order to prepare it, the plaster is first calcined, to deprive it of its water of crystallization, and then immediately thrown into a water-bath saturated with alum. In six hours, it is withdrawn, and, after having been dried in the air, is again calcined at a dull red-heat, and then ground. This plaster may be used like common plaster, but is frequently tempered with a solution of alum instead of pure water. Alumed plaster does not set immediately, like ordinary plaster, but retains its softness for several hours. It may be advantageously substituted for stucco. Mixed with an equal quantity of sand, it produces a substance possessing extreme hardness, and fitted for making flag-stones.

Carbonate of Lime.

§ 563. Carbonate of lime is one of the most extensively diffused substances on the surface of the globe. It is sometimes found in isolated and perfectly terminated crystals, when it assumes one of two incompatible forms, and is one of the first ascertained instances of dimorphism. Its most frequent form is that of a rhombohedron having an angle of 105° ; but a very considerable number of forms, derived from this, is met with, all presenting three very easy cleavages, which lead to the rhombohedron of 105°. Very large and perfectly transparent rhombohedral fragments of carbonate of lime are frequently found in Iceland, hence called *Iceland spar*, and are highly prized by opticians. The second dimorphic form of carbonate of lime is a right prism with a rectangular base, belonging to the fourth system of crystallization, and is called by mineralogists *arragonite.* Both forms of the carbonate may be artificially obtained. If an alkaline carbonate be added to a cold solution of a salt of lime, a copious precipitate is formed, which, after some time, becomes granular, and the microscope detects in it small rhombohedrons. If, on the contrary, a boiling solution of a salt of lime be poured into a hot solution of carbonate of ammonia, a dense powder is immediately obtained, in which the microscope shows small crystals of arragonite. If small pieces of arragonite be carefully heated, they soon separate suddenly and fall into powder, and if the temperature has not been raised to redness, the substance undergoes no change of composition, but presents the same weight as before calcination. The disaggregation has been produced solely by a change in the system of crystallization, and the microscope discovers the existence of small rhombohedral crystals in the disaggregated matter.

A solution of sugar dissolves a large quantity of hydrated lime; and if the solution be exposed to the air, it absorbs carbonic acid, and deposits carbonate of lime in the form of small rhombohedral crystals, perfectly transparent. If this experiment be made at a low temperature, crystals of hydrated carbonate of lime are deposited; but these crystals are soon converted into ordinary carbonate of lime, at a temperature above 32°.

§ 564. The waters of a great number of natural springs contain carbonate of lime, dissolved by the assistance of an excess of carbonic acid. These waters, on reaching the air, soon part with their carbonic acid, and the carbonate of lime separates. Calcareous incrustations are thus formed, which, after a time, become very large. The fountain of Saint-Allyre near Clermont, produces these incrustations in a short space of time; for if an object be exposed for a few days to the falling water, it becomes covered with a calcareous crust. In this manner the calcareous *stalactites* and *stalagmites* are formed (fig. 371) which line the walls of certain grottos. The water, traversing fissures in the rocks, drops from the roof, but as each drop remains suspended for some time before falling, it parts with a portion of its carbonic acid, and, consequently, of its carbonate of lime. The same drop, falling on the floor, deposits another portion of calcareous carbonate. As the dropping continues in the same spot, a dependent calcareous incrustation, or stalactite, is formed, which gradually increases toward the earth. Immediately beneath this suspended incrustation, a similar one, or a stalagmite, rises from the earth. These incrustations sometimes join each other, and form a continuous column. The carbonate of lime is crystallized in these incrustations, as can be easily ascertained by their fracture.

Fig. 371.

§ 565. In saccharoidal marble, the carbonate of lime is likewise crystallized, but the crystals are strongly aggregated to each other. The various limestones formed in all the sedimentary rocks, constituting frequently strata of great thickness, exhibit carbonate of lime in very various degrees of compactness. The limestones of transition rocks are, in general, less compact. The majority of these limestones contain the impressions of shells, and some are wholly formed of them. Chalk is a calcareous rock but slightly aggregated, and belonging to the secondary formations.

The shells of the molluscæ, and of birds' eggs, the carapaces of the crustaceæ, are formed of nearly pure carbonate of lime, and the bones of man and animals also contain a considerable proportion of it.

§ 566. Carbonate of lime, subjected to heat, decomposes before fusing; but if it be heated in a gun-barrel hermetically sealed, the high pressure in the tube prevents the escape of carbonic acid, and the carbonate fuses without decomposing. If the barrel be allowed to cool slowly, the fused limestone assumes a crystalline texture, and then resembles exactly saccharoidal marble.

Carbonate of lime does not appreciably dissolve in pure water, while water charged with carbonic acid dissolves it in considerable quantity.

Nitrate of Lime.

§ 567. Nitrate of lime is obtained by dissolving carbonate of lime in nitric acid, and concentrating the liquid by heat, when it assumes, on cooling, a crystalline form. It is a deliquescent salt.

Phosphates of Lime.

§ 568. The phosphates of lime corresponding to trihydrated or ordinary phosphoric acid, are those which are best known. When bone-ashes are treated with sulphuric acid, sulphate of lime is formed, and separates because it is but slightly soluble. The liquid contains a phosphate of lime, improperly called *biphosphate*, which separates in the form of crystalline spangles, if the liquid is sufficiently concentrated. The formula of the salt is $(CaO+2HO)PO_5$. It was stated (§ 205) that this product is used in the manufacture of phosphorus.

If a solution of ordinary phosphate of soda $(2NaO+HO)PO_5+24HO$ be poured into a solution of a salt of lime, a white gelatinous precipitate is obtained, having the formula $(2CaO+HO)PO_5+4HO$. If this precipitate be digested with ammonia, it parts with a portion of its phosphoric acid, and a precipitate remains of which the formula is $3CaO,PO_5$. The same phosphate $3CaO,PO_5$ is immediately precipitated when an excess of phosphoric acid is poured into a solution of chloride of calcium and the liquid supersaturated with ammonia.

Bone-ashes are composed of $\frac{4}{5}$ phosphate of lime, and $\frac{1}{5}$ carbonate of lime. The formula of the phosphate of lime of bones is $3CaO,PO_5$.

These various phosphates of lime, with the exception of the biphosphate, are insoluble in water, but readily soluble in an acid liquid.

Phosphate of lime is found crystallized in nature in a mineral called *apatite;* the phosphate $3CaO,PO_5$ found in it being combined with a small quantity of chloride and fluoride of calcium.

If the biphosphate $(CaO+2HO)PO_5$ be heated to redness, it fuses into a substance which remains vitreous after cooling; and its nature is entirely changed, for it has become insoluble in water. Heat has caused the phosphate to pass from the tribasic to the monobasic modification, and the ignited product is *metaphosphate of lime* CaO,PO_5.

Chlorate of Lime.

§ 569. This salt is obtained mixed with chloride of calcium by passing a current of chlorine through milk of lime. There are formed, at first, hypochlorite of lime and chloride of calcium; but, if the chlorine be continued, after the lime is entirely converted into these two products, a new reaction takes place, and chlorate of lime is formed, particularly if the temperature be raised. This liquid may be used for the manufacture of chlorate of potassa, by merely pouring chloride of potassium into it, when a double decomposition takes place, and chlorate of potassa is deposited.

Hypochlorite of Lime.

§ 570. This salt is very important on account of its application to bleaching. It is obtained in a state of purity, by adding a solution of hypochlorous acid to milk of lime; but there must be an excess of lime, for as soon as hypochlorous acid predominates, the hypochlorite is decomposed into chlorate of lime and chloride of calcium:

$$3(CaO,ClO)=CaO,ClO_5+2CaCl.$$

A solution of hypochlorite of lime, at first blues the tincture of litmus reddened by an acid; but soon destroys its colour.

Chlorine does not act on quicklime; but, if passed slowly over hydrated lime, hypochlorite of lime and chloride of calcium are formed:

$$2CaO+2Cl=CaO,ClO+CaCl.$$

It is essential to leave always an excess of lime; for, if the current of chlorine be continued after the lime is completely converted into hypochlorite of lime and chloride of calcium, a new reaction ensues, by which the hypochlorite is converted into chlorate of lime and chloride of calcium. This reaction manifests itself, particularly if the temperature be elevated, either from a too copious supply of chlorine or from the substance being too much heated.

§ 571. The name of *chloride of lime* is commercially given to a mixture of hypochlorite of lime, chloride of calcium, and hydrated lime, which is obtained by imperfectly saturating slaked lime by chlorine. It is manufactured in large quantities, for it is almost exclusively employed in bleaching.

Chlorine is prepared by the reaction of a mixture of sea-salt, peroxide of manganese, and dilute sulphuric acid, at a gentle heat, in a leaden apparatus, composed of a still *abcd* (fig. 372), enclosed in a casing of sheet iron. Steam is carried between the casing and still, through the pipe *o*, so as to maintain the temperature at about 140°. The pipe *s* serves to withdraw the substances when all their chlorine is disengaged. The cap or top of the still has several tubulures; one at *e*, through which the materials are introduced; one at *f*, for the escape of the gas; another at *g*, to which is soldered a safety-tube, furnished with a funnel, through which the acid is poured gradually; and lastly, a tubulure *h*, traversed by an iron rod, covered with lead and terminating in a large paddle *mn*, also covered with lead, which is used to stir the mixture. The tubulures are constructed with small leaden grooves, into which sulphuric acid is poured in order to seal the joints hermetically. The arrangement is easily understood by reference to fig. 372.

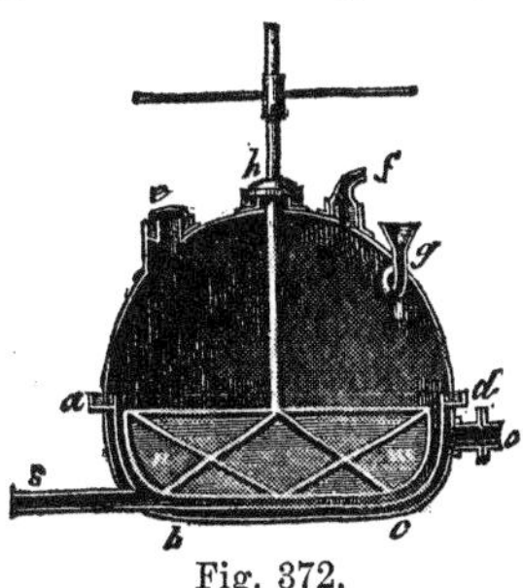

Fig. 372.

The chlorine is conveyed into large chambers of masonry, in which are arranged a great number of wooden shelves, covered by a layer of hydrate of lime about ¾ inch thick. Where the chambers are very low, the hydrate is simply spread over the floor to the thickness of about 2 inches; in which case, it must be constantly stirred with rakes to renew the surface. When the lime has absorbed a sufficient quantity of chlorine, it is withdrawn and packed in casks.

By treating chloride of lime with water, the hypochlorite of lime and the chloride of calcium are dissolved, and the excess of hydrated lime remains in the form of a pulp. The clear liquid may be separated by filtering or decanting.

The chloride is often prepared, in the workshops in which it is to be used, in solution, by conveying chlorine into cylinders half filled with lime, which is constantly stirred in order to promote the absorption of chlorine.

Hypochlorite of lime is decomposed by the most feeble acids, even by carbonic, and from this property it always exhales the odour of hypochlorous acid, which is expelled by the carbonic acid of the air.

An aqueous solution of chlorine exerts an oxidizing agency on all substances capable of higher oxidation, many examples of which have been already presented. By virtue of this oxidizing agency, a solution of chlorine destroys the colour of coloured organic bodies, acting in a similar manner to oxygenated water. Water is decomposed, its hydrogen combining with chlorine, and its oxygen, in the nascent state, oxidizing the organic matter, which is usually converted into a new colourless body. Moreover, it will be shown hereafter that organic substances, subjected to oxidizing agencies, are finally converted into acids, which may be easily removed by alkalies. The coloured organic substances printed on cloths or muslins by virtue of special affinity, and which, in this state, are insoluble in water and alkaline lyes, are therefore converted, by an oxidizing action, into other substances possessing acid properties, and which can be readily removed by alkaline lyes. It will be readily seen, that 1 equiv. of hypochlorous acid, or 1 equiv. of hypochlorite of lime, in the presence of an acid, must exert the same oxidizing and decolourizing action as 2 equivs. of oxygen in the nascent state, or 2 equivs. of chlorine dissolved in water; for free hypochlorous acid is readily decomposed into 1 equiv. of chlorine and 1 equiv. of oxygen. Now, to obtain 1 equiv. of hypochlorite of lime, 2 equivs. of chlorine are required to act on 2 equivs. of hydrated lime; so that the liquid obtained by treating chloride of lime with water should exert the same bleaching power as the quantity of chlorine used to produce this chloride of lime.

In order to bleach a piece of goods, it is first dipped into a weak solution of chlorohydric acid; then passed through a vat containing chloride of lime; and lastly, washed with some alkaline liquid.

Chloride of lime is also used as a disinfecting agent, and to destroy disagreeable odours. The hypochlorous acid is gradually driven off by the carbonic acid of the air, and, like chlorine, it destroys the substances which evolve those odours. The best method of employing it consists in impregnating linen with a strong solution of the chloride, and hanging it up in the place where the air is to be purified.

§ 572. Commercial chloride of lime necessarily presenting various degrees of strength, it is important to the purchaser to be able to ascertain with ease and accuracy its bleaching power, as that alone gives it value. The determination is made by means of the *chlorometric analysis* about to be described with some minuteness.

In order to compare the merchantable values of the various qualities of chloride of lime found in commerce, the weights of the different chlorides are ascertained which will bleach the same volume of a standard solution of organic colouring matter. The values of the chlorides will be in the inverse ratio of these weights.

The colouring matter chosen, is a solution of indigo in sulphuric acid. In order to prepare it, the indigo of commerce is treated with Nordhausen oil of vitriol or fuming sulphuric acid, which dissolves a considerable quantity of it when it is diluted with water, and produces a deep-blue liquid. The bleaching of this liquid by chlorine is very marked, for the colour passes immediately from a deep-blue to a yellow. The solution of indigo is diluted with water, until 1 litre of it is exactly bleached by 1 litre of dry chlorine, at the temperature of 32°, and under a pressure of 0.76 m. (29.92 inches.)

To effect this, a normal solution of chlorine is first prepared, by means of which the solution of indigo is rated. The normal solution may be prepared in various ways, of which we shall describe the most simple. A ground-stoppered bottle is filled with dry chlorine (§ 168, fig. 223), and the temperature and barometric pressure noted at the same time. The inverted bottle is immersed in a dilute solution of potassa (fig. 373), the stopper withdrawn a very little, in order to allow a small quantity of the alkaline liquid to enter the bottle, and then replaced. After shaking the bottle without removing it from the solution, a vacuum is formed by the absorption of the chlorine; when the cork is again removed to allow the entrance of a small quantity of the alkaline solution. The bottle is again shaken, and the operation repeated until the absorption of the chlorine is completed. If the bottle contained originally nothing but chlorine, it is evident that it will be entirely filled with the solution of potassa; but if it contained air mixed with the chlorine, the air will remain after the absorption of the chlorine. In all cases, the volume of alkaline liquid which has entered the bottle is exactly equal to the volume of chlorine absorbed. If, therefore, the chlorine, at the moment of closing the bottle, were under the normal conditions of temperature and pressure, that is to say, at 32°, and under a barometric pressure of 0.760 m., the solution of potassa would contain its normal volume of chlorine, and we will call its standard 100. But, if the surrounding temperature were t, at the moment of closing the bottle, and the pressure H, the solution of potassa would only contain a volume of chlorine represented by $\frac{1}{1+0.00367.t} \cdot \frac{H}{760}$ of chlorine under normal conditions, and its standard is represented by $100 \cdot \frac{1}{1+0.00367.t} \cdot \frac{H}{760}$.

Fig. 373.

The solution of indigo must now be diluted with water, so that 50 cub. centim. of the solution shall be exactly bleached by $50\frac{1}{1+0.00367.t} \cdot \frac{H}{760}$ of the bleaching solution of potassa. To avoid repetition, a preliminary test of the solution of indigo is made, by taking 50 cub. centim. of the solution with the pipette D (fig. 374), which has a mark γ at the level of 50 cub. centim., and pouring them into a glass placed on a sheet of paper. The chlorimeter (fig. 375) is filled up to 0 with the standard bleaching liquid, which is poured out slowly until the moment of discolouration. Let n be the number

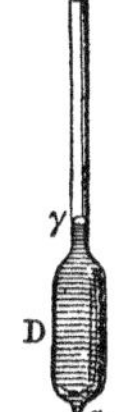

Fig. 374.

of divisions poured out: it will represent $\frac{n}{2}$ cub. centim., as the chlorimeter is divided into cubic demicentimetres. The standard of the solution of indigo is therefore $n \frac{1}{1+0.00367.t} \cdot \frac{H}{760}$, and must be diluted with water so as to bring it to 100. Supposing that the preceding expression, calculated in numbers, gives 175, sufficient water is added to 100 parts of the solution of indigo to bring the volume to 175, which will make it a normal solution of indigo of the standard of 100. The standard should, however, be verified by another experiment, and corrected, if necessary. The normal coloured liquid should then be preserved in a well-stoppered bottle.

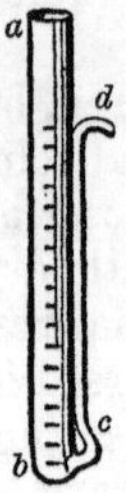

a d c b

Fig. 375.

In order to test a bleaching chloride, small samples of the chloride are taken from various parts of the mass to be tested, so as to make a sample which may be considered as representing the average of the whole. 10 gm. of this sample being rubbed in a porcelain or glass mortar with a small quantity of water, more water is added and decanted into a filter placed in the vessel A (fig.. 376) of 1 litre content. This process is repeated several times, and lastly the vessel A is filled with water to the level of the mark *a*. Filtration may be avoided by employing careful decantation.

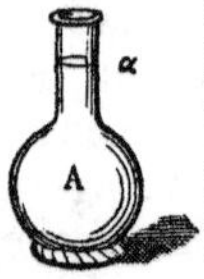

α A

Fig. 376.

The liquid, being cleared by repose or filtration, is poured into the chlorimeter as far as the division 0. On the other hand, 50 cub. centim. of the normal solution of indigo, taken up with the pipette D, are poured into a vessel B (fig. 377) placed on a sheet of white paper; and while shaking this vessel with the left hand, the solution of the bleaching chloride is poured slowly into it. When approaching the moment of discoloration, the chloride should be added by drops. Supposing that it required 115 divisions of the chlorimeter to effect the discoloration, the standard of the chloride will be $\frac{100}{115}=86.9°$.

B

Fig. 377.

If the inverse method of testing could be made, by pouring the normal solution of indigo, from the alkalimeter into a volume of 50 cubic centimetres of a solution of the bleaching chloride, until the latter assumed a blue colour, it is evident that the standard of the chloride would be immediately given by the number of cubic demicentimetres of the solution of indigo poured out. But this cannot be done, because the solution of indigo contains a large quantity of acid, and because the first portions poured into the bleaching liquid would disengage a quantity of chlorine greater than that necessary to decolorize the indigo with which they immediately come into contact. We would thus be liable to the loss of chlorine. But, when the chloride is poured into the solution of indigo, the chloride is always in the presence of an excess of indigo, and is not subject to loss.

§ 573. The solution of indigo is liable to serious objection which has caused it to be abandoned. It soon changes, and may be the cause of error, when a solution is employed which has been made for some time.

A standard solution of arsenious acid in chlorohydric acid is now substituted for the normal blue liquid: the chlorine set free converts the arsenious into arsenic acid, and it is easy to ascertain the moment at which the transformation occurs; for experience shows that if a solution of arsenious acid be coloured by a few drops of a solution of indigo, chlorine does not bleach it until it has entirely converted the arsenious into arsenic acid.

In order to prepare the normal arsenious solution, 4.439 gm. of pure arsenious acid are weighed out, dissolved in chlorohydric acid diluted with its volume of water, and water then added, so that it shall occupy the volume of 1 litre. If doubts exist as to the purity of the arsenious acid, the standard of the arsenious solution must be verified by means of the normal chlorine liquid previously mentioned.

The first test should be regarded as only an approximation. A second is made, by pouring immediately into the 50 cub. cntim. of uncoloured arsenious solution, a volume of the solution of chloride, somewhat less than that which effected the decolorization in the first test. A few drops of the solution of indigo are then first added, to colour the liquid, after which the chloride is added, drop by drop, so that the moment of discoloration can be ascertained with precision.

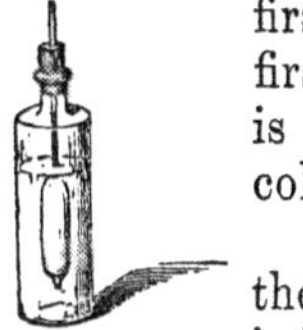
Fig. 378.

As there is some danger in filling the pipette D with the arsenious solution by sucking it with the mouth, it is better to fill it by immersion, as in fig. 378.*

* The method commonly practised in England and the United States for ascertaining the strength of bleaching-salt is to dissolve a given weight of crystallized copperas, protosulphate of iron, in water, and add to it a solution of a given quantity of the bleaching-salt, from an alkalimeter, until all the protoxide is converted into peroxide of iron. A salt of iron fully peroxidized will not give prussian blue with red prussiate of potash, (ferrid cyanide of potassium,) but the least trace of protoxide yields a blue colour instantly. To determine the complete peroxidation of the copperas by the bleaching-salt, many small drops of a solution of red prussiate are put upon a surface of porcelain, and a drop of the copperas solution touched to one of them by a glass rod. If the colour be blue, more chloride is added to the copperas solution, when a drop is again taken out and tried with another drop of the red prussiate. This operation is repeated until the yellow drop of red prussiate is no longer blued. A preliminary experiment followed by one more exact makes the whole test shorter than by employing a single test; and the approach of the point of peroxidation is recognised by greenish-blue, green, and light-green colours successively.—*J. C. B.*

A still more exact method, for which less time is required than for either of those mentioned in the text and in the note by Prof. Booth, is the following:—A solution of a given quantity of the bleaching-powder is added to a measured solution of pure protosulphate of iron, in such quantity that only a part of the protoxide of iron will be oxidized by the chlorine; the remaining protoxide is then very accurately determined with permanganate of potassa, according to the me-

COMPOUNDS OF CALCIUM WITH SULPHUR.

§ 574. Calcium forms a great number of compounds with sulphur. By calcining sulphate of lime with charcoal, it is converted into monosulphide of calcium CaS, a white substance, nearly insoluble in water. If milk of lime be boiled with the flowers of sulphur, more sulphuretted sulphides are obtained, which remain in solution with the hyposulphite of lime. If the sulphur is in great excess, and the ebullition prolonged, the protosulphide CaS_5 is obtained, which remains in the solution, and is not deposited by the cooling of the liquid. If it is boiled for a shorter time, and the hot liquid filtered, the yellow solution deposits, on cooling, orange-coloured circular crystals of the bisulphide CaS_2, but little soluble in cold water, which dissolves only about $\frac{1}{400}$ of its weight.

COMPOUND OF CALCIUM WITH CHLORINE.

§ 575. Only one compound of calcium with chlorine is known, and is prepared by dissolving hydrate or carbonate of lime in chlorohydric acid. Chloride of calcium is produced in large quantities in the preparation of ammonia, which is made by heating a mixture of chlorohydrate of ammonia and lime in large cast-iron cylinders (§ 123). The residue from the operation is chloride of calcium, mixed with a small quantity of lime in excess, from which the chloride is extracted by treatment with cold water. The liquid, highly concentrated by evaporation, and allowed to cool, deposits large crystals of the hydrated chloride, the formula of which is $CaCl+6HO$. These crystals are very deliquescent, and produce a great degree of cold by solution in water; but the greatest depression of temperature is obtained by mixing them with pounded ice, when, as was stated (§ 374), the temperature could thus be reduced to —49°. Hydrated chloride of calcium fuses readily in its water of crystallization, and, when heated to 400°, parts with 4 equivalents of water, leaving a porous mass, which absorbs water with great avidity, and is well fitted for drying gases. Heated still further, it parts with the balance of its water, and then fuses at a red-heat. The fused chloride is generally cast in the form of flat cakes, which are broken up and preserved in a well-stoppered bottle. It is frequently used in the laboratory, either for drying gases or for removing the water which is mixed with liquids of organic origin.

The anhydrous chloride dissolves in water with such an elevation

---

thod described in § 804; the quantity of protoxide thus found, subtracted from that contained in the measured solution employed, gives the quantity oxidized by the chlorine, from which the percentage of the latter is found by a simple and easy calculation.— *W. L. Faber.*

of temperature that the heat evolved by its combination is greater than that which becomes latent by the act of solution of the hydrated chloride. It dissolves in large proportion in water, and is also quite soluble in absolute alcohol. The alcoholic solution made by heat deposits, on cooling, crystals of a combination of the chloride with alcohol, an *alcoholate* of chloride of calcium.

If a concentrated solution of chloride of calcium be boiled with an excess of hydrated lime, a considerable proportion of the hydrate is dissolved; and the filtered liquid deposits, on cooling, a crystallized compound of chloride of calcium and lime, the formula of which is $CaCl+3CaO+15HO$.

COMPOUND OF CALCIUM WITH FLUORINE.

§ 576. Fluoride of calcium is found in nature, either in compact masses of various hues, or in well-defined crystals, which are cubes, sometimes modified by the facets of the octahedron. Mineralogists call it *fluor-spar*. It presents a remarkable phenomenon of phosphorescence. When its powder is heated in an iron spoon, it becomes luminous long before reaching a red-heat, and evolves a violet or green light, according to the specimen. It is used in the laboratory in the preparation of fluohydric acid (§ 204).

DISTINCTIVE CHARACTERS OF THE SALTS OF LIME.

§ 577. The salts of lime are not precipitated by ammonia, which distinguishes them from the earthy metals, and from the second class of metals, properly so called (§ 276). They are precipitated by the alkaline carbonates, a character which distinguishes them from the salts furnished by the alkaline metals.

If sulphuric acid or a sulphate be poured into a very dilute solution of a salt of lime, no precipitate is formed; in which case the salts of baryta and strontia would yield a precipitate. If the solution of the salt of lime is more concentrated, a precipitate of hydrated sulphate of lime is formed, which, if left to itself for some time, collects in the form of small crystalline spangles, easily recognisable by the microscope.

Salts of lime yield, with oxalic acid and the oxalates, a granular precipitate of oxalate of lime, nearly insoluble in water, and soluble with great difficulty in an excess of acid. Advantage is taken of this property, not only to detect the presence of lime, but also in chemical analyses, to precipitate it from the liquids which contain it.

MAGNESIUM.

EQUIVALENT = 12.1.

§ 578. Magnesium* is obtained by decomposing the anhydrous chloride of magnesium by potassium or sodium. A few globules of potassium or sodium are placed at the bottom of a platinum crucible, and above them the chloride of magnesium broken in pieces. The crucible is covered with its lid, which is fastened down by iron wire, and the temperature then raised by an alcohol lamp. Reaction takes place at a red-heat, with a violent deflagration, which would throw off the lid of the crucible were it not firmly fixed. The potassium combines with the chlorine, and the magnesium is set free. The crucible being allowed to cool, the substance is treated with water as cold as possible, which dissolves the chloride of potassium and the unaltered chloride of magnesium, leaving the magnesium in the form of metallic globules.

Magnesium possesses a certain degree of ductility, and presents the colour and lustre of silver. It changes more slowly in the air than the preceding metals, and is not sensibly decomposed by very cold water; but at a temperature above 86° the decomposition commences, and at about 212° is very active. Heated to a dull red, either in the air or in oxygen, the metal ignites. It becomes equally incandescent in chlorine.

COMPOUND OF MAGNESIUM WITH OXYGEN.

§ 579. Only one compound of magnesium with oxygen is known, the protoxide, or *magnesia*, which is prepared by calcining the hydrocarbonate of magnesia, or the *white magnesia* of the pharmaceutist. As this hydrocarbonate is very light, the magnesia produced by it is also very light, and considerable bulk is required for any ordinary weight of matter. This circumstance is very inconvenient in several chemical processes, particularly in those which are effected, in the dry way, in vessels of limited dimensions. For these peculiar cases, magnesia is prepared by calcining the nitrate of magnesia, which yields a much heavier oxide. Magnesia is a white powder, infusible at the highest temperatures of our furnaces. It is slightly soluble in water, requiring about 5000 times its weight of that liquid; and yet this solubility is sufficient to enable moistened magnesia to blue the tincture of litmus reddened by an acid. It is a powerful base, perfectly saturating

* Magnesium was first isolated by M. Bussy, by adopting a process by which Wœhler has already succeeded in preparing aluminum and glucinum.

acids. It is precipitated by lime, but the chief cause of the precipitation is the fact that magnesia is still less soluble in water than lime.

Anhydrous magnesia does not produce any sensible degree of heat with water; for, although it forms a combination with it, the action is so slow that evolution of heat is inappreciable. A monohydrate of magnesia MgO+HO is formed in this case, and easily restored to the anhydrous state by heat. The same hydrate is precipitated when a solution of potassa is poured into that of a magnesian salt.

Caustic magnesia is a powerful antidote in poisoning by arsenious acid, with which it combines to form an insoluble compound free from any poisonous effect.* The magnesia for this purpose should be in the hydrated state, or but slightly calcined, nor can its carbonate be substituted for it.

§ 580. The composition of magnesia may be obtained by the synthesis of sulphate of magnesia, that is, by ascertaining, as in the case of lime (§ 552), the weight of sulphate of magnesia yielded by a given weight of magnesia. It may also be deduced from the direct analysis of the sulphate, by determining the weight of sulphate of baryta yielded by a known weight of sulphate of magnesia when its solution is precipitated by chloride of barium.

SALTS OF MAGNESIA.

Sulphate of Magnesia.

§ 581. Sulphate of magnesia, or Epsom salt, exists in several mineral springs, particularly in those of Epsom, in England, Seidlitz and Pullna, in Bohemia. These waters are used in medicine as a purgative, and owe their efficacy to the sulphate of magnesia which they contain. This sulphate, in mineral springs, appears to arise from the reaction of sulphate of lime in solution on the magnesian limestone which constitutes the formation. The water, charged with sulphate of lime, remaining for a long time on the magnesian soil, reacts on the carbonate of magnesia, carbonate of lime being deposited, and sulphate of magnesia dissolved. The mineral waters, collected in shallow basins, concentrate by evaporation, and their complete evaporation yields crystallized sulphate of magnesia.

Such a formation of sulphate of magnesia, by the reaction of sulphate of lime in solution on carbonate of magnesia, may be proved by direct experiment, by filtering slowly and repeatedly water saturated with sulphate of lime through a thick stratum of magnesian limestone, when the water will finally contain only sulphate of magnesia. But an inverse decomposition can likewise be effected by operating at a high temperature. If carbonate of lime

* Hydrated oxide of iron, made up into a thin mud with water, serves the same purpose, and is preferable on account of its cheapness.—*W. L. Faber.*

and a solution of sulphate of magnesia be heated to about 400° in a thick glass tube closed at both ends, sulphate of lime and carbonate of magnesia are formed. The inverse reaction is an important fact in geology, as it serves to explain the formation of native magnesian limestone. It is admitted that carbonate of magnesia has been formed by the reaction of carbonate of lime on sulphate of magnesia dissolved in the hot waters which covered the globe to a great depth, the lower strata of which, consequently, might have attained a very high temperature.

The sulphate may also be obtained by adding sulphuric acid to the native carbonate of magnesia or magnesian limestones, such as dolomite, very rich in this carbonate; whereby it would form sulphate of lime, but slightly soluble in water, and sulphate of magnesia, which is very soluble, particularly in hot water.

Lastly, it was stated (§ 498 and § 501) that the mother waters of the salines contained considerable quantities of this salt; so that all the Epsom salt used in medicine might be obtained from these waters at a cheap rate.

§ 582. Sulphate of magnesia crystallizes, at ordinary temperatures, in small elongated prisms, having the formula MgO,SO_3+7HO. If the crystallization takes place at an elevated temperature, the salt deposited contains only 6 equivalents of water, but if at several degrees below 32°, large crystals are obtained, of which the formula is MgO,SO_3+12HO. Epsom salt, heated to 464°, still retains 1 equiv. of water, which it loses at a higher temperature. The anhydrous sulphate fuses at a red-heat. At 32°, 100 parts of water dissolve about 26 parts of the salt. The plate at page 407 contains its curve of solubility for the temperatures comprised between 32° and 212°.

Sulphate of magnesia combines with the alkaline sulphates and with that of ammonia, forming double salts which readily crystallize. The formula of the double sulphate of magnesia and potassa is MgO,SO_3+KO,SO_3+6HO. Considerable quantities of this salt are deposited during the evaporation of the mother waters of salines (§ 502). The formula of the double sulphate of magnesia and ammonia is $MgO,SO_3+(NH_3,HO)SO_3+6HO$: it is isomorphous with the double salt of potassa.

Nitrate of Magnesia.

§ 583. This salt is prepared by dissolving magnesia in nitric acid. It is very soluble in water and deliquescent, and is entirely decomposed at a red-heat, yielding a residue of pure magnesia.

Carbonate of Magnesia.

§ 584. Carbonate of magnesia is found in nature, generally in compact masses, but sometimes crystallized in rhombohedrons. It also exists in nature in combination with carbonate of lime, which is isomorphous with it, and nearly all limestones contain a small quantity of magnesia. The *dolomite* of mineralogists, which constitutes large formations in some countries, particularly in the Alps, is a double carbonate of lime and magnesia, with the formula CaO,CO_2+MgO,CO_2.

When an alkaline carbonate is poured into the solution of a magnesian salt, a white gelatinous precipitate is formed, which is a hydrocarbonate of magnesia, that is, a compound of the hydrate and carbonate of magnesia. The proportions of the two compounds vary, according to the quantity of alkaline carbonate used, the state of concentration of the liquids, and their temperature. It is manufactured on a large scale for medicinal purposes, and is called in pharmacy *white magnesia*, (*alba.*) It is made as light as possible, for which purpose dilute and hot solutions of sulphate of magnesia and carbonate of soda are mixed together. The liquid is then filtered in rectangular baskets lined with muslin, which retains the precipitate. The hydrocarbonate, well washed and dried, presents the shape of square blocks of excessive lightness.

White magnesia dissolves in considerable quantity in water charged with carbonic acid. The solution, exposed to the air, loses its carbonic acid, and the hydrated carbonate of magnesia MgO,CO_2+3HO is deposited.*

Phosphates of Magnesia.

§ 585. A neutral phosphate of magnesia is obtained by decomposing the hydrocarbonate by phosphoric acid. It is soluble in from 15 to 20 parts of water. Phosphate of magnesia forms, with phosphate of ammonia, double phosphates of very slight solubility. If a solution of phosphate of ammonia be added to a hot solution of sulphate of magnesia, small prismatic crystals of a double phosphate are deposited on cooling, of the formula

$$[2(NH_3,HO)+HO]PO_5+(2MgO+HO)PO_5+6HO.$$

If, on the contrary, we add to the solution of sulphate of magnesia, first chlorohydrate of ammonia, and afterward ammonia, which then forms no precipitate, as we shall see (§ 589), and lastly phosphate of ammonia, a granular precipitate is deposited, insoluble in the liquid in which the precipitation took place, and of which the formula is $(NH_3,HO+2MgO)PO_5+6HO$. But since this precipitate is somewhat soluble in pure water, it must be washed with the smallest quantity of water possible.† This double phosphate possesses great interest; for it is often in this state of combination that, in chemical analyses, magnesia is precipitated from its solu-

---

* Beautiful crystals are sometimes formed in well-corked bottles containing the bicarbonated solution.—*J. C. B.*

† It should always be washed with ammoniacal water.—*J. C. B.*

tions. The same phosphate is likewise occasionally found in the animal economy, forming calculi in the bladder, and is called *ammoniaco-magnesian phosphate.*

Silicates of Magnesia.

§ 586. Silicates of magnesia are found in nature, generally combined with water, constituting, in some localities, entire rocks, or veins. The mineral called *magnesite*, or *meerschaum*, and *talc*, are composed of silicate of magnesia MgO,SiO_3, combined with water.* *Serpentine* is also formed of silicate of magnesia combined with the hydrate of magnesia, its formula being $2(3MgO,2SiO_3)+MgO,2HO$. Serpentine, which constitutes large masses in certain primitive rocks, is easily attacked by acids, and may be used in the preparation of sulphate of magnesia. It can be worked in a turning-lathe, into various ornamental objects remarkable for their beautiful colours. Silicate of magnesia, combined with other silicates, forms a great number of minerals constituting several primary rocks, such as chrysolite, augite, and hornblende.

COMPOUND OF MAGNESIUM WITH SULPHUR.

§ 587. A *monosulphide of magnesium* is obtained by heating a mixture of sulphate of magnesia and charcoal in a crucible; but the product is always mixed with magnesia. A purer product is obtained by adding to the preceding mixture an alkaline polysulphide, or a mixture of carbonate of soda and an excess of sulphur. Sulphide of magnesium is not obtained in the humid way, by boiling magnesia and sulphur with water; a behaviour which distinguishes magnesia from the other alkaline earths and approximates it to the earths. Magnesia in fact forms a transition between the alkaline earths and the earths.

COMPOUND OF MAGNESIUM WITH CHLORINE.

§ 588. Chloride of magnesium is obtained in solution in water, by treating white magnesia with chlorohydric acid. When the solution is evaporated to a high degree of concentration, it deposits, on cooling, crystals of a hydrated chloride with the formula $MgCl+5HO$; but if the evaporation be continued to dryness, the chloride is decomposed, chlorohydric acid being disengaged, and free magnesia remaining. In this decomposition, likewise, magnesia resembles the earths, the chlorides of which undergo a similar alteration. Anhydrous chloride of magnesium is obtained by heating a mixture of magnesia and charcoal in a porcelain tube, through which a current of dry chlorine is passed; but, the chloride having very slight volatility, remains mixed with charcoal.

---

* Water is often wanting in talc.—*J. C. B.*

To obtain the chloride pure, white magnesia is dissolved in concentrated chlorohydric acid, sal ammoniac added thereto, and the whole evaporated to dryness. The residue is placed in a platinum crucible, and heated to redness over an alcohol-lamp. The chloride of magnesium combines with the chlorohydrate of ammonia, and acquires sufficient stability to allow the water to be driven off by heat before reacting on the chloride. Heat then decomposes the dried double chloride, disengaging chlorohydrate of ammonia, and leaving chloride of magnesium in a melted state, which, on cooling, solidifies in a crystalline mass. This anhydrous chloride of magnesium is used (§ 578) in the preparation of metallic magnesium.

Chloride of magnesium exists in sea-water, and the mother waters of the salines (§ 503) contain considerable quantities of it, which they deposit in the form of the double chloride of magnesium and potassium.

DISTINCTIVE CHARACTERS OF THE SALTS OF MAGNESIA.

§ 589. The salts of magnesia yield white gelatinous precipitates with the alkaline carbonates, which distinguishes them from the alkaline salts.

Ammonia, poured into a solution of a salt of magnesia which does not contain an excess of acid, nor any ammoniacal salt, yields a white precipitate, which the salts of baryta, strontia, and lime, do not yield under like circumstances. But if the magnesian liquid contains a sufficient quantity of any ammoniacal salt, it is no longer precipitable by ammonia, because the magnesian salt forms a double ammoniacal salt, not decomposable by ammonia. Nor is a precipitate produced if the liquid contains a great excess of acid; for, by adding ammonia to neutralize the liquid, a quantity of ammoniacal salt is formed, sufficient to produce the double magnesian salt not decomposable by ammonia. The same phenomenon is manifest when the magnesian salt exists in the neutral state in the liquid, a portion only of the magnesia being precipitated by the ammonia; for the acid transferred to the ammonia by the precipitated magnesia, forms a quantity of ammoniacal salt, sufficient to produce, with the magnesian salt which remains in the liquid, the double salt undecomposable by ammonia. This property likewise places magnesia between the alkaline earths and the earths.

The salts of magnesia are precipitated by lime-water.

They are never precipitated by the alkaline sulphates, unless the magnesian liquid be extremely concentrated, in which case, sulphate of magnesia might crystallize; but it is always easy to prove that these crystals are very soluble in water. The salts of baryta and strontian are, on the contrary, precipitated by the sulphates, even when their solutions are very dilute; the salts of lime themselves yield a precipitate of sulphate of lime, easily recognised by its appearance, unless the liquid is extremely dilute.

The salts of magnesia, heated before the blowpipe with a small quantity of nitrate of cobalt, yield a rose-coloured residue.

DETERMINATION OF THE ALKALINE EARTHS, AND METHODS OF SEPARATING THEM FROM EACH OTHER, AND FROM THE ALKALIES.

§ 590. Baryta and strontia are always determined in the state of sulphates. When they are in solution, the liquid is boiled, a few drops of chlorohydric acid added to it, and then a solution of chloride of barium is poured in. The sulphates are deposited in the form of a granular powder, which is collected on a small filter, well washed with hot water, and dried on the filter. After desiccation, the precipitate separates readily from the filter, and is carefully dropped into a platinum crucible, which is heated to redness over an alcohol-lamp. The filter being suspended by a platinum wire over the crucible, is inflamed, and as it burns in the air, its ashes fall into the crucible. The crucible, with its contents, being weighed, the contents are removed, and the crucible cleaned. The crucible being replaced over the lamp, a second filter, of the same size as the first, and made from the same sheet of paper, is burned. This filter, to resemble the first as closely as possible, should have been washed with water acidulated with chlorohydric acid. The crucible is again weighed, and the weights necessary to restore the equilibrium of the scales represent the weight of the sulphate. The sulphate, enclosed in its filter, should not be calcined in the crucible, because a certain quantity of sulphide of barium is always formed, and in order to have only the sulphate, it would be necessary to sprinkle it with sulphuric acid, and calcine it anew.*

§ 591. When a solution contains only lime, combined with a volatile acid or with sulphuric acid, the lime may be determined in the state of sulphate. To effect this, the liquid is evaporated to dryness in a porcelain, or still better, in a platinum capsule, the residue sprinkled with sulphuric acid, the excess of acid evaporated, and the substance heated to redness. The sulphate of lime

* It is generally advisable to remove all the contents of a filter, and burn the latter separately, where it can be safely done without loss; but the method of burning the filter in the air over the crucible is objectionable, from the danger of losing particles of ashes of the filter, or of the substance adhering to it, from heated currents of air. A much better method is to burn the filter on the cover of the crucible, or to incline the crucible and burn the filter in it a little in front of the powder; and in either case to begin at a low red-heat, and finish it at a full red. By managing the heat properly, there is no danger of reducing the sulphate of baryta to a sulphide, for even sulphate of lead is burned in the same manner without the slightest detriment to the crucible, which would certainly be injured if sulphuret of lead were formed.—*J. C. B.*

which remains is weighed. At other times, the liquid is evaporated to dryness with a small quantity of sulphuric acid, and treated with dilute alcohol, which does not sensibly dissolve the sulphate of lime, but which can dissolve other saline substances existing in the liquid with the sulphate. The sulphate of lime is washed with alcohol, and weighed after calcination.*

Lime may also be precipitated by an alkaline carbonate, or still better, by an oxalate, the oxalate of lime being still more insoluble than the carbonate, provided the liquid be made alkaline by the addition of a small quantity of ammonia. The precipitate may be determined either as caustic lime, as carbonate, or as sulphate of lime. If it is to be determined as caustic lime, the oxalate is calcined at a white-heat, and, after being weighed, it is ascertained whether the lime has become completely caustic, by sprinkling it with nitric acid, which should produce no effervescence. It is well, for the sake of exactness, to sprinkle the calcined matter with sulphuric acid, and determine the lime in the state of a sulphate, after a new calcination.

In order to determine lime as carbonate, add carbonate of ammonia to the matter calcined in a platinum crucible, and heat it only to a dull red-heat, to drive off the excess of carbonate of ammonia.

§ 592. When magnesia exists alone in a liquid, combined with a volatile acid or with sulphuric acid, it may be determined as sulphate by proceeding exactly as with lime. It may also be precipitated as carbonate by an alkaline carbonate; but it is advisable to evaporate the liquid to dryness and treat the residue with water. The carbonate of magnesia then separates completely: the precipitate is calcined at a red-heat, and weighed in the state of caustic magnesia.

Magnesia is often determined in the state of phosphate. In this case, ammonia is first added to the liquid, and afterward a solution of phosphate of ammonia. The precipitate of phosphate of magnesia and ammonia is collected on a filter, quickly washed with water containing a little ammonia, and weighed after calcination. The phosphate of magnesia thus obtained contains 36.6 pr. ct. of magnesia.

§ 593. Let us now suppose a liquid to contain at the same time alkaline bases, potassa or soda, and the four alkaline earths, baryta, strontia, lime, and magnesia, only volatile acids being present. By adding an excess of carbonate of ammonia, the alkaline earths will be precipitated in the state of carbonates, leaving the alkalies alone in solution. This liquid is evaporated to dryness, after the addition of a small quantity of sulphuric acid. The residue, when calcined to redness and melted in a platinum crucible, will be com-

* The best strength of alcohol is a mixture of about 6 measures of commercial alcohol (80 per cent.) with 5 measures of water, in which sulphate of lime is wholly insoluble, while the sulphates of magnesia and of the alkalies are soluble in it.—*J. C. B.*

posed only of the alkaline sulphates, the ammoniacal salts having been driven off by the heat. The alkaline sulphates are weighed, and the proportions of potassa and soda they contain determined by the processes described (§ 525 *bis*, 526, and 527).

The alkaline carbonates are dissolved in chlorohydric acid, the liquid is sufficiently diluted, heated to ebullition, and sulphuric acid or sulphate of ammonia added, by which baryta and strontia only are precipitated in the state of sulphates. They are weighed after calcination. To ascertain the proportions of these two bases, they are fused in a platinum crucible with three times their weight of pure carbonate of soda, and then treated with water. Baryta and strontia remain in the state of insoluble carbonates, while the sulphuric acid of the sulphates is found in the alkaline liquids, from which, after adding an excess of chlorohydric acid, it is precipitated by chloride of barium. The weight of sulphuric acid thus obtained, compared with the weight of the sulphates of baryta and strontia with which it was combined, often permits a calcination of the proportions of these two bases to be made with sufficient accuracy, at least when they exist in nearly equal quantities in the solution. The proceeding is, in this case, similar to that explained (§ 525 *bis*) in the analysis of the sulphates of potassa and soda.

The carbonates of baryta and strontia are, after being converted into chlorides by adding chlorohydric acid, evaporated to dryness, and treated with concentrated alcohol, which does not sensibly dissolve the chloride of barium, but readily takes the chloride of strontium into solution; thus the two bases are separated, and may be afterward determined in the state of sulphates.

The liquid from which the baryta and strontia have been eliminated, now contains only lime and magnesia. It is saturated with ammonia until a decided alkaline reaction takes place; oxalate of ammonia is then added, which gives a precipitate of oxalate of lime. In this case, the presence of a large quantity of ammoniacal salts in the liquid prevents the precipitation of the magnesia. The oxalate of lime is determined according to § 591.

The liquid, then containing only magnesia and ammoniacal salts, is evaporated to dryness, and the residue is heated to redness, after a small quantity of sulphuric acid has been added; by this operation the ammoniacal salts are driven off, and sulphate of magnesia alone remains. The magnesia may also be precipitated by phosphate of ammonia, and the phosphate of magnesia and ammonia weighed after calcination.

§ 594. A mixture of the salts of potassa, soda, baryta, strontia, lime, and magnesia, may also be analyzed by separating the bases in a rather different order. Precipitating the baryta and strontia by sulphuric acid, the lime by oxalate of ammonia, the magnesia by carbonate of ammonia, and afterward evaporating the liquid, the residue will contain only alkalies.

III. EARTHY METALS.

ALUMINUM.

EQUIVALENT = 13.67; (170.9; O = 100).

§ 595. Aluminum* is one of the substances most extensively spread over the surface of the globe: its oxide, combined with silicic acid and a certain quantity of water, forms the clays. The silicate of alumina, combined with other silicates, constitutes several minerals, the most important of which are feldspar and mica, two constituent minerals of the granites, that is, of the primitive rocks forming the inner crust of the globe accessible to our means of observation. The name *aluminum*, given to this metal, is derived from *alum*, a double sulphate of alumina and potassa, which has for a long time been used in the arts.

Aluminum is obtained by decomposing the anhydrous chloride of aluminum by potassium; the process is the same as that described for magnesium (§ 578). After the cooling of the crucible in which the chloride of aluminum has been heated with potassium, the substance is treated with cold water, which dissolving the chloride of potassium, leaves the aluminum in the form of a gray powder, showing a metallic lustre when burnished.

Aluminum ignites when heated in contact with the air; it does not decompose water at the ordinary temperature, but at 212° the decomposition is very manifest. Aluminum causes an evolution of hydrogen, on being dissolved in dilute acids or treated with a solution of potassa or soda; in other words, it decomposes water in the presence of acids or of powerful bases; a circumstance owing to the fact that this substance acts at the same time the part of an acid and a base.

COMPOUND OF ALUMINUM WITH OXYGEN.

§ 596. Only one combination of aluminum with oxygen is known; it is obtained by precipitating a solution of alum by an excess of carbonate of ammonia: the white gelatinous precipitate, after being well washed with boiling water, dried and calcined, yields anhydrous alumina. It may also be obtained directly, by heating ammoniacal alum to a strong red-heat; but it often retains, when thus prepared, a small quantity of sulphuric acid. Alumina is a white powder, insoluble in water, readily soluble in a solution of potassa, soda, baryta, and strontia, except after being heated to

* Aluminum was first isolated by M. Wœhler.

redness, and slightly soluble in a concentrated solution of ammonia: in the latter cases, it plays the part of a true acid, and several aluminates may be procured in a crystallized state. It also dissolves in the acids, yielding salts which invariably show a strong acid reaction. Calcined alumina, on the contrary, is with difficulty dissolved in potassa and the acids. The combination of alumina with the alkalies takes place, in all cases, at a red-heat.

Alumina is found crystallized in nature, in the form of minerals, often possessing brilliant colours, which are used by jewellers as precious stones. The crystalline form of these minerals belongs to the rhombohedric system; their most ordinary form is that of the primitive rhombohedron, or six-sided prism. The names of these minerals vary with their colour; thus, native alumina, when blue, is called *sapphire*, and when red, takes the name of *ruby*. These colours are often owing to very minute quantities of colouring metallic oxides. Colourless and transparent alumina is known by the name of *hyaline corundum*. Lastly, it is most frequently met with in the form of opaque six-sided prisms, or even of rounded pebbles, coloured brown by oxide of iron. The density of mineral alumina is considerable, being about 3.9; it is, moreover, after the diamond, the hardest substance occurring in nature. On account of this property, opaque corundum, called *emery*, is used to polish precious stones and glass. It is finely powdered, and separated into several sorts, according to its fineness; the powdered emery being suspended in water, the large particles fall to the bottom of the vessel, while the liquid, when allowed to rest for some time, holds the finer emery in suspension.

Alumina is infusible in the heat of our furnaces; but it melts before the oxyhydrogen blowpipe, forming colourless and transparent globules, which often, on cooling, assume a crystalline texture. In order to obtain artificially fused alumina, it is sufficient to heat common potassic alum, after having previously dishydrated it by heat in the oxyhydrogen blowpipe; the sulphate of alumina is decomposed, the sulphate of potassa is volatilized at this high temperature, and there remains only alumina, which fuses when the temperature is sufficiently elevated. An addition of a small quantity of chromate of potassa to the alum imparts a red colour to the melted alumina, which then forms a perfect imitation of natural ruby.

Alumina, precipitated from a solution of alum by carbonate of ammonia in excess, forms a gelatinous substance, hydrate of alumina, which is readily soluble in acids and alkaline liquids, but will not, however, combine with very feeble acids, such as carbonic. It does not lose its water by exposure in a dry vacuum, nor at the heat of boiling water, but must be heated to redness to be obtained perfectly anhydrous. Calcined alumina no longer combines with water, but it is a hygrometric substance, readily condensing the moisture of the atmosphere. Hydrated alumina is found in nature: *diaspose* is one of these crystallized hydrates, with the formula Al_2O_3+3HO; *gibbsite* is also a hydrate of alumina.

By subjecting a solution of hydrate of alumina in potassa to slow evaporation, an aluminate of potassa is obtained in crystalline grains, of the formula KO,Al_2O_3. Baryta gives a similar compound. The mineral called *spinell* is an aluminate of magnesia, of which the formula is MgO,Al_2O_3. Several of these crystallized aluminates may be obtained by mixing together suitable proportions of alumina and the metallic oxides we wish to combine, adding to the mixture 5 or 6 times its weight of boracic acid, stirring it well, and exposing the whole, placed in a platinum crucible, for several days to a high temperature in a porcelain furnace. The boracic acid first melts and dissolves the alumina and the other metallic oxides, but the tension of vapour of the boracic acid at this temperature being very great, it is evaporated but slowly. The alumina and the metallic bases, being in presence of the same solvent, combine with each other. In proportion as the solvent evaporates, the compound separates, and forms, as it is slowly deposited, small well-terminated crystals. By the same process, several other compounds found in the mineral kingdom, which are infusible in the heat of our furnaces, may be obtained crystallized.

§ 597. The composition of alumina has been deduced from the analysis of alum. Potassic alum is a double sulphate of alumina and potassa, containing water of crystallization, which it loses at a moderate heat. 10 gr. of anhydrous potassic alum are dissolved in hot water, and the alumina is precipitated by an excess of carbonate of ammonia: the precipitate, when collected on a filter, is well washed, and then weighed after calcination. 1.986 gr. of alumina are obtained. The liquids are evaporated: the residue, when calcined to redness in a platinum crucible, is composed of sulphate of potassa alone, the ammoniacal salts having been volatilized by heat. The sulphate of potassa thus obtained weighs 3.373 gr.

10 other grains of anhydrous alum are then dissolved in boiling water, and the sulphuric acid precipitated by an excess of chloride of barium: in this case, 18.044 gr. of sulphate of baryta are found, which contain 6.188 gr. of sulphuric acid. Now, the 3.378 gr. of sulphate of potassa contain 1.547 gr. of sulphuric acid; the weight 1.986 gr. of alumina is therefore combined with the weight 4.641 gr. of sulphuric acid.

This sulphate of alumina is regarded as a neutral sulphate; knowing the oxygen of the sulphuric acid to be treble that of the oxygen contained in the base, and finding the weight of that contained in 4.641 gr. of sulphuric acid to be 2.784 gr., one-third of this weight, that is 0.928, is combined with the 1.986 gr. of alumina. Alumina is therefore composed of

Aluminum	1.058	53.27
Oxygen	0.928	46.73
Alumina	1.986	100.00

It now remains for us to discover the formula suitable to alumina. If we suppose that this base presents the same formula as the bases previously studied, the formula should be written AlO, and the equivalent of alumina would be given by the proportion,

$$46.73 : 53.27 :: 100 : x, \text{ whence } x = 113.99.$$

But this formula AlO is contradicted by considerations founded on isomorphism. Alumina never appears as isomorphous with an oxide of the formula RO, but is, on the contrary, always isomorphous with certain oxides R_2O_3, of which the formulæ are certain. Thus, a series of alums, having the same crystalline form and very analogous properties, are obtained by combining sulphate of potassa with the sulphates of sesquioxide of iron Fe_2O_3, sesquioxide of manganese Mn_2O_3, and oxide of chrome Cr_2O_3. Native crystallized alumina, or corundum, presents also the same crystalline form as the native sesquioxide of iron, or *specular iron*, and the sesquioxide of chrome. The formula of alumina, therefore, should undoubtedly be written Al_2O_3; consequently the neutral sulphate of alumina must take the formula $Al_2O_3,3SO_3$.

The equivalent of alumina is then obtained by the proportion,

$$46.73 : 53.27 :: 300 : 2x, \text{ whence } x = 170.98.$$

SALTS FORMED BY ALUMINA.

Sulphate of Alumina.

§ 598. The neutral sulphate of alumina has for a long time been manufactured on a large scale, being employed in dyeing, and advantageously substituted for alum. It is obtained by treating clay with sulphuric acid, for which purpose the clays containing the smallest quantity of iron possible, the kaolins, for example, are selected. They are calcined at a dull red-heat in ovens, then ground to powder, and mixed with one-half of their weight of sulphuric acid of the density 1.45: this mixture is heated in another oven, until sulphuric acid begins to be driven off. It is then withdrawn and allowed to rest for several days, when the mass, treated with water, yields a solution of sulphate of alumina. But as this solution almost always contains some traces of a salt of iron, which would destroy its use in dyeing, it is important to separate this ingredient, which is effected by precipitation with prussiate of potash, added to the liquid until a blue precipitate is no longer formed. It is then evaporated; the sirupy residue is poured into small leaden basins, where it solidifies in the form of a white mass. Sulphate of alumina is soluble in double its weight of water. A solution saturated when hot deposits the salt in the form of small crystalline spangles, of which the formula is $Al_2O_3,3SO_3+18HO$.

A solution of neutral sulphate of alumina can dissolve an additional proportion of alumina when digested with hydrated alumina: a basic sulphate of alumina, of the formula $2Al_2O_3,3SO_3$ is then formed.

Lastly, by pouring ammonia into a solution of sulphate of alumina, a tribasic sulphate of alumina is precipitated in the form of a crystalline powder, having for its formula Al_2O_3,SO_3+9HO —a compound occurring in nature.

§ 599. Sulphate of alumina is very important on account of the double salts which it forms with the alkaline sulphates and with that of ammonia, a class of salts comprised under the general name of *alums*. Most frequently, however, this name is given to the double sulphate of alumina and potassa. These combinations are easily prepared by mixing together the solutions of the two sulphates, and evaporating the liquid to allow the double salt to crystallize. Potassic and ammoniacal alum are very slightly soluble in cold water, and readily crystallize: sodic alum, on the contrary, is very soluble. The best mode of obtaining sodic alum in crystals is by pouring a layer of absolute alcohol on a concentrated solution of the salt, and allowing it to rest for several days; the alcohol gradually combining with the water, allows the sodic alum to be deposited in the form of beautiful octahedral crystals.

These three alums follow the regular system of crystallization: their ordinary forms are the octahedron and cube, or combinations of the two, in which sometimes the octahedron, and sometimes the cube predominates. Their composition is also similar; thus, the formula of

Potassic alum is........................$KO,SO_3+Al_2O_3,3SO_3+24HO$.
Sodic alum.............................$NaO,SO_3+Al_2O_3,3SO_3+24HO$.
Ammoniacal alum...............$(NH_3,HO)SO_3+Al_2O_3,3SO_3+24HO$.

The basic sesquioxides which are isomorphous with alumina, form, with the sulphates of potassa, soda, and ammonia, perfectly similar salts, also called *alums*. These new alums crystallize in octahedrons or in cubes, like those formed by the sulphate of alumina, and have similar formulas; thus, the sulphate of sesquioxide of iron, $Fe_2O_3,3SO_3$, yields:

A ferri-potassic alum..................$KO,SO_3+Fe_2O_3,3SO_3+24HO$.
A ferri-sodic alum ....$NaO,SO_3+Fe_2O_3,3SO_3+24HO$.
A ferri-ammoniacal alum.....$(NH_3,HO)SO_3+Fe_2O_3,3SO_3+24HO$.

The sulphate of sesquioxide of manganese $Mn_2O_3,3SO_3$ gives, in the same manner,

A mangani-potassic alum ....$KO,SO_3+Mn_2O_3,3SO_3+24HO$.

A mangani-sodic alum..............$NaO,SO_3+Mn_2O_3,3SO_3+24HO$.

A mangani-ammoniacal alum $(NH_3,HO)SO_3+Mn_2O_3,3SO_3+24HO$.

Finally, the sesquioxide of chrome gives the following alums:

A chromi-potassic alum...............$KO,SO_3+Cr_2O_3,3SO_3+24HO$.

A chromi-sodic alum................$NaO,SO_3+Cr_2O_3,3SO_3+24HO$.

A chromi-ammoniacal alum...$(NH_3,HO)SO_3+Cr_2O_3,3SO_2+24HO$.

We shall frequently refer to the existence of the isomorphous alums in proof of the isomorphism of the sesquioxides.

Potassic alum is the one most used in the arts: it is employed in dyeing, and its manufacture has received great attention in all countries.

Potassic alum dissolves in 18.4 parts of cold, and in only 0.75 of boiling water; its curve of solubility may be seen in the plate at page 407. It is deposited, on cooling, in beautiful octahedrons, the angles of which are often terminated by the faces of the cube, and is then called *octahedral alum;* but it may also be obtained crystallized in cubes by pouring carbonate of potassa into an ordinary solution of alum, saturated at 122°: a sub-sulphate of alumina is precipitated, which redissolves if the liquid be shaken. On allowing the liquid afterward to cool, the alum crystallizes in its ordinary form, but it then takes the form of cubes, sometimes modified by the faces of the octahedron, the cube, however, always predominating. This alum is called *cubic-alum*, and is more esteemed in commerce than the octahedral, the latter frequently containing some sulphate of iron, which, as it changes the shades of colours, is very injurious in dyeing. Now, as alum crystallizes in cubes only in liquids containing an excess of alumina, and consequently deprived of oxide of iron, the cubic form of alum is a proof of its purity.

The taste of alum is, at first, sweet, and like sugar, but it soon becomes very astringent. When heated, it first melts in its water of crystallization; then, on cooling, solidifies into vitreous masses, called *rock-alum.* Heated still further, it gradually loses its water and becomes anhydrous. When alum is heated in a crucible, the substance, at first liquid, becomes more and more doughy, as it loses its water; it swells considerably, rising above the crucible, and if it be gradually heated, the anhydrous alum assumes the form of a spongy mass, which rises in a mushroom-shape above the crucible (fig. 379). Dishydrated alum is used in medicine as a caustic: it is called *burnt alum.* Lastly, alum decomposes when heated to redness, disengaging a mixture of sulphurous acid and oxygen, and leaving as a residue free alumina and unaltered sulphate of potassa, which latter salt may be separated by dissolving in water. Alum calcined with charcoal, or better, with lamp-black, yields a very finely-divided residue, consisting of alumina, sulphuret of potassium, and charcoal. This residue is a true pyrophorus: it ignites when exposed to a damp atmosphere.

Fig. 379.

§ 600. For the manufacture of alum, several methods are employed:

1st. To a solution of sulphate of alumina obtained by the action of sulphuric acid on clay, as stated in § 598, sulphate of potassa or chloride of potassium is added, and the liquids are allowed to cool, being constantly shaken. The alum is precipitated in the form of small granular crystals, which, after being perfectly drained, are washed with a small quantity of cold water: from a solution of these crystals in boiling water, octahedral masses of alum are deposited on cooling. Chloride of potassium is preferable to sulphate of potassa, because it converts the salts of iron mixed with the sulphate of alumina into chloride of iron, which, being much more soluble than the sulphate, is consequently not precipitated with the alum. This method is, however, generally too expensive to be adopted in the manufacture of alum.

2d. The greater portion of alum is obtained by the spontaneous or artificial roasting of certain argillaceous rocks, strongly impregnated with small crystals of sulphurets of iron. The most common is the bisulphuret FeS_2, or *pyrites;* it is sometimes, however, a sulphuret Fe_2S_3, or *magnetic pyrites.* These argillaceous and pyritous rocks are met with in great abundance in two geological formations: they are found in the transition rocks, where they form schists, which commonly are bituminous, and also occur in the formation of the tertiary rocks, immediately above the chalk. These latter aluminous schists are much less aggregated: their roasting is more easy, and frequently takes place spontaneously in the air.

The aluminous schists are placed in large prismatic heaps on a layer of combustible matter laid on an impervious hearth, which is slightly inclined. The combustible is fired, which soon causes the sulphur of the pyrites and the bituminous matter with which the schist is impregnated to ignite also. The combustion must be carefully regulated, so that the temperature may not rise too high in certain parts of the mass: this is done by covering the heaps with powdered schist already calcined, or, on the other hand, by poking up the parts where the combustion is going on too slowly. Small quantities of water are from time to time poured upon the heap. The combustion ceases after a period of five or six months: the heaps, which then are much reduced in size, are demolished, the substance sprinkled with small quantities of water, and exposed to the air for some time. The solutions arising from these washings, or from the rain fallen on the heap, are conducted into watertight reservoirs. Lastly, the substance, subjected to a methodic system of lixiviation, yields solutions sufficiently concentrated to be evaporated by fire.

The aluminous schists of the tertiary rocks are much more changeable: it suffices to expose them to the air and wet them from time to time, to effect their spontaneous oxidation. Iron pyrites absorbs the oxygen of the air, and is converted into sulphate of iron and sulphuric acid, which, combining gradually with the alumina of the schist, form sulphate of alumina:

$$FeS_2+7O=FeO,SO_3+SO_3.$$

In Picardy, large quantities of alum are obtained from the tertiary schists, which rapidly decompose in the air. They are made into heaps, which are turned from time to time, and occasionally wetted, if the season be very dry. Oxidation goes on rapidly, and sometimes the heat evolved is even sufficient to fire the mass, which, however, must be avoided, as in this case a considerable quantity of sulphurous acid is disengaged. When the sulphatization is sufficiently advanced, the matter is lixiviated, and the washings, which mark 18° or 20° on the areometer, are subjected to evaporation: on being allowed to cool, they deposit a large quantity of sulphate of protoxide of iron, while the mother liquid contains the sulphate of alumina. Chloride of potassium is poured into the hot solutions, and they then are allowed to cool; when alum begins to be deposited, the crystallization is disturbed by constant stirring. The alum then precipitates in a crystalline sand, which is gradually withdrawn by a rake, and allowed to drain on an inclined plane, from which the solution is conducted into the crystallizing vessel. The washed schists may yield an additional quantity of sulphates, but then the roasting must be assisted by artificial heat, by arranging them in large prismatic heaps on a layer of brushwood which is ignited. The pyrites and the bituminous matter taking fire, soon extend the combustion through the whole mass: the temperature is regulated by making openings in the almost impervious covering of the mass. Soluble sulphates, but principally sulphate of alumina, are again formed, as the greater portion of the sulphate of iron passes into the state of an insoluble sub-sulphate of sesquioxide of iron. By treating the roasted schists, which present an ochrous colour, with water, the sulphate of alumina and a certain quantity of the sulphate of protoxide of iron are dissolved; the solution is evaporated to a proper degree of concentration, and then treated in the same manner as the first lixiviation, to obtain the alum.

The alum thus obtained requires to be purified by recrystallization, to effect which the impure crystalline sand is washed with a small quantity of cold water, and then dissolved in boiling water. The hot solution, on being allowed to cool in casks, deposits alum in large crystals on the sides of the casks. When the solution is completely cooled, and deposits no more crystals, the mother liquid is run off, the casks are taken to pieces by removing the iron hoops which hold the staves, and a crystalline mass of alum, shaped like the inside of the cask, is removed. This, after being broken into large pieces, and washed with a small quantity of cold water, is ready for sale.

3d. In some localities, principally at Tolfa, near Rome, a rock, called *alunite*, or *alum-stone*, is found, from which a highly-valued alum, called *Roman alum*, is obtained. The formula of alunite is $KO,SO_3+Al_2O_3,SO_3$. It is heated in ovens until sulphuric acid begins to be disengaged; by subsequent treatment with water, the ordinary alum is dissolved, leaving a residue of alumina. The liquid, when evaporated, yields cubic crystals of alum, generally tinged to a rose-colour by a small quantity of peroxide of iron, which, however, is not injurious in dyeing, on account of its insolubility in water. Roman alum is more valuable than the ordinary kind, as it is certain to contain no soluble iron; but this alum is now made artificially, by adding carbonate of potassa, which precipitates a certain quantity of subsulphate of alumina, to a solution of ordinary alum. By shaking the liquid, and exposing it for some time to the air, the subsulphate is redissolved, and hydrated peroxide of iron remains: by evaporating the liquid, cubic alum deposits. This alum is colourless, but, for a long time, dyers would not make use of it. To make it resemble Roman alum, the manufacturers then introduced it into casks with a small quantity of pounded brick: by letting the casks revolve for a few minutes, the ordinary colour of Roman alum was imparted to the article.

If carbonate of potassa be poured into a boiling solution of alum, a subsulphate of alumina is at first precipitated, but immediately redissolves in the liquid; however, if the addition of the carbonate of potassa be continued, a granular precipitate, which does not dissolve by agitation, is soon formed: the composition of this precipitate is the same as that of the alunite of Tolfa, and it is called *insoluble alum.*

Silicates of Alumina.

§ 601. The silicates of alumina exist in great abundance in nature, and possess a high degree of interest. They are sometimes found crystallized, but are chiefly important in their hydrated state. Thus, our ordinary clays, porcelain-earth, or kaolin, and the halloysites are merely hydrosilicates of alumina, containing, however, a small quantity of silicate of potassa. These substances are evidently produced by decomposition of the primitive rocks, chiefly the granites: the alkaline silicate of the constituent minerals of these have been dissolved, silicate of alumina, more or less pure, has remained, and was drifted off by water, forming deposits in new basins.

The feldspars are double silicates, formed by an alkaline silicate and that of alumina: the formula of ordinary or *orthose feldspar* is $KO,SiO_3+Al_2O_3,3SiO_3$. Frequently, however, lime or magnesia takes the place of a part of the potassa.

Minerals which have been for a long time confounded with feldspar, on account of the resemblance of their external characters, or a certain analogy in their chemical composition, are also known. They have been called *albite*, *petalite*, *triphan*, and *labradorite*, according as soda, lithine, or lime takes the place of a part of the potassa.

The clays are found in the various geological formations of rocks. The purest clay is that constituting kaolin, or porcelain-earth: it is found in white, amorphous, friable masses, forming with water merely a slightly cohesive paste. Kaolin generally is the result of the decomposition of a feldspathic rock *in situ*. In some localities, this alteration may be traced from the intact feldspar forming the interior of the rock to the most friable kaolin on the surface. This clay frequently contains small fragments of unaltered feldspar, which are easily separated by levigation. The formula of kaolin, thus washed, approaches closely that of Al_2O_3,SiO_3+2HO.

§ 602. The ordinary clays do not differ greatly from this composition; but they are frequently mixed with various proportions of quartzose sand, oxide of iron, and carbonate of lime, which affect considerably the physical and chemical qualities of the clay. Pure clay is eminently *plastic*, that is, it forms a very pliant paste with water, which may be moulded and kneaded into any shape. This is called *fat clay;* but when it contains any considerable proportion of foreign matters, its plasticity is greatly diminished, and it is then said to be *poor*. Clay mixed with a considerable proportion of carbonate of lime is called *marl*. The chemical properties of clay are not less affected than their physical by the admixture of foreign matters; thus, pure clay, which is completely infusible in the highest heat of our furnaces, or also when mixed with sand, becomes fusible when it contains any considerable proportion of oxide of iron or carbonate of lime.

Certain kinds of clay, known by the name of *fuller's earth*, are used in the scouring of woollen stuffs. These clays are first levigated, to separate the quartzose particles they may contain, the fuller's earth, well dried, is then powdered and spread over the cloth to be scoured, and the whole passed over a cylinder. By its capillarity, the clay absorbs all the grease in the cloth.

The intimate mixture of clay with hydrated peroxide of iron is called *ochre*, or *ochrous earth*. Ochres are used in painting; their shades vary with the quantity of oxide of iron they contain. An addition of hydrate of sesquioxide of manganese imparts a brown hue to them. *Sienna earth* is a clay of this kind.

COMPOUND OF ALUMINUM WITH SULPHUR.

§ 603. Hitherto sulphuret of aluminum has been obtained only by heating aluminum in the vapour of sulphur, as a blackish gray mass, assuming, when burnished, a slightly metallic lustre: it cannot be obtained in the moist way. When sulfhydrate of ammonia is added to a solution of a salt of alumina, sulphohydric acid gas is evolved, and the alumina is precipitated in the state of a hydrate.

COMPOUND OF ALUMINUM WITH CHLORINE.

§ 604. By dissolving aluminum in aqueous chlorohydric acid, a solution of chloride of aluminum is obtained, which may be crystallized in a dry vacuum; very deliquescent crystals, of which the formula is Al_2Cl_3+12HO, are deposited. Their water of crystallization cannot be expelled by heat without decomposition: chlorohydric acid is disengaged, and the isolated alumina remains. Anhydrous chloride of aluminum may, however, be prepared by allowing dry chlorine to act on a mixture of alumina and charcoal heated to redness in a porcelain tube. The chlorine will not attack alumina when alone; but, when the alumina is mixed with charcoal, oxide of carbon gas is evolved, and chloride of aluminum, being volatile, condenses in a receiver placed in front of the porcelain tube. In order to obtain an intimate mixture of alumina and carbon, alumina and lampblack are ground together, a small

Fig. 380.

quantity of oil is added, and the pasty mixture rolled into small balls, which are calcined in an earthenware crucible. These small porous masses are introduced into a porcelain tube, arranged in a reverberatory furnace (fig. 380). Through one end of the tube a current of dry chlorine is passed, while the other enters an allonge which communicates with a well-copled bottle; the chloride of aluminum condenses in the allonge and receiver, in the form of small crystalline laminæ, of a yellowish-white colour. Larger quantities of this substance may be obtained, by replacing the porcelain tube by a tubulated stone-ware retort, which will contain a larger quantity of the mixture of carbon and alumina. The apparatus must be then arranged as represented in fig. 265. Chloride of aluminum volatilizes at a temperature slightly above 212°: it fumes in the air, and rapidly attracts moisture, and should therefore be kept in a ground-stoppered bottle.

DISTINCTIVE CHARACTERS OF THE SALTS OF ALUMINA.

§ 605. The solutions of the salts of alumina are precipitated by ammonia, a characteristic distinguishing them from the alkaline and alkalino-earthy salts, but which may, nevertheless, confound them with the salts of magnesia. We have seen (§ 589) that if a sufficient quantity of an ammoniacal salt be added to a magnesian salt, the latter is no longer precipitated by ammonia: a salt of alumina, however, is always precipitated.

Caustic potassa and soda precipitate the salts of alumina, but an excess of either of these reagents immediately redissolves the precipitate. This character distinguishes with great accuracy the salts of alumina from those of the alkalies and alkaline earths.

The salts of alumina are precipitated by lime-water. The alkaline carbonates and carbonate of ammonia, poured into the solution of a salt of alumina, precipitate hydrated alumina, which, when well washed, will redissolve in acids without effervescence. The sulfhydrates also precipitate hydrated alumina.

If sulphate of potassa be added to a concentrated and hot solution of a salt of alumina, octahedral crystals of alum are deposited on cooling: from a dilute solution, the crystals of alum are also deposited by evaporation.

The salts of alumina, heated before the blowpipe with a small quantity of nitrate of cobalt, give a substance of a beautiful characteristic blue colour.

GLUCINUM.

EQUIVALENT=6.96.

§ 606. The oxide of glucinum, or *glucina*,* exists in several minerals in combination with silicic acid. Of these, the most common is the emerald, a combination of silicate of alumina and silicate of glucina, of the formula $Gl_2O_3,SiO_3+Al_2O_3,SiO_3$. The crystalline form of the emerald is the regular 6-sided prism, belonging to the rhombohedric system: the mineral is found in the state of a stone, but presenting a very evident crystallization, in the environs of Limoges. The emerald is rarely found in the transparent state; sometimes it exhibits beautiful colours, and possesses great value as a precious stone. The transparent and green emerald alone is called *emerald* in jewelry. When it exhibits only a pale-green hue, it is called *beryl;* and lastly, when it is bluish-green, bears the name of *aqua marina.*

Glucinum is obtained, like aluminum, by heating in a closed platinum crucible a mixture of anhydrous chloride of glucinum with potassium: the same process is followed as in the preparation of aluminum and magnesium. Glucinum appears in the form of a grayish powder, which acquires a metallic lustre by burnishing: it decomposes water only at the boiling point. Heated in the air, it becomes incandescent, and is converted into an oxide: in acid or alkaline liquids it dissolves with the evolution of hydrogen gas.

COMPOUND OF GLUCINUM WITH OXYGEN.

§ 607. Only one compound of glucinum with oxygen is known: it is called *glucina.* Glucina is obtained from the Limoges emerald, by finely powdering the mineral, and melting it in a platinum crucible with treble its weight of carbonate of potassa. The substance is afterwards treated with sulphuric acid, and then with water, which dissolves the sulphates of alumina, potassa, and glucina, leaving the silex, which is easily separated by filtration. The liquid is evaporated by boiling: on being allowed to cool, the greater portion of the alumina separates in the state of crystallized alum. An excess of ammonia added to the mother liquid diluted with water, precipitates at once the balance of alumina, sesquioxide of iron, and glucina. The moist precipitate is left to digest with a concentrated solution of carbonate of ammonia, which dissolves only the glucina, from which the residue of alumina and sesquioxide of iron are separated by filtration: the glucina then

* Glucina was discovered in 1797, by Vauquelin. M. Wœhler first isolated glucinum.

precipitates by boiling, as a carbonate, which, when calcined, leaves pure anhydrous glucina.

Glucina presents the appearance of a white powder, soft to the touch, insoluble in water, infusible in the heat of our furnaces, of the specific gravity 3.0. It is soluble in a solution of caustic potassa and soda, but ammonia will not sensibly dissolve it.

§ 608. The composition of glucina has been deduced from the analysis of the chloride of glucinum. It has been found that 10 gr. of chloride of glucinum contain 8.842 of chlorine. The proper formula of glucina still remains to be known. If the formula GlO be assigned to it, and consequently, the formula of GlCl to the chloride of glucinum, the equivalent of glucinum will be calculated by the proportion,

$$8.842 : 1.158 :: 443.2 : x, \text{ whence } x = 58.04.$$

Assuming, on the contrary, that the composition of glucina is analogous to that of alumina, that is, if its formula is assumed as Gl_2O_3, the equivalent will be given by the proportion,

$$8.842 : 1.158 :: 1329.6 : 2x, \text{ whence } x = 87.06.$$

The question is here much more difficult to decide than in the case of aluminum, as, in the case of the latter metal, we had isomorphism for a guide, while, for glucinum, no isomorphism of any of its combinations with a corresponding compound of aluminum, or with any such formed by the oxides RO, has been discovered. Thus, chemists do not agree upon the formula of glucina; and, while some assign to this base the formula GlO, and place it aside of magnesia, others give it the formula Gl_2O_3, and rank glucinum with aluminum.

SALTS FORMED BY GLUCINA.

§ 609. Glucina has a stronger affinity for acids than alumina. Its salts have a sweet taste, from which it has derived the name of *glucina*, (from γλυκυς, "sweet.")

The hydrate of glucina is obtained by precipitating the salt of glucina by ammonia: it is a white gelatinous substance, readily parting with its water when heated.

Glucina forms several compounds with sulphuric acid: the neutral sulphate $Gl_2O_3,3SO_3+12HO$ yields beautiful crystals.

COMBINATION OF GLUCINA WITH CHLORINE.

§ 610. Hydrated glucina dissolves readily in chlorohydric acid: the solution, when evaporated, deposits crystals of hydrated chloride of the formula Gl_2Cl_3+12HO.

Anhydrous chloride of glucinum is obtained by the process described (§ 604) for the chloride of aluminum. It volatilizes in the shape of small white crystalline spangles.

DISTINCTIVE CHARACTERS OF THE SALTS OF GLUCINA.

§ 611. The salts of glucina are precipitated by ammonia, even in the presence of an excess of ammoniacal salt: solutions of potassa and soda also precipitate them, but an excess of alkali redissolves the precipitate. These two properties distinguish the salts of glucina from the alkaline and alkalino-earthy salts, but confound them with the salts of alumina.

The salts of glucina are distinguished from those of alumina by not forming, like the latter, an alum with the sulphate of potassa, and by the property of carbonate of ammonia in excess dissolving the precipitate of carbonate of glucina, which it, at first, produces in glucinic solutions.

The alkaline carbonates likewise precipitate the salts of glucina, but the carbonate of glucina is sensibly soluble in an excess of the reagent.

The salts of glucina do not turn blue when heated before the blowpipe with a small quantity of nitrate of cobalt.

ZIRCONIUM.

EQUIVALENT = 34.0.

§ 612. The oxide of zirconium, or zirconia,* exists in considerable quantity in a well-crystallized mineral called *zircon*, a silicate of zirconia $2Zr_2O_3,SiO_3$, containing most frequently a small quantity of oxide of iron. In order to extract the zirconia, the zircons are heated in a crucible and thrown red-hot into cold water: by this sudden cooling, they become friable, and may be finely pulverized. The powdered zircon is heated to a strong white-heat in a platinum crucible, with thrice its weight of carbonate of potassa: the mass, when calcined, is treated with chlorohydric acid, the solution is evaporated to dryness, and again treated with water. The silex is evaporated by filtering, and sulfhydrate of ammonia is added to the liquid, which precipitates the zirconia in the state of a hydrate, and the iron as protosulphuret. The clear liquid is decanted off after settling, and the precipitate allowed to digest for several hours with a solution of sulphuric acid, by which the sulphuret of iron is dissolved in the state of a hyposulphite, while the zirconia remains perfectly white: it is calcined after being well washed.

Zirconia is a white powder, insoluble in water, and infusible at the temperature of our furnaces. When calcined, it dissolves with great difficulty in the acids: it is, however, readily dissolved in them when in the state of a hydrate.

Zirconium is obtained by decomposing the fluoride of zirconium by potassium; the metal appears in the form of a grayish powder, which assumes, when burnished, a metallic lustre.

DISTINCTIVE CHARACTERS OF THE SALTS OF ZIRCONIA.

§ 613. The solutions of the salts of zirconia are precipitated by caustic potassa and soda; but the precipitate is not redissolved in an excess of the reagent: a characteristic which distinguishes zirconia from alumina and glucina. Ammonia behaves with solutions of zirconia like as with those of potassa and soda.

A concentrated solution of sulphate of zirconia yields, with sulphate of potassa, a white crystalline precipitate, which completely separates when the liquid is saturated with sulphate of potassa.

---

* Zirconia was discovered by Klaproth, in 1789.

THORIUM.

§ 614. The oxide of thorium, or *thorina*,* has hitherto been discovered only in two very rare minerals, called *thorite* and *pyrochlore.* Thorina is chiefly obtained from thorite by reducing this mineral to a fine powder, and boiling it with chlorohydric acid; chlorine is disengaged; the solution is evaporated to dryness and treated with water. The liquid, when filtered, is subjected to a current of sulphuretted hydrogen, which precipitates a small quantity of sulphuret of tin and lead, which is separated by filtration. A solution of ammonia is then added to the liquid, which precipitates the thorina mixed with oxides of iron and manganese. The precipitate is then redissolved in sulphuric acid, and the liquid rapidly concentrated by ebullition, when the sulphate of thorina, which is very slightly soluble in hot water, is soon precipitated; it is collected on a filter and washed with boiling water.

Sulphate of thorina is remarkable for being more soluble in cold than in boiling water. Calcined, it yields pure thorina.

Thorina is a very heavy white powder: its specific gravity is about 9.4, greatly surpassing that of baryta. Thorina contains 11.84 per cent. of oxygen.

YTTRIUM, ERBIUM, TERBIUM.

§ 615. These three metals have been discovered in some rare minerals, to which mineralogists have assigned the names of *gadolinite*, *orthite*, and *yttrotantalite.* Their properties are but little known, and we shall not stop to consider them. The oxides of these metals are called *yttria*, *erbia*, and *terbia.*†

CERIUM, LANTHANIUM, DIDYMIUM.

§ 616. These three metals have been found together in several minerals, the most important of which is *cerite.*‡ The three metallic oxides exist in it, in combination with silicic acid. We shall not describe the combinations of these metals, as they are but little known, and have hitherto received no application.

---

* Thorina was discovered by Berzelius.

† Yttria was discovered in 1794, by Gadolin. Erbia and terbia have been recently discovered by M. Mosander.

‡ Cerium was discovered in 1809, by Berzelius and Hisinger. Lanthanium and didymium have been recently discovered by M. Mosander.

DETERMINATION OF THE EARTHS: THEIR SEPARATION FROM THE ALKALIES AND ALKALINE EARTHS.

§ 617. We shall here treat only of alumina and glucina; the other earths being so rare that nothing need be said concerning the methods of determining them.

Alumina and glucina are always determined in the state of anhydrous alumina and glucina. To effect this, the bases are calcined to redness in a platinum crucible: it is advisable to allow the substance to cool in a closed crucible, and weigh it rapidly, as it soon absorbs the moisture of the air.

Alumina and glucina are generally precipitated from their solutions by ammonia; but it is important not to forget that these two hydrated bases are sensibly soluble in liquids highly charged with ammonia; it is therefore better, when possible, to effect the precipitation by sulfhydrate of ammonia.

§ 618. When the alumina and glucina have been weighed together after calcination, they are separated by treatment with concentrated sulphuric acid, which dissolves them when assisted by heat, although but slowly if the substance has been strongly calcined. It is evaporated to dryness, treated with water, and then precipitated by carbonate of ammonia, in which the glucina redissolves. The precipitate of alumina should be digested several times with a solution of carbonate of ammonia, if the glucina is to be dissolved.

§ 619. When alumina and glucina exist together in a solution with alkalies and alkaline earths, they are separated by supersaturating the liquid with highly caustic ammonia, which precipitates only alumina and glucina. Sometimes, however, if the liquid contains a great deal of magnesia, a part of this base is deposited, because then a quantity of ammoniacal salt sufficient completely to prevent the precipitation of the magnesia by ammonia has not formed during the saturation. In this case, the moist precipitate is redissolved in chlorohydric acid, and an excess of ammonia is added; the magnesia then remains in the liquid.

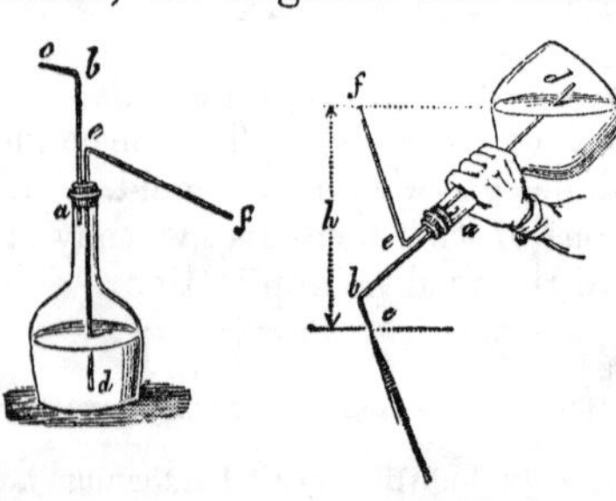

Fig. 381. Fig. 382.

Alumina and the majority of the earths, precipitated from their solutions, form gelatinous substances, which it is very difficult to wash completely. For this purpose, the *washing-bottle* represented in figs. 381 and 382 is generally used. This bottle is composed of a flat-bottomed balloon (fig. 381), the neck of which is closed by a cork pierced by two tubes—the tube *abc*, which opens in the upper part of the balloon, is drawn out at *c*, and the tube *def*, open at both ends, and descending to the bottom of the balloon. When the bottle rests on its bottom, it communicates with the external air by the tube *abc*; when, on the contrary, it is inverted, as in fig. 382, the air enters by the tube *def*, and the water escapes by the tube *abc* in a fine stream, which may be directed on the several parts of the precipitate deposited on the filter. The rapidity of the stream may be increased by giving a greater length to the tube *abc*, thus increasing the difference of the level *h*, under the influence of which the water flows. Precipitates are, generally, more effectually washed with hot than with cold water.

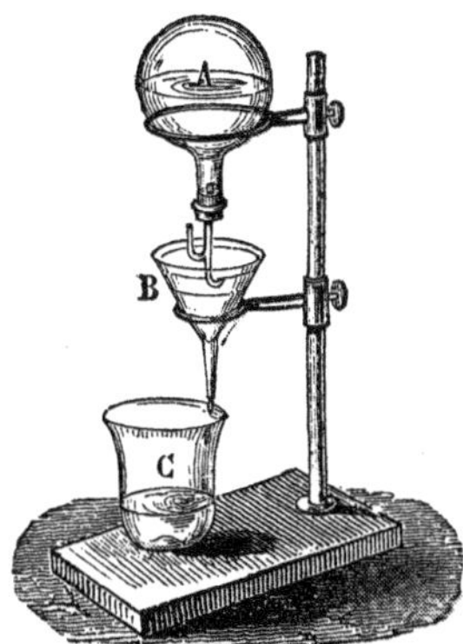

Fig. 383.

Fig. 383 represents an apparatus by which the washing may be performed without constant manipulation on the part of the operator. This apparatus, which is frequently used for washing precipitates in chemical analyses, is composed of a washing-bottle, the cork of which is traversed by a tube *abcd* arranged as seen in fig. 384. The filter being completely filled with water, the balloon A, also filled with water, is inverted, so that the delicate and curved end *d* may dip to the distance of about 1 centimetre into the water of the filter: it is kept in this position by means of a stand. The pressure of the atmosphere acts on the liquid of the small lateral tube *bc*, and also on the level of the liquid in the filter, and consequently on the water of the tube *abd*. The water of the bottle receives an impulse from the weight of the liquid column comprised between the level of the liquid in the filter and that of the liquid in the lateral tube *cb*; but the lateral tube *cb* being very small, capillary action prevents the air from entering it, and equals the pressure of a small column of water. The water will therefore not flow from the washing-bottle, as long as the capillary action in *ab* surpasses the hydrostatic pressure exerted by the column *h*. But in proportion as the water escapes from the filter, its level falls, the height of the column *h* increases, and this very soon overcoming the capillary action in *cb*, water will flow from the bottle into the filter, air will pass in by the lateral tube *cb*, and a new equilibrium will be established in consequence of the rise of the level in the filter. By means of this apparatus, the liquid is kept at nearly a constant height in the filter, and the

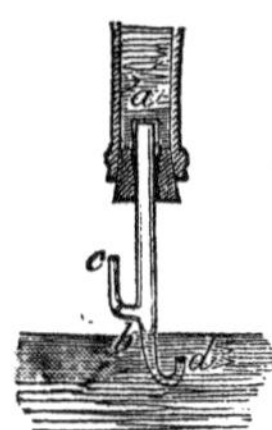

Fig. 384.

upper stratum is always pure water, which is a condition very favourable to efficacious washing.

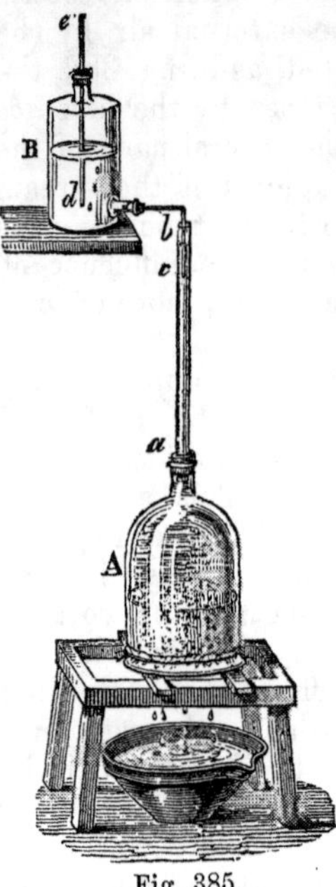

Fig. 385.

When the quantity of gelatinous precipitate is considerable, it is almost impracticable to wash it in an ordinary filter, and then it is advisable to employ the arrangement represented in fig. 385. The large opening of the tubulated bell-glass A is closed with a doubled sheet of filtering-paper, kept in its place by a cloth tied around the border of the bell-glass. The bell-glass being placed on a stand over a dish, the liquid holding the precipitate in suspension is gradually poured into it. When the whole of it has been introduced into the bell-glass, a long tube *ab* is filled to the opening *a*, through which the water for washing is poured. A large pervious surface is thus offered for filtration, which takes place through a precipitate forming a layer of equal thickness, and under the pressure of a column of water which may be increased at will by increasing the length of the tube *ab*. The washing may be made continuous by passing into the bottle a curved tube *ab* fitted to the lower aperture of a Mariotte's bottle B; the level of the liquid is thus kept at a constant height in the tube *ab*, and a continuous washing is effected under very favourable circumstances, because the pure water, arriving slowly from above, has no tendency to mix with the inferior strata which have become impure by their contact with the precipitate.

---

§ 620. In connection with the particular study of the alkaline, alkalino-earthy, and earthy metals, we shall enter with some minuteness into the description of the manufacture of several important products which contain the compounds of these metals, namely, the manufacture of gunpowder, that of lime and mortars used in building, the manufacture of glass, and of earthenware.

GUNPOWDER.

§ 621. By mixing intimately saltpetre with charcoal or with sulphur, we obtain substances which, when subjected to a high temperature, deflagrate and suddenly develop a large volume of gas. When the combustion takes place in a contracted space, considerable pressure is exerted on the surrounding walls of this space, and if one of these be movable, it may be projected with more or less force.

If, for example, 1 equivalent of nitre KO,NO_5 is mixed with 1 equivalent of carbon, there are produced, by detonation, 1 equivalent of carbonate of potassa, 1 equivalent of nitrogen, and 3 equivalents of oxygen:

$$KO,NO_5+C=KO,CO_2+N+3O;$$

2 volumes of nitrogen and 3 of oxygen will therefore be disengaged.

We may calculate by approximation the volume of gas developed by one volume of the detonating mixture. 1 equivalent of nitrate of potassa weighing 1264.3, and 1 equivalent of carbon weighing 25.0, the weight of the mixture will therefore be 1339.3. Assuming that this pulverized mixture occupies the same volume as an equal weight of water, we can admit that a weight 1339.3 gm. of the mixture will occupy a volume of 1.339 lit. Now, this weight of the mixture develops 1 equiv. = 175 of nitrogen, and 3 equiv. = 300 of oxygen.

1 lit. of nitrogen at 32°, under a pressure of 0.760 m. weighs 1.257 gm.
1 " of oxygen " " " " 1.429

The volume occupied by the nitrogen at 32°, and under a pressure of 0.760 m., will be given by the proportion,

$$1.257 : 1.000 :: 175 : x, \text{ whence } x = 139.2 \text{ lit.}$$

The volume occupied by the disengaged oxygen under the same circumstances will be deduced from the proportion,

$$1.429 : 1.000 :: 300 : y, \text{ whence } y = 209.9 \text{ lit.}$$

Thus a volume of detonating mixture represented by 1.339 lit., yields 349.1 lit. of gas at 32°, and under a pressure of 0.760 m.: a volume 253 times greater than that of the explosive substance. The volume of gas, at the moment of development, is really much larger than we have just found, being strongly dilated by the high temperature produced by the combustion; and we may safely admit that the expansion is at least three times greater than that given by calculation, when the gas was supposed to have a temperature of 32°.

If 1 equivalent of nitrate of potassa is mixed with 2 equivalents of carbon, then 1 equivalent of carbonate of potassa, 1 equivalent of nitrogen, 1 of carbonic acid, and 1 of oxygen are formed:

$$KO,NO_5+2C=KO,CO_2+N+CO_2+O.$$

The equivalent of carbonic acid being represented by 2 volumes, it will be seen that 5 volumes of gas are still disengaged; that is, that the expansion is the same as in the preceding case. The projectile force may, however, be greater, if a high temperature be developed during the combustion.

Lastly, if 4 equivalents of carbon are added to 1 equivalent of nitre, then 1 equivalent of nitrogen and 3 equivalents of oxide of carbon are disengaged:

$$KO,NO_5+4C=KO,CO_2+N+3CO.$$

1 volume of oxide of carbon containing only a $\frac{1}{2}$ volume of oxygen, it is evident that 6 volumes of oxide of carbon will be developed: the gaseous volume will therefore be equal to 8. Thus, there will be a greater production of gas than in the two preceding cases. The projectile force might, however, be less, if the heat developed be not so great. Moreover, in the mixture we have just supposed, a great portion of the carbon does not ignite.

Mixtures of nitre and sulphur also produce, by detonation, considerable volumes of gas. Thus, a mixture of 1 equivalent of nitre and 1 equivalent of sulphur yields 1 equivalent of sulphate of potassa, 1 equivalent of nitrogen, and 2 equivalents of oxygen:

$$KO,NO_5+S=KO,SO_3+N+2O;$$

4 volumes of gas will therefore be formed.

With 1 equivalent of nitre and 2 equivalents of sulphur we have

$$KO,NO_5+2S=KO,SO_3+N+SO_2,$$

that is, again 4 volumes of gas; for the equiv. of sulphurous acid is represented by 2 volumes.

A mixture of 1 equiv. of nitre with 4 equivs. of sulphur gives

$$KO,NO_5+4S=KS+N+3SO_2;$$

2 volumes of nitrogen and 6 volumes of sulphurous acid will therefore be disengaged; in all, 8 volumes of gas. In fact, however, the gaseous volume is less considerable, owing to the incomplete combustion of the sulphur.

Mixtures of nitre and carbon generally produce a greater volume of gas than mixtures of nitre and sulphur; but the latter have the advantage of being more combustible.

§ 622. Experiments have proved that the mixtures possessing the greatest projectile force consist of nitre, carbon, and sulphur.

A mixture of			
1 eq. of nitre	1264		66.0
1 " sulphur	200		10.5
6 " carbon	450		23.5
	1914		100.0

gives $KO,No_5+S+6C=KS+N+6CO$;

that is, 14 volumes of gas. But in reality the gaseous volume is less considerable, because a large portion of the carbon escapes combustion, and the temperature does not rise very high.

The following mixture possesses a greater projectile force:

1 eq. of nitre	1264	74.8
1 " sulphur	200	11.9
3 " carbon	225	13.3
	1689	100.0

We then have $KO,NO_5+S+3C=KS+N+3CO_2$,

with the disengagement of 8 volumes of gas.

We may calculate by approximation the volume of gas produced by a volume 1 of this mixture. Let us again admit that the mixture occupies the same volume as an equal weight of water. We shall say that 1689 gm. of the mixture, or a volume of 1.689 lit. disengages 175 gm. of nitrogen = 139.2 lit., and 825 gm. of carbonic acid = 417.3 lit.; total gaseous volume = 556.5 lit. A volume 1 of the detonating mixture will therefore produce 329 times its volume of gas at 32° and under a pressure 0.760 m.

§ 623. The numerous experiments made in all countries to discover empirically the best composition for powder, show that it should be as approximate as possible to that just now theoretically developed.

In France, three different compositions are in use:

For war powder	Saltpetre	75.0
	Sulphur	12.5
	Charcoal	12.5
		100.0
For sporting powder	Saltpetre	76.9
	Sulphur	9.6
	Charcoal	13.5
		100.0
For blasting powder	Saltpetre	62.0
	Sulphur	20.0
	Charcoal	18.0
		100.0

Prussian war powder shows the following composition:

Saltpetre	75.0
Sulphur	11.5
Charcoal	13.5
	100.0

English and Austrian war powder:

Saltpetre	75.0
Sulphur	10.0
Charcoal	15.0
	100.0

Swedish war powder:

Saltpetre	75.0
Sulphur	16.0
Charcoal	9.0
	100.0

Chinese powder:

Saltpetre	75.7
Sulphur	14.4
Charcoal	9.9
	100.0

French blasting powder is the only one which differs remarkably from the theoretical composition just indicated: this is, because a great projectile force is not required; and the government, which imposes a considerable tax on sporting powder, endeavours to manufacture a blasting powder such that it cannot be substituted for the former. This powder has, indeed, less strength, and fouls the gun very rapidly.

§ 624. Powder should satisfy several conditions, which vary according to the weapon in which it is to be used. When it is very explosive, and the explosion of the charge is instantaneous, the reaction on the walls of the weapon is sudden and violent, frequently causing the weapon to burst: the powder is then said to be too *explosive*. If the powder is not sufficiently explosive, the projectile is thrown from the weapon before all the charge is burned; a portion of the latter, therefore, is uselessly inserted and wasted. The powder most suitable for any given weapon is that which, burning perfectly whilst the projectile passes through the chamber of the piece, communicates to it, gradually, and not instantaneously, the whole projectile force of which it is capable. Hence the quality of the powder must vary according to the nature of the piece in which it is used. With equal quantities of the ingredients, the quality of the powder can still be altered, by using charcoal more or less carbonized, by giving the substance a greater or less degree of compactness, or by varying the size of the grain.

Before proceeding to study the manufacture of the various kinds of powder, we shall investigate the preparation of its primary components.

Choice and preparation of the primary components.

§ 625. *Saltpetre.*—The saltpetre used in the manufacture of powder is the refined nitre of which we spoke (§ 450). This nitre is remarkably pure, and rarely contains more than 2 or 3 thousandths of sea-salt. It comes from the refinery in very small crystalline grains, and in this state is used in the manufacture of powder.

§ 626. *Sulphur.*—Powder-mills purchase the refined sulphur in rolls. It must be reduced to an impalpable powder, which is effected in wooden drums (figs. 386 and 387) having on the inside wooden brackets *a*, *b*, arranged along the edges of the cylinder. These drums are cylindrical, and about 1.10 m. long, with a diameter of about 1.15 m.: they revolve on a horizontal iron axis OO′. Through a door *abcd*, which is furnished with iron handles *m′ m*, the material is introduced. Pulverization is effected by means of small brass balls, of about 5 or 8 millimetres in diameter, of which each drum contains 150 kilogrammes: 30 or 40 kilogrammes of sulphur are added, and the drum is made to revolve for 6 hours, during which time the balls, rolling with the sulphur, crush it and reduce it to extreme fineness. In order to withdraw the sulphur, the door of the drum is removed, and replaced by a similar door *abcd*, the panels of which are of wire-gauze (fig. 388); by causing the drum to revolve 5 or 6 times, the sulphur escapes through this door, leaving the balls in the drum.

Fig. 386. Fig. 387.

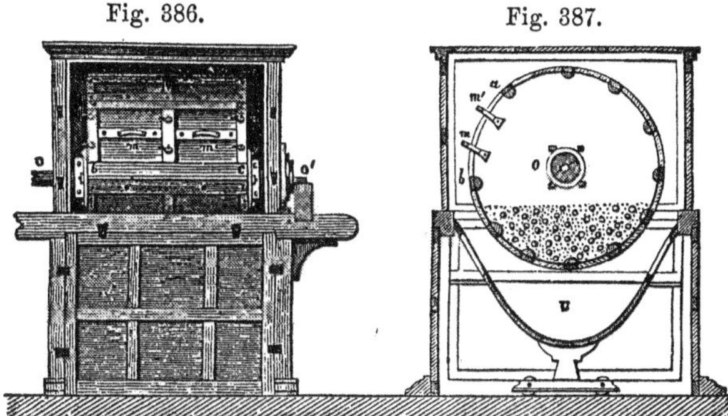

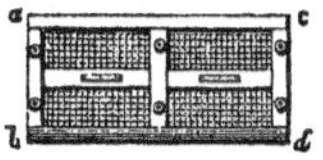

Fig. 388.

The powdered sulphur is sifted in a bolting-machine, similar to that used for bolting flour; the particles which have not been sufficiently pulverized are thus separated, as well as any small grains of sand, which might occasion accidents in the manufacture of the powder.

§ 627. The charcoal destined for the fabrication of powder must be most carefully selected. All kinds of wood are not suitable for the preparation of this charcoal: the tender and light woods, which yield a friable, porous charcoal, leaving very little ash, are preferred.

The woods most esteemed are the black alder and spindle-tree: poplar and chestnut may also be used. Hemp-stalks likewise yield a very good charcoal.

The wood of the black alder is exclusively used in France. The branches of about 15 or 20 millimetres in diameter are preferred; and if larger branches are used, they are first split. The bark is always removed, as it gives too much ash. These branches are cut into lengths of from 1.5 to 2 metres, and tied in bundles weighing from 12 to 15 kilogrammes.

The carbonization is never effected in kilns, as common charcoal is made, but in pits or in cylinders.

§ 628. *Carbonization in pits.*—Cylindrical pits, about 1.5 m. in diameter and 1.2 m. in depth, are excavated in the earth and lined with bricks, and filled with the wood, cut into pieces of 0.30 m. in length, until the heap rises to the height of a few decimetres above the mouth of the pit. Fire is communicated through a hole at the bottom; and as the combustion advances, the branches are raised with a fork, so as to allow the fire to be regularly distributed. The pile gradually sinks, and fresh wood must be added to keep the pit full. When a flame is no longer seen, the mouth of the pit is hermetically closed by a sheet-iron lid, and the carbonization is then finished without access of air. The pit remains closed for three or four days, in order entirely to extinguish and cool the charcoal. It is then opened, the charcoal removed, and conveyed to the sorting-room, where it is most carefully sorted by hand; such branches as have not been sufficiently carbonized and the half-burnt pieces are rejected, as also those which are too much carbonized, and therefore would make bad powder. The good charcoal should be used immediately, as it sensibly deteriorates by exposure to the moist air.

By carbonization in pits, about 18 to 20 per cent. of charcoal are obtained.

§ 629. *Carbonization in cylinders.*—This process yields a much larger proportion of charcoal; its quality is also more constant and uniform, because the fire can be regulated at will, and the carbonization can be arrested at the proper moment.

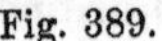

Fig. 389.

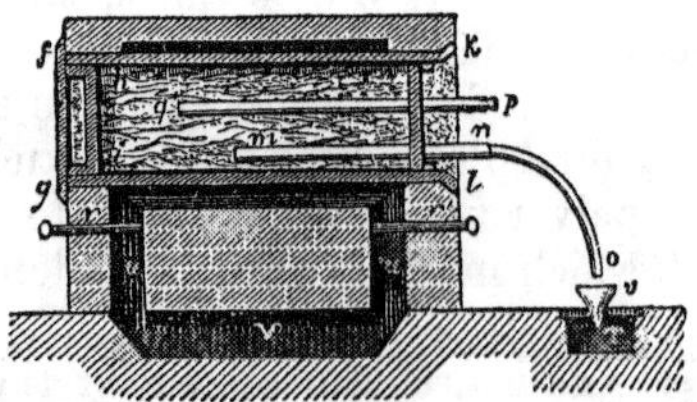

Fig. 390.

The cylinders C, C (figs. 389 and 390) are arranged in pairs in the same furnace: they are made of cast iron, having 2 metres in length and about 0.70 m. in diameter. One end of the cylinder is closed by a cast-iron lid, having four circular openings, through which pass four sheet-iron tubes, as *pq*, *mn*. Three of these tubes, which serve for the introduction of sticks of wood, are closed externally with wooden plugs, which can be withdrawn from time to time, so as to observe the progress of the carbonization. The fourth is open, and gives exit to the gases which are evolved during the process. A curved copper tube *no* is fitted to one end of it, opening above a funnel *v*, which communicates with a horizontal canal T, ranging along the furnace and opening into the chimney. There are generally twelve furnaces arranged in the same masonwork.

The combustible is placed on the grate *d*, the flame and smoke ascend between the two cylinders, surround them, and descend by vertical pipes *u* and *u'* into a horizontal canal VV', which extends under all the furnaces, and opens into a chimney built in the middle of the room. The heat around each cylinder is regulated by registers *r* and *r'*, in the vertical pipes *u* and *u'*. The part *abc* of the cylinders, which is more immediately exposed to the action of the fire, is covered with a luting of broken tiles and clay. The maximum of temperature is thus found at the top of the cylinders, favouring greatly the progress of the operation.

The sticks of wood to be carbonized are about 1.5 m. in length: when the cylinders are filled with them, the movable end *fghi* is replaced. This end is made of two sheets of iron, the space between which is filled with ashes: assay sticks are then introduced into the tubes *pq*, *mn*.

When the cylinders are charged, fire is kindled on the grate: turf is the fuel generally used. Active decomposition of the wood does not begin under four or five hours. The progress of the operation is estimated by the quantity and colour of the smoke which escapes from the pipe *no*. When the carbonization is supposed to be advancing, the assay-sticks are withdrawn, and an opinion formed from their appearance of the progress of decomposition in the various parts of the cylinders: if it be more advanced in some parts than in others, the combustible is pushed to the side where the carbonization is slowest. The heat is also regulated by the registers *r* and *r'*. In 11 or 12 hours, no vapour escapes any longer from the pipe *no;* the operation is then terminated, the registers are closed, and the carbonization is completed without further aid. On the following day, the charcoal is withdrawn and placed in sheet-iron extinguishers, (étouffoirs.)

Carbonization in cylinders yields from 35 to 40 per cent. of charcoal, which is sorted by hand, and broken into small pieces.

The carbonization is not carried so far when the charcoal is intended for sporting powder: it is then withdrawn in the state of *red charcoal* (charbon roux); its colour then is brown. For war powder the carbonization is pushed further, to the state of *black charcoal*,* (charbon noir.) Powder made with red charcoal would be too explosive for muskets or artillery.

MANUFACTURE OF POWDER.

§ 630. The principal processes of the many used in the manufacture of powder are the following:

1st. Powder-mills with stampers.

2d. The pulverizing drum and hydraulic press, called also the *revolutionary process*.

3d. Powder-mills with edge-stones.

4th. The Bernese, or process of Champy, by which round powder is made.

1st. *Powder-mills with stampers.*

§ 631. These are the oldest; they make good powder, and are still in use in France for the manufacture of war powder.

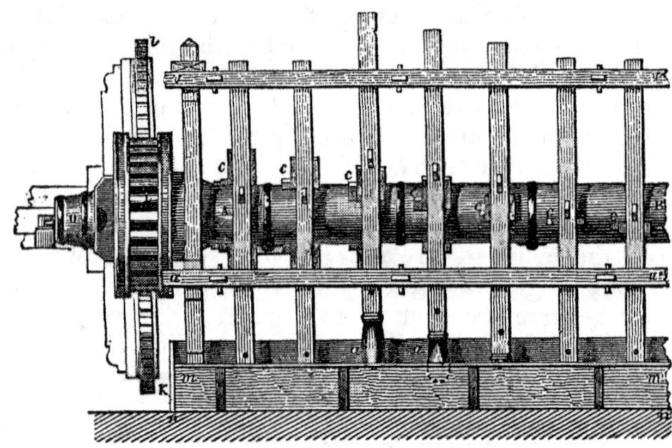

Fig. 391.

A battery of pestles (fig. 391) is generally composed of two parallel rows of ten pestles, each of which falls into its own mortar. The pestles are made of square pieces of wood (fig. 392) 2.5 m. in length and 0.10 m. square, terminating in a rounded part which fits into a pyriform brass box *a*. Their weight is about 40 kilogrammes.

The mortars are hollowed out of a large block of chestnut-wood

* Called also "*distilled charcoal.*"—*Trans.*

mm', about 0.60 m. square; their shape is that represented in fig. 393. The material, under the blows of the pestle, rises along the sides, but soon falls to the bottom, on account of the shape of the mortar. From the position of the latter, the blows of the pestle, falling on the length of the grain of the wood, would very soon destroy the mortars; and to prevent this, a piece of hard wood *z* is inserted at the bottom.

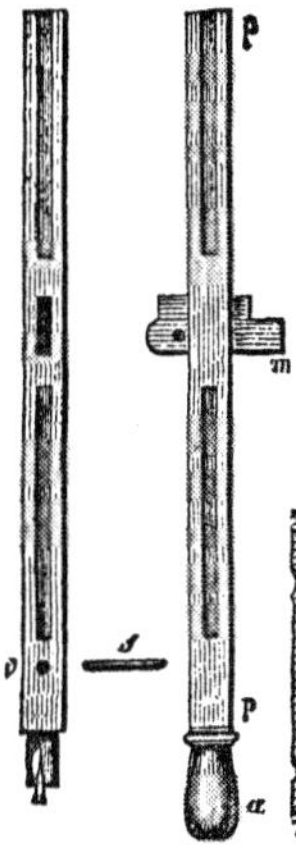

Each row of pestles is set in motion by its own shaft OAB, furnished with cogs C (fig. 391). The two parallel shafts are thrown into gear by two wooden wheels L and the wheel IK, attached to the shaft of the water-wheel, which moves the whole machine. The shafts OAB thus make four revolutions while the water-wheel makes but one. Each pestle has a crosspiece *m* (fig. 392), by which the cogs elevate it. The latter are arranged spirally around the shafts, so that the same number of pestles is always raised, and the machine has constantly the same work to do. Horizontal crossbeams *uu'*, *vv'* regulate the movements of the pestles. The lower crossbeam *uu'* also serves to hold the pestles suspended while the workman is engaged with the mortars. To suspend the pestle, the workman raises it until the hole *o* is above the crossbeam *uu'*, and then inserts into this hole a pin *s* which rests on the crossbeam.

Fig. 392.

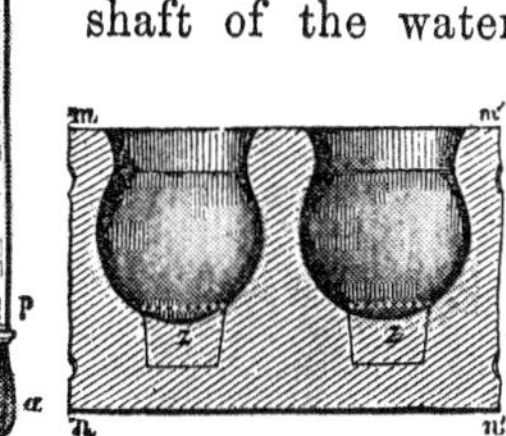

Fig. 393.

The charge of each mortar is 10 kilogrammes. On the one hand, 1.25 kilog. of charcoal in pieces are weighed, and placed in a small wooden bucket; and on the other, 1.25 kilog. of sulphur and 7.50 kilog. of saltpetre, which are likewise placed in another bucket, are accurately weighed and carried to the mill.

The charcoal is placed in each mortar, and wetted with one litre of water: the pins *s* are then removed, and the pestles lowered. They are instantly set to work, by letting water on the wheel. The pestles are allowed to stamp the charcoal for 30 minutes; the wheel is then stopped, the pestles fastened with the pins, and the sulphur and saltpetre placed in the mortars. The three substances are then mixed with the hand, moistened with a half-litre of water, and again mixed. The pestles are lowered, and the battery set in motion. The workman ascertains in a few moments if the material is behaving properly under the pestles. If the external temperature is too great, an additional quantity of water sometimes becomes necessary.

After stamping for half an hour, the material in the mortar is changed. After the battery is stopped and the pestles are fastened by the pins, the workman removes, with a copper ladle (fig. 394), the material from the first mortar and deposits it in a small wooden box called a *trough*. In the same way he removes the material from the second mortar, depositing it in the first, which he has just emptied: the material in the third is received by the second, that of the fourth by the third, and that of the fifth by the fourth. Lastly, the fifth mortar receives the material taken from the first. Each workman superintending only five mortars, four men are required for the battery.

Fig. 394.

The pestles are set in motion, and allowed to stamp for an hour: a second exchange is then made precisely like the first. This is continued for 12 hours, an exchange being made every hour; from time to time, the material is moistened, in order to preserve the proper degree of dampness. After the last exchange, the battery is allowed to work for two hours, to give additional consistency to the material.

During these fourteen hours, the material has received about 30,000 blows with the pestle: this number has been ascertained to be necessary to give the powder the proper degree of density. Wherever it has been reduced, a powder has resulted which would not bear transportation.

§ 632. The material, when removed from the mortars, is deposited in wooden buckets, called *tubs*, and sent to the graining-house.

The object of graining powder is to bring the material which comes from the mill into the shape of grains of a given size. This process is effected in sieves (fig. 395) of 0.60 m. in diameter, the bottom of which is made of leather pierced with circular holes. The sieves are named differently according to the diameter of their holes. The holes of the *guillaume* are from 5 to 10 millimetres in diameter. Those of the *common powder sieve* are 4 millimetres, while the diameter of those of the *musket powder sieve* is only 2 millimetres.

Fig. 395.

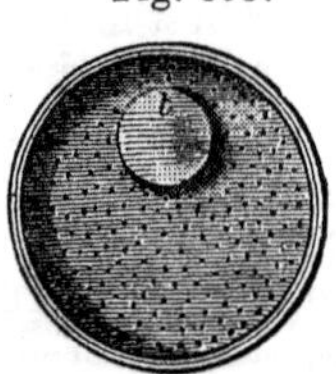

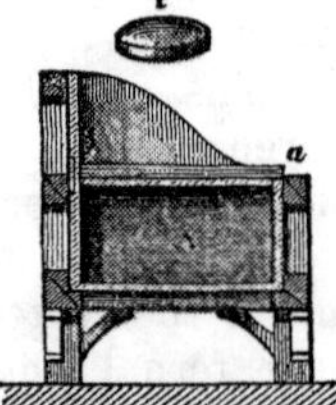

Fig. 396.

Around the graining-house are arranged wooden boxes called *maies* (fig. 396), through which wooden bars *ab* are passed for the support of the sieves.

The workman places the material in the guillaume, rests this sieve on the bar *ab*, and moves it backward and forward in a horizontal position. A portion of the material passes through the holes; but as the motion alone would not suffice to drive all through the apertures, the larger pieces are broken by placing in the sieve a lenticular disk of hard wood *t* (fig. 395), called a *cake*. This cake is 21 centimetres in diameter, 55 millimetres in thickness at the centre, and only 45 at the circumference.

The material which has passed through this sieve is deposited in the common powder or in the musket-powder sieve, according to the quantity to be manufactured. This sieve is handled in the same way as the first, the cake always being used. The material which has passed through the sieve is composed of grains of the requisite size, of smaller grains, and of dust, or meal. The separation of common powder is effected by pouring it over the musket-powder sieve, without using the cake; the fine grains falling through, leaving the common powder to remain in the sieve. The material which has passed through being composed of musket powder and meal, is passed through another sieve, the holes of which are smaller than those of the musket-powder sieve, thus separating the meal. Still finer grains may be obtained of a uniform size by using a finer sieve: a certain quantity is thus separated, and sold as sporting powder. The meal is carried back to the mill and again stamped, after having been moistened with water.

§ 633. The grains of powder thus obtained are small angular fragments: they are called *angular* or *green powder* (poudre verte). This powder must be dried or glazed, for which two processes are adopted: drying by exposure to the air, or by the application of artificial heat.

Drying in the open air can of course only be done in fine weather. The damp powder is spread, 3 or 4 millimetres in thickness on cloths, which are arranged on tables, along a wall having a southern exposure and sheltered from the north. A different surface of the grains of powder is occasionally exposed by stirring. The drying is pretty rapidly effected during the summer, but in spring and autumn is much slower.

Drying by artificial heat has the advantage of being more regular, and capable of being performed at all seasons. The powder is spread in thin layers, on cloths stretched over wooden frames, between which a current of warm air passes, heated by means of long tubes in wooden closets, through which a current of hot water is constantly passing.

2d. *Revolving process.*

§ 634. This process was adopted for the manufacture of a large quantity of powder in a short time; it is now, however, no longer employed, as the quantity of powder obtained is of an inferior kind.

In the first place, the nitre alone, and then the mixture of sulphur and charcoal, were finely powdered in drums with brass balls. The materials were then properly proportioned, and the mixture deposited in revolving drums, containing balls of tin, which effected an intimate admixture of the ingredients.

A moist cloth was then placed on a square copper plate, over which was arranged a wooden frame, intended to hold the powder: this frame was then filled with the preceding mixture. The frame was then removed, and the mixture covered with a second damp cloth, on which a second copper plate was placed, another moist cloth and another layer of material was added, and so on. When the mass was sufficiently thick, it was compressed by a hydraulic press, thus diffusing the water in the cloths through the material, and moistening it uniformly.

The cakes arising from this operation were exposed for some time to the air, to dry them, and then grained in the ordinary manner.

3d. *Mills with edge-stones.*

§ 635. This process is applied in France to the manufacture of sporting powder, and produces a very compact and superior article. The proportions adopted are the following:

Saltpetre	80.0	or	76.9
Sulphur	10.0	...	9.6
Charcoal	14.0	...	13.5
	104.0	...	100.0

The charcoal and sulphur are first reduced to powder in revolving drums with brass balls, as stated in § 626; but the charcoal, being pulverized with more difficulty, requires a longer time for this operation. The charcoal is therefore first pulverized alone, and the sulphur is not added for some time. 21 kilogrammes of red charcoal, as it comes from the sorting-room, are allowed to revolve for 12 hours in the drum; then 15 kilogrammes of sulphur, in pieces, are added, and the operation is continued for 6 hours. The mixture is then withdrawn in the state of an impalpable and perfectly homogeneous mixture, by operating as was stated for the pulverization of sulphur alone.

The proper quantity of saltpetre is then added to the binary compound, and the whole deposited in another drum, called the *mixing-drum* (mélangeoir), in which the three ingredients are intimately mixed together. The drum is divided into 3 compartments by oak partitions, which are kept asunder by 12 wooden ribs on the interior; the latter, being covered with a piece of cow-hide, form a cylinder, the convex surface of which is of leather. The material is introduced and withdrawn through a door held in its place by copper screws. In order to effect the mixing, 60 kilogrammes of bronze balls of 5 millimetres in diameter, and 26 kilog. of mixture, are allowed to revolve in the drum for 12 hours, at the rate of 25 or 30 revolutions per minute. The material is then withdrawn, as from the other drum, by substituting for the door another of which the panels are of wire-gauze.

Fifty kilog. of this mixture are then placed in a box called a *maie*, and continually stirred, while one litre of water is poured on it with a watering-pot, the rose of which is pierced with very fine holes. In summer, double this quantity of water is sometimes used. It is then carried to the grinding-mill.

This mill consists of two vertical cast-iron millstones M, M (fig. 397), weighing 5500 kilog. and resting on a cast-iron platform AB, supported by solid mason-work. The diameter of these stones is 1.50 m.; their thickness at their circumference 0.50 m. The diameter of the horizontal platform is 2.0 m. Each stone is traversed by an iron axis CDC′, which runs on one side into a vertical cast-iron shaft EF, and on the other into a framework GHIH′G′, firmly fastened to the vertical shaft EF. A horizontal shaft KL, below the floor and communicating with the water-wheel, moves the vertical shaft by means of conical gearing. Two small wooden scrapers s, s', shod with copper, are fastened on iron arms t, t' fixed to the movable shaft, and follow the course of the stones. Their object is to push into the track of the wheels any portions of the material which the pressure might drive toward the edges of the platform. Scratchers r, r', shod with copper, rub continually against each wheel, and detach any material which may adhere to it.

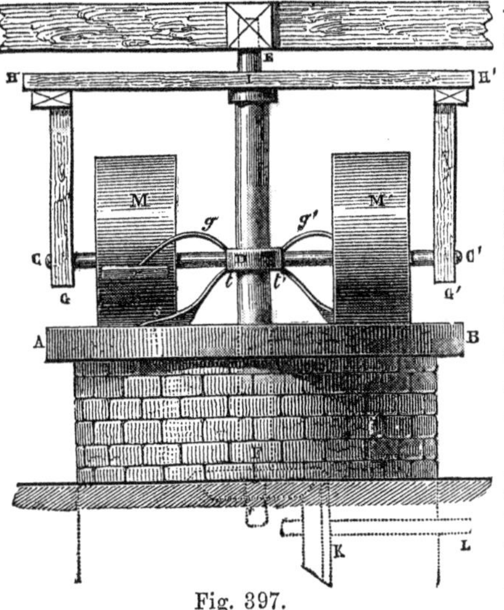

Fig. 397.

Fifty kilog. of material are spread evenly on the platform: the mill is then set in motion, the rapidity increasing gradually until the shaft EF makes about 8 revolutions per minute. In about an hour the greater portion of the water added has evaporated, through the considerable rise of temperature during the operation; the material has become dry, and requires again to be moistened. In order to effect a uniform moistening throughout the whole mass, a receiver V (fig. 398), terminating in a horizontal tube *ab* pierced with very small holes, is fastened behind one of the millstones: into this receiver 1 litre of water is poured, and allowed to flow at pleasure, by means of a stopcock in the vertical tube. The workman also cleans the track of the millstones with a copper scraper, without stopping the mill. After an hour's operation, he stops

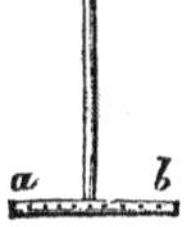

Fig. 398.

the mill; and having very accurately examined the material along the track, he turns the mill very slowly, so as to require 8 or 10 minutes for a single revolution of the platform. The stones, thus resting for a long time on one point, forcibly compress the material, thus effecting a great density. This terminates the operation: the cake is removed and sent to the graining-house.

§ 636. The graining-machine now used consists of a wooden frame AB (fig. 399), of octagonal form, and 2.50 m. in diameter, suspended horizontally by 8 ropes. In the centre is a collar, shod with copper, through which passes the curved iron *defgh*, called a *signole*, making at the same time a part of the vertical axis KH, of which the upper end H turns in a socket set in a joint. The lower end K is furnished with a horizontal bevelled cog-wheel, running into a vertical bevelled cog-wheel on the axis MN, by means of which the whole machine is set in motion. It is evident that during the rotary movement of the axis KH, the signole communicates a similar motion to the frame AB.

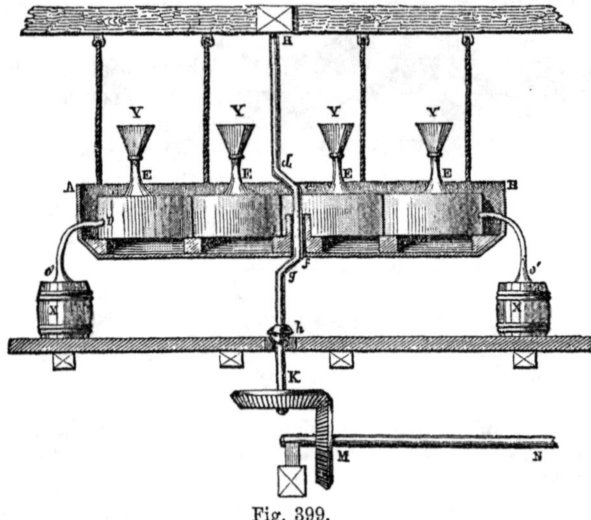

Fig. 399.

Eight graining-machines, having 3 compartments each (fig. 400), are fixed on the frame. The bottom AB of the first is of walnut, 2 centimetres in thickness, pierced with small holes rimed out from below.

A wooden plate C, weighing 2 kilog., and made of the service-tree, rests on this bottom; and, at the two opposite points, are two openings of 1 decimeter in width, to which are fitted two inclined copper planes, in the shape of small troughs, the lower extremities of which touch the surface of the second bottom FG. This bottom, 3 centimetres distant from the first, is made of

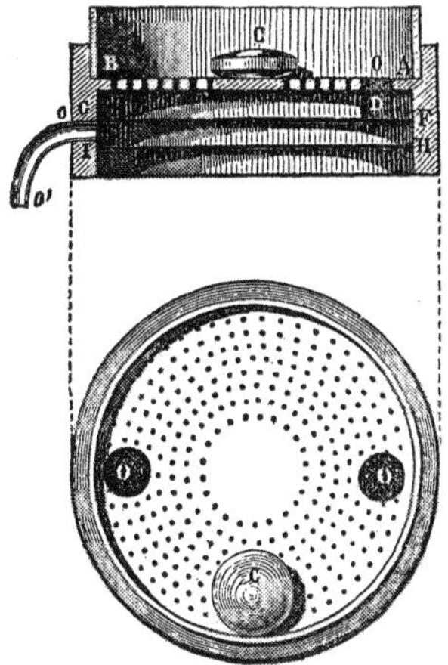
Fig. 400.

metallic gauze, the meshes of which allow sporting powder to pass through. Lastly, at 3 centim. from this second bottom, there is a third HI of silk bolting-cloth, intended to receive the meal powder. The lower part of the graining-machine, which rests on the surface of the frame, is covered with leather: the upper surface is covered by cloth furnished with a leather tube E for the introduction of the material. On the side of the sieve there are two openings O, O′, each also provided with a leather tube, intended to convey the grained and meal powder into small light boxes X, X′.

The graining-sieve being arranged on the suspended frame, the material is introduced by the small troughs Y, Y′, and the frame is set in motion. The plate in the sieve then moving circularly over the wooden plate, breaks up the material, which, after passing through the holes of the wooden bottom AB, falls on the metallic gauze FG. All that part which is fine enough to escape through the meshes falls, and the larger particles which remain, on meeting the inclined plane of the troughs, ascend along these troughs to the first plate, by virtue of its circular motion, and are again subjected to the action of the plate. While this is taking place in the two upper compartments, the mixture of grained and meal powder, which has passed through the metallic gauze, falls on the silk bolter, and is bolted. The meal, which passes through the bolting-cloth, falls on the leather bottom of the frame, whence it is conveyed by a leather tube into a small tight box, while the clean grains, which remain on the silk, escape by an opposite opening and fall into a small barrel.

The meal is sent to the mill, to be again pulverized: the cake produced is grained as before.

§ 637. Sporting powder undergoes another operation, called *glazing*, the object of which is to give it a polished and brilliant surface, which insures its preservation and renders it more dense.

The glazing-machine is a cylindrical wooden drum (fig. 401) of 2.70 m. in length, and 1.20 m. in diameter, divided internally into five compartments, by intermediate partitions. Each compartment has its own door. A wooden shaft traverses the drum, and receives its movement by proper gearing: the inside of the drum contains, like the mixing-machines, 12 projecting wooden ribs.

Above the glazing-machine is a large hopper, divided into five

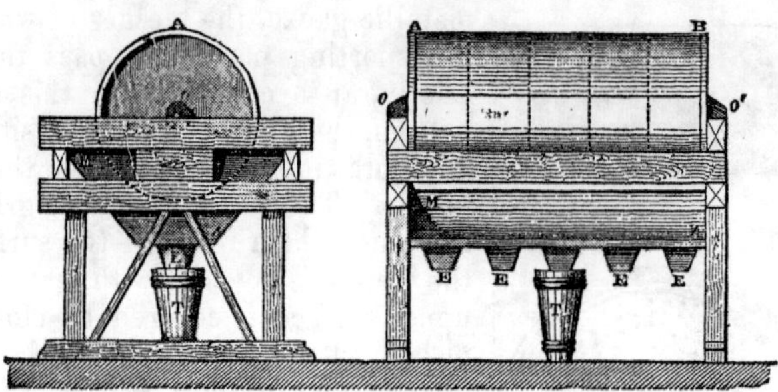

Fig. 401.

compartments corresponding to those of the drum, each of which terminates in a leather tube serving to convey the material into a barrel beneath. 100 kilog. of grains being placed in each compartment of the drum, it is made to revolve slowly for the first 12 hours. The powder thus rolls continually on itself: the wooden ribs renewing the points of contact, the grains wear off their angles against each other, and become polished. The drum is then made to revolve faster, and in 36 or 40 hours the glazing is terminated.

Powder taken from the glazing-machine is dried as usual.

Glazing gives powder greater density, but diminishes its inflammability: it must, therefore, not be pushed too far, and should be stopped when the grains are sufficiently hard to bear transportation, and are free from dust.

§ 638. A quality of sporting powder, superior to the preceding, is obtained by again grinding the grained powder by the process just described, subjecting it to a second pulverization and graining. This powder, after glazing, is known by the name of *poudre royale* (royal powder), and is superior to the best foreign powders.

4th. *Manufacture of Round Powder by the Bernese process, or the process of Champy.*

§ 639. Blasting-powder is made in France by a peculiar process, first used at Berne, whence it has obtained the name of *Bernese process.* It is also called the *process of Champy*, in honour of the inspector of powder, to whom great improvements in its working are due. This process is also applied to the manufacture of cannon and musket powder.

For blasting powder, the more highly-burned charcoal, which is unfit for other powder, is used: the great degree of calcination is in this case not injurious to the quality of the powder, as blasting powder should not possess too great an inflammability.

Six different operations may be distinguished in the manufacture: pulverization, mixing, graining, equalization, glazing, and drying.

The pulverization is effected by bronze balls in iron drums, exactly as has been previously described, with the only difference that at the same time balls of 4.5 m. in diameter, and some varying from 7 to 15 mm. are used, the charcoal being more difficult to grind. The drum contains 120 kilog. of these balls, with 30 kilog. of sulphur and 27 of charcoal, which is the proportion for 150 kilog. of powder. The door is closed, and the drum made to revolve for 4 hours, at the rate of from 25 to 28 revolutions per minute: the binary mixture, being then sufficiently ground, is removed from the drum.

The further mixture is then made as follows:—14.25 kilog. of the substance taken from the drum, exactly weighed, are placed in a barrel, and 23.25 kilog. of saltpetre added. Each barrel then contains 37.50 kilog. of the compound, viz:

Saltpetre	23.25	62.0
Sulphur	7.50	20.0
Charcoal	6.75	18.0
	37.50	100.0

This compound is carried to the mixing-machine, which are leather drums, containing 60 kilog. of bronze balls of 4.5 mm. in diameter. The 37.50 kilog. of it are introduced, and the machine made to revolve at the rate of 25 or 30 revolutions per minute. After four hours' working, the compound is well mixed; the material is then conveyed into a maie, and placed in barrels to be carried to the graining-house.

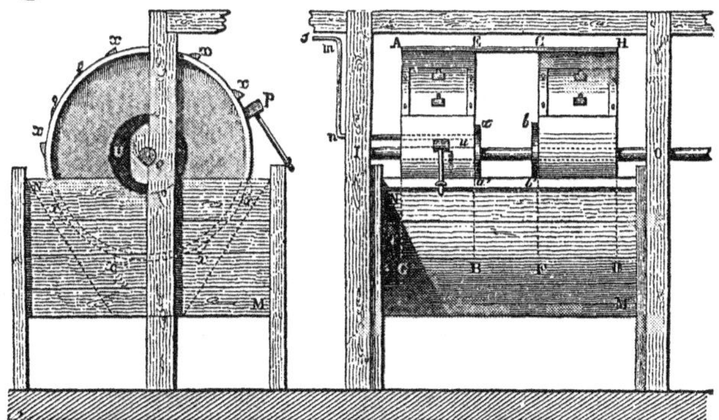

Fig. 402.

§ 640. The machine (fig. 402) used for the manufacture of round grains consists of two large oak drums AEGB, CHFD, 1.75 m. in diameter, and 0.63 m. in height. Each of them has only one entire end BE, CF: the opposite end AG, HD being furnished with a circular opening U of 0.60 m. diameter in the centre. The two drums are traversed by the same iron axes IO, supported between two strong vertical beams by two copper chains. Two copper disks *aa'*, *bb'*, fixed on the iron axis, connect the transverse iron axis IO with the ends EB and CF of the drum, while four strong cross-pieces, as AB, keep the whole steady. Each drum has a door M, of 0.35 m. by 0.60 m., closed with four copper screws, and used for introducing and withdrawing the material. All the lower part of the machine is surrounded by a large trough N, furnished with inclined copper planes, intended to receive the material when withdrawn by the doors, and conduct it into barrels placed beneath.

The drum AEGB is used for graining, and the other CHFD for glazing the powder.

The outer periphery of the granulator AEGB is furnished with 12 small cleats *x*, *x*, *x*, which, during the movement of the drum, move, and cause a small wooden hammer *p*, fastened by a cord to the side of the trough N, to strike constantly on its surface, detaching, by its blows, any portion of the material which might adhere to the drum. A copper watering-tube *nu*, 2 centim. in diameter, and 0.40 m. in length, having one side pierced with very minute holes, enters the granulating machine, a little above its axis, and communicates, by a curved copper tube *nms*, with a forcing-pump. This pump (fig. 403) is composed of a copper pump-tree P, in which a perfectly well-fitting piston moves: an iron rod *tt'*, fastened to the upper part of the piston, works between two wooden uprights. The piston is set in motion by means of a winch and a rope which passes over a pulley fixed to the iron rod. The lower part of the pump-tree communicates, on the one hand, with a reservoir of water, and, on the other, with the injecting-tube *smnu*; two stopcocks *r*, *r'* closing at will the communicating tubes. When the stopcock *r* is opened and the piston raised, the lower part of the pump fills with water: if this stopcock be closed and that at *r'* opened, the piston descends by its own weight, allowing the water to escape through the watering-tube *smnu*.

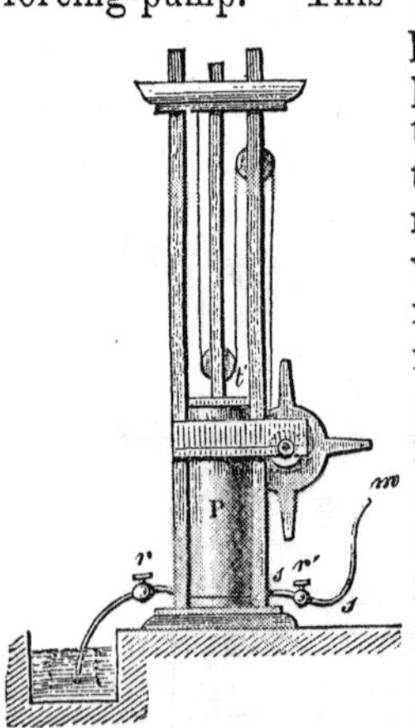

Fig. 403.

In order to introduce a charge of the material, the workman removes the door M of the granulating-machine, and pours in 100 kilog. of powder already grained, called the *nucleus* (noyau), the origin of which will be hereafter explained; he replaces the door, and sets the machine in motion at the rate of 10 revolutions per minute. During this motion, the first sprinkling, of 5 per cent.

of water, is made; the fluid thus wetting the nucleus which occupies the lower part of the granulating-machine in the form of a fine rain, and the rotary motion of the drum constantly renewing the surface, all the grains are uniformly moistened.

When the first sprinkling is over, he introduces, through the opening U, 50 kilog. of the mixture, as it comes from the mixing-machine, inserting 1 kilog. at a time with a wooden shovel, spreading it as evenly as possible in the drum. The movement of the machine rolling the damp grains constantly among the dry meal-powder, causes the latter to adhere to their surface, and each grain thus to increase by concentric layers.

Immediately after, a second sprinkling is made, and then 50 kilog. of the ternary mixture are gradually added. After allowing the machine to revolve for a quarter of an hour, the workman ascertains if the meal powder is entirely absorbed; he then empties the machine, by dropping the material into barrels placed beneath. These operations last from 35 to 40 minutes.

§ 641. The material, when taken from the machine, is composed of variously-sized grains, which require to be separated, or *equalized.*

This is done by shaking the grains over two leather sieves; the first, called the *equalizer* (égalisoir), separates those grains which are too large, while the second, the *subequalizer*, allows those which are too fine to pass through. The holes in the equalizer are 3.4 mm. in diameter. The grains and irregular pieces which do not pass through are set aside; those which pass through are sifted on the sub-equalizer, the holes of which are 1.2 mm. in diameter. There remain on the latter sieve those grains the diameter of which are comprised between 1.2 mm. and 3.4 mm. and which are suitable for blasting: they are deposited in a barrel to undergo a subsequent operation. All which passes through the sub-equalizer is composed of grains smaller than 1.20 mm.: it is considered as a *nucleus*, because this grain need only be increased in the granulating-machine to make it of the proper size. As each operation yields the quantity of nucleus necessary for a succeeding operation, it is sufficient to obtain some for the first operation, for which the angular powder, of the size of musket powder prepared in the stamping-machine, is employed.

The grains which are too large and the irregular pieces, which remained on the equalizer, are broken by means of the cake, and used as a nucleus for the succeeding operation.

Blasting powder is glazed as well as sporting powder, in order to increase its density. This operation is effected in the second drum CHFD. 200 kilog. of equalized grains are introduced, and it is turned for 4 hours: by direct experiment it is ascertained when the grain has acquired sufficient density. For this purpose 60 gm. of the glazed grains are poured into a graduated test-glass: the grain is considered as sufficiently glazed when the level of the material rises to a certain division in the instrument.

The glazed grain is dried in the ordinary way.

§ 642. Round war powder is manufactured by the same method, the usual proportion of the ingredients for war powder, 25 of saltpetre, 12.5 of sulphur, and 12.5 of charcoal being employed. Two kinds of equalized grains are separated: those of which the diameter is between 1.2 mm. and 2.1 mm. constituting cannon powder; and musket powder, the diameter of the grains of which varies from 1.0 mm. to 1.20 mm.

METHODS OF TESTING THE FORCE OF POWDER.

§ 643. In the French powder-mills, powder is subjected to a series of experiments, intended to ascertain the physical qualities and the ballistic force of each kind of powder.

War powder must fulfil the following conditions:

The grain must be angular, hard, dry, and equal; the size varying from 2.5 mm. to 1.4 mm. for cannon powder, and from 1.4 mm. to 0.6 mm. for musket powder. It should resist moderate pressure, and leave no dust when rubbed between the hands. The apparent density of powder is measured by a peculiar apparatus, called a *gravimeter*. It is a measure holding exactly 1 cubic decimetre: it is filled by means of a valved funnel, which fits thereon, and spreads the powder uniformly. The weight of the litre of powder, not heaped up, contained in this measure, is its *gravimetric density*. For war powder, this density is from 0.820 kilog. to 0.830 kilog.

§ 644. The ballistic force of powder is measured at the same by the *eprouvette mortar*, or *testing-mortar*, and the *pendulum-gun* or *pendulum-test*.

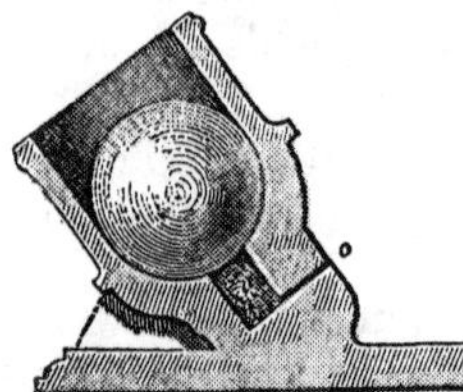

Fig. 404.

The eprouvette-mortar is a cast iron mortar (fig. 404), the axis of which has an inclination of 45°; its internal diameter is 191.2 mm. By means of a bent funnel, 92 gm. of powder are introduced into the chamber *a* of the mortar, and a bronze ball of 189.5 mm. in diameter, weighing 29.4 kilog. is placed thereon. To be satisfactory, the ball must be thrown at least 220 metres.

§ 645. The pendulum-gun (fig. 405) is composed of two parts—the pendulum-gun AB, properly so called, and the receiver, or *ballistic pendulum*, CD. The pendulum-gun is made of a musket-barrel *ab*, the breech of which is replaced by a piece of iron supported at the bottom of an iron frame *omn*, terminated at its upper part by two gudgeons *o*, shaped like knife-blades, forming a horizontal axis. Below the pendulum is an axis *mn*, sustaining a movable mass of lead *p*, which may be made to slide on a horizontal rod, capable of being itself fixed at different heights. This mass is placed in such a position that the centre of oscillation of the compound pendulum is over the axis of the gun, and over the vertical axis which passes through the centre of gravity. The pendulum-gun has a rod *i*, which drives a movable slider over a graduated arc *cd*: this slider marks the recoil of the pendulum.

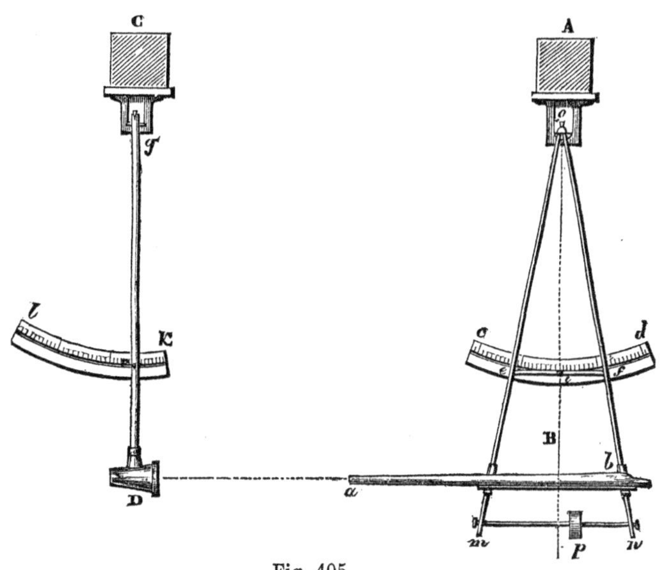

Fig. 405.

The ballistic-pendulum is composed of a conical bronze box D suspended to an iron frame-work *gh*, which terminates itself, at the upper part, in a horizontal axis made of two knife-shaped gudgeons. This system therefore forms a second pendulum, as movable as the first. The axis of suspension of these pendulums should be accurately parallel. The box contains a mass of lead, into which the ball penetrates; it has also an appendage *r*, which moves on a graduated arc *kl*, and drives a slider over the arc. The distance to which the slider is driven by the impinging of the ball measures the momentum communicated by the ball to the pendulum. The apparatus is so arranged that the centre of oscillation of the pendulum is over the axis of the conical box. Mathematical formulæ permit a calculation of the initial rapidity of the ball, either by the space traversed by the slider of the ballistic pendulum, or by that of the slider of the gun-pendulum.

The weight of each of these pendulums, when mounted, is 25 kilogrammes.

The charge of powder in the gun weighs 10 gm.; the diameter of the ball is 16.3 mm. The initial rapidity of the ball, inferred from the two observations just indicated, should be 450 metres per second.

For sporting powder only 5 gm. are used: they should give the following initial degrees of rapidity:

For fine powder	330	metres
" superfine	350	"
" royal	375	"

In many French powder-mills, a *cannon-pendulum*,* arranged on exactly the same principles as the gun-pendulum, is used.

§ 646. War powder is likewise subjected, from time to time, to several other experiments, intended to test its hardness, its capability of transportation, or the more or less rapid changes it undergoes by exposure to the moisture of the atmosphere.

ANALYSIS OF POWDER.

§ 647. The analysis of powder is a tedious and delicate operation, when the proportions and nature of its components are to be ascertained very exactly. The first operation is to determine the proportion of hygrometric water the powder contains; for which purpose a known weight of powder is exposed for several days in a dry vacuum, and the loss it experiences ascertained; or else the substance is placed in a U-shaped tube, kept at a temperature of 60° or 70° and traversed by a current of dry air. The apparatus is arranged as described (§ 261) for oxalic acid.

Ten gm. of dry powder are then treated with hot water, which dissolves the nitrate of potassa. The insoluble residue, composed of sulphur and charcoal, is collected on a small filter, which has been previously dried and weighed. When this residue has been properly washed, it is dried with the filter at a moderate temperature, and weighed: by subtracting from this weight that of the filter above, the weight of the sulphur and charcoal is obtained. After separating, as carefully and completely as possible, the substance from the filter, it is again weighed in a small bottle and treated with sulphuret of carbon, which may be mixed with an equal volume of ether, without too much impairing its solvent power. The charcoal which remains isolated is collected on a small filter previously dried, and weighed after a second desiccation, after hav-

---

* This method, the invention of the Citizen Regnier, made in the year VII. of the republic, still bears his name.—*Translator.*

ing been well washed in a mixture of sulphuret of carbon and ether. The weight of the sulphur is thus obtained by the difference. It may, however, also be weighed directly after evaporating, at a low temperature, the solvent which contains it. The charcoal of the powder is not pure carbon: it contains, as the carbonization is always imperfect, a considerable proportion of oxygen and hydrogen; but, as the chemical nature of the charcoal exerts great influence on the quality of the powder, it is important, in an accurate analysis, to ascertain the amount of carbon exactly. Charcoal is analyzed, like organic substances in general, according to the process explained (§ 260) for the analysis of oxalic acid. An idea may be formed of the composition of charcoal by the following numbers, obtained from the analysis of the red charcoal used in the manufacture of sporting powder:

Carbon	71.42
Hydrogen	4.85
Oxygen and Nitrogen	22.91
Ashes	0.82
	100.00

§ 648. The quantity of sulphur contained in powder may also be determined by operating directly on the powder itself. To effect this, 10 grammes of dry powder are dissolved in a small quantity of hot water, nitric acid is added, and, after allowing the fluid to boil, small quantities of chlorate of potassa are gradually introduced. Under the influence of these oxidizing agents, the sulphur is dissolved in the state of sulphuric acid, which is precipitated, after the liquid is filtered, by chloride of barium. The precipitate is allowed to settle, the clear liquid poured on a filter, and the precipitate, after being boiled for a few moments with chlorohydric acid, to dissolve the nitrates it might contain (§ 536), is collected on the same filter and weighed after calcination.

Ten grammes of dry powder may also be mixed with an equal weight of nitrate of potassa and four or five times its weight of chloride of sodium: the mixture being thrown, in small quantities at a time, into a platinum crucible, deflagrates slowly, without any loss of the material. It is subsequently treated with water, and the sulphuric acid is precipitated by chloride of barium, after supersaturating the liquid with chlorohydric acid.

It has also been proposed to dissolve the sulphur of the mixture of sulphur and charcoal, by a solution of monosulphide of sodium, or of hyposulphite of soda; but this process is useless, because the charcoal, being always considerably attacked by these alkaline liquids, gives off a peculiar acid, called *ulmic acid.*

§ 649. Very frequently, only the quantity of saltpetre contained in powder is to be ascertained. This is easily done by treating

50 grammes of powder with 200 grammes of hot water, and filtering the liquid into a test-glass having a mark at the level corresponding to 500 cubic centimetres. The material is washed with water on a filter, until the filtrate reaches the level. The liquid is then cooled to 60°, the contraction it undergoes by cooling being compensated by the addition of a small quantity of water: it is then well shaken to render it homogeneous, and a peculiar areometer, graduated so that its level will mark immediately the hundredths of nitrate of potassa contained in the 50 grammes of powder, is dipped in. In this manner the proportion of nitrate of potassa may easily be determined, to very nearly a half-hundredth.

LIME AND MORTARS.

BUILDING MATERIALS.

§ 650. The material used in building is of two kinds: natural, or building-stones, and artificial, or bricks. We shall now study only the natural material, and return to the artificial when treating of earthenware.

Generally speaking, those stones are selected for building which are the cheapest, and possess at the same time sufficient resistance to the action of rain and frost. Very often the preference is given to those which are light, easily worked, and will well bind with the mortar.

The preference given to any kind of stone depends essentially on the use for which it is intended; thus moles, breakwaters, etc., which are constantly washed by the waters of the ocean, can be built only of very hard stone, capable of resisting the corroding action of salt-water. For the foundation of houses in damp locations, a hard stone, not likely to nitrify, is required.

Building-stones may be divided into three classes, according to their chemical nature:

1st. The stones formed by the alkaline and earthy silicates, such as granite, porphyry, certain trachytes, and basalts. As these stones are very difficult to cut, being extremely hard, they are used, in the form of hewn stone, only for special constructions, demanding great solidity and subject to continual wear, such as sea-dikes, footways, pavements, etc. Moreover, they do not bind well with mortar. Being capable of a fine polish, and often presenting beautiful shades of colour, they are used for pedestals, obelisks, columns, and other large architectural ornaments.

Many volcanic rocks also furnish a material highly valued as building-stone, as possessing lightness combined with great solidity. Certain volcanic pumice-stones and scoriæ yield a light material, very valuable in the construction of inside arches.

2d. The quartzose rocks found in various geological formations also yield a good material for building. The most important of these are the sandstones. Graywacke, the old red sandstone, and the variegated sandstone furnish excellent stone for cutting.

In the tertiary formation in the environs of Paris, a quartzose rock, called *millstone* (meulière,) which, being porous and light, is nevertheless very solid, is frequently used for the foundation of houses, because it arrests with great efficacy the dampness of the earth, and cannot nitrify. The quartzose pebbles found in layers in the various strata of cretaceous rocks are also sometimes used.

3d. The limestones furnish very valuable building material. White marble and certain coloured and veined transition limestones are used for ornamental purposes, such as mantel-pieces, hall-floors, etc., or for monumental and artistic purposes.

The tertiary limestones and those of the jurassic formation furnish a material highly prized for cutting. They may be divided into compact and granular limestone; the first, being hard, resists wear, nitrifies with difficulty, and is susceptible of a high polish. The limestone of Château-Landon is of this class, and is extensively used in Paris for monuments, especially in those parts intended to be sculptured.

The ordinary building-stone of Paris is a conchiferous limestone, called *coarse limestone.* The different strata of this rock yield stones varying in value, the inferior qualities and their strata are used for *ashlar-work.*

The chalk formation also yields a moderately good building-stone: the chalk tufa of Touraine is used for building throughout a large portion of central France.

The famous *travertin* in the environs of Rome, which has been used in the construction of the greater portion of the monuments of Italy, is a fresh-water calcareous tuff, belonging to the tertiary formation.

The compact limestones may be used in building immediately after being quarried, which is not the case with the other limestones: as they are more or less porous, they must be exposed to the atmosphere for several months, or even years, in order to evaporate their *quarry water.* These stones are often very soft when taken from the quarry, and harden in the air: chalk tuff, which, when recently extracted, may easily be cut with a knife, does not become hard until after several years' exposure.

§ 651. Building materials are divided into two classes, according to their form: regular material, such as hewn stone, bricks, etc., and irregular material, as rubble stones and large pebbles.

Buildings may be constructed, with regular materials, without the interposition of any substance to unite their surfaces, provided these surfaces be hewn so as to be in pretty close contact. Walls constructed in this manner are called *dry walls.* But, with irregular materials, a solid building can only be erected by interposing a substance called *mortar*, intended to fill the interstices, and bind the materials to each other. It is necessary that the mortar should acquire, after some time, sufficient hardness and adhesion to prevent its falling off, or being washed out by rain. Even with regular materials, a thin coat of mortar is interposed to close the interstices; but in this case the mortar is not required to fulfil the same conditions as when used with the irregular materials: it need not require the same hardness, at least with regular materials of large size.

We shall divide mortars into three classes:

1st. Common mortar, made with non-hydraulic lime.

2d. Hydraulic mortars.

3d. Mortars eminently hydraulic, or cements.

COMMON MORTARS, MADE OF FAT LIME.

§ 652. A paste of lime and water, exposed to the air, will dry after some time; the greater part of the water evaporating, leaves a cracked and friable mass of hydrated lime. But if a very thin layer of this paste be laid between well-dressed and porous stones, the greater part of the water soaks into the stones, and the thin layer of hydrated lime which remains becomes consistent and adheres strongly to the stones. The water should not soak up too rapidly, for in this case the lime sets too quickly, and never becomes very hard: for this reason the stone is moistened before applying the diluted lime. As the adhesion of the hydrated lime with the stone is greater than that with its own particles, the layer must not be too thickly spread. A much more consistent material is obtained by mixing slaked lime with two or three times its weight of quartzose sand, or some ground stone, and tempering the whole with water. This mixture is applied, with a trowel, on the moistened stone: another stone is laid thereon, pressing it down as much as possible, so as to squeeze out the superfluous cement, and obtain only a very thin layer of mortar. Each grain of sand is thus enveloped in a small pellicle of lime, and adheres to it strongly. The addition of the sand presents another advantage, in preventing a too great contraction of the substance on drying, which would thereby split and become too friable. The solidification of this kind of mortar does not depend on the evaporation of the water alone, but also on the combination of the lime with the carbonic acid of the air. The portions in immediate contact with the air are entirely converted into carbonate of lime; but the inner parts only reach the condition of a compound of carbonate and hydrate of lime, which acquires a great degree of hardness (§ 551). This change requires a long lapse of time, for, after many years, the lime in walls is still found almost entirely hydrated: these mortars, therefore, should not be used in the interior of thick walls, where no opportunity of drying is afforded them.

It will readily be understood that the quartzose sand mixed with lime has exerted no chemical action; for if the solidified mortar be dissolved in an acid, no gelatinous silex is separated, which would probably take place if the sand had partially combined with the lime, forming a silicate.

The quality of the mortar depends greatly on its mode of preparation, the quality of the sand, the quantity of water used, and the more or less perfect mixing of the compound. Sharp sand is preferable to smooth. In all cases, the mortar should solidify slowly: it even has been remarked to become more consistent when laid in the fall than when used in summer, when the water evaporates too rapidly.

Common mortar, made with fat lime, is used not only for regular materials, such as hewn stone or bricks, but also for rubble-stone. Care must be taken, however, to insert small pieces of stone between the others, when the spaces are too large.

In dry places, common mortar, made with fat lime, does not set until after some time; but it solidifies with difficulty in any case, and not at all in water. In this last case, the mortar is soon diluted with water, and in a short time entirely washed away. For buildings in damp locations or under water, peculiar mortars are necessary, which set, not in consequence of their desiccation, but by virtue of a special chemical action. These are known by the name of *hydraulic mortars*.

HYDRAULIC MORTARS AND CEMENTS.

§ 653. We have seen (§ 553) that pure carbonate of lime, or that containing only a few hundredths of foreign substances, yields on calcination a lime, the properties of which are closely allied to those of pure lime. This lime, called fat lime, develops a great degree of heat with water, and swells considerably, its volume becoming three or four times that of anhydrous lime. But when the limestone contains a greater proportion of foreign substances, its properties are remarkably changed, and it acquires new ones, which have been turned to good advantage in the art of building. If of the impurities occurring in carbonate of lime, the most prominent are the oxides of iron and of manganese, or quartzose sand, such a limestone yields, when burned, a lime which swells but little, and will form no adhesive paste with water: when tempered, it hardens in time, but falls to pieces in the water. If the foreign substance mixed with the limestone be clay, or silex in a certain state of division, and if its proportion is as much as 10 or 15 per cent. of the limestone, the lime produced from it is a poor lime, but possesses the remarkable quality of setting under water after a longer or shorter time, provided it has not been too strongly calcined. This kind of lime is called *hydraulic lime*. The setting of hydraulic lime is owing to a chemical combination between the lime and the silex of the clay: the manner in which these two substances communicate this property to the lime becomes manifest from the following experiments:

If we preserve for some time, in a bottle well corked, lime-water and dried clay at a temperature of 300° or 400°, the clay will be found to abstract the lime from the water; and, if the contact be sufficiently prolonged, the water no longer turns tincture of litmus blue. Gelatinous silex, when substituted for the clay, also takes up the lime, though less actively than the clay. Hydrated alumina likewise removes some of the lime, while magnesia, the oxides of iron, and manganese are nearly inert. This experiment shows that alumina, silex, and particularly clay, have an affinity for lime sufficient to separate it from the water, and form with it an insoluble compound, while magnesia and oxide of iron do not possess this property. Silex, in the state of quartzose sand, is equally inert.

If a gelatinous silex, previously dried to the state of a mealy powder, is mixed with lime, the whole worked up with water, allowing the paste to stand for some time, a portion of the lime combines with the silex, as the water no longer dissolves the whole of the lime; and, if the substance be treated with an acid, a portion of the silex separates in the gelatinous state, which proves it to have been in combination with the lime.

Lastly, by subjecting a very intimate mixture of carbonate of lime and clay to a moderate heat, a substance which hardens after some time with water is obtained, in which the greater portion of the lime is combined with silicate of alumina; for it is only partially soluble in water, and leaves a residue of gelatinous silex when dissolved in a weak acid. The clay is attacked by the weak acid by being burned in contact with carbonate of lime, while in its original state it is unaffected by them.

These experiments show that the solidification of hydraulic lime under water is caused by the combination of the hydrate of lime with the silicates of alumina and lime: a new aggregation of the material is thus effected, and at the same time the lime is rendered insoluble in water.

§ 654. Intimate mixtures of limestone and clay are found in nature, argillaceous limestones, which yield hydraulic lime immediately on burning. Experiment has shown that a limestone must contain at least 10 or 12 per cent. of clay in order to possess hydraulic properties. The lime produced by such a stone, when tempered with water, hardens in moist places, or under water, in about twenty days; but the hydraulic properties are much greater when the limestone contains 20 to 25 per cent. of clay: then the tempered lime acts in two or three days. Lastly, if the limestone contains 25 to 30 per cent. of clay, it sets in a few hours: this last kind of lime has been called *Roman cement*, or *lime cement*.

The nature of the clay exerts a great influence on the hydraulic qualities of lime: a fine division of the clay and a slight combination of the silex with the alumina are indispensable conditions. The best clays are those which give off a portion of their silex to a solution of caustic potassa.

The first Roman cements were made at London, from the pebblestones found in the bed of the Thames: precisely similar pebbles have since been found on the seacoast, in the vicinity of Boulogne. Subsequently, thick strata of limestone, belonging to the jurassic rocks, and yielding an excellent cement, have been discovered in Burgundy, in the vicinity of Pouilly and Vassy. In those countries where the jurassic rocks are abundant, chemical analysis has led to the discovery of similar limestones.

We here subjoin the analysis of the principal limestones containing hydraulic lime, and cements, which are used in building.

Moderately Hydraulic Limestones.

	Of Macon.	Of St. Germain (Ain).	Of Bigna.
Carbonate of lime	89.2	85.8	83.0
" of magnesia	3.0	0.4	2.0
" of iron	—	6.2	—
Clay or silex	7.8	7.6	15.0
	100.0	100.0	100.0

Highly Hydraulic Limestones.

	Of Metz.	Of Senonches.	Of Lezoux (Puy-de-Dôme).
Carbonate of lime	77.3	80.0	72.5
" of magnesia	3.0	1.5	4.5
" of iron	3.0	—	—
" of manganese	1.5	—	—
Clay or silex	15.2	18.5	23.0
	100.0	100.0	100.0

The limestone of Senonches contains only very finely divided silex.

Limestones containing Cement.

	Of Boulogne-sur-mer.	Of London.	Of Pouilly (Côte-d'Or).	Of Argenteuil, near Paris.
Carbonate of lime	63.6	65.7	57.2	63.0
" of magnesia	—	0.5	3.6	4.0
" of iron	6.0	6.0	6.6	—
" of manganese	—	1.9	—	—
Clay	23.8	24.6	25.2	27.0
Water	6.6	1.3	7.4	6.0
	100.0	100.0	100.0	100.0

When limestones contain more than 30 per cent. of clay, they do not yield cement by burning, as in that case the substance does not form a sufficiently adhesive paste.

The burning of hydraulic limestone, and especially that of the cements, requires peculiar care. If the temperature be too elevated, the material becomes too compact, in consequence of too intimate a combination of the lime with the silicate of alumina, and no new compound is formed when it is mixed with water. The heat should be as low as possible, and only sufficient to drive off the greater part of the carbonic acid of the carbonate of lime and the water in the clay.

§ 655. Slightly aggregated silex and clay are not the only substances which impart hydraulic qualities to lime. Magnesia, to a certain extent, though in a less degree, has the same property: thus many of the magnesian limestones, some of the dolomites for example, yield, on burning, an inferior quality of hydraulic lime. The hydraulic properties of these magnesian limes depend evidently on a chemical combination which takes place, in water, between the hydrate of lime and the hydrate of magnesia. It has even been ascertained that a very intimate mixture of quicklime and carbonate of lime possess, in a low degree, hydraulic properties: thus limestone, burned at a moderate temperature, so that a great portion of it remains in the state of carbonate, yields a feebly hydraulic lime: in burning lime, pieces imperfectly calcined, and possessing this property, are always found: lime-burners call these the *core*. The hydraulic quality of an intimate mixture of quicklime and carbonate of lime should be attributed to the formation, in water, of a compound of carbonate of lime and hydrate of lime, which we have mentioned (§ 551).

Quartzose sands are frequently mixed with cements, and especially with hydraulic limes, so as to increase their hardness, and give greater volume to the mortar.

§ 656. Hydraulic limes are made artificially by calcining intimate mixtures of fat lime and clay. Lime of this nature has been used for the construction of the majority of the buildings in Paris, it being cheaper than the native hydraulic lime brought from a distance. Artificial hydraulic lime is made at Paris, by diluting, in water, a mixture of 4 parts of chalk of Mendon with 1 part of clay from the same locality, and grinding the whole by vertical wheels revolving in a circular track. The pulp, partly dried, is moulded into bricks, which are dried in the air, and then calcined in furnaces at a proper degree of heat.

HYDRAULIC MORTARS MADE WITH FAT LIME.

§ 657. *Hydraulic mortars* are also made by mixing fat lime with burnt clay, or certain porous rocks resembling, in composition, burnt clay. In the environs of Pozzuoli, near Naples, is found a porous rock, of volcanic origin, which possesses in an eminent degree the property of forming hydraulic mortar with fat lime: it is called *pozzuolana*, and was formerly extensively imported from Italy. Now, several formations of similar rocks are known: the majority of the volcanic tufas, found on the borders of the Rhine, in Auvergne, etc., possess similar properties. The name *pozzuolana* has been given to all these substances. It is, moreover, well known, that the greater part of burnt clay, when not too highly calcined, is an excellent substitute for the pozzuolana of Italy. Common bricks, tiles, and ordinary earthenware give, when pounded, a very good artificial pozzuolana.

The chemical reaction by which a mixture of fat lime and pozzuolana acquires hydraulic properties is shown by the following experiment:—The surface of a common brick, left for some time in lime-water, turns completely white, by becoming covered with a pellicle of caustic lime, which the water cannot dissolve. If finely powdered pozzuolana be left for some days in a well-corked bottle filled with lime-water, it seizes on all the lime, and, after some time, the water evinces no alkaline reaction on the red tincture of litmus. These experiments show the affinity of pozzuolana for hydrated lime. Therefore, if a mortar made with an intimate mixture of powdered pozzuolana and water sets, it is because the hydrated lime attaches itself strongly to the pozzuolana, by virtue of a special affinity, and thus becomes insoluble in water.

Mortars made of fat lime and pozzuolana acquire, in time, an intense degree of hardness. This may be seen in the remaining ruins of Roman edifices, in which these mortars were exclusively used, and in which the durability of the cement is frequently found to have outlived that of the building material used in their construction.

CONCRETE.

§ 658. In moist situations, we are frequently obliged to make an artificial impervious soil, to receive the foundation of buildings, by mixing hydraulic mortar with small stones. Two or three parts of broken, angular stones are generally used for 1 part of mortar. This mixture, called *concrete*, is spread over a level surface, on which the hewn stones can easily rest. It sets in a few days, and becomes perfectly impervious to moisture.

ANALYSIS OF LIMESTONES.

§ 659. We have said that an idea could be formed, from the chemical composition of a limestone, of the nature of the lime it would yield after burning. The analysis of limestone is therefore very important, and inquirers cannot be too earnestly recommended to analyze the various limestone strata in the vicinity of the works they are constructing: they may thus discover lime similar to that they are obliged to transport, at a heavy expense, from a distance.

Limestone is readily analyzed. What is chiefly to be determined is the carbonate of lime and that of magnesia, the oxides of iron and manganese, the clay, and the proportion of water combined with the clay and the metallic oxides.

Ten grammes of limestone, broken into small pieces, are calcined at a strong white-heat in a platinum crucible: the loss of weight p then represents the carbonic acid and the water. Ten other grammes of powdered limestone are then dissolved in weak chlorohydric acid, which, taking into solution the carbonates of lime and magnesia and the metallic oxides, leave only the clay and qüartzose sand. This residue is collected on a small filter and calcined, after having been washed with a small quantity of boiling water: its weight p' represents the anhydrous clay and the quartz. The appearance of this residue at once shows it to be composed of clay alone, because it then forms a light soft powder: any grains of sand it may contain are easily recognised by the touch; and these quartzose particles may be separated by levigation in a glass. The chlorohydric solution, added to the water of the washing, is evaporated at a moderate heat to drive off the excess of acid, is again treated with water, and the liquid introduced into a bottle holding 2 litres, which can be corked. This bottle is filled with perfectly clear lime-water, well shaken, and then allowed to rest; the oxides of iron and manganese and the magnesia are thus precipitated. The clear fluid is drawn off with a siphon, after having ascertained that it possesses a decided alkaline reaction, to be sure that an excess of lime-water has been employed: the precipitate is quickly collected on a filter, washed, and then recalcined.

In general, it suffices to ascertain the weight p'' of the precipitate, and judge from its colour whether it is formed chiefly of the hydrate or sesquioxide of iron. When limestone is analyzed merely with a view to its technical application, the separation is carried no further. It is evident that if the weight p' be subtracted from the weight $(10-p)$, the difference $(10-p-p')$ will represent the weight of the lime: it is easy then to determine by calculation, 1st, the weight q of carbonic acid which forms carbonate of lime with this quantity of lime; 2dly, the weight q' of this same acid, which forms carbonate of magnesia with the precipitate p'' given by the lime-water, if this precipitate be considered as magnesia, $(q+q')$ then represents the weight of the carbonic acid in the limestone, and consequently $p-(q+q')$ represents the water combined with the clay.

But if the composition of the limestone is to be ascertained more exactly, the precipitate yielded by the lime-water must be analyzed. This precipitate, in addition to the oxides of iron, manganese, and magnesia, may contain a small quantity of alumina, arising from the circumstance of the clay of the limestone having been attacked by the chlorohydric acid, if the latter has been too concentrated. The precipitate is dissolved in chlorohydric acid, and a slight excess of ammonia is added to the liquid: the quantity of sal ammoniac formed by the saturation is sufficient to prevent the precipitation of the magnesia and the oxide of manganese, and the oxides of iron and alumina are alone precipitated. They are collected on a small filter, in order to separate the liquid, and immediately redissolved, by sprinkling on the filter a few drops of weak chlorohydric acid: an excess of caustic potash, which precipitates the hydrate of peroxide of iron and redissolves the alumina, is then added. The peroxide of iron should be well washed with boiling water, because it obstinately retains a small quantity of potassa. The alkaline liquid containing the alumina is supersaturated by chlorohydric acid, and the alumina is precipitated hot by carbonate or sulfhydrate of ammonia. In order to separate the magnesia and oxide of manganese in the same solution, sulfhydrate of ammonia is added, which precipitates sulphuret of manganese, and, after the separation of this precipitate, the magnesia is obtained as ammoniaco-phosphate of magnesia by an addition of ammonia and phosphate of ammonia.

§ 660. Magnesian limestone may be analyzed in another way, by determining the lime directly instead of ascertaining its weight by a difference, as in the preceding method. The limestone is dissolved in weak chlorohydric acid, the insoluble clay separated, and the liquid saturated with ammonia, which precipitates the oxide of iron and the alumina, the large proportion of ammoniacal salts contained in the liquid preventing the precipitation of both the magnesia and the oxide of manganese. The precipitate is allowed to settle, keeping the vessel corked: the fluid is poured off, and the precipitate collected on a filter. It is important to operate quickly, in order to prevent the ammonia from absorbing carbonic acid from the air, and precipitating the lime as carbonate. Oxalate of ammonia is added to the filtered liquid, giving a precipitate of oxalate of lime, the ammoniacal salts existing in the solution again preventing the precipitation of the magnesia. The oxide of manganese and the magnesia are then separated successively, as in the preceding method.

VARIOUS MASTICS.

§ 661. We shall here indicate the composition of the principal mastics used in building, in the manufacture of different chemical products, and also in the laboratory, where they are used for luting and rendering chemical apparatus impervious to gases.

Bitumen or asphaltum is one of the chief mastics used in building: it is employed for foot-walks, terraces, etc. It is prepared by mixing native or artificial bitumen, melted, with sand. This mastic is run into sheets; it is made very smooth, and in a few hours acquires great consistency. The effect of the sand is to render the bitumen less friable, and prevent it from wearing away too rapidly. The origin and composition of bitumen will be treated of under the head of organic chemistry.

A very hard mastic is made by mixing eight or ten parts of pounded bricks with one part of litharge and linseed oil. This is called *Dhil's mastic*: it is used for mending and pointing stone walls. The stones should be moistened before applying the mastic, so as not to absorb the oil contained in the composition. After a few days, Dhil's mastic becomes as hard as stone: it is impervious to water.

Another mastic, which becomes very hard, and is hydraulic, is prepared by mixing ten parts of sand with one part of lime, or with four or five parts of chalk, and tempering the mixture with linseed oil rendered drying by boiling with litharge.

For repairing stones, and particularly marble, a mastic called *mastic of white of eggs* is frequently employed, which is made by tempering powdered quicklime with albumen of eggs. A similar mastic is prepared by substituting white cheese for the white of eggs.

In order to fasten cast-iron pipes, laminæ of lead are generally used, strongly compressed by screws between the flanges of the pipe. Sometimes the pipes enter each other, and then a mastic is interposed, which soon adheres with great tenacity and becomes very hard: this consists of 50 parts of iron filings, or still better of cast iron, 1 part of sal ammoniac and 1 part of sulphur: the mixture is moistened with water at the moment of application. After some time a chemical reaction takes place, in consequence of the combination of the surface of the iron filings with the sulphur and the chlorine of the sal ammoniac, and the mixture becomes solid.

To join the various parts of machines, a mastic prepared of minium and linseed oil is used. This mastic is compressed between the pieces to be joined, and becomes very hard after some time. When the spaces to be closed are large, rolls of hemp soaked in this mastic are used.

Glazier's putty is a mixture of carbonate of lead and a drying oil.

In chemical laboratories, several mastics are used to close hermetically the joints of various apparatus. The best is the *plumber's mastic*, made of a mixture of resin, tallow, and colcothar, to to which pounded brick is frequently added. This mastic is applied hot, and may be made as fusible as may be necessary by an addition of a suitable quantity of resin and wax. Sealing-wax may be used for the same purpose, especially for covering corks, which thus become impervious to gases. Ordinary sealing-wax is however too brittle, and should be mixed with a small quantity of wax and tallow.

The luting generally used in the laboratory for covering the stoppers of tubes is prepared by pounding almond paste with starch paste.

In the manufacture of chemical products, lutings formed of quicklime, clay, and white of egg are used; they are kept on the joints by a cloth. Sometimes, a mixture of calcined plaster and starch, tempered with water, is used.

For joining parts of philosophical apparatus, a mastic of melted caoutchouc or a mixture of wax and tallow is generally used.

§ 662. The disengaging-tubes of chemical apparatus are generally fastened by means of corks: for this purpose, only the finest and softest corks should be chosen. They are pierced by means of a round file, slightly conical, called a *rat-tail file*, and made to fit tightly around the tube.

When it is desired to render the joint absolutely impervious to gases, the corks must be covered with resin mastic; a precaution which is indispensable for apparatus used in analysis, the weight of which should not vary with the external conditions of the atmosphere. Mastic applied to the corks preserves them from the contact of the air.

Glass tubes are joined together by caoutchouc tubing, fastened with silk thread or fine wire: an hermetically closed joint is thus obtained, which resists the action of the majority of gases, provided the internal pressure does not greatly exceed that of the atmosphere. Ready-made caoutchouc tubes can be bought. In the laboratory, however, they are most frequently made with sheet caoutchouc (fig. 406), because then any required size can be given to them. To make them, a small sheet of caoutchouc is applied to the glass tube, and with long, sharp, and *clean* scissors, the edges are divided, and will immediately unite at the cut on being gently pressed together, forming a tube exactly fitting the glass.

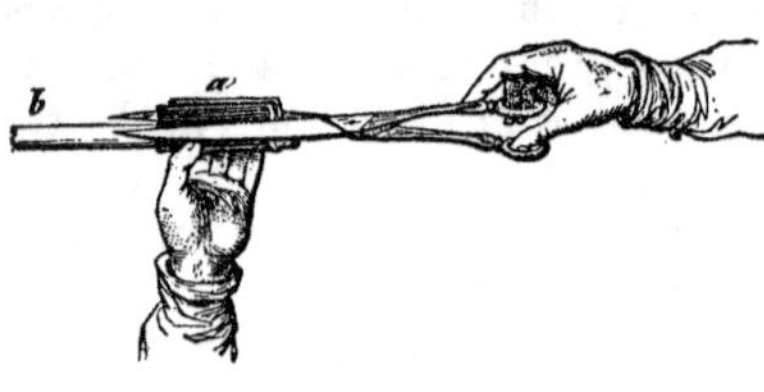

Fig. 406.

When the gas in the apparatus is very elastic, caoutchouc tubes cannot be used, as they would soon swell and burst. In order to join the two tubes in such a case, their ends *a* and *c* (fig. 407) are ground until they accurately fit each other, and then covered with a copper tube *ef*, which is fastened with resin mastic applied hot, as seen in fig. 408. It is well to cover the ends of the tubes with melted mastic before passing the copper tube over them: in this way a tight joint is certain to be obtained, and the action of the gas, if of a corrosive nature, on the metallic tube is effectually prevented.

Fig. 407.
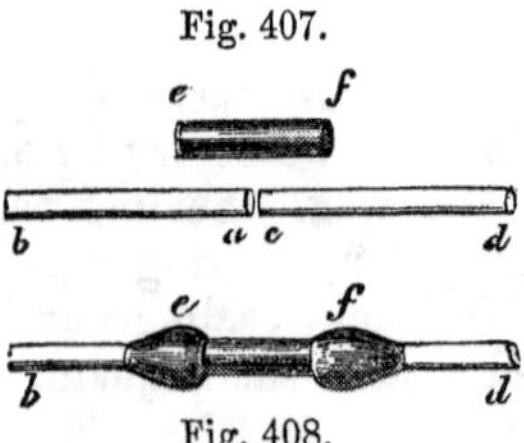

Fig. 408.

GLASS.

§ 663. The appellation of *glass* is given to hard substances endowed with a certain degree of transparency and presenting a peculiar kind of fracture, called *vitreous*. In this point of view, many fusible substances which, on cooling, do not crystallize easily, such as phosphoric and boracic acids, should be classed among the *glasses;* but, in common parlance, the name *glass* is exclusively applied to double transparent silicates, which are worked when hot by blowing, and which are unchangeable in water.

Glass is generally composed of a double silicate of lime and potassa or soda. In many kinds, as in bottle-glass, the alkaline silicates are partly replaced by very fusible metallic silicates, such as the silicates of iron; in some, oxide of lead is also substituted for the lime. This last kind bears the name of *crystal*.

Before treating of the properties and composition of the various kinds of glass used in the arts, it is necessary to examine, more in detail than we have hitherto done, the properties of the simple silicates which enter into its composition.

ALKALINE SILICATES.

§ 664. The only silicates used in the manufacture of glass are the silicates of potassa and soda, the most fusible of all the silicates; their degree of fusibility greatly varying, however, with the proportion of the base. In order to express clearly the composition of the simple or multiple silicates, the ratio existing between the oxygen of the silicic acid and that of the united bases is generally indicated, as well as the proportion of the quantities of oxygen contained in the several bases.

If silicic acid is fused with 2 or 3 times its weight of potassa or soda, a substance is obtained apparently homogeneous, melting at a red-heat, and completely soluble in cold water. Silex, fused with an equal weight of potassa or soda, also produces a homogeneous substance, readily fusible, but no longer completely soluble in water. As the proportion of alkali diminishes, the vitreous mass becomes more difficult of fusion: an alkaline silicate, in which the oxygen of the alkali is to that of the silicic acid as 1 : 18, fuses only at the highest temperature of a forge-fire.

Soluble glass is a vitreous product obtained by melting together, in an earthen crucible, 15 parts of sand, 10 of carbonate of potassa, and 1 of charcoal. This substance, treated with cold water, parts only with the foreign salts which were mixed with the carbonate of potassa; but is itself completely dissolved in 4 or 5 times its weight of boiling water. It has been proposed to use this substance to render cloth, and particularly theatrical decorations, incombustible.* In fact, if a coat of this solution be applied to any stuff, it remains covered, after drying, with a transparent and fusible varnish, which preserves it from the air; and it burns with difficulty, because the silicate prevents the access of the air. The stuff merely carbonizes, and does not favour the progress of the fire, as would be the case if its surface were free. Many fusible and non-efflorescent salts, among which are the phosphate and borate of ammonia, would produce the same effect.

The silicates of potassa and soda are distinguished by the property of not crystallizing on cooling after fusion, owing to their passing from the state of perfect liquidity to that of a solid, not suddenly, but through all the intermediate doughey conditions. This property accompanies the alkaline silicates in their combination with the other metallic silicates, and is very important, as it facilitates the working of these multiple silicates by blowing; and, moreover, the substance retains its transparency after cooling.

Silicates of Lime.

§ 665. The silicates of lime melt at only very high temperatures. The most fusible compound is that resulting from the union of silicic acid with lime, in such proportions that the oxygen of the lime is to that of the silicic acid as 1 : 3; this silicate melts in a strong forge fire, and becomes crystalline on cooling. The silicates of lime, having a ratio of 1 : 4 or 1 : 1 between the oxygen of the base and that of the acid, do not fuse completely, only softening in the highest heat that can be produced in a forge-fire.

Silicates of Magnesia.

§ 666. The silicates of magnesia are as difficult of fusion as those of lime. The most fusible is that of which the formula is MgO,SiO_3; it melts in a strong forge-fire.

Silicates of Alumina.

§ 667. The silicates of alumina are still more infusible than those of lime and magnesia. The silicate $Al_2O_3,3SiO_3$, which appears the

---

* In Germany, this combination, known by the name of *wasserglas*, a large manufactory of which is at Prague, is extensively employed for rendering especially the wooden work of buildings incombustible, and protecting them at the same time from decomposition, (rotting.) In England it is used for the same purpose, made up with various pigments, as *silica colours*. It probably would also make an excellent artificial marble, capable of being moulded into architectural ornaments, or spread as a plaster on walls, when made up with proper proportions of porcelain-clay, or, perhaps, even chalk or plaster of Paris, with a slight admixture of borax. It was first obtained by Fuchs, at Munich.— *W. L. F.*

most fusible, merely softens in a forge-fire. All these silicates melt easily in the oxy-hydrogen blowpipe; for we have seen (§ 596 and § 243) that alumina and silex melt separately in the powerful heat produced by this apparatus.

Silicates of the Protoxide of Iron and Manganese.

§ 668. These silicates, which enter into the composition of some kinds of glass, melt much more readily than the silicates of the earths and those of the alkaline earths. The silicates FeO,SiO_3 and MnO,SiO_3 may be melted in the common furnaces of our laboratories: they all crystallize easily by slow cooling.

Silicates of Lead.

§ 669. The silicates of lead are fusible in proportion to the quantity of oxide of lead they contain; that showing the composition PbO,SiO_3 melts at a strong red-heat. The silicates of lead crystallize with difficulty; the cooling must take place very slowly in order to obtain any indices of crystallization in the mass.

Multiple Silicates, formed by the Alkalies, the Alkaline Earths, the Earths, and Metallic Oxides.

§ 670. Several multiple silicates, in the form of beautiful crystals, are found in nature. We have seen (§ 601) that feldspar is a double silicate of alumina and potassa, of the formula $KO,SiO_3 + Al_2O_3,3SiO_3$. This mineral melts in a forge-fire, and does not crystallize during the very slow cooling of a porcelain-furnace; but crystals of this compound have been found in the fissures of iron blast-furnaces, showing the same form as those of native feldspar.

When the alkaline silicates are melted with other metallic silicates, vitreous substances are generally obtained after cooling, which appear homogeneous, and crystallize only when the cooling is extremely slow. But it is difficult to decide whether these substances are formed by a homogeneous chemical combination, or whether they merely result from a solution of various silicates in each other; a solution which has set in mass, without crystallizing during the process of cooling.

The temperature at which a multiple silicate fuses is almost always below the medium temperature of fusion of the various simple silicates which compose it; sometimes it is even below that of the most fusible silicate entering into the combination. Thus, the simple silicates of alumina and lime are nearly infusible in our forge-fires, but they form, when combined, double silicates which readily melt in these fires.

By adding to a silicate which crystallizes easily on cooling, one which has not this tendency, for example an alkaline silicate, double silicates are obtained, which crystallize with great difficulty, and preserve their vitreous appearance after cooling. Thus the double silicates of potassa or soda, combined with those of lime or oxide of iron, do not crystallize after fusion. Silicate of alumina likewise opposes the crystallization of the multiple silicates into which it enters, although less effectually than the alkaline silicates.

The silicates of potassa and soda lose by volatilization a large proportion of their bases. Thus it may be explained how the multiple silicates containing alkaline silicates become less and less fusible as these are allowed to remain for a longer time in furnaces at a very high temperature, and acquire, with time, the property of crystallizing by slow cooling, at the same time losing their vitreous appearance.

We have seen that the alkaline silicates which contain a large proportion of alkali are soluble in water. When they contain more silex, they are not attacked by this fluid, but they may be by powerful acids; but when they are still richer in silex, even acids do not affect them. The silicates of lime, alumina, and oxide of lead are attacked by acids when they contain a large proportion of base, but they are intangible when rich in silex. Fluohydric acid, however, decomposes every silicate, whatever proportion of silicic acid it may contain, for it attacks quartz itself (§ 243).

By combining the alkaline silicates with silicate of lime, double silicates are obtained sufficiently fusible to be worked by blowing, and nevertheless containing enough silicic acid to resist the action of acids.

§ 671. We shall divide the various kinds of glass into three grand classes:

1st. Common colourless glass, which is a double silicate of lime and potassa or soda.

2d. Common coloured glass, or bottle-glass, a multiple silicate of lime, oxide of iron, alumina, and potassa or soda.

3d. Crystal, which is a double silicate of potassa and oxide of lead.

1st. *Colourless Glass.*

§ 672. Common colourless or white glass, which is used for making tumblers, window-glass, and looking-glasses, is a double silicate of lime and potassa or soda, either of these being preferred according to its price. Carbonate of soda being much cheaper in France than carbonate of potassa, is almost exclusively employed in the manufacture of white glass; in Germany and the north of Europe the potassa, being cheaper, is preferred. The selection of these bases is not a matter of indifference. Soda yields a more fusible and easily worked glass, but it is always more or less coloured by a greenish-yellow tinge, not perceptible when the glass is very thin, but very decided when it is thicker, as, for example, in a window-pane.

§ 673. The most beautiful glass having a base of potassa and lime is the Bohemian. This glass, made with the utmost care from choice materials, is remarkable for its lightness, its brilliant transparency, and permanency. The ratio between the oxygen of the silicic acid and that of the bases is at 4 : 1, sometimes rising to 6 : 1; the oxygen of the lime is to that of the potassa as 1 : $\frac{2}{3}$ in the most esteemed tumbler-glass of Bohemia. This proportion is as 1 : 1 in the glass used for mirrors, in which great fusibility is required. The proportion of silex is increased in order to make hard and infusible glass; in this way the Bohemian glass tubes for chemical purposes are made, as they are much less fusible than the French glass, and therefore preferable for organic analysis.

The silex used in Bohemia is the hyalin quartz of the old rocks, found in the form of large pebbles in the fields or the beds of the mountain streams. This quartz is heated to a strong red-heat in a reverberatory furnace, and then thrown into cold water, by which it becomes very friable, and is then, without difficulty, finely powdered by stampers, or ground by edge-stones.

The carbonate of potassa used in the manufacture of Bohemian glass is the refined carbonate; nevertheless, this salt is never pure, some carbonate of soda always being mixed with it. The crude potashes are carefully selected and refined by solution: the crude potash, on being treated with one-half its weight of water, leaves the foreign salts, as well as a considerable quantity of carbonate of potassa, as a residue. The solution yields, when evaporated, potassa for the manufacture of first-quality glass, while the remainder serves for that of an inferior quality.

The lime is obtained by subjecting a very pure and often perfectly white saccharoid carbonate of lime to calcination in a reverberatory furnace.

§ 674. When these materials, however carefully they may have been selected, contain a small quantity of protoxide of iron, a greenish tinge, which greatly lessens its commercial value, is imparted to the glass. This discoloration is remarkably destroyed by adding to the mixture a small quantity of peroxide of manganese. The protoxide of iron imparts a deep green colour to glass, when present in any quantity; but, if converted into a sesquioxide, it gives a scarcely perceptible yellow tinge. Sesquioxide of manganese colours the glass violet; but a corresponding quantity of protoxide scarcely produces a sensible change. If, therefore, to a mixture to which protoxide of iron would give a high colour, a quantity of peroxide of manganese sufficient to transform the protoxide of iron into a sesquioxide, by passing itself into the state of a protoxide of manganese, is added, a nearly white glass is obtained; for the colour it then has is due only to the sesquioxide of iron, which produces a scarcely perceptible yellow tinge, the protoxide of manganese effecting no colouring at all. But it is important not to use an excess of peroxide of manganese, because the glass would have a violet shade, owing to the formation of sesquioxide of manganese. Peroxide of manganese, on account of this special use, is called the *glass-maker's soap*, (savon des verriers.)

Frequently, also, a small quantity of arsenious acid is added to the mixture: as this acid is completely volatilized during the melting of the glass, none of it remains in the objects manufactured: its object is merely to render the mixture more homogeneous, or to facilitate the *refining* of the glass. By volatilizing at a high temperature, it forms bubbles of gas, which, on traversing the fluid mass, mix its several particles together, and precipitate the solid material scattered through it.

§ 675. The fuel used in Bohemia is a resinous wood, burning with a bright flame and causing a very rapid fusion. The air of the furnace being always oxidizing, no alteration of the glass need be feared by the carbonaceous dust or other particles contained in the smoke. An admixture of carbon would considerably injure the quality of the glass and discolour it; but when it exists in small quantity, the glass assumes a beautiful yellow colour: these coloured glasses are often made expressly. When it is present in somewhat greater quantity, the glass assumes a purple-red colour. Peroxide of manganese opposes also this discoloration of glass by carbon, an accident which frequently happens when the furnace has no proper draught. In some glass-houses, it is prevented by the addition of a small quantity of nitrate of potassa.

A white glass of first quality is made, by melting together

110 parts of pulverized quartz;
64 " refined carbonate of potassa;
24 " caustic lime.

In other glass-factories in Bohemia, beautiful tumbler-glass is made of a mixture of

120 parts of pulverized quartz;
60 " refined carbonate of potassa;
25 " caustic lime;
½ " arsenious acid;
2 " peroxide of manganese;
2 " nitre.

§ 676. First-quality white glass is made in France of white quartzose sand, artificial soda, quicklime, and a certain proportion of fragments of glass: in this glass the ratio of the oxygen of the silicic acid to that of the united bases is ordinarily as 4 : 1. This composition gives an easily fusible, but slightly tender glass: when a harder glass is desired, the proportion of silicic acid is increased.

A fine sand, as white as possible, is selected, and sometimes made more friable, by heating it to redness, and throwing it in that state into cold water. The sands from Aumont, near Senlis, from Etampes and Fontainebleau are highly esteemed, and are exclusively used in the glass-factories in the environs of Paris. The lime is obtained from a limestone as pure as possible, and previously calcined in an oven to drive off the carbonic acid; it is then exposed to the air, and falls to dust. It is sometimes used in the state of carbonate of lime, finely powdered. Very white chalk, as that from Bougival, near Paris, is perfectly adapted to this purpose.

For first-quality white glass, the carbonate of soda obtained in the manufacture of artificial soda is used. For the inferior qualities, sulphate of soda, which is cheaper than the carbonate, is substituted; but, as the sulphate of soda is decomposed by silicic acid only at a very high temperature, at which the crucibles would soon be destroyed, a certain quantity of charcoal is added: this facilitates its decomposition, by abstracting a portion of the oxygen from the sulphuric acid, thus causing it to pass into the state of sulphurous acid, for which the affinity of soda is much more feeble. One part of charcoal is generally mixed with 12 or 14 of sulphate of soda.

§ 677. The materials, intimately mixed, undergo a preliminary calcination called *frit*, before being placed in the melting-pots, intended to commence the combination, and at the same time to allow the substance to be introduced into the melting-pots already heated to redness. The breaking of the pots by sudden cooling is thus avoided, and the fusion is more rapid.

Figs. 409 and 410 represent a glass furnace for the manufacture of window-glass. Fig. 410 gives a horizontal section made at the height of the line AB of fig. 409: fig. 409 represents a vertical section of the oven, in the direction of the line CD of fig. 410. The oven is composed of an arched space M, in the middle of which is the grate G above the ash-hole. On each side of the grate are two shelves F, of strong mason-work, on which the pots I, I are placed: the pots are introduced through several doors in the upright wall of the oven, which are subsequently closed up with bricks. A circular opening *o* is preserved above each pot, large enough to allow the material to be withdrawn and to introduce into the oven the object to be manufactured. The flame of the fuel on the grate G rises in the oven M: it is then conducted by openings into the lateral ovens N, N, called *arches*, in which the preliminary preparation is made, the *frit* of the mixture: in these same arches, the new pots are kept for a long while before introducing them into the principal oven, in order gradually to

Fig. 409.

Fig. 410.

prepare them to bear the high temperature of the ovens, and render them stronger. The flame and smoke, having passed through the ovens N, escape by the flues.

Each pot is attended by two workmen, a master glass-blower and an assistant. The master-blower, standing on a small wooden bridge L, raised from 1 to 1½ metre above the ground, is thus enabled to dip into the pots and handle the pieces he is about to blow. Small walls *n*, *n* separate the working-spaces of each pot, in order that the blower may not be inconvenienced by the heat of the adjoining working-hole.

§ 678. Great care is required in the manufacture of the melting-pots: only the most infusible clays can be used: the process will be described under the head of earthenware. They are generally 0.7 m. to 0.9. m. in depth, and will hold about 400 or 500 kilog. of melted material.

The pots, when newly made, are kept for several months in hot rooms, so as to dry slowly. They are then introduced into the arches of an oven, the temperature of which is not very high, and are gradually and slowly brought nearer to those parts of the arch where the heat is greatest. They are introduced into the principal furnace only after having been subjected to a very high temperature. Each pot should serve for several meltings: it is rarely necessary to replace all the pots of a furnace by new ones. They are thrown aside, as they wear out, and a sufficient supply should always be kept in the arches, to replace those which are destroyed.

§ 679. The mixture of the material is generally composed of

100 parts of sand;		
35 to 40	"	chalk;
30 to 35	"	carbonate of soda, or an equivalent quantity of a mixture of sulphate of soda and charcoal;
50 to 150	"	broken glass, or *cullet*.

These materials, intimately mixed, are set to frit in an arch of the furnace; where they are turned from time to time, in order to render the mixture more uniform. The fire on the grate is made to burn actively after the working-holes of the furnace have been closed. The workman deposits the frit in the pots, removing it red-hot from the arch with a shovel: after the addition of each shovelful, he waits until the material is melted before adding another, and so on until the pot is filled. He then leaves it to itself for several hours, in order to clear it of bubbles of air and foreign substances which rise to the surface. These substances, called *glassgall*,* are formed by alkaline salts in excess, which have not been decomposed by the silicic acid: they are particularly numerous when impure carbonate of soda has been used, or when a mixture of sulphate of soda and charcoal has been substituted for it. The workman generally removes them with an iron ladle. From time to time he extracts a small quantity of melted glass, and judges of its quality by its appearance after solidification.

§ 680. When the glass is sufficiently fused, the temperature of the furnace is lowered, in order to bring the glass to a consistency fit for working. We shall not attempt to describe the processes of glass-blowing in detail, but merely that adopted in France for the making of window-glass.

§ 681. The *pipe* (fig. 411) is the principal tool of the master-blower. It is an iron tube, 1.50 m. in length, having a perforation through its long axis of 3 millimetres in diameter: it is covered externally, to a distance of about 35 centimetres, by a wooden tube *cd*, to protect the workman's hand from the intense heat.

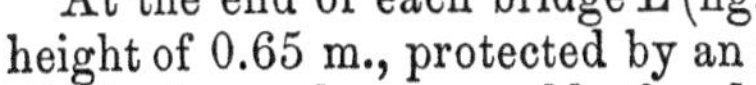

b c d a

Fig. 411.

At the end of each bridge L (fig. 410) is a small platform, of the height of 0.65 m., protected by an iron plate, called the *marver*, on which the workman moulds the doughey glass (fig. 412) adhering

* Also called *sandiver* or, commonly, *salts*.—*Trans.*

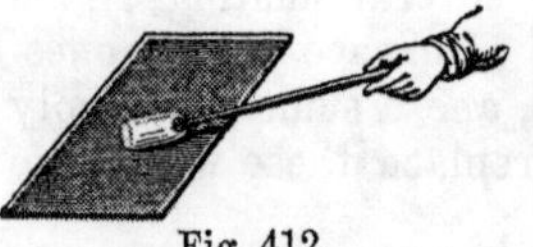

Fig. 412.

to the end of the pipe into the proper shape for blowing. Near the *marver* is a wooden block, containing several hemispherical or pear-shaped cavities, which are kept constantly moist.

The pipes are heated in a small opening at the base of the furnace. The workman, taking one, dips it into the glass, collects a certain quantity, withdraws it, and turns it so that the fluid glass may not separate, then collects an additional quantity, and hands the pipe thus charged to the master-blower. The latter, having received it, rests it on the iron platform, always turning it, dips it again into the pot, and then returns quickly to the platform with a mass of red-hot glass, and rests it, still keeping up the rotary motion, in the water which fills the cavity of the block. He then draws the greater portion of the glass which envelops the sides toward the end of the pipe, by means of a sheet-iron blade (fig. 413).

Fig. 413.

The mass of glass, cooled by the water, but adhering to the end of the pipe, is carried back to the working-hole to be softened. When the workman thinks it is soft enough, he withdraws the pipe, and recommences the same manipulation in the water, but at the same time blows in the pipe, so as to give the glass the shape of a sphere of about 3 decimetres in diameter (fig. 414), and then suddenly lifts the pipe into the air, and blows the sphere above his head. The upper part of the sphere then sinks by its own weight, and the bulb spreads horizontally (fig. 415). By suddenly dipping the pipe, the sphere assumes the shape of fig. 416. The workman then swings the pipe backward and forward, like the pendulum of a clock, blowing from time to time through the pipe while making this movement, so that, by the simultaneous action of weight and blowing, the glass balloon elongates and assumes the shape of a cylinder (fig. 417). The glass cylinder can rarely be brought to the proper dimensions by one operation, but generally must be heated several times in the oven. When the cylinder is finished, the master-blower rests the pipe on a portable hook which the assistant arranges in the direction of the working-hole, and introducing the cylinder into the furnace so that its end becomes excessively heated, blows through the pipe with the whole force of his lungs, until the cylinder is pierced. The piercing of the cylinder is also often effected in another manner: the assistant fastens, by means of a pipe, a small quantity of very hot glass to the extremity *o* of the cylinder; this end the workman dips into the oven, and blows forcibly through the pipe, or simply stops its orifice with his finger. The pressure of the internal air bursts the end *o*, where the glass has been softened by the drop

Fig. 414.

Fig. 415.

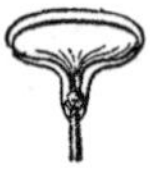

Fig. 416.

of hot glass (fig. 418). The workman then removes the cylinder from the fire, and the assistant cuts off with scissors the convexity of the cylinder, so as to open it entirely (fig. 419); the blower then moves the pipe with great rapidity, either by swinging it or causing it to revolve completely. This manœuvre cools the glass rapidly, at the same time preventing the object being made from becoming misshaped. When the glass is solid, the blower gives the pipe to the assistant, who, resting it on a trestle, at the same time applies a drop of water, taken up with a bent iron rod, to the point of junction of the pipe and cylinder, and, by a slight blow on the middle of the pipe, detaches the cylinder.

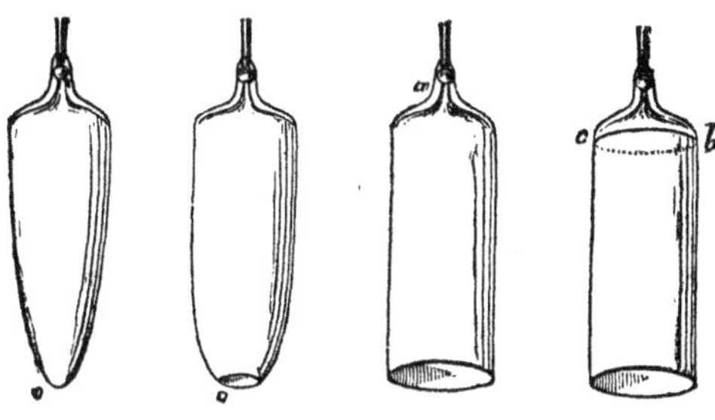

Fig. 417. Fig. 418. Fig. 419. Fig. 420.

The cylinders thus prepared are intended for window-glass; but, being as yet open at one end and closed at the other, this end must also be opened. As the panes must have a given size, the workman applies to the upper edge of the cylinder a stick on which the size of the pane is marked; then, without moving the stick, he dips from the pot, with an iron rod, a drop of glass, which is elongated by drawing out: by applying this red-hot glass thread to the circumference *cb* of the cylinder (fig. 420), at the line to be separated, a very accurate division is immediately effected.

§ 682. The glass cylinders are then carried to the *flattening* furnace (figs. 421 and 422), which is composed of two adjacent ovens V, U, separated only by a very small thin brick wall, extending from the floor to the roof. Beneath this partition-wall is an opening *ii*, of 1 metre in breadth, and a few centimetres only in height, serving for the passage of the panes, which having been flattened in the first compartment V, are reheated and slowly cooled in the chamber U. Both compartments are heated by furnaces beneath. The cylinders to be flattened are laid on a table: a drop of water is passed over the upper edge

Fig. 421.

Fig. 422.

ed (fig. 423), followed by a red-hot iron, which effects a clean fracture throughout the whole length: after this the cylinders are presented to the opening O (fig. 422) of the flattening furnace, being gradually introduced into it by means of two grooves, which regulate their progress; thus avoiding a too sudden heating, which might crack them. When the workman sees that the cylinders are about bending on themselves, he takes the hottest on the end of an iron rule, and draws it into the middle of the furnace, near the flatting plate V (fig. 422), which is often made of cast-iron, and sometimes of thick plate-glass, dusted with a little plaster to prevent adhesion. This plate is placed immediately in front of the longitudinal opening *ii*, through which the pane must pass to enter the baking furnace U: its upper surface should also be exactly on a level with the floor of the furnace, so that the pane of glass may meet with no impediment in its progress.

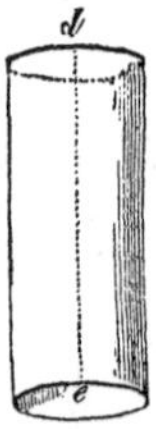

Fig. 423.

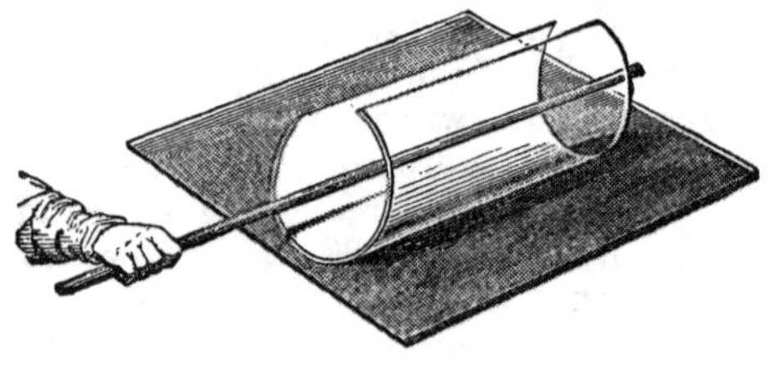

Fig. 424.

Fig. 425.

The cylinder having reached the plate, the workman, armed with his rule, presses down to the right and left the two sides, which yield readily to the weight of the rule (fig. 424). He then takes another iron bar (fig. 425), terminating in a highly polished piece, and applying this polished part on the glass, passes it rapidly over the surface, so as to flatten it perfectly.

The pane, properly flattened, is pushed through the longitudinal opening *ii* into the second compartment U, where the temperature is much lower; a workman passes beneath it a thin iron rule, terminating in a fork (fig. 426), and raising the pane, which is already firm enough not to bend, rests it in a vertical position against an iron bar *ff* (fig. 422), which passes through the whole length of the

Fig. 426.

oven. A number of panes are thus heaped on each other, until the workman deems it sufficient. A second horizontal bar is then arranged, on which additional panes are disposed, and so on until the compartment U is nearly filled. The furnace is then allowed to cool; and the glass, when withdrawn, is ready for sale.

Clock-shades, decanters, tumblers, etc. are made of the same glass.

Inferior glass articles, such as common window-glass, apothecaries' phials, etc., are made of less pure materials: they are commonly coloured green by protoxide of iron.

§ 683. In France, the base of plate-glass is a mixture of soda and lime, and the oxygen of the silicic acid is to that of the united bases as 6 : 1. For the same quantity of lime, a quantity of carbonate of soda is added double of that contained in window-glass, because it is necessary to give greater fusibility to plate-glass.

In the plate-glass factory of Saint-Gobain, which is the largest in France, the mixture is made of

300	parts of	very white quartzose sand,
100	"	dried carbonate of soda,
43	"	lime slaked in the air (fallen lime),
300	"	cullet.

The materials are most carefully selected and purified; for it is essential to obtain as white and perfect a glass as possible. Melting-furnaces similar to those described (§ 677) are used, but they are always heated by wood. The material passes successively into two pots: it is first melted in a conical one, into which it is gradually poured, until the pot is nearly filled. This fusion requires 15 to 16 hours: it is then allowed to fine, by rest, at a high temperature. Workmen then remove the liquid glass with copper ladles, and transfer it to smaller square pots, called *cuvettes*, placed in the furnace on the same shelf and alongside of the melting-pots. When the transfer has been effected, the working-holes are closed, to restore fluidity to the glass: the cuvettes are then removed on a peculiar kind of cart, and brought above a very smooth bronze table, previously heated by red-hot coals laid thereon. The fluid glass is poured on this table, spread out, and smoothed by means of a cylinder or roller: when cooled, it is placed in a furnace and again heated, in order that it may easily bear changes of temperature. It is then divided into pieces of the requisite size, leaving out the defective portions, and *polished*, by fixing the glass on a stone table with plaster, and rubbing it with quartzose sand, by means of a second piece of glass smaller than the first. In making large glasses, several pieces, set in motion by a machine, are used at once. The surface of the glass thus becomes perfectly smooth, and is *rough-ground*, but as yet unpolished. The final *polish* is given by rubbing the surface first with finer emery, diluted with water, and then rubbing it with colcothar, also diluted with water, by means of heavy polishers covered with felt.

2d. *Bottle-glass.*

§ 684. Bottles are made of cheap materials, because it is important that their price should be low, and the peculiar colour is not a matter of much importance. The most ochrous sands are frequently preferred, because the oxide of iron they contain imparts fusibility to the glass. Pure alkaline carbonates being too expensive, the alkaline material is furnished by the crude sea-soda and wood-ashes. A considerable portion of washed ashes, called *spent ashes,* is added, which introduces the silicates of alumina and potassa. Lastly, a large quantity of cullet is poured into the mixture. In bottle-glass, the oxygen of the silicicacid is double or treble that of the united bases.

The following is the composition of a mixture used for bottle-glass:

Ochrous sand	100
Soda from seaweed	40 to 60
Fresh ashes	30 to 40
Spent ashes	150 to 180
Ochrous clay	80 to 100
Cullet	100 to 150

Bottle-glass is of various colours. That of French bottles is a deep green, owing to protoxide of iron; those made in certain parts of Germany have a brownish-yellow hue, produced by a mixture of the sesquioxides of iron and manganese.

Bottle-glass furnaces generally contain 6 pots of the largest size. The fusion should be rapid, to economize the fuel. The pots being entirely filled with the mixture, the fire is stirred up to effect the fusion, and when the material is liquid, a fresh quantity is added: seven or eight hours are required thus to fill the pots with melted glass, after which the work is begun immediately, the sandiver first being removed. The furnace is allowed to cool until the material has acquired the degree of consistency proper for working.

§ 685. The pipes having been heated in the holes at the bottom of the furnace, an assistant dips one into the melted glass, collecting as much of it as he can, and withdraws it by a continuous rotary motion. When the glass has become sufficiently consistent not to bend on itself, he collects some more, and so on: when he has gathered enough to finish a bottle, he passes it to the blower, who applies the glass to the left face of the marver, turning the pipe constantly, in order to fashion the neck of the bottle; at the same time he compresses the glass at the end of the pipe by means

Fig. 427. of the sheet-iron plate (fig. 413), and then blows through the pipe, so as to give the glass an egg-like form (fig. 427). He then rests the glass against the edge of the marver, marks the neck of the bottle, heats the piece in the furnace, withdraws it, and blows it, after having introduced it into a bronze or earthen mould of the proper size. When the bottle is formed, the blower withdraws it from the mould, and by a seesaw motion raises it on high (fig. 428), and indents the bottom of the bottle, by means of an instrument (fig. 429) called the *punty* or *pontil*, consisting of a small square piece of sheet-iron, the angle of which rests on the centre of the bottom of the bottle, while it revolves on the pipe. Then, taking a drop of water with the punty, he applies it to the neck of the bottle, which is immediately carried to a small cavity in the side of the furnace, and separated from the pipe by a dexterous jerk.

Fig. 428. Fig. 429.

Fig. 430.

The bottle being thus prepared, the blower turns it, and fastening the pipe to its base (fig. 430), extracts from the pot with another pipe a small quantity of melted glass, which elongates like a thread: the end of this he brings to the neck of the bottle, and by a rotary motion surrounds the mouth with a small glass cord: he then introduces the neck into the working-hole, and finishes the mouth with pincers. The bottle being completed, an assistant takes it from the hands of the master-workman, carries it to the annealing-furnace, and detaches the pipe by a dexterous blow.

The bottles are arranged in rows, upon each other, in the annealing-furnace, the heat of which should be kept below a dull red. When it is filled, the working-holes are closed, and it is allowed to cool. Modern annealing-furnaces are composed of a long gallery, heated by a furnace in the centre, and terminating by doors at either end. This longitudinal furnace is traversed by an endless iron chain, to which iron carts are attached containing the objects to be annealed. They enter at one end, and are withdrawn at the other, after having remained in the furnace long enough to be properly annealed.

3*d*. *Crystal.*

§ 686. Crystal is a kind of glass used only for the fabrication of articles of luxury; it must therefore be very transparent, perfectly homogeneous and colourless, and the greatest care must be exercised in the selection of the materials for its composition. Crystal is a double silicate of potassa and oxide of lead, the composition varying greatly in the different factories: the proportion of the oxygen of the silicic acid to that of the united bases ranges from 6 : 1 to 9 : 1. The ratio of the oxygen of the potassa to that of the oxide of lead ranges between still wider limits, viz. from 1 : 1 to 1 : 2.5. By increasing the proportion of oxide of lead, greater density and higher refracting and dispersing powers are imparted to the crystal, which produce in cut-glass the beautiful effects of colour by transmitted light. But the proportion of the oxide of lead cannot be increased indefinitely, because the crystal, in that case, acquires a yellowish tinge.

The finest and purest sand is chosen for the manufacture of crystal: the carbonate of potassa employed is refined; and the ordinary oxide of lead or *litharge* is not used, because it always contains some particles of metallic lead, which would be scattered through and injure the glass. Minium, an oxide of lead of a degree of oxidation superior to the protoxide, only is used: this oxide cannot contain metallic lead, and the oxygen it evolves when heated prevents the reduction of any lead by the carbonaceous dust or particles of other substances which may fall into the pot.

The ordinary proportions for tumblers, decanters, &c., are

300 parts of pure sand,
200 " minium,
100 " purified carbonate of potassa.

Crystal-glass furnaces are generally heated with wood; in some, however, coal is burned, but in that case the shape of the pots must be changed. Coal produces a very fuliginous smoke, the deoxidizing action of which it would be very difficult to prevent, if the glass were melted in open pots; peculiarly shaped pots (fig. 431), called *covered crucibles*, or *muffles*, are therefore used: their vertical opening is placed in front of the working-hole of the furnace.

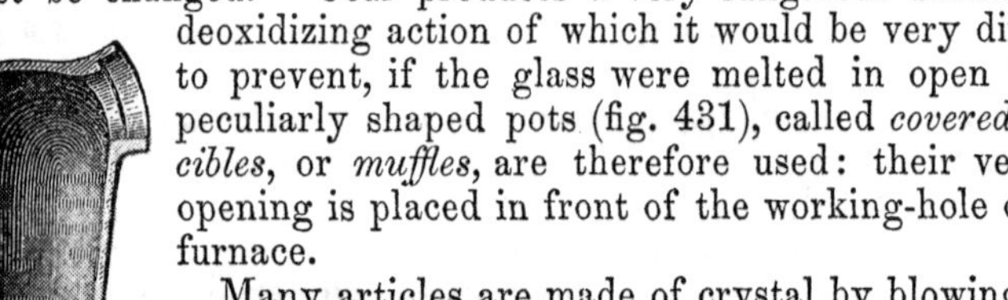

Fig. 431.

Many articles are made of crystal by blowing, but it is also cast in great quantities in bronze or wooden moulds, which latter are kept moist, so as not to carbonize too rapidly.

§ 687. The glass tubes used by chemists, and also thermometer-tubes are made by a particular process, which we shall briefly describe. The workman gathers on the end of his pipe a certain quantity of glass prepared as usual; he then blows it into the shape of a pear (fig. 432), which he makes larger or smaller, thicker or thinner, according to the size and thickness of the tube required. Another workman has also gathered some melted glass on the end of a pipe, and applies it to the bottom of the bottle (fig. 433); the two workmen then recede rapidly from each other. The

Fig. 432.

Fig. 433.

glass pear is then drawn out, as seen in figs. 434 and 435, and is converted into a tube terminating into two swollen extremities.

Fig. 434. Fig. 435.

Tubes of 30 or 40 metres in length are thus made: they are laid on a wooden floor, and divided into lengths of 1 metre each. It will be seen that the external diameter of these tubes is not equal throughout its whole length, being generally smallest toward the centre; neither is the internal calibre more regular, and it is rare to find a tube possessing the same internal diameter throughout its whole length.

MANUFACTURE OF GLASS FOR OPTICAL PURPOSES.

Crown-glass and Flint-glass.

§ 688. Two kinds of glass are used for optical instruments: one, called *crown-glass*, is analogous in its composition to Bohemian glass, while the other, called *flint-glass*, is a species of crystal. This glass must be as colourless as possible, and perfectly homogeneous: great care is therefore required in the choice of the materials entering into its composition, and they must be refined expressly.

Ordinary flint-glass is manufactured of

100	parts of	white sand,
100	"	minium,
30	"	very pure carbonate of potassa.

The density of this flint is about 3.5. A more refracting flint, but one slightly coloured yellow, is made of

225	parts of	white sand,
225	"	minium,
52	"	carbonate of potassa,
4	"	borax,
3	"	nitre,
1	"	peroxide of manganese,
1	"	arsenious acid,
89	"	cullet of the preceding flint.

The melting-furnace (fig. 436) contains only one covered crucible or pot, into which the mixture is gradually introduced by small portions at a time, always waiting until the preceding charge has become perfectly fluid. Eight or ten hours are required for the whole charge of a pot. A strong blast is then applied, and kept up for four hours, to render the mixture perfectly fluid. When this is effected, a hollow cylinder *ab*, made of fire-clay, previously heated to redness, and which does not sink in the melted glass, on

Fig. 436.

account of its greater lightness, is introduced into the pot. Into the cavity of this cylinder a curved iron bar *fe* is passed, the end of which is heated to redness: by resting this bar on an iron gallows *kl*, the clay cylinder may be moved in any direction, so as to mix intimately the various parts of the liquid mass. The bubbles of air are thus driven out, and the whole rendered perfectly homogeneous: this operation must be frequently repeated, to make the glass as perfect as possible. The clay cylinder is then removed, and the furnace allowed to cool slowly for 8 days.

The pot is then taken out, and is broken after cooling, to retract the glass, on which small polished facets are cut, here and there, so as to judge of its quality in various parts. This mass is then broken into pieces, and those that are perfect are selected, and heated in a muffle to soften them; they are then rolled into balls with pincers, and afterward carried to moulds which give them a lenticular shape. Lastly, they are allowed to cool slowly in an annealing-furnace.

Crown-glass is made exactly in the same way, of

120	parts of	white sand,
35	"	carbonate of potassa,
20	"	carbonate of soda,
20	"	chalk,
1	"	arsenious acid.

By joining two lenses, properly cut, one of crown, and the other of flint-glass, *achromatic lenses* are obtained, which are remarkable for their property of giving the same convergence to all the coloured rays, so that a colourless object produces, in the focus of the compound lens, an image equally colourless, the edges of which are free from the coloured fringes always presented by images seen through simple lenses. This property, however, is very manifest only in those rays which do not depart very far from the axis of the lens.

Strass.

§ 689. A peculiar kind of crystal is sometimes made, very dense and refracting, resembling the diamond, when it has been properly cut. By colouring this glass with various metallic oxides, coloured glasses closely imitating the precious stones are obtained. This crystal, called *strass*, should be made of the purest materials, and requires great care in fining: generally, a certain quantity of borax is added. The manufacture of artificial jewels has in modern times reached great excellence.

Enamel.

§ 690. The name of *enamel* is given to a species of glass, rendered opake by an addition of certain metallic oxides. Peroxide of tin or stannic acid is generally used for this purpose: however, arsenious acid, phosphate of lime, or antimoniate of oxide of antimony may also be employed. Enamel is generally made of a very fusible crystal. An alloy of 15 parts of tin and 100 parts of lead are oxidized in a reverberatory furnace, by which a stannate of oxide of lead is formed, which is purified by levigation. 100 parts of this plumbeous stannate are then mixed with 100 parts of very pure sand and 80 parts of carbonate of potassa: an addition of small quantities of certain metallic oxides to this mixture gives coloured enamels.

OF THE IMPERFECTIONS AND ALTERATIONS TO WHICH GLASS IS SUBJECT.

§ 691. We have seen that objects made of glass are kept for some time in a furnace at a dull red-heat, and then allowed to cool slowly: this process, called *annealing*, is a very essential operation, for glass cooled suddenly after blowing, is so brittle as to be useless. It frequently happens that common tumblers, which are imperfectly annealed, break suddenly on a slight change of temperature: such glass sometimes, also, is fractured when exposed to the current of air from an open door.

This property is highly developed in the *lachrymæ Batavicæ*, or *Prince Rupert's drops*. These are drops of glass suddenly cooled, and made by allowing drops of melted glass to fall into cold water: they thus become suddenly solid, in the form of tears, (fig. 437), terminating in a long tail; and as the outer surface solidifies while the interior is still at a high temperature, it retains nearly the shape it had in the liquid state. The internal particles are kept in an abnormal condition by those of the surface surrounding them: if this resistance of the surface particles be removed, at only one point, the whole mass bursts with noise, and falls into dust. This occurs, for example, if the tail of the drop be broken off.

Fig. 437.

A similar effect is produced in a small glass apparatus, long known as the *philosopher's phial*, a kind of glass tube, thick, and of a pyriform shape: the master-blower frequently makes them on his pipe, when trying the metal in the pot. If any hard substance, a small ball for example, be dropped into this phial, which has not been annealed, the shock is sufficient to reduce the phial to dust.

The workmen apply this tendency of glass to break in a given direction when touched with a cold body, to detach the pipe from the objects blown, or to crack the glass in any direction required.

§ 692. When glass has been exposed for a long time to a high temperature, it loses, by volatilization, a considerable portion of its alkali, and becomes less and less fusible, at the same time acquiring the property of readily crystallizing by slow cooling. Thus masses of glass of a crystalline structure are often found in the worn-out pots which have been for a long time in the furnace and cooled slowly: at other times, the crystallization is developed only in some parts of it, the remainder being vitreous; the vitreous portion always containing more alkali than that rendered opake by crystallization. This alteration of the glass takes place not only at its fusing point, but also at a lower temperature. If a glass bottle be left for several days in a furnace, at a degree of heat approaching that which effects the softening of the glass, it entirely loses its transparency and resembles a porcelain bottle. The glass thus altered, *devitrified*, is much less fusible than when transparent. A peculiar art was attempted to be founded on this property, which consisted in making objects of blown glass, and then destroying their fusibility by devitrification. This devitrified glass was called *Réaumur's porcelain;* but the manufacture of it has been abandoned.

§ 693. Glass containing a large proportion of alkali changes by exposure to moist air, its surface becoming rugose and cracked. Frequently an excessively thin pellicle of altered glass forms on it, producing the same play of colours as a soap-bubble, or a drop of oil on a large surface of water; an alteration produced by the surface of the glass parting, after a long time, with a portion of its alkali: it is particularly remarkable in pieces of glass which have remained buried for years in a damp soil. These pieces are sometimes found to have entirely lost their transparency, to be swollen, and cleavable into very thin lamellæ: then they exhibit the same play of colours as mother-of-pearl.

OF GLASS-WORKING IN THE LABORATORY.

§ 694. Various small objects are made of the glass tubes of commerce; for this purpose, an oil-lamp, generally made of tin (fig. 438), fed by a bellows, and called an *enameller's lamp*, is used. The wick is of cotton, and does not project very high. The bellows is worked with the foot: the blast of air is conveyed by a pipe which

Fig. 438.

can be turned in various directions. By properly arranging the wick, and modifying the inclination of the pipe, and adapting a proper aperture to it, a flame of any size may be obtained at pleasure. When working with a plumbeous glass, or crystal, the flame must be made oxidizing by admitting a greater quantity of air; for, if the flame were reducing, oxide of lead would be brought to the surface of the glass in the state of metallic lead, and the glass would be blackened. It is important not to heat the glass too suddenly, lest it should break; it is therefore first held for a few moments before the flame, and brought by degrees into the hottest part.

§ 695. In order to bend a glass tube, it is heated to the distance of 3 or 4 centimetres on each side of the point of flexion, turning it constantly, so that its whole periphery may be uniformly heated. As soon as the tube is sufficiently soft to yield to a slight force, it is bent; but it is important not to make the curve too short, because the tube would be misshaped and brittle. The tube is therefore not heated at the point where it was begun to be bent, but the flame is directed on the adjacent part, so as to make a small arc of a circle. Tubes can be bent in an alcohol-lamp even more readily than in an enameller's lamp, for it is better not to have the glass too hot.

§ 696. In order to close a tube at one end, a longer tube is heated in the enameller's lamp, at the point of closure, turning it constantly in the flame: as soon as it is perfectly soft both ends are gently drawn out, still turning it. The tube thus takes the shape of fig. 439. The point of the flame is then directed to the point *a* of the narrow part, and the two halves of the tube are separated, each of which will furnish a tube closed at one end; the ends are then rounded and made more uniform in thickness. To do this, the end is again heated in the lamp, blowing into it occasionally, to round it. Lastly, a *border* is only required to complete it; which is made by simply heating the sharp edges until they are rounded by fusion. If the edges are to be widened, or a mouth made to pour liquids, it is done by applying an iron wire against the softened edges, by which means the aperture can be fashioned at will (fig. 440).

Fig. 439.

Fig 440.

When the end is to be closed, this end is heated in the lamp, and the heated end of another tube applied to it. The two tubes are soldered together, and the operation is then continued as just described.

§ 697. It is frequently necessary to solder a smaller tube *cd* (fig. 441) to the end of a larger one *ab*. The larger tube is then drawn out, in the lamp, till it is of the size of the smaller one, and

Fig. 441.

the tube *ab* is next closed at the point *b* of the narrow part, by placing the part *b* in the point of the flame, and turning the tube between the fingers. Then, after having heated the closed end to soften it, a very thin sphere, which bursts by blowing through the opening *a*, is formed at the end *b*. By means of a file, the glass is separated so as to leave only a widened edge-border at the end *b*. The same is done to the end *c* of the small tube; the ends *b* and *c* are then exposed to the flame, opposite to each other, turning them constantly, after having previously closed the end *a* with a cork. When these ends are sufficiently softened, they are pressed firmly against each other, the joint is equally heated throughout, and from time to time the operator blows through the small tube, in order to prevent the solder from forming a ring. Lastly, it is drawn out slightly, so that no swelling may exist at the point of union.

§ 698. If a narrow tube *cd* (fig. 443) is to be soldered to the side of a larger tube *ab*, the point of the flame, after having rendered it as sharp as possible by a proper arrangement of the pipe and lamp-wick, is directed on the point *e* (fig. 442) of the tube *ab*. When it is sufficiently softened, the end of a glass point, also heated, is fastened and drawn quickly forward: thus a point *ef* is formed on the tube *ab*. This point is closed in the lamp; then, having stopped the end *K* with wax, the point *ef* is again introduced into the flame, and when it is in fusion, a very thin sphere, which bursts, is formed by blowing through the open end *l*.

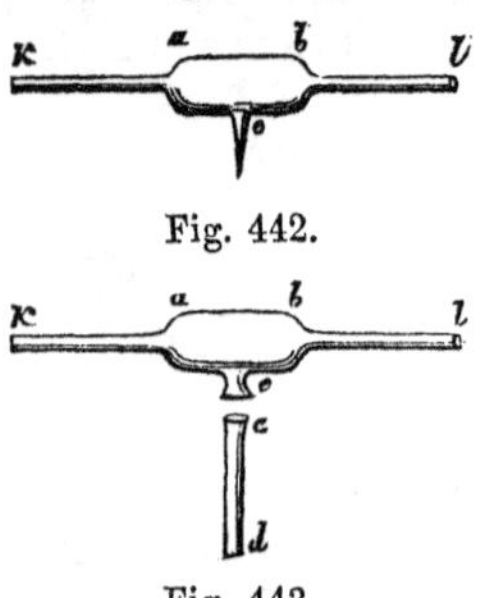

Fig. 442.

Fig. 443.

A portion of the glass is filed off, the edges of the aperture are melted (fig. 443), and after having closed the end *l* with wax, the end *e* of the small tube, also heated, is brought in contact with the opening *e*. The joint is formed by gradually heating all its parts, and blowing from time to time through the opening *d*.

§ 699. If a globe is to be blown at the end of a tube, the tube is closed in the lamp, and by continuing the action of the flame a mass of glass, large enough to make the globe required, is collected at this end. This mass of glass being very soft, the tube is gradually extended by blowing gently into it. It is then heated again uniformly, and afterward, by constantly turning the tube and blowing gently, a globe of any size may be produced at pleasure.

When the globe is to be large, and still be at the end of a narrow and thin tube, it is better to blow the globe separately on a larger tube, and then solder it to the narrow one. To do this, the

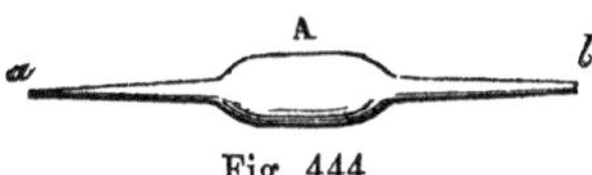

Fig. 444.

larger tube is drawn out between two points (fig. 444), by the process stated in § 696; one end *a* is closed in the lamp, and then the part A heated in the flame so as to soften it completely. Lastly, the operator blows through the end *b*, turning it constantly, until the globe has attained the size required: the globe is then soldered to the tube, as described (§ 697). But as the globe is still terminated by a point, the latter is placed in the flame, and, by blowing gently after having softened this part of the globe, it is distended so as to cause the small piece of glass to disappear. The bottles which are to contain the volatile liquids intended for analysis (§ 269) are blown in the same way.

§ 700. In order to fashion a funnel at the end of a tube, as, for example, on safety-tubes, a globe drawn out between two points (fig. 445) is soldered to the end of the tube, as in § 699, and then the point *ab* is detached (fig. 446). The part *a*, as well as the end of

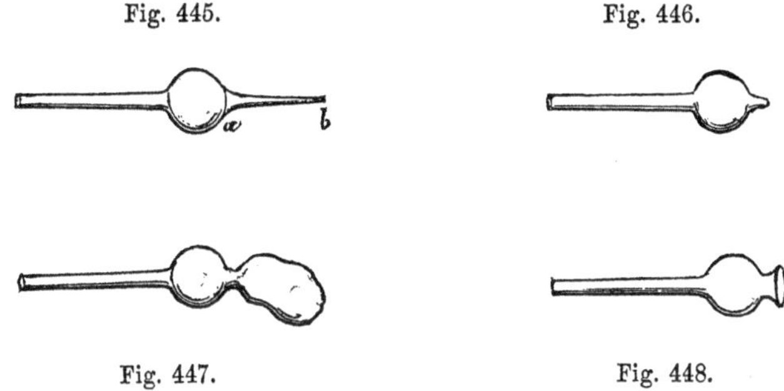

Fig. 445. Fig. 446.

Fig. 447. Fig. 448.

the globe, is heated, and when they are very soft, a smart blow of wind through the tube is given: thus a second irregular and very thin globe (fig. 447), fastened to the first, is produced; this is broken and the glass detached by means of a file (fig. 448), so as to leave only an edge, which is melted in the lamp, and properly widened by an iron rod (fig. 449).

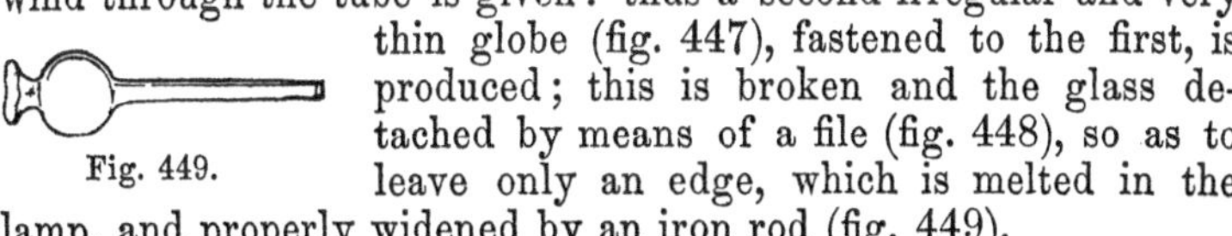
Fig. 449.

Small bottles, intended to hold definite quantities of volatile liquids for analysis (§ 269), are made as in § 690, but of narrow and thin tubes.

§ 701. In order to break a glass tube at any given point, a mark is made on it with a gun-flint or a very sharp three-edged file; the tube is then pulled in the direction of its length, and it separates at the mark. If the tube be large, it must be slightly bent at the same time.

In order to separate thicker and larger portions, as, for example, to shorten the neck of a retort or flask, a mark with a file is made at the proper point, and followed with a point of red-hot iron;* it then cracks in the direction of the mark.†

COLOURED GLASS AND PAINTING ON GLASS.

§ 702. Glass dissolves the greater part of the metallic oxides, and while it preserves its transparency, is often tinged with the most beautiful hues: on this property the manufacture of coloured glass is founded. It suffices to mix intimately with the metal of which the glass is to be made, a given quantity of the metallic oxide, to produce coloured melted glass: with certain metallic oxides, however, peculiar care is required.

Protoxide of iron FeO imparts to glass a deep or bottle-green colour, while the sesquioxide Fe_2O_3 produces a yellow tinge. Oxide of copper CuO and oxide of chrome Cr_2O_3 yield a beautiful green, but of different shades. Oxide of cobalt CoO gives a brilliant blue; sesquioxide of manganese Mn_2O_3 a violet. A mixture of equal parts of oxide of cobalt and oxide of iron colours the glass black. Protoxide of copper Cu_2O yields a very beautiful red colour, but so intense that the glass nearly loses its transparency if the oxide be in the proportion of a few hundredths.

A fine purple is obtained by mixing a certain quantity of oxide of tin with finely powdered crystal, soaking the mass in a solution of chloride of gold, and melting it, when dried, in a crucible.

When the metallic oxide to be used as a colouring agent can be deoxidized in the furnace, as, for example, the sesquioxide

---

* A red-hot coal, held with a forceps, carried round the intended line of separation, answers the same purpose: care must only be taken to blow away the ashes as soon as they form by contact with the cold glass, so as always to present a red-hot point to the surface of the glass.—*W. L. F.*

† The process of dividing a tube by friction, described in Hare's Chemistry, is so much superior to that adopted by our author, that the translator has not hesitated to substitute it for the French mode:—

"Some years ago, Mr. Isaiah Lukens showed me that a small phial or tube might be separated into two parts, if subjected to cold water, after having been heated by the friction of a cord made to circulate about it, by two persons alternately pulling in opposite directions. I was subsequently enabled to employ this process for dividing large vessels, of four or five inches in diameter; and likewise to render it in every case more easy and certain, by means of a piece of plank forked like a boot-jack, and also having a kerf or slit cut by a saw, parallel to and nearly equidistant from the principal surface of the plank, and at right angles to the incision forming the fork.

"By means of the fork, the glass is held steady by the hand of the operator. By means of the kerf, the string, while circulating about the glass, is confined to the part where the separation is desired. As soon as the cord smokes, the glass is plunged into water, or if too large to be easily immersed, the water must be thrown upon it. This method is always preferable when the glass vessel is so open that, on being immersed, the water can reach the inner surface. As plunging is the most effectual method of employing the water, I usually, in the case of a tube, close the end which is to be sunk in the water, so as to restrict the refrigeration to the outside."—*Hare's Compendium, ed. 4th, p.* 60.

of manganese can be, a small quantity of nitre is added to the mixture.

A beautiful yellow glass is made by adding lampblack to a mixture which would produce common white glass. By varying the proportion of lampblack, several intermediate shades between a bright and a purple yellow can be produced.

§ 703. When it is wished to make glass of clear colours with metallic oxides which possess powerful colouring action, it is difficult to obtain the shade desired by adding the proper quantity of the colouring oxide to the mixture in the pot. Glass is then set in layers, (*verre plaqué*,) so that it is formed of white glass throughout the greater part of its thickness, and has one face only formed by a thin layer of coloured glass; and in order to vary at will the intensity of the colour, the layers are made of suitable thickness. This kind of glass is made as follows:—Two pots are placed in the oven, one filled with white, and the other with coloured glass. The workman first takes up with his pipe a certain quantity of white-glass; then, when it begins to assume the proper degree of consistency, he dips it into the coloured glass, and thus fastens a layer of this on the white mass. He then blows the whole into cylinders, in order to make muffs for flatting (§ 688). The inside of the cylinder is necessarily white, the layer of coloured glass being only external.

Painting on glass is done with very fusible and finely powdered coloured glass. The composition of this glass varies with the nature of the colouring oxide; for the majority of them, a mixture of 2 parts of quartz, 2½ of oxide of lead, and one of bismuth is used; but as certain colouring oxides are altered by the oxides of lead and bismuth, in this case a mixture of 2 parts of quartz, 1½ of melted borax, ¼ of nitre, and ¼ of carbonate of lime is used. The colouring oxide is added to these mixtures, and they are melted in a muffle-furnace; the glass obtained is reduced to an impalpable powder, ground in turpentine, and the paint thus prepared is applied with a pencil. The painted glass is then heated in a muffle, at a temperature sufficient to melt the coloured glass, but not to affect the object on which the painting has been made.

In order to form the groundwork of the picture, glass coloured in the paste is generally used, the outlines and shades being painted on one of the surfaces. The various pieces of glass are then dexterously fitted together by means of small sheets of lead, each small pane harmonizing with the outline and shades of the figure designed. The painted surface of the glass is placed outside, so that the picture is seen through the coloured glass.

The numbers and divisions marked on enamel dial-plates are applied in the same way.

ANALYSIS OF GLASS.

§ 704. We will suppose that the glass to be analyzed contains, or may contain, silex, potassa, soda, lime, manganese, alumina, oxide of iron, oxide of manganese, and oxide of lead.

Five grammes of the glass, reduced to an impalpable powder, are intimately mixed with about three times its weight of pure carbonate of soda: the mixture having been weighed in a platinum crucible, the latter is covered with its lid, and heated in an alcohol-lamp having a double current of air, so as to completely melt the carbonate of soda. For this purpose, it is well to surround the crucible with a small sheet-iron chimney extending a few centimetres beyond it: the chimney, at the same time increasing the draught, forces the flame completely to envelop the crucible. The carbonate of soda is kept melted for at least 20 minutes, and then allowed to cool. By using a thin crucible, the alkaline cup may be detached by the pressure of the fingers, and is received in a porcelain saucer, containing a certain quantity of water, and covered by an inverted funnel. Water, acidulated with nitric acid, being poured into the platinum crucible, and then into the saucer, the alkaline cup dissolves with effervescence, the funnel preventing any loss of substance, by the projection of the small liquid pellicles surrounding the gaseous bubbles which burst on the surface of the fluid. Toward the close the liquid is acidulated with an excess of nitric acid, and evaporated to dryness at a moderate heat. Hot water, acidulated with nitric acid, is poured on the dried matter: it is allowed to digest for some time hot, and then diluted with water: all the metallic oxides then dissolving, leave the silex alone as an insoluble residue. It is collected on a filter, calcined after being well washed, and weighed.

A current of sulphuretted hydrogen is passed through the liquid, which precipitates only the lead in the state of a sulphuret; and finally, the liquid is heated to ebullition, still keeping up the current of sulphuretted hydrogen, in order to facilitate the deposit of sulphur. The sulphuret of lead is collected on a filter, and, after having washed it, the filter is burned in a platinum crucible, and the substance sprinkled with nitric acid, mixed with a small quantity of sulphuric, in order to convert it into sulphate of lead: lastly, it is calcined to redness. The weight of the oxide of lead is deduced by calculation from the weight of the sulphate of lead obtained.

Sulfhydrate of ammonia is then poured into the liquid to precipitate the alumina and the sulphurets of iron and manganese; the wet precipitate is redissolved in chlorohydric acid, and the separation of the two oxides effected by the process described in § 659.

The liquid, which then contains only lime, magnesia, and the alkaline salts, is boiled to drive off the excess of sulfhydrate of ammonia, and chlorohydric acid added to decompose that which still remains. Lastly, it is supersaturated with ammonia, and the lime precipitated in the state of oxalate of lime by oxalate of ammonia; the presence of ammoniacal salts in the liquid (§ 589) keeping all the magnesia in solution.

The solution is then concentrated by evaporation, an excess of carbonate of soda added, and it is evaporated to dryness, to decompose the ammoniacal salts, and drive off the ammonia as carbonate: it is then treated with water, which leaves the magnesia in the state of insoluble carbonate.

§ 705. In the analysis just described, the proportions of all the various components of the glass have been ascertained successively, with the exception of those of the alkalies, which must be found by a particular process. The glass is first dissolved in fluohydric acid. As this acid is difficult of preservation, it is better to prepare it freshly for each analysis, which is done in the following manner: Into a small platinum retort (fig. 450) made of two pieces, very finely

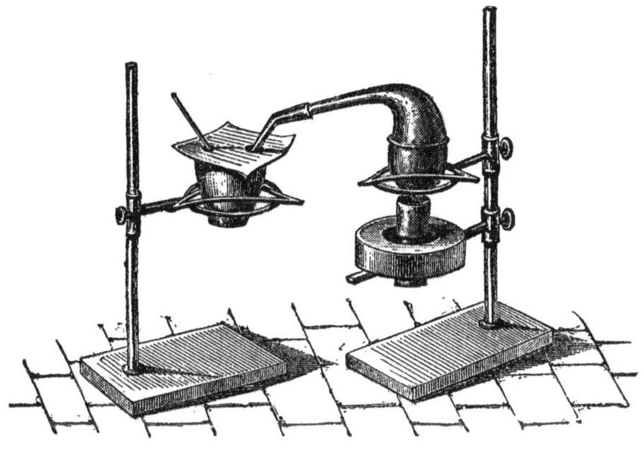

Fig. 450.

powdered fluor-spar is introduced and sulphuric acid added: on the other hand, 5 gm. of glass in impalpable powder are placed in a large platinum crucible, with a certain quantity of water, and covered with a sheet of platinum pierced with two openings. The neck of the platinum retort passes through one of those openings; the other, much smaller, is traversed by a platinum wire, flattened into a spoon at its end, and used for stirring the material in the crucible. On gently heating the retort the fluohydric acid dissolves in the water of the crucible, attacks the vitreous matter, and a large quantity of fluoride of silicium is disengaged. The material is stirred from time to time with the platinum spoon, and when the glass is entirely dissolved, the crucible is gently heated, to drive off the excess of acid and evaporate the water; sulphuric acid is then poured upon the residue, completely to expel the fluohydric acid and convert all the oxides into sulphates. When the greater part of the sulphuric acid has been driven off by heat, the substance is treated with water, which leaves the silex and sulphate of lead as a residue. The liquid is filtered and an excess of carbonate of ammonia added, which precipitates the alumina, the lime, the oxide of iron, a part of the oxide of manganese, and the magnesia: an addition of a small quantity of sulfhydrate of ammonia completes the precipitation of the manganese. The liquid, when filtered, contains only the alkaline salts, a small quantity of magnesia, and salts of ammonia: it is evaporated to dryness, the residue calcined at a strong red-heat, and the alkaline bases are weighed in the state of sulphates. The magnesia is overlooked for the moment, until the termination of the analysis; the potassa is separated by perchloride of platinum (§ 527), and the soda is determined by calculation from the difference obtained.

The magnesia must be sought in the solution remaining after the precipitation of the double chloride of potassium and platinum. The platinum is then precipitated by sulfhydrate of ammonia, and the liquid, filtered with an excess of carbonate of soda, is evaporated: the carbonate of magnesia is then separated by treatment with water. This base may also be precipitated by phosphate of ammonia (§ 592).*

---

* A much better method of separating the magnesia from the alkalies is the following, when the bases can easily be obtained as chlorides:—The liquid containing magnesia and the alkalies is evaporated to dryness in a platinum crucible, after having condensed its volume by evaporation in a porcelain capsule, out of which the very concentrated solution is carefully washed, with as little water as possible, into the platinum vessel; a small quantity of pure red oxide of mercury is then added, and the crucible subjected to a strong white-heat over a spirit-lamp, until all the mercury is volatilized. Care must be taken not to inhale the fumes. The magnesia then all remaining as insoluble caustic magnesia, is separated by filtration from the alkalies, which then may be determined by weighing them together, determining the potassa by precipitation with chloride of platinum, and finding the weight of the soda by the difference.

Phosphate of soda, with the addition of some ammonia, effects the precipitation of magnesia much more perfectly than phosphate of ammonia.—*W. L. F.*

POTTERY.

§ 706. The term *pottery* is applied to all objects made of an argillaceous earth, to which a certain consistency is given by burning. The art of pottery is also called the *ceramic* art*, and the earthy pastes used in the manufacture are termed *ceramic pastes*. Clay is the base of all the ceramic pastes, and is plastic in the highest degree: when reduced to a proper state by water, it may be kneaded, fashioned, and moulded to any form, and when, by drying, it has become more consistent, may be worked on the lathe and cut with edged tools; and lastly, burning gives it a great degree of hardness. These various properties render clay highly adapted to the manufacture of hollow-ware.

Burnt or merely dried clay adheres strongly to the tongue: this physical property is owing to the fact that the substance is traversed by innumerable capillary canals, which rapidly absorb the moisture of the tongue, so that it sticks closely to the clay. In consequence of this porosity, vessels of baked clay allow water to soak through them, and must, therefore, to be rendered impervious to fluids, be covered by a varnish, called *glaze*. The glaze of fine pottery, as porcelain, is always formed of a vitreous substance, very analogous in composition to the material of the paste itself: it should not be very fusible, and still should melt at a temperature below that at which the vessel would lose its shape: the glaze incorporates itself so closely with the paste, that the line of separation cannot be seen, if a piece of burnt porcelain be broken. To produce this effect, however, a very high temperature and a large quantity of fuel are required, so that such a glazing is applicable only for high-priced ware. The glaze of common earthenware is much more fusible.

Fine pottery, such as porcelain, is made of very carefully selected materials, and should be colourless after burning, so that the glaze may retain its transparency. Common pottery, on the contrary, is made of impure clays, which are frequently ochreous, and much less rare than pure and colourless clay. As this pottery, after burning, becomes red, the colour is hidden by making the glaze opake, or giving it a very deep colour: in this kind of ware, the varnish is not incorporated with the material, but forms a distinct layer, which is readily seen by breaking a piece.

Pure clay, diluted in water, forms a paste eminently plastic and

---

* Derived from κεραμος, "potter's clay," *as if from* κεω, "to burn," and ἔρα, "earth."—*Trans.*

easily worked; but it shrinks greatly on burning, and it is difficult to prevent the vessels made of it from losing their shape and cracking. This inconvenience is remedied by adding another material, called *cement*, to the clay, which is then said to be *scoured.* In common pottery, the cement is generally a more or less ferruginous quartzose sand: powdered brick, or any powdered baked earth, is sometimes used. The addition of this material diminishes greatly the plasticity of the paste, renders it more difficult to work, and at the same time more porous. The glazing is therefore more necessary if the vessel is intended to hold water.

If a substance which begins to fuse at the temperature of burning pottery, be intimately mixed with clay, a substance which remains translucid after fusion is obtained: the vessel, however, has not lost its shape, because it has not softened much at that temperature, and only the material added has undergone fusion. A similar phenomenon ensues when melted wax is dropped upon paper, the latter remaining translucid after the solidification of the wax. The aggregation of the paste by burning renders it hard and compact, and it would be unnecessary to add glazing to make it water-tight; but it is generally glazed, to improve its appearance and remove the roughness of its surface. The vitrifiable material added is often feldspar; at other times, lime, which, by combining with a part of the clay, forms a double silicate of alumina and lime, more fusible than the simple silicate. Oxide of iron produces the same effect; but, as it discolours the paste, is only used for common pottery. The proportion of vitrifiable material which can be mixed with the clay is limited, because it greatly diminishes the plasticity of the paste, and makes it harder to work.

§ 707. We shall divide earthenware into two grand classes: the first will contain that of which the paste softens by burning, and thus becomes compact and impervious to liquids; to this class belong the various kinds of porcelain* and stone-ware. The second will comprise those kinds of which the paste remains porous after burning: this class includes earthenware, *fayence*,† delft-ware, etc.

POTTERY THE PASTE OF WHICH BECOMES COMPACT BY BURNING.

§ 708. Let us first examine porcelain: being the most expensive and beautiful of all the various kinds of pottery, its manufacture requires the greatest care.

Porcelain.

§ 709. The clay used in the manufacture of porcelain, called

* Porcelain, from *porcelana*, the Portuguese word for a cup.

† Fayence, from Fayenza, in Italy, where this ware was first made.

*kaolin,** is a product of decomposition of the igneous rocks of primitive origin, and, as it always proceeds from the change of a feldspathic rock, is most generally yielded by granites very rich in feldspar, though sometimes also by the porphyries, rarely by the trachytes. In these rocks, the feldspar has been more or less altered: in some, the silicate of potassa has entirely disappeared, while in others a small quantity still remains: in the latter case, fragments of unaltered feldspar, increasing the fusibility of the material, are frequently found in the midst of the earthy mass. To separate these fragments, as well as the quartzose particles, the material is washed in a vat: as the kaolin is generally very friable, this operation is easy; were it otherwise, it would be necessary to grind it previously, either in a mill or by stamping. The material is mixed with the water, by means of paddles moved by machinery: the largest particles fall to the bottom of the vat. The liquid mud is poured into a second vat below the first, where it is allowed to rest for a few moments, that the quartzose or feldspathic particles may settle: it is then transmitted into a third vat still lower, where the water is allowed to settle for a long time, and deposit all the clay it holds in suspension: lastly, the clear water is drawn off, and the argillaceous mud at the bottom of the vat dried.

The kaolin of Saint-Yrieix, near Limoges, which is almost exclusively used in the porcelain manufactories of France, presents, on an average, the following composition, after the levigation just described:

Silex	48.00
Alumina	37.00
Potassa	2.50
Water	12.50
	100.00

The washed kaolin of Morl, near Halle in Saxony, which is used in the porcelain-factories of Berlin, and which is produced by the decomposition of a quartziferous porphyry, contains, after calcination—

Silex	71.42
Alumina	26.07
Peroxide of iron	1.93
Lime	0.13
Potassa	0.45
	100.00

It is easily seen, with a lens, that this latter kaolin is not homogeneous, and that it contains a large quantity of pure sili-

* Kaolin, from *kao* and *lin*, two Chinese words signifying *porcelain-clay*.—*Trans*

ceous particles. In order to convert it into porcelain-clay, the addition of a certain quantity of finely powdered feldspar is required.

The kaolin of Saint-Yrieix must, on the contrary, be mixed with quartzose sand, reduced to an impalpable powder, and a certain quantity of carbonate of lime. At the porcelain factory of Sèvres, near Paris, different proportions are used, according to the quality of the porcelain to be made:

	For domestic purposes.	For ornamental purposes.
Washed kaolin	64.0	62.0
Chalk from Bougival	6.0	5.0
Sand from Aumont	20.0	17.0
Fine or feldspathic sand	10.0	—
Quartzose feldspar	—	17.0
	100.0	100.0

§ 710. The feldspar and quartz which are to be mixed with the clay, must be first rendered more friable, by being heated to redness and thrown into cold water: they are then reduced to an impalpable powder in a mill with edge-stones, and afterward levigated in order to separate the grosser particles.

The paste of kaolin and that of the quartz and feldspar are mixed wet, and as intimately as possible: it is then dried, in order to give it the degree of consistency fit for further working. This desiccation is effected, either by compressing the liquid pap in a press, in muslin bags, or by heating it in peculiar ovens, or by leaving it for a long time in plaster-boxes, the porosity of which assists the evaporation.

The paste which has become more consistent should be worked for a long time, in order to effect a more uniform mixture of the ingredients. This operation is generally effected by *tramping* in round vats, that is to say, by letting a man stamp it with his naked feet: it is then pounded with wooden stampers, after being rolled into balls. This paste is sufficiently worked when no bubbles of air can be seen on breaking it.

These various mechanical operations require great care and cleanliness on the part of the workman. He must prevent the introduction of dust or any organic matter into the paste; for a single hair will effectually destroy a piece of porcelain, as the gas disengaged by the decomposition of the organic matter produces blisters or cracks.

Porcelain may be made of the paste thus prepared; but it has been found to improve by being kept for several years in damp places. It then undergoes what is called *rotting;* it becomes black inside, and disengages an appreciable smell of sulphuretted hydrogen. The small quantity of organic matter in the paste is destroyed by spontaneous combustion, in the damp air: it reacts at the same time on some traces of the sulphates, which are also found in it, and transforms them into sulphurets, which, in their turn, disengage sulphuretted hydrogen while changing into carbonates at the expense of the surrounding carbonic acid.

§ 711. Before working up the paste, it is again mixed with the hand, and squeezed into balls, which are forcibly thrown on the table on which this work is done. The air-bubbles which formed in the paste during the rotting are, in this way, driven out.

It is formed into articles of various forms, by several processes, of which we shall distinguish:

1. Throwing on the potter's lathe.
2. Press-work.
3. Moulding, properly so called, or casting.

The potter's lathe (fig. 451) consists of a vertical axis, inserted at its lower part into a disk of wood, which the workman moves

Fig. 451.

with his foot: on the upper end of this axis is a smaller disk, supporting the paste to be worked. The workman, seated on a bench, places a certain quantity of paste on the upper disk, causes it to revolve by means of his foot, and fashions it into the form intended: when the piece is large, he adds an additional quantity of paste, and so on, until the proper size is attained. He generally uses a pattern and several measures to guide him in shaping the piece.

This first operation is called *hollowing out the stuff* (ébauchage), and rarely produces a shape sufficiently regular to be immediately burned. The process is completed by *shaping* (tournassage), an operation frequently performed on the same lathe. The article hollowed out is in this case allowed to dry spontaneously for some time, in order to acquire more consistency; it is then made to revolve on the lathe, and worked with a cutting-tool, precisely like turning in wood. Its outlines thus become well defined, and it is reduced to the proper thickness. Fig. 451 represents a workman in the act of finishing a vase by throwing. The fragments of paste detached during the operation are called *turnings;* they are mixed with fresh paste, to which they impart peculiar qualities.

§ 712. These operations may often be abridged by combining the moulding with press-work: let us, for example, study the manufacture of a dinner-plate. The workman, having deposited a proper quantity of paste on the upper disk of the lathe, fashions it with his fingers into a cylindrical vase of no great height; he then brings down the upper edges of the vase, and shapes out roughly the form of a plate. He stops the lathe, and, by means of a brass wire (fig. 452), cuts off the base of the plate, and detaches it from the platform of the lathe: after allowing the rough plate to dry for a short time in the air, to become more consistent, he inverts it on a plaster mould (fig. 453), which exhibits in relief the shape of the inside

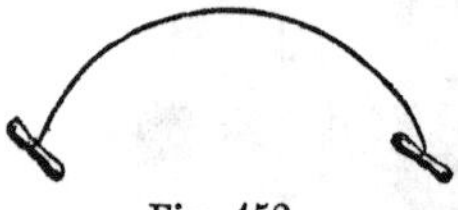

Fig. 452.

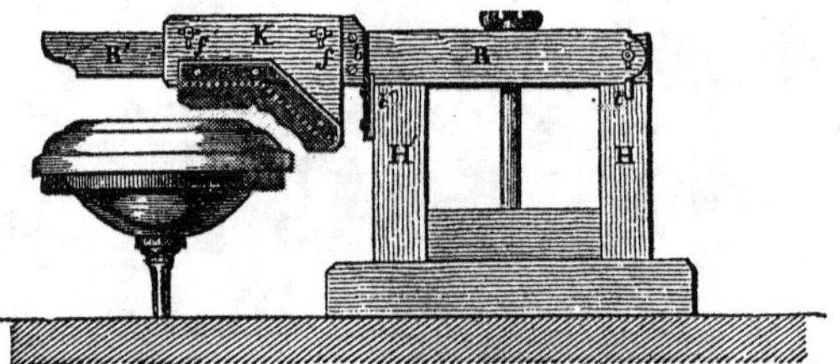

Fig. 453.

of the plate. By compressing the paste forcibly against the mould, so as to effect an exact impression, and then giving the wheel a circular concentric motion, he brings it under a brass or steel knife *c*, the edge of which presents the semi-profile of the outer surface of the plate. He gradually depresses this knife, so that it cuts into the plate to the proper thickness, of which he judges by marks on the knife. In some factories, the workman simply prepares a plate of paste, of proper thickness, compresses it by a sponge, on the plaster mould (fig. 453), and completes it by means of the knife, as has just been described.

§ 713. In moulding, the ceramic paste is applied to the mould, the shape of which it is to take: these moulds, which are generally made of plaster, and always of some porous substance, are fashioned on a plaster, earthen, or even a metal pattern, when many are required. The mould is often composed of several pieces, which can be separated in order to remove the article made: they are held, until that time, in a kind of plaster box, moulded itself on the outside of the mould, and called a *coat*. As the ceramic paste must contract somewhat in consequence of the absorption of its water by the porous walls of the mould, the article moulded is easily extracted, provided the sections of the mould are so combined as to present no obstacles themselves. The projections at the lines of junction of the various parts of the mould are removed by a sharp instrument: these lines must be judiciously disposed, so as not to be too apparent, as they sometimes show on the pieces after burning.

Moulds intended for the making of round objects, as handles and columns, are made of two equal parts which fit each other exactly. Half of the object is moulded in each of these parts, and, while the paste is yet soft enough to adhere, the two halves are united. The workman waits for a few moments, until the paste is partly dried by the absorption of the water through the porous sides of the mould, and then separates the two parts of the latter.

§ 714. In order to unite the various component parts of an object, the workman generally does not wait until they are thoroughly dried, but marks on the principal pieces the points of junction of the pieces to be added, and engraves thereon cross-cuts, to render them rough: he then applies with a pencil a thick pap, formed of the ceramic paste suspended in water, and called *slip* (barbotine); and then quickly applies the pieces. It requires a skilful workman to do this. In fact, ceramic objects, turned in the lathe, experience a contractive influence by the circular motion by which they were made, and even by the direction in which the pressure was applied. The piece, in burning, contracts concentrically on itself; and if the handle of a vase has been accurately applied in the vertical position, it leans to one side on the burned piece: therefore, in order to obtain a vertical position after burning, the handle must be slightly inclined, so as to counteract the effect of this twisting motion. The proper inclination depends on the length of the handle, and, to a certain degree, on the shape of the vase. The workman must foresee all these effects.

§ 715. A certain number of pieces of a peculiar shape is made by *casting*. If a liquid pap of ceramic paste thinned with water is poured into a mould of porous plaster, the mould absorbs a great portion of the water of the pap, and part of the paste adheres to the internal surface of the mould. In four or five minutes, the fluid pap is allowed to run off: the layer of paste adhering to the mould, to the thickness of 2 or 3 millimetres, becomes more consistent in consequence of the absorption of the water by the sides of the mould. In a few moments, this layer is sufficiently dried to act as an absorbent on an additional quantity of slip. If, therefore, the mould be filled anew, a second coat of paste is formed, which adheres closely to the first, and this process is continued until the sides of the object are sufficiently thick.

In this way the porcelain tubes and retorts are made which are used in chemical laboratories, and also many hollow pieces, such as the spouts of tea-pots. As an exemplification, we shall select a porcelain tube. The mould is formed of two equal parts (fig. 454), each presenting a semi-cylindrical canal, terminating into two small canals *a*, *b*. The two parts of the mould are joined by screw-collars *l*, *l* (fig. 455), and a cylindrical canal is thus formed, terminating by apertures. A coating of very clear slip is painted over each part of the mould, with a badger's-hair pencil, and the two halves are fitted together.

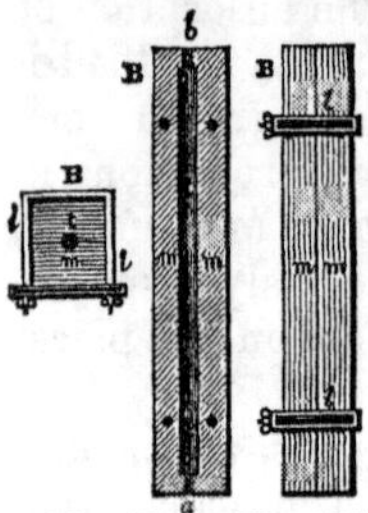

Fig. 454. Fig. 455.

The slip intended for casting is contained in a bucket furnished with a stopcock, above another bucket having a cross-piece, in the middle of which is a conical leather bung. The lower end of the mould is then rested on the bung, which closes it exactly, the upper opening being, of course, just beneath the stopcock. As the latter is opened, and the canal filled with slip, the level soon sinks in the mould in consequence of the absorption of the water, and is restored by an additional quantity of slip; the mould is then removed from the bung, and the non-adherent slip falls off. As the adherent layer is not sufficiently thick, it is set aside for a few moments, long enough to fill three or four other moulds; the first is then filled anew, after having inverted it. If the tube is not yet thick enough, a third casting must be performed, always inverting the mould. In 3 or 4 hours, the mould may be separated: the beard and blisters on the tube are then removed with a sharp instrument.

§ 716. The porcelain articles made by these various processes are first baked, so as to dry them completely and impart to them a certain degree of consistency; but the material is still very porous. They are then *glazed*, and finally burned.

We spoke, in § 706, of the glaze applied to porcelain, and the principal conditions it must fulfil. We saw that the material of the glaze must have a certain affinity for the ceramic paste, in order to cover the pieces perfectly and leave no part exposed; this affinity, however, must not be too great, or the glaze would penetrate into the paste, and not leave enough on the surface. The glaze must be more fusible than the ceramic paste; but the difference of fusibility again must not be too marked, for if the glaze should melt before the paste was burned, it would flow toward the bottom of the pieces, or enter the substance of the paste. A last condition, and one of the most difficult to fulfil for pottery in general, is to give the glaze nearly the same dilatability by heat as the paste, as otherwise it would crack, and start in every direction.

The glaze of Sèvres porcelain is made of a feldspathic rock, mixed with a certain quantity of quartz. No other substance is added to it, but the rock is selected with regard to the quantity of quartz it contains, and the degree of fusibility of the glaze required.

The glazing is generally done by *immersion*. The feldspathic rock is ground in water in mills, and then purified by levigation: the material, very finely divided, is suspended in water, to which a small quantity of vinegar is added, because this acid effectually prevents the precipitation of the powdered matter. This clear pap, called *slip*, is placed in large buckets, into which the workman dips quickly and dexterously the piece to be glazed: the piece, from its porosity, absorbs the water, and the vitrifiable matter suspended in the water is deposited on its surface. By this rapid and simple process, the thickness of the glazing becomes uniform throughout, if one part of the piece has not been allowed to remain longer in the liquid than another. With a knife and a piece of felt, the glaze is removed from those parts which do not require its application. As the part by which the workman holds the piece is necessarily not glazed, it is afterward painted over with slip.

In order that *biscuit* porcelain should be properly glazed, its surface must be perfectly clear, and especially free from all greasy substances; hence the workman should avoid touching them with his hands. Advantage is sometimes taken of this property to prevent certain parts of the piece from taking the glazing; they are covered with a mixture of wax and tallow. Lastly, when it is desired that a piece, or a portion of it, be less highly glazed than another, it is more or less soaked with water with a pencil, before glazing; the absorbent action of the paste is thus diminished, and a thinner coat of glaze deposited.

Glazing by immersion can only be done on porous pieces, such as biscuit porcelain; but if it is required to glaze pieces which, having been highly burnt, are no longer sufficiently porous, it is done either with a brush or by sprinkling.

§ 717. Porcelain-kilns are generally composed of 2 or 3 stories. In the upper story, where the temperature is lowest, the biscuit is burned, and in the lower, or two lower stories, if there be three, the last burning of the porcelain is effected.

Figs. 456 and 457 represent a three-storied kiln, in the manufactory at Sèvres. Fig. 456 gives an external view, and fig. 457 represents a vertical section through the axis of the kiln. In the two stories L and L′ the porcelain is burned, and in L″ the biscuit is baked. Each of the compartments L, L′ is heated by four outer

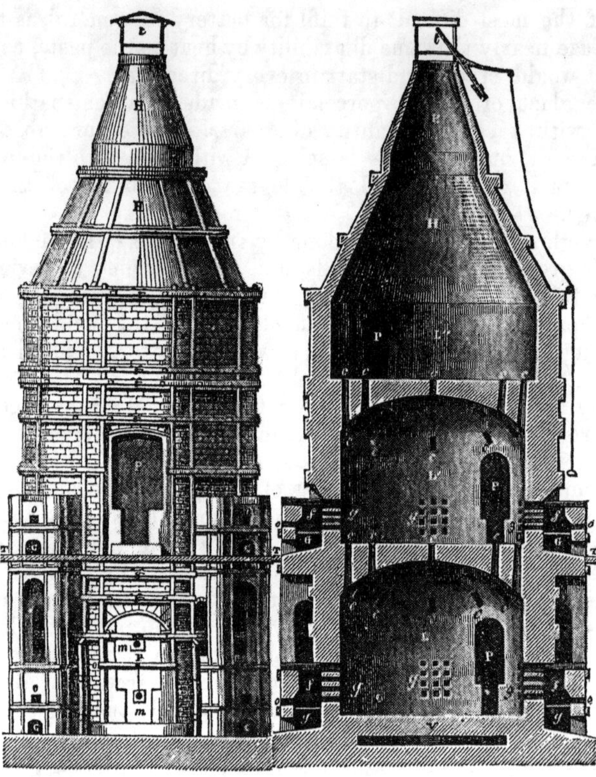

Fig. 456. Fig. 457.

furnaces immediately adjoining the kiln, and called *alandiers*. The flame in these furnaces is inverted: they are composed of a rectangular vat *f*, terminating below in a grate. The face they have in common with the kiln has several rectangular holes *g*, through which the flame enters the kiln; the ash-holes, as well as the openings *o*, may be closed internally. When the porcelain is deposited in the kiln, in the manner to be described, a few live coals are placed upon the grate, and above that, wood split into short pieces: the door of the ash-hole is then closed. The draught of air is through the kiln itself, which acts as a chimney; the fresh air enters through the upper hole of the alandier, which is open, and the inverted flame passes into the oven through the openings *g*. The flame and current of hot air pass from the lower to the upper story, through the holes *c* made in the roof, and escape through the upper aperture *t*, which can be regulated at will by a register. Birch and aspen wood are used in the alandiers; pit-coal has not yet been successfully employed, at least for fine porcelain, as it makes too fierce a fire in front of the working-holes *g*, and it is very difficult to render, with this fuel, the temperature of each compartment nearly uniform. Pit-coal, also, burns with a smoky flame, which frequently discolours the porcelain and diminishes its value.

The kiln, made of refractory bricks, is firmly held together by an iron framework, which will be easily understood by an inspection of fig. 456. In each compartment there is a large door P for charging the kiln, which is closed by brick-work during the burning. In this temporary mason-work several small holes *m* (fig. 456) are made, through which small fragments of glazed porcelain, called time-pieces or watches (*montres*), are introduced: these are intended to be withdrawn from time to time, in order to judge of the progress of the baking.

§ 718. The porcelain articles cannot be placed unprotected in the kiln, for they would be exposed immediately to the current of hot air, carrying with it a considerable quantity of ashes, which would stick to the melted glaze. The various pieces must also not touch each other at any point, as otherwise they would adhere; each piece must, therefore, be placed in a vessel called a *seggar* (cazette, or gazette).

The seggars are made of refractory clay; they should be less fusible than the porcelain. Their paste should be coarse, that they may resist the immediate and unequal action of the fire without breaking, and can be used several times. They are composed of very pure plastic clay, carefully levigated, and freed from all particles of quartz, limestone, or pyrites: to this clay a certain quantity of fragments of broken seggars, reduced to an impalpable powder, is added as a cement. At Sèvres the proportions are generally 40 parts of washed plastic clay and 60 of cement.

The seggars and supports are made in the same way as the pieces, but more roughly. The paste is stamped, in order to incorporate the cement with the various clays of which it is composed; it is then fashioned on the potter's lathe, and turned, but only hollowed out. Seggars are generally made of two pieces: an external covering, usually cylindrical, and a flat bottom, on which the porcelain rests; but their form varies with the use to which they are to be applied. Fig. 458 represents a series of plates; each seggar will be seen to be composed of two parts, a cylindrical covering *t* and a kind of vessel *i*, having nearly the shape of the plate, and on the bottom of which the bottom of the plate rests. The seggars are arranged

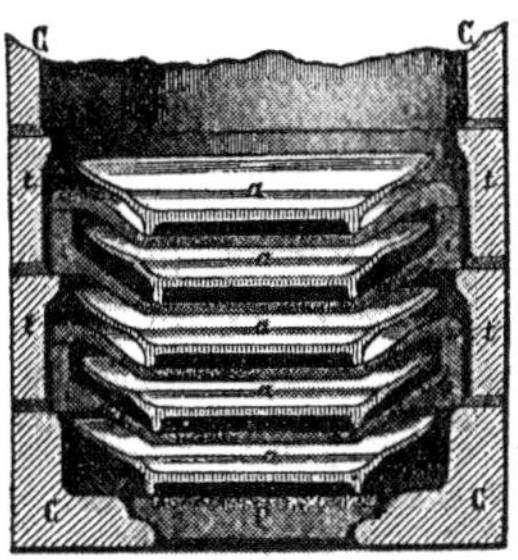

Fig. 458.

above each other, so as to form a perfectly vertical pile, called a *bung*.

The *charging* of the furnace requires particular care on the part of the workman. He should endeavour to fill the kiln as completely as possible, without closing the working-holes, and still to preserve between the pieces the spaces necessary for a proper distribution of the flame through the furnace: he places near the working-holes *g*, those pieces which, from their size or peculiar nature, require the highest temperature. The piles of seggars are fastened to each other by small caps of burnt clay.

§ 719. Fig. 459 represents very accurately the arrangement of the pieces in a kiln: some of the seggars are supposed to be divided, in order to show the porcelain inside.

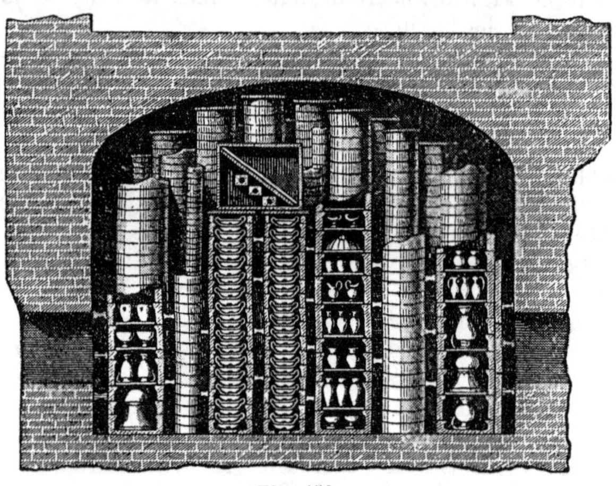

Fig. 459.

Although the glazing may be removed with great care and very perfectly from those parts which come in contact with the supports, the porcelain paste might adhere at certain points, if, between the support and the part denuded of glazing, sandy argillaceous coating were not interposed, of such composition as to prevent all adhesion: this is called the *terrage* of the supports.

The spaces between the seggars are closed with an argillaceous luting, composed of 30 parts of plastic clay, and 70 of quartzose sand.

The biscuit itself is placed in the seggars; but their arrangement is more simple, because there is no fear of their adhering to the seggars, and a great number of pieces may be placed in the kiln.

The kiln being charged, the doors are walled up and the firing commenced. First the alandiers of the upper chamber are closed, and only those of the lower story heated. When the porcelain in the first compartment is supposed to be burned, the alandiers of the second story are opened, and a small fire kept up for about an hour, without completely extinguishing the fire below. All the apertures of the lower alandiers are then closed hermetically, and those of the second story are partially, and afterwards entirely, stopped. The fire is carefully managed, until the pieces in the second story are perfectly baked; the furnace is then allowed to cool, and after having removed the brick walls which closed the doors P, the porcelain pieces are removed from the kiln.

The baked porcelain is very carefully sorted: while the faultless pieces are considered as of first quality, the others are divided into several classes, according to the nature of their defects.

§ 720. The porcelain, the manufacture of which we have just described, is called *hard*, or *Chinese porcelain.* Other qualities are made, called *tender*, or *French china*, which require a lower temperature, and may be sold at a cheaper rate: the paste of this porcelain should be more fusible than that of the hard porcelain, a character which is easily given to it by introducing larger proportions of alkaline material, either in the state of feldspar, or even in that of alkaline carbonates and nitrates. The glaze of this porcelain should also be much more fusible than that of hard porcelain: with this intention, a certain quantity of oxide of lead is introduced.

Sometimes, in the manufacture of the paste of tender porcelain, the clay which is the essential base of the hard porcelains is not used. Thus, the paste of tender porcelain formerly made at Sèvres, and now called *Old Sèvres china*, was made by first fritting in an oven,

Sand from Fontainebleau	60.0
Fused nitrate of potassa	22.0
Sea-salt	7.2
Alum	3.6
Alicant soda	3.6
Gypsum from Montmartre	3.6
	100.0

Seventy-five parts of this frit were mixed with 17 of white chalk and 8 of marly limestone from Argenteuil, and black soap or gum was added to the paste, to make it more binding.

The glaze was made of

Calcined sand from Fontainebleau	27
Calcined silex	11
Carbonate of potassa	15
" soda	9
Litharge	38

Stoneware.

§ 721. This is a kind of porcelain, which differs from the finer sort merely in the paste being always more or less discoloured, and less carefully worked. The base of this ware is clay, which in general contains a large proportion of oxide of iron, and is thus more fusible than kaolin: sometimes the fusibility is still further increased by the addition of a certain quantity of lime, or of alkaline salts. Baked clays or quartzose sand are added as cement. The clay is scarcely ever washed, except for fine pottery; the larger pieces of quartz or limestone are merely separated by hand. The paste is fashioned on the potter's lathe; and the pieces, dried in the air, are baked in furnaces, at a temperature nearly equal to that used for the turning of porcelain. This kind of pottery is seldom glazed, but an ingenious substitute is employed: when the pottery has attained a very high temperature, a few handfuls of damp sea-salt are thrown into the furnace. This salt volatilizes, the vapour is decomposed by the presence of the water and the contact of the argillaceous walls, chlorohydric acid is disengaged, and the sides of the pieces are covered with a silicate of soda, which, by combining with the silicate of alumina, produces a very fusible double silicate, forming a varnish over the surface of the pieces.

The paste of stoneware is of itself impervious after burning; therefore the only use of glazing is to give it a better finish. Some of this ware, however, merely dried in the air, is glazed, either with a brush or by sprinkling, with the scoriæ of blast-furnaces or very fusible volcanic lava.

POTTERY THE PASTE OF WHICH REMAINS POROUS AFTER BURNING.

§ 722. This division comprises several kinds, such as the various fayences and earthenwares used in cooking.

Earthenware, or Fayence.

§ 723. The clays belonging generally to the secondary formations are used for the manufacture of fine earthenware. When these clays do not contain any colouring metallic oxides, as the oxides of iron and manganese, the paste remains white after burning; but as they often contain large proportions of these oxides, the paste generally becomes red or brown by burning. Earthenware is always glazed, and subjected successively to two fires: they are first burnt at a high temperature, lower however than that for burning hard porcelain; and, after this first burning, they are covered, by immersion, with an easily fusible glaze, and exposed to a second fire, generally much less intense than the one first used.

As the paste of earthenware should not soften in the first fire, it must be very slightly fusible: it is made of a plastic clay which has been carefully levigated for fine earthenware, and to which a greater or less proportion of quartz, reduced to an impalpable powder, has been added. The proportion of quartz is often greater than that of the clay, for in certain kinds of earthenware, a mixture of 70 parts of quartz and 30 of clay is used. The paste of earthenware is more easily worked than that of porcelain, being more plastic; in other respects it is moulded nearly in the same way. Earthenware is burned in kilns similar to those used for porcelain, but the charging is more simple: a much greater number of pieces can be introduced, because the paste does not soften, and there is no danger of their becoming misshaped. Thus, in the first firing of plaster, they may be placed on each other, and the whole pile surrounded by a cylindrical seggar. More care is requisite for the second firing of glazed earthenwares, because the pieces would adhere to each other. They must be supported by three points; and for this purpose the seggars have three holes, disposed in the same horizontal circle, through which small pieces of baked earth are introduced, on which the edges of the plates rest.

Fine earthenware is glazed with a glass of alkalies and oxide of lead, the proportion of the latter being increased when a very fusible glaze is required, combined with economy of fuel; but the glaze is, in that case, very tender, and can be scraped off with a knife, so that the plates soon become scratched. The highly plumbeous glasses are, moreover, easily attacked by chemical agents, especially at the parts injured by the knife; they also soon blacken when in contact with substances which disengage sulphuretted hydrogen. It is sufficient to cook stale eggs or fish in these vessels to give them a brown tinge. Therefore, in fine earthenware, the proportion of the oxide of lead should be diminished as much as possible: but the glaze being the less fusible, the price of the ware is greatly increased, and approximates that of common porcelain, which is always preferable.

The glaze of common French earthenware is made by melting together in a crucible,

Quartzose sand	100
Carbonate of potassa or soda	80
Red-lead	120 to 150

One or two parts of smalt, or glaze coloured blue by oxide of cobalt, are commonly added to the mixture, in order to give a slight blueish tinge to the glaze, more agreeable to the eye than dead white.

For a very fine article, such as the English earthenware, a very small proportion of oxide of lead is used.

The glaze of coloured earthenware should be opake, in order to conceal the disagreeable colour of the paste: the opacity is produced by the addition of a certain quantity of oxide of tin. This glaze, a true enamel (§ 690), is then frequently coloured with metallic oxides.

Earthenware is much less patient of fire than porcelain; the glaze cracks and blisters very readily, as, for instance, when the vessels are washed in hot water.

Common Earthenware.

§ 724. Very common pottery, such as flower-pots, is made of impure clays, often very ochreous, and mixed with more or less sand. These clays are more generally used as they are taken from the earth, after merely separating the pebbles and lumps which are not easily crushed. They are rarely levigated, as this operation would render them too costly, but are stamped, and frequently allowed to moulder for years in pits, to increase their plasticity. The pieces are fashioned on the potter's lathe, dried in the air, and then burned at a low temperature, without being glazed.

§ 725. The common earthenware used in cooking is made of clay, to which a certain quantity of lime in the state of marl, and also quartzose sand, is added. This ware is glazed generally with a plumbeous glass, coloured by some metallic oxide. The glaze is composed of 6 or 7 parts of litharge and 4 or 5 of clay.

§ 726. In warm countries, chiefly in Spain, a very porous kind of pottery is made with clay mixed with large quantities of sand or of baked clay. In this way the bottles called *alcarazas* are made, which, when filled with water, are easily permeated by this fluid, and present an outer surface constantly moist and exposed to the drying agency of the air. When these vessels are suspended in a current of air, the water evaporates so rapidly from their surface that the temperature of the water falls several degrees below that of the surrounding air: alcarazas are therefore used in hot countries to cool water; but they are not of much use in temperate climates, in which, during the summer, the temperature of the cellars is lower than that produced by the spontaneous evaporation of water.

Common Building-bricks.—Tiles.

§ 727. Common bricks are made of clay burned at very various temperatures. In hot countries, they are merely dried in the sun; but, in that case, they are always very friable, and can only be used in buildings where great solidity is not required. Most frequently, they are burned in a kiln, and sometimes the temperature is high enough to effect a sort of superficial fusion of the material. Burned bricks are generally of a reddish colour, owing to the oxide of iron which frequently abounds in the clay.

Nearly all the sedimentary and alluvial earths, containing argillaceous strata, are adapted to the manufacture of common bricks. When the clay is too fat, sand is added: the clay, when dug out of the earth, is left for some time in pits, and then stamped. The bricks are either made by hand, or in rectangular wooden frames, or sometimes by machinery: they are dried in the air, and then burned in kilns, with some cheap fuel. Roofing and paving tiles are made in the same way.

Fire-bricks for the construction of furnaces; and Crucibles.

§ 728. Refractory clays, which consequently should contain no large quantity of oxide of iron, nor of carbonate of lime, are used in the manufacture of these bricks. These clays are not common, and fire-bricks can therefore be made only in certain favoured localities, the best of which in France is Burgundy. The clay is coloured with quartzose sand.

The greatest care is required in the selection of the clay for melting-pots; for example, those used in glass-houses. These clays are nicely levigated, and scoured by the addition of a considerable proportion of cement, generally yielded by the broken pots, carefully sorted to exclude all pieces of glass. The paste frequently contains more than $\frac{1}{2}$, and sometimes $\frac{2}{3}$, of this cement. In the same way excellent crucibles are made, which resist a forge-fire as well as the small earthen furnaces used in chemical laboratories.

Hessian crucibles, for a long time the most esteemed for the melting of metals, are made of a refractory clay, mixed with a coarse quartzose sand occurring in the tertiary formation near Almerode. These crucibles readily resist sudden changes of temperature without cracking.

Crucibles highly valued for the melting of steel are also made of 1 part of fire-clay, and 2 of graphite or plumbago. This paste can be easily worked, and the crucible is susceptible of a high polish. During the burning of the crucibles, it undergoes no change internally, as only the surface of the graphite burns. Plumbago is found only in a few localities: within the last few years, it has been replaced by very finely powdered coke, and crucibles of good quality have been thus made.

ORNAMENTS AND PAINTING.

§ 729. Fine pottery is often ornamented by the application of colours or metallic coatings to their surface: sometimes they are painted, thus adding greatly to their value.

The colours applied to porcelain are made of colouring metallic oxides, mixed with more or less fusible vitreous substances. The mixture, when melted, is reduced to an impalpable powder, and then ground with essence of turpentine or lavender: these pastes are applied with a brush, and the pottery is then subjected to a temperature high enough to vitrify the colours. These colours must fulfil several conditions; we shall enumerate some of the most important:

1. They must melt at a temperature which is not sufficiently elevated to effect a chemical decomposition, which would change the colour: in other words, the fusibility of the vitreous flux must be in proportion to the fixedness of the colouring matter, and the temperature to which the painted piece is subjected must be such as not to injure the most fugitive colour present.

2. They must adhere with sufficient firmness to the pottery after burning, to resist friction.

3. They must retain a vitreous aspect after burning.

4. They must be unchangeable by water, atmospheric air, and even by the liquids intended to be contained in the vessel.

5. They must bear a proper ratio of dilatability with the paste of the pottery, and especially with its glaze.

§ 730. The colouring materials may be divided into four classes:

The first, comprising the most important and numerous colours, includes the metallic oxides.

The second is composed of those mineral substances which retain an earthy and opake aspect after burning, and which obtain their lustre only from the general glazing which covers them. They are called *engobes*.

The third class contains the metals; chiefly gold, silver, and platinum. They are applied in the metallic state, mixed merely with a small quantity of some fusible material, to cause them to adhere to the surface of the pottery. They are then polished by burnishing.

The fourth class comprehends the metallic lustres. These are very finely divided metals, applied in excessively thin layers, and often produce a fine play of colours.

Two kinds of vitrifiable colours are distinguished, according to the temperature at which the pottery is burned: *refractory colours*, which do not change even at the high temperature at which glazed porcelain is burnt; and *muffle colours*, which do not bear this temperature without alteration. The latter are vitrified at much lower temperatures in peculiar furnaces, called *muffle-furnaces*.

Refractory colours may be applied under the glaze, or may be mixed with it, and then burned immediately in the high fire of the porcelain-kiln. Muffle colours, on the contrary, are only applied to glazed porcelain.

Refractory colours are not very numerous: they consist of the cobalt blue yielded by the oxide of cobalt CoO; chrome-green, produced by the oxide of chrome Cr_2O_3; the browns, made from the sesquioxides of iron and manganese; the yellow, obtained from oxide of titanium; and the blacks, furnished by protoxide of uranium.

Muffle colours are more numerous, and the palette of the porcelain-painter is nearly as richly provided as that of the portrait-painter. These colours are made by mixing in a crucible the metallic oxides with colourless glasses, called *fluxes*, the fusibility of which is regulated by the temperature to which the paintings may be exposed without detriment to the most fugitive colour. The components of these fluxes are quartz, feldspar, borax or boracic acid, nitre, the carbonates of potassa and soda, red-lead and litharge, and oxide of bismuth. At Sèvres, seven kinds of fluxes, which suffice for all colours, are used, the majority of which are composed of quartz, oxide of lead, and boracic acid; to some, a small quantity of carbonate of soda is added. The flux for metals is composed of oxide of bismuth mixed with one-tenth of its weight of melted borax.

We shall not here enter into the composition and mode of preparation of the various colours used in porcelain-painting, but merely indicate the chemical nature of the principal colouring substances.

The blues are always produced by oxide of cobalt, their shades being varied by an addition of oxide of zinc, or by that of small quantities of colouring metallic oxides.

The greens are furnished by the oxide of chrome Cr_2O_3 and by protoxide of copper CuO, the shades being varied by adding other colouring oxides: they are rendered yellow by the oxides of antimony and lead; brown, by the sesquioxides of iron and manganese; blue, by the oxide of cobalt, etc. etc.

The yellows are given by oxide of uranium U_2O_3, chromate of lead PbO,CrO_3, sesquioxide of iron and antimoniate of potassa: they are mixed with the oxides of lead, zinc, and tin.

The reds are produced by protoxide of copper Cu_2O, and by sesquioxide of iron.

The violets and rose-colours are obtained from the *purple of Cassius*, which is an intimate mixture of metallic gold and peroxide of tin in various proportions.

The blacks are furnished by protoxide of uranium, or by the metallic oxides of cobalt and manganese.

The whites are produced by ordinary enamel (§ 690).

The gold is prepared by precipitating a solution of perchloride of gold by protosulphate of iron: the pulverulent gold is mixed with one-twelfth of its weight of oxide of bismuth, to which a little borax has been added; the whole is diluted with some essential oil, and painted on the glazed porcelain. After burning, the gold assumes a metallic lustre, but it is dead: it is polished by rubbing it, first with an agate, and then with a blood-stone burnisher.

Gold lustre is obtained by precipitating a solution of gold in aqua regia by ammonia. The precipitate, called *fulminating gold*, is mixed when moist with essence of turpentine; it is spread without any flux over the surface of the porcelain. The piece is exposed to the fire, and the lustre of the gold brought out by friction with a piece of linen or muslin.

A lustre, remarkable for its beautiful play of colours, and called *cantharides lustre*, is obtained from chloride of silver, which is partially decomposed by combustible vapours. A mixture of plumbeous glass, a small quantity of oxide of bismuth, and chloride of silver is applied with a pencil, and the piece is heated in a muffle; and when it is red-hot, a smoky vapour is introduced into the muffle, by which the chloride of silver is partially decomposed.

The burning of painted porcelain is an extremely delicate operation: it is done in *muffle-furnaces* (fig. 460), the fire of which is regulated with the utmost care. The workman is governed in the management of the fire, by the examination of small *watches* of porcelain, introduced into the muffle with the porcelain, and withdrawn from time to time: on these watches some of the most fugitive colours on the porcelain are painted, the rose-colour, for example; and also the substances which would not adhere unless exposed to a sufficiently high temperature, the gold coating, for instance, are applied on them. The workman must therefore so manage the fire, as to cause the gold to adhere firmly, without changing the shades of the most delicate colours.

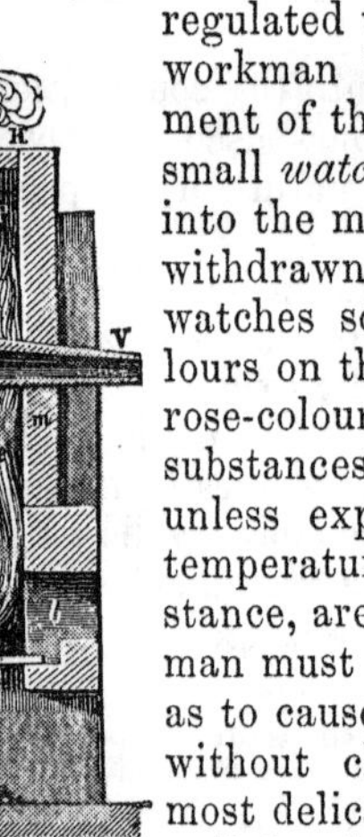

Fig. 460.

Painted porcelain is always exposed to two firings: after the first, which is considered only as biscuit, the painter retouches it, to correct any faults in the colouring; it is then subjected to the second heating. Very highly finished paintings are often burned a greater number of times.

Only fine pottery, such as porcelain, is painted; but engravings are transferred on earthenware, even of the commoner sorts. An ordinary engraved copperplate is used for this, and the ink employed consists of glass, coloured brown, black, red, or blue, etc., reduced to an impalpable powder, and ground in linseed-oil. The engraving is printed on a sheet of thin paper, the engraved side of which, after moistening the sheet, is impressed on the dry pottery; by carefully removing the paper, the design is left on the vessel. The oil is then driven off by heat, and the glazing done in the ordinary way.

CHEMICAL ANALYSIS OF EARTHENWARE.

§ 731. The paste of earthenware contains the same elementary substances as glass, and differs from the latter only in the proportions of its components: the ceramic pastes are therefore analyzed by the processes indicated in § 704.

END OF VOL. I.

www.ingramcontent.com/pod-product-compliance
Lightning Source LLC
LaVergne TN
LVHW021049110826
845150LV00001B/25

* 9 7 8 1 4 2 5 5 6 8 3 1 3 *